CORPUS JURIS HUMOROUS

A Compilation Of

HUMOROUS, EXTRAORDINARY, OUTRAGEOUS,
UNUSUAL, COLORFUL, INFAMOUS, CLEVER
AND WITTY REPORTED JUDICIAL OPINIONS AND
RELATED MATERIALS DATING FROM
1256 A.D. TO THE PRESENT

———————

Compiled and Edited By

JOHN B. MCCLAY
ATTORNEY AT LAW

&

WENDY L. MATTHEWS
ATTORNEY AT LAW

ISBN # 0-9631488-0-X
Library of Congress Catalog Number: 91-91457
Printed in the United States of America

by

MAC-MAT
c/o
McCLAY & ALANI
A Professional Law Corporation

1630 East Palm Avenue
Santa Ana, California 92701

Telephone: (714) 558-1535

Telecopier: (714) 558-8024

ABOUT THE EDITORS

JOHN B. McCLAY
ATTORNEY-AT-LAW

John B. McClay has practiced law in Orange County, California since 1980 and is co-founder and co-lead counsel of McCLAY & ALANI, a Professional Law Corporation. The firm emphasizes real property litigation and commercial asset management law, representing developers, commercial landlords and asset management companies throughout Southern California. John B. McClay is a graduate of the University of California at Berkeley (B.S., Business Administration, 1976) and Pepperdine University School of Law, (J.D., 1979) where he was named to the Dean's Honor List and served on the Pepperdine Law Review.

ABOUT THE EDITORS

WENDY L. MATTHEWS
ATTORNEY-AT-LAW

Wendy L. Matthews has practiced law in Orange County, California since 1989, and established the Law Offices of Wendy L. Matthews in 1991. Her firm emphasizes serious injury litigation and probate/estate planning law. Wendy L. Matthews studied geology at Monterey Peninsula College, transferring to the Gemological Institute of America (G.G., 1978). As a gemologist, she has served as a consultant and expert witness in connection with litigation involving gem fraud. She has completed post-graduate studies at the University of Cambridge and is a graduate of Western State University College of Law (B.S.L., 1986; J.D., 1988).

ACKNOWLEDGEMENTS

The editors wish to express their profound gratitude and appreciation to the many persons who have assisted in the preparation of this work, including but not limited to the following:

JON A. DIERINGER
Western State University College of Law
Class of 1992
(Research)

J. MARK SUGARS, B.S. (Bio. Sci.), B.A. (Classics)
Candidate for Ph.D. (Classics)
University of California, Irvine
(Latin and Norman-French Translations)

THOMAS W. BOSSE
University of Notre Dame School of Law, J.D. 1991
(Research and Citations)

CHRISTOPHER D. LEWIS
Western State University College of Law
Class of 1994
(Research)

DARLA JEAN LANGFORD-PIROOZ
Fullerton College - Candidate for Paralegal Certificate, 1992
(Computer Technician & Manuscript Preparation)

MARTY LONGÉ
Penguin Productions - Desktop Publishing, Graphic Design

Janet S. Fohrman, Laura E. Stephens, Ardelis Malone, Jeanine Briggs, Eleanor Wahl, Denise P. McCall, Geri R. Grissom, Lynda M. Durham, Andrew Y. Nahm, Victoria A. Halliday, Ross Steiber, Kathleen Traeger, Brandee D. Turner, Maren E. Agnew, Kwang (Paul) Lee, Brian Kim; Eldridge Suggs IV, Sonya A. Webster, Barbara Martin, Kathy Derby, Linda Huth, Melanie Brown, Alessandra Capella, Joanne J. El Kareh, Susan H. Pruner, Julie L. Carrell, Anne Monaghan.

A special acknowledgement and thanks is extended to Douglas D. Alani, Esq., co-founder and co-lead counsel of MCCLAY & ALANI, a Professional Law Corporation, for his patience, tolerance, and support throughout the duration of this project.

A further special acknowledgement and thanks is extended to the Honorable George Rose Smith (Associate Justice, Arkansas Supreme Court, 1949-1987) for his excellent sense of humor and valuable assistance in the preparation of this work.

This work is also specially dedicated by John B. McClay to his parents, Robert H. McClay and Virginia C. McClay and by Wendy L. Matthews to her parents, Eugene C. Matthews and Shirley E. Matthews.

DEDICATION

THIS BOOK IS DEDICATED
TO THE JUDGES AND COMMISSIONERS
SERVING IN JUDICIAL SYSTEMS
THROUGHOUT THE WORLD

. . . A judge's life, like every other, has in it much of drudgery, senseless bickerings, stupid obstinacies, captious pettifogging, all disguising and obstructing the only sane purpose which can justify the whole endeavor. These take an inordinate part of his time; they harass and befog the unhappy wretch, and at times almost drive him from that bench where like any other workman he must do his work. If that were all, his life would be mere misery, and he a distracted arbiter between irreconcilable extremes. But there is something else that makes it--anyway to those curious creatures who persist in it--a delectable calling. For when the case is all in, and the turmoil stops, and after he is left alone, things begin to take form. From his pen or in his head, slowly or swiftly as his capacities admit, out of the murk the pattern emerges, his pattern, the expression of what he has seen and what he has therefor made, the impress of his self upon the not-self, upon the hitherto formless material of which he was once but a part and over which he has now become the master. That is a pleasure which nobody who has felt it will be likely to underrate. . . .

- Learned Hand,[1]

---

[1] "The Preservation of Personality," presented as a commencement address at Bryn Mawr College, Bryn Mawr, Pennsylvania, June 2, 1927. [from Dilliard, Irving; *The Spirit of Liberty; Papers and Addresses of Learned Hand*, The University of Chicago Press, p. 43 (1952).]

INTRODUCTION

. . . The law has always been a hard task-master and requires of its advocates a serious approach and stern visaged application. When it comes face to face with life, as it unfolds in the drama of the courtroom, the law sometimes reaches its serious, stern results from facts which have been compiled with humor. So--while the end results of the law are deadly serious--there is about the lawyer (and even judges, occasionally) a spark of the humor of life--and a need for it. So let it be . . . for, while the end result is most serious to both plaintiff and defendant, what has brought about the necessity for the end result, is most humorous. . .

- Randolph H. Weber,[1]
United States District Judge

The cases and materials presented in this compilation represent the culmination of more than a decade and a half of ardent, resolute and purposeful research and collection. The process was both tedious and inherently gratifying. The real work, of course, was performed by the judges who wrote the opinions. Their wit, humor, and literary acumen is self-evident. The cases and materials are reproduced in as complete a form as possible to enable the reader to appreciate the fabric of the judicial humor within a meaningful factual and legal context. They are presented *verbatim et literatim*, exactly as reported. The original language, grammar and spelling have all been retained, notwithstanding any obvious or technical improprieties. In many cases, the grammatical errors and arcane usages constitute an integral part of the humor of the writing. The judicial opinions are genuine and all have been reported, published and/or otherwise preserved in written form, generally in one or more of the officially-recognized reporters. The opinions are drawn from a variety of judicial systems, each having its origin in the English common law tradition, including the United States, England, Canada and South Africa. Citations, and parallel citations where available, are provided.

For the most part, the cases and materials are self-explanatory. Where deemed helpful or appropriate, summaries of the court record and/or prior proceedings, as well as explanatory references, translations of Latin and Norman-French phrases and editorial comments are offset in brackets. Internal abbreviations and deletions from the original text are denoted by triple dot (. . .) ellipses.

---

[1] From *Aetna Insurance Company v. Sachs*, 186 F. Supp. 105, 106 (1960).

In certain cases, paragraphing was added to enhance readability. Such editing as was required reflects the subjective judgment of the compilers. Our objective was to retain as much of the structural cohesiveness and logical sense of the opinions as possible and not merely to provide a compilation of humorous excerpts. The materials are not presented in chronological order, but rather, are loosely organized within the broad categories outlined by the chapter titles. Where ascertainable, we have set forth the full name of the judge authoring each of the judicial opinions included within the compilation, rather than simply noting his or her surname, as is the usual custom. In cases where it was impossible to identify the judge involved, particularly in the ancient opinions, the author is simply designated as "Anonymous."

In addition to the judicial opinions, we have included a number of the Statutes of the Realm of England, consisting primarily of laws enacted by the English Parliament during the reign of Henry VIII (1509 - 1547). As editors, we considered these "Actes" to be sufficiently humorous, extraordinary and/or outrageous as to be consistent with the primary theme of the compilation.

Perhaps the most difficult editorial task we encountered was deciding which of the many cases and materials assembled should be included within this volume. The process was entirely subjective, involving the admittedly personal judgment and discretion of the editors. We did our utmost to include the best and most representative works within each of the broad subject matter categories outlined by the chapter titles. Many excellent cases and materials could not be included in this collection due to the inherent spatial constraints, and must await our follow-up volume, Corpus Juris Humorous II, which is currently being compiled and edited.

J.B.M.

Santa Ana, California
October 20, 1991

SUMMARY OF CHAPTERS

TABLE OF CONTENTS

CHAPTER I:

CANINE, EQUINE, FELINE, BOVINE, MURINE, PORCINE, ANSERINE, AVIAN, MULINE, VESPINE, PISCINE, CERVINE, CIMICINE, LEPIDOPTERINE AND GRYLLINE LAW

CHAPTER II:

LAW, LAWYERS, JUDGES, LEGAL PROCEDURES, PROCESSES, INTERPRETATIONS, SUBTLETIES, DISTINCTIONS, LOOPHOLES, TECHNICALITIES, NUANCES & INTRICACIES

CHAPTER III:

ALCOHOL, DRUGS, GAMBLING,
VICE, PROFANITY, LEWDNESS, OBSCENITY,
INDOLENCE, SLOTH, VAGRANCY
AND OTHER ASSORTED PREVALENT EVILS

CHAPTER IV:

BUSINESS, TRADE, COMMERCE, CONTRACTS,
PROPERTY, PROFESSIONS, CORPORATIONS, REGULATION,
TAXATION AND RELATED MERCANTILE MATTERS

CHAPTER V:

*PASSION, ROMANCE, LOVE, LUST,
LICENTIOUSNESS, FORNICATION, MARRIAGE,
INTRIGUE, INDIFFERENCE, DISENCHANTMENT,
DISGRACE, DISSOLUTION AND DIVORCE*

CHAPTER VI:

CLEVER SCHEMES, BIZARRE CLAIMS, RIDICULOUS CONTENTIONS, NOVEL DEMANDS, STRANGE LAWSUITS AND GOOD OLD-FASHIONED FRAUD AND DECEIT

CHAPTER VII:

*SCOUNDRELS, CROOKS, OUTLAWS,
RENEGADES, ROGUES, KNAVES AND OTHER MISCREANTS;
THEIR CRIMES, GRAND AND PETTY; AND THE PROCESSES AND PRO-
CEDURES RELATED THERETO*

CHAPTER VIII:

WILLS, TRUSTS, PROBATE AND RELIGION
AND OTHER MATTERS CONCERNING THE HEREAFTER

CHAPTER IX:

ACCIDENTS, SLIPS, FALLS, CRASHES, CRUNCHES, WRECKS, BUMPS, THUMPS AND LUMPS

CHAPTER X:

SCURRILOUS, SCANDALOUS, ARBITRARY,
CAPRICIOUS, WILLFUL, DELIBERATE,
INTENTIONAL, MALICIOUS, OPPRESSIVE, OBSTINATE,
DESPICABLE, OUTRAGEOUS, LOATHSOME, EGREGIOUS,
AND REPREHENSIBLE TORTIOUS ACTS AND CONDUCT

CHAPTER I

CANINE, EQUINE, FELINE, BOVINE, MURINE, PORCINE, ANSERINE, AVIAN, MULINE, VESPINE, PISCINE, CERVINE, CIMICINE, LEPIDOPTERINE AND GRYLLINE LAW [1]

Judicial Humor. . . Again the advice must be a flat Never. Judicial humor is neither judicial nor humorous. . .

1967 - Hon. George Rose Smith
From "A Primer of Opinion Writing for Four New Judges" [2]

In judicial language, that part of the Primer disapproving judicial humor is hereby overruled, set aside, held for naught, and stomped on!

1990 - Hon. George Rose Smith
From "A Critique of Judicial Humor" [3]

---

[1] Dog, horse, cat, cow, rodent, pig, goose, bird, mule, wasp, fish, deer, bedbug, butterfly and cricket law.

[2] Hon. George Rose Smith, "A Primer of Opinion Writing, For Four New Judges," 21 *Ark. Law Rev.* 197, 210 (1967).

[3] Hon. George Rose Smith, (Footnote 60) "A Critique of Judicial Humor," 43 *Ark. Law Rev.* 1, 25 (1990).

CHAPTER I: CANINE, EQUINE & FELINE

IN RE SIRUS JOD
Justice Court of California, Tuolumne County
Case No. 515 (1851)

R. C. BARRY, Justice Peace.

This were a crimminel caze or suite in which one Sirus Yod or Jod butcher were indited by me fur cruelity to animules. The only testimmony projuced were that of Bill Foarde and Arkansaw who planely prooved that Cirus Jod had tied up a oxe in the sunshine all day without water or feade which were a shame and a outrage on the public morrels and desency. Jod defended hisself by sayeing the oxe was not his property nor did he owne him that he only tied him up so his owner could git him. I found Jod gilty and fined him the costs of Court 2-1/2 ounzes and 1/2 ounce for feading and wattearing the said oxe and the trubble the Constable has been att.

Sonora, Aug 20, 1851
John Luney, Constable.

UNITED STATES v. DOWDEN
United States District Court, W. D. Louisiana
139 F. Supp. 781 (1956)

BENJAMIN CORNWELL DAWKINS, Jr., Chief Judge

A tiny tempest in a tinier teapot has brought forth here all the ponderous powers of the Federal Government, mounted on a Clydesdale in hot pursuit of a private citizen who shot a full-grown deer in a National Forest.

Not content with embarrassing defendant by this prosecution, and putting him to the not inconsiderable expense of employing counsel, the Government has compounded calumny by calling the poor dead creature a "fawn". Otherwise fully equipped with all the accouterments of virile masculinity, the deceased, alas, was a "muley". Unlike other young bucks, who could proudly preen their points in the forest glades or the open meadows, this poor fellow was foredoomed to hide his head in shame: by some queer quirk of Nature's caprice, he had no horns, only "nubbins", less than an inch in length.

Instead of giving him a quiet, private interment and a *requiescat in pace* [may he rest in peace], which decency should have dictated as his due, the Government has filed his blushing head in evidence for all to see. Pointing to the lack of points, to prove its point, it now insists that, whatever his status may have been in other climes, in Louisiana our departed friend is officially puerile.

All this - requiring the services of five game agents, two biologists, the opposing attorneys, the United States Marshal and three Deputies, the Clerk, Court Reporter, and a Federal Judge who is a little tired of such matters - stems at least partly from the failure of the Louisiana Legislature to reckon wisely with the exceptional or unusual.

Prosecution proceeds upon 18 U.S.C. §13 which provides:

> "Whoever within or upon any of the places now existing or hereafter reserved or acquired as provided in section 7 of this title, is guilty of any act or omission which, although not made punishable by any enactment of Congress, would be punishable if committed or omitted within the jurisdiction of the State, Territory, Possession, or District in which such place is situated, by the laws thereof in force at the time of such act or omission, shall be guilty of a like offense and subject to a like punishment."

The Louisiana Statutes Annotated - Revised Statutes, Title 56:124(1), stipulate, in pertinent part:

> "No person shall:
> "(1) Take any *fawn (a deer with horns less than three inches long)* or any doe (a female wild deer), at any time; or a wild deer at any time when driven to the high lands by overflow or high water." (Emphasis supplied).

Evidently relying on some uncanny prescience instead of his eyesight for his judgment of the deer, or perhaps having trusted to luck - which was with him - or a proper profile view, defendant slew the animal at some forty paces in the Kisatchie National Forest on December 10, 1953. Soon the law had him in its clutches, but because the authorities obviously were unsure of their ground, formal charges were not filed here until February 24, 1955. Meanwhile, a State Grand Jury, having jurisdiction over the heinous offense, had refused to indict. Trial in this Court has been delayed until now by slightly weightier matters and by several continuances engendered by fruitless efforts of counsel to stipulate the facts.

Finally and inexorably, jury trial having been formally waived and that expense at least avoided, Nimrod's case has been heard and he is found not wanting:

1. The object of our inspection was not less than sixteen months, nor more than eighteen months, old. His teeth told the tale.
2. He was no doe, or pseudo-doe. *All* witnesses agree on this.

3. Except for his unfortunate looks, which he couldn't help, he was "all man". He could have and may have become the father of a fawn.

4. He weighed some 90 to 100 pounds on his cloven hooves, and 57 pounds dressed, or rather, undressed. Deer on Government lands apparently aren't as well nourished, and don't grow as large as elsewhere.

5. Biologically he was a buck, not a fawn, who in strictly female company would have had to bow to no critic. His handicap actually was one only upon having to fight for the affections of the distaff side. What he lacked in weapons, he could have made up for in celerity, dexterity or finesse.

In all *important* respects, therefore, notwithstanding the Louisiana Legislature, which may be forgiven for its ignorance, Buck has been grossly slandered. He never should have been dubbed arbitrarily as a "fawn". He was no baby and was not even a sissy.

It necessarily follows that if Buck is not guilty, neither is Alvin, who is acquitted and discharged *sine die* [without assigning a day for a further hearing.]

AETNA INSURANCE COMPANY v. SACHS
United States District Court, E.D. Missouri
186 F. Supp. 105 (1960)

RANDOLPH H. WEBER, District Judge.

This matter arises upon plaintiff insurance company's Complaint for Declaratory Judgment. It seeks determination of liability under its policy No. PPF-Mo 1-242411, issued to defendant January 29, 1956, for a term of 3 years and which policy contained an attached personal property rider. This rider, with a $25 deductible provision, insured certain listed property against loss or damage. The defendant had made a claim against plaintiff for damage caused to carpeting and after plaintiff's complaint was filed he answered and filed a counterclaim in which he sought to recover $7,500 plus damages for vexatious delay and reasonable attorney's fee. The cause was tried before the Court, without a jury.

The law has always been a hard taskmaster and requires of its advocates a serious approach and stern visaged application. When it comes face to face with life, as it unfolds in the drama of the courtroom, the law sometimes reaches its serious, stern results from facts which have been compiled with humor. So —

while the end results of the law are deadly serious — there is about the lawyer (and even judges, occasionally) a spark of the humor of life — and a need for it. So let it be with this opinion; for, while the end result is most serious to both plaintiff and defendant, what has brought about the necessity for the end result, is most humorous.

Our factual situation obviously had its inception when defendant obtained the insurance policy from plaintiff. If all had proceeded in the normal course of human events from that point on, this suit would never have been brought, for plaintiff insured against and was prepared for the usual expectancies of fire, wind and rain. But, defendant purchased, and plaintiff issued, the rider, known commonly in the trade as a "floater". Now, "floater" provisions are covered by (and in this instance, rightly so) the rules of "maritime" law, for the risks are sometimes unusual.

In any event, the policy in question provided generally for damages and loss to the furnishings and personal property of the defendant for reasons other than fire, wind and rain, to-wit, theft and other fortuitous circumstances. What subsequently transpired after issuance brings into play the "floater" provisions of this policy.

Defendant and wife purchased in October 1957 a "French Poodle", which they appropriately and fascinatingly named "André ". According to defendant, André was properly trained and "broke" and life was pleasant for the defendant and his wife until defendant and wife went on vacation and left André at a kennel for the duration. When they returned their first thoughts were of André and they promptly brought him back to their chateau, blissful in the reunion. But the home-like serenity was soon shattered, for madam soon spied André with his leg hoisted in masculine canine fashion and his purpose has been, and was being, accomplished. Madam did not testify, but defendant said she told him of the occurrence and he promptly surveyed the living room, dining room and hall and found signs of André's misfeasance. His next step was to notify his insurance agent and make claim under the "floater" provisions of this policy.

There was some dispute between the parties as to whether proper notice was given and claim made, but the Court is convinced that defendant gave notice within the terms and provisions of the policy and plaintiff cannot escape liability on that point. Plaintiff did send an adjuster to the premises to survey the effects of where André, the French Poodle, had popped in, piddled and popped out. In fact, he testified that André gave a "command performance" while he was there.

Also, a rug specialist was sent to the premises and he too made a survey. He found spots ranging in diameter from the size of a "dime" to nine inches, and in number from 75 to 80. He testified that one or two could have been repaired, but not that many, for it would have been impossible to match the yarn in the rug and the patches and repairs would have been as obvious as André's tell-tale marks. He also said that the spots would have been readily noticeable from the time they dried and that they extended throughout the living room, dining room, hall, stairway and were on the rug, furniture and drapes; which gives rise to the conclusion that André had the run of the house.

The owner of the kennel, where André spent just two weeks, gave as his opinion that a dog with good habits would not lose them in two weeks; that he properly cared for the dog and had provisions for outside relief facilities for the dogs in his kennels; and, that four to five times a day would be a maximum amount of calls to nature for any dog, including André.

Plaintiff brought this declaratory judgment suit to determine its liability for threatened prosecution by the defendant and contended that this was just too many incidents to be liable for. Defendant answered and denied, claiming surprise in André's change of habits and further contended that there were but four or five incidents and the rest of the spots were pure dribbles, and he counterclaimed for total loss of carpeting and for damages in the amount of $7,500 therefor.

At the rate of four or five calls per day, at best it would have taken André about sixteen days to make all the spots. But, on the theory that each incident is entitled to a dribble or two, it could probably be said, without fear of contradiction, that the spotting represents ten to twelve incidents and probably over a period of a week. In that length of time if the spots had not been seen, they at least should have been recognized by other sensory perception.

A review of the search books to the law reveals no cases in point. Either there never was a poodle as prolific as André, or, before such insurance, people caught them, put their nose in it and threw them outside. Thus, we have a case of first impression. The testimony is that André met his demise, by truck, some few weeks after his prolific, piddlin' propensities were discovered and he, therefore, can never be made aware of his place in history unless he rests in some Valhalla from whence he can eat, sleep and answer his calls to nature, while still permitted to glance back occasionally to review the results, devastation, chaos and the indecision caused by his handiwork.

The unprecedented problem requires some decision, for the law, right or wrong, must conclude litigation. I would conclude this episode in the following manner:

For one or two occasions of André's imprudence we might expect the plaintiff to be liable, even though it is stretching the credulity of any sage of the law to put permission and right upon liability where a person gives a canine pet the right to perambulate and pounce unrestrained throughout the house. Such privileges, even to a poodle, seem more the part of valor than of wisdom, especially where the play pen is a $7,500 rug and expensive furniture and drapes.

The law has always allowed each dog its first bite, for then the owner is put on notice of its dangerous tendencies. I would even go one or two better in incidents such as this and would have allowed recovery for two or three incidents. This would give the insured some opportunity, through sight or smell, to discover the occurrence, prevent its repetition and make claim for that which seems a fortuitous circumstance or event. But, to allow for such prolific indiscretions, ad infinitum, is beyond credulity and borders onto wanton recklessness and disregard for which a person should not be rewarded.

While André might not be expected to know the terms and conditions of plaintiff's policy, it seems most fantastic that defendant should be able to contend that André's indiscretion was fortuitous. Judge Hand, in Mellon v. Federal Ins. Co., [citation omitted] said "* * *, even in an 'all risk' policy, there must be a fortuitous event — a casualty — to give rise to any liability for insurance."

In the law, "fortuitous" means "by chance" and "by accident". It seems to me that it is just "by accident" that André didn't do what he did, much before the alleged occurrence, and, if "by chance" he didn't, it was just too much, and too often, to require plaintiff to pay for it.

One cannot stand by and see damage being done, allow it to be done and then collect for the total loss. In other words, one cannot be present and see a fire when it first originates and at a time when something could be done to extinguish it, then go off and allow the damage to be done and attempt to collect for the total damage. Such conduct constitutes culpable negligence and precludes a recovery. Fleisch v. Insurance Co. of North America, [citation omitted].

An insurer is not liable for reckless and inexcusable negligence. Vol. 5, Appelman Insurance Law and Practice, § 3114; Vol. 6, Couch Cyclopedia of Insurance Law, § 1492. Neither is an insurer liable for loses resulting from inherent vice, defect, or infirmity in the subject matter insured. Chute v. North River Ins. Co., [citation omitted]. Further, defendant had an obligation under Paragraph 20 of the policy in question to safeguard the property insured thereunder. Under the terms of the policy defendant cannot recover where he discovered, or should have discovered, the damage long before it reached its final extent, in time thereafter to have safeguarded the property and have kept the damage to a minimum. See Yellin, et al. v. National Surety Co.,[citation omitted].

In the case at bar, defendant allowed and permitted the damage to become so extensive that he is now claiming a total loss, whereas, plaintiff, if liable at all, should have been exposed only to a minimal loss.

I would say that defendant, because of such gross negligence and indiscretion in permitting André to roam the house at will, hoisting his leg at random, probably yipping and yiping in his canine Utopia, should not be allowed to recover. Certainly, a dog can be controlled by his master, and while a master cannot expect perfection from a dog, even a poodle, he should ever be aware to keep him from expensive parts of the house where he might do damage with either end. Further, defendant here should not be allowed to collect for a total loss which he himself could have kept at a minimum by the exercise of a little discretion, observance or care.

So, in the Eastern District of Missouri, while we love our dogs, let it be the law that we don't collect for so many puddles made by poodles, even under the "floater" provisions of a policy with "maritime" law as precedent. It is this Court's conclusion that judgment should be entered declaring the plaintiff is not liable under the terms and provisions of its policy of insurance for the damage caused to the carpeting in question under the circumstances proven and existing in this case. Further, that defendant should not be allowed to recover upon his counterclaim against the plaintiff.

In other words, I am saying to the defendant, "You cannot recover"; to the plaintiff, "You may continue your policy in peace"; and to the beloved little French poodle, the proximate cause of this litigation and discourse, I say, "*Paix a toi aussi, André* [Peace to you too, André.]"

This Memorandum Opinion shall be filed as the findings of fact and conclusions of the Court herein and judgment will be entered in accordance herewith.

STATE OF KANSAS v. JACKSON
Court of Appeals of Kansas
5 Kan. App.2d 170; 613 P.2d 398 (1980)

J. RICHARD FOTH, Chief Judge.

The issue in this case is whether an animal constitutes "traffic" subject to police regulation. If so, the owner of the animal in this case was guilty of refusing to comply with the lawful order of an officer directing traffic, in violation of K.S.A. 8-1503, and was properly fined $25.00. If an animal is *not* traffic, and the statute deals only with vehicular traffic, then the defendant owner is not guilty and must prevail in his appeal.

The animal involved here was named Frieda. Frieda's mother apparently had an impeccable equine pedigree -- indeed, the events of the case suggest origins in the hunt country of Maryland or Virginia, with strains of hunter, Morgan, or perhaps saddle-bred in her background. Unfortunately, like many young ladies of breeding she made a love match far below her station. Her mate may have had charm, and clearly had animal magnetism, but he was also indisputably a jackass. Frieda, the product of this unhappy union, was a mule.

She was no ordinary mule, however. Although genealogy and geography had conspired together to deprive her of her rightful heritage, Frieda could not be content with a mule's customary plodding fate shackled to a plow or wagon, with no hope of pleasure in youth or even progeny to comfort her in old age. Encouraged by her owner and by a coonhound named Buck - reportedly valued at $1500 - Frieda took up that nocturnal ritual known as coon-hunting. She was an apt pupil. From her father she had inherited a surefootedness which proved advantageous on rough and rocky ground. From her mother she had acquired talents which, with a little practice, enabled her to clear a four-foot fence with ease. It was this latter ability that precipitated the case at bar.

It was in April of 1979, while returning from one of her favorite evening outings, that Frieda had her present brush with the law. It was almost midnight and Frieda, tired from the chase, was riding in the back of her owner's pickup, swaying gently between the stock racks and looking forward to spending the rest of the night peacefully in her pasture on the banks of the Verdigris River. Buck was in the cab with their mutual owner, the defendant. They had proceeded up the River Road to a point less than half a mile from Frieda's pasture when they encountered a police barricade and Deputy Lee Coltharp of the Montgomery County sheriff's office.

Coltharp advised defendant that that portion of the River Road was restricted and no unauthorized traffic could go through. The sheriff's office was dragging the river for a reported drowning victim, and the area contained a command center in a large tent, portable generators and flood lights, and numerous official vehicles. Although he had been allowed through some six hours earlier when he had picked Frieda up, this time the defendant was ordered to turn around and go back. He protested that doing so would mean eight or ten miles of driving to reach the nearby pasture, but Coltharp was adamant; it was "Sheriff's orders."

Defendant pulled his truck just past the barricade and off the road as if to turn around. Instead, he parked, got out, and signaled to Frieda. Obediently, Frieda jumped out of the truck. Before Coltharp could react, defendant mounted and rode off into the night, up the River Road, through the restricted area, to the pasture. There Frieda made her last jump of the night, over the fence and into the familiar safety of her home grounds.

Defendant returned down the River road afoot, again through the restricted area, to his truck and the waiting Buck. Also waiting was Deputy Coltharp, citation in hand. The citation was later replaced by a complaint, charging a violation of K.S.A. 8-1503:

> "No person shall willfully fail or refuse to comply
> with any lawful order or direction of any police
> officer or fireman invested by law with authority
> to direct, control or regulate traffic."

Defendant was convicted after trial to the court, and appeals contending that the statute is directed only at vehicular traffic, and not at jumping mules and pedestrians. The contention must fail.

The statute under which the charge was made is part of the uniform act to regulate traffic on the highways, enacted as Laws 1974, ch.33. Definitions of the terms used in that act are now found in Article 14 of Chapter 8 of the statutes, and include K.S.A. 8-1477;

> "'Traffic' means pedestrians, ridden or herded
> animals, vehicles and other conveyances either
> singly or together while using any highway for
> purposes of travel."

Thus both Frieda when ridden up the highway and defendant when walking back down the highway were "traffic" subject to police traffic control. There being no contention that the police order forbidding access to the River Road was not "lawful," defendant's violation of the order contravened the statute.

Trial counsel for the defendant urged to the trial court that the incident should be regarded as an essentially humorous affair, not deserving of criminal sanction. The argument is repeated in the brief on appeal. The trial court rebuffed that suggestion, and so do we. The untrammeled passage of civilians through an area marked off for police investigation has a potential for mischief which is obvious. Although all participants except Frieda may have exhibited a certain amount of stubbornness the law did not require Deputy Coltharp to make an exception for the defendant and Frieda.

Affirmed.

CALLEJA v. WILEY
District Court of Appeals of Florida, Second District
290 So. 2d 123 (1974)

ROBERT T. MANN, Chief Judge.

Tony, (formerly Toni) is a cat, and the focal point of this dogfight between three utterly human beings. To explain why a cat's tale is pending in the Court of Appeal, we must begin at the beginning.

Mrs. Calleja brought Tony to Dr. Wiley to be spayed. As she put it, "We wanted to make sure we didn't have any baby kittens around the house." Dr. Wiley undertook the operation, but after making the supposedly necessary incision found no female organs. Assuming that, without inquiring whether, the Callejas' concern about the feline population explosion extended to the neighbors' houses, he castrated Tony. The operation cost $15, which was paid.

A few days later, Tony developed a urinary blockage. Dr Wiley performed more surgery, and charged $20, which Mrs Calleja wasn't happy about, but it would have cost $4 more to leave Tony overnight and let her husband handle it, so she gave a check for $20 on the account of Calleja Construction. When he learned what had happened, Mr. Calleja thought he had been shabbily dealt with, and stopped payment. He wrote letters to Dr. Wiley and to the South West Florida Veterinary Medical Association. The Association did not attribute the urinary obstruction to the surgery, and dismissed the mistake as to the cat's gender as something "most all practitioners have done." Dr. Wiley's attribution of the dispute to a failure of communication in a letter suggesting further discussions was followed by a statement that "The check will be processed in accordance with Florida law after a reasonable wait for your reply, approximately one week."

Dr. Wiley went to the Court House and signed an affidavit charging Sandra Calleja with uttering a worthless check "with intent to injure and defraud." Her complaint for malicious prosecution which followed the dismissal of the charge alleges that she was "arrested, imprisoned, booked, mugged (sic) and fingerprinted."

The trial judge granted Dr. Wiley a summary judgment, and Mrs. Calleja appeals. We reverse.

Reversed and remanded.

WILEY v. SLATER
New York Supreme Court, Appellate Division
22 Barb. 506 (1856)

WILLIAM F. ALLEN, J.

[An action was brought in the justice court of Oneida County, New York, to recover damages for alleged injuries to the plaintiff's dog inflicted by the defendant's dog in a fight, as a result of which the plaintiff's dog died. The justice court rendered a judgment in favor of the plaintiff for $25 damages and $5 costs, and the county court affirmed the judgment. The defendant then appealed.]

This is the first time I have been called upon to administer the law in the case of a pure dog fight, or a fight in which the dogs, instead of the owners, were the principal actors. I have had occasion to preside upon the trial of actions for assaults and batteries originating in affrays in which the masters of dogs have borne a conspicuous part, and acquitted themselves in a manner which might well have aroused the envy of their canine dependents. The branch of the law, therefore, applicable to direct conflicts and collisions between dog and dog is entirely new to me, and this case opens up to me an entire new field of investigation.

I am constrained to admit total ignorance of the *code duello* [dueling code] among dogs, or what constitutes a just cause of offense and justifies a resort to the *ultima ratio regum* [last resort of kings], a resort to arms, or rather to teeth, for redress; whether jealousy is a just cause of war, or what different degrees and kinds of insult or slight, or what violation of the rules of etiquette entitle the injured or offended beast to insist upon prompt and appropriate satisfaction, I know not, and am glad to know that no nice question upon the conduct of the conflict on the part of the principal actors arises in this case.

It is not claimed, upon either side, that the struggle was not in all respects dog-like and fair. Indeed I was not before aware that it was claimed that any law, human or divine, moral or ceremonial, common or statute, undertook to regulate and control these matters, but supposed that this was one of the few privileges which this class of animals still retained in the domesticated institution, to settle and avenge, in their own way, all individual wrongs and insults, without regard to what Blackstone or any other jurist might write, speak or think of the "rights

36

of persons" or "rights of things." I have been a firm believer with the poet in the instructive if not semi-divine right of dogs to fight; and with him would say

> *"Let the dogs delight to bark and bite,*
> *For God hath made them so;*
> *Let bears and lions growl and fight,*
> *For 'tis their nature to."*

It is possible that had the owners of both dogs been present the belligerents would have been charged and the familiar questions growing out of *son assault* [his own assault] and *molliter manus imposuit* [he gently laid hands upon] would have been presented, but no such questions are made here.

The defense is not rested upon the principle of self-defense, or defense of the possession of the master of the victorious dog. Had this defense been interposed, a serious and novel question would have arisen, as to the liability of the offending dog for excess of force, and whether he would be held to the same rules which are applied to human beings in like cases offending; whether he would be held strictly to the proof of the necessity and reasonableness of all the force exerted, under the plea that in defense of his carcase or the premises committed to his watch and care, "he did necessarily a little bite, scratch, wound, tear, devour and kill the plaintiff's dog, doing no unnecessary damage to the body or hide of the said dog."

Addressing myself to the question really made in the case then, the first difficulty I meet with is the want of proof of ownership by the defendant of the offending dog. The plaintiff made a *prima facie* case, by proving an apparent possession of the dog, but the appearances were entirely explained by the witness Nowell, who testifies that the dog was not owned by the defendant, nor kept nor harbored by him, but was really a trespasser on the premises, being kept at the shop adjoining. . . .

Whatever may have been the character and habits of the dog, there is no evidence that he was the aggressor, or in the wrong, in this particular fight. The plaintiff's dog may have provoked the quarrel and have caused the fight; and if so, the owner of the victor dog, whoever he may be, cannot be made responsible for the consequences. . . .

There is no evidence that the dog alleged to belong to the defendant was a dangerous animal, or one unfit to be kept. The cases cited, in which dogs have attacked human beings, although trespassers, and the owners have been held liable, are not applicable. It is one thing for a dog to be dangerous to human life, and quite another to be unwilling to have strange dogs upon the master's premises. To attack and drive off dogs thus suffered to go at large, to the annoyance if not to the detriment and danger of the public, would be a virtue, and that is all that can be claimed, upon the evidence, was done in this case. Owners of valuable dogs should take care of them proportioned to their value, and keep them within their own precincts or under their own eye.

It is very proper to invest dogs with some discretion while upon their master's premises, in regard to other dogs, while it is palpably wrong to allow a man to keep a dog, who may or will, under any circumstances, of his own volition, attack a human being. If owners of dogs, whether valuable or not, suffer them to visit others of their species, particularly if they go uninvited, they must be content to have them put up with dogfare, and that their reception and treatment shall be hospitable or inhospitable, according to the nature or the particular mood and temper at the time, of the dog visited. The courtesies and hospitalities of dog life cannot well be regulated by the judicial tribunals of the land. . . .

Evidence is slight that the dog died in consequence of this fight. I should infer, from the evidence, that he continued his annoying visitations until someone who did not own a white dog with black spots on his head, made use of a shot gun or "Sharpe's rifle," or some other substitute, to abate the nuisance. But as this question is left in doubt by the evidence, the judgment of the justice is conclusive as to the cause of death. I can, however, see no just grounds for the judgment. It can only be supported upon the broad ground that when two dogs fight and one is killed, the owner can have satisfaction for his loss from the owner of the victorious dog; and I know of no such rule. The owner of the dead dog would, I think, be very clearly entitled to the skin, although some, less liberal, would be disposed to award it as a trophy to the victor, and this rule would ordinarily be a full equivalent for the loss; and with that unless the evidence differ materially from that in this case he should be content.

The judgment of the county court, and of the justice, reversed.

LUSSAN v. GRAIN DEALERS MUTUAL INSURANCE COMPANY
United States Court of Appeals, Fifth Circuit
280 F.2d 491 (1960)

JOHN R. BROWN, Circuit Judge.

This case presents the question whether an action which a human being would normally take may be considered by a jury to be that which the law's ordinary prudent person would have taken under such circumstances.

What brings this all about was a wasp — or a bee — it really doesn't matter for bees and wasps are both of the order hymenoptera, and while a wasp, unlike the bee, is predacious in habit, both sting human beings, or humans fear they will. The wasp did not intrude upon a pastoral scene or disturb the tranquility of nature's order. What this wasp did — perhaps innocently while wafted by convection or the force of unnatural currents generated by the ceaseless motion of man's nearby machines — was to find itself an unwelcome passenger in an automobile then moving toward, of all places, Elysian Fields — not on the banks of Oceanus, but a major thoroughfare in the City of New Orleans on the Mississippi.

With the wasp was the defendant — owner and driver of the vehicle. Two others were with him in the front seat as his mobile guests. The wasp flew in — or his presence was suddenly discovered. Like thousands of others confronted with the imminent fear of a sting by such air-borne agents, the defendant driver swatted at the wasp. Whether he hit the wasp, no one knows. But momentarily the defendant driver apparently thought this menace had flown his coupe. The wasp, however, was not yet through. One of the passengers suddenly looked down and hollered out "watch out, it's still alive." Instinctively the defendant driver looked down at the floorboard and simultaneously made a sweeping swat at the wasp or where the wasp was thought to be. The wasp with all his capacity for harm scarcely could have thought itself so powerful. For without ever stinging anyone, or perhaps for that matter even being there at all, this anonymous bug brought substantial damage to one of the guests. Unconscious probably that it had set in motion the law's but-for chain reaction of causation, the wasp was the blame in fact. For when the driver by involuntary reflex took the swat, he lurched just enough to pull the steering wheel over to crash the moving car into a vehicle parked at the curb.

The traditional twelve good men performing their function in the jury system by which men drawn from all walks of life pass upon behavior of their fellow men, heard these uncontradicted facts. Instructed by the judge in a clear fashion on the law of due care in a charge to which no exception was taken, the jury in nine minutes returned a verdict for the driver. The plaintiff, appellant here, injured substantially by this combination of natural, human and mechanical forces has a single aim, and hope and necessity: convincing us that the trial court erred in not granting the plaintiff's motions for instructed verdict and j.n.o.v.

His surprise or even disappointment in this adverse verdict, actually returned in favor of a direct action insurer-defendant, is not sufficient to give to this incident the quality essential to a directed verdict. Variously stated, restated, repeated and reiterated, the legal standard to be met is that no reasonable man could infer than the prudent man would have acted this way. Marsh v. Illinois Central R. [citation omitted]. In the determination of this, little instruction comes from prior cases involving a Connecticut bee in Rindge v. Holbrook [citation omitted] or a diversity Eighth Circuit Iowa wasp, Heerman v. Burke, [citation omitted].

Asserting this negative imperative — no reasonable man could hold as the jury did — inescapably puts the reviewing judge, trial or appellate, in the position of a silent witness in behalf of mankind. In assaying the scope of the specific record, we inevitably measure it in terms of the general experience of mankind including our own. Charles Alan Wright, The Doubtful Omniscience of Appellate Courts, 41 Minn.L.Rev. 751 (1957). We draw on what we and what all others constituting that composite reasonable man have come to know. The sources of this knowledge are as variable as are the subjects of inquiry.

In this simple case in the search for the negative limits of the inferences open to the so-called reasonable man, we deal with a situation known and experienced by all — the involuntary reflex responses by which nature protects life from harm or apprehended harm. In a philosophical way it may be that nature has here elevated the instinct of self-preservation to a plane above the duty to refrain from harming others. It is here where man through law and ordered society steps in. But in stepping in, man, through law, has erected as the standard of performance, not what had to be done to avoid damage, but that which prudent human beings would have done or not done.

At times the judgment of the common man — voiced through the jury or other trier of fact — on what the prudent man should have done will be to deny to the individual concerned a legal justification for his perfectly human instinctive response. At other times what is actually usual may be equated with that which is legally prudent.

That is what occurred here. A wasp became the object of apprehended harm. Protective responses were instinctive and natural and swift. True, this diverted driver and his attention from other harm and other duties. But the jury in these circumstances under unchallenged instruction on legal standards concluded that this was normal and prudent human conduct. What better way is there to judge of this?

Affirmed.

LYONS v. STILLS
Supreme Court of Tennessee
97 Tenn. 514; 37 S.W. 280 (1896)

JOHN S. WILKES, J.

This case involves the life and death of a Texas pony. The plaintiff, Lyons, sold the pony to the defendant for $65, and took his note, retaining the title to the pony until she was paid for. Suit was brought on the note before a justice of peace, and he gave judgment for the plaintiff. The circuit judge on appeal reversed the judgment, and the plaintiff has appealed to this court and assigned errors.

It appears that the plaintiff, Lyons, was a trader in Texas ponies, and sold the animal to the defendant, who was a farmer. The defendant was in the act of leading the pony away to carry her home, with an ordinary halter upon her, when the plaintiff suggested that a "slip halter' would suit the temperament and disposition of the animal better. He thereupon furnished the defendant with a slip halter, and had one of his experienced helpers to put it on the pony, and adjust it properly. He then advised the defendant to lead the pony home by the "slip halter," and not to turn her loose, or put her into a stable, but to tie her to a post until she was gentle. Defendant obeyed the instructions, and, following the direction of plaintiff, carried the pony home, and hitched her to a post, gave her some corn and fodder, and left her for the night.

The next morning the defendant came around to see if the pony was making any progress towards getting gentle, and found her very quiet; in fact she was dead. He says that he does not certainly know what caused her death, but thinks it was because "she could not get her breath." This seems quite probable, as the "slip halter" was found to have "slipped" down and become tightened around her nostrils. It does not appear that she had any disease; certainly was full of life the evening before, and showed no signs of any ailment. She was a small pony mare, well formed, with bright eyes, and a remarkably active pair of heels.

The defendant was sued on the note. He defended on the ground that he only took the pony on "probation" for six months, and by the contract had the right, at any time he was dissatisfied, to rescind the trade and deliver up the pony. It does not appear that he made any effort to return the animal. His counsel excuse this on the ground that he was prevented by the "act of God." Defendant, in his proof, however, says he was prevented from making the return by the "act of the pony." We think the formal tender or delivery back of the pony was, under the circumstances, an immaterial matter, not going to the merits of the case. Defendant states that when he saw that the pony had committed suicide he did not care to keep her any longer, and he therefore exercised his option to rescind the trade. His theory, after the pony died, was that she belonged to the vendor, and had never become his property, and hence it was not his loss. He also set up that there was a total failure of consideration.

The circuit judge, trying the case without a jury, took this latter view of the case, and under the evidence, we think he was clearly correct as to the fact of there being a total failure of the consideration. The trial judge was of the opinion this would relieve the defendant from the payment of the note. The evidence offered by the defendant that he took the pony on probation was objected to, and the circuit judge rejected it. We think the trial judge was in error in discarding this testimony. It does not contradict the note, but sets up an independent agreement, made at the same time, that upon a contingency or condition the note was to become void. This was competent as between the parties. . . . We think the weight of the proof was that the defendant was to have the right to rescind the trade at any time within six months, if he became displeased with his bargain; and, having exercised his option, we cannot say that he acted arbitrarily in becoming displeased after the pony had put an end to her further usefulness by means of the device furnished by the plaintiff. The judgment of the court below is affirmed, with costs.

KOPLIN v. QUADE
Supreme Court of Wisconsin
145 Wis. 454; 130 N.W. 511 (1911)

JOHN BARNES, J.

On September 14, 1907, the plaintiff was the owner of a thoroughbred Holstein-Friesian heifer, which was born on January 8, 1906, and had been thereafter duly christened "Martha Pietertje Pauline." The name is neither euphonious nor musical, but there is not much in a name anyway. Notwithstanding any handicap she may have had in the way of a cognomen, Martha Pietertje Pauline was a genuine "highbrow," having a pedigree as long and at least as well authenticated as that of the ordinary scion of effete European nobility who breaks into this land of democracy and equality, and offers his title to the highest bidder at the matrimonial bargain counter. The defendant was the owner of a bull about one year old, lowly born and nameless as far as the record discloses. This plebeian, having aspirations beyond his humble station in life, wandered beyond the confines of his own pastures, and sought the society of the adolescent and unsophisticated Martha, contrary to the provisions of section 1482, St. 1898, as amended by chapter 14, Laws 1903. As a result of this somewhat morganatic mesalliance, a calf was born July 5, 1908. Plaintiff brought this action to recover resulting damages and secured a verdict for $75, upon which judgment was entered, and defendant appeals therefrom.

The case was apparently tried without any clear conception of what the appropriate rule of damages applicable to such an unusual situation was. The charge of the court on the subject was not illuminating or helpful to the jury, but no exception was taken thereto. The defendant requested an instruction which was not accurate, and no exception was taken to the refusal of the court to give it. At the close of the testimony, the defendant moved for a directed verdict and excepted to the ruling of the court denying such motion. The correctness of this ruling can be reviewed without any motion for a new trial having been made.

If on the evidence before the court the plaintiff was entitled to recover any amount, then the court properly denied the motion. The plaintiff offered testimony tending to show that he kept and intended to keep Martha for breeding purposes and for the milk which she might produce, and not for sale. It also showed that plaintiff was the owner of a blue blooded bull of the Holstein-Friesian variety, to which he intended to breed Martha some three months later than the date of the unfortunate occurrence related. There was evidence tending to show that a thoroughbred calf would be worth all the way from $22.50 to $150, depending on its sex, markings, and other characteristics. Its sinister birth disqualified the hybrid calf born from becoming a candidate for pink ribbons at county fairs, and it was sold to a Chicago butcher for $7, and was probably served up as pressed chicken to the epicures in some Chicago boarding house.

Numerous witnesses testified that a thoroughbred calf had a much greater value than a grade calf, and this evidence is not contradicted in any way. True, the witnesses vary widely as to the amount of such difference in value, but the matter of arriving at an exact amount of compensation in most tort actions is involved in uncertainty and difficulty, and it was for the jury to say on all the testimony what sum would reasonably compensate the plaintiff. This element of damages was direct and proximate and the objection to it on the ground of remoteness is not well taken.

The true measure of damages was the difference between the value of the heifer to the plaintiff before and after the trespass, in view of the uses which the plaintiff intended to make of the heifer. Such a rule furnishes compensation, and this is what the law aims at. One of [the] elements [of damage] would be the difference between the value of the calf dropped and the value of a calf from the heifer if bred to a registered Holstein-Friesian bull. It is apparent that there was some competent evidence before the jury from which it might properly return a verdict for substantial damages, and that, therefore, the motion to direct a verdict was properly denied. Indeed, this result might well follow if the plaintiff were entitled to recover nominal damages only.

Judgment affirmed.

UNITED STATES v. BYRNES
United States Court of Appeals, Second Circuit
644 F.2d 107 (1981)

WILLIAM HUGHES MULLIGAN, Circuit Judge:

Who knows what evil lurks in the hearts of men? Although the public is generally aware of the sordid trafficking of drugs and aliens across our borders, this litigation alerts us to a nefarious practice hitherto unsuspected even by this rather calloused bench -- rare bird smuggling. The appeal is therefore accurately designated as *rara avis* [a rare bird]. While Canadian geese have been regularly crossing, exiting, reentering and departing our borders with impunity, and apparently without documentation, to enjoy more salubrious climes, those unwilling or unable to make the flight either because of inadequate wing spans, lack of fuel or fear of buckshot, have become prey to unscrupulous traffickers who put them in crates and ship them to American ports of entry with fraudulent documentation in violation of a host of federal statutes. [1] The traffic has been egregious enough to warrant the empaneling of a special grand jury in 1979 in the Northern District of New York to conduct a broad investigation of these activities. Even the services of the Royal Canadian Mounted Police were mustered to aid the inquiry.

A principal target of the grand jury investigation was Kenneth Clare, a Canadian, who was believed to be in the business of shipping exotic birds into the United States, misrepresenting on import documents the value, the species and even the number of birds in the containers, thus avoiding the payment of United States Customs duties, inspection and quarantine. When one learns that an adult swan stands some four and a half feet tall and is normally ill tempered, the reluctance of a border inspector to make a head count is understandable. In this case Clare even had the audacity to pass off as Canadians, birds whose country of origin was England! Another target of the investigation was a California attorney, Edward R. Fitzsimmons, whose hobbies included the collection of horses, llamas

---

[1] E.g., 18 U.S.C §§43 (transportation of wildlife taken in violation of state, national or foreign laws), 542 (entry of goods by false statements), 1001 (false or fraudulent statements to federal agencies); Food & Drugs Act, 21 U.S.C. §111 (prevention of contagious diseases); Endangered Species Act, 16 U.S.C. §1538 (regulating import and export of endangered species).

and exotic birds. It was believed that Fitzsimmons and Clare worked together hand or claw in glove.

In February 1975, Fitzsimmons allegedly purchased from Clare four trumpeter swans and two red-breasted geese.[2] The crated birds were brought from Canada through Massena, New York, a Port of Entry in the Northern District of New York. Their entry papers were spurious. The trumpeter swans (cygnus buccinator) were described in the shipping documents as mute swans which are a less valuable variety. The birds were then airlifted to San Francisco by the Flying Tiger where they were picked up by Janet Leslie Cooper Byrnes, the appellant, who was employed as a secretary by Fitzsimmons. Byrnes was a *quondam* [one-time, former] zoologist at the London Zoo and knowledgeable about ornithological matters.

When called before the grand jury on February 7, 1979, Byrnes testified that she did pick up the birds in 1975 but further stated that after driving away from the airport for ten or fifteen minutes, when she heard no noises from the crates.[3] She stated that she stopped at a gas station, pried open the crates and discovered that all the birds were dead and in fact so stiff that she assumed they had been dead for some time. (D.O.A.). She promptly drove to a municipal dump where the birds were interred in unconsecrated ground.

By reason of this testimony the appellant was indicted on May 8, 1980 on four counts of false declarations before a grand jury in violation of 18 U.S.C. §1623.[4] After a three day jury trial before Hon. Neal McCurn, Northern District of New York, Byrnes was convicted on two counts on July 18, 1980.[5] She was sentenced to be committed to the custody of the Attorney General for a period of six months and fined $5,000 on each count. Execution of the prison sentence was suspended and the defendant was placed on probation for a period of one year on each count, the sentences to be served concurrently. This appeal followed.

---

[2] No birds have been indicted and there is no indication in the record that they were even aware of, much less participated in, the criminal activity unearthed by the grand jury. They were at least as innocent as the horses whose jockeys were bribed to discourage their best efforts at Pocono Downs.

[3] The trumpeter swan makes a noise described by a trial witness, Cherie Perie, as "weird." The appellant, on the other hand, in her grand jury testimony, stated that the male trumpeter during courtship "struts around with his neck and head held high and makes this marvelous little trumpeting sound." Transcript at 29. De gustibus. The mute apparently courts in silence.

[4] Title 18 U.S.C. §1623(a) provides in pertinent part:
"Whoever under oath . . . in any proceeding before a grand jury of the United States knowingly makes any false material declaration
. . . shall be fined not more than $10,000 or imprisoned not more than five years, or both."

[5] Two of the four counts of the indictment, including appellant's testimony that the swans were mute rather than trumpeter (Count II) and that Fitzsimmons had no business relationship with Clare (Count IV) were dismissed by the trial court prior to submission to the jury. The remaining counts related to appellant's testimony that the swans and geese were dead (Count I) and that she disposed of the allegedly dead birds at a landfill (Count IV).

CHAPTER I: CANINE, EQUINE & FELINE

I.

Appellant does not challenge the sufficiency of the Government's proof to support the conviction. Ida Meffert, who had emigrated from Germany and had obvious difficulty with the English language, was one of four government witnesses brought from California to Syracuse, New York for this momentous trial. She testified that she was a collector of Australian parrots in Hayward, California and described these parrots as "citizens." The court interjected: "A citizen bird?" The witness answered: "Yeah, the whole birds is citizen." [6] More pointedly Mrs. Meffert testified that in February 1975 the appellant delivered four live swans and two live red breasted geese to her pursuant to an arrangement with Fitzsimmons whereby Mrs. Meffert and her husband provided room and board for some of his exotic wildlife. Mrs. Meffert was subjected to a grueling cross examination by counsel for appellant that was apparently aimed at her ornithological qualifications. Mrs. Meffert testified that after a few days one of the swans died and she preserved his leg in her freezer to establish his demise. [7]

> "Q. Are sparrows birds?
> A. I think so, sure.
> Q. Is a crow a bird?
> A. I think so.
> Q. Is a parrot a bird?
> A. Not to me.
> Q. How about a seagull, is that a bird?
> A. To me it is a seagull. I don't know what it is to other people.
> Q. Is it a bird to you as well or not?
> A. To me it is a seagull. I don't know any other definition for it.
> Q. Is an eagle a bird?
> A. I guess so.

---

[6] There are various record references to "citizen" birds which was confusing since those at issue here were aliens. We are persuaded, however, that the word spoken was "psittacines" (parrots) and not citizens. The confusion of the scrivener is understandable.

[7] The difficulty of establishing that swans and geese were birds, a proposition not accepted by Mrs. Meffert, was obviated by a Government stipulation that both were birds.

> *"Let the long contention cease!*
> *Geese are swans, and swans are geese."*
> The Scholar Gypsy, The Last Word,
> Stanza 2, Matthew Arnold.

The trial judge, perhaps to relieve the tension, observed that while he had enjoyed goose dinners he had never consumed swan - some indication of the limited cuisine available in the Northern District. The swan leg was not offered in evidence as an exhibit.

> Q. Is a swallow a bird?
> A. I don't know what a swallow is, sir.
> Q. Is a duck a bird?
> A. Not to me, it is a duck.
> Q. But not a bird.
> A. No, to other people maybe.
> Q. Where is your husband now, ma'am?
> A. Up in the room."

Transcript at 400-01.

"Man comes and tills the field and lies beneath,
And after many a summer dies the swan."
Tithonus, Alfred Lord Tennyson.

The principal argument on appeal is not that Byrnes had truthfully testified to the grand jury, but rather that her testimony was not "material" within 18 U.S.C. §1623(a). That statute is violated only when the false statements bear upon issues under investigation by the grand jury. Appellant argues that her testimony that the birds were dead upon arrival and buried rather than delivered to Mrs. Meffert, was totally irrelevant to the grand jury investigation. The District Court rejected this contention and we affirm its finding of materiality. The leading case in this circuit addressing the question of materiality of false declarations before a grand jury is *United States v. Berardi,* [citation omitted]... Both parties rely upon Berardi as did the District Court in finding the materiality of Byrnes' declarations. All of the elements of materiality set forth in Berardi are met here.

As we explained in that case, the Government has the burden of establishing that the perjury was committed in response to a question within the purview of the grand jury investigation. That nexus need not be established beyond a reasonable doubt [citation omitted]. It is normally satisfied by introducing into evidence the grand jury minutes or the testimony of the foreperson of that jury. This enables the district court to determine the scope of the grand jury investigation and the relationship of the questions which elicited the perjury... Here Judge McCurn had the benefit of the minutes as well as the testimony of the deputy foreperson and the United States Attorney in charge of the investigation.

Materiality is broadly construed:

> "Materiality is thus demonstrated if the question
> posed is such that a truthful answer could help the
> inquiry, or a false response hinder it, and these
> effects are weighed in terms of potentiality
> rather than probability... "

... Measured by this broad test it is clear that the appellant's perjury here was material. The grand jury investigation was prolonged and broad in scope. Appellant's argument that it was simply limited to the importation of wildlife and had nothing to do with matters subsequent to importation is not accurate.

Fitzsimmons was a target of the investigation and appellant's testimony that he had not received the birds shielded Fitzsimmons from the conspiracy charge relating to his role in the transactions in which he and Clare were allegedly involved. Moreover, had the truth been told Ida Meffert would have been identified months before her role in the matter was actually discovered. Appellant's false testimony clearly impeded and hindered the investigative efforts of the grand jury. Her perjury was therefore material within the meaning of the statute. . .

Finally, appellant urges that the trial judge committed reversible error by not taking judicial notice of Migratory Bird Permit Regulations, 50 C.F.R. Part 21 (1979) which require the registration of trumpeter swans and the obtaining of permits for their possession and disposal. Mrs. Meffert admitted that she had never registered the swans but also stated that she was unaware that any such regulations were in existence. Appellant argues that since they were not registered Mrs. Meffert never possessed the trumpeter swans. The argument is totally unpersuasive.

Count II, charging appellant with false testimony that the swans were mute rather than trumpeters, was withdrawn from the jury. Thus, the relevance of the registration was minimal. Furthermore, Mrs. Meffert admitted that the swans weren't registered. Therefore, the point was made and her conceded ignorance of the Migratory Bird regulations hardly establishes that she didn't possess the swans which she didn't consider birds in any event. [8] The existence of the regulations was irrelevant and whether or not Mrs. Meffert violated them would only confuse the issue before the jury. The trial judge has broad discretion in these matters and he committed no abuse of discretion in refusing to take judicial notice of the regulations or submitting them to the jury. . .

The judgment of conviction is affirmed, justice has triumphed and this is my swan song.

---

[8] For a liberal construction of the term "birds," by a Canadian court see *Regina v. Ojibway*, 8 Criminal Law Quarterly 137 (1965-66) (Op. Blue, J.), holding that an Indian who shot a pony which had broken a leg and was saddled with a downy pillow had violated the Small Birds Act which defined a "bird" as "a two legged animal covered with feathers." The court reasoned that the statutory definition:

> "does not imply that only two-legged animals qualify, for the legislative intent is to make two legs merely the minimum requirement. . . Counsel submits that having regard to the purpose of the statute only small animals 'naturally covered' with feathers could have been contemplated. However, had this been the intention of the legislature, I am certain that the phrase 'naturally covered' would have been expressly inserted just as 'Long' was inserted in the Longshoreman's Act.

> "Therefore, a horse with feathers on its back must be deemed for the purpose of this Act to be a bird, *a fortiori*, a pony with feathers on its back is a small bird." Id. at 139.

AKERS v. SELLERS
Appellate Court of Indiana, en banc
114 Ind. App. 660; 54 N.E. 2d 779 (1944)

HARRY L. CRUMPACKER, Chief Judge.

This is a controversy over the ownership and possession of a Boston bull terrier dog upon which the appellant, while declining to measure its true value to him in mere money, has placed an arbitrary value of $25. Were we to judge the importance of these proceedings by such a fictitious standard of value we would be inclined to resent this appeal as a trespass on the court's time and an imposition on our patience, of which quality we trust we are possessed to a reasonable degree. But we have in mind Senator Vest's immortal eulogy on the noble instincts of a dog so we approach the question involved without any feeling of injured dignity but with a full realization that no man can be censured for the prosecution of his rights to the full limit of the law when such rights involve the comfort derived from the companionship of man's best friend.

The parties to this litigation were at one time husband and wife. We conclude from the record that their union was not blessed with children, but some seven years ago there came into their lives the Boston terrier which is the subject of this controversy. He was the gift of a doctor of veterinary medicine with whom he been left to board by a former owner who had never sought his return. What his age may have been at the time is not disclosed, but, assuming that he was then a pup, it is apparent that he is now about to enter the mellow years when those qualities most to be desired in a dog are at their peak, and the natural springtime inclination to roam, common to all males of whatever specie, is on the wane.

Despite the tie and cementing influence of this little Boston terrier, the marriage of the parties proved not to have been made in heaven and the appellee sought and obtained a divorce. The court wherein such divorce was decreed, feeling perhaps that the care and custody of the dog of the parties was not an inescapable appendage to their domestic controversy, failed to make any order in reference to the same and the wife, being left in the possession of the domicile on separation from her husband, just naturally came into the custody of the dog.

Whether the learned judge who heard the appellant's petition for divorce would have made such disposition of the dog had the matter been called to his attention, we are, of course, unable to say. Whether the interests and desires of the dog, in such a situation, should be the polar star pointing the way to a just and wise decision, or whether the matter should be determined on the brutal and unfeeling basis of legal title, is a problem concerning which we express no opinion. We recognize, however, the tragedy of his consignment to the appellee if, in fact, his love, affection and loyalty are for the appellant.

However that may be, the appellant, insisting that legal title and the dog's best interests are in accord and both rest in him, brought this suit in replevin and upon the trial thereof was unsuccessful. The record presents that no question for our consideration except that the evidence is insufficient to sustain the decision of the court and that the same is contrary to law. We find evidence tending to prove that the dog in controversy was first given to the appellant and by him, in turn, given to the appellee. This is sufficient to support the decision, and as there is no reason shown why possession should not accompany ownership such decision is not contrary to law.

We feel that had the trial court seen fit to apply Solomon's test and offered to cut the dog in halves, awarding one part to each claimant, the decision might have been for the appellant, as the appellee has failed to show sufficient interest in the controversy, or its subject, to file an answer below or favor us with a brief on appeal. The fact, however, that we may possibly have more confidence in the wisdom of Solomon than we do in that of the trial court hardly justifies us in disturbing its judgement.

Affirmed.

JACKSON COCA COLA BOTTLING CO. v. CHAPMAN
Supreme Court of Mississippi
106 Miss. 864; 64 So. 791 (1914)

RICHARD F. REED, J.

A "sma'mousie" caused the trouble in this case. The "wee, sleekit, cow'rin,' tim'rous beastie" drowned in a bottle of coca cola. How it happened is not told.

There is evidence for appellant that its system for cleansing and filling bottles is complete, and that there is watchfulness to prevent the introduction of foreign substances. Nevertheless the little creature was in the bottle. It had been there long enough to be swollen and undergoing decomposition when the bottle was purchased from the grocer and opened by appellee. Its presence in the bottle was not discovered until appellee had taken several swallows. An odor led to the discovery. Further events need not be detailed. Appellee says he got sick. Suffice it to say he did not get joy from the anticipated refreshing drink. He was in the frame of mind to approve the poet's[1] words:

> *"The best-laid schemes o' mice an' men*
> *Gang aft aglay*
> *An' lea'e us nought but grief an' pain,*
> *For promis'd joy!"*

---

[1] [Ed. Note: The poem is "To a Mouse, on Turning Her Up in Her Nest, with the Plough, November 1785" by Robert Burns.]

The record discloses sufficient evidence to sustain the jury's verdict for appellee. There is no error for reversal. Appellant company bottled the coca-cola for the retail trade to be sold to the general public as a beverage refreshing and harmless. The bottle in this case as purchased by the grocer from appellant.

We find the law pertinent to this case clearly stated . . . in the case of *Watson v. Augusta Brewing Company*, [citation omitted] . . . , as follows: "When a manufacturer makes, bottles and sells to the retail trade, to be again sold to the general public, a beverage represented to be refreshing and harmless, he is under a legal duty to see to it that in the process of bottling no foreign substance shall be mixed with the beverage, which, if taken into the human stomach will be injurious." . . .

Affirmed.

COAKER v. WILCOCKS
Supreme Court of Judicature, King's Bench Division
[1911] 1 K.B. 649

SIR CHARLES JOHN DARLING, J.

[Early in the year 1904 one Lamb was the occupier of the defendant Wilcocks' newtake. Lamb kept a number of Scotch sheep. At the time of his occupation the fences of the newtake were dilapidated. On the death of Lamb his widow gave up the farm and sold the sheep, including some of the Scotch sheep, to the plaintiff, Coaker, who turned them onto the enclosed Forest of Dartmoor. Forty-two of these Scotch sheep jumped the fences enclosing the defendant's newtake, whereupon defendant promptly seized and impounded them for trespassing. Plaintiff sued to recover damages for this seizure, alleging that the sheep had escaped from the moor onto defendants newtake as a result of the defective condition of defendant's fences. The court found for the defendant and plaintiff appealed.]

In this case it appears that the defendant was the occupier of enclosed land which was originally part of the Forest of Dartmoor; when this land was enclosed, other land unenclosed was left outside its area. It has long been the custom to turn sheep out upon this unenclosed land.

Now ordinarily sheep are not commonable animals on forest lands; but by prescription they may become so; and on these lands sheep are and long have been commonable. For the purposes of this case the defendant is to be taken as bound to fence his land against commonable animals. . . The plaintiff had the right to put sheep upon the unenclosed land, and the defendant was bound to fence his enclosed land against sheep; but that does not mean every kind and description of sheep. No doubt a sheep may be commonable although it comes from Scotland. . .

. . . The evidence in the present case proves that these Scotch sheep are of a peculiarly wandering and saltative disposition, straying and jumping in a way which distinguishes them from sheep which have hitherto been turned on to the unenclosed land, wandering as other sheep do not and jumping as other sheep cannot. In my judgment the defendant was not bound to fence his land from sheep of this description; it was the duty of the plaintiff, if he chose to own such sheep, to keep them from trespassing on the defendant's land; and as the plaintiff failed to do this, the defendant was entitled to distrain them damage feasant.

. . . For these reasons I think that this appeal should be dismissed..

ROOS v. LOESER
California Court of Appeal, First Appellate District
41 Cal. App. 782 (1919)

FRANK H. KERRIGAN, J.

This is an action for damages alleged to have been sustained by plaintiff by reason of the killing of her dog, of the variety known as Pomeranian, by an Airedale belonging to the defendants. A jury trial was had, and judgment went for the plaintiff in the sum of five hundred dollars. Defendant made a motion for a new trial, which was denied, and he now appeals from the judgment.

The complaint alleges that on the sixteenth of May, 1917, the plaintiff was the owner of a Pomeranian dog of the value of one thousand dollars; that the defendant was the owner of an Airedale, of vicious disposition and dangerous character, which on said date and for a long time prior thereto was evilly disposed toward other dogs and was accustomed to attack them without provocation, all of which matters were well known to the defendant; that nevertheless, the defendant carelessly and negligently permitted said Airedale to go upon the public streets of San Francisco unleashed and free from restraint, and that on the day mentioned, without provocation and while the plaintiff's dog was proceeding peaceably along the public street, said Airedale attacked it from behind, the attack resulting in breaking the neck of the Pomeranian, from which its death immediately ensued.

From the evidence it appears that on said day the Pomeranian, attended by two maids, was pursuing the even tenor of its way upon the street, "tarrying" now and then and occupied with matters entirely its own, when the Airedale, an arrogant bully, domineering and dogmatic, being beyond the reach of the sound of his master's voice and having evaded the vigilance of his keeper (for the maids and the man were vigilant), dashed upon the scene, and with destruction in his heart and mayhem in his teeth pounced upon the Pomeranian with the result already regretfully recorded; the plaintiff's dog had had its day. It crossed to that shore from which none, not even a good dog, ever returns.

Leaving this painful subject and turning to the considerations elaborately discussed in the briefs of able counsel, we remark that there was a time in history of the law when, as is said in one of the early cases, "dog law" was as hard to define as "dog Latin." As Blackstone puts it, dogs were the subject of property to a very limited and qualified degree, they had no intrinsic value, and were regarded as being kept only through the whim or caprice of their owner. They were not the subject of larceny. (2 Blackstone's Commentaries, 393.) But that day has passed, and dogs now have a well-established status before the law. Considerable sums of money are invested in dogs, and they are the subject of extensive trade. Aside from their pecuniary value their worth is recognized by writers and jurists. Cuvier has asserted that the dog was perhaps necessary for the establishment of civil society, and that a little reflection will convince one that barbarous nations owe much of their subsequently acquired civilization to the dog. From the building of the pyramids to the present day, from the frozen poles to the torrid zone, wherever man has wandered there has been his dog.

In the case of State v. Harriman, . . . he is eulogized in the following language: "He is the friend and companion of his master, accompanying him on his walks; his servant aiding him in his hunting; the playmate of his children, an inmate of his home, protecting it against all assailants."

In his well-known tribute to the dog, United States Senator Vest characterizes him as "the one absolutely unselfish friend a man may have in this selfish world, the one that never deserts him, never fails him, the one that never proves ungrateful or treacherous. . . ."

The Pomeranian was small, weighing about four and a half pounds, but history discloses that the small dog, perhaps oftener than his bigger brother, has rendered modest but heroic service and by his fidelity has influenced the course of history. . . .

As already indicated, the law now recognizes that dogs have pecuniary value, and constitute property of their owners, as much so as horses and cattle or other domestic animals. . . . The plaintiff's dog was the proud possessor of the kennel name Encliffe-Masterpiece; his pedigree and reputation entitled him to be regarded in dog circles as possessing the bluest of blood; in short, in canine society he belonged to the inner circle of the four hundred. In West and East he had won the first prize in every bench show at which he had been exhibited. He was middle-aged and in good health. Experts testifying placed his monetary value at one thousand dollars.

The owner of a dog is not liable for the injuries caused by it unless it is vicious and the owner has notice of this fact. . . . But we think the evidence in this case shows, by inference at least, that while the defendant's dog was an estimable animal in many respects, he was, nevertheless, prone to attack without provocation other dogs irrespective of size, and that such an assault upon a dog of the weight and physical characteristics of that owned by the plaintiff was likely to prove harmful, if not fatal, to the object of the attack. As to the defendant's prior knowledge of the vicious propensities of his Airedale, while the evidence may not clearly show that he was personally aware of them, it sufficiently demonstrates than his employee, in charge of him at the time of the attack, and whose custom it was to exercise it on the public streets, knew of its dangerous character, which knowledge the law charges to the employer. The knowledge of a servant or agent of an animal's vicious propensity will be imputed to the master when such agent or servant has charge of or control over the animal. . . .

It is urged by the appellant that the court erred in refusing to instruct the jury, as requested, that the plaintiff was guilty of contributory negligence arising from the fact that her dog was upon the public streets without being licensed — unlike the defendant's Airedale, whose master had ornamented his favorite with a tag entitling him to roam the city's streets secure from interference by the poundkeeper or his myrmidons. The appellant's contention in this respect would be well grounded if the plaintiff's omission to comply with the ordinance requiring dogs to be licensed had contributed to the incident resulting in the Pomeranian's untimely end. But for aught that appears the absence of a tag from the collar of plaintiff's dog was unnoticed by the Airedale, and was not the matter that aroused his ire or induced him to make the attack. His was the canine point of view and not that of the license collector. When the violation of an ordinance has no causal connection with the injury, as contributing thereto, the rule has no application. . . .

Judgment affirmed.

NASHVILLE & K. R. CO. v. DAVIS
Supreme Court of Tennessee
78 S.W. 1050 (1902)

JOHN S. WILKES, J.

This is an action for damages against the railroad company for running over and killing three geese of the value of $1.50. The owner of the geese lived about one mile from the railroad, but permitted them to run at large, and they went upon the railroad track near a public crossing. The engineer blew the whistle and rang the bell for the crossing, but there is no proof that he rang the bell or sounded the alarm for the geese. Whether the geese knew of this failure to whistle for them does not appear. We think there is no evidence of recklessness or common-law negligence shown in the case, and the only question is whether a goose is an animal or obstruction in the sense of the statute (section 1574, subsec. 4, Shannon's Compilation), which requires the alarm whistle to be sounded, and brakes put down, and every possible means employed to stop the train and prevent an accident when an animal or obstruction appears on the track. It is evident that this provision is designed, not only to protect animals on the track, but also the passengers and employees upon the train from accidents and injury.

It would not seem that a goose was such an obstruction as would cause the derailment of a train, if run over. It is true, a goose has animal life, and, in the broadest sense, is an animal; but we think the statute does not require the stopping of trains to prevent running over birds, such as geese, chickens, ducks, pigeons, canaries, or other birds that may be kept for pleasure or profit. Birds have wings to move them quickly from places of danger, and it is presumed that they will use them (a violent presumption, perhaps, in the case of a goose, an animal which appears to be loath to stoop from its dignity to even escape a passing train). But the line must be drawn somewhere, and we are of the opinion that the goose is a proper bird to draw it at. We do not mean to say that in the case of recklessness and common-law negligence there might not be a recovery for killing geese, chickens, ducks, or other fowls, for that case is not presented. Snakes, frogs, and fishing worms, when upon railroad tracks, are, to some extent, obstructions; but it was not contemplated by the statute that for such obstructions as these trains should be stopped, and passengers delayed.

We are of the opinion that there is error in the court below giving judgment for the plaintiff, and the judgment is reversed, and, the case having been heard without a jury, the suit is dismissed, at the plaintiff's cost.

GEORGIA SOUTHERN & FLORIDA RAILWAY COMPANY v. THOMPSON
Supreme Court of Georgia
111 Ga. 731; 36 S.E. 955 (1900)

SAMUEL E. LUMPKIN, J.

There was a head-end collision between a moving locomotive and a stationary bull, the latter showing fight and manifesting total ignorance of the doctrine of impenetrability. The company's servants in charge of the locomotive were better versed in the principles of natural philosophy, and according to their testimony, did their best to save the animal from the consequences of his rashness; but in spite of all their well-directed efforts, the crash came with its inevitable result. They were the only eye-witnesses. At the trial the plaintiff proved certain circumstances which were consistent with his contention that the defendant's witnesses did not state accurately the details of the catastrophe but these circumstances were also perfectly consistent with the company's contention that its witnesses gave an entirely correct version of what occurred. Under the well-settled rules of evidence applicable to such a case, it must be held that the defendant's witnesses were in no legal or fair sense discredited, and that the verdict in the plaintiff's favor can not lawfully stand.

Judgment reversed.

CHAPTER I: CANINE, EQUINE & FELINE

MONTGOMERY v. MARYLAND CASUALTY COMPANY
Supreme Court of Georgia
169 Ga. 746; 151 S.E. 363 (1929)

STIRLING PRICE GILBERT, J.

[James A. Rourke Machine Company operated on the Savannah River a plant where it engaged in repairing boats. Under the workmen's compensation act the Maryland Casualty Company had underwritten its liability for injury to employees. John Montgomery was employed as custodian or watchman of the property. He was accidentally drowned on the premises of the employer at attempting to rescue his dog which had fallen into the river, and his widow applied to the industrial commission for compensation. The application was denied, and that finding was upheld by the superior court of Chatham County. On appeal the judgment was affirmed by the Court of Appeals.]

From the dawn of primal history the dog has loomed large in the art and literature of the world, including judicial literature. So it doubtless will be until the "crack of doom." In metal and in stone his noble image has been perpetuated, but the dog's chief monument is in the heart of his friend, "man." As a house pet, a watchdog, a herder of sheep and cattle, in the field of sport, and as the motive power of transportation, especially in the ice fields of the far north as well as in the Antarctics, the dog has ever been a faithful companion and helper of man. In the trackless forests of the new world he was on the firing line of civilization in the task of subduing all enemies, whether savage man or wild beast.

We find in astrology the dog star is "the brightest star in the heavens; the Alpha of the constellation Canis Major;" and in Greek mythology Cerberus is the watchdog at the entrance of the infernal regions. Diana, the goddess, had her deer-hounds, and literature is enriched by the story of Odysseus's (Ulysses) dog Argos. After twenty years of war and wandering this king of Ithaca returned, unrecognized in his beggar rags even by Penelope, but as he entered the courtyard, "Lo! a hound raised up his head and pricked his ears. In times past the men used to lead the hound against wild goats and deer and hares, but as then despised he lay in the deep dung of mules and kine. There lay the dog Argos, full of fleas. Yet even now, when he was aware of Odysseus standing by, he wagged his tail and dropped both his ears, but nearer to his lord he had not strength to draw. Odysseus looked aside and brushed away a tear. Therewith he passed into the fairlying house and went straight to the hall, to the company of the proud wooers. But upon Argos came black death, even in the hour that he beheld his master again, in the twentieth year." Masters of the brush have pictured the dog on canvas everlasting, among them Landseer, Blake, Tracy and Andrea del Sarto. The last named painted "Tobias accompanied by the angel Raphael."

Among many of the most beautiful of nature's plants and trees, we have the dog-wood, dog-daisy, dog-laurel, dog-rose, dog-violet, and the like; there are dog days, the dog watch (on ship board); there is dogma, doggery, dog-latin, and the "dogged," as Shakespeare wrote: "Doth dogged war bristle his angry crest and snarl in the gentle eyes of peace." King John, act IV, scene 3. Holy writ abounds with his mention, as, "A living dog is better than a dead lion." Ecclesiastes, IX: 4. "Who loves me loves my dog" is a French proverb of the thirteenth century, and in substance has figured in the literature of many writers, including St. Bernard, of Clairvaux and Erasmus. Poets great and small, their pens inspired by the Olympic maid, have paid tribute to the dog. Lord Byron who was devoted to his "Boatswain," wrote of him:

> *"But the poor dog, in life the firmest friend,*
> *The first to welcome, foremost to defend,*
> *Whose honest heart is still his master's own,*
> *Who labors, fights, lives, breathes for him alone."*

And again:

> *"'Tis sweet to hear the watch dog's honest bark.*
> *Bay deep mouthed welcome as we draw near home."*

The great bard of Avon, in his Julius Caesar, makes Brutus say "I had rather be a dog and bay the moon, than such a Roman;" and in Macbeth Shakespeare gives us quite a catalogue of dogs: "hounds and greyhounds, mongrels, spaniels, shoughs, water-rugs and demi-wolves; the swift, the slow, the subtle, the housekeeper, the hunter;" and in Midsummer Night's Dream, speaking of hounds, he says: "Their heads are hung/With ears that sweep away the morning dew;/Crook-knee'd and dew-lapp'd like Thessalian bulls;/Slow in pursuit, but match'd in mouth like bells, each unto each:

> *Such gallant chiding; for beside the groves,*
> *The skies, the fountains, every region near*
> *Seem'd all one mutual cry. I never heard*
> *So musical a discord, such sweet thunder."*

In modern times Thompson in "Major Jones' Courtship" makes his hero to boast of owning two of the best coon dogs in the settlement, describes the music they make in pursuit, and concludes:

> *"It puts me in mind of what Shakespeare sez about dogs:*
> *I have herd sich powerful discord,*
> *Sich sweet thunder."*

Sir John Lucas in a poem "To a Dog" pictures his "wraith in a canine paradise" where the

CHAPTER I: CANINE, EQUINE & FELINE

". . . little faithful barking ghost
May leap to lick my phantom hand."

And so with other poets almost without number, among whom are Chaucer, Sir Walter Scott, Alexander Pope, Kipling, Trowbridge, Ruskin, and of course Stephen O. Foster, the author of so many beautiful southern melodies. It was he who wrote of "Old Dog Tray":

"Old dog Tray's ever faithful;
Grief can not drive him away;
He is gentle, he is kind --
I shall never never find
A better friend than old dog Tray."

Some three thousand years before Christ, Socrates[1] wrote: "When I see some men, I love my dog the more."

Baron Curvier considered the dog "the most complete, the most singular, and the most useful conquest man has gained in the animal world."

Xanthippus, father of Pericles, had a dog, which leaped into the sea and swam along the galley side to follow his master, but finally fainted and died away near the island of Salamis; and Plutarch says: "That spot in the island which is still called the Dog's Grave is said to be his."

It is said that dogs bore their part in the siege of Troy, at Marathon, and in the battle of Salamis.

Herodotus said[2]: "In whatsoever house a cat has died by a natural death, all those who dwell in this house shave their eyebrows only; but those in whose house a dog has died shave their whole bodies."

Alcibiades' dog is now represented in marble at Duncombe Hall, England.

There was Prince Llewellyn and his greyhound "Gelert;" Sir Isaac Newton and his "Diamond;" Mirabeau and his "Chico;" "Diomed,"about whom his master, John S. Wise, wrote a book; Josephine and her "Fortune" that left a scar on Napoleon's leg; and Sir Walter Scott and his dozens of dogs.

Relics of dogs were found among the ruins of Herculaneum beside the forms of Roman sentries. In the late world war the dog shared the dangers of their soldier-masters in flood and field and trench.

---

[1] [Ed. Note: According to our history books, Socrates was made to drink hemlock in 399 B.C. so this reference may be chronologically imprecise. Furthermore, the Oxford Dictionary of Quotations, 2nd Ed., attributes the remark, or one similar to it, to Madame Roland, who died in A.D. 1793.]

[2] [Ed. Note: in his account of Egyptian customs.]

Lord Byron had graven on a marble shaft his tribute to his dog: "Near this spot is deposited the remains of one who possessed beauty without vanity, strength without insolence, courage without ferocity, and all the virtues of man without his vices." This praise, which would be but meaningless flattery if inscribed over human ashes, is but a just tribute to the memory of Boatswain, a dog, who was born at Newfoundland, 1803, and died at Newstead Abbey, November 18, 1803.

In like vein Alexander H. Stephens wrote for his sagacious poodle Rio: "Here rest the remains of what in life was a satire on the human race, and an honor to his own -- a faithful dog."

Senator George Graham Vest said: "The one, absolute, unselfish friend that man can have in this selfish world, the one that never deserts him, the one that never proves ungrateful or treacherous, is his dog."

Tributes might be multiplied almost without number. Like man, not all dogs are good dogs. They have left behind them records showing every degree of good and bad. One poet's commentary has been judicially recognized in Woodbridge v. Marks, 36 N.Y. Supp. 82:

> *"That dogs delight to bark and bite,*
> *For God hath made them so."*

In the case just cited it was said: "Conceding the highest place here or hereinafter to this companion of man which is claimed by any one, even to the faith of the Indian: *'That in the happy hunting grounds/His faithful dog shall bear him company.'* Still in the walks of life he must give way to the interests of man." . . .

For many of the facts stated above credit is due to "Pippa Passes, and Rather Doggily" (Sewanee Review), a little classic by William C. Jones, from which I quote as follows: "When the house is still and only the wind is abroad, Pippa muses by the fire at her master's feet, black muzzle on white paws, and in her eyes that question which troubled the soul of Tamas Carlyle, 'Is the universe friendly or nay?' The hearth is red, fleecy the rug, the shadows flickering warm; but Pippa is too staunch a terrier to leave danger or doubt unchallenged. She sniffs the unseen, then turns a more disquieted glance to the being in the chair. That damp, twitching nose senses truth beyond the oracle of his book, news beyond his radio's find. A growl, snarls, a rush to the window, a dash to the locked door. She lunges and scratches and leaps, back bristled, flanks heaving, teeth snapping, in her throat a hubbub that would rejoice the heart of three-headed Cerberus. The master is roused. What skulker, what power of darkness? A witch, perchance. Worse! It is that ancient anathema of a good dog's world, the dragon that would upset all seven of the tailwagging heavens; it is Grimalkin, the Stray Cat. A wild charge to the back fence, followed by a ferreting of every nook which might harbor the foe, so placates Pippa that she returns with tail as high as a bobbed tail well could be, and soon is aslumber on the rug . . . When a dutiful fox dies, no epitaph is writ; rather he is flayed for the parsimonious tanner. When a mule goes the way of all flesh, no mound is reared, serviceful though his years have been. When a lambkin lies still and stark on the trencher, even the poet who was wont to rhyme on the pretty innocent will regale himself with one of its chops. But when a certain little creature, having a bark at one end and a bit of tail at the other, with a flea or two between, takes leave for the isles of the blest, the lords of earth look foolish while their ladies weep, and humanity feels a tug at the heart."

A recent story, "Hound of Heaven," tells of a fox terrier after death, floating through the clouds, the cold winds blowing through his whiskers, finally landing at the pearly gates of canine heaven, and fresh upon his admission he is engaged in mortal combat with "Hodge," the famous cat, pet of Samuel Johnson.

From what has been said it will not be difficult to ascertain where the sentiment and inclination of the court would lead. The court, however, is a court for the correction of errors, and we must be guided by law. The law of the case [is set forth below]:

Under the terms of the workmen's compensation act, in order for compensation to be due, the injury to the employee must arise both out of and in the course of the employment. Neither alone is enough. . . .

Under the law and the evidence of this case, the dog was not a part of the watchman's "equipment," even though it be conceded that the dog was useful as a watchdog and companion. .. .

The dog can not legally be classified as a "fellow workman" falling under the principle ruled in Ocean Accident &c. Co. v. Evans (Texas) [citation omitted]. . . .

The act of the watchman in attempting to rescue the dog, which had jumped or fallen into the river, was not an emergency so as to constitute the act one performed in behalf of the employer, arising out of and within the scope of the employment. . . .

Judgment affirmed.

CORSO v. CRAWFORD DOG AND CAT HOSPITAL, INC.
Civil Court of the City of New York
97 Misc. 2d 530; 415 N.Y.S. 2d 182 (1979)

SEYMOUR FRIEDMAN, J.

The facts in this case are not in dispute.

On or about January 28, 1978, the plaintiff brought her 15-year-old poodle into the defendant's premises for treatment. After examining the dog, the defendant recommended euthanasia and shortly thereafter the dog was put to death. The plaintiff and the defendant agreed that the dog's body would be turned over to Bide-A-Wee, an organization that would arrange a funeral for the dog. The plaintiff alleged that the defendant wrongfully disposed of her dog, and failed to turn over the remains of the dog to the plaintiff for the funeral. The plaintiff had arranged an elaborate funeral for the dog including a head stone, an epitaph, and attendance by plaintiff's two sisters and a friend. A casket was delivered to the funeral in which, upon opening the casket, instead of the dog's body, the plaintiff found the body of a dead cat. The plaintiff described during the nonjury trial, her mental distress and anguish, in detail, and indicated that she still feels distress and anguish. The plaintiff sustained no special damages.

The question before the court now is twofold. (1) Is it an actionable tort that was committed? (2) If there was an actionable tort, is the plaintiff entitled to damages beyond the market value of the dog?

Before answering these questions, the court must first decide whether a pet such as a dog is only an item of personal property as prior cases have held (Smith v. Palace Transp. Co. [citation omitted]). This court now overrules prior precedent and holds that a pet is not just a thing but occupies a special place somewhere in between a person and a piece of personal property.

As in the case where a human body is withheld (Zaslowsky v. Nassau County Public Gen. Hosp. [citation omitted]; Diebler v. American Radiator & Std. Sanitary Corp., [citation omitted], the wrongfully withholding or, as here, the destruction of the dog's body gives rise to an actionable tort.

In ruling that a pet such as a dog is not just a thing, I believe the plaintiff is entitled to damages beyond the market value of the dog. A pet is not an inanimate thing that just receives affection; it also returns it. I find that plaintiff Ms. Corso did suffer shock, mental anguish and despondency due to the wrongful destruction and loss of the dog's body. She had an elaborate funeral scheduled and planned to visit the grave in the years to come. She was deprived of this right.

This decision is not to be construed to include an award for the loss of a family heirloom which would also cause great mental anguish. An heirloom, while it might be the source of good feelings, is merely an inanimate object and is not capable of returning love and affection. It does not respond to human stimulation; it has no brain capable of displaying emotion which in turn causes a human response. Losing the right to memorialize a pet rock, or a pet tree or losing a family picture album is not actionable. But a dog — that is something else. To say it is a piece of personal property and not more is a repudiation of our humaneness. This I cannot accept.

Accordingly, the court finds the sum of $700 to be reasonable compensation for the loss suffered by the plaintiff.

UNITED STATES v. SPROED
United States District Court, D. Oregon
628 F. Supp. 1234 (1986)

JAMES M. BURNS, District Judge.

Judges seldom get a chance to wax lyrical. Rarer still does a judge have an opportunity to see a case centered around a butterfly.[1] Those who read this opinion will, therefore, recognize that this case presented me with a temptation which I obviously count not resist. This case charges defendant Sproed with catching butterflies in a National Park.

Sproed and his son were at Rim Village of Crater Lake National Park on the afternoon of August 23, 1985 apparently doing just that - namely, catching butterflies! Along came a Park Ranger who had apparently taken keenly to heart the "Law and Order" rhetoric which some say has been a hallmark of the current administration. Responding to this Petty Offense[2] the Ranger issued to Sproed what became enshrined in judicial records as Citation P127482.

It would not be surprising to find that most of our citizens would be embittered if accused of such a heinous crime. Sproed is no exception. For reasons which appear below, I do not have to decide whether Sproed was, in fact, guilty of a crime. If his letter is to be believed, he and his young son may well have been moved by somewhat the same poetic spirit as the "aged, aged man" invented and immortalized by Lewis Carroll:

> *I saw an aged, aged man,*
> *A-sitting on a gate.*
> *'Who are you, aged man?' I said,*
> *'And how is it you live?'*

---

[1] Butterflies are normally grist for the poet's mill, not that of the judge. Occasionally, even the august Court of Appeals finds itself cerebrating over butterfly related causes, Friends of the Endangered Species v. Jantzen, 760 R.2d 976 (9th Cir. 1985)

[2] Petty offenses, a species of criminal offense established by the congress (18 U.S.C. §1) used to carry a maximum penalty of six months in jail or a $500 fine or both. (Actually, the maximum fine for the offense charged here would have been $5,000; last year in the comprehensive Crime Control Act of 1984, Congress "upped the ante" for petty offense fines to $5,000.) Under applicable statutes, regulations are promulgated by the various federal agencies - Department of Interior and so forth; violation of such regulations - after they are published in the Code of Federal Regulations is a petty offense. When a Park Ranger - or some other agency enforcement officer comes across a violation, a citation is issued. The citation normally provides a specified sum as collateral, i.e. bail. If the accused does not wish to contest the matter, he or she sends in the bail amount and the matter is closed. The accused may demand a trial, usually before a U.S. Magistrate; the accused, however, as a matter of right, can have the case heard by a District Judge. Occasionally a sort of third option is chosen by the accused, as happened here. He will send in a letter of explanation with a request, usually explicit, that the matter be dismissed, or otherwise be disposed of.

And his answer tickled through my head
Like water through a sieve.
He said, 'I look for butterflies
That sleep among the wheat;
I make them into mutton-pies,
And sell them in the street.'
Through the Looking Glass, Ch. 8.

Or Mr. Sproed may have believed, along with the German poet Heine that:

With the rose the butterfly's deep in love
A thousand times hovering round;
But round himself, all tender like gold,
The sun's sweet ray is hovering found.

Mr. Sproed may even have been mulling over the lines written by Oregon's own "poet", Joaquin Miller.

The gold-barr'd butterflies to and fro
And over the waterside wander'd and wove
As heedless and idle as clouds that rove
And drift by the peaks of perpetual snow.

In any event, alas, no trial will ever occur to sort these things out. The reader should be made aware of why the judicial machinery never geared up for a full trial of this case. When Sproed's letter [3] arrived at the Clerk's office, it was referred to Magistrate Hogan, along with a touching note suggesting this might be a case in which judge Hogan would want to exercise his judicial discretion. Shortly thereafter, Assistant U.S. Attorney Kent filed a motion to dismiss pursuant to Rule 48(a) of the Federal Rules of Criminal Procedure Judge Hogan dismissed the case. Fortunately (or otherwise), I became aware, shortly afterward, of this case of lepidopteral *lese majeste* [injured majesty, i.e., high treason]. I chose to exercise my supervisory power as a District Judge to review the ruling

---

[3] I have reproduced, in typewritten form, Mr. Sproed's handwritten letter received by the Clerk's office on September 9, 1985, and it is attached as Appendix A to this opinion.

of the Magistrate, 28 U.S.C. §636. [4]

In his letter to the Court, Sproed says that he and his son "have always loved and enjoyed the out-of-doors and never knowingly disregard laws. . . [W]e were out catching butterflies. We have a collection and wherever we go we try to add to it. It never entered my mind that it was unlawful to catch a butterfly in the park."

Sproed said he and his son "saw no signs and there was nothing even hinting [that butterfly-catching was a crime] in the paper given to us when we entered the park." Thus, he felt "that a friendly explanation and a warning was all that was necessary - it would have made this a learning experience instead of a bitter remembrance." He said that "It will take some time for me to restore my boy's previous respect for park rangers. I trust that your decision will make that job easier for me."

---

[4]Judge Hogan had no need, in view of the government's motion, to look more closely at the citation. The Park Ranger may have been on shaky legal as well as entomological grounds. The description of the violation alleged was "Preservation of Natural, Cultural & Archeological Resources." The Ranger filled in, as the regulation he felt had been trampled upon, 36 C.F.R. 2.1(a)(1). That section provides as follows:

2.1 Preservation of Natural, Cultural and Archeological Resources:
    (a) Except as otherwise provided in this chapter, the following is prohibited:
        (1) Possessing, destroying, injuring, removing, digging, or disturbing its natural state:
            (i) Living or dead wildlife or fish, or the parts of products thereof, such as antlers or nests.
            (ii) Plants or the parts of products thereof.
            (iii) Nonfossilized and fossilized paleontological specimens, cultural or archeological resources, or the parts thereof.

Wildlife is defined by 36 C.F.R. § 1.5 to mean:

"any member of the animal kingdom and includes a part, product, egg or offspring thereof, or the dead body or part thereof, except fish."

Actually, one could read Mr. Sproed's second paragraph as the functional equivalent of a Rule 12 Motion to Dismiss on the ground that the citation fails to state a claim. Under well settled constitutional principles, a criminal charge, under the Fifth Amendment must be specific enough in its charging language to notify the accused of the nature of his alleged offense so he may prepare a defense and plead double jeopardy in the event of conviction or acquittal. Under these circumstances, however, I doubt that the Park Ranger would want to pursue the charge. He would presumably, take to heart Wordsworth's dictum in his poem "To A Butterfly", which may not be entirely inapplicable here:

> *Much converse do I find in thee,*
> *Historian of my infancy!*
> *Float near me; do not yet depart!*
> *Dead times revive in thee;*
> *Thou bring'st, gay creature as thou art!*
> *a solemn image to my heart . . .*

The Sproed's experience exemplifies the axiom "Nature Imitates Art," as one can see from Appendix B. It is a copy of a recent strip from the widely syndicated comic "BLOOM COUNTY." Permission to reproduce this copyrighted strip has been graciously granted by the Washington Post Writers Group, which syndicates this comic strip.

Judge Hogan, AUSA Kent, the sharp-eyed young lady in the Clerk's office and I have now done our bit. Restoring the younger Sproed's respect - if this will help somewhat in achieving that worthy aim - seems, somehow, a fitting way to close the year 1985. It is a small victory, perhaps, but well worth the effort.

Mr. Sproed's young son, as a part of the process of having his respect restored, is urged not to take too literally the accompanying panel strip of "Bloom County."

For the foregoing reasons, I approve, affirm and adopt the Magistrate's order of dismissal.

APPENDIX "A"

Your Honor:

Since it is neither reasonable nor practical to appear in court, I am writing this letter of explanation. I don't like to use the courts time on such matters but $50 represents a lot of time and hard work to me and more important is this decision in my boys mind.

I plead not guilty to the charge of "Destruction of Natural Cultural & Archeological Resources." The park ranger spent about 30 minutes on his C.B. and looking through his book but never did find anything against collecting insects. So he just included it in the above class.

My boy and I have always loved and enjoyed the out-of-doors and never knowingly disregard laws. In this case we were out catching butterflies. We have a collection and wherever we go we try to add to it. It never entered my mind that it was unlawful to catch a butterfly in the park. We saw no signs and there was nothing even hinting at such a thing in the paper given to us when we entered the park (which I have enclosed). It does state that it is o.k. to catch fish.

It is this kind of incident that destroys young peoples' respect for the law. I felt that a friendly explanation and a warning was all that was necessary - it would have made this a learning experience instead of a bitter remembrance. We do not have the opportunity to travel a lot and I am afraid this "special occasion" may be remembered only by the outcome of this incident.

It will take some time for me to restore my boy's previous respect for park rangers. I trust that your decision will make that job easier for me.

Very Sincerely,

(s)

David Sproed

STEVENS v. THE STATE OF GEORGIA
Supreme Court of Georgia
77 Ga. 310 (1886)

LOGAN E. BLECKLEY, Chief Justice.

[The Defendant, Stevens, was indicted for the larceny of a black sow-hog, the property of Rowland. At the trial, the following facts emerged: The hog was a pet, and was in the habit of going up to the house and did not run away. It was found missing from Roland's property on Sunday, and he suspected the defendant, who lived about three hundred yards away. With two others, Roland went to the Stevens' house, looking for his hog as a "stolen hog". He asked Stevens to allow him to search the house, but the defendant declined. Roland then went to town to obtain a search warrant. After he was gone, the defendant said he, too, was going to town to see if the owner had a right to a warrant. He did not return. On searching Steven's premises, some hog bones were found in the house; hog hair and entrails were found buried in one hole in the garden and fresh hog meat in another. The meat was equivalent in size and the hair was the same color as that of the missing hog. Stevens was found and arrested several years later at a place more than fifty miles away. The jury convicted the defendant.]

In the house hog bones, in the garden hog hair, hog entrails, hog meat, buried in the earth, refusal of the occupant of the premises to permit a search without legal warrant, his abrupt departure from home whilst the warrant was being procured, his flight or retreat to a point more than fifty miles distant, and his continuous absence until arrested and brought back for trial, are strongly suggestive of a suspicious intercourse on his part with some hog or other. The jury were of opinion that it was the hog described in the indictment; and as he was a near neighbor to that hog, and as it disappeared about that time and its owner went in search of it as a stolen hog, and as the hair and the meat found buried in the garden looked like the hair and meat of that hog, it is highly probable that the jury were not mistaken.

Complaint is made that a witness was allowed to testify that the owner was hunting for the animal "as a stolen hog." And so he was, undoubtedly. He would not want to look in a dwelling-house, or under the ground in a garden, for a strayed hog; and such were the places searched. How the witness ascertained that the owner regarded it as stolen, whether from acts alone, or from declarations and acts together, does not appear; but if the prisoner or his counsel had wanted to learn this, the witness ought to have been interrogated on the sources of his knowledge. He testified as if he knew the fact somehow, and if he knew it, he could state if as explanatory of the mode and purpose of the search. He was present at the search and assisted in conducting it on the owner's behalf. Moreover, the prisoner himself was present, face to face with the owner, when the investigation began, and when steps were taken to enter upon the search with due legal authority. He could have had no doubt that the owner was looking for stolen property. Any man who inters his pork may expect the late departed hog to be hunted for as stolen, if it is hunted for at all, on his premises.

Judgment affirmed.

LYMAN v. DALE
Supreme Court of Missouri
262 Mo. 353; 171 S.W. 352 (1914)

WALLER W. GRAVES, J.

This case involves the magnificent sum of $5. It reaches us under a certification from the Springfield Court of Appeals. We are enlightened by three well-written opinions from the three respective members of that court. The facts we shall state for ourselves. Plaintiff, having had one wheel of an old buggy somewhat demolished by coming in contact with a mule belonging to defendant, but being led by an employé of defendant, sought damages therefor before a justice of the peace in October, 1909. He thus challenges his enemy in an amended petition filed before such justice:

"Plaintiff, for an amended petition, states that on the 2d day of October, 1909, at the county and state of Missouri, he was driving a horse and buggy along Walnut street, between South and Jefferson streets, in the city of Springfield, on the right-hand side of the street; that defendant's agent and employé, on the aforesaid date, was leading a wild and unruly mule along the aforesaid street in such a careless and negligent manner as to permit said mule to run into and against plaintiff's said buggy, thereby injuring and breaking the wheel and axle of said buggy and damaging the same to the extent of $5. Plaintiff further states that, at the time of the accident aforesaid, defendant's agent and employé leading said mule was acting in the scope of his employment. Wherefore plaintiff prays judgment in the sum of $5."

CHAPTER I: CANINE, EQUINE & FELINE

As we gather the facts, plaintiff has been successful throughout from the justice's court up to the present. In the Court of Appeals his success was by a divided court. In this court he stands behind the fortification erected by his judgment, and submits his case here without brief. A yellow slip of paper found in the files here bears the ominous inscription, "The Celebrated Mule Case," and nothing more. Why we were thus enlightened by this otherwise silent monitor we know not. It at least admonishes to look well to the facts.

Plaintiff and his brother and father-in-law were driving east on Walnut street in Springfield, Mo., in plaintiff's buggy, and, at a point where there was some digging in the street and some brick piled up in the street, met defendant's employé, James S. Parker, who was riding one mule and leading another. Both mules were of good size, and the one being led was gray in color, if the color is material. According to plaintiff's evidence, the halter strap by which the mule was led was five or six feet long; two witnesses say five and another says five or six feet. It was being held near the end. In passing the bricks the mule shied across to the buggy and got his hind leg between the shaft and the wheel, and in extricating itself damaged the wheel. . .

. . . There is no evidence in the case to the effect that the mule in question was wild and unruly, or that defendant had any knowledge of the animal being unruly or wild, if it was so, in fact. Defendant said that the mule was well broke, but a little high-lifed, and this is as far as the evidence in behalf of the defendant adds to plaintiff's case. Defendant demurred to the evidence at the close of the plaintiff's case. Plaintiff's right to recover under the pleadings and under the evidence is thus squarely presented.

I. There are at least two reasons why this judgment should be reversed. It is true that in justice's courts the same strict formalities of pleadings are not required as in the circuit court; but it is further true that, if the plaintiff elects to plead in strictness in such court, he is bound by his pleadings there as he would be elsewhere. By this we mean, if he is suing in tort, and specifically states the negligence upon which he relies to recover, he must recover for that negligence and none other. In the case at bar, what is the negligence upon which the plaintiff seeks to recover? Is it the negligent handling of a mule, an ordinary average mule, or is it the negligent handling of a wild and unruly mule? And, if the latter, has there been a case made? This is the first proposition in the case. We have set out in full the plaintiff's statement of his cause of action. A reading of that statement shows that the plaintiff was undertaking to charge the careless and negligent handling of "a wild and unruly mule." This was the case defendant was called upon to meet. When, therefore, it was made to appear that the defendant had not handled "a wild and unruly mule" at all, the case stated had failed. Under the pleadings, the defendant was not required to come prepared to meet the question of a negligent handling of an ordinary mule, but, on the other hand, the plaintiff, if permitted to recover, must recover upon the case made by his pleadings. Under the case pleaded, his proof failed, and the court should have directed a verdict for the defendant.

II. But even grant it that the petition in this case is in such form and substance as to permit a recovery upon the proof of a negligent handling of a mule, without reference to the "wild and unruly" characteristic of the animal, as two of the judges of the Court of Appeals thought, yet should there have been a recovery under the evidence? We think not.

Plaintiff's theory is that the leading of a mule, somewhat "high-lifed" or high-spirited, upon a street, where a portion of the street was torn up by digging, and in which was piled bricks in a long continuous row or pile, by a halter, with a rope of five feet long, was negligence. There is no question but that there was ample of the obstructed street for the safe passage of both the buggy and the mules. It is true that plaintiff's witnesses say that the mules should have been haltered together, or something of that kind. This is their expert view of the situation, but we hardly think that the question is one calling for opinion evidence; and, although such was admitted without objection, the case here is not changed by reason of that fact. . . .

The use of a halter with a rein of five or six feet for the leading of both horses and mules upon the public highway is one of such long standing that expert testimony has no place in such a case. Not only so, but such a leading is not negligence; at least it is not negligence unless some vicious propensity of the animal be pleaded and shown. In this case we have no vicious propensity pleaded or proven. It is true that the petition charges that the mule was "wild and unruly" (not strictly a vicious propensity), but even that was not shown. Without some proof of vicious propensities, the trial court should have said that the mere proof that the defendant led the mule by a halter rein five or six feet long was no evidence of negligence upon his part. To hold that such conduct amounted to negligence is to overthrow all common knowledge as to the handling of animals upon the public highways. Courts must not blind themselves to common knowledge. The proof made in this case failed to show negligence in any degree, and the judgment from start to finish should have been for defendant. Eddy v. Union R. Co., 25 R. I. 451, 56 Atl. 677, 105 Am. St. Rep. 897, 1 Ann. Cas. 204.

We regret to feel constrained to thus abruptly terminate "The Celebrated Mule Case," but it should have been so determined long since.

Let the judgment of the circuit court be simply reversed, so that there will be an end to the controversy. All Concur.

HENRY LAMM, J. (concurring)

It was Dr. Johnson (was it not?) who observed that Oliver Goldsmith had "contributed to the innocent gayety of mankind." (Note bene: If, as a pundit tells me, it was Garrick, and not Goldsmith, Johnson spoke of, and if, in quoting, I misquote, then memory has played a trick upon me, and a learned bar will correct me. Time and weightier matters press me to go on and leave the "quotation"? stand.) The function of this suit is somewhat the same. Beginning with the "J.P.'s" it has reached the "P. J.'s" and in its journey has run the gamut of three courts, one above the other. Now, *secundum regulam* [in accordance with the rule] it, a fuss over $5, has reached the highest court in the state for final disposition—all this because (1) of divergence of opinion among our learned brethren of the Springfield Court of Appeals, and (2) the provisions of the Constitution in that behalf made and provided. However, if the amount at stake is small, the value of the case for doctrine's sake is great.

As I see it, the case is this: Dale, a man of substance, a farmer, owned a brown and a gray mule, both young and of fine growth; one saddlewise, the other otherwise. Both, used to the plow and wagon, were entitled to the designation, "well broke and gentle." One Parker was Dale's manservant, and in the usual course of his employment had charge of these mules. On a day certain he had driven them to a water wagon in the humble office of supplying water to a clover huller in the Ozark region hard by its metropolis, to wit, Springfield. Eventide had fallen; i.e., the poetical time of day had come when the beetle wheels his droning flight, drowsy tinkling lulls the distant folds, and all the air a solemn stillness holds. In other words, dropping into the vernacular, it was time to "take out." Accordingly, Parker took out with his mind fixed on the watchdog's honest bark baying deep-mouthed welcome as he drew near home; he mounted the ridable mule. He says he tied the other to the hames of the harness on the ridden one by a four or five foot halter rope, and was plodding his weary way homeward à la the plowman in the Elegy.

The vicissitudes of the journey in due course brought him to Walnut street in said city of Springfield. At a certain place in the street the city fathers had broken the pavement and made a "rick of brick" aside a long hole or ditch. Hard by this rick of brick was a ridge of fresh earth capped by a display of red lantern danger signals. It seems the unridden mule crowded against the ridden one and harassed Parker by coming in scraping contact with his circumjacent leg. Any boy who ever rode the lead horse in harrowing his father's field will get the idea. In this pickle he took hold of the halter rope, still fastened to the hames, to keep the unridden mule from rasping his said leg. It might as well be said at this point that witnesses for plaintiff did not observe that the end of the rope was attached to the hames of the ridden mule. As they saw it, Parker was leading the mule. As will be seen a bit further on, at this point a grave question arises, to wit: Is it negligence to lead a mule by hand, or should he be fastened "neck and neck" to his fellow? But we anticipate.

Going back a little, it seems as follows: At about the time Parker had reached said part of Walnut street, plaintiff and two other were in a buggy pulled by a single horse and on their own way home to the country. So equipped, these several parties met face to face. At this point it will do to say that, while the mules were used to being on the water wagon, it is not so clear that these travelers three were. There are signs of that artificial elation in the vehicle party that in the evening springs from drinking ("breathing freely"), but on the morning after produces the condition of involuntary expiation Dr. Von Ihring calls "Katzenjammer." They disavow being half seas over or drunk. Their chief spokesman, as descriptive of the situation, in part told his story mathematically in this fashion:

> "I had not drank so much but what I kept count. I
> can keep count until I take three, and hadn't quit
> counting yet. * * *"

In the course of their journey they, too, came to the brick rick, the ditch, the ridge of dirt, and the red lights on Walnut street. There they met, as said, the gray and brown mule and Parker face to face. When mules and rider approached and passed the three travelers, all on the same side of the ditch, the led mule (whether scared by the hole in the ground, the rick of brick, or the ridge is dark) shied from his fellow ("spread" himself), and presently his hind leg was mixed up with the shafts and wheel of the buggy. When the status quo ante was re-established, both leg and wheel were found damaged. Subsequently a blacksmith offered to repair the damages to the wheel for, say, a dollar and a half. This sum defendant, though denying liability, was willing and offered to pay; but plaintiff's dander was up, and he, as buggy owner, demanded a new wheel worth $5 and sued. In the justice court defendant lost outright and appealed. In the circuit court the same. The learned judges of the Court of Appeals could not agree (the *furor scribendi* [frenzied desire to write] being much in evidence, and three learned opinions falling from their several pens) and sent the case here—and here it is.

My Brother GRAVES has well disposed of it on certain grounds, but the theme being the Missouri mule, and state pride calling for further exposition, the said *furor scribendi* has seized me—witness:

(a) It is argued that it was negligence to ride one mule and lead its fellow by hand. That they should be halter-yoked "neck and neck." Parker says he necked them in a way, but plaintiff takes issue on the fact. Allowing credit to plaintiff's evidence, two questions spring, viz: First. Is the neck-and-neck theory "mule law" in this jurisdiction? Second. If so, then was the absence of the neck-and-neck adjustment the proximate cause of the injury? We may let the first question be settled in some other mule case and pass to the second as more important. It will be observed that the neck and forequarters of the mule did not do the damage. Contra, the hindquarters or "business end" of the mule were in fault. We take judicial notice of facts of nature. Hence we know that haltering a mule neck and neck to another will not prevent his hind parts spreading. His neck might be on one line, but his hind legs and heels might be on another—a divergent one. True, the mental concept relating to shying or spreading would naturally originate in the mule's head. But it must be allowed as a sound psychological proposition that haltering his head or neck can in no wise control the mule's thoughts or control the hinder parts affected by those thoughts. So much, I think is clear and is due to be said of the Missouri mule whose bones, in attestation of his activity and worth, lie bleaching from Shiloh to Spion Kop, from San Juan to Przemysl (pronounced, I am told by a scholar, as it is spelled). It results that the causal connection between the negligence in hand and the injury is broken, and recovery cannot go on the neck-and-neck theory. This because it is plain, under the distances disclosed by the evidence, that the mule's hind legs could reach the buggy wheel in spike of a neck-and-neck attachment.

(b) The next question is a bit elusive, but seems lodged in the case. It runs thus: There being no evidence tending to show the mule was "wild and unruly" as charged, is such a mule *per se* a nuisance, a vicious animal, has he a heart devoid of social duty and fatally bent on mischief when led by a halter on the street of a town, and must his owner answer for his acts on that theory? Attend to that view of it:

(1) There are sporadic instances of mules behaving badly. That one that Absalom rode and "went from under" him at a crisis in his fate, for instance. So it has been intimated in fireside precepts that the mule is unexpected in his heel action, and has other faults. In Spanish folk lore it is said: He who wants a mule without fault must walk. So, at the French chimney corner the adage runs: The mule long keeps a kick in reserve for his master. "The mule don't kick according to no rule," saith the American Negro. His voice has been a matter of derision, and there be those who put their tongue in their cheek when speaking of it. Witness the German proverb: Mules make a great fuss about their ancestors having been asses. And so on, and so on. But none of these things are factors in the instant case, for here there was no kicking and no braying standing in the relation of *causa causans* to the injury to the wheel. Moreover the rule of logic is that induction which proceeds by merely citing instances is a childish affair, and, being without any certain principle of inference, it may be overthrown by contrary instances. Accordingly the faithfulness, the dependableness, the surefootedness, the endurance, the strength, and the good sense of the mule (all matters of common knowledge) may be allowed to stand over against his faults and create either an equilibrium or a preponderance in the scales in his favor. He then, as a domestic animal, is entitled to the doctrine that, if he become vicious, guilty knowledge (the *scienter*) must be brought home to his master, precisely as it must be on the dog or ox. The rule of the master's liability for acts of the ox is old. Ex. 21:29. That for the acts of the dog is put this way: The law allows the dog his first bite. Lord Cockburn's dictum covers the master's liability on a kindred phase of liability for sheep killing, to wit: Every dog is entitled to at least one worry. So with this mule. Absent proof of the bad habit of "spreading" when led and the *scienter*, liability did not spring from the mere fact his hind leg (he being scared) got over the wheel while he was led by a five-foot halter rope, for it must be held that a led mule is not a nuisance *per se*, unless he is to be condemned on that score out and out because of his ancestry and some law of heredity, some asinine rule, so to speak— a question we take next.

(2) Some care should be taken not to allow such scornful remarks as that "the mule has no pride of ancestry or hope of posterity" to press upon our judgment. He inherits his father's ears; but what of that? The asses' ears, presented by an angry Apollo, were an affliction to King Midas, but not to the mule. He is a hybrid, but that was man's invention centuries gone in some

province of Asia Minor, and the fact is not chargeable to the mule. So the slowness of the domestic ass does not descend as a trait to the Missouri mule. It is said that a thistle is a fat salad for an ass' mouth. Maybe it is also in a mule's, but, be it so, surely his penchant for homely fare cannot so far condemn him that he does not stand *rectus in curia* [upright in the court]. Moreover, if his sire stands in satire as an emblem of sleepy stupidity, yet that avails nought, for the authorities (on which I cannot put my finger at this moment) agree that the Missouri mule takes after his dam and not his sire in that regard. All asses are not four-footed, the adage saith, and yet to call a man an "ass" is quite a different thing than to call him "mulish." *Vide* [see] the lexicographers.

Furthermore, the very word "jackass" is a term of reproach everywhere, as in the literature of the law. Do we not all know that a certain phase of the law of negligence, the humanitarian rule, first announced, it has been said, in a donkey case (Davis v. Mann, 10 Mees, & W. 545) has been called, by those who deride it, the "jackass doctrine?" This on the doctrine of the adage: Call a dog a bad name and then hang him. But, on the other hand, to sum up fairly, it was an ass that saw the heavenly vision even Balaam, the seer, could not see and first raised a voice against cruelty to animals. Num. 22: 23 et seq. So, did not Sancho Panza by meditation gather the sparks of wisdom while ambling along on the back of one, that radiated in his wonderful judgments pronounced in his decision by the common-sense rule of knotty cases in the Island of Barataria? Did not Samson use the jawbone of one effectually on a thousand Philistines? Is not his name imperishably preserved in that of the fifth proposition of the first book of Euclid—the *pons asinorum* [the asses' bridge][1]? But we shall pursue the subject no farther. Enough has been said to show that the ass is not without some rights in the courts even on sentimental grounds; ergo if his hybrid son, tracing his lineage as he does to the Jacks of Kentucky and Andalusia, inherits some of his traits, he cannot be held bad *per se*. Q.E.D.

It is meet that a $5 case, having its tap root in anger (and possibly in liquor), should not drag its slow lengths through the courts for more than five years, even if it has earned the soubriquet of "the celebrated mule case."

The premises herein and in the opinion of Brother GRAVES all in mind, I concur.

HANCOCK CONSTRUCTION CO. v. BASSINGER.
New York Supreme Court, Appellate Division
198 N.Y.S. 614 (1923)

RICHARD P. LYDON, J.

The plaintiff as landlord and the defendant as tenant entered into a lease of an apartment at 540 Manhattan Avenue, New York City, for a term of 16 months, to wit, from June 1, 1921 to September 20, 1922, at a total rental of

---

[1] [Ed. Note: i.e., "The angles opposite the equal side of an isosceles triangle are equal."]

$1,220, payable $90 monthly in advance; the premises to be occupied by the defendant, his wife, and grown daughter. The defendant, prior to the execution of the lease in question, and been a tenant of the plaintiff in another apartment in the same group of buildings. Defendant entered into possession of the new apartment, and remained in possession until March, 1922, when he vacated the premises, and he paid no rent for the four months -- April, May, June and July, 1922. This action is brought to recover said 4 months' rent, as well as $121.67 attorney's fees and $5.75 for telephone charges. . .

The contest on the trial centered around the defense of constructive eviction because of vermin. It appears that, prior to defendant's taking possession, the plaintiff had redecorated and refurnished the apartment; the new paper having been placed on the former wall paper. After defendant and his family were in possession about a week, bedbugs began to appear in all the rooms, and they gradually increased in numbers, notwithstanding the numerous complaints defendant made to the landlord, and the numerous attempts of the exterminators whom the landlord sent to the apartment to try to drive the vermin out. After each visit of these exterminators, there would be relief for a day or two, but then the reinforced army would come forth again with renewed vigor, and the defendant and his family would spend sleepless nights, as they were unable to get a resting place in the apartment where solitude and sleep could be enjoyed. Defendant's wife purchased from the exterminators a fluid that they used, and in the interval between visits she spread same in the cracks in the walls and behind the moldings. The bugs came from behind the molding on the wall, out of the cracks, and from behind the wooden panels on the wall. They became so numerous that they got into defendant's clothes, and, at times while he was in his office at business, an inquisitive bedbug which had accompanied him downtown would come forth from some secret place, much to defendant's embarrassment. The defendant and his family remained in the apartment during the ten months that plaintiff was making efforts to rid it of the vermin, but finally they could stand it no longer and vacated the premises. . .

It may well be that the presence of bugs and ants in an apartment can, within certain limits, be controlled and removed by the tenant, and which would not warrant the claim that the condition amounted to a constructive eviction, but that rule should not be extended to cover offensive and unbearable nuisances outside of the apartment. This tenant could not pull down the walls or the ceilings. He and his family ought not to be compelled to pay rent for an apartment in which they could not live. . .

The instant case is an aggravated condition, evidently the result of negligence on the part of the plaintiff in not properly caring for its property. The condition existing in that apartment, as shown by the testimony, was not caused by the tenant, and he could not remedy it. The landlord tried to, and failed. . .

Judgment reversed, and new trial ordered . . .

MATTER OF SADWIN
United States Bankruptcy Court, M.D. Florida
3 B.R. 581 (1980)

ALEXANDER L. PASKAY, Bankruptcy Judge.

When man bites dog, that is news. When dog bites man, it is not news unless the victim of the bite is a veterinarian and he is bitten by his patient. This is not unusual either and would not be noteworthy by itself except where the owner of the patient is sued by the veterinarian. That is not only news, but no doubt adds an unusual twist to an old but otherwise very interesting encounter between man and beast.

At this point one should wonder what this has to do with the bankruptcy court, especially since neither the vet, nor the dog named Hashish has ever had any financial difficulties as far as it appears from the record. However, since the owner of Hashish decided to seek relief in the bankruptcy court, most notably an absolution from the burden imposed upon him by a state court through a judgment as a result of the unfortunate encounter of the vet with Hashish, the matter immediately became the concern of this Court.

This is so because the victim of the not overly affectionate behavior of Hashish had the gall to escape the legal consequences of the judgment obtained by the vet against them through the discharge generally available to bankrupts, filed a complaint to determine the dischargeability of the debt pursuant to § 17c of the Bankruptcy Act. The claim of non-dischargeability is based on § 17a(8) of the Bankruptcy Act and asserts that the judgment against the bankrupts represent a liability for a willful and malicious injury to the person.

The underlying state court judgment was entered by default in the amount of $77,829. The plaintiff initially contended that the state court default judgment was *res judicata* and that this Court was confined to a review of the state court judgment. . . .

The salient facts of this controversy are basically without dispute, although two matters will be discussed below in greater detail, both of which are supposed to be relevant to the controversy, according to the Defendant.

At the time of this controversy, Howard Brent Sadwin and his wife, Linda Pauline Sadwin, resided in Seattle, Washington and were the owners of a German Shepherd who, according to the Plaintiff, is appropriately named Hashish since Hashish means "assassin" in Arabic. The Plaintiff, Dr. Thomas A. Gornall, III is a veterinarian residing in Seattle, Washington. In May of 1976, the Sadwins, who lived in an apartment house, were charged and subsequently found guilty of maintaining an animal nuisance in violation of the City Code of Belleview, a suburb of Seattle, Washington. This charge was based on certain complaints made by neighbors that Hashish barks, and at times jumps at persons while restrained on a leash. However, there is no evidence in this record which indicates that Hashish has bitten anyone prior to the instance which is the crux of this present controversy. There is evidence in this record to the contrary, that is, Hashish has never bitten anyone other than Dr. Gornall, the Plaintiff involved in this controversy.

Hashish having developed a skin rash on his underbelly and an ear infection, was taken by the Sadwins to Dr. Gornall in June of 1976. According to Mr. Sadwin, at this time they discussed the animal nuisance charge with Dr. Gornall who first denied and then stated that he did not recall such a conversation. Dr. Gornall examined Hashish at this occasion, who showed no vicious tendencies and behaved properly during the examination. Dr. Gornall prescribed some ointment for the rash, but since the rash did not subside, on October 2, 1976, the Sadwins took Hashish back to Dr. Gornall for additional treatment. Inasmuch as the rash was located primarily on the underbelly of Hashish, Dr. Gornall instructed the Sadwins to have Hashish lie down on his side on the floor of the examining room in order to enable Dr. Gornall to inspect the rash more closely. To accomplish this, Mr. Sadwin held the head of Hashish while Dr. Gornall knelt on the back of the animal and commenced to examine the skin rash on the stomach of the dog. While Dr. Gornall was in the process of examining Hashish, the dog suddenly freed its head and struck Dr. Gornall in the face and bit him in the lip area. There is a strong dispute whether or not the dog merely reacted to an offensive and painful pressure in a sensitive area or jumped at the vet without any provocation and for no reason at all. The first possibility is supported by Mr. Sadwin's testimony and the second is, of course, supported by the vet who denies that he touched the genitalia of the dog.

Shortly thereafter, Dr. Gornall filed a civil suit for damages and obtained a judgment in the amount of $77,829 by default. Subsequently, the Sadwins moved to Florida and on November 7, 1978, filed a voluntary petition for bankruptcy, duly scheduling the obligation owed by them to Dr. Gornall by virtue of the default judgment. The evidence further indicates through the testimony of an expert witness that, while dog bites are occupational hazards in the profession of the vet, they are primarily considered to be acceptable only if the bites are on the hand and not if they are on the face.

Since the issue of liability has already been resolved in order to sustain the claim of non-dischargeability under § 17a(8) of the Bankruptcy Act, the Plaintiff must show that the liability is the result of willful and malicious conduct on the part of the Bankrupts.

In considering these elements the Supreme Court in the case of Tinker v. Colwell, 193 U.S. 473, 24 S.Ct. 505, 48 L.Ed. 754 (1904) stated that:

> "It is not necessary in the construction we give to the language of the exception in the statute to hold every willful act which is wrong implies malice. . . ."

The Court defined "wantonly" as:

> "Means without reasonable excuse and implies turpitude, and an act to be done wantonly must be done intentionally and with design, without excuse and under circumstances evidencing a lawless destructive spirit. . . . "

The Court is not unmindful of a series of cases cited by Plaintiff which held that debts created by judgments obtained against dog owners for injuries sustained from dog bites were liabilities for willful and malicious injuries within the meaning of § 17a(8) of the Bankruptcy Act. . . . Furthermore, in the cases cited, unlike the instant case, the dog owners had knowledge of the dog's vicious nature. To establish absolute liability either by common law or by virtue of a statute as to the owner of a dog is not the same as to establish the elements of willfulness and malice which are indispensable elements of a claim of non-dischargeability under § 17a(8). To sustain a claim of dischargeability non-dischargeability, the Plaintiff must establish either that the Bankrupts actually harbored an ill will and malice toward the injured party and in furtherance of his hostility exposed the third party to the dog knowing that the dog would bite the third party whether excited or not or the owner willfully and knowingly put the dog in the position in which he knew that there was a great likelihood that he would harm others.

In the present instance, the record is totally devoid of any evidence that these Bankrupts harbored any ill will toward the Plaintiff or that they brought Hashish to the Plaintiff knowing that the vet will not be able to handle Hashish and being aware of the dog's vicious propensities, were reasonably certain that the dog would attack the Plaintiff during the treatment. Even if the Sadwins were aware of the unpredictability of Hashish, they were perfectly justified in assuming that the proper place to take a sick dog is to a vet and that he will know how to treat and handle the dog. Obviously, a vet is supposed to be trained to handle his patients and if a vet does not know how to handle an animal during treatment, the treatment of which he accepted, he should not be heard to complain if the animal causes injuries to the vet during his treatment. Animals, even with known vicious propensities, are entitled to treatment and if a vet is apprehensive that a dog that is known to have vicious tendencies might harm him, he is free to decline to render the services requested and should restrict his practice to treating small, docile animals such as canaries, hamsters and the like.

In light of the foregoing, just because the Bankrupts may be liable to the vet for the injuries he suffered, this liability cannot be characterized as a result of willful and malicious conduct on their part within the meaning of the excepted provision of § 17a(8) and, therefore, the claim of non-dischargeability cannot be sustained.

A separate final judgment in accordance with the foregoing will be entered.

BOSLEY v. ANDREWS
Supreme Court of Pennsylvania.
393 Pa. 161; 142 A.2d 263 (1958)

JOHN C. BELL, JR., Justice.

Defendant's cattle strayed onto plaintiffs' farm and injured their crops, for which the jury gave plaintiffs a verdict of $179.99. Mrs. Mary Louise Bosley, the wife-plaintiff, sought to recover damages for a heart disability which resulted from her fright and shock upon being chased by a Hereford bull owned by defendant. The bull did not strike or touch plaintiff, and plaintiff suffered no physical injury. The Superior Court sustained the entry of a nonsuit. . .

. . . Plaintiff was a very nervous woman and had on a number of occasions after this episode fainted from coronary or cardiac insufficiency without any outside or known cause. She fainted when she was being examined in 1953 by defendant's doctor, and she also fainted in the courtroom. Dr. Diehl ascribed these fainting spells to a combination of nervousness and cardiac insufficiency.

The rule is long and well established in Pennsylvania that there can be no recovery of damages for injuries resulting from fright or nervous shock or mental or emotional disturbances or distress, unless they are accompanied by physical injury or physical impact. . .

. . . To allow recovery for fright, fear, nervous shock, humiliation, mental or emotional distress--with all the disturbances and illnesses which accompany or result therefrom--where there has been no physical injury or impact, would open a Pandora's box. A plaintiff might be driving her car alertly or with her mind preoccupied, when a sudden or unexpected or exceptionally loud noise of an automobile horn behind or parallel with her car, or a sudden loud and unexpected fire engine bell or siren, or a sudden unexpected frightening buzz-sawing noise, or an unexpected explosion from blasting or dynamiting, or an unexpected nerve-wracking noise produced by riveting on a street, or the shrill and unexpected blast of a train at a spot far from a crossing, or the witnessing of a horrifying accident, or the approach of a car near or over the middle line, even though it is withdrawn to its own side in ample time to avoid an accident, or any one of a dozen other every-day events, can cause or aggravate fright or nervous shock or emotional distress or nervous tension or mental disturbance.

Such an event, if compensable, may cause normal people, as well as nervous persons and persons who are mentally disturbed or mentally ill, to honestly believe that the sudden and unexpected event caused them fright or nervous shock or nervous tension with subsequent emotional distress or suffering or pain or miscarriage or heart attack, or some kind of disease. In most cases, it would be impossible for medical science to prove that these subjective symptoms could not possibly have resulted from or been aggravated or precipitated by fright or nervous shock or nervous tension or emotional disturbance or distress, each of which can in turn produce an ulcer or headaches or fainting spells or, under some circumstances, a heart attack, or a serious disease. For every wholly genuine and deserving claim, there would likely be a tremendous number of illusory or imaginative or "faked" ones. Medical science, we repeat, could not prove that these could not have been caused or precipitated or aggravated by defendant's alleged negligent act. . .

. . . The judgment of the Superior Court is affirmed.

MICHAEL A. MUSMANNO, Justice (dissenting).

Like those human beings who believe that fame and fortune always lie in some land distant from their own, the cows of the Dale Andrews farm in West Salem, Mercer County, were not satisfied to browse and chew their cuds in their own pasture. They were certain that in the fields across the highway which bordered their owner's domain, the grass was greener, the earth fresher, the trees shadier, and the skies above bluer. Thus from time to time they would leave their own preserves and invade the Bosley farm on the other side of the road where, with the spirit of bovine buccaneers, they devoured their neighbor's corn and wheat, destroyed his vegetable gardens, knocked over young peach trees, damaged the apple orchard, mangled berry bushes, and eventually departed, leaving behind them a wide swath of ruin and destruction. They sometimes went away of their own accord, but frequently they had to be driven back to their home territory by the Bosleys.

On the morning of April 10, 1950, at about 9 o'clock they ambled over to the Bosley farm to breakfast in the fields which were the scene of former invasions but before they reached the regurgitation stage, Mrs. Evelyn Turner (married daughter of the Bosleys), assisted by a trained cattle dog, which was half collie and half of indeterminate breed, headed them off and sent them mooing back to their own pastures. By noon, however, they forgot their defeat of the morning and decided to visit the Bosleys for lunch. This time they came, eight of them, with reinforcements. They brought along their boy friend, a 1500-pound Hereford white-faced bull.

Inspirited and encouraged by their horned escort, the female bovines overran the peach trees and apple orchard when Mrs. Turner, who was in the field with her 6-year old son and the dog, sounded the alarm to her mother, Mrs. Bosley, then in the house. Mrs. Turner at once rang up the Andrews on the telephone to tell them to call off their cloven-hoofed trespassers, and then hurried outside to assist her daughter, not knowing of the presence of Mr. Hereford. Mr. Hereford and Mrs. Bosley saw each other at the same time. Mrs. Bosley screamed, and the truculent Hereford lowered his head to charge. Terror-stricken, Mrs. Bosley tried to run, but, as in a bad dream one cannot flee although disaster is at one's heels, she froze to the spot. As she later described the agonizing moment:

> "I turned around and looked, and he was coming
> at me with his head down, and I started to run, but

CHAPTER I: CANINE, EQUINE & FELINE

I thought I could not get my legs to go and I
choked up and I collapsed, and momentarily, I
though he was going to get me, I could just even
feel that he was on top of me."

In the meantime, the collie-mongrel dog, who was to become the
unwreathed hero of the episode, bounded into the space between the bull and the
terror-stricken woman. The bull then, as dull-witted as his brothers in the shouting
arenas of Spain who pursue an innocuous red rag, took after the dog, and Mrs.
Bosley was saved from a leaden-footed toreador's end.

After managing some five stumbling steps, Mrs. Bosley fainted. Upon
regaining consciousness, her daughter was rubbing her wrists and her grandson
was crying: "Nan, Nan, are you breathing?" From this point she was helped to
the barn some 150 feet away where she remained for half an hour. From here she
was assisted to a milk house between the barn and the family dwelling. Finally
she was taken home where she was at once put to bed. A doctor was summoned
and he found her suffering from "an attack of coronary insufficiency and some
heart failure."

Following ten days' confinement to bed she was taken to the Greenville
Hospital where she remained 17 days. Since then her health has never been good.
She suffers sinking spells and blackouts, she is weak and exhausted and she has
become a periodical guest of clinics and hospitals. It is the medical opinion of Dr.
G. H. Diehl, who treated her from the day of the bull episode, that the angina
pectoris, with which she is at present afflicted, was precipitated by "the running,
the chasing and the fear that was caused when the bull chased her." It is his opinion
further that Mrs. Bosley "will probably always have angina pectoris and cardiac
insufficiency in the future."

Oliver H. Bosley, husband to Mrs. Mary Bosley, and Mrs. Bosley in her
own right, brought suit in trespass against Dale Andrews on three counts: (1) for
damages done to Bosley's crops, (2) for injuries to Mrs. Bosley, and (3) for
expenses incurred by Mr. Bosley on account of his wife's injuries. The plaintiffs
recovered a verdict on the first count, but the Trial Judge directed a verdict for the
defendant on the second and third counts. The plaintiffs appealed . . .

. . . The Majority Opinion of this Court states at the outset that Mrs.
Bosley "sought to recover damages for a heart disability which resulted from her
fright and shock upon being chased by a Hereford bull owned by defendant." The
Majority thus admits that Mrs. Bosley's heart disability is a result of the fright and
shock caused by the aggressiveness of the defendant's bull. Although the bull was
about 25 feet away from Mrs. Bosley when she first beheld him charging toward
her, she ran some "five steps" before she collapsed. Allowing for at least two feet
for each step, it becomes evident that the bull was within 10 to 15 feet of Mrs.
Bosley before his course was diverted. It is enough merely to visualize a snorting,
charging bull with impaling horns only a dozen feet away, to grasp at once the

magnitude of Mrs. Bosley's fright and the extent of the terror to which she was subjected.

Although there is evidence that Mrs. Bosley did suffer from arteriosclerosis prior to April 10, 1950, it was the charge by the bull which, as another doctor (Dr. Ernstene) testified, "constituted the trigger mechanism that brought the symptoms into clinical prominence. . . "

. . . But this Court says that even if we conclude that Mrs Bosley's present physical disablement is the result of the fright, shock, and strain she experienced when the defendant's bull chased her, she is not entitled to a verdict because it would be bad policy to allow her to recover. The Majority says:

> "To allow recovery from fright, fear, nervous shock, humiliation, mental or emotional distress--with all the disturbances and illnesses which accompany or result therefrom--where there has been non physical injury or impact, would open a Pandora's box."

What is in Pandora's box which would apply to cases of this character? The Majority does not specify, but presumably it fears that from Pandora's box there would issue forth what it recounts in the immediately following sentence, namely:

> "A plaintiff might be driving her car alertly or with her mind preoccupied, when a sudden or unexpected or exceptionally loud noise of an automobile horn behind or parallel with her car, or a sudden loud and unexpected fire engine bell or siren, or a sudden unexpected frightening buzz-sawing noise, or an unexpected explosion from blasting or dynamiting, or an unexpected nerve-wracking noise produced by riveting on a street, or the shrill and unexpected blast of a train at a spot far from a crossing, or the witnessing of a horrifying accident, [which was caused by the negligence of the defendant], or the approach of a car near or over the middle line, even though it is withdrawn to its own side in ample time to avoid an accident, or any one of a dozen other every-day events, can cause or aggravate fright or nervous shock or emotional distress or nervous tension or mental disturbance."

CHAPTER I: CANINE, EQUINE & FELINE

I would say that a woman who could run the gamut of such a potential succession of blasts, shrills, dynamitings, nervewracking rivetings, explosions, buzzings, horn blowings, siren wailings and bell tollings, and emerge alive at the end-- a trip more fraught with wild excitement and adventure than Vice President Nixon's journey through South America--should be compensated in some fashion, if not in a lawsuit, at least by public subscription.

The great feat of the Majority seem to be that if we should allow the plaintiff in this case to submit her case to a jury, and, incidentally, *that is all she is seeking*, the courts would be besieged with "faked" cases. The majority prophesies with alarm:

> "For every wholly genuine and deserving claim,
> there would likely be a tremendous number of
> illusory or imaginative or 'faked' ones."

But are our courts so naive, are they so gullible, are they so devoid of worldly knowledge, are they so childlike in their approach to realities that they can be deceived and hoodwinked by claims that have no factual, medical, or legalistic basis? If they are, then all our proud boasts of the worthiness of our judicial system are empty and vapid indeed.

The Majority's apprehension that if we should allow the instant case to go to a jury for factual determination, the Courts would be engulfed in a tidal wave of lawsuits, is to look upon a raindrop and visualize an inundation. Many jurisdictions now permit recovery where physical disablement tortiously caused is not made manifest through visible trauma, and I have seen no report that in those States the Courts are awash in trumped-up cases. Many States at one time followed the non-liability doctrine but later abandoned it. . .

. . . *Stare decisis* is the viaduct over which the law travels in transporting the precious cargo of justice. Prudence and a sense of safety dictates that the piers of that viaduct should be examined and tested from time to time to make certain that they are sound, strong and capable of supporting the weight above. . .

. . . It is objected that the effect of fright is subjective, imaginative, conjectural, and speculative, and therefore easily simulated and feigned, so that its actual existence is difficult to ascertain, and, if found to exist, is inherently insusceptible of compensation by any precise pecuniary standard. These considerations undeniably tend to multiply fictitious or speculative claims, and to open to unscrupulous litigants a wide field for exploitation, but these difficulties are common, are surmountable, and *so should not prevent the operation of the general and fundamental theory of the common law that there is a remedy for every substantial wrong*. . .

. . . It seems to me that it is a violation of the living spirit of the law to adhere to an ancient rule which has no pragmatic application to realities of today. A precedent, in law, in order to be binding, should appeal to logic and a genuine sense of justice. What leads dignity to the law founded on precedent is that, if analyzed, the particularly cited case wields authority by the sheer force of its self-integrated honesty, integrity, and rationale. A precedent can not, and should not, control, if its strength depends alone on the fact that it is old, but may crumble at the slightest probing touch of instinctive reason and natural justice. With such criteria in mind, it is difficult to understand how this Court can allow damages for mental and nervous disability if incurred at the same time that a finger is bruised, but will deny compensation of any kind to the victim who sustains no outer mutilation but will be invalidated for life because his inner mechanism has been shattered beyond repair. . .

. . . What is the difference, in point of liability, on the part of a railroad company, between a case where a passenger's arm is cut in a train wreck, and a case where a passenger suffers a broken heart valve as a result of the fear he experience in expecting death as a car passed over him? Is the negligence and responsibility of the tortfeasor any less marked toward the living man than to the dead man's family when, after the throb of the overturned locomotive has ceased and the hissing of the punctured air brakes has faded away, then lie on the ground, next to one another, the body of a stark dead passenger and the body of a living passenger, unconscious, but unblemished by a single scratch? To determine liability by what follows rather than by what precedes and accompanies a catastrophe is like concluding that no earthquake has occurred because no one was killed even though the earth gaped and the houses danced as if doing a grisly quadrille . . .

. . . The heart has been so excessively the subject of poetic rhapsodizing that it would seem we may have lost sight of the fact that it is objectively a physical organ with mechanical functions as rigidly followed as the metallic movements of the village pump. Mrs. Bosley's ailment is not be to equated with intangible grieving or sentimental lamenting. Her heart condition is as much a matter of muscle and tissue as traumatic neuritis. However, while Mrs. Bosley's condition is tangible and palpable, it was caused by a force which did not touch her except through operation of the mind. But that does not mean that the application of the distant force was any less realistic. When a person whitens with fear, blushes with shame, shivers from apprehension, or petrifies with horror, there is no immediate bodily contact with the force which produces those definite physical reactions. But can we say that there is no actual bond between the emotion-creating phenomenon and the organism of the person who responds to the phenomenon? To answer that question in the negative would be to deny the most elementary certainties of human experience.

What provokes laughter? Is laughing not the result of a mental appraisement? But laughter itself is not mental. Abdominal, facial, and labial muscles, vocal cords, larynx and pharynx must all operate and coordinate in order to produce a hearty guffaw. What are tears? Except when they are concomitant with torture or whipping, they are the result purely of intangible thought. One thinks of a lost relative, a departed friend, a tragic event, and a saline solution forms in the eyes. A great deal of physical machinery goes into action to manufacture those drops of water, and it would be sheer perversity to say that there is no connection between the item of grief and the distillation of the resulting tears.

Can laughter and weeping ever by physically injurious? It is no figure of speech that people have actually laughed themselves to death. It is no rhetorical exaggeration to say that people have died of weeping and grief. [1] There is, therefore, an objective linking--of cause and effect--between outer phenomenon and physical reaction. Thus, if one can die with laughing, perish with weeping and freeze from fear, how can it be said that there is no tie of contact between the terror if immediate death caused by the charging of a ferocious beast and a heart ailment which contemporaneously occurs and thereafter unceasingly continues?. . .

. . . This Court finds difficulty in attaching liability to the defendant in this case because of the gap between the bull's nose and Mrs. Bosley's prostrate body, which measured no more than 10 to 15 feet. If the animal's charging horns had advanced closer and had just grazed, without seriously harming Mrs. Bosley, then, according to [Pennsylvania law], she would be entitled to recover. . . .

. . Let us suppose the following situation: Mr. A. maliciously designs to visit serious harm upon Mrs. B. who is frail, of a highly nervous disposition, and has a weak heart. As Mrs. B. is walking along a dark lane at night, Mr. A. steps out before her, wearing a lighted hideous mask and makes blood-curdling noises. Mrs. B. collapses from fright but sustains no physical injury, nor is there any impact between her and Mr. A. However she never gets over the shock and is invalided for life. To deny Mrs. B. the right to recovery for the harm inflicted upon her in such a case would not only be an injustice but a monstrous wrong.

Let us take another case. Mr. A. is a court physician who on an extremely cold night is summoned to attend a patient who lives 12 miles away. He travels in a top buggy drawn by a pair of horses. After treating the sick man he starts back home. Arriving at a railroad crossing he is held up for a period of from 45 to 50 minutes by a freight train. (It is admitted that there was negligence here on the part of the railroad company.) The cold freezes his hands and penetrates his body. When he finally reaches home he is so numb and chilled that he has difficulty in removing his clothing. Articulate rheumatism sets in and he is invalided thereby

---

[1]King Richard II, Act III, Scene iii:

> *"Aumerle, thou weep'st, my tender-hearted cousin!*
> *We'll make foul weather with despised tears;*
> *Our sighs and they shall lodge the summer corn,*
> *And make a dearth in this revolting land.*
> *Or shall we play the wanton with our woes,*
> *And make some pretty match with shedding tears?*
> *As thus, to drop them still upon one place,*
> *Till they have fretted us a pair of graves*
> *Within the earth; and, therein laid--there lies*
> *Two kinsmen digg'd their graves with weeping eyes."*

for a long time. It is quite evident that his illness is the result of the exposure caused by the long wait at the railroad crossing. Does he have a good cause of action against the railroad company? This Court indubitably would say No, but our sister appellate Court has already answered that very question in the affirmative because this case is not, like the previous illustration, a hypothetical one. This is the actual case of Cowdrick v. New York Central R. Co., 65 Pa.Super. 416, where a verdict won against the railroad company was affirmed by the Superior Court. . .

. . . Is not this entire problem simply one of ascertaining effect from cause? Dr. Cosdrick was not struck by a railroad train, he was not bowled over by a piece of mental flung off from a passing locomotive. He was hurt by the arctic weather from which he would have been insulated, had it not been for the negligence of the railroad company which exposed him to its frigid temperature for almost an hour. In the case at bar, Mrs. Bosley would not have been hurt had it not been of the negligence of Dale Andrews in exposing her to the bellicosity of his bull, which can be seen more damaging than the blast of a winter's wind.

I would not recommend that the Supreme Court of Pennsylvania change one of its rules which is venerable with age, if it were one which appeals to reason, fairness, and justice. But when the rule defended by the Majority stands on such slippery ground as has been indicated in this case, should we not look to other jurisdictions to see how they are treating the same problem? The Majority Opinion does not lift binoculars to look across our borders into other States. It does not even apply spectacles to the Restatement on Torts. Section 436(2) of that magnificent compendium of legal principles states:

> "If the actor's conduct is negligent as creating an unreasonable risk of causing bodily harm to another otherwise than by subjecting him to fright, shock or other similar and immediate emotional disturbance the fact that such harm results solely from the internal operation of fright or other emotional disturbance does not protect the actor from liability. . . "

. . . The heart may be injured by a blow as easily as the lungs, liver, or any other internal organ. And that blow may be administered through the application of force against the outer walls or through the channels of the senses. It is a matter of common knowledge that persons afflicted with certain ailments must avoid excitement, not only the excitement of physical movement but that which is felt through the sense of sight, hearing, and possibly smell. The interlinking between sensory excitation and physiological reaction is such a historical, demonstrable, and everyday reality that to dwell on it at length would be like carrying the proverbial coals to Newcastle or crocodiles to the Nile.

Although afflicted with arteriosclerosis, Mrs. Bosley could have relished life in all its beneficial fullness. By observing whatever limitations doctors might have placed on her activities, there is no reason why she could not have looked forward to a reasonable long existence, enjoying with full flavor the many sweetnesses that normal living affords. The books are filled with cases of people who, because of an arterial burden, may not run as fast as athletes run for a train, bus, or street car, but who adjust themselves admirable to a less rapid pace and find more time to breathe in the fragrance of the garden of good, wholesome living. Mrs. Bosley had every reason to look forward to that prospect.

A trespasser came to her home and struck her down. The bull belonging to the defendant was as much a trespasser and invader as a robber breaking through a window at night. As soon as the bull crossed the frontiers of the Bosley farm, its owner, Dale Andrews, was guilty of a trespass. Whatever damage succeeded that invasion, and because of that invasion, was Dale Andrews' responsibility. Under the law of *quare clausum fregit* [wherefore he broke the close], Andrews' liability was almost automatic. . .

. . .To say that to grant what the law allows in this case might create an untoward situation in other cases is like saying that the fountain of justice should be boarded up because of the possibility that someone might drown in its salutary waters.

I would have the fountain flowing at all times, assured that the established safeguards of the law will keep away those who would defile its pure and refreshing essence just as those same safeguards are prepared, if not shackled, to hold responsible those who allow ferocious animals to roam at large to the hurt and grievous loss of the innocent and the unsuspecting, in the tranquil enjoyment of their homes, their gardens, and the prospect of a safe and cloudless future.

In recapitulation I wish to go on record that the policy of non-liability announced by the Majority in this type of case is insupportable in law, logic, and elementary justice--and I shall continue to dissent from it until the cows come home.

MILES v. CITY COUNCIL OF AUGUSTA, GEORGIA [CASE 1]
United States District Court, S.D. Georgia
551 F. Supp. 349 (1982)

DUDLEY H. BOWEN, District Judge.

This case is before the Court on the cross-motions for summary judgment of plaintiffs Carl and Elaine Miles and defendant City Council of Augusta, Georgia. For the reasons to follow, summary judgment is GRANTED IN FAVOR OF DEFENDANT AND DENIED AS TO THE PLAINTIFFS. The plaintiffs' motion will be discussed first.

I. PLAINTIFFS' MOTION

In this case, the attack upon the power of the City of Augusta to levy an occupation tax arises under somewhat unusual circumstances. The pertinent facts, as gleaned from the record,[1] are as follows:

A. The Cat

Carl and Elaine Miles are an unemployed, married couple who own "Blackie, The Talking Cat." Trained by Carl Miles, Blackie allegedly is able to speak several words and phrases of the English language. On June 22, 1981, plaintiffs were required by defendant to obtain a business license. From May 15, to June 22, 1981, plaintiffs had accepted contributions from pedestrians in the downtown Augusta area who wanted to hear the cat speak. People would stop the plaintiffs who strolled the streets with the cat. Upon being stopped, plaintiffs would ask for a contribution. There is, however, evidence of the plaintiffs soliciting an off-duty policeman for money in exchange for a performance. Plaintiffs dispute this allegation. It is undisputed that plaintiffs would ask for, and lived off, the contributions received for Blackie's orations. Several complaints were received by the August Police Department regarding the plaintiffs' solicitations. Plaintiffs were warned by the police not to solicit unless they first obtained a business license.

Through their exploit of his talents, Blackie has provided his owners with at least the minimal necessities of life.[2] Plaintiff Carl Miles has entered into several contracts with talent agents in Georgia, South Carolina and North Carolina. These agents have paid, at least in part, the Miles' living expenses over a period of time. The evidence does not clearly show that this support was provided during the relevant time period of May 15th to June 22nd. It does, however, permit the inference that prior to the plaintiffs' arrival in Augusta, they intended to commercially exploit Blackie's ability.

---

[1] In ruling on the motions for summary judgment, the Court has considered only the evidence in the file. However, it should be disclosed that I have seen and heard a demonstration of Blackie's abilities. The point in time of the Court's view was late summer, 1982, well after the events contended in this lawsuit. One afternoon when crossing Greene Street in an automobile, I spotted in the median, a man accompanied by a cat and a woman. The black cat was draped over his left shoulder. Knowing the matter to be in litigation, and suspecting that the cat was Blackie, I thought twice before stopping. Observing, however, that counsel for neither side was present and that any citizen on the street could have happened by chance upon this scene, I spoke, and the man with the cat eagerly responded to my greeting. I asked him if his cat could talk. He said he could, and if I would pull over on the side street he would show me. I did, and he did. The cat was wearing a collar, two harnesses and a leash. Held and stroked by the man Blackie said "I love you" and "I want my Mama." The man then explained that the cat was the sole source of income for him and his wife and requested a donation which was provided. I felt that my dollar was well spent. The cat was entertaining as was its owner. Some questions occurred to me about the necessity for the multiple means of restraint and the way in

B. The Ordinance

Under its charter the City of Augusta is empowered to impose license taxes. Section 139 of the charter states, in pertinent part:

> The City Council of Augusta, by ordinance, may require any person, firm or corporation to pay a license tax upon any occupation, trade or business followed or carried on within the corporate limits of the City of Augusta . . .

Pursuant to this enabling provision, the City Council enacted Ordinance No. 5006, the 1981-1982 business license ordinance. The ordinance exhaustively lists the trades, businesses and occupations subject to the ordinance and the amount of tax to be paid. Although the ordinance does not provide for the licensing of a talking cat,[3] section 2 of the ordinance does require any "Agent or Agency not specifically mentioned" to pay a $50.00 tax.

---

which the man held the cat's paw when the cat was asked to talk. However, these are not matters before the Court and are beyond the purview of a federal judge. I do not know if the man whom I saw with the cat was the plaintiff Mr. Miles.

This sequence has not been considered as evidence or as an uncontroverted fact in the case. It is simply stated for the purpose of a disclosure to the parties of the chance contact.

[2] That a talking cat could generate interest and income is not surprising. Man's fascination with the domestic feline is perennial. People of western cultures usually fall into two categories. Generally, they are ailurophiles or ailurophobes. Cats are ubiquitous in the literature, lore and fiber of our society and language. The ruthless Garfield commands the comic strips, the Cat in the Hat exasperates even Dr. Seuss, and who hasn't heard of Heathcliff, Felix, or Sylvester? Historically, calico cats have eaten gingham dogs, we are taught that "a cat can look at a king" and at least one cat has "been to London to see the Queen."

It is often said that imitation is the sincerest form of flattery. To the animal world, I am sure that the sincerest form is anthropomorphosis. The ailurophobes contend that anthropomorphosis abounds, and that it is the work of ailurophiles. The ailurophiles say that they do not anthropomorphize cats but, rather, that cats have such human qualities as they may condescend to adopt for their own selfish purposes. Perhaps such was the case with Saki's ill-fated Tobermory, the cat who knew too much and told all, who, when asked if the human language had been difficult to learn, ". . . looked squarely at [Miss Resker] for a moment and then fixed his gaze serenely on the middle distance. It was obvious that boring questions lay outside his scheme of life."

For hundreds, perhaps thousands of years, people have carried on conversations with cats. Most often, these are one-sided and range from cloying, mawkish nonsense to topics of science and the liberal arts. Apparently Blackie's pride does not prevent him from making an occasional response to this great gush of human verbiage, much to the satisfaction and benefit of his "owners." Apparently, some cats do talk. Others just grin.

[3] It seems doubtful that the city fathers would anticipate the need for a specific category of this sort.

C. The Attack

Plaintiffs attack the ordinance as being unconstitutionally vague and overbroad in contravention of the Due Process clauses of the fourteenth amendment to the United States Constitution and of the Georgia Constitution. They contend they are not required to obtain a license and that requiring them to do so before they may solicit on the streets violates their first amendment rights of speech and association as well as the right to equal protection secured by the fourteenth amendment. . .

. . . The purpose behind the ordinance questioned in this case is to generate revenue. It is a tax on occupations and businesses. The preamble to Ordinance No. 5006 (the ordinance) states, in part, "An ordinance to fix the annual and specific taxes and licenses of the City of Augusta on Business Occupations and Professions . . . Clearly, the ordinance does not have as its sole purpose the regulation of solicitation per se. The thrust of the ordinance is directed, not at speech and association, but at the generation of revenue through the imposition of an occupation tax.

The power of the defendant to levy an occupation tax is unquestionable. The city charter authorizes the very ordinance passed by the defendant council. The taxing power, as embodied in a municipality's charter, is well recognized as a means for raising revenue. The ordinance is not one designed to regulate speech or association, but merely to raise revenue. The ordinance does not subject anyone's speech or associational activity to any penalty unless committed within the context of one's occupation for which a tax has not been paid. Thus, the ordinance does not tread upon plaintiffs' fundamental constitutional rights.

[I]t is noted an exhaustive list of businesses, occupations and trades subject to taxation is contained in the ordinance. Equally important to note is the practical impossibility of specifying, with particularity, each and every occupation, trade or business, that would conceivably come within the ambit of the ordinance. Plaintiffs cannot reasonably argue that before the defendant can require a business license for a talking cat, it must specifically provide for such an occupation in its ordinance. The self-evident thrust of the ordinance is to tax occupations, businesses and trades that derive income from the practice of that occupation, business and trade in the marketplace.

Plaintiff's contention that they are not required to obtain a license carries the implication that they are not engaged in an occupation. In their brief, plaintiffs cite several definitions of the terms "occupation" and "business." The general import of these definitions is that one is engaged in an occupation or business when that work or activity occupies one's time or attention on a regular basis for profit or support. Inasmuch as the ordinance does not define "occupation" or "business", the common definition cited above applies. Plaintiffs' activity, regardless of its peculiarity, falls within this definition.

Carl Miles, in his deposition of April 23, 1982, stated at pages 35-36 that prior to June 22, 1981, he would ask for a contribution when people asked to hear his cat talk. From May 15, 1981, to June 22nd, he received enough contributions, usually $.25 or $.50 each, to pay his weekly rent of $35.00 and purchase other necessities, except for a two-week period in which he used money from his savings. Miles Deposition, at p. 38. He and his wife were otherwise unemployed, with no other income. Plaintiffs would walk, with the cat, in the vicinity of Broad and Greene Streets, major avenues of motorized and pedestrian traffic, for several hours a day. Deposition of Elaine Miles, at p. 13. Thus, they were regularly engaged in a pursuit yielding income however small.

The plaintiffs' commercial interest in Blackie is well established. It is undisputed that before they moved to Augusta and after the business license was obtained, Carl Miles entered into several agreements with talent, or booking, agencies in South Carolina, North Carolina and Georgia. Carl Miles Deposition, at pp. 6-7, 21-23. Prior to June 22nd, Blackie appeared on television and radio. For example, in 1980 Blackie appeared on "That's Incredible," a nationally televised program, for $500.00. Also, plaintiffs' living expenses have been paid in part by at least one promotional agency who had contracted with Carl Miles. Although the activity recounted here occurred either prior to the plaintiffs' move to Augusta or after June 22nd, it is relevant to show the interest plaintiffs had in exploiting Blackie on a commercial basis. This interest coupled with the near daily receipt of contributions requested by the plaintiffs for performances by the cat brings them well within the definition of occupation.

Furthermore, the question of obtaining a business license was not new to Carl Miles. He had on previous occasions, in Charlotte and Columbia, inquired as to the necessity of a license. Deposition, at pp. 19-20. He, therefore, viewed his exploitation of the cat as a business activity for which a license might be required. The fact that those cities did not require a license does not alter the nature of his activity or prevent the City of Augusta from requiring one. Since they did not hold themselves out as a charity, the plaintiffs cannot persuasively argue that their activity did not require a license. The ordinance is not impermissibly vague.

As demonstrated in both motions for summary judgment, there is no genuine issue of material fact existing in this case. Consideration was limited, therefore, to entitlement of judgment as a matter of law. Under the facts and the applicable law, defendant prevails. The ordinance challenged by the plaintiffs is constitutionally valid depriving them of neither due process nor equal protection. The ordinance is a legitimate, rational means for the generation of revenue for the benefit of the defendant. It does not trammel the fundamental rights of the plaintiffs as guaranteed by the state and federal constitutions.

Accordingly, in consideration of the foregoing findings and conclusions, plaintiffs' motion for summary judgment is DENIED. Judgment is, however, granted in favor of the defendant City Council of Augusta on all issues.

MILES v. CITY COUNCIL OF AUGUSTA, GEORGIA [CASE 2]
United States Court of Appeals, Eleventh Circuit.
710 F.2d 1542 (1983)

Before GERALD BARD TJOFLAT, FRANK M. JOHNSON, JR. and JOSEPH W. HATCHETT, Circuit Judges.

PER CURIAM:

Plaintiffs Carl and Elaine Miles, owners and promoters of "Blackie the Talking Cat," brought this suit in the United States District Court of the Southern District of Georgia, challenging the constitutionality of the Augusta, Georgia, Business License Ordinance. Their complaint alleged that the ordinance is inapplicable in this case or is otherwise void for vagueness and overbroad, and that the ordinance violates rights of speech and association. The district court granted summary judgment in favor of the defendant City Council of Augusta. *Miles v. City of Augusta,* 551 F.Supp. 349 (S.D.Ga 1982). We affirm.

The partnership between Blackie and the Mileses began somewhat auspiciously in a South Carolina rooming house. According to the deposition of Carl Miles:

> Well, a girl come around with a box of kittens, and she asked us did we want one. I said no, that we did not want one. As I was walking away from the box of kittens, a voice spoke to me and said "Take the black kitten." I took the black kitten, knowing nothing else unusual or nothing else strange about the black kitten. When Blackie was about five months old, I had him on my lap playing with him, talking to him, saying I love you. The voice spoke to me saying, "The cat is trying to talk to you." To me, the voice was the voice of God.

Mr. Miles set out to fulfill his divination by developing a rigorous course of speech therapy.

> I would tape the sounds the cat would make, the voice sounds he would make when he was trying to talk to me, and I would play those sounds back to him three and four hours a day, and I would let him watch my lips, and he just got to where he could do it.

CHAPTER I: CANINE, EQUINE & FELINE

Blackie's catechism soon began to pay off. According to Mr. Miles:

> He was talking when he was six months old, but
> I could not prove it them. It was where I could
> understand him, but you can't understand him. It
> took me altogether a year and half before I had
> him talking real plain where you could understand
> him.

Ineluctably, Blackie's talents were taken to the marketplace, and the rest is history. Blackie catapulted into public prominence when he spoke, for a fee, on radio and on television shows such as "That's Incredible." Appellants capitalized on Blackie's linguistic skills through agreements with agents in South Carolina, North Carolina and Georgia. The public's affection for Blackie was the catalyst for his success, and Blackie loved his fans. As the District Judge observed in his published opinion, Blackie even purred "I love you" to him when he encountered Blackie one day on the street.[1]

Sadly, Blackie's cataclysmic rise to fame crested and began to subside. The Miles family moved temporarily to Augusta, Georgia, receiving "contributions" that Augusta passersby paid to hear Blackie talk. After receiving complaints from several of Augusta's ailurophobes, the Augusta police - obviously no ailurophiles themselves[2] - doggedly insisted that appellants would have to purchase a business license. Eventually, on threat of incarceration, Mr. and Mrs. Miles acceded to the demands of the police and paid $50 for a business license.

The gist of appellant's argument is that the Augusta business ordinance contains no category for speaking animals. The ordinance exhaustively lists trades, businesses, and occupations subject to the tax and the amount of the tax to be paid, but it nowhere lists cats with forensic prowess. However, section 2 of Augusta's Business Ordinance No. 5006 specifies that a $50 license shall be paid by any "Agent or Agency not specifically mentioned." Appellants insist that the drafters of section 2 could not have meant to include Blackie the Talking Cat and, if they did, appellants assert that section 2, as drafted, is vague and overbroad and hence unconstitutional.

Upon review of appellants' claims, we agree with the district court's detailed analysis of the Augusta ordinance. The assertion that Blackie's speaking engagements do not constitute an "occupation" or "business" within the meaning of the catchall provision of the Augusta ordinance is wholly without merit. Although the Miles family called what they received for Blackie's performances "contributions," these elocutionary endeavors were entirely intended for pecuni-

---

[1] We note that this affectionate encounter occurred before the Judge ruled against Blackie. See Miles, supra, 551 F.Supp. at 350 n.1.

[2] See 551 F.Supp. at 351 n.2.

ary enrichment and were indubitably commercial. [3] Moreover, we refuse to require that Augusta define "business" in order to avoid problems of vagueness. The word has a common sense meaning that Mr. Miles undoubtedly understood [4] ... Finally, we agree with the district court that appellants have not made out a case of overbreadth with respect to section 2 of the ordinance. Appellants fail to show any illegal infringement of First Amendment rights of free speech [5] or assembly. The overbreadth of a statute must be "judged in relation to the statute's plainly legitimate sweep." [citation omitted] Appellants' activities plainly come within the legitimate exercise of the city's taxing power.

AFFIRMED.

MINCEY v. BRADBURN
Supreme Court of Tennessee
103 Tenn. 407; 56 S.W. 273 (1899)

JOHN S. WILKES, J.

This is a lawsuit arising out of the unlawful acts of a disorderly mule. He was found loitering about the streets of Knoxville, without any apparent business, no visible means of support, and no evidence of ownership, except a yoke on his neck. This yoke was evidence that the mule had been at some time in a state of subjection, but did not indicate to whom. Although he does not appear to have been drunk or boisterous, a vigilant officer of the police of the city arrested him and took him to the lockup. The policeman was authorized to do this by a city ordinance, which was no doubt intended and well calculated to preserve the lives of the people and the good order of the city by prohibiting mules from being loose in the streets.

The mule was arrested on the 7th of September, and was locked up (in) the city pound. The poundkeeper did not know who he belonged to, and the mule made no disclosures of his ownership. The poundkeeper, it appears, went to the market house, and inquired of the butchers if a mule had escaped from any one of them. Why he should suppose that a butcher's stall should be an appropriate place to find out the owner of a live mule does not appear. The poundkeeper further

---

[3] This conclusion is supported by the undisputed evidence in the record that appellants solicited contributions. Blackie would become catatonic and refuse to speak whenever his audience neglected to make a contribution.

[4] As found by the district court, Mr. Miles had previously inquired as to the necessity of obtaining a business license in Charlotte, North Carolina, and in Columbia, South Carolina. 551 F.Supp. at 353.

[5] This Court will not hear a claim that Blackie's right to free speech has been infringed. First, although Blackie arguably possesses a very unusual ability, he cannot be considered a "person" and is therefore not protected by the Bill of Rights. Second, even if Blackie had such a right, we see no need for appellants to assert his right *jus tertii*. Blackie can clearly speak for himself.

inquired of such country people as he could find if they knew of any one who had lost a mule. A farmer, who lived out about three miles from the city, said that one of his neighbors had lost a mule, and requested that no advertisement be made until he could see if the mule was his neighbor's. When the farmer asked his neighbor if he had lost a mule, he was told that unfortunately he had not. In this way five days elapsed before any advertisement was made.

In the meantime the mule was kept in close confinement, and refused to be interviewed. On the 12th of September, or five days after the mule was arrested, the poundmaster advertised in the Knoxville Journal & Tribune that the mule would be sold on the 14th, unless called for and charges paid; and no one calling, the mule was sold publicly, for case, for $20, and one O. T. Smith became the purchaser. The costs and charges were paid out of the proceeds of sale, and the balance was left in the city treasury to be called for by the owner. What this balance was docs not appear. It is stated in the record that it was ($____) blank dollars. Whether this means that there was no balance, or that the amount was unknown and not material, is left in doubt.

Mr. Smith, the purchaser, sold the mule to Mincey, but for what sum does not appear. Mincey, it appears, bought the mule in good faith, and did not know that he had ever been arrested or confined in the city lockup, or that he had been sold by the city. So far as he knew, the mule had the usual good reputation of his species.

In the meantime, Mr. Bradburn, to whom the mule belonged, missed him from his corncrib, and supposed he had gone to Sevier county, where he came from originally. He made inquiries, however, and among other things went to a telephone station to inquire of the poundkeeper if he had such a mule. It appeared, however, that "Central" was busy or gone to dinner, and Mr. Bradburn could not reach the poundkeeper. He thereupon asked Mr. Clark to telephone for him. Mr. Clark reported that word came back to him from the other end of the line that there was no mule there. It does not appear who was at the other end of the line, so that the truth of this answer is not verified. The mule, however, did not return to Sevier county, but preferred to be locked up in Knoxville. Mr. Bradburn did not see the advertisement in the Journal & Tribune. Probably he did not take that paper, but read the Sentinel. Counsel says that the advertisement was put in an obscure place. Exactly what he means the court to infer from that we are unable to see. The court cannot judicially know there is anything obscure in any Knoxville paper, unless it be in the reports of supreme court opinions, and these appear to be obscure only to the lawyers who lose their cases.

After the sale, and plaintiff found out where his mule was, he replevied him. The case was tried before the court and jury in the court below, and plaintiff was successful, and defendant has appealed; but he has been paid back the money he paid for the mule, and the further proceedings do not appear to interest him. The city comes in, however, by counsel, and complains earnestly of the charge of the circuit judge.

The learned trial judge charged that an ordinance of the city which provided for a sale of animals impounded after only two days' advertisement was unreasonable and invalid; that two days was not sufficient notice to give, and a sale under such advertisement would be void, and confer no title on the purchaser, and he could communicate none to a party who bought from him, even without notice. The learned trial judge also charged that the proceeding by the municipality to sell impounded stock, being a summary proceeding, must be strictly pursued; that the poundmaster should immediately, upon impounding the animal, make the advertisement, and that if the mule was impounded on the 7th, and not advertised till the 12th, it was not a compliance with the ordinance, and a sale thereunder would be null and void, and communicate no title to the purchaser, and he could convey none to his vendee; that, no matter if the poundmaster made the delay with good intentions, hoping to find the owner, it would furnish no excuse.

The city attorney insists that this is requiring too great a degree of diligence on the part of the poundmaster, and that a reasonable delay will not vitiate his sale, especially when that delay is caused by trying to find the owner. The argument is that the work "immediately," as used in the ordinance, does not mean "instantaneously"; that the poundkeeper must have sufficient time to shut the pound gate, so as to keep the mule in, before he starts to the printing office; that, after he does start, he may proceed in a brisk walk, and is not required to run; that after he gets there time must be allowed to set up the matter in type, and there must then be a delay until the hour when the paper is printed, and ready for distribution; and that the poundkeeper is not required to get out an extra.

We are satisfied the learned trial judge did not mean to require such dispatch as this, and, without undertaking to say how rapidly the poundmaster must proceed, we are of opinion that, under all the facts of this case, there was no such unreasonable delay as would render the sale void.

Now, if the mule was the party complaining, the court would feel disposed to say the delay was too great, as it does not appear that the mule had anything to eat during his stay as the city's guest. But neither the city nor the owner has any ground of complaint.

It is said by counsel that the other question presented is an exceedingly important one, and we approach it with a deep feeling of responsibility. Counsel for plaintiff says that the ordinance is unreasonable, and the charge was necessary to correct a great and growing evil. What this evil is the record does not disclose. It is not alleged that any great trust or combine is being formed in impounded mules, and it is not shown that any trust at all exists as to mules running loose. The attorney for the city has furnished us a printed brief, which we have read with much interest and profit, and have filed away for future reference. In it a case is cited from North Carolina, where the supreme court of that state held that three days' advertisement of an impounded hog was sufficient. Shaw v. Kennedy, 4 N.C. 591; Hellen v. Noe, 25 N.C. 493. Also a case from Missouri, holding that three days' advertisement of impounded cattle was sufficient. White v. Haworth, 21 Mo. App. 439.

Under a former ordinance of the city of Knoxville, it was held that five days' notice by posters at the court-house door was sufficient. Mayer, etc., v. King 7 Lea 44. In the case of Moore v. State, 11 Lea 35, it was held that an ordinance of the taxing district of Memphis, providing that impounded stock might be sold on four days' advertisement, was valid. Now, if it would take four days to affect the city of Memphis with notice, it is said it would not require less time to reach the public in Knoxville.

The argument of the city attorney seems to be that, if a hog may be sold in three days, a mule might be sold in two days, since he is much more of a nuisance, and much more dangerous to keep, and the city ought not to be expected to remain forever on guard. Now, we do not desire to say anything disrespectful of or derogatory to the mule. He has no posterity to protect and keep alive his memory. The ordinance applies to all animals, and we are of the opinion that two days' advertisement is not enough. No owner would feel any great sense of loss in so short a time. We feel constrained, upon the ground stated, that the time is too short, and declare the ordinance unreasonable, and the judgment must be affirmed. The defendant must pay all costs. We would tax the city with it, as it loses one of its ordinances, but we are unable to tell from the partial transcript whether the city is a party or not.

HAMPTON v. NORTH CAROLINA PULP CO.
United States District Court, E.D. North Carolina
49 F. Supp. 625 (1943)

ISAAC M. MEEKINS, District Judge.
This is a civil action at law brought by the plaintiff against the defendant in which the plaintiff seeks to recover from the defendant damages in the sum of $30,000 for the alleged wrongful diversion and destruction of fish in the navigable waters of the Roanoke River near Plymouth, North Carolina. A motion to dismiss the cause for failure of the complaint "to state a claim upon which relief can be granted" was heard by me at Raleigh in Term and thereafter briefs were filed in due course.

Well, . . . Fish is the subject of this story. From the fifth day of the Creation down through the centuries, some of which lie behind us like a hideous dream, fish have been a substantial factor in the affairs of men. After giving man dominion over all the Earth, God gave him dominion over the fish in particular, naming them first in order, reserving unto Himself only one certain fruit tree in the midst of the Garden,[1] and Satan smeared that - the wretch! Whatever else we may think of the Devil, as a business man he is working success. He sat in the original game, not with one fruit tree, but with the cash capital of one snake, and now he

---

[1] Gen. 1:26, 28; 2:17; 3:3, 4.

has half the world grabbed and a diamond hitch on the other half. [2]

Great hunters lived before Nimrod who was a mighty one before the Lord,[3] and great fishermen before Izaak Walton, whose followers are as numberless as the sands of the sea - not counting the leaves of the forest, as if anybody ever did, or could, except the quondam Literary Digest, which polled itself to death in the late Summer and middle Fall of 1936.

The most notable group of fishermen of all time was that headed by Peter, the impulsive Apostle, and his followers Thomas, Nathaniel, the sons of Zebedee, and two other Disciples, seven fishermen in all - a working majority of The Twelve.[4]

Considered solely as a food product, fish have unlimited possibilities - quantitative and qualitative. We are told that a few little fishes and seven loaves, five loaves and two fishes, according to St. Luke, were more than sufficient to feed a hungry multitude of four thousand men, together with the women and children present, and of the fragments there were seven baskets full of fish.[5] Quantitative.

Professor Agassiz, the eminent Harvard scientist said: "Fish is a good brain food." One wrote to know "in what quantities should it be taken?" The great scientist wrote back: "In your case, a whale a day for thirty days." Qualitative.

Fish have their place in song and story. In song, from the nursery rime: "Little Fishes in the Brook," to the huge leviathans that forsake unsounded deeps to dance on sands.[6] In story, since the dawn of civilization and the imagination of man began to build romances and tall tales, full and fruity. He was more wag than skeptic who said: "In all the world there are only three really great fish stories - Admiral Noah, Commodore Jonah and Captain John Smith." Herbert Hoover added the fourth when, fishing in Nevada, he pulled a twenty-five pound trout from the green waters of Pyramid Lake.[7]

Noah built an ark so many cubits high, wide and long. It had one door in the side, and one window in the top twenty-two inches square.[8] What ventilation! We are told it rained forty days and forty nights and all the mountains were covered with water.[9] We know that Mount Everest is 29,140 feet high.[10] Since it was covered by the flood, the water reached an altitude of more than 29,140 feet. Divide the altitude by forty and we find that the average rainfall was more than 700 feet per day. How's that for dampness!

---

[2] The eminent American Modernist.
[3] Gen. 10:9.
[4] John 21:2, 3.
[5] Matthew 15:36.
[6] Two Gentlemen of Verona.
[7] Desert Challenge - Lillard.
[8] Gen. 6:14, 15, 16.
[9] Gen. 7:12, 20.
[10] Encyclopedia Brittanica.

CHAPTER I: CANINE, EQUINE & FELINE

Apart from the Biblical account of the flood, many nations have vivid accounts of floods in which all the people except a chosen few, were destroyed. One account, that points this story, is a fable about a flood in ancient India. A fish warned Manu that a flood was coming. Manu built a ship and the fish towed it to a mountain and thus saved everybody.[11] We can laugh at this fable without fear of condemnation here and damnation hereafter. That was not *our* flood.

Jonah, like all the orthodox Jews of his time, thought Jehovah was a local Deity. Jonah did not like his assignment to Nineveh and in an effort to side-step it he took passage on a ship at Joppa for Tarshish and fled from the presence of the Lord.[12] The Prophet thought that if he could get into another jurisdiction he would be safe. However, before he crossed the boundary line into Tarshish, Jehovah pulled down on him with a double-barrel tempest and a muzzle-loading leviathan.[13] When he found himself a prisoner, for three days and three nights, in the belly of the great fish that the Lord had prepared, Jonah began to think things over. We all do when our "take a chance" does not pan out as we hoped. The net result was that the Prophet, after repenting of his disobedience and praying forgiveness, was allowed to go ashore. "The Lord spake unto the fish, and it vomited out Jonah upon the dry land."[14] This was before the advent of the camera enthusiast, else we might have been fortified with an authentic photograph of the minor Prophet walking ashore with the lower jaw of the whale for gang-plank. The eminent American Modernist said he was rather inclined to think that Jonah proved too tough for his whaleship's digestion and that in a fit of acute ptomaine poisoning, the cantankerous old Prophet was cast forth.

Captain John Smith, in the minds of many people, is more a joke than a myth. However, patient and interesting investigation has led me to the conclusion that he was not only a great Englishman, but a very great Englishman; that he was not only a great man, but a very great man; that he was good, useful and sane and did a very great World Service. Measured by all the standards of constructive achievement he was essentially a World Man. That Captain John Smith is less a myth than a joke is one of the glaring anomalies of history. Perhaps the raconteur had it in mind to emphasize his facetiousness by fact; to contrast his shadow with substance - his fancy with truth.

The Skeptic may scoff and the Modernist may moderate, but the story of Noah and the story of Jonah are enduring torches that lighted the way of man in his struggle upward through the immensity of the Shadow, and now as then guide the fumbling fingers of the trembling hand as with the establishment and strength of Jachin and Boas.[15]

---

[11] Encyclopedia Brittanica.
[12] Jonah 1:3.
[13] Jonah 1:4, 17.
[14] Jonah 2:10.
[15] I Kings 7:21.

Divested of the insistence of the Fundamentalists on the Verbal Inspiration and Infallibility of the Bible, and accepted in the light of reason, which examines and explains, the story of Noah is the greatest statement on the importance of preparation ever penned by mortal hand. In thunder tones we are warned; in time of peace, prepare for war; in the days of ease and luxury and laissez-faire, remember that evil days are ahead; in the fat years, prepare for the lean ones just around the corner - always be ready "to flee from the wrath to come!"[16]

Likewise, the story of Jonah is the greatest statement on fidelity to duty, hard and inexorable, that ever fell from the lips of man. It shouts forth the consequences that follow lapses from duty through wilful disobedience or otherwise. "Duty," said General Lee, "is the most sublime word in the English language."

The fish industry is among the foremost in World Trade. Indeed, in some countries it is the chief occupation of the people and the main source of national income. Through the ages it has developed a lore and nomenclature peculiar unto itself. What is more expressive of failure than, "A Water Haul?" What more charming password for an Ananias Club than, "What A Whopper?" What better synonym for discomfort and disgust than, "Fisherman's Luck," though coarse in translation - classic in application? And where is the Lawyer who has never gone on a "Fishing Expedition?" Who wants to "Fish in Troubled Waters?" A whale of a bargain is a big one. Land Shark suggests Shylock, and Shylock is a type. They are synonymous and offer a perfect illustration of a distinction without a difference. "It sounds Fishy," means "It's a Lie on Its Face," and much more diplomatic. Everybody knows that "Fishy Smell" as well as the man "With the Codfish Eye." All these terms are as well understood by the Public as are the terms Bulls and Bears of the Stock Exchange. Codfish Tongues and Codfish Sounds mean one and the same thing and are interchangeable terms in the Trade.

As it is the biggest fish that always breaks the hook or bites the line in two, so, here, the huge sum of thirty thousand dollars is asked as compensation for fish that were never caught. I can remember when that sum would buy a lot of fish. I have seen six-pound roe shad retail for five cents apiece and cured herrings sell for two dollars a thousand - one hundred and twenty pounds of shad for one dollar and five herrings for one cent.

And this large sum is now asked for whose Fish? Certainly not the plaintiff's because he never owned them. I repeat the question, *whose* Fish? The answer is plain: they belonged to the Public.

Yes, I am fully aware that my fall from the Woolsack, and my break over time's old barrier growth of right and fit;[17] my reluctance to plod on with the solemn brood of care,[18] and my impatience of professional solemnity,[19] may cause

---

[16] Matthew 3:7.

[17] Browning.

[18] Gray.

[19] Chesterton.

the Big Wigs of the Bar to scowl down their displeasure. So be it. Permit me to interrupt myself:

Wigs were introduced in the Courts of England in 1670. A little more than a century ago the modern article was invented, and is made of the manes and tails of horses in the ratio of five white strands to one of black. The advantage is that it maintains its permanent wave without the aid of curling irons and oil. The disadvantage is that they are almost prohibitively expensive.[20] I resume.

I have often observed that the bigger the wig, the smaller the wigger, and the louder the roar and thunder in the index.[21] With majestic mien, wrinkled front and prone brow, oppressive with its mind,[22] one Big Wig, with a slight shiver, asks another: "Influenza?" Then another with emphatic sniff asks: "John Barleycorn?" The answer is, "Neither!" I am sound in limb, wind and withers and as dry as Shadrach, Meshach and Abednego when, with their hair unsinged and with no smell of fire passed on them, they walked out of Nebuchadnezzar's burning fiery furnace and were each forthwith raised to an high estate in the Province of Babylon.[23]

Oh, well, now, yes, of course, the Circuit Court gives me a lot of trouble. But "hit ain't as bad as it mought be." If I am not reversed in more than nine cases out of ten, I feel from fair to middling. And if I draw ten straight, that does not send me to bed as even one reversal does some of the gentlemen of the Bench, State and Federal, so I have heard. Nor do I waste time explaining how and wherein the Circuit Court "got all balled up" and reversed me. That is what Circuit Courts are for - to correct the mistakes of District Judges - otherwise there would have been no compelling need to justify their establishment, except, the need to protect the Supreme Court against a deluge of appeals.

When I see a Big Wig infused with self and vain conceit, as if this flesh which walls about our life were brass impregnable,[24] I think of Charles James Fox, who, when looking at a portrait of Lord Chancellor Thurlow, his full-bottomed wig falling bountifully to his shoulders and giving him that appearance of sagacity for which he is remembered, said: "No man ever was so wise as Thurlow looks," and but for the unimpeachable integrity of Charles Lamb I might well doubt his observation that, "lawyers were children once."[25]

There is a good story going around about a plaintiff who sued his city in Tort. A manhole on the sidewalk was left open and unguarded. The plaintiff fell into it and was severely injured. The city interposed the plea of Contributory Negligence for that the plaintiff was drunk when he fell into the hold. On Cross-examination the plaintiff admitted that he had had one or two, possible three, small

---

[20] Newton on Blackstone.

[21] Hamlet.

[22] Browning.

[23] Daniel 3:26, 27, 30.

[24] Richard II.

[25] Newton on Blackstone.

ones (the usual maximum on the witness stand) and that he might have been feeling good. When the plaintiff rested, the defendant moved for judgment as of Non-Suit. The *nisi prius* Judge promptly granted the motion and signed judgment accordingly. An Appellate Justice, speaking for the Court in a reversal opinion, precisely one sentence long, said: "A drunken man is as much entitled to a safe street as a sober one, and much more in need of it." This equals: "You can't unscramble the eggs," as said North Carolina's great Chief Justice, Ruffin.

Far be it from me to bandy civilities with my superiors in learning, but after a round with the May Act I think a Judge is entitled to chuckle if he can; that it is pardonable now and then to intersperse a little human interest in the tedious search for judicial maxims and precedents that bind. "One laugh," said Charles Lamb, "is worth a hundred groans in any state of the market."

I invoke Equity, which does not depend upon the length of the chancellor's foot, notwithstanding the learned John Selden said it did, and set up: the weight of years and the weariness of service, and that this remains a fish story whichever way it is twisted. I shall not further prolong this prologue, but here upon this bank and shoal of time, I'll jump the life to come[26] and proceed to consider the questions involved in the cause before me for determination.

The plaintiff, in substance, alleges that he is now, and has been since 1911, the owner and in possession of those two certain tracts of land, situated on opposite sides of the Roanoke River, and known respectively as the "Kitty Hawk" and "Slade" Fisheries; that the properties are ideally located for the business of fishing, and have for a number of years, during the fishing season, been operated for that purpose by the plaintiff and his ancestors in title, expensive equipment having been placed and maintained thereon for the proper and profitable conduct of such business; that, from time immemorial, great quantities of fish of the kinds specified have been accustomed, during the Spring of each year, to make their way from the Ocean through Albemarle Sound, and thence into the fresh-water spawning grounds in the upper reaches of the Roanoke River; and that, by reason of this annual migration of fish, plaintiff's fishing business, and his "Kitty Hawk" and "Slade" Fisheries, have been "principally and particularly valuable."

It is alleged that the defendant is the owner of a boundary on the Roanoke River situate below the plaintiff's property which the fish, entering the river in their annual migration to the spawning grounds, are compelled to pass before reaching that portion of the river running between the plaintiff's properties; that, during the period referred to in the complaint, the defendant has maintained upon the boundary a plant for the manufacture of sulphate pulp, bleached and unbleached; that, in the course of the manufacturing operation, during the three years immediately preceding the institution of this action, the defendant has from day to day discharged into the waters of the Roanoke River, opposite its plant, a large volume of poisonous and deleterious waste and matter injurious to the fish then

---

[26] Macbeth.

in passage to the spawning grounds, with the result that the annual migration of the fish upstream has been interrupted or diverted and large quantities of them have been destroyed; and that, as a natural consequence thereof, the plaintiff's business, and the usufruct of his property, during each of the three years have greatly diminished - all to the plaintiff's great and lasting damage in the sum of $30,000.

Measured by these allegations, it is not open to question that the acts of the defendant were palpably wrongful. They were, indeed, in violation of various criminal statutes of the State, designed to conserve the public good. If, then, upon indictment, the acts charged were admitted or established, no Court could hesitate to pronounce the defendant guilty of the creation and maintenance of a public nuisance and impose the maximum penalties of the statutes as are therein provided. But the right of the plaintiff to recover damages for this alleged wrong presents a far different question. In a case of pure tort, the wrong-doer is responsible for all the damages directly caused by his misconduct, and for all indirect and consequential damages, resulting naturally and probable from the wrongful acts, which are susceptible to ascertainment with a reasonable degree of certainty. Damages which are not the natural and probable result of the act complained of, but which are contingent or merely possible, or based upon a conjectural probability of future loss, and so beyond the scope of reasonable determination are too remote and are not recoverable. [citation omitted]. It is well settled that in actions by private individuals, based upon the creation or maintenance of a public nuisance, there can be no recovery, even of nominal damages, upon the mere establishment of the wrongful act. In such cases it is essential to the plaintiff's cause of action that he show an appreciable injury. [citation omitted].

At the outset, therefore, I am confronted with the inquiry as to whether, in his allegations of injury and damage, the plaintiff has brought himself within the requirements of these rules. In other words, are the damages alleged by the plaintiff the natural and probable consequences of defendant's wrongful act, capable of ascertainment with reasonable certainty, or are they merely contingent or possible consequences based upon a conjectural apprehension of events?

If it be assumed that a portion of the fish diverted or destroyed would otherwise have been caught by the plaintiff, the question still remains as to the proportion and kinds of these oviparous denizens of the silent deep which would have made their way into plaintiff's seines or nets. The answer to this question is more than difficult; it is obviously impossible with any reasonable degree of certainty. The plaintiff, doubtless would be able to show his catch during preceding seasons. But experience joins with common sense in teaching that the result in one season affords no criterion of the result in others. The truth is that nothing in the field of industry is more uncertain or variable than the business of fishing, or the profits to be derived therefrom in any given period. Success or failure depends upon such a variety and diversity of contingencies - the eccentricities of climate, unanticipated seasonal changes, the clarity and temperature of inland streams, the whims and vagaries of sun and wind and tide, as is illustrated by what happened on the Sea of Tiberias in obedience to the command: "Cast the net on the other side of the ship."[27] Through the operation of these natural forces millions of shad and herring, which may have spawned in one season in the upper Roanoke River, may spawn the next in some other freshwater stream far removed from the menace of plaintiff's reticulated snares. By reason thereof, many a promising and hopeful season has ended in disaster, and the business of fishing, in any give stream during any given period, has been reduced to an unpredictable gamble.

As previously stated, in actions in tort, the damages recoverable, whether direct or consequential, must flow naturally and reasonably from the wrongful act alleged. I am of the opinion that the attempt to so estimate and segregate the damages in this case would involve a misty maze of conjecture and speculation as unprofitable as calculating the mechanical value of a cubic mile of pea-soup fog off the Grand Banks of Newfoundland.

While these considerations seem to point unerringly to the solution of the question considered, I am not disposed to rest my decision upon this weakness in the plaintiff's case. For there is, I think, an even more patent and fundamental defect. It is uniformly held in North Carolina, and generally elsewhere, that, in order for a private citizen to sustain an action predicted upon a public nuisance, he must establish an injury, which is not only appreciable, but special and peculiar to himself, differing not only in degree, but in kind from that common to the public. . . And, while the Courts of North Carolina have been alert in such cases to administer relief where an injury peculiar to the complainant has been shown, they have been equally zealous and alert in denying relief, where the injury alleged, upon studious consideration, has been held to be merely of the kind suffered by all citizens alike. Particularly is this true where the nuisance considered was initially of a public nature, and did not become so merely by reason of an aggregation of private injuries so widespread or so long continued as to constitute a public menace. [citation omitted]. The rule is that no private individual may have relief in law or equity from the actual or threatened consequences of a public nuisance: the exception relates only to those who are able to show an appreciable injury peculiar to themselves.

This case falls, I think, within the rule and not within the exception. The plaintiff alleges no invasion of his soil, no obstruction of his right of ingress or egress, no interference with the movement or installation of his nets, seines or other fishing equipment, no dissemination of noxious odors or disease-bearing insects destructive of health or comfort, no corruption of the surrounding atmosphere or of his private wells or springs, nor other injury of a kind recognized as warranting a recovery in an action based upon a public nuisance. . .

---

[27] John 21:6.

True, it is alleged that defendant's wrongful acts constitute a trespass, as well as a nuisance, and that the usufruct of plaintiff's business and property has been seriously impaired "usufruct" being used, manifestly, in the sense of profit. But the first of these allegations is obviously a conclusion of the pleader, while the latter must of necessity be referred to defendant's wrongful diversion or destruction of the fish. Otherwise no casual connection is discernible between the wrongdoing alleged and the consequences experienced, and the complaint is fatally defective. . .

Stated concisely, the alleged injury consists in the diminution of annual revenues from the plaintiff's business and property; the alleged wrong in defendant's diversion or destruction of fish in the Roanoke River, through the daily discharge into that stream of poisonous and deleterious matter.

The complaint is fatally defective for the reason that the plaintiff did not own either the River or the fish therein. Both, upon the allegations and implications of the complaint, belonged to the State. It is true that the plaintiff had the right to fish in the River, and to appropriate to his own use the fish so taken therefrom. But the plaintiff had not reclaimed the fish in question. Moreover, his right of fishery was neither several nor exclusive. Nor was it incidental to his riparian ownership, but a right held in common with the public. [citation omitted]. To illustrate: A trapper operating muskrat traps in the Great Dismal Swamp may maintain an action for damage to or destruction of his traps by reason of fire wrongfully set out by another. But it can hardly be said that the trapper could maintain a claim for diminution of profits by reason of the actual destruction or the necessitated change of range of the rats. He has no right of property in any rat until he reclaims it by reducing it to actual possession. Here, the plaintiff does not seek damage for injury to and loss of his traps, that is to say, injury to and loss of his nets, seines, boats, lands, buildings and other necessary equipment, and for the obvious reason that the wrong he complains of, by the very nature of it, could not produce such injury or loss. The plaintiff seeks only to recover for diminution of his profits by reason of the alleged wrongful diversion and destruction of fish in which he had no right of property, and precisely for the same reason that the trapper had none in the rats. It seems to me the analogy is perfect.

If, therefore, the plaintiff has sustained an injury, then so has every citizen of the State. If the plaintiff may maintain this action, every citizen of the State may maintain a like action for the same wrong.

Careful consideration of the briefs and authorities cited, supplemented by independent research, constrains the conclusion that the plaintiff may not recover for an injury to property in which he had no vestige of special interest. Having failed to bring himself within the terms of the exception, he is bound by the rule.

This conclusion is further necessitated by the decisional law of the State. In Dunn v. Stone, 4 N.C. 241, after stating the general principle by which actions of this character are controlled, the Court expressly held that the plaintiff, a riparian owner on the Neuse River, was not entitled to maintain the action for the reason that he had sustained no peculiar injury through the obstruction of fish in their upstream passage to his fishery.

I cannot agree that this decision has been rendered obsolete by statutory prescription of a right to sue in like cases. N.C.Code, §894.

In many cases, concededly, the North Carolina Courts have sustained recoveries, upon dissimilar facts, based upon a public nuisance. But no case has been cited, nor has research revealed one, in which the application of the rule in Dunn v. Stone has been questioned. On the contrary, as well since as before the enactment of this Statute, Dunn v. Stone has been cited by the North Carolina Courts as embodying the law in actions of like character.

I am not impressed by the argument that the authority of this decision is destroyed by its hoar austerity. As to its age: The chief evidence offered by the Fundamentalists in the defense of the Verity of the Bible is its antiquity - that it has withstood the assaults of unbelievers for two thousand years, unshaken and unmodified.

I am loath to renounce the Old in order to accept the New. I believe in the fine-grained truths that have been established by the world's best life - sacred and secular. We use them without a thought of their antiquity, although countless epochs and generations of men went to make them. There is a beautiful ivory mammoth tusk sticking seven feet out of the frozen ground in Alaska which the Indians have used for centuries as a hitching post. We, too, hitch up to the solid truths which serve our daily convenience, although embedded in the past - firm as the Rock of Ages.

Moreover, the plaintiff seems to find no fault with the law of property in animals *ferae naturae* because of its antiquity. When all the animals, except fish which, for obvious reasons, did not take passage in the Ark, were safely on board and the door close and barred, Noah had them under subjection, having reduced them to possession. After a cruise of one hundred and fifty days,[28] Noah let them all out, in the six hundred and first year, on the twenty-seventh day of the second month thereof, and they scattered over the face of the earth, each after its kind. From then until Dunn v. Stone was decided, and even until now, the legal right in and to animals *ferae naturae* has been and is precisely the same - no change. Should Dunn v. Stone therefore be ignored because of its age, and the law itself which it upholds, dating back to the very beginning of recorded events, be given a coat of many colors? To do so would be much like a physician who eases the pain but ignores the cause.

As to its austerity: The plaintiff in his reply brief cites State v. Oliver, 70 N.C. 60, and says: "So far as this plaintiff is concerned it is immaterial whether Dunn v. Stone be considered as overruled entirely and expressly * * * or simply ignored in its implications denying damages to riparian owners. The result is the same and it is manifest, as said by the late Judge Settle in State v. Oliver, 70 N.C.

---

[28] Gen. 7:24; 8:3.

61, 'the Courts have advanced from that barbarism.'"

Upon examination I found that State v. Oliver was a criminal case dealing with a defendant for wife-beating. He interposed the defense that he used a whip no larger than his thumb. He was convicted and sentenced. He appealed. The Supreme Court affirmed, and Mr. Justice Settle, speaking for the Court, in an opinion about as long as a marble, said: "We may assume that the old doctrine, that a husband had a right to whip his wife, provided he used a switch no larger than his thumb, is not law in North Carolina. Indeed, the Courts have advanced from that barbarism until they have reached the position, that the husband has no right to chastise his wife, under any circumstances."

It is a far cry from the barbarism of wife-beating to the diversion of fish, which have next to no nervous system, swimming in the navigable waters of the Roanoke River. To insist that State v. Oliver has any point here is as useless as an effort to create a hiatus in a hole. And I see nothing in the present case that impedes the world's advance or that suggests the repeal of the laws that in our fathers' day were best.

Nor am I impressed with the suggestion that Dunn v. Stone is rendered negligible by the fact that it emanated from a one-man Court - Chief Justice Taylor. It is nevertheless the pronouncement of the highest Court of North Carolina and therefore binding in this jurisdiction. [citation omitted].

I am of the opinion the motion should be allowed and the action dismissed. It is so ordered and judgment will be entered accordingly.

N. B. The footnotes are merely references and are not intended to indicate quotations.

STATE OF SOUTH CAROLINA v. LANGFORD
Supreme Court of South Carolina
55 S.C. 322; 33 S.E. 355 (1899)

IRA B. JONES, J.

[George Langford was indicted for stealing a dog, and for burglary in breaking into and stealing from a dog house. From an order quashing the indictment on the demurrer of defendant, the State of Georgia appealed.]

In this case the State appeals from an order quashing an indictment, containing two counts-- one charging burglary of a dog house within 200 yards of and appurtenant to the dwelling of Mary Nichols, with intent to steal, &c., the goods and chattels of Mary Nichols in the said dog house; the other count charging larceny of a dog of the value of $10 of the proper goods and chattels of Mary Nichols, then and there being found in the said dog house. . . .

. . . 1. The first and principal question presented is whether a dog is the subject of larceny. By the old common law, larceny could not be committed of a dog. The reasons assigned for this were the baseness of the nature of such creature; that it was kept for mere whim and pleasure; that being unfit for food, it was of no intrinsic value; that the penalty for the felony of larceny was too severe to apply for the stealing of so contemptible a creature. By the Statute of 10 George III., ch. 18 (George III. was fond of stag hunting), the taking and carrying away of a dog was made punishable, but not as larceny. Under the reasoning satisfactory at that day, it was larceny to steal a tame hawk, but not larceny to steal a tame dog, although it was larceny to steal the hide of a dead dog. Yet by the common law dogs were held to be such property as would sustain an action of trover for their recovery. Civil remedies were permitted for injury to or loss of dogs, and they would go to the executors and administrators as property.

The reason for the outlawry of dogs in favor of thieves can hardly be regarded as persuasive at this day and here, and such crude application of the principles of the common law must yield to common sense. The fitness of an animal for food is not the only test of its value to mankind; its capacity for useful service in other ways is often the real test of value. Nor is the fact that an animal is kept for the whim and pleasure of its owner any sort of reason for excluding it from the law of larceny as a thing of no value, for amusement has its valuable uses to man. Neither is it just to say of the dog that its nature is so base as to render it unworthy of protection as absolute property, for Baron Cuvier says the dog is the "completest, the most singular, and the most useful conquest ever made by man."

When we are told that the Greeks and Romans employed dogs in war, armed with spiked collars, and that Corinth was saved by war dogs which attacked and checked the enemy until the sleeping garrison were aroused, we better understand Shakespeare's Antony when he said, "Cry havoc, and let slip the dogs of war." We should not let our contempt for sheep-killing dogs and our dread of hydrophobia do injustice to the noble Newfoundland, that braves the water to rescue the drowning child; to the Esquimaux dog, the burden bearer of the arctic regions; the sheep dog, that guards the shepherd's flocks and makes sheep raising possible in some countries; to the St. Bernard dog, trained to rescue travelers lost or buried in the snows of the Alps; to the swift and docile greyhound; to the package carrying spaniel; to the sagacious setters and pointers, through whose eager aid our tables are supplied with the game of the season; to the fleet fox hounds, whose music when opening on the fleeing fox is sweet to many ears; to the faithful watch dog, whose honest bark, as Byron says, bays "deep-mouthed welcome as we draw near home;" to the rat-exterminating terrier; to the wakeful fice, which the burglar dreads more than he does the sleeping master; to even the pug, whose very ugliness inspires the adoration of the mistress; to the brag 'possum and coon dog, for which the owner will fight if imposed upon; and lastly to the pet dog, the playmate of the American boy, to say nothing of the "yaller dog," that defies legislatures.

Of all animals the dog is most domestic. Its intelligence, docility and devotion make it the servant, the companion and the faithful friend of man. The raising and training of dogs are now pursued by many as a business, large sums of money are invested in them, and they are bought and sold as other property. In this State, by statute, dogs are and have long been taxed as personal property, according to value and for revenue. As stated in *Salley v. R.R., 54 S.C., 484:* "What the law taxes as personal property it will protect as such." This legislation is potent in two ways: (1) If the common law rule, notwithstanding the fallacy of the reasoning upon which it is based, as applied to present conditions, should be held of force in this State, in the absence of modification by statute, then the statute taxing dogs as personal property ad valorem and for revenue is a modification of the common law rule. (2) It brings dogs as personal property and things of value within the meaning of "chattels" in our State as to simple larceny -- see 160 Criminal Code, the term "chattel" including all kinds of *property* except freehold, or things parcel thereof, and perhaps choses in action. . .

. . . The judgment of the Circuit Court is reversed, and the case remanded for further proceedings.

THE GEORGIA RAILROAD AND BANKING COMPANY v. NEELY
Supreme Court of Georgia
56 Ga. 540 (1876)

LOGAN E. BLECKLEY, Judge.

[Plaintiff brought an action against the Georgia Railroad and Banking Company for damages resulting from the killing of a mule and the disabling of a colt, both the property of the plaintiff. The evidence showed that the Plaintiff, having made his crop, turned his mule out, having first hobbled her. The mule, by grazing, would feed herself, saving the plaintiff the expense of keeping her. The colt was also turned out. Both went upon the track of defendant at night, and were struck by a passing train. The mule was killed and the colt ruined. The jury found for the plaintiff, awarding $48.00 damages. The defendant moved for a new trial.]

Georgia, for the most part is unfenced. For purposes of mere transit, unenclosed territory is here scarcely less common to things that go upon land than are the high seas to ships and steamers. Cattle have, in this state, generally, license to range at large at the will of their owners. And, with the right of way secured, railroad trains may run along their prepared and pre-established paths, through forest as well as field. Corporations are not bound to fence their lines, nor farmers to confine their ordinary domestic animals. Nor is it incumbent upon either to prevent trains and animals from crossing each other's track.

A locomotive and a mule may well pass over the same ground, so that they pass at different moments of time. If, however, they contend for the same place at the same instant, and a collision ensues, with damage to either, the diligence of their respective owners may be challenged and compared. In two respects the comparison will influence the pecuniary consequences of the collision; it will decide whether any compensation is due to the owner of the injured property, and if any, whether it should be full or only partial. . .

On scrutinizing the evidence before us we are of opinion that the company's agents were not wanting in ordinary care or reasonable diligence; and that the verdict which was rendered on the basis of contributory negligence cannot be upheld. The evidence is not conflicting nor inadequate. The burden of proof cast by law on the defendant, has been successfully carried. . . Let a new trial be granted.

Judgment reversed.

STARRY v. HORACE MANN INS. CO.
Supreme Court of Alaska
649 P.2d 937 (1982)

ALLEN T. COMPTON, Justice.

Presented in the guise of a simple problem of insurance coverage, this peculiarly "Alaskan" controversy raises a profound, albeit hairy question: Is a "bear hide wall mount" a "fur" within the scope of an insurance exclusionary clause? Differently stated, "When is a fur not a Fur?" [1]

I. BEAR FACTS

The bear hide wall mount in dispute was displayed on the living room wall in James F. Starry's home. The hide was prepared as a rug, in a stretched-out fashion with the head and claws attached. [2] A burglar, as it were, left the wall bare, as it wasn't. Starry filed a claim with his insurer, Horace Mann Insurance Co. (Horace Mann) to recover $5,000.00, the value of the bear hide mount, and for incidental damages to the home resulting from the unlawful entry.

Horace Mann, baring claws of its own, invoked the policy's exclusionary clause and offered only partial compensation for the bear hide. The exclusionary clause provided:

> This Company shall not be liable for loss in any one occurrence with respect to the following property for more than ... (4) $500.00 in the aggregate for loss by theft of jewelry, watches,

---

[1] We disclaim responsibility for this characterization. See 5 The Alaska Bar Rag, Nos. 5 & 6, at p. 4 (1982).

[2] Another, albeit far different bear hide mount was described in *Green v. Koslosky,* 384 P.2d 951 (Alaska 1963). In that case a taxidermist attempted to prepare a full size standing mount of a polar bear. The flawed result purportedly bore no resemblance to a polar bear, and was instead described as an "albino grizzly."

> necklaces, bracelets, gems, precious and semi-
> precious stones, gold, platinum and *furs includ-*
> *ing articles containing fur which represents its*
> *principal value*;. . . (Emphasis added).

Perhaps estimating the difficulty of convincing another brown bear to trade a life in the wilderness for posterity in the Starry home, Starry initiated this suit against Horace Mann, seeking recovery of the full value of the bear hide and an award of punitive damages.

The parties filed cross motions for summary judgment. In an affidavit in support of his motion, Starry contended that he did not obtain supplemental insurance for the bear hide mount, as he did for other items subject to the exclusionary clause, because he did not "understand a bear hide to be a fur." His understanding was that the bear hide mount was "a trophy, and not a fur."

Starry submitted the affidavit of Perry Green, an Anchorage furrier, stating that "Brown bear rugs and mounts are not furs, anymore than a moose head mounted on a board would be considered a fur. A Brown Bear rug is a trophy... A Brown Bear is a hair animal and not a fur."

In contrast, Horace Mann submitted the affidavit of Gerald A. Victor, another furrier in Alaska, who stated in part:

> It is well known that bears have fur. The quality
> of the fur on a bear rug is an integral factor in
> determining its worth. It is certainly true that the
> existence of fur on a bear rug represents its
> principal value. If one were to remove all of the
> fur from a bear rug it would be virtually worthless.
> It is well known that hunters who wish to bag a
> bear for the purposes of making it into a rug are
> very concerned with the quality of the bear's fur
> coat. For this reason bears who are being hunted
> for this purpose are often taken in the Spring
> when their coats are at their richest.

The court entered partial summary judgment on the contract claim in favor of Horace Mann. The judgment was certified as final pursuant to Civil Rule 54(b) and this appeal followed.

II. BEAR COVERAGE

An insurance policy "is construed so as to provide that coverage which a layman would reasonably have expected given his lay interpretation of the policy terms." *Continental Insurance Co. v. Bussell*, [citation omitted]. We have also recognized "the rule that provisions of coverage should be construed broadly while exclusions are interpreted narrowly against the insured." *Hahn v. Alaska Title Guaranty Co.* [citation omitted]. Ambiguities are resolved against the insurer. . . Of course, the preference due an insured's interpretation is only applicable where the insurance provision in dispute is ambiguous. . .

The question raised by Starry on appeal is whether a layperson, viewing the contract as a whole, would reasonably expect that a bear hide wall mount is a fur article "containing fur which represents its principal value" within the meaning of the exclusionary clause. In support of his position that a bear hide wall mount is not subject to the exclusion, Starry points to the definition of a fur animal by the Alaska Department of Fish and Game.[3] Horace Mann, in contrast, submits that the phrase is not ambiguous and, by common understanding, would be read as including a bear hide wall mount. The insurer points to the dictionary definition of fur,[4] the Encyclopedia Americana, and state and federal statutes and regulations allegedly including brown bear hides within the purview of a "fur."

Horace Mann also refers to *Seeberger v. Schlesinger* [citation omitted] in which the Supreme Court decided that Chinese goat skins are furs for the purposes of custom duties, even though "goat skins are not ordinarily classified as furs - a term usually reserved for the short fine hair of certain animals, whose skins are largely used for clothing."

The other articles named in the exclusionary clause all consist of decorative personal apparel, and would suggest to a reasonable layperson that the scope of the clause is restricted to items of that genre. While the furriers' affidavits and the various references to statutory and regulatory definitions of the term "fur" suggest that the term may have a specialized meaning in a variety of other contexts, this case involves the interpretation of a homeowner's insurance policy, not a customs' regulation, fish and game laws, a workers' compensation statute, or a commercial trade dispute. We think a reasonable homeowner could view the exclusionary clause in question as restricted to common, everyday effects in the nature of jewelry and furbearing garments. With such an interpretation in mind, we think it plain that a reasonable person would not conclude that a bear hide wall mount is subject to the exclusionary clause. One, we suspect, would have nearly as much difficulty using the brown bear hide as a garment in its mounted condition as one would before the bear's demise.

In sum, we conclude that recovery for the bear hide wall mount is not limited by the exclusionary clause. We REVERSE and REMAND for the entry of summary judgment in Starry's favor.

---

[3] 5 AAC 90.020(8) states:
(8) "fur animals" includes beaver, coyote, arctic fox, red fox, lynx, marten, mink and weasel, muskrat, land otter, sea otter, raccoon, red squirrel, flying squirrel, ground squirrel and marmot, wolf and wolverine.

[4] According to Horace Mann, Webster's Third New International Dictionary, defines "fur" as "the fine, soft, thick covering or coat of a mammal." However, several secondary dictionary meanings define "fur" with reference to garments. See Webster's New World Dictionary.

BOORSE v. SPRINGFIELD TOWNSHIP
Supreme Court of Pennsylvania
377 Pa. 109; 103 A.2d 708 (1954)

HORACE STERN, Chief Justice.

Shortly after midnight a valuable racing mare was discovered in a helpless condition with one leg wedged in a culvert draining into a gutter at the edge of a public highway in Montgomery County. Whether it was partly on the shoulder of the highway or entirely on private property does not appear. Two police officers, one employed by Springfield Township and the other by Upper Dublin Township, both of which townships border on his highway, arrived on the scene and shot and killed the mare. Plaintiff, the owner of the mare, brought action against the townships to recover the value of the animal. In his complaint he alleged that the officers knew that the mare was his property but they did not notify him or give him any opportunity to extricate the animal, nor did they make any effort to determine whether the condition of the mare made it necessary to destroy her. . .

. . . Plaintiff's case cannot surmount the barrier of the rule establishing the immunity of municipalities from liability for torts committed by their employes in the course of performance of a governmental function, unless a right of recovery is expressly granted by statute. . .

. . . Judgment affirmed.

MICHAEL A. MUSMANNO, Justice (dissenting).

In the darkness of early morning on October 3, 1953, a valuable thoroughbred racing horse named "All's Over," strayed from an enclosure on the land of its proprietor, and, doubtlessly excited over an unexpected freedom, headed for distant highways. At a point close to the boundary line between Springfield Township and Upper Dublin Township, "All's Over" unwaringly entered into a culvert and there became wedged at a spot 200 yards south of Dresherton Road. Shortly after this involuntary halting of movement, two policemen arrived--one from Springfield Township and the other from Upper Dublin. Without making any effort to dislodge the imprisoned but uninjured animal, and without seeking counsel of its well-known owner, the two policemen fired ten revolver shots into the horse.

For "All's Over," it was now indeed all over.

After their brave deed had been accomplished, the police officers notified the owner, Herbet C. Boorse, who made arrangements to have the horse transported to the University of Pennsylvania Veterinary Hospital where an autopsy was performed. With an unintentional caprice that only added to the tragedy of the occurrence, the examining doctor reported that there was absolutely nothing wrong with the horse except ten bullets holes in its head.

Boorse brought an action of trespass against Springfield and Upper Dublin Townships, asking for $25,000 damages for the loss of his private property. The defendants filed preliminary objections on the ground that townships, being governmental subdivisions, were immune from tort actions for the acts of their policemen. The lower Court sustained the objections and entered judgment for the defendants. The plaintiff appealed to this Court which has affirmed the action of the lower Court.

A citizen of the United States has been deprived of a valued possession worth $25,000 under circumstances of undoubted wanton negligence, and yet he may not even be heard in Court. The first principle a student encounters as he prepares to fit himself for the practice of the law is that there is no right without a remedy, or stated in another manner, there is no wrong that may not be corrected in law. But his case presents a wrong which no one can deny, and yet the plaintiff pleads in vain for a hearing.

The defendant municipality Springfield Township resists liability on the ground that it is not responsible for any act of "misfeasance or non-feasance" of its policemen. The Complaint, however, describes an act of malfeasance, specifically charging the two policemen with conduct which was "both wilful and wanton," exhibiting a "reckless disregard of the property rights of the plaintiff."

In the year 1876, the mayor of Philadelphia was sued for ordering the destruction of property which the mayor claimed was a nuisance and a fire hazard. The jury returned a verdict for the defendant, and the property-owner appealed. Although this Court affirmed the verdict, it specifically declared, through Chief Justice Sharswood, "that the case properly submitted to the determination of the jury." Fields v. Stokley, [citation omitted]. It could well be that even in this case the jury would return a verdict for the defendants, but the plaintiff has the right to have a jury pass upon the issue he presents.

But no jury has here justified the action of the police officers employed by the two defendant townships.

As the mayor in the Fields v. Stokley case pleaded a fire hazard, so also the defendant municipalities here pleaded a traffic hazard. But it is not clear how the police removed an alleged traffic hazard by substituting for an erect live horse an inert and enormous carcass spread flatly over a thoroughfare. Nor is it apparent how the defendants justify the use of firearms for the removal of a "traffic hazard". We presume that one effective way to prevent traffic congestion would be to set up machine guns at busy intersections, but such a procedure would scarcely be acceptable to the law.

It is the theory of the Majority Opinion, affirming the lower Court which sustained preliminary objections to the plaintiff's Complaint, that a citizen suffering a loss of the character here described is without remedy because the principle of immunity for sovereign power is so imbedded in law that we are powerless to change it. In support of this position, the majority cites the case of Fox v. Northern Liberties, [citation omitted] where a superintendent of police, (in 1841) under the guise of enforcing an ordinance, appropriated the plaintiff's horse and sold it. Upon appeal to this Court it was held that the owner of the horse was without remedy because the municipal corporation could not be held responsible for the act of its agent.

The Majority Opinion also cited Elliott v. City of Pittsburgh, [citation omitted] (decided in 1874), another horse case. There, police officers of the City of Philadelphia seized the plaintiff's horse because of an asserted violation of a speed limit and then so negligently cared for it that the horse broke away and was killed. The plaintiff sued the City, the City demurred on the grounds of non-suitability, the lower Court granted judgment on the demurrer, and this Court, on appeal, affirmed the judgment.

For decades now the ghosts of these precedents have been clattering down the highways of the law, and it is about time that some Court stopped them and led them to pasture. Their usefulness on the thoroughfare of logic and true justice is over. It is not consonant with twentieth century American justice to say that property may be destroyed by any one, much less the State (the very symbol of correctness in organized society), with legal impunity. The law of nature, compounded of the dictates of the Supreme Lawmaker and reason emanating from untrammeled intellect, rebels against this antiquated doctrine of irresponsibility, no matter by whom or by what exercised.

The theory of governmental immunity for the tortious acts of governmental representatives, employees and agents is founded upon the presumption that a sovereign power cannot be adjudged in error, and this idea in turn stems from the meretricious formula that a king can do no wrong. The history of kings has been the history of usurpation of power through wars, conquest, assassination, oppression and treachery. Once having climbed to the throne and seized the scepter of absolute jurisdiction the kings announced that their authority derived from God and that, being divinely appointed and anointed they of course could do no wrong. Through the operation of this bold and mendacious theorem, the kings immunized themselves from prosecution for past treason, present offenses and contemplated future crimes. Since the king created the courts and selected the judges, the proposition that the monarch was infallible acquired the sanction of law.

However, despite the supposed protection of God, kings were poisoned, waylaid, beheaded and otherwise murdered. Their successors then denounced the acts of the dead sovereigns and they themselves set up a new series of "divinely" inspired acts of robbery and murder. Mankind can stand so much, whereupon the people of a given kingdom rebel, and the divine right of kings is shown to be what it always was, the emptiest pretension and the sheerest nonsense. But even with dethronement and beheadings, there has still lingered around the figure of a king an intangible awe springing from the memory of his absolutism which opened and locked prison gates and which carried sword points in his words. No one approaches even a dead lion with indifference. Thus, despite the fact that America discarded kings nearly two centuries ago and that the English monarch is now but an innocuous geniality, the common law deriving from British sovereigns still proclaims that the sovereign power can do no wrong.

The time has come to bury this legal charlatanry in the grave of its discredited monarchical grandsires. From time to time courageous judges have thrown spadefuls of earth in this direction, but there has not been a concerted collective effort to entomb this fiction which is recognized by a goodly portion of the judiciary as sheer fantasy. Our own Court has on many occasions repudiated in individual cases the doctrine of governmental immunity but it has also paid obeisance to this discredited theory, merely because there are cases in the books which support it. I myself refuse to admit that a palpable error in law must be persisted in simply because it is an old error.

The Fox case, supra, was decided in 1841. Many horses have entered the eternal grazing ground of the Last Roundup since that decision. The outer world presents methods of transportation entirely undreamed of by the judges of 1841. Many locomotives of judicial adjudication have demolished the precedent in the Fox case. Nonetheless, it continues to lift its equine head from time to time in presumed authority to decide facts and circumstances in a society of 1953 as far removed and as changed from 1841 as television is removed from the magic lantern. . .

. . . As a matter of fact, it is not even true that you cannot sue the government. We know that the government, in one form or another, is sued every day. Allegheny County is the defendant in scores of lawsuits each year. And so is the City in Pittsburgh. And, for that matter, so also is the Commonwealth of Pennsylvania.

The fact that the Commonwealth in civil cases can and does initiate suits as a plaintiff is evidence that it can appear also as a defendant because if it had absolute power it would not need to pass through the medium of the Courts to assert its absolutism. Certainly the Soviet Union never sues to take property. Of course, if the Constitution of Pennsylvania declared that neither the State, nor its subdivisions, was subject to lawsuit, that would end the matter because the Constitution, being the will of the people, can declare anything. But the Constitution has not so stated. If anything, the Constitution would seem to invite the people to redress of grievances against tortfeasors regardless of identity. In fact, it would be strange indeed if, although one can sue a corporation, bank, railroad, his neighbor, even his brother, sister, father or mother, he could not sue the government. In a government founded on the proposition that all men are created equal, it would be an anomaly that one can obtain redress from every one but the entity supposed and intended to be answerable to all its citizens. . .

. . . Advocates of the immunity doctrine have argued that to hold the government responsible in tort actions would impose a great burden on the government's treasury. Such an argument offends against logic almost as much as it does against honorable conduct in the affairs of man. To say that every one should be held liable for his wrongs except the government is to argue for a double standard of morality that is simply intolerable in a democracy.

It has even been suggested that with governmental tort responsibility, the number of suable accidents would increase. Allowing for a certain amount of cupidity and covetousness in mankind, (a fact no one denies) I refuse to accept that, because of a newly acquired right to recover for personal and crippling injuries, a large segment of the population would throw itself in front of garbage trucks, tumble into incinerating plants and stand under roof-discharging ice avalanches so as to obtain money for pain and crutches for broken legs.

A grave and solemn responsibility rests, as I view it, on the Supreme Court of Pennsylvania, to bring order out of confusion, logic out of sophistry, reason out of pedantry, law out of dogma, and justice out of injustice. . .

. . . The plaintiff in this case, Herbert C. Boorse, is entitled to know how and why two men carrying every indicia of authority of their respective masters, specifically, Springfield Township and Upper Dublin Township, destroyed his property. . .The action of the lower Court in sustaining the preliminary objections . . . summarily ousted the plaintiff from Court. It was not only Herbert C. Boorse who was rebuffed by that eviction. The rights of personal property generally have sustained an equally staggering blow by the decision in this case.

BEN HAR HOLDING CORPORATION v. FOX
Municipal Court of City of New York, Borough of Queens
147 Misc. 300; 263 N.Y.S. 695 (1933)

NICHOLAS M. PETTE, Justice

This is an action to recover the sum of $135 as rent for an apartment on the first floor of the building, No. 215-37 Lawrence boulevard, Bayside, N.Y., for the months of October, November and December, 1932, under a written lease entered between the parties on December 31, 1931.

Upon the trial, the defendant stipulated that the only defense to be passed upon by the court was that of constructive eviction. Therefore, the initial question of whether the defendant is liable for the October rent is resolved against him, since he admits that he occupied the premises until October 25th, the rent having become due on October 1st.

In support of said defense, the defendant contends that he was compelled to move because the apartment was infested with crickets that they caused annoyance and discomfort to him and his family. His wife testified that she became ill and nervous by reason of the presence of these insects, which were described by her and other witnesses as being black, green, and silver in color, about an inch and a half long, and that they caused sleeplessness. One witness testified that she saw them crawling up the wall, and that they resembled beetles. It was testified that several of these insects were found in defendant's bed.

The landlord submitted, in rebuttal, that although complaints had been made of the existence of insects, an investigation by its exterminator had revealed the presence of only three dead crickets. An interesting letter sent by the landlord to the tenant, as far as material, reads as follows:

"You mention in your letter the existence of a plague of insects which has become unbearable. The insects you complain of are crickets and no doubt found in most of the houses and apartments in Bayside. They are harmless and many people enjoy their chirping. In fact, there was a poem dedicated to the Cricket on the Hearth, and in China they put them in cages to hear them sing. The little creatures enter the house though the doors as people enter so that if they are unwelcome they are removed by the tenant, which also removes the dust tracked in on one's feet. However, as you know we had the exterminator attend to your apartment and as a result you found three dead crickets so we thought that ended the matter. If it is your desire to give up the apartment on some other account you should not blame it on the crickets or call them a plague of insects."

It is well settled that eviction discharges the duty to pay rent [citation omitted]. The law of constructive eviction is of comparatively modern origin. The early common law did not recognize constructive eviction, actual eviction being necessary to relieve the tenant from the liability for rent [citation omitted]. The cases seem confused as to what facts may constitute a constructive eviction. However, it is generally held that if there be (a) an injurious interference with the tenant's possession; (b) a substantial deprivation of the tenant's beneficial use of the premises or some part thereof; or (c) a material impairment of the tenant's beneficial enjoyment of the premises so that he is compelled to vacate, then constructive eviction is thereby constituted. But the underlying, essential element which must be present is an affirmative act or omission on the part of the landlord. . .

In this situation, it becomes the duty of the court to determine whether the presence of crickets amounted to a constructive eviction. It has been held that: "An eviction depends upon the materiality of the deprivation. If trifling, and producing no substantial discomfort or serious inconvenience, it will be disregarded, and will not afford cause for the termination of the relation of landlord and tenant." . . .

In the case at bar, the court is merely concerned with the proposition of whether a few crickets in the tenant's premises, under the circumstances testified to, may be legally classified among the various types of creatures known to be noxious or mischievous, and commonly referred to as vermin or pests, the presence of which will in law, constitute a constructive eviction.

The solution of the problem requires an examination which leads into the fields of entomology where nature asserts its majesty, and man must bow in reverence. A cricket is defined as a "Saltatorial Gryllid Orthopterous insect," of which there are several species, the most common in this region being the house cricket (*Gryllus domesticus*). Whatever the variety, the cricket's most conspicuous means of locomotion is an habitual leaping, which at times is so frequent as to suggest dancing. Hence, the term "Saltatorial."

Webster's Dictionary defines vermin as including "noxious little animals, or insects, collectively, as squirrels, rats, mice, worms, flies, bugs," etc. The term "bug" would seem to be the nearest reference to a particular type of insect. Is a cricket a bug? The same lexicographer has this to say: "According to present popular usage in England, and among housekeepers in America, bug, when not joined with some qualifying word, is used specifically for bedbug. As a general term it is used very loosely in America."

That a bedbug, "a wingless, bloodsucking insect especially infesting beds" is malodorous and repulsive, is within common observation, and therefore may easily be qualified as one of the vermin class. Whether an assemblage of cockroaches, which are bugs performing and scurrying about the household, constitutes a nuisance, is not in point. But, it is difficult to consign a cricket to such lowly levels, even though there is testimony here that some were found in defendant's bed. We are dealing with crickets as a particular genus of the lower animal kingdom, of the order orthoptera, which includes grasshoppers, cockroaches, locusts and allied genera, and we may not therefore, pause to take cognizance of a mere few of some species of the genus, whose individual characteristics or propensities may be quite distinct and independent from the rest of the species, to hibernate in bed on a par with a human being, especially since the testimony fails to show the particular circumstances under which the creatures came to be in the bed, unless it be due to the "retiring" disposition spoken of in Chamber's Encyclopedia.

Assuming that the cricket may be tersely described as a bug, the question still remains whether he is noxious, and hence, one of the vermin class. The defendant's contention that the creatures were plague of insects," may readily be disposed of as not sustained by the facts. A plague, which is a calamity, may be said to exist in cases where a multitude of insects, such as the locust species, unexpectedly invade a territory, destroying the crops, and causing untold suffering. But, crickets in a house, in a rural community, are nothing out of the ordinary.

While a cricket is technically an insect and a bug, it would appear from a study of his life, that instead of being obnoxious, he is an intellectual little fellow, with certain attainments of refinement and an indefatigable musician par excellence. Besides the great leaping powers common to both male and female, the male of the species is provided with a stridulating apparatus by which he produces the chirping sound which may be heard nightly in the open fields, and in country districts, in the neighborhood of the fireplace, since it is particularly fond of warmth. Chambers' Encyclopedia says that the cricket "hides in nooks and crevices, and loves the neighborhood of the fire, especially in winter. Its merry note has become associated with ideas of domesticity, as in Dickens' 'Cricket on the Hearth.' * * * It remains quiet during the day, but hunts about actively at night for crumbs and other scraps. * * * Is well known for the sound by means of which the male captivates his mate. The loudest noise made by the cricket is probably the Sicilian species (*Gryllus megalocephalus*), which is said to make itself heard at a distance of a mile." We may be thankful that such a species does not inhabit these parts.

The sound is produced by a file-like ledge on one wing which is rubbed on the rough upper surface of the nervures of the chitinous cover of the other wing. This ledge is used instinctively as a sort of manubrium for the emission of sound, much after the fashion in which the violinist applies his bow. Undoubtedly, then, here is a naturalistic musician, endowed with an instrumentation than which there appears to be no equal for endurance and fortitude.

That the resonant sound produced, whether it be called chirping, stridulation, or singing, is music nevertheless, and that it has received its classical definition and allocation, is attested by its frequent mention in poetry and literature. Clarence Weed, a naturalist and entomologist, speaking of the observation of crickets in a glass jar, etc, says: "If you watch them carefully, you will see that they sing with the fiddles on their wings. Our American crickets are by no means lacking in interest. They are the most abundant and familiar of our insect musicians, and they give the warm evenings of the late summer and early autumn a special charm which would be greatly missed without their notes. They are the easiest insects to observe in musical action, for they can be kept in confinement where they will continue singing with apparently as much freedom as when in the open field."

At his point, it is proper to note that the practice of keeping crickets in vivariums is widespread in Japan, where, from time to time, the government has had to pass regulations controlling their sale and propagation. It appears that in that country, as well as in China, the crickets are prized according to the quality of their song.

Weed goes on the say that the songs are "among the most pleasing and characteristic sounds of the late summer and early autumn. This insect music is undoubtedly primarily for the purpose of attracting the female, but it also seems soon to become an instinctive habit, kept up hour after hour and night after night throughout weeks of adult life.

The evidence at bar shows that the crickets were black, green and silvery. The silvery cricket was probably one of the four or five species of tree crickets of whose delectable notes Weed makes a special mention as follows: "Listeners who study them carefully find that there is a rhythmic quality in the notes of the snowy tree cricket which varies from the more continuous tones of the striped tree cricket. The song of the former has well been described as 'a series of clear, high-pitched trills, rhythmically repeated for an indefinite length of time.' The quality is that of a clear whistle, and has best been described by the word 're-treat.' The pitch varies somewhat with the temperature, but on an ordinary evening it is about C, two octaves above middle C, or on a warm evening, it may reach as high as D."

CHAPTER I: CANINE, EQUINE & FELINE

As demonstrating the intellectual capacity of these creatures, we see that they possess the power of organization for the purpose of producing harmonic or symphonic results. Continuing from Weed: "So far as known, these crickets are the only insects that have the instinct to organize themselves into orchestras. It has been noted by many observers that all the crickets in a given patch of weeds or raspberries are likely to be performing upon their instruments with such distinct regularity of time that all sound in unison in what may fairly be called an orchestral concert."

Burrows characterizes the crickets' merry "re-treat" as a "rhythmic beat"; Thoreau says it is a "slumberous breathing"; Hawthorne terms it as "audible silence," and adds: "If moonlight could be heard, it would sound like that." The "World Book" says that this little insect has "become associated with the crackling fire and the steaming kettle," and reference is made to Cowper's description of the tune as:

> "Sounds inharmonious in themselves and harsh,
> Yet, heard in scenes where peace forever reigns,
> And only there please highly for their sake."

Dickens, in his beautiful Christmas tale, "The Cricket on the Hearth" has immortalized the chirping of these creatures as a symbol of peace and contentment. Indeed, in that story, the cricket sings only when things are running smoothly, but in times of sadness and trouble it is silent.

It is singular that a musician should complain about another musician. The tenant with his tuba, which is similar to the ancient bombardon, is able in an artificial band or orchestra, to dispense all the music within its compass, nearly four octaves, including all the chromatic tones. The cricket, with his musical armature, is capable of emitting his intermittent notes, though mainly for selfish purposes in love-making, yet in obedience to its natural instinct. Bates observes that the ground cricket (*Gryllus campestris*) after burrowing for his home, sits at the mouth of his hole in the evenings "noisily stridulating until the female approaches, when the louder notes are succeeded by a more subdued tone, whilst the successful musician caresses with his antennae the mate he has won."

This is typical of the romance of all forms of life. The cricket is thus revealed to be not only a histrionic performer and a singer, but a romantic lover as well. His strains, by whatever nomenclature known, may be really likened to the familiar crooning so endearing and entertaining to the gentle sex of the human family, and his unique adaptability for orchestral renditions, as Weed remarks, makes of him a member of the musical fraternity, and so a confrere of defendant. That there was, in this case, what may be termed a unilateral affinity between the crickets and the tuba player is demonstrated by the fact that not only were they attracted by the tuba's deep notes, but they wished to be his personal companions, each a concomitant adjunct in the production of orchestral melody.

Dickens' prototype cricket lay still in times of adversity. Here there was trouble indeed. The tuba player's non-reciprocating attitude towards the crickets' attachment must have caused dismay among them, and if the hosts would leave the premises it would mean misery for them. A loss of habitation and appurtenances in these days is a disastrous event, and three of the crickets must have become so melancholy that, to use a bit of criminal phraseology, they suffered pains of which they languished, and languishing did live until of said pains they did die.

Upon the above considerations, I am constrained to reject defendant's theory of constructive eviction, the facts being quite unsubstantial.

The crickets gained access to the premises through no act or omission on the landlord's part. The court must take care lest a situation such as here presented, which in rural communities can easily involve bullfrogs, crickets, locusts, grasshoppers, katydids, et similia, may, in the words of Judge MacLean (dissenting), "become a convenient precedent throughout the wide municipality for tenants who would have themselves evicted by incidents easy for them to bring about and impossible for the landlord to forefend." Madden v. Bullock [citation omitted].

Judgment will be entered for the plaintiff for the full amount demanded.

LUMPKIN v. PROVIDENT LOAN SOCIETY INCORPORATED
Court of Appeals of Georgia
15 Ga. App. 816 (1915)

NASH R. BROYLES, J.

The Provident Loan Society Incorporated sued out a distress warrant for rent against T. B. Lumpkin, in the municipal court of Atlanta. The trial judge, sitting without a jury, gave a judgment for the plaintiff, and refused to grant a new trial; and the appellate division of that court sustained his judgment; to which the defendant excepts.

The undisputed testimony showed that the office leased and occupied by the plaintiff in error was narrow, with no ventilation whatever except a door in the front, opening from the street, and a small transom in the rear, which opened into a dark unoccupied storeroom. The evidence showed, however, that he leased this office with full knowledge of its condition and arrangement, and remained there for more than a year without suffering any discomfort. And he can not now complain of defects which were in existence, and known to him, at the time of the lease. . .

This is a unique case. We have been unable to find another like it in any of the books. In the celebrated case of Smith v. Marrable [citation omitted] it was held that where a house, at the time it was leased, was so greatly infested with bugs as not to be reasonably suitable for habitation, the tenant could quit it without notice; there being an implied condition of law that the house was reasonably fitted for habitation. There is, however, a vital distinction between that case and the case at bar, for here the office was not infested with rats until more than a year subsequent to the making of the lease.

In another English case Collins v. Barrow [citation omitted] it was held that the tenant was justified in quitting without notice premises which were noxious and unwholesome for want of proper sewerage. In that case it is clear that it was the landlord's duty, and one that he could easily have performed, to supply proper sewerage for the premises. . . In Paradise v. Jane, [citation omitted] the defendant pleaded that "Prince Rupert and his army of aliens entered upon the demised premises and did drive away the defendants cattle and expelled him from the lands let to him by the plaintiff, and kept him out, so that he could not enjoy the lands during the term; and it was holden that the plea was insufficient, and the defendant must pay the rent; for where a party by his own contract creates a duty or charge upon himself, he is bound to make it good, notwithstanding any accident by inevitable necessity, because he might have provided against it by his contract, and the rent is a duty created by the parties upon the reservation." . . .

. . . None of these authorities, however, control this case, for here no repairs were needed; the undisputed evidence being that the physical condition of the premises was exactly the same as when they were leased, and there was no evidence whatever that any repairs were required.

Our Georgia statute, however, does not render the landlord liable for extraordinary and unforeseen occurrences. In fact, the whole trouble of the plaintiff in error can be summed up in one word -- rats! It is true that the evidence discloses that the office was badly ventilated, and one witness for the defendant in error testified that was the cause of the bad odor; but the plaintiff in error himself makes no such complaint; he puts the bad odors, and the consequent untenantability of his office, squarely upon the "offending heads" of the rats. There is no contention that the rodents disturbed the office force by unseemly squeaking or squealing, or that they otherwise conducted themselves in any ungentlemanly or unladylike manner, or that they gnawed his furniture, or that they themselves had a bad odor; but the sole contention is that they brought in food, presumably from an adjoining restaurant (which was established about a year after the plaintiff in error leased his office), and that this food alone caused the offensive odors.

The plaintiff in error, not being an object of charity, but a man of considerable means, strongly objected to having food thus brought in to him from his neighbors, and especially the kind that was furnished, he not being especially fond of "chicken bones," "fish heads," "scraps of cheese," "tripe," and such like delicacies. He testified that he disinfected the premises, but all in vain. He set traps, and every day caught scores of rats "as big as squirrels," but their numbers were no more diminished by his captures than were the ranks of the allies or the Germans by the "Battle of the Aisne." No traps, no disinfectants, "no nothing" could stop the onslaught of these hungry and persistent vermin; they were imbued with the true "Atlanta spirit," and continued with undiminished ardor their kindly meant but misunderstood attentions. Finally, in despair, the plaintiff in error, having no "pied piper" to entice them by the witchery of his music to their destruction in the "rolling waters of the river Weser" (or the Chattahoochee), cut the "Gordian knot" by breaking his lease and moving to another distinct building.

We do not think that, under the law and the evidence, the landlord can be held responsible for the action of the rats. It is clearly established that there was no bad odor in the premises of the plaintiff in error until after the adjoining restaurant was opened (about a year after the plaintiff in error leased his office), and that the odor was caused entirely by food brought in, presumably from that restaurant, by rats. There was no evidence to show that the restaurant was a nuisance, or that it was improperly conducted. The plaintiff in error himself declared in his testimony that he could not swear that it was a nuisance, and that he did not desire it closed up, as it was not responsible for his troubles, and the landlord offered to remove the restaurant if the plaintiff in error would swear that it was a nuisance, and the plaintiff in error declined to do so, saying it was not to blame. If the restaurant which caused the influx of the rats, and was thereby indirectly responsible for the odor, was not to blame, how could the landlord be held responsible for the actions of these pests?

There is, however, another plea which the plaintiff in error might have set up by way of recoupment, which would have received our careful and sympathetic consideration. The fear of rats, and even of mice, entertained by the fair sex, is proverbial, and this court will take judicial cognizance of the fact that any real-estate office overrun by such vermin would lose all patronage of the ladies, and would be entirely deprived of the refining and elevating influence of their presence, to say nothing of the more substantial emoluments derived from business dealings with them. If the plaintiff in error had rested his case on this ground, at once solid and sentimental, this court (though all of its members are staid and settled married men, but, like all men of intelligence and discernment, fond of the beautiful) would have diligently sought to find a way to relieve him, if not by the harsh and inflexible rules of law, then by the softer and more pliant ones of equity. But the plaintiff in error (possibly through fear of his better half) not having made this plea, the only thing we can do, while affirming the judgment against him, is to tender our congratulations upon the fact that at last he has escaped from his too attentive friends (?) -- the rats.

Judgment affirmed.

JORDACHE ENTERPRISES, INC. v. HOGG WYLD, LTD.
United States Court of Appeals, Tenth Circuit
828 F.2d 1482 (1987)

DEANELL REECE TACHA, Circuit Judge.

This case, a trademark infringement action brought against a manufacturer that identifies its blue jeans for larger women with a smiling pig and the word "Lardashe" on the seat of the pants, reminds us that "you can't make a silk purse

---

[1] The first appearance of this proverb in its present form is attributed to Jonathan Swift. *See* J. Swift, *A Complete Collection of Genteel and Ingenious Conversation, According to the Most Polite Mode and Method Now Used at Court, and in the Best Companies of England* 181 (London 1738).

out of a sow's ear."[1] Appellant Jordache Enterprises, Inc., alleges error in a district court decision finding no likelihood of confusion between the Jordache and Lardashe trademarks and finding no violation of New Mexico's antidilution statute. We affirm.

Appellant, a New York corporation formed by three immigrant brothers in 1978, is the fourth largest bluejeans manufacturer in the United States. It produces and markets all types of apparel for men, women, and children, the principal product being designer blue jeans. Most items are identified by one of appellant's several registered trademarks, including the word "Jordache" printed in block letters, the word "Jordache" printed in block letters and superimposed over a drawing of a horse's head, and a drawing of a horse's head alone. Some products are identified by the word "Jordache" written in script letter, a mark which has not been registered.

An intensive advertising campaign has created great customer awareness of Jordache products. In 1984, for example, appellant spent about thirty million dollars annually on television, radio, newspaper, and magazine advertisements and other promotional efforts. The message of this advertising has been that Jordache jeans convey "the look of the good life." Jordache jeans are now sold in retail outlets throughout the world.

Appellant has licensed Shaker Sport to manufacture and market Jordache jeans for larger women. Shaker Sport has expended substantial resources in advertising these jeans, and it had sold between 33,000 and 60,000 pairs by 1985.

In 1984, appellees Marsha Stafford and Susan Duran formed Hogg Wyld, Ltd., now Oink, Inc., for the purpose of marketing designer blue jeans for larger women. In an operation conducted out of their homes in New Mexico, the two women designed a product, selected a manufacturer, and ultimately sold over 1,000 pairs of jeans. Sales were limited to specialty shops in several southwestern states and to acquaintances or others who heard of the product. The women have not directly advertised their jeans, although several retailers have done so.

The name of the Oink, Inc. blue jeans gave rise to this suit. Names suggested at one time or another for the jeans by Stafford, Duran, or others, included "Thunder Thighs," "Buffalo Buns," "Seambusters," "Rino Asirus," "Hippo Hoggers," "Vidal Sowsoon," and "Calvin Swine." Other names and marks were suggested as a take-off on Stafford's childhood nickname, "Lardass." This nickname inspired ideas such as "Wiseashe" with a picture of an owl, "Dumbashe" with a picture of a donkey, "Horseashe" with a picture of a horse, and "Helium Ash" with a picture of a balloon. The women decided to name their jeans "Lardashe."

Appellant first became aware of Lardashe jeans after an Albuquerque TV station broadcast a news segment, which was also broadcast nationally by NBC, highlighting the new product. Jordache brought suit against Stafford, Duran, and their corporation, alleging trademark infringement in violation of the Lanham Trade-Mark Act, 15 U.S.C. §§ 1051-1127, the new Mexico Trademark Act, N.M.Stat.Ann. §§ 57-3-1 to -14 (1987), and common law. The district court, after a three-day bench trial, held that no trademark infringement had occurred on any of the alternative claims. . . Jordache now appeals this court.

I.

The Lanham Act prohibits the unauthorized use of a reproduction, copy, or imitation of a registered trademark in a way that "is likely to cause confusion" with the registered mark. . . (similar test for infringement of an unregistered trademark by a junior user). "Confusion occurs when consumers make an incorrect mental association between the involved commercial products or their producers". . . This court has identified several factors, originally set forth in Restatement of Torts §729 (1938), that are relevant to whether there is a likelihood of confusion between two marks:

(a) the degree of similarity between the designation and the trade-mark or trade name in
   (i)   appearance;
   (ii)   pronunciation of the words used;
   (iii) verbal translation of the pictures or designs involved;
   (iv) suggestion;
(b) the intent of the actor in adopting the designation;
(c) the relation in use and manner of marketing between the goods or services marketed by the actor and those marked by the other;
(d) the degree of care likely to be exercised by purchasers" . . .

This list is not exhaustive. All of the factors are interrelated, and no one factor is dispositive . . . The party alleging infringement has the burden of proving likelihood of confusion . . .

The district court found that the Jordache mark and the Lardashe mark are not confusingly similar. Appellant argues that the court employed an improper legal construction . . . in reaching this result . . .

Trademarks may be confusingly similar if they suggest the same idea or meaning. For example, this court has held that a trademark consisting of an overflowing stein with the words "Brew Nuts" conveys the same meaning as a trademark consisting of the words "Beer Nuts" [citation omitted].

The court found the *words* "Jordache" and "Lardashe" similar, but not the horse and pig *designs*. The court did not find the word "Jordache" has an inherent meaning. Rather the "meaning" described by the court referred to the "relatively subtle and refined" horse design that is employed in the Jordache trademarks. The district court did not attach an improper "meaning" to the Jordache marks.

Appellant further argues that the district court erred in finding the trademarks are not confusingly similar. Similarities between trademarks are to be given more weight than differences . . . The district court found that "[t]he overall differences between the two marks greatly overcomes the similarity in spelling and pronunciation of the names Jordache and Lardashe" . . .

Our review of the evidence shows that the marks, and their suggested images, are obviously different. Many of the Jordache jeans are identified by a small brown patch with the word "Jordache" written in white in block letters with a gold horse's head superimposed over the lettering. In other instances, the patch is white with blue block lettering and no horse. Sometimes "Jordache" is written in script or only the horse's head is used.

In contrast, the Lardashe jeans have a large, brightly colored pig head and two hooves, giving the appearance that a pig is peering over the back pocket. The word "Lardashe" is written in script beneath the pig's head, below which is an upside down embroidered heart. We agree with the district court that the "striking, brightly colored, and far from subtle" pig design is "humorous, or 'cute,' or facetious" . . . we agree with the district court's finding that the striking dissimilarities in the designs used in the marks greatly outweigh any similarities . . .

The district court found the appellees' "intent was to employ a name that, to some extent, parodied or played upon the established trademark Jordache"; appellees "did not intend to 'palm off' their jeans as Jordache jeans; that is, to confuse the public into believing it was buying a Jordache product" . . . Appellants contend the court erred in its analysis of intent and the relevance of parody.

The "deliberate adoption of a similar mark may lead to an inference of intent to pass off goods as those of another which in turn supports a finding of likelihood of confusion" . . . "The proper focus is whether defendant had the intent to derive benefit from the reputation or goodwill of plaintiff" . . .

Given the unlimited number of possible names and symbols that could serve as a trademark, it is understandable that a court generally presumes one who chooses a mark similar to an existing mark intends to confuse the public. However, where a party chooses a mark as a parody of an existing mark, the intent is not necessarily to confuse the public but rather to amuse . . . the purpose of a parody is "to create a comic or satiric contrast to a serious work".

In one sense, a parody is an attempt "to derive benefit from the reputation" of the owner of the mark, . . . if only because no parody could be made without the initial mark. The benefit to the one making the parody, however, arises from the humorous association, not from public confusion as to the source of the marks. A parody relies upon a difference from the original mark, presumably a humorous difference, in order to produce its desired effect.

"Now everything is funny as long as it is happening to somebody Else, but when it happens to you, why it seems to lose some of its Humor, and if it keeps on happening, why the entire laughter kinder Fades out of it." W. Rogers, *Warning to Jokers: Lay Off the Prince*, in *The Illiterate Digest*, I-3 *The Writings of Will Rogers* 75 (1974). The same is true in trademark law. As McCarthy writes, "No one likes to be the butt of a joke, not even a trademark. But the requirement of trademark law is that a likely confusion of source, sponsorship or affiliation must be proven, which is not the same thing as 'right' not to be made fun of." 2 J. McCarthy, *Trademarks and Unfair Competition* § 31:38 at 670 (2d ed. 1984)...

The district court found the appellee's explanation for their adoption of the Lardashe mark not credible.[2] The court found that their real intent was to parody Jordache ...

C.

Another factor to be considered in determining whether there is a likelihood of confusion is "the degree of care likely to be exercised by purchasers." ... The district court found that customers are likely to exercise a high degree of care in purchasing clothing that costs between fifteen and sixty dollars. . . Appellant says that "[o]ne can just as easily surmise" that a lesser degree of care

---

[2] Stafford and Duran testified at trial that they had not heard of Jordache jeans when they selected the Lardashe name. Stafford explained that "Lardashe" was meant to be a more polite version of "lardass," her childhood nickname. She testified to the meaning of "ashe" as an alternative spelling by saying that "if you'll look in your Bible, it's the goddess of fertility. It's the goddess of womanhood which I've known about for a long time and which meant quite a bit to me." Further testimony revealed that Stafford was referring to several goddesses, but was unable to locate any of them in the Bible.* Finally, Stafford testified that the "e" at the end of "Lardashe" is meant to appear like a pig's tail when the word is written in script.

"In cases where defendant concocts an elaborate fantastic and strained scenario of how it 'coincidentally' hit upon its symbol, judges are not amused when asked to swallow fantastic fabrications about coincidental, unknowing usage." 2 J. McCarthy, *Trademarks and Unfair Competition* § 23:35 at 156 (2d ed. 1984) (see cases cited in n. 8 and in 1986 supplement). In one case, Sears, Roebuck & Co., the owner of the trademark "SEARS" for its Sears Financial Network sued an individual who had established a corporation called Sears Financial Services. The defendant explained how he had chosen that particular name: "Realizing that the Corporation needed a name, I began considering my options. I had long ago been smitten with a Miss Patricia Sears and, upon parting, promised to memorialize her through one of my endeavors. Remembering this promise, I named the company Sears Financial Services." *Sears, Roebuck & Co. v. Sears Fin. Network*, 576 F.Supp. 857, 863 (D.D.D.1983). The court said that it had difficulty in accepting this story, and "it can thus be preliminarily inferred that the defendant's intent was to trade off the plaintiff's well-known name and marks SEARS." *Id.*

Similarly, the district court in this case correctly looked beyond appellees' stated explanation in determining their true purpose in selecting the Lardashe mark. Indeed, Duran testified that the reason for rejection of "Horseashe" with a picture of a horse's head as a possible mark was that the appellees wanted to stay away from Jordache's horse mark. This awareness of the Jordache mark belies Stafford's explanation for choosing "Lardashe" and supports the district court's finding that "Lardashe" was intended to be a parody.

*[Ed. Note: Stafford perhaps was thinking of Ashtoreth, a fertility goddess also known as Astarte and Ishtar.]

will be used in selecting a pair of blue jeans. Brief of Appellant at 27. Appellant has offered only a guess, not any evidence of the degree of care that would satisfy its burden of proof. The district court's finding of a high degree of care is not clearly erroneous.

D.

Obviously, the best evidence of a likelihood of confusion in the marketplace is actual confusion . . . Appellant offered evidence that it believed showed actual confusion, but the district court did not find this evidence compelling. Appellant challenges the court's findings.

Paul Ornstein, Executive Vice President of Shaker Sports, testified that he was called by associates who asked whether Lardashe jeans were affiliated with Jordache. The district court ruled that this testimony was hearsay and that even if it was admissible, it was not evidence of actual confusion by consumers in the marketplace. . . We hold that Ornstein's testimony was admissible because it was offered to show the then existing state of mind of Ornstein's associates. *See* Fed.R.Evid. 803(3).

Although Ornstein's testimony was admissible, the district court correctly gave it little weight. . .

Dilution of a trademark can also occur if the challenged mark blurs the mental image conveyed by the original mark. The statutorily protective distinctive quality of a trademark is diluted as the mark's propensity to bring to mind a particular product or source is weakened. . .

In the present case, the district court found that "[b]ecause of the parody aspect of Lardashe, it is not likely that public identification of JORDACHE with the plaintiff will be eroded; indeed, parody tends to increase public identification of a plaintiff's mark with the plaintiff" [citation omitted]. The court further found that "[u]nder all the circumstances, the continued existence of LARDASHE jeans imply will not cause JORDACHE to lose its distinctiveness as a strong trademark for jeans and other apparel." *Id.* We hold these findings are not clearly erroneous.

The third element of dilution law is tarnishment. A mark can be tarnished if it is used in an unwholesome context. Precisely what suffices as an unwholesome context is not immediately evident [citation omitted]. (Use of "Bagzilla" mark on garbage bags not "unsavory or degrading") [citation omitted]; ("Petley Flea Bags" does not tarnish "Tetley Tea Bags") [citation omitted]; (use of "Be Prepared" slogan on poster portraying a pregnant girl in a Girl Scout uniform does not injure the Girl Scouts) [citation omitted]; (Use of Dallas Cowboys Cheerleaders uniforms in "sexually depraved" movie improperly injures plaintiff's business reputation) [citation omitted]; and (use of Coca-Cola design in "Enjoy Cocaine" poster improper tarnishment). The district court found that while LARDASHE "might be considered to be in poor taste by some consumers . . . it is not likely to create in the mind of consumers a particularly unwholesome, unsavory, or degrading association with plaintiff's name and marks" [citation omitted].

This argument presumes that the public will associate the manufacturer of Lardashe jeans with the manufacturer of Jordache jeans, thereby causing damage to the high quality image of Jordache. Because we find that the Lardashe mark was an intentional parody of the Jordache mark, we assume that the public will to some extent associate the two marks. To be actionable, however, the association of the two marks must tarnish or appropriate the good will and reputation of the owner of the mark. If the public associates the two marks for parody purposes only and does not associate the two sources of the products, appellant suffers no actionable injury. . . Association of marks for parody purposes without corresponding association of manufacturers does not tarnish or appropriate the good will of the manufacturer of the high quality similar product. . .

The cases finding a trademark had been tarnished even though there was no unwholesome context all involve the use of identical, or almost identical, trade names on different products [citation omitted]; (Steinway pianos and Stein-Way clip-on beverage can handles) [citation omitted]; (Cartier jewelry, china, and silver and Cattier cosmetics and toiletries) [citation omitted]; (Black Label beer and Black Label cigarettes) [citation omitted]; (Tiffany jewelry, china, silverware, and glassware and Tiffany's Restaurant and Lounge) [citation omitted]; (Yale locks and Yale flashlights). In each of these cases the public could readily associate one product with the manufacturer of the other product on the assumption that the manufacturer is in the business of producing two separate and distinct products. This is not the case here. It is unlikely that the public would assume that the same manufacturer would use quite different marks on substantially the same product. . . . Our review of the records convinces us that the public will not associate Lardashe jeans with the appellant or, if they do, they will only make the association because they believe Jordache Enterprises, Inc. manufactures Lardashe jeans. Therefore, there is no likelihood of an injury to appellant, and its dilution claim must fail.

III.

"If it had grown up,' she said to herself, 'it would have been a dreadfully ugly child; but it makes rather a handsome pig, I think.'" L. Carroll, *Alice's Adventures in Wonderland* 78-79 (1892).

The judgment of the district court is affirmed.

APPENDIX

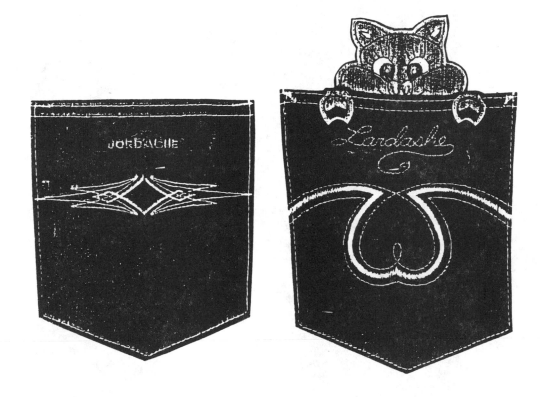

CHAPTER II

LAW, LAWYERS, JUDGES, LEGAL PROCEDURES, PROCESSES, INTERPRETATIONS, SUBTLETIES, DISTINCTIONS, LOOPHOLES, TECHNICALITIES, NUANCES & INTRICACIES

Mr. Leach made a speech,
Angry, neat, but wrong;
Mr. Hart, on the other part,
Was prosy, dull, and long.

Mr. Bell spoke very well,
Though nobody knew about what;
Mr. Trower talk'd for an hour,
Sat down, fatigued, and hot.

Mr. Parker made the case darker,
Which was dark enough without;
Mr. Cooke quoted his book,
And the Chancellor said, I doubt.

- Anonymous[1]

. . . I should apologize, perhaps, for the style of this bill. I dislike the verbose and intricate style of the English statutes, and in our revised code I endeavored to restore it to the simple one of the ancient statutes, in such original bills as I drew in the work. I suppose the reformation has not been acceptable, as it has been little followed. You, however, can easily correct this bill to the taste of my brother lawyers, by making every other word a "said" or "aforesaid," and saying everything over two or three times, so that nobody but we of the craft can untwist the diction, and find out what it means; and that, too, not so plainly but that we may conscientiously divide one half on each side. . .

- Thomas Jefferson[2]

---

[1] Anon. Poem, *A Second Miscellany at Law*, Sir Robert Megarry, p. 4 (1973) quoting from Oxford Book of Light Verse, p. 272 (1938).

[2] Thomas Jefferson, Letter to Joseph Carrington Cabell [1778-1856], dated Sept. 9, 1817, written from Poplar Forest [regarding a plan for elementary schools] from The *Writings of Thomas Jefferson*, Vol. XVII, *Definitive Edition*, pp. 417-418 (1905).

IN RE JESUS RAMIREZ
Justice Court of California, Tuolumne County
Case No. 516 (1851)

R. C. BARRY, J.P.

This is a suit fore Mule Steeling in which Jesus Ramirez is indited for steeling one black mare mule, branded 0 with a 5 in it from Sheriff Werk. George swarcs the mulc in question is hisn and I beleeve so to on hearing the caze I found Jesus Ramirez gilty of feloaniusly and against the law made and provided and the dignity of the people of Sonora steelin the aforesade mare mule sentenced him to pay the costs of Coort $10 and fined him $100 more as a terrour to all evil dooers. Jesus Ramirez not having any munney to pay with I rooled that George Werk shuld pay the costs of coort, as well as the fine, and in defalt of payment that the said one mare mule be sold by the Constable John Luney or other officer of the Court to meet the expenses of the Costs of the Coort, and also the payment of the fine aforesaid.

H.P. Barber the lawyer for George Werk insolently told me there were no law for me to rool so, I told him that I didn't care a damn for his booklaw, that I was the law myself. He continued to jaw back I told him to shut up but he wouldn't I fined him $50 and committeed him to gaol for 5 days for comtempt of Coort in bringing my roolings and dississions into disreputableness end as a warning to unrooly persons not to contradict this Coort.

Aug. 21, 1851
John Luney, Constable.

MYLWARD V. WELDON
Chancery Court of England
Reg Lib-A 1596, fol. 672 (1596)
Reprinted in Monroe's *Acta Cancellariae 1545 - 1625*, Vol. 1, p. 692

ANONYMOUS, Judge

Forasmuch as it now appeared to this court by a report made by the now Lord Keeper being then Master of the Rolls, upon consideration had of the plaintiff's Replication[1] according to an order of the 7th of May, of Anno 37 Reginæ, that the said Replication doth amount to six score[2] sheets of paper, and yet all the matter thereof which is pertinent might have been well contrived in sixteen sheets of paper, wherefore the plaintiff was appointed to be examined to find out who drew

---

[1] [Ed. Note: a "replication" is a reply made by the plaintiff to the defendent's answer in a suit in chancery.]

[2] [Ed. Note: one hundred twenty.]

the same Replication, and by whose advice it was done, to the end that the offender might, for example's sake, not only be punished, but also be fined to her Majesty for that offence; and that the defendant might have his charges sustained thereby. (The execution of which order was, by a later order made by the late Lord Keeper the 26th of June, Anno 37th Reginæ, suspended without any express cause, shewed thereof in that order, and was never since called upon until the mater came to be heard on Tuesday last, before the Lord Keeper, at which time some mention was again made of the same Replication);

And for that it now appeared to his Lordship, by the confession of Richard Mylward, alias Alexander, the plaintiff's son, that the said Richard himself did both draw, devise, and engross the same Replication, and because his Lordship is of opinion that such an abuse is not in any sort to be tolerated -- proceeding of a malicious purpose to increase the defendant's charge, and being fraught with much impertinent matter not fit for the court;

It is therefore ordered, that the warden of the Fleet shall take the said Richard Mylward, alias Alexander, into his custody, and shall bring him into Westminster Hall on Saturday next, about 10 of the clock in the forenoon, and then and there shall cut a hole in the midst of the same engrossed Replication which is delivered unto him for that purpose, and put the said Richard's head through the same hole, and so let the same Replication hang about his shoulders with the written side outward, and then, the same so hanging, shall lead the said Richard bareheaded and barefaced round about Westminster Hall, whilst the Courts are sitting, and shall shew him at the Bar of every of the three Courts within the Hall, and then shall take him back again to the Fleet, and keep him prisoner until he shall have paid £10 to her Majesty for a fine, and 20 nobles to the defendant for his costs in respect of the aforesaid abuse, which fine and costs are now adjudged and imposed upon him by this court for the abuse aforesaid.

MACKENSWORTH v. AMERICAN TRADING TRANSPORTATION COMPANY
United States District Court, E. D. Pennsylvania
367 F. Supp. 373 (1973)

EDWARD R. BECKER, District Judge.

The motion now before us
has stirred up a terrible fuss.
And what is considerably worse,
it has spawned some preposterous doggerel verse.

The plaintiff, a man of the sea,
after paying his lawyer a fee,
filed a complaint of several pages
to recover statutory wages.[1]

The pleaded facts remind us
      of a tale that is endless.
A seaman whom for centuries
      the law has called "friendless"
is discharged from the ship before
      voyage's end
and sues for lost wages, his finances
      to mend.

The defendant shipping company's
      office is based in New York City,
and to get right down to the nitty
      gritty,
it has been brought to this Court by
      long arm service, [2]
which has made it extremely nervous.

Long arm service is a procedural tool
      founded upon a "doing business"rule.
But defendant has no office here,
      and says it has no mania
to do any business in Pennsylvania.

Plaintiff found defendant had a ship
      here in June '72.
but defendant says that ship's business
      is through.
Asserting that process is amiss,
it has filed a motion to dismiss.

Plaintiff's counsel, whose name is
      Harry Lore,
read defendant's brief and found it
      a bore.

---

[1] In nautical terms, the wage statute is stowed
    at § 594 of 46 U.S.Code.
[2] Long arm service is effected, not by stealth,
    but through the Secretary of the Commonwealth.

Instead of a reply brief, he acted
      pretty quick
and responded with a clever
      limerick:

      " Admiralty process is hoary
        With pleadings that tell a sad story
        Of Libels in Rem
        The bane of sea-faring men
        The moral:
        Better personally served than be sorry."

Not to be outdone, the defense took
      the time
to reply with their own clever rhyme.
The defense counsel team of Mahoney,
      Roberts & Smith
drafted a poem cutting right to the pith:

      " Admiralty lawyers like Harry
        Both current and those known from lore
        Be they straight types, mixed or fairy
        Must learn how to sidestep our bore.

        For Smith, not known for his mirth
        With his knife out for Mackensworth
        With Writs, papers or Motions to Quash
        Knows that dear Harry's position don't wash."

Overwhelmed by this outburst of
      pure creativity.
we determined to show an equal
      proclivity.
Hence this opinion in the form of
      verse,
even if not of the calibre of Saint-
      John Perse.

The first question is whether, under
      the facts,
defendant has done business here to
      come under Pennsylvania's long
      arm acts. [3]

---

[3] Designed to relieve the plaintiff's service burdens,
    Pennsylvania's latest long arm law may be found at § 8309 of 43 Purdon's.

If we find it has, we must reach
        question two,
whether that act so applied is con-
        stitutional under Washington
        v. International Shoe. [4]

Defendant runs a ship known as
        the SS Washington Trader,
whose travels plaintiff tracked
        as GM is said to have followed Nader
He found that in June '72 that ship
        rested its keel
and took on a load of cargo here
        which was quite a big business deal.

In order for extraterritorial
        jurisdiction to obtain.
it is enough that defendant do a single
        act in Pa. for pecuniary gain.
And we hold that the recent visit of
        defendant's ship to Philadelphia's port
is doing business enough to bring it
        before this Court.

We note, however, that the
        amended act's grammar [5]
is enough to make any thoughtful
        lawyer stammer.
The particular problem which
        deserves mention
is whether a single act done for
        pecuniary gain also requires
        future intention.

---

[4] That decision of the Supreme Court of Courts,
    may be found at page 310 of 326 U.S. Reports. [66 S.Ct. 154, 90 L.Ed.95].

[5] The words of the statute are overly terse,
    still we will quote them, though not in verse:
    (a) General rule. - - Any of the following shall constitute "doing business" for the purposes of this chapter:
    . . . (2) The doing of a single act in this Commonwealth for the purpose of thereby realizing pecuniary benefit or otherwise accomplishing an object with the intention of initiating a series of such acts.
    (3) The shipping of merchandise directly or indirectly into or through this Commonwealth.
    42 Pa. § 8309.

As our holding suggests, we
        believe the answer is no,
and feel that is how the Pa. appellate
        cases will go.
Further, concerning § (a) (3)'s
        "shipping of merchandise"
the future intention doctrine has
        already had its demise. [6]

We do not yet rest our inquiry,
        for as is a judge's bent,
we must look to see if there is
        precedent. [7]
And we found one written in '68 by
        three big wheels
on the Third Circuit Court of
        Appeals.

The case, a longshoreman's personal
        injury suit, is Kane v. USSR,
and it controls the case at bar.
It's a case with which defendants
        had not reckoned,
and may be found at page 131 of 394
        F.2d.

In Kane, a ship came but once to
        pick up stores
and hired as agents to do its chores
        a firm of local stevedores.

---

[6] See Aquarium Pharmaceuticals Inc. v. Industrial Pressing and Packaging (E.D.Pa.1973).
    Prospects for suit on a single goods shipment
        are decidedly greener
    because of the *Aquarium* decision of Judge
        Charles R. Weiner,
    holding that, in a goods shipment case no future
        intention is needed;
    the message of *Aquarium* we surely have
        heeded.
    Anyone who wishes to look *Aquarium* up
        can find it at P. 441 of 358 F.Supp.
[7] We thus reject the contention that one of the judicial vices
    is too much reliance on *stare decisis*.

Since the Court upheld service on
    the agents,
      the case is nearly on all fours,
and to defendant's statutory argument
    Kane closes the doors.

Despite defendant's claim that
    plaintiff's process is silly,
there have been three other seamen's
    actions against defendant, with
    service in Philly.
And although they might have tried
    to get the service corrected,
the fact of the matter is they've
    never objected.[8]

We turn then to the constitu-
    tional point,
and lest the issue come out of joint,
it is important that one thought be
    first appended:
the reason the long arm statute was
    amended.

The amendment's purpose was to
    eliminate guess
and to extend long arm service
    to the full reach of due process.
And so we now must look to the facts
to see if due process is met by
sufficient "minimum contacts."

The visit of defendant's ship
    is not yet very old,
and so we feel constrained to hold

---

[8] Berrios v. American Trading & Production Co. (AT&P) (defendant's predecessor), C.A. 68-47; Gibson v. AT&P, C.A. 68-1466.
    And in Battles v. AT&P., C.A. 73-102
      in this very annum,
    service on the Secretary of the Common-
      wealth
    was authorized by Judge John B. Hannum.

that under traditional notions of
          substantial justice and fair play,
defendant's constitutional argument
          does not carry the day.

This Opinion has now reached its
          final border,
and the time has come to enter an
          Order,
which, in a sense, is its ultimate
          crux,
but alas, plaintiff claims under a
          thousand bucks.

So, while trial counsel are doubtless
          in fine fettle,
with many fine fish in their trial
          kettle,
we urge them not to test their
          mettle,
because, for the small sum involved,
          it makes more sense to settle.

In view of the foregoing Opinion, at
          this time
we enter the following Order, also
          in rhyme.

ORDER

Finding that service of process is
          bona fide,
the motion to dismiss is hereby
          denied.
So that this case can now get about
          its ways,
defendant shall file an answer within
          21 days.

IN THE MATTER OF THE MOTION TO ADMIT
MISS LAVINIA GOODELL TO THE BAR OF THIS COURT
Supreme Court of Wisconsin
39 Wis. 232 (1875)

EDWARD G. RYAN, C.J.

In courts proceeding according to the course of the common law, a bar is almost as essential as a bench. And a good bar may be said to be a necessity of a good court. This is not always understood, perhaps not fully by the bar itself. On the bench, the lesson is soon learned that the facility and accuracy of judicial labor are largely dependent on the learning and ability of the bar. And it well becomes every court to be careful of its bar and jealous of the rule of admission to it, with the view of fostering in it the highest order of professional excellence.

The constitution makes no express provision for the bar. But it establishes courts, amongst which it distributes all the jurisdiction of all the courts of Westminster Hall, in equity and at common law. *Putnam v. Sweet,* 2 Pin., 302. And it vests in the courts all the judicial power of the state. The constitutional establishment of such courts appears to carry with it the power to establish a bar to practice in them. And admission to the bar appears to be a judicial power. It may therefore become a very grave question for adjudication here, whether the constitution does not entrust the rule of admissions to the bar, as well as of expulsion from it, exclusively to the discretion of the courts.

The legislature has, indeed, from time to time, assumed power to prescribe rules for the admission of attorneys to practice. When these have seemed reasonable and just, it has generally, we think, been the pleasure of the courts to act upon such statutes, in deference to the wishes of a coordinate branch of the government, without considering the question of power. We do not understand that the circuit courts generally yielded to the unwise and unseemly act of 1849, which assumed to force upon the courts as attorneys, any persons of good moral character, however unlearned or illiterate; however disqualified, by nature, education or habit, for the important trusts of the profession. We learn from the clerk of this court that no application under that statute was ever made here. The good sense of the legislature has long since led to its repeal. And we have too much reliance on the judgment of the legislature to apprehend another such attempt to degrade the courts.

The state suffers essentially by every such assault on one branch of the government upon another; and it is the duty of all the coordinate branches scrupulously to avoid even all seeming of such. If, unfortunately, such an attack upon the dignity of the courts should again be made, it will be time for them to inquire whether the rule of admission be within the legislative or judicial power. But we will not anticipate such an unwise and unbecoming interference in what so peculiarly concerns the courts, whether the power to make it exists or not. In the meantime, it is a pleasure to defer to all reasonable statutes on the subject. And we will decide this motion on the present statutes, without passing on their binding force.

This is the first application for admission of a female to the bar of this court. And it is just matter for congratulation that it is made in favor of a lady whose character raises no personal objection; something perhaps not always to be looked for in women who forsake the ways of their sex for the ways of ours.

The statute provides for admission of attorneys in a circuit court upon examination to the satisfaction of the judge, and for the right of persons so admitted to practice in all courts here except this; but that to entitle any one to practice in this court he shall be licensed by order of this court. Tay. Stats., ch. 119, §§ 31, 32, 33. While these sections give a rule to the circuit courts, they avoid giving any to this court, leaving admission here, as it ought to be, in the discretion of the court. This is, perhaps, a sufficient answer to the present application, which is not addressed to our discretion, but proceeds on assumed right founded on admission in a circuit court. But the novel positions on which the motion was pressed appear to call for a broader answer.

The language of the statute, of itself, confessedly applies to males only. But it is insisted that the rule of construction, found in subd. 2, sec. 1, ch. 5, R.S., necessarily extends the terms of the statute to females. The rule is that words in the singular number may be construed plural, and in the plural, singular; and that words of the masculine gender may be applied to females; unless, in either case, such construction would be inconsistent with the manifest intention of the legislature.

This was pressed upon us, as if it were a new rule of construction, of peculiar application to our statutes. We do not so understand it. It appears to be but a particular application of the general rule this stated by Tindall, C.J.: "The only rule for the construction of acts of parliament is, that they should be construed according to the intent of the parliament which passed the act." And it is not new or peculiar here. Potter's Dwarris, 111. The last clause of the rule, relating to sex, seems to be almost as old as Magna Charta. Coke 2 Inst., 45. We apprehend that, unless in the construction of penal statutes, it has been little questioned since the much considered case of *King v. Wiseman*, Fortescue, 91.

The rule is permissive only, as an aid in giving effect to the true intent of the legislature. Even of a statutory rule positive in terms, Lord Denman said: "It is not to be taken as substituting one set of words for another, nor as strictly defining what the meaning of a word must be under all circumstances. We rather think that it merely declares what persons may be included within a term, when the circumstances require that they should." *Queen v. Justices, etc.*, 7 A.&E., 480. So, *a fortiori*, of the permissive rule here.

And the argument for this motion is simply this: that the application of this permissive rule of construction to a provision applicable in terms to males only, has effect, without other sign of legislative intent, to admit females to the bar from which the common law has excluded them ever since courts have administered the common law. This is sufficiently startling. But the argument cannot stop there. Its logic goes far beyond the bar. The same peremptory rule of construction would reach all or nearly all the functions of the state government, would obliterate almost all distinction of sex in our statutory *corpus juris*, and make females eligible to almost all offices under our statutes, municipal and state, executive, legislative and judicial, except so far as the constitution may interpose a virile qualification.

Indeed the argument appears to overrule even this exception. For we were referred to a case in Iowa, which unfortunately we do not find in the reports of that state, holding a woman not excluded by the statutory description of "any white male person." If we should follow that authority in ignoring the distinction of sex, we do not perceive why it should not emasculate the constitution itself and include females in the constitutional right of male suffrage and male qualification.

Such a rule would be one of judicial revolution, not of judicial construction. There is not sign nor symptom in our statute law of any legislative imagination of such a radical change in the economy of the state government. There are many the other way; an irresistible presumption that the legislature never contemplated such confusion of functions between the sexes. The application of the permissive rule of construction here would not be in aid of the legislative intention, but in open defiance of it. We cannot stultify the court by holding that the legislature intended to bring about *per ambages* [in a roundabout way], a sweeping revolution of social order, by adopting a very innocent rule of statutory construction. . .

So we find no statutory authority for the admission of females to the bar of any court of this state. And, with all the respect and sympathy for this lady which all men owe to all good women, we cannot regret that we do not. We cannot but think the common law wise in excluding women from the profession of the law. The profession enters largely into the well being of society; and, to be honorably filled and safely to society, exacts the devotion of life. The law of nature destines and qualifies the female sex for the bearing and nurture of the children of our race and for the custody of the homes of the world and their maintenance in love and honor. And all life-long callings of women, inconsistent with these radical and sacred duties of their sex, as is the profession of the law, are departures from the order of nature; and when voluntary, treason against it.

The cruel chances of life sometimes baffle both sexes, and may leave women free from the peculiar duties of their sex. These may need employment, and should be welcome to any not derogatory to their sex and its proprieties, or inconsistent with the good order of society. But it is public policy to provide for the sex, not for its superfluous members; and not to tempt women from the proper duties of their sex by opening to them duties peculiar to ours. There are many employments in life not unfit for female character. The profession of the law is surely not one of these.

The peculiar qualities of womanhood, its gentle graces, its quick sensibility, its tender susceptibility, its purity, its delicacy, its emotional impulses, its subordination of hard reason to sympathetic feeling, are surely not qualifications for forensic strife. Nature has tempered woman as little for the juridical conflicts of the court room, as for the physical conflicts of the battle-field. Womanhood is moulded for gentler and better things. And it is not the saints of the world who chiefly give employment to our profession. It has essentially and habitually to do with all that is selfish and malicious, knavish and criminal, coarse and brutal, repulsive and obscene, in human life.

It would be revolting to all female sense of the innocence and sanctity of their sex, shocking to man's reverence for womanhood and faith in woman, on which hinge all the better affections and humanities of life, that woman should be permitted to mix professionally in all the nastiness of the world which finds its way into courts of justice; all the unclean issues, all the collateral questions of sodomy, incest, rape, seduction, fornication, adultery, pregnancy, bastardy, legitimacy, prostitution, lascivious cohabitation, abortion, infanticide, obscene publications, libel and slander of sex, impotence, divorce: all the nameless catalogue of indecencies, *la chronique scandaleuse* [the scandalous chronicle] of all the vices and all the infirmities of all society, with which the profession has to deal, and which go towards filling judicial reports which must be read for accurate knowledge of the law. This is bad enough for men.

We hold in too high reverence the sex without which, as is truly and beautifully written, *le commencement de la vie est sans secours, le milieu sans plaisir, et le fin sans consolation* [the beginning of life is without assistance, the middle is without pleasure, and the end without consolation], voluntarily to commit it to such studies and such occupations. *Non tali auxilio nec defensoribus istis* [Not with such help or with those defenders], should judicial contests be upheld. Reverence for all womanhood would suffer in the public spectacle of woman so instructed and so engaged.

This motion gives appropriate evidence of this truth. No modest woman could read without pain and self abasement, no woman could so overcome the instincts of sex as publicly to discuss, the case which we had occasion to cite *supra, King v. Wiseman*.[1] And when counsel was arguing for this lady that the word, person, in sec. 32, ch. 119, necessarily includes females, her presence made it impossible to suggest to him as *reductio ad absurdum* [a reduction to an absurdity] of his position, that the same construction of the same word in sec. 1, ch. 37, would subject woman to prosecution for the paternity of a bastard, and in secs. 39, 40, ch. 164, to prosecution for rape. Discussions are habitually necessary in courts of justice, which are unfit for female ears. The habitual presence of women at these would tend to relax the public sense of decency and propriety. If, as counsel threatened, these things are to come, we will take no voluntary part in bringing them about.

By the Court. — The motion is denied.

---

[1] [Ed. Note: In that case, the defendent was charged with committing sodomy on an eleven year old girl.]

CHAPTER II: LAW, LAWYERS & JUDGES

IN RE ROBIN E. LOVE
United States Bankruptcy Court, S. D. Florida
61 B. R. 558 (1968)

A. JAY CRISTOL, Bankruptcy Judge.

This cause came on to be heard sua sponte upon the court's own motion to dismiss this chapter 7 petition pursuant to 11 U.S.C. § 707(b) and the court having received the inspiration for the motion from a little old ebony bird and not from any party in interest or any other person and having considered the presumption in favor of debtor provided in 11 U.S.C. § 707(b) and not deeming it appropriate to take evidence, the court finds:

Once upon a midnight dreary, while I pondered weak and weary
Over many quaint and curious files of chapter seven lore
While I nodded nearly napping, suddenly there came a tapping
As of some one gently rapping, rapping at my chamber door,

"Tis some debtor" I muttered, "tapping at my chamber door--
Only this and nothing more."

Ah distinctly I recall, it was in the early fall
And the file still was small
The Code provided I could use it
If someone tried to substantially abuse it

No party asked that it be heard.
"Sua sponte" whispered a small black bird.
The bird himself, my only maven, strongly looked to be a raven.

Upon the words the bird had uttered
I gazed at all the files cluttered
"Sua sponte," I recall, had no meaning; none at all.

And the cluttered files sprawl, drove a thought into my brain.
Eagerly I wished the morrow--vainly I had sought to borrow

From BAFJA, surcease of sorrow--and an order quick and plain
That this case would not remain as a source of further pain.
The procedure, it seemed plain.

As the case grew older, I perceived I must be bolder.
And must sua sponte act, to determine every fact,
If primarily consumer debts, are faced,

Perhaps this case is wrongly placed.
This is a thought that I must face, perhaps I should
      dismiss this case.

I moved sua sponte to dismiss it for I knew
      I would not miss it
The Code said I could, I knew it.
But not exactly how to do it, or perhaps
      some day I'd rue it.

I leaped up and struck my gavel.
For the mystery to unravel
Could I? Should I? Sua sponte, grant my motion to dismiss?
While it seemed the thing to do, suddenly I thought of this.

Looking, looking towards the future and to what
      there was to see
If my motion, it was granted and an appeal
      came to be,
Who would file, but pray tell me,
      a learned brief for the appellee
The District Judge would not do so
At least this much I do know.
Tell me raven, how to go.

As I with the ruling wrestled
In the statute I saw nestled
A presumption with a flavor clearly in the debtor's favor.
No evidence had I taken
Sua sponte appeared foresaken.
Now my motion caused me terror
A dismissal would be error.
Upon consideration of § 707(b), in anguish, loud I cried
The court's sua sponte motion to dismiss
      under §707 (b) is denied.

IN RE RAYMOND, DEBTOR.
United States Bankruptcy Court, E.D. Virginia
12 B.R. 906 (1981)

HAL J. BONNEY, Jr., Bankruptcy Judge

When Godfrey Marks penned that rousing popular nautical chorus: *"Sailing, sailing over the bounding main; For many a stormy wind shall blow ere Jack comes home again,"* he never considered that the stormy wind to which he referred might not be tempestuous billows or stormy blasts but bankruptcy. Alas!

Jack is David Ernest Raymond of the United States Navy aboard the USS America (CV66). His wife is Susan Lucille known to the Court as debtor 81-00831-N. Interestingly, she also seeks to file Jack's bankruptcy petition by virtue of his power of attorney which she holds.

There is an issue. May [or is it can?] one file bankruptcy for another under a power of attorney which one holds?

There is an answer. No.

Jack is out to sea and shall not return for several months. The couple's "severe financial situation," the application says, requires immediate relief.

An appeal has been encouraged, something we do not always do. It is hoped that an appellate court will consider the issue head on and simply answer the issue rather than suggest alternatives.

There are alternatives and they usually suffice. Unfortunately, these fellows with "severe financial situations" run into the lawyer's office just as the ship is leaving Pier 12 for an extended cruise rather than anticipating their needs. They expect miracles; we dispense few. We are not very good at it.

The alternatives are utilization of the Soldiers' and Sailors' Relief Act in state courts to forestall creditors. Or they sign the bankruptcy papers just before going up the gangplank, but the Court dismisses the petition without prejudice preserving the right to reopen the case, without payment of additional fees, when the petitioner is available to perform the duties incumbent upon a debtor. *In re Ehly*, [citation omitted]. Or if the fellow is already on the bounding main, the attorney will prepare the papers and send them to the ship there to be executed and returned.

But these alternatives won't work here and we must face the issue as to whether or not one might find authority to use a power of attorney for these purposes. Jack is away, cannot be easily reached and his wife wishes to do this for him.

The power of attorney before us is a typical, well-drafted, general one regularly utilized by service personnel. There is no mistake about it, it bestows many a power. The missus can dispose of, collect, endorse, borrow and on and on. The document is shocking and one wonders why anyone would sign such a far-reaching thing. It reposes a lot of trust.

The use of powers of attorney is a part of the law of agency. Virginia does not require that they be recorded, but it is permissible. Code of Virginia [as amended] § 55-107. Indeed, a power of attorney is to be strictly construed. 3 Am.Jur.2d, Agency § 28...

Obviously, agency law obtains, but it is not all that crucial here, as noted below, and we shall not lengthen an opinion by reciting it all for no good purpose. One certainly has the power to constitute another as his attorney, and one has the power to exercise the power. No question about it and we do not quarrel with it. But does it extend to such a personal act as taking bankruptcy status? The Court thinks not.

Bankruptcy is a personal exercise of a privilege and due to the seriousness of it, it may not be exercised by another. Can one exercise a power of attorney

1 - to enlist another in the armed forces,
2 - to exercise the franchise for another,
3 - to file for divorce for another,
4 - to offer for office for another, or
5 - to enter into a personal employment contract for another?

No! There is a difference between exercising the power granted to sell land or dispose of property and exercising a very personal, psychic act. There is indeed a limit as to what might be done by power of attorney.

Is bankruptcy such a personal thing? I think it is. It is not an administrative procedure that one seeks before a federal agency. It is a judicial process. 1 Collier on Bankruptcy [14th Ed.] § 1.09, 1.10. . . .

Bankruptcy is a serious step; it holds its stigmas still. It is a unique judicial process where one is laid bare, financially. And remember this — it results in a court record for future employers, creditors, friends, relatives and the public to see. Would you grant a security clearance to one who cannot manage his financial affairs and files bankruptcy? I only ask the question. Some would and some would not.

We perceive bankruptcy to be a very personal matter which only the individual can voluntarily exercise.

The law? There is none. A Third Circuit case, *In re Paul A. Closkey, Inc.*, [citation omitted] would permit creditors use of the power of attorney in involuntary cases, but it truly does not come to grips with our issue. *Eitel v. Schmidlapp*, [citation omitted] while it does not touch upon bankruptcy, is an excellent case on the law of principal and agent.

Too, one feels compelled to cite *U.S. v. Kras*, [citation omitted] for the proposition that bankruptcy is not a right and it carries with it certain obligations. No pay, no go. A fortiori, no show, no go.

The application for authority for the wife to exercise her power of attorney and file bankruptcy for her husband is hereby denied.

Much ado about nothing? That possibility has rung in our ears throughout the writing of this wisdom. Some would say what difference does it make. Others would say he is but one of hundreds of thousands and what difference does it make. Still others would say that the poor fellow needs help, give it to him. What difference does it make?

I grant that were this judge flown to the USS America to question Jack, he would readily endorse his wife's filing of bankruptcy for him. We detest, utterly detest, a dot the i's and cross the t's approach. Rigidity of the system is to be avoided and we are usually to be found in that camp.

However, we stick by our guns on two grounds. Use of the power for this purpose could open you know whose box. Relative to service personnel, we see all too frequently the abuse of the power in other respects while Jack is away. It is, frequently, a tool for insolvency. If allowed here, it will be misused.

Secondly, it is a deep personal action which only the individual should make. We must keep it that way, purely. This crucial step he must take himself.

IT IS SO ORDERED.

LUKENS v. FORD
Supreme Court of Georgia
87 Ga. 541; 13 S.E. 949 (1891)

LOGAN E. BLECKLEY, Chief Justice

In the ornithology of litigation this case is a tomtit, furnished with a garb of feathers ample enough for a turkey. Measured by the verdict, its tiny body has only the bulk of twenty-five dollars, but it struts with a display of record expanded into eighty-three pages of manuscript. It seems to us that a more contracted plumage might serve for so small a bird, but perhaps we are mistaken. In every forensic season, we have a considerable flock of such cases, to be stripped and dissected for the cabinets of jurisprudence. We endeavor to pick our overfledged poultry with judicial assiduity and patience.

The motion for a new trial contains eight grounds, five of them alleging error in the charge of the court. The full charge is set out in the record, and we have examined it minutely. Reading it all together, and construing it as a whole, it is free from material error. . . .Why the defendant should have requested the court to instruct that he, the defendant, had no right to dig down and lower the spring, and that the plaintiff had a right to keep the water in it as it stood at the date of the contract, if it was not below the natural height, we are at some loss to conjecture; but we cannot order a new trial because the defendant requested instructions apparently favorable to his adversary, and the court gave them in compliance with the request.

Perhaps the object of the defendant was to curry favor with the jury by showing them that he was willing to make concessions, and was not disposed to controvert what was of no consequence to the merits of the dispute. But we do not know this to be so; and if we did, we hardly think that such a light touch in currying favor would vitiate the trial. . . .There is a strong flavor of afterthought in what the motion for a new trial has to say touching the form of the verdict.. . .

To reopen this fierce but petty litigation because of a slight error, would not be wholesome practice. This is the second of the spring and fish-pond cases. . . .

In so far as our duty requires us to verify the correctness of the verdict, we regard it as sound enough to be upheld by the presiding judge in the exercise of his discretion.

Judgment Affirmed.

IN RE JOSE
Justice Court of California, Tuolumne County
Case No. 101 (1851)

R. C. BARRY, J.P.

This is a caze where one James Knowlton brings sute again Jose _____ for feloniously, and surreptitiously, taking, steeling, and robing him the said James Knowlton late of San Francisco, One Bucskin purs or sacke of goold dust of the valu of 4000 dolars.

After heering the evidense projuced in the case. I demanded of Jose whether he was going to pleed guilty or not. Jose answered me thus, you find out. For which insulent, and abominable contempt of coort I fined him 3 ounces, and adjuged him guilty, I sentesed him to restore the goold dust to the Court and to receive well lade on 40 lashes on his bear back, and to pay the Costs of the Court.

Costs of Court 5 ounces which Jose not having I rooled that James Knowlton should pay. Deducted the amount and returned the balanse to the owner James Knowlton.

July 9th, 1851
U. H. Brown, Constable

WARREN v. PURTELL
Supreme Court of Georgia
64 Georgia Reports 428 (1879)

LOGAN E. BLECKLEY, Justice

[This case involved the assertion of a claim of marital exemption to certain personal property levied upon by plaintiff pursuant to a judgment obtained against claimant's husband. The case was on the black-board for trial while the criminal docket was being called, and the court had been occupied with criminal business on the day the verdict was rendered, and no notice had been given during the morning that the cases on the civil trial calendar would be called later that day. Thus neither the attorney for plaintiff nor for claimant knew that the case would be taken up for trial. The case was called for trial and disposed of adversely to claimant in the absence of claimant's attorney.]

The claimant's counsel no doubt reasoned well. The circumstances indicated that the case would not be reached, or if reached, that it would not be tried so early in the term. But the presence or absence of parties and counsel when their cases are called in their order for trial, cannot be left to sound reasoning. Probability cannot be made the measure of progress in the dispatch of business. As we all know, sometimes there is a drag and sometimes a run; and those having business to attend to in court must bear in mind that a wide variation from the average rate of progress may occur. Indeed, it is always probable that something improbable will happen. . .

Judgment affirmed.

LOWE v. MORRIS
Supreme Court of Georgia
13 Ga. 147 (1853)

HIRAM WARNER, J.

This is a motion to dismiss the writ of error, on the ground that the Clerk of this Court has omitted to annex the seal of the Court thereto, as required by the 20th rule of practice. That rule requires, "that writs of error shall issue in the *name of the Governor of the State,* shall bear teste in the *name of the Judges of this Court,* shall be *signed by the Clerk,* and *sealed with the seal of this Court,* and shall be returnable to the *next succeeding term.*" . . .

By the 22d rule of practice, it is made the duty of the Clerk of this Court, "to keep on hand for the use of the bar, blank writs of error, *according to the form adopted by this Court,* duly by him *signed* and *sealed,* to be furnished to the bar on application therefor."

This writ of error has been issued by the Clerk in exact conformity with the rule, except the *omission* to attach the seal of the Court to it. The Clerk of the Superior Court has obeyed it by sending up the record to this Court, and the parties have acted in obedience to it. . .

Has there been a *writ of error filed* in this case, as contemplated by the Constitution? . . . *Blackstone* defines a writ of error to be, a writ which lies for some supposed mistake in the proceedings of a Court of Record, and which only lies upon matter of *law* arising upon the face of the proceedings.

I am. . . of the opinion, that a *writ of error* has been *filed,* as contemplated by the Constitution and the Act of 1852, and that the *clerical omission* of not attaching the seal of the Court thereto may be *amended instanter.*

JOSEPH H. LUMPKIN, J., concurring.

Is a writ of error a nullity without a seal?

My first impression was, that this defect was fatal. Upon reflection, my final conclusion is, the other way. I am not entirely satisfied, however, that I am right, for the reason that my brother Nisbet thinks differently. And a life-long friendship, with an endeared official intimacy of seven years, has inspired me with the most unfeigned respect for the head as well as the heart of my colleague. . .

He has authority on his side, both ancient and modern, sacred and profane.

His signet or seal was the pledge of *identity* and fidelity, exacted by Tamar of Lord Judah, one of the twelve Princes of Israel. *Moses' Reports, Book Genesis, c 38, v. 18.* See also, *Esther, c. 8*, v. 8 and 10. It would seem from this last case, that even at this early period *Monarchs* as well as *Courts* at this day, could only act through their official seal. And the reason given is, that the precept issued in the King's name and sealed with his ring, by his Clerk Mordecai the Jew, *may no man reverse*. And this is the strong position of my learned brother. (M. anciently, as now, I would remark, was a favorite *initial* for the name of Court Clerks, from *Mordecai the Jew, even down to Martin, the Gentile.*) Whatever else there may be that is new under the sun, it is very evident, from this last authority, that *mails* are not. For we are told that these letters mandatory of Ahasuerus were sent by *post*, on horseback, and riders on mules, camels and young dromedaries.

So much for the antiquity and importance of seals. It will be found, upon further investigation, that modern decision adhere very strictly to these patriarchal precedents. . . .

In *Lessee of Beal et al. vs. King et al.* [citation omitted] the Court say, "No principle is more definitely settled, than that process of a Court having a seal, can only be evidenced by its seal, which is the appointed mode of showing its authority.". . .

In *Hall vs. Jones,* [citation omitted] where an original writ, like the one before us, had the seal of the Common Pleas instead of that of the Supreme Court, to which it was returnable, the plaintiff having made use of a blank writ of the common Pleas, he moved that the writ should be amended by affixing the proper seal; but the Court decided that it could not be done. . .

Fearing lest my dissenting brother may not be as industrious in citing cases *against* himself as I have been for him, let the foregoing suffice.

Those who are curious to investigate the subject of seals, will find the best account of them in the writings of *Lord Hale* and *Baron Gilbert*.

The earliest mode of commerce, being by barter or exchange of a cow or sheep for some other commodity, it is supposed that the image of these and other animals stamped upon leather or other yielding substance, by wood or metal, constituted the first currency as well as the first use of seals; next, the impression was made upon the metals, certain superscriptions, indicating the value of the coin, as a Napoleon or a Washington. The latter, without weighing, is universally taken in the United States, to denote twenty dollars. Next, contracts were attested by seals, either where chirography was not known, or where the party could not write his name.

Lord Coke defines a seal to be, wax with an impression, [citation omitted] *"Sigillum"* says he, *"est cera impressa, quia cera sine impressione non est sigillum."* [A seal is wax with an impression, because wax without an impression is not a seal.] Common Law definition of a seal . . . But it is a curious fact, that there is neither an Act of Parliament nor an adjudged case, up to *Lord Coke's* day, to bind the Courts as to what constitutes a seal. His opinion was probably founded upon the practice of the country in his day.

New York, and most of the States North, have held that a seal is an impression upon wax, wafer or some other tenacious substance, capable of being impressed. . . . But in Pennsylvania, New Jersey, and the Southern and Western States generally, the impression upon wax has been disused and a circular, oval or square mark, opposite the name of the signer, is held to have the same effect as a seal, the shape of it being altogether indifferent. It is usually written with a pen, sometimes printed. . . .

The truth is, that this whole subject, like many others, is founded on the usage of the times, and of the country. A scroll is just as good as an impression on wax, wafer, or parchment, by metal, engraved with the arms of a prince, potentate or private person. Both are now utterly worthless, and the only wonder is, that all technical distinctions growing out of the use of seals, such as the Statute of Limitations, plea to the consideration, &c. are not at once universally abolished. The only reason ever urged at this day, why a seal should give greater evidence and dignity to writing is, that it evidences greater deliberation, and therefore should impart greater solemnity to instruments. Practically we know that the art of printing has done away with this argument. For not only are all official, and most individual deeds, with the seals appended, *printed* previously, and filled up at the time of their execution, but even merchants and business men are adopting the same practice, as it respects their notes.

Once the seal was everything, and the signature was nothing. Now the very reverse is true: the signature is everything, and the seal nothing. Thanks to the advancing intelligence of the age! In the days of ignorance, to be able to read and write, would save a felon's neck. Many of the educated gentry now, who are too lazy to work, and prefer to live by their wits, are the fellows upon whom the penalties of the law are visited in their utmost severity.

So long as seals distinguished identity, there was propriety in preserving them. And as a striking illustration, see the signatures and seals to the death warrant of Charles the First, as late as January, 1648. They are 49 in number, and no two of them alike. But to recognize the waving, oval circumflex of a pen, with those mystic letters to the uninitiated, L. S. imprisoned in its serpentine folds, as equipotent with the coats of arms taken from the devices engraved on the shields of knights and noblemen; shades of Eustace, Roger de Beaumont, and Goeffry Gifford, what a desecration! The reason of the usage has ceased; let the custom be dispensed with altogether.

In *Jones & Temple vs. Logwood,* [citation omitted] President Pendleton states, that there was a period, when the impression was made with the eye-tooth, and thinks there was some utility in the custom, since the tooth's impression was the man's own, and presented a test in case of forgery. But this reason, however applicable in Virginia in 1791, does not hold true in this epoch of dentistry, when no man's tooth is his own, but teeth, like almost everything else, are artificial.

Another learned Judge, adverting to this same fact, traces to it the phrase, "I will prove it to your teeth, or by your teeth." He also supposes that "the cutting of the eye tooth" had an allusion to this, whether the eye-tooth being cut at a certain age, it might denote the being of the age of discretion, so as to be capable of contracting, or whether it related to the impression of that tooth as a mark, being a tooth of signal and singular impression.

What magic, I ask, is there in our own seal? True, the Clerk has attested this writ of error in his official name, and by his private seal, and in obedience to it, the Clerk of the Circuit Court has certified and transmitted to this Court all the records and papers of file in the Court below, which are necessary to enable us to hear and determine properly, this cause, upon its merits. But then we look in vain on this writ, for the three pillars supporting an arch, with the word Constitution engraved within the same, emblematic of the Constitution, supported by the three departments of Government; Legislative, Judicial and Executive. The first having engraved on its base, Wisdom, the second, Justice, and the third, Moderation, and then on the right of the Executive column, a man standing with a drawn sword, and resembling most striking in figure and attitude our most worthy and excellent Chief Magistrate. But I forbear.

Illi robur et aes triplex [He has strength and triple brass.] He would be a bold Judge indeed, who would venture to decide *an issue of law* in the absence of this *speaking* device! There is a charm in that arch--a spell in those pillars--an inspiration in the eye of that fierce-looking swordsman, which guarantees a faithful administration of justice, although simply and but very imperfectly impressed on the foolscap paper on which the writ of error is printed, instead of wax or some other tenacious substance.

To whom we are indebted for the change in our seal, I am not antiquarian enough to state. The old devices, I always venerated; the one side the scroll on which was engraved the Constitution of the State of Georgia and the motto, *pro bono publico* [For the public good.] On the other side, an elegant house and other buildings, fields of corn, and meadows covered with sheep and cattle; a river running through the same, with a ship under full sail and the motto, *Deus nobis haec otia fecit* [God has made these delights for us.] The Latinity as well as the piety of this seal, commend themselves to my hearty admiration. They will challenge a comparison, even on the score of architectural taste too, with the *arch* resting on *three pillars*. But then the capital defect in the old seal--who does not anticipate me?--was the absence of that *cocked-hat swordsman*. Without this *addendum,* it is difficult to decide that any public document can impart absolute verity. This, it is, I am sure, that has exerted such a controlling influence over the judgment of my dissenting brother, with his well-known military propensities.

CHAPTER II: LAW, LAWYERS & JUDGES

The Act of 1845 authorizes this Court to establish and procure a seal. My recollection does not serve me whether the State Coat of Arms was selected as the device. I take it for granted it was. If so, where, upon any seal attached to any writ of error or citation returnable to this Court, are those three potent and cabalistic words: wisdom, justice, and moderation? Do not these constitute a part of the seal just as much as the seal does a part of the writ of error? Is it the seal of this Court without them? If so, how much, and what portions of it may be omitted and still leave a good seal? Would it be a seal without the arch, without the pillars, without the motto? I forbear even to put the question whether it would be a seal without the *military effigy?* without that *cocked-hat swordsman?* Of course it would be a nullity. As well talk of a *man* without a *body!*

For myself, I am free to confess, that I despise all forms having no sense or substance in them. And I can scarcely suppress a smile, I will not say "grimace irresistible," when I see so much importance attached to such trifles. I would cast away at once and forever, all law not founded in some reason--natural, moral or political. I scorn to be a *"cerf adscript"* [1] to things obsolete, or thoroughly deserving to be so. And for the "gladsome *lights* of jurisprudence" I would sooner far, go to the reports of *Hartly,* (Texas,) and of *Pike* and *English,* (Arkansas,) than cross an ocean, three thousand miles in width, and then travel up the stream of time for three or four centuries, to the ponderous tome of *Sindefin and Keble, Finch and Popham,* to search for legal wisdom. The world is changed. Our own situation greatly changed. And that Court and that country is behind the age that stands still while all around is in motion.

I would as soon go back to the age of monkery--to the good *old* times when the sanguinary *Mary* lighted up the fires of Smithfield, to learn true religion; or to *Henry VIII,* the British Blue-Beard, or to his successors, *Elizabeth,* the two *James's* and two *Charles's*, the good old era of butchery and blood, whose emblems were the pillory, the gibbet and the axe, to study constitutional liberty, as to search the records of black-letter for rules to regulate the formularies to be observed by Courts at this day.

I admit that many *old* things may be *good* things--as old wine, old wives, ay, and an old world too. But the world is older, and consequently wiser now than it ever was before, Our English ancestors lived comparatively in the adolescence, if not the infancy of the world. It is true that *Coke,* and *Hale,* and *Holt,* caught a glimpse of the latter-day glory, but died without the sight. The best and wisest men of their generation were unable to rise above the ignorance and superstition which pressed like a night-mare upon the intellect of nations. And yet we, who are "making lightning run messages, chemistry polish boots and steam deliver parcels and packages," are forever going back to the good *old* days of witchcraft and astrology, to discover precedents for regulating the proceedings of Courts, for upholding seals and all the tremendous doctrines consequent upon the distinction

---

[1] [Ed. Note: An ornamental stroke or projection added to a letter in printing.]

between sealed and unsealed papers, when *seals de facto* no longer exist! Let the judicial and legislative axe be laid to the root of the tree; cut it down; why cumbreth it, any longer, *courts and contracts?*

Having treated this subject scripturally and historically, though very discursively, I propose to add a word or two upon the physiological aspect of the question. And I repeat the interrogatory propounded at the beginning of this opinion, namely, what defect will make a writ of error void? And I answer the query by proposing another: what defect, original or supervenient, will reduce man from the genus *homo?*

Will the amputation of the feet and legs disfranchise a descendant of Adam of his title to manhood? It will not be denied but that he may lose every limb of the body and leave nothing but the naked trunk, and yet be a *man* "for a' that."[2] And is the seal, though it be constituted of the arch, and pillars and swordsman, more essential to the writ of error or a pedestal to support it, than legs and feet and arms are to manhood? Common sense will decide.

By the XXth rule, the writ of error is required to issue in the name of the Governor of the State, bear teste in the name of the Judges of this Court, be signed by the Clerk and sealed with the seal of this Court, and be made returnable to its next succeeding term.

The XXIVth rule prescribes imperatively the form of the writ, "the following shall be the form of writs of error," &c. Supreme Court Manual 33. The provisions of this latter rule, it would seem, should be no less binding than those of the former. And any departure from either would be equally incurable or alike amendable. And yet we have not hesitated to allow writs of error to be amended as to dates, names of the parties, and other important particulars prescribed by the form. . . .

Neither at Common Law nor by any of the Statutes of Amendments and Jeofails was the writ of error amendable in England till the Statute of *5 George I.* was passed, and the reason assigned for this exclusion was like much of the other technical folly to be found everywhere in all the *old* English books, to-wit, that amendments were granted for the *support* of judgments, but that the principal design of the writ of error is to *reverse* them. But by the 13th chapter of the Act referred to, it is declared, "that all writs of error, whenever there shall be any variance from the original record, *or other defect*, may and *shall* be amended by the respective Courts where such writ or writs of error shall be made returnable.". . .

With these desultory remarks, I am content to leave the law, learning, and logic of the case to my brother *Warner*, to whom it legitimately belongs, and who, I have no doubt, will do ample justice to the argument, and with whom I *concur,* in *retaining* the writ of error.

---

[2] [Ed. Note: From Robert Burns', "For A' That and A' That."]

MARTIN v. KIESBEAMPTE
Supreme Court of South Africa, Durban and Coast Local Division
[1958] 2 S. A. Rep 649

G. N. HOLMES, J.

[The Applicant, an election agent of a candidate in the Newcastle division in the general election held on April 18, 1958, filed for an order restraining the issuance of absentee voting papers to respondent. The court below issued the restraining order.]

In this case the applicant's affidavits were in English and his counsel addressed the Court in English. The first respondent's affidavit was in Afrikaans and counsel for the respondents addressed the Court in Afrikaans. In which language then should the Court give judgment? One's experience is that the winner is usually content to know merely that he has won. But the loser likes to know the reasons why he has lost. I proceed therefore to give judgment in the language of the losers.

Dit is die keerdag van 'n bevel *nisi* wat op 26 Maart 1958 uitgereik is. Daar is 'n beroep op die respondente gedoen om redes aan te voer waarom die Hof nie die eerste respondent sou verbied om 'n stembrief aan die tweede respondent uit te reik nie, waardeur hy in die naderende algemene verkiesing as 'n afwesige kieser mag stem nie. Die bevel het as 'n tussentydse interdik gegeld. . . .

[Affirmed]

DACY v. THE STATE OF GEORGIA
Supreme Court of Georgia
17 Ga. 439 (1855)

JOSEPH H. LUMPKIN, J.

[This was an indictment against defendant Dacy for illegally receiving corn from a slave, charged in the indictment to have been committed on *May* 1, 1852. When the case was called for trial, defendant moved a continuance, on the ground of the absence of certain witnesses, by whom he expected to prove an *alibi* on the day named in the indictment. The Soliciter General stated that he did not expect to prove the offence on that day, the Court refused the continuance, which decision was assigned as error.

The defendant's Counsel then asked for time to plead a former acquittal; and took half an hour to look for the record, but was unable to find it, and the Soliciter General having examined his papers, into whose custody the indictment was traced, and not finding the former indictment, the Court ordered the trial to proceed. The Counsel for defendant objected on the ground that there was such an indictment and order of acquittal, which could be found, if time were allowed.

The State introduced one witness, who proved the receipt of corn from a slave by the defendant, in the early part of May, 1852. The witness did not recollect the day, but said it was not the 1st. No other testimony was introduced. The Jury returned a verdict of guilty.

Afterwards, the defendant's Counsel moved in arrest of judgment, and for a new trial, and produced an order of Court, granted at May Term, 1853, granting an acquittal to the defendant, predicated on two successive demands for trial under the Penal Code. He produced also the bill of indictment, on which said order was granted (which was found among the Soliciter General's papers) and which was word for word with the present indictment, except that the other charged the offence on *June* 1, 1852. . . . The Court refused the motions, holding the proof of identity in the offences charged in the two indictments was not sufficient, and sentenced the defendant to thirty days' imprisonment, and payment of costs.]

. . .The Court was right in refusing to continue the case. The defendant proposed to prove an *alibi* by the witnesses who were absent; that is, that on the 1st day of May, 1852, the time stated in the presentment, when the offence was committed, he was absent from home during the whole day. To this, the Solicitor General replied, that he did not expect to show that the misdemeanor was committed on the 1st, but on a subsequent day in May.

. . .This he was entitled to do, as the time need not be proved as laid, unless where it is of the essence of the offence. And the facts may be proved to have occurred on any other day previous to the preferring of the indictment. . . .

In view of the incalculable importance of *time* to the Courts, and the unparalleled exigencies of this busy-working age, when the habit of wine-bibbing even is discontinued, not so much from any moral conviction as to its danger or inutility, as from the simple fact, that men can not afford, as formerly, "to tarry *long* at the table!" I repeat, that in view of all this, we may concede, perhaps, that some degree of *laches* was imputable to the party. We are called upon by Counsel to rebuke, indignantly, the idea, that the profession are to become absolute drudges in hunting up papers belonging to the offices, &c. Let such appeals be addressed to those who lounge in castles of indolence. We confess *ourselves* incapable of appreciating them. *Everybody must learn to labor*. This is the fundamental law of the universe.

> "*Nought is sleeping,*
> *From the worm of painful creeping*
> *To the cherub on the throne.*"

It is true, that our sturdy ancestors held it beneath the condition of a freeman to appear at the return day of the writ, *or to do any other act at the precise time appointed*. [citation omitted] But those good old days of ease and indulgence are gone forever. And it is a vain struggle to attempt to retain or revive them.

. . .Conceding, as we do then, that Courts are and should be disinclined to relieve against verdicts occasioned by the negligence of parties; still, where justice imperatively demands it, it will be done. No earthly doubt exists but that the defendant has been convicted and sentenced to a month's imprisonment in the common jail of the county, for an offence from which he had been fully acquitted and discharged. Negligence or no negligence, can justice demand such, the sacrifice of the liberty of a citizen, in order to preserve a rule? We cannot sanction such a doctrine, especially as the State was not without fault in this matter.

Had the books of the Clerk been paged and indexed as they should have been, the order on the minutes could have been referred to instantly. And then again, the indictment in the former case, was found in the possession of the Solicitor General, who, when applied to, as the record states, *before* the trial, denied having it, having overlooked it in the hurried examination of his papers.

Under all the circumstances, odious as the crime may be for which Dacy has been convicted, and notwithstanding he escaped through a loop in the Statute, without having been tried upon the merits; still, shielded as he is under the immunity of the laws of the land, the judgment against him must be reversed and a new trial awarded.

LOWER MERION TOWNSHIP v. TURKELSON
Supreme Court of Pennsylvania
403 Pa. 72; 169 A.2d 97 (1961)

BENJAMIN R. JONES, Justice

Glenn A. Turkelson, a member of the Lower Merion Township police department, on March 7, 1958 was suspended from duty on a charge of having failed to account for money received by him in his official capacity. After hearing, the Civil Service Commission of Lower Merion Township found Turkelson guilty of a violation of the Police Code of Discipline and directed that he be removed from the police force as of March 7, 1958. . . .

Turkelson then appealed to the Court of Common Pleas of Montgomery County and . . . that court reinstated Turkelson as a police officer as of June 1, 1958 "with pay from that date." The township then appealed to this court and we affirmed Turkelson's reinstatement as of June 1, 1958. . . .

Subsequent to the decision of this Court, Turkelson, on July 9, 1959 reported for duty and then submitted his resignation as a police officer without prejudice. Turkelson then demanded that the Township pay him his salary of $5,534.03 from June 1, 1958 [the date of his reinstatement] to July 9, 1959 [the date of his resignation]. The township refused payment upon the ground that during the period Turkelson was off the police force he had been employed by the Post Office Department at which employment he earned $5,690.60 and that such sum constituted a set-off against Turkelson's claim for salary. . . .

The only question before us is whether Turkelson was entitled to be paid his salary as a police officer during the period of his improper dismissal without the deduction of any moneys earned in other employment by him during the same period of time. . . . On reconsideration, we fully affirm the ruling in Vega [v. Bergettstown], a ruling which negatives Turkelson's present claim.

Order affirmed

MICHAEL A. MUSMANNO, Justice (dissenting).

One of the specious lay criticisms (sometimes advanced semi-humorously) against the law is that it speaks and employs a language which is often unintelligible to the public. Thus, the average nonprofessional might have difficulty in understanding what a Court means when it says: *Benigne faciendae sunt interpretationes, propter simplicitatem laicorum, ut res magis valeat quam pereat; et verba intentioni, non e contra, debent inservire* [Interpretations of written instruments must be made liberally, because of the simplicity of the common people, so that the subject-matter may stand rather than become void; and words ought to be subject to the intent, and not the other way around.]

Fortunately, in recent years, lawyers and judges have been using less Latin and overly formalistic phrases, and this is commendable and desirable. However, there is still a deplorable tendency on the part of the Courts to "interpret" the English language in a way which not only mystifies the non-legal population but confuses even lawyers and others trained to understand the medieval abracadabra of the law. This case is in point.

Glenn A. Turkelson, a policeman in Lower Merion Township, Montgomery County, was dismissed as of March 7, 1958 because of alleged violation of the Police Code of Discipline. He appealed the dismissal to the Court of Common Pleas of Montgomery County which reversed the order of the Civil Service Commission and reinstated Turkelson as of June 1, 1958, "with pay from that date." The township appealed to this Court which affirmed the decision of the Court of Common Pleas [citation omitted]. In accordance with that affirmance Turkelson reported for work and later made claim for the salary which was not paid to him during the time he was under suspension and his case was in the Courts.

The Township Code under which Turkelson was suspended provides that in the event a suspended or removed policeman shall be reinstated, he "shall be reinstated with *full pay* for the period during which he was suspended.[1]

What does "full pay" mean? Does it require an education beyond the third grade to answer that question? No matter how one strains and stretches the English language, no matter on what Procrustean bed the English vocabulary is laid for violent elongation or shortening, "full pay" cannot mean anything less than whole, entire, complete pay. Pour the words through a colander, place them in an alembic, study them under a microscope, reproduce them in capitals, italics or the minutest type, they will always come out the same--full pay.

---

[1] Italics throughout mine.

Lord Macaulay, the great British essayist, said that "the first law of writing, that law to which all other laws are subordinate, is this, that the words employed shall be such as convey to the reader the meaning of the writer." What did the Legislature of Pennsylvania mean when it said "full pay"? Did it mean half pay, one-third pay, part pay, or did it mean full pay? The Majority says that it meant full pay less whatever amounts the police officer may have earned while suspended. But if the Legislature meant to convey that meaning, why would it not have said "full pay less whatever amounts the police officer may have earned while suspended"?

The Legislature, busy as it is, and concerned, as it must be, with the multitudinous problems confronting the Commonwealth, is not so parsimonious with its time and so distraught over its responsibilities that it would omit a phrase highly essential to an understanding of its intention, when that phrase was available at the time of the original drafting of the bill, in committee, and when the bill was being considered on the floor of the House or Senate.

When this Court interprets "full pay" to mean part pay, it is doing exactly what the Legislature decided not to do, and, to that extent, it is becoming a third House on Capitol Hill, to amend, change, rewrite, veto or even nullify what the constitutional two houses, plus the approval of the Governor, have constitutionally enacted.

Even more than that, this Court is telling the Legislature that it does not know the meaning of words. And still more than that, it is amending the dictionary. One can leaf through the dictionaries bearing the reliable imprints of Webster, Oxford, Funk and Wagnalls, New Century, Mirriam-Webster, Random House, Simon and Schuster, World, Thorndike-Barnhart, and Winston, and in none of them will one find that the word "full" can under any circumstances mean not full, half, part. In each and every volume dedicated to the definition of words, one will find that full means the cup filled to the brim, the glass with wine reaching the rim, the barrel loaded to the barrelhead, the reservoir with water lapping at the high water mark, the bottle with its liquid pushing at the cork. This Court, thus, in denying Turkelson full pay, defies every dictionary instructing the English-speaking people on the use of the language. . . .

But there is another and equally important reason why the Majority opinion in the case at hand is fallacious. It not only linguistically defies the Legislature but it proceeds to take further liberties with the vocabulary of the nation by repudiating words which the Majority of this Court has *itself* used. As already mentioned, the present case was before this Court on a previous occasion. [citation omitted] Section 645, art. VI, 53 P.S. § 55645, of the Township Code, under which Turkelson was suspended provides:

> "* * * the person suspended * * * shall have
> immediate right of appeal to the court of common
> pleas of the county and the case * * * be deter-
> mined *as the court deems proper*."

The Court of Common Pleas of Montgomery County, after a hearing on the subject of suspension or dismissal, ordered Lower Merion Township to reinstate Turkelson to his position as of June 1, 1958, "with pay from that date." ...

After saying that the Court below had full discretion, this Court now proceeds to modify that fullness. It says that the Court below did not have discretion to reinstate Turkelson as of June 1, 1958, "with pay from that date." What kind of discretion did the Court below have if it did not have full discretion? Is there half discretion, partial discretion, fragmentary discretion? If by "full discretion," this Court means anything less than full, I can see that our State reports are being launched on a wild, tempestuous and uncontrolled lexicographical sea. If this Court can make "full pay" permanently mean incomplete pay, I can see the Borough Code soon awash in a verbal Sargasso Sea. ...

Repeatedly this Court, when asked to make some change in the law to bring it closer to changed social and economic conditions has said that if a change is to be made, it must be made by the Legislature. But in the case at bar, this Court repudiates the Legislature, ignores the dictionary-makers, and turns its back on its own words.

Might this not tempt lay critics to say: *"Allegans contraria non est audiendus"* [Someone who makes contradictory statements should not be listened to]?

BENDHEIM BROTHERS & COMPANY v. BALDWIN
Supreme Court of Georgia
73 Ga. 594 (1884)

M. H. BLANDFORD, Justice

This case tried in a justice's court on appeal before a jury, the Honorable R.G. Riggins, justice of the peace, presiding. His honor charged the jury as follows: "Gentlemen, this is a case which has been tried by me before, and I decided in favor of defendant; I further charge you, gentlemen, that if you find that any settlement has been made, you find for defendant; retire and make up your verdict."

The law does not require a justice of the peace to charge the jury at all; his ignorance of the law, as well as propriety, would seem to demand that he should not, but if he undertakes to instruct the jury, he must do it correctly and in accordance with law. A justice of the peace is generally a man of consequence in his neighborhood; he writes the wills, draws the deeds and pulls the teeth of the people; also he performs divers surgical operations on the animals of his neighbors.

The justice has played his part on the busy stage of life from the time of Mr. Justice Shallow down to the time of Mr. Justice Riggins. Who has not seen the gaping, listening crowd assembled around his honor, the justice, on tiptoe to catch the words of wisdom as they fell from his venerated lips?

> *"And still they gazed,*
> *and still the wonder grew,*
> *that one small head*
> *Could carry all he knew."*

The instructions given in this case exercised an undue and unwarrantable influence upon the jury. Such is to be inferred from the fact that they found for defendant, when the evidence was overwhelmingly in favor of the plaintiff. The judge of the superior court should have granted the writ of *certiorari* in this case, and it was error to have refused the same.

Judgment reversed.

YATES v. CARLISLE
Kings Bench, Hilary Term, 1 George III
96 E. R. 150; 1 Black W. 270 (1761)

ANONYMOUS, Judge

Reference to the Master, to report, by whose fault the pleadings were extended to so enormous a length. He reported this to be an action of trespass, battery, and false imprisonment, against eight defendants, commenced A. D. 1751: That in the declaration there were three counts for the trespass, and two for false imprisonment: That there were twenty-seven several pleas of justification by these several defendants; which, with replications, traverses, novel assignments, and other engines of pleading, amounted at length to a paper book of near two thousand sheets, which was brought into Court.

He was of opinion, that the fault lay principally in the length and intricacy of the declaration; the action being only brought to try, whether the freeholders and copyholders of the manor of Ellerton in Yorkshire (whereof Luke Robinson, Esq., a barrister, was lord, in right of his wife) were entitled to common in a ground called the inclosure; That the declaration was catching, by running changes upon the several defendants, and the several names of this ground, that it was necessary for the defendants to guard every loophole, which made their pleas so various and so long; That Robinson had declared, he had drawn the declaration in this manner on purpose to catch the defendants, and that he would scourge them with a rod of iron; That in another cause for the same question, brought against the same defendants (in Robinson's own name), the art was so far improved, that the paper book would amount to three thousand sheets.

Robinson, in propriâ personâ, shewed cause against this report, no other counsel caring to be employed; and insisted, he had a right to do what he had done, and that he thought the whole declaration necessary. The Court strongly inclined to fix some heavy censure upon him, but desired that, previously, the question of right might be tried: and it was recommended by the Court to Serjeant Hewit, ex parte Robinson, and Mr. Winn, for the defendants, to settle an issue for that purpose; which they did the next day, in a quarter of a sheet of paper; and it went down to be tried on the northern circuit.

GOOD'S CASE

Kings Bench, Hilary Term, 2 Charles I
79 E.R. 1300; 1 Popham 211 (1627)

ANONYMOUS, Judge

Good and his Wife brought a Writ of Error upon a Judgement, given in the Court of the Castle of Windsor, in an Action of Debt there, which was entered Trin. Mich. 2 Car. Rot. 119, 120. and two Errors were assigned.

1. Because the Judgement there is given in these words, *ideo consideratum adjudicatum, & assessum est* [accordingly, it has been determined, decided, and assessed], whereas it ought to be onely by the word *consideratum* [determined], and the Judgement being the act of the Court, the Law is precise in it, and therefore it hath been resolved, that a Judgement given by the word *concessum* [conceded] is not good, but it ought to be by the word *consideratum* [determined].

2. The costs *ex incremento* [by way of increase], are not said to be given, *ad petitionem quaerentis* [at the request of the plaintiff], as it ought to be, for *beneficium nemini obtruditur* [a benefit is thrust upon no one], and therefore it hath been resolved in this Court, that an alien born shall not have *medietatem linguae*, [moiety of tongue[1]], if he does not request it, and as to this it was answered of the other side, that costs ought always to be assessed *ex petitione quaerentis* [by way of a request of the plaintiff], and albeit here the request of the Plaintiff was not precisely put to increase of the costs, yet at the beginning of the Judgement it is said, *Ideo ad petitionem quaerentis consideratum &c.* [Accordingly, it has been determined, etc., at the request of the plaintiff]. And that costs shall be given *ex incremento* [by way of increase], so that this request goes to all the Sentence.

. . . and by the unanimous opinion of all the Court, the Judgement was reversed for both the Errourrs, for

1. *Ideo considerat. adjudicat. &c.* [accordingly, it has been determined, decided, etc.] is not good, the Judgement being the Act of the Court, and the Law hath appointed in what words it shall be given, and if other words should be suffered, great uncertainty and confusion would ensue, and needlesse verbosity is the mother of difficulty.

---

[1] [Ed. Note: "Moiety of tongue" refers to the right of a foreigner on trial to a special jury consisting of six native Englishmen and six of his fellow countrymen.]

2. The increase of costs ought to be give *ad petitionem quaerentis* [at the request of the plaintiff], and the words *ad petitionem quaerentis* [at the request of the plaintiff] being misplaced, will not supply this defect, and Dammages *ex incremento* [by way of increase] is alwayes given *ad petitionem quaerentis* [at the request of the plaintiff] for as Bracton saith, *Omne judicium est trinis actus trium personarum, judicis, actor, et rei* [Every judgement is a threefold act of three persons, the judge, the pleader of the case, and the criminal], and if in this case, the usuall form should not be observed, all would be in a confusion, and in as much as the words are misplaced, it is as if they had not been put in at all, and therefore void, like to a case put in Walsinghams case in Plowden, where an averrement misplaced, is, as if there were none: In this case the Judgement was reversed. . .

CENTRAL OF GEORGIA RAILWAY COMPANY v. MINOR
Appeals Court of Georgia
2 Ga. App. 804; 59 S.E. 81 (1907)

ARTHUR GRAY POWELL, J.

[Minor, the husband of the plaintiff, was employed by the defendant company to work in its yards at Macon in the capacity of "hostler helper," an understudy to the man who sees that locomotives are properly prepared and furnished for use in actual service, and was electrocuted when he pulled upon a cable attached to a conveyor for loading coal into a locomotive. A current of electricity escaped from a wire against which the cable came into contact. The wire was part of an arc-light circuit which supplied a lamp burning in front of the chute. The jury returned a verdict of $10,715 for the plaintiff. The motion for a new trial, which was overruled, complains that the verdict is contrary to the evidence; also that it is excessive.]

. . . As to the contention that the verdict is contrary to the evidence, that no negligence on the part of the master is shown, that the death of the deceased came about by reason of an accident, unforeseeable by ordinary care, it is necessary to say only that the evidence was such that a verdict either way could have been legally justified. Whether the wires were unsafely located in the beginning, whether the railroad company by ordinary care could have discovered this fact, whether an inspection reasonable under all the circumstances would have disclosed the probability of danger, were questions involved; and as to these things there was evidence pro et con. Possibly, the members of this court, if they had been upon the jury which tried the case, would not have come to the conclusion reached by the jury; yet we can not say that the inferences were not issuable.

> *"Now, who shall arbitrate?*
> *Ten men love what I hate,*
> *Shun what I follow, slight what I receive;*

Ten, who in ears and eyes
Match me; we all surmise,
They this thing, and I, that."

Under the law of the land the jury, the "ten men" and two, must, as to these questions, arbitrate; not we. . . .

Judgment affirmed.

LEE v. PORTER
Supreme Court of Georgia
63 Ga. 345 (1879)

LOGAN E. BLECKLEY, Justice.

In the court below, this was a rule for the distribution of money. The parties to the present writ of error were competing creditors, each claiming a judgment lien upon the fund. This issue as to both law and fact was, by consent, tried by the court without a jury, and the judgment is excepted to generally, with no specification as to whether the error intended to be alleged was a mistaken finding upon the facts, or an erroneous ruling on some point of law.

A material part of the evidence was documentary, such as exemplifications from the records of other courts, and no copy of the documents is brought up, nor does any recital of their contents appear. The bill of exceptions merely represents that this and that writing showed so and so, stating the supposed legal effect, but not in a way to enable this court to determine for itself what conclusions ought to have been drawn from them. At the call of the case here, the defendant in error moved to dismiss the writ of error for this deficiency in the record. The assignment of error being general, we cannot review the judgment without going into the facts, just as the court below did. For this purpose, we ought to have the evidence, and not merely the inferences which the counsel for the plaintiff in error, with the judge's sanction, drew from it in preparing the bill of exceptions.

It may be that we would draw very different inferences, and these differences might go to uphold the judgment; for many steps in the reasoning of the court below might be defective, and still its ultimate conclusion be correct. It not infrequently happens that a judgment is affirmed upon a theory of the case which did not occur to the court that rendered it, or which did occur and was expressly repudiated. The human mind is so constituted that in may instances it *finds the truth* when wholly unable to *find the way* that leads to it.

The pupil of impulse, it forc'd him along.
His conduct still right, with his argument wrong;
Still aiming at honor, yet fearing to roam,
The coachman was tipsy, the chariot drove home.

Writ dismissed.

CHAPTER II: LAW, LAWYERS & JUDGES

WILLIAMS v. JOHNS
Chancery Court of England
21 E.R. 355; Dick. 477 (1773)

SIR HENRY BATHURST, J.

This was an application without notice, to commit the defendant for a contempt, in making the person, who served him with a subpoena to appear and answer, eat the same, and otherwise ill treating him; the defendant ordered to stand committed, unless cause; but by reason of his ferocious, and terrible disposition, no one being willing to hazard serving him, leaving the order at his house, was to be deemed good service.

ANONYMOUS
Queens Bench, Hilary Term, 9 Anne
91 E.R. 79; 1 Salk. 84 (1711)

ANONYMOUS, Judge

MOTION was made for an attachment against the defendant on affidavit, that being served with a rule of Court to shew cause why an information should not be filed against him, he said, He did not care a fart for the rule of Court. And Northery Attorney General insisted, he ought to be first heard to shew cause against it. *Et per totam Cur* [And by the whole Court]: He shall answer in custody, for it is to no purpose to serve him with a second rule, that has slighted and despised the first. It is to expose the court to a further contempt. And accordingly the defendant was brought in, and entered into a recognizance to answer interrogatories. Which is all that can be had thereupon; and if he forswear himself, he is subject to a prosecution for perjury.

DENNY v. RADAR INDUSTRIES, INC.
Court of Appeals of Michigan
28 Mich. App. 294; 184 N.W.2d 289 (1970)

JOHN H. GILLIS, JUDGE.

The appellant has attempted to distinguish the factual situation in this case from that in Renfroe v. Higgins Rack Coating and Manufacturing Co., Inc. (1969), 17 Mich. App. 259, 169 N.W.2d 326. He didn't. We couldn't.

Affirmed. Costs to appellee.

FERGUSON v. MOORE
Supreme Court of Tennessee
98 Tenn. 342; 39 S.W. 341 (1897)

JOHN S. WILKES, J.

This is an action for damages. The declaration has two counts, — one for breach of contract to marry, and the second for seduction accomplished by reason of such contract. The cause was heard before a court and a jury of Lincoln county, and a verdict for $2,000 was rendered upon the first count, and of $12,700 upon the second, and for the aggregate sum of $14,700 judgment was rendered for plaintiff, and defendant has appealed, and assigned errors. . . .

It is further assigned as error that plaintiff's counsel, in his closing argument, called defendant hard names, such as "villain," "scoundrel," "fiend," "hell hound," etc., which, it is alleged, was calculated to prejudice defendant before the jury. It must be admitted these are rather harsh terms, and other language could have been used, no doubt, equally as descriptive, and not so vituperative; but it does not appear that defendant asked the court to interpose, and we cannot put the trial judge in error under these circumstances.

It is true the trial judge, in his discretion, might have checked the counsel on his own motion; but, inasmuch as defendant and his counsel did not object, the court did not probably feel called upon to act. It is not reversible error.

It is next assigned as error that counsel for plaintiff, in his closing argument, in the midst of a very eloquent and impassioned appeal to the jury, shed tears, and unduly excited the sympathies of the jury in favor of the plaintiff, and greatly prejudiced them against defendant. Bearing upon this assignment of error we have been cited to no authority, and after diligent search we have been able to find none ourselves.

The conduct of counsel in presenting their cases to juries is a matter which must be left largely to the ethics of the profession and the discretion of the trial judge. Perhaps no two counsel observe the same rules in presenting their cases to the jury. Some deal wholly in logic, — argument without embellishments of any kind. Others use rhetoric, and occasional flights of fancy and imagination. Others employ only noise and gesticulation, relying upon their earnestness and vehemence instead of logic and rhetoric. Others appeal to the sympathies -- it may be the passions and peculiarities -- of the jurors. Others combine all these with variations and accompaniments of different kinds. No cast-iron rule can or should be laid down.

Tears have always been considered legitimate arguments before a jury, and, while the question has never arisen out of any such behavior in this court, we know of no rule or jurisdiction in the court below to check them. It would appear to be one of the natural rights of counsel which no court or constitution could take away. It is certainly, if no more, a matter of the highest personal privilege. Indeed, if counsel has them at command, it may be seriously questioned whether it is not his professional duty to shed them whenever proper occasion arises, and the trial judge would not feel constrained to interfere unless they were indulged in to such excess as to impede or delay the business of the court. This must be left largely to the discretion of the trial judge, who has all the counsel and parties before him, and can see their demeanor as well as the demeanor of the jury.

In this case the trial judge was not asked to check the tears, and it was, we think, an eminently proper occasion for their use, and we cannot reverse for this. But for the other errors indicated the judgment must be reversed, and the cause remanded for a new trial. Plaintiff will pay the costs of the appeal.

BRINSON v. FAIRCLOTH.
Supreme Court of Georgia
82 Ga. 185; 7 S.E. 923 (1888)

LOGAN E. BLECKLEY, C.J.

Brinson, the plaintiff in error, is the step-son of the defendant in error, Mrs. Faircloth, formerly Mrs. Brinson. He was the administrator upon his father's estate, in which she, as widow of the deceased, took dower. Before the commissioners made their return, he purchased her dower estate, paid her the price agreed upon, $400, and took her deed of conveyance. She afterwards became dissatisfied with the bargain and filed her bill for a rescission of the contract, and for cancellation of the deed, alleging fraud and misrepresentation on his part in making the purchase. The jury found in her favor, and he moved for a new trial, which motion the court overruled. . .

One of the counsel for Mrs. Faircloth was her brother-in-law, and kept the hotel in the county town where the court was held. While the jury were charged with the case, the court sent them to the hotel, duly attended by a sworn bailiff, to take a meal at the public expense. They had, so far as appears, no improper communication with any one, and neither said nor heard anything touching the case. The record is silent as to any other inn or public house at which the jury could have been entertained, and we take it for granted there was no other. No impropriety, or even irregularity, appears in what the court did.

In this degenerate age, jurors must eat. It follows that they are to be sent when necessary to where they can get something to eat, and to the only place of that kind, when there is but one in town. It was said in the argument that the very atmosphere of the hotel was charged with influence in favor of the landlord's kinswoman and client. If the jury were hungry, most likely the table neutralized the atmosphere during the short time they were exposed to its influence.

In the other grounds of the motion for a new trial we discover nothing calling for separate notice. If Mrs. Faircloth testified truly,—and the jury certainly believed her,—the verdict was warranted. It is of doubtful public policy to uphold the purchase by an administrator of a dower estate, made before the return of the commissioners has been filed and finally acted upon by the court.

Judgment affirmed.

DAVIS v. KIRKLAND
Court of Appeals of Georgia
1 Ga. App. 5; 58 S.E. 209 (1907)

RICHARD BREVARD RUSSELL, J.

H. Kirkland brought suit against Mrs. R. B. Hall. He asked to recover money paid to her for timber for turpentine purposes. He alleges that he parted with his money upon condition that it should be repaid to him or to the party who might gain a certain mentioned case, then pending in the superior court. He averred that Mrs. Hall (now Davis) lost in that suit and refused to pay him as agreed. . . .

The defendant, in her answer, though she did not remember the exact amount of money paid her, admitted all of the plaintiff's allegations, except as to the promise to repay. She denied absolutely that there was ever such an agreement on her part as was alleged by the plaintiff upon that subject. The controlling, and indeed only, issue of fact raised by the pleadings was whether the defendant promised to return the money to the plaintiff upon the terms and conditions he set up. The judge directed a verdict for the plaintiff, and the defendant excepted.

There was evidence in behalf of the contentions of both parties. The legal quarrel, begun in the pleadings, warmed into a well-drawn battle in the testimony. And the lines of the two armies of fact at issue did not harmonize or fraternize any more after the heavy cannonading of the witnesses than they did at first in the desultory firing along the picket lines of the pleadings. For this reason, we think the judge erred in directing a verdict. In a Georgia trial the judge is the impersonation of the law he expounds, construes, and enforces. The jury is the sole arbiter -- the only god of battles -- to still the conflict and decide the victor, in the struggle between antagonistic testimony marshaled under opposing leaders, each contending for supremacy. After the legal battle lines have, by the permission of the judge, moved from the skirmishing of the pleadings into full action and real conflict between contending statements of fact, he is transformed into a mere representative of a neutral power, friendly alike to both belligerents, -- the law, -- who will see that there is no violation of those rules of war, enforced by law, and that neither combatant shall smuggle or receive from the territories of law any contraband of war in the form of illegal evidence. The law, whose representative he is, is friendly to both.

But he can not stop the conflict as long as it proceeds under law's rules of war. Should the two armies meet, panoplied in their pleadings, and either fail to fight, for the total lack of the ammunition of evidence, then, as the representative of his country, the law, he declines to recognize a state of war, and makes no protest when the victor overruns and absorbs his opponent's territory. If they fight until the arbiter of battles of fact, the jury, decides the conflict and acclaims the victor, the judge then only embodies in his judgment proclamation to the world at large of the law's recognition and approval of the substantial results accruing to the victorious party.

CHAPTER II: LAW, LAWYERS & JUDGES

In the justly ordered universe of jurisprudence there has never been friction between these separate nationalities, the law and the evidence. Law has ever held a protectorate over facts, and guarantees its autonomy. These nations differ greatly in intrinsic characteristics. The law is serene and conservative through the ages, and peace and order are universal in her wide domain. The territory of facts is in well-nigh constant revolution, and its every inhabitant is volatile, erratic, or capricious, and especially inclined to change his costume or disguise himself at the behest of each new forensic tailor. The law does not exercise her suzerainty over the domain of evidence with an iron hand with a view of enforcing absolute peace among its inhabitants, because the very reason for her sovereignty is found in certain, continual, and irrepressible feuds and dissensions. Frequent as are these contentions, and however well calculated to tax the patience of law's ministers, the law will not allow her judge to enter the domain of evidence while it is unsettled, nor even to express an opinion as to which side should win.

Since the birth of Magna Charta, -- one of law's leading citizens, -- whenever internal dissension or revolution arises in the territory of evidence, to determine which contending faction shall be entitled to the jewel truth, she calls in, as sole arbiter to settle the dispute, the jury, who under law's irrevocable appointment shall settle, in every nook and corner of law's protectorate, --the domain of facts, -- all issues, great and small. The wisdom of all men most enlightened, the experience of those most familiar with the practice, the innate sense of justice, all concur in the opinion that disputes between such varying and variable characters as visit and inhabit the domain of facts can not be satisfactorily adjusted and finally determined by any umpire more absolutely reliable and just than the jury.

In the very beginning of its official existence this court desires to place itself on record as standing for the exclusive right of the jury to determine every issue of fact in the trial of every case in Georgia. And we so willingly and cordially follow the decisions of the Supreme Court in [citation omitted] that we quote from them, not only as an expression of our views, but also, if possible, to emphasize them as a proper construction and analysis of the separate functions of our judicial system. . . . "The evidence is not conclusive. It pushes the mind into that great pitfall called doubt, and there leaves it. The jury are the best doctors of doubt, and there leaves it. The jury are the best doctors of doubt that we know of." . . . Courts must take the verdicts of juries, when proper from the evidence, as a right conclusion as to what is the truth of a case. . . Whoever has had any experience with juries must concede that they endeavor to do right. They take questions of fact in a practical way, unimpeded by the legal fetters that restrain a professional mind. They may not find sometimes as a court would find. If they do their work fairly under the rules, courts ought not to disturb their verdicts. . .

No principle is better settled in Georgia than that a verdict should not be directed, unless there is no issue of fact; or unless the proved facts, viewed from every possible legal point of view, can sustain no other finding than that directed. . . .

In view of the fact that we hold that the directing of a verdict in the case was such error as demanded a new trial, it becomes unnecessary to consider the various other assignments of error. If error was committed as to any of these, the learned trial judge will no doubt correct it on the next hearing.

Judgment reversed

SKIPPER v. THE STATE OF GEORGIA
Supreme Court of Georgia
59 Ga. 63 (1877)

LOGAN E. BLECKLEY, Judge

The larceny was of three cows. The corpus delicti was clearly proven. One cow had been recovered. The hides of the other two had bccn found and identified. All three of the animals had been driven into Alabama and sold. The prisoner's brother had sold them. He was jointly indicted with the prisoner for the larceny, and, at the time of the prisoner's trial had been convicted. He was a witness for the state on the prisoner's trial, and if his testimony was true, the prisoner was undoubtedly guilty as charged. There was some appearance of self-contradiction in a part of his evidence. Some of it was contradicted by another witness introduced by the state. Still, the main facts implicating the prisoner stood uncontradicted, and as to all of them that were essential, he was strongly corroborated by another witness, who testified to seeing the prisoner, with some other person, engaged in driving the cattle, near the place from whence they were stolen, and about the time the larceny was committed. This second witness was a female, who admitted that she had prosecuted the prisoner for stealing some of her property.

. . .Another request to charge, which was also refused by the court, was in these terms, 'If you believe from the evidence that either one or more of the witnesses has ill-will or unkind feelings to prisoner, that is one of the methods of impeaching a witness, and that weakens the testimony of the witness." Ill-will in a witness does not, ipso facto, work an impeachment, nor does it necessarily weaken the force of his testimony. It may weaken it, and is proper to be considered by the jury.. . .

. . . Witnesses may be scarce who can do full justice to their enemies, but certainly there are some. For my own part, I think there are multitudes of people who are trustworthy and reliable in all situations and under all circumstances. Declaim against the world as we may, it abounds in truth, purity and integrity. The law brands no witness as impeached just because he is not at peace with the scoundrel against whom he testifies. It recognizes the possibility of bias in his evidence, but it does not go further, and convert the possibility into a certainty. It leaves that for the jury to do, in the event they shall believe, on their oaths, that it ought to be done, under all the circumstances of the particular case. The jury may discount for ill-will, but here is no rule that they must.. . .

Judgment affirmed.

GORDON v. GREEN
United States Court of Appeals, Fifth Circuit
602 F.2d 743 (1979)

JOHN R. BROWN, Chief Judge:

As we see it, the only issue currently before the Court in these five consolidated cases is whether verbose, confusing, scandalous, and repetitious pleadings totaling into the thousands of pages comply with the requirement of "a short and plain statement" set forth in F.R.Civ.P. 8. We think that the mere description of the issue provides the answer:[1] we direct the District Court to dismiss the complaints — with leave to amend — because of appellant's failure to comply with F.R.Civ.P. 8(a) and (e).

The Pleadings: Gobbledygook

The appellant, Edwin F. Gordon, invested several million dollars in a series of Florida real estate syndications. When the promises of substantial profits failed to materialize, appellant filed suit against the sellers and promoters of the syndications, claiming various violations of the federal securities laws.

Under F.R.Civ.P. 8, a party seeking relief must submit a pleading containing "a short and plain statement of they grounds upon which the court's jurisdiction depends," F.R.Civ.P. 8(a)(1), and "a short and plain statement of the claim showing that the pleader is entitled to relief." F.R.Civ.P. 8(a)(2). In addition, F.R.Civ.P. 8(e)(1) states that "[e]ach averment of a pleading shall be simple, concise, and direct." As the following factual account demonstrates, nothing was further from the minds of the appellant and his lawyer than the clear directions contained in F.R.Civ.P. 8(a) and (e).

These five consolidated cases were originally brought in the Southern District of New York in March and April of 1976. At this initial stage, appellant filed five separate long, verbose, and confusing verified complaints containing a total of 165 typewritten pages and an additional 413 pages of exhibits. In one of the five cases, appellant filed an amendment to the verified complaint (8 pages plus 39 pages of exhibits). . .

In September 1976, . . . appellant filed an "Amendment to Verified Complaint" for each of the actions. Each "Amendment to Verified Complaint" was 19 pages. On September 30, 1976, the Trial Court dismissed the action, but not for failure to comply with Rule 8. Rather, after combing through the mountain of pages before him, the Trial Judge concluded that appellant failed to establish federal court jurisdiction. Subsequently, appellant topped his mountain of legal papers with a fourth set of complaints and a motion for leave to amend. The motion was summarily denied.

---

[1] The Trial Judge apparently did not, since he struggled and strained to decipher plaintiff's mountain of papers, ultimately holding that the Court lacked jurisdiction.

"Let Thy Speech Be Short,
Comprehending Much In Few Words" [2]

The various complaints, amendments, amended amendments, amendments to amended amendments, and other related papers are anything but short, totaling over 4,000 pages, occupying 18 volumes, and requiring a hand truck or cart to move.[3] They are not plain, either. The Trial Court described the pleadings as being "extremely long and combin[ing] into single counts detailed recitation of evidence and legal arguments complete with extensive citations of authority." The Court also observed that a paragraph from one typical complaint was single spaced, "extend[ed] the full length of a legal page and constitute[d] a single sentence." Much of the pleadings are scandalous as well.[4] Moreover, we cannot tell whether complaints filed earlier in time are to be read in conjunction with those filed later or whether the amended versions supersede previous pleadings.

One option before us is to struggle through the thousands of pages of pleadings in an effort to determine (assuming we possibly could) whether the Trial Court correctly dismissed for lack of jurisdiction. However, such a course of action would be unwise from the standpoint of sound judicial administration. All would know that there is no longer any necessity for paying the least bit of heed to F.R.Civ.P. 8(a) in its demand for "a short and plain statement" reiterated by the 8(e) requirement that each averment "be simple, concise, and direct." Lawyers would

---

[2] Ecclesiasticus 32:8.

[3] Appellant's filings demonstrate once and for all that history does in fact repeat itself. In discussing Dr. J.H. Baker's second volume of Spelman's Reports, the 1978 Report of the Council and Abstract of the Accounts of the Selden Society reveals (p. 6): "It is in the 16th century that the sheer physical bulk of the [plea] rolls [became] truly daunting, with a mile or two of parchment used in a term." If every party filed the massive pleadings submitted here, we would only hasten the speed at which our country's trees are being transformed into sheets of legal jargon. Moreover, we would need to build another courthouse simply to store legal documents.

[4] At the risk of further polluting the legal waters by immortalizing this gibberish in the annals of the Federal Reporter, we quote some typically scandalous language from one of appellant's many filings:

> Green and Broberg worked closely together to keep their grandiose "Money making monster" scheme in operation . . . concept in this scheme that can only be described as diabolical and monstrous. . . . by not only failing to register this securities investment scheme to bring it under the supervision and censure of the S.E.C. but to openly operate in what was, in fact, an outlaw fashion, based on the spurious so-called "legal opinion" of Attorney Broberg, rendered to investors and potential investors, to the effect that this scheme did not constitute securities but that, on the contrary, it was simple country-style real estate with lots of country-style profit in it for all collaborators, but destruction for the defector who will be cannibalized by the rest of the group, again based on the so-called "legal opinion" of Broberg to the effect that the failure to make payments for whatever reason constitutes a breach of the so-called "trust agreement" and subjects the defector to losing his entire interest and having it assumed (cannibalized) by the remaining investors. . . .

see that in the face of even gross violations of Rule 8, we would undertake the burden of trying to parse out 18 volumes of words, disorganized and sometimes conflicting, with a mish-mash of so-called evidentiary materials, citations of authority, and other things that a pleader, aware of and faithful to the command of the Federal Rules of Civil Procedure, knows to be completely extraneous. And the District Courts who come on the firing line are the first victims of this paper mill. We think that the Trial Court should have dismissed the complaints with leave to amend. While a Trial Court is and should be given great leeway in determining whether a party has complied with Rule 8, we think that as a matter of law, verbose and scandalous pleadings of over 4,000 pages violate Rule 8.

In finding a violation of Rule 8, we do not recede even one inch from the position expressed by this Court in [citations omitted] and a host of other cases sounding an approach of liberality under F.R.Civ.P. 12 in reading a pleading as an adequate statement or claim. Appellant asks not that we adopt a liberal approach, but that we stand liberality on its head by accepting 4,000 pages of chaotic legal jargon in lieu of a short and plain statement. We would be hindering, not promoting, the underlying purpose of Rule 8, which is "to eliminate prolixity in pleading and to achieve brevity, simplicity, and clarity." . . . We fully agree with the observation of the District Court for the Eastern District of Michigan that "the law does not require, nor does justice demand, that a judge must grope through [thousands of] pages of irrational, prolix and redundant pleadings. . . ." [citation omitted]

Our view—that flagrant violations of Rule 8 should not be tolerated—is shared by Courts throughout the country. There are numerous cases in which complaints have been dismissed as being contrary to the letter and spirit of the Rule. . . .

As previously stated, in ordering the suits dismissed we do so with leave to amend. Appellant may file a short and plain statement in lieu of the 18 volumes of papers currently before us. . .

If our holding results in more time and expense to appellant, that would be fair recompense for these marked, unjustifiable violations of the letter and spirit of the Federal Rules of Civil Procedure and an indifference as though they had never been adopted 41 years ago.[5]

. . . VACATED and REMANDED.

---

[5] Counsel as scrivener would have been fair game for the discipline meted out by the Chancellor in 1596. As Professor Richard C. Wydick of Davis Law School reports:

> In 1596 an English chancellor decided to make an example of a particularly prolix document filed in his court. The chancellor first ordered a hole cut through the center of the document, all 120 pages of it. Then he ordered that the person who wrote it should have his head stuffed through the hole, and the unfortunate fellow was led around to be exhibited to all those attending court at West Minster Hall.

Wydick, Plain English for Lawyers, 1978, 66 Calif.L.Rev. 727.

Obviously this applies only to counsel who filed the papers, not to the appellate counsel who briefed and argued the case here.

McDOUGALD v. WILLIFORD
Supreme Court of Georgia
14 Ga. 665 (1854)

JOSEPH H. LUMPKIN, J.

An action of ejectment was brought in the superior Court of Muscogee county, by [Williford] the heir of Brooks, to recover Lots Nos. 72 and 76, in the City of Columbus. The defendants were the tenants of Daniel McDougald, deceased. Mrs. Ann E. McDougald, as the administratrix of her husband, Daniel McDougald, filed her [complaint] representing, amongst other things, that her intestate, in his life-time [on April 20, 1840], executed a deed to the lots in dispute, to Brooks, the ancestor of the plaintiffs, to enable Brooks to claim these lots for McDougald, during his temporary absence from the State, provided any attempt should be made to disturb the property. And she charges, that the conveyance was intended merely to operate as a power of attorney, for this purpose, and for none other. . . The [complaint] prayed that the deed might be canceled, and the action of ejectment perpetually enjoined.

[Later, Mrs. McDougald] by her solicitor, moved the Court to make an amendment to the bill, the main feature and object of which was to allege, that the deed made to this property, never was delivered to Brooks, the feoffee; that it was lodged with Alexander McDougald, one of the subscribing witnesses, and brother of the feoffer, to be kept by him, until the exigency might arise, which would render it necessary to hand it over to Brooks; and that the crisis never having happened, the deed never was delivered, but had been, by the said witness, deposited in the Clerk's office for registration only; and that in this way, a copy had been obtained by the heirs of Brooks--the original never having been in the possession, power or control, either of the plaintiff's or their ancestor.

The defendants' solicitor moved to strike out this amendment, on the grounds. . . That it was contradictory to the original bill [and] the Court sustained the [defendant's] motion,. . .

In Courts of Justice, Equity and common Law the time will come, *and now is*, when mis-pleading will never be allowed to prejudice any party; but every case will be ultimately tried upon its real and substantial merits.

Under the modern doctrine, amendments are more a question of cost than anything else. Where a different case is made by the amendment, the plaintiff should be taxed with the costs, and the defendant made to pay no more than he would have been put to had the bill been brought right originally.

Thank God that the night of pedantry and quibble is passing away, and the morning of reason and common sense is breaking brightly upon the world! The men of 1799 disdained to invoke the spirits of departed oracles, in search for rules for our Courts of Justice. But a *middle age* intervened, and in spite of our Act of 1818, and other Statutes of amendments, we have been bandied "from Coke to Cooke--from Year Books to Dome Books--from *ignotum* [the unknown] to *ignotius* [the more unknown]," until we had become the most *law-ridden* people upon the face of the earth. Modern law reform is sweeping away all of these miserable cobwebs of antiquated nonsense, and life, liberty, reputation and property are appreciated too highly to allow them to rest on "legal riddles and paradoxes." Forms are no longer anything--substance is everything. . .

Judgment reversed.

MEHAFFEY v. HAMBRICK
Supreme Court of Georgia
83 Ga. 597; 10 S.E. 274 (1889)

LOGAN E. BLECKLEY, Chief Justice

Under the law applicable to this case as a whole at the present stage of it, no examination of the grounds of the motion for a new trial is needful or would be proper, for the court below should not have adjudicated upon the motion either to grant or deny it, without having before it a proper brief of evidence.. . .

. . . Tested by several deliverances from this bench, the report of a trial consisting in part of dialogue between counsel and witnesses concerning the facts, and in part of extraneous matter, is not a brief of the evidence.. . .

. . . Of course the testimony, pure and simple, should be admitted into the document without admixture with extraneous matter, such as remarks by court or counsel. It is not the province of the brief to report the trial, but to present a synopsis of the evidence.

. . . In the oral examination of witnesses during almost any trial, many trivial and immaterial questions are asked and answered, and during a lengthy trial this worthless lumber accumulates to an enormous mass. In briefing the evidence all such stuff should be omitted. . .

As a sample of this kind of matter, we now transcribe from the report under examination the following questions and answers: "Q. George Washington, if he was living, with his little hatchet could mark them, couldn't he? A. Yes sir, I suppose so." p. 106. "By the court: What is the name of the creek? A. Bob O'Shelly. Q. Do you know how it is spelled? A. No sir, I don't know as I never saw it spelled." p. 163. "By the court: Did you ever eat any mulberries off that tree? A. No sir, I never ate any mulberries off of that tree in my life." p. 171. "By Mr. Alexander: Did that tree bear mulberries? A. I think it did. Q. Pretty fair eating? A. Pretty good, I think. Q. What were they worth a quart? A. We didn't sell them by the peck, quart or gallon either. We just ate all we got." p. 173. This mulberry tree was killed by the plaintiff five years before the trial, and three years before the trespass, the alleged cause of action, was committed. . .

. . . In so far as the brief consisted of a mere copy of the stenographic notes after being written out in ordinary character by the reporter, it is in no proper legal sense a brief of the oral evidence; for only an abstract or abridgment of the oral testimony can rightly be considered a brief of it. . . . The substance only of the material testimony should be set out in succinct narrative form. Questions put to witnesses should be reproduced in the brief only when necessary either to clearness or brevity, and then they should be as much abbreviated as practicable. . .

Here the immaterial is blended with the material; every question, however verbose, is repeated at full length, and the examination of witnesses sprawls over one hundred and sixty-one pages, though the whole case involves less than that many dollars. The condensing powers of any ordinary lawyer faithfully applied to the task would serve to compress all the material testimony contained in the report within a dozen or two pages. Why, then, should the time of courts, and the money of suitors by increased costs, be taxed with the whole text, *verbatim et literatim* [word-for-word and letter-for-letter], of the stenographic report? Condensation is a duty no less of the bar than of the bench.

Suppose the members of this court should dump into their opinions the whole contents of the records upon which they adjudicate, or the reporter of the court should state literally *all* of the facts, whether material or not, with what profit or patience would the profession receive and use the Georgia Reports? The crude and shapeless materials which form the rudiments of a case should be worked into order as much as possible by the learned counsel most familiar with them; and in each stage of its progress the case should be made to throw off as much as may be of the irrelevant and immaterial baggage with which it is incumbered. Only by being freed somewhere from the *impedimenta* with which it set out can it reach the goal of justice.

Such a document as we are reviewing is not a brief of evidence, nor can the decision of any court make it one except in name. Were we to pronounce it a brief, our judgment would be a legal lie. Even a solemn act of the General Assembly could not change its nature by impressing it with a new appellation, any more than it could give a family to a man by calling him the head of a family. We venture the opinion that every member of the legal profession, without exception, who suffers himself to think candidly, knows or is capable of knowing that a literal stenographic report by question and answer, covering one hundred and sixty pages, and embracing every word of the testimony, with no discrimination of what is material or immaterial, is not a brief of evidence. No thoughtful lawyer seriously addressing his mind to the subject would any more confound the two things than he would his argument and his brief.

We are not to be understood as reflecting in any degree upon our learned brother of the circuit bench, for we well know that a recent practice, fostered by the indolence of some counsel, and the overwork of others, has grown up of substituting the stenographer's report for the brief of evidence, and he but followed this practice in the present instance. His decision was doubtless the result of bad precedents, rather than the offspring of his own deliberate, independent thought. Moreover, some of the cases which we have cited above had not been ruled when his decision was made. Nor even in them is there any direct authoritative ruling upon the precise question now presented. Not heretofore, so far as we know, has the decision approving such a report as a brief of evidence been directly excepted to. Such an exception is quite distinct from a motion to dismiss the motion for a new trial. We have held that a motion to dismiss is not available, whilst the order approving the brief is intact. And so we again hold. But here the decision which resulted in the order of approval is directly assailed, and having no doubt that it was erroneous we so pronounce it. The effect of this is to render vain and valueless all the subsequent proceedings on the motion for a new trial. . .

Judgment on main bill of exceptions affirmed.

GOLDEN PANAGIA STEAMSHIP, INC. v. THE PANAMA CANAL COMMISSION
United States Court of Appeals, Fifth Circuit
791 F.2d 1191 (1986)

IRVING L. GOLDBERG, Circuit Judge:

It is sometimes said that "two ships passing in the night" is a bad thing. This case proves that the opposite result -- two ships colliding in broad daylight -- may not always be desirable either. When such a meeting of minds, men, and machinery occurs in the Panama Canal, the situation becomes even more complicated than usual.

Appellant Golden Panagia sued the responsible American authorities in the U.S. District Court in Panama for $300,000 in damages to its ship -- only to have its attorney "settle" the case for $195,000 and pocket the cash, never to be heard from again.... Golden Panagia got to the bottom of this affair about a year later, but by then the courts of the United States had also vanished from the Panamanian scene. Undeterred, Golden Panagia filed two further suits against the U.S. Government in the Eastern District of Louisiana, the first to reopen the case supposedly settled in Panama, the second for another $195,000 check to replace the one stolen by its attorney. The district court dismissed the first case on jurisdictional grounds and ruled against Golden Panagia in the second because it found no negligence on the Government's part. We affirm both decisions.

I. FACTUAL AND PROCEDURAL BACKGROUND

On February 1, 1979, the good ship M/V Golden Panagia, owned and operated by plaintiff-appellant Golden Panagia Steamship, Inc. ("Golden Panagia"), collided with the equally good ship M/V World Agamemnon in the Panama Canal. At the time of the collision each ship was under the command of a pilot employed by the Panama Canal Company, as required by regulations then in effect. . . .[1]

Golden Panagia retained as counsel Henry L. Newell, a Panamanian attorney, and on September 18, 1979, Newell filed suit against the Panama Canal Company in the United States District Court for the District of the Canal Zone for damages of $303,797.11 sustained by the M/V Golden Panagia. *Golden Panagia Steamship, Inc. v. Panama Canal Company*, No. 79-343-B (D.C.Z.1979) ("Golden Panagia I"). On October 1, 1979, the Panama Canal Treaty of 1977 went into effect, which provided for the Panama Canal Company to cease operations in Panama; in its place congress substituted the Panama Canal Commission as an agency in the Executive Branch of the United States Government. . . .

In June, 1981, Newell entered into a settlement agreement with the United States, and the parties submitted to the court, Sear, J., a Consent Judgment, which stated in part:

> . . . having agreed to settle the claims asserted herein, it is hereby ORDERED, ADJUDGED, AND DECREED:
>
> That Henry L. Newell, as attorney for Plaintiff, Golden Panagia Steamship, Inc., receive from the Defendant the sum of one hundred ninety-five thousand three hundred eighteen dollars and fifty cents ($195,318.50) without interest and without costs....

Violanti, Newell, and Judge Sear signed the Consent Judgment, which was entered June 15, 1981. Thereafter the Government gave Newell a United States Treasury check in the amount of $195,318.50 made payable to "Henry L. Newell as Attorney for Golden Panagia Steamship Inc." Newell acknowledged receipt of the funds in a Satisfaction of Judgment executed by him and filed in the court on July 20, 1981.

On March 31, 1982, the jurisdiction of the United States Courts in the Republic of Panama ended and the district court ceased operations. When the Panama Canal Treaty of 1977 went into effect on October 1, 1979, U.S. courts in Panama were denied jurisdiction over new cases; however, art. XI, ¶ 6, granted

---

[1] The Panama Canal Company was a federally chartered company created by Congress to operate the Canal. Act of September 26, 1950, 64 Stat. 1041; . . .

See LeMoyne, *Is Panama Set to Run the Canal?*, N.Y. Times, May 8, 1986 at 6, col. 1 (national ed.):

Among the most important tasks in the waterway is that of the 230 pilots who guide the ships through the narrow locks from ocean to ocean. At present, almost all are North americans. But under a special program Panamanians are being trained for the tricky work in which a misjudgment of a few feet can result in dented hulls, crushed piers *and costly lawsuits*. (emphasis added).

them full jurisdiction for thirty months (i.e., until March 31, 1982) to dispose of cases "already instituted and pending before the courts prior to the entry into force of [the] Treaty."

On April 23, 1982, Golden Panagia attempted to re-open its case by bringing an action against the Panama Canal Commission and the United States in the United States District Court for the Eastern district of Louisiana. *Golden Panagia Steamship, Inc. v. Panama Canal Commission, the United States of America,* 557 F.Supp. 340 (E.D.La.1983) ("Golden Panagia II"). In its complaint Golden Panagia alleged in part:

VIII.

The United States of America negligently issued a check payable to Henry Newell as attorney for the M/V GOLDEN PANAGIA rather than issuing the check for settlement to plaintiff.

IX.

Attorney Newell then obtained the funds, executed satisfaction of judgment, and stole the funds.

X.

Plaintiff had no knowledge of the settlement negotiations and extended no authority to attorney Newell to settle the case.

Golden Panagia sought by motion to "set aside the aforementioned settlement and judgment entered into fraudulently and without authority by attorney Newell and reinstate said suit" in order to relitigate its original claim. In the alternative, Golden Panagia demanded judgment against the United States and the Panama Canal Commission in the amount of $195,318.50, for the alleged negligence of the U.S. Attorney in paying the settlement amount directly to Newell. The district court, Sear, J., found that it lacked jurisdiction to consider these claims and granted the government's motion to dismiss on February 11, 1983. . . .

On January 3, 1984, Golden Panagia brought another action in the United States District Court for the Eastern District of Louisiana, this time against the United States Department of Justice and the United States. *Golden Panagia Steamship, Inc., v. The United States Department of Justice, et al.,* No. 84-22 (E.D.La) ("Golden Panagia III"). . . . The case proceeded to trial and was submitted to the district court, Sear, J., on depositions, exhibits, and briefs. The court found that Newell had acted with "apparent authority" at all times and that the United

States had no reason to foresee that he would steal the settlement funds. Finding no negligence, the court rendered judgment in favor of the United States on February 26, 1985. . . .

II. THE ACTION FOR REINSTATEMENT (GOLDEN PANAGIA II)

. . . Reading the pleadings charitably, however, the district court construed them as either a motion or an independent action for relief from judgment under Fed.R.Civ.P. 60(b). Considered as a motion for reinstatement, the suit had to be dismissed because it was not brought "in the court and in the action in which the judgment was rendered." . . . Considered as an independent action, the suit had to be dismissed because the district court lacked subject matter jurisdiction. . . . We adopt the opinion of the district court . . . affirming its dismissal of Golden Panagia's action for reinstatement. . . .

III. THE FEDERAL TORT CLAIMS ACTION (GOLDEN PANAGIA III)

A. *Authority, Actual and Apparent*

Golden Panagia's central contention is that "Newell did not have authority to settle the claim or enter into a consent judgment" on Golden Panagia's behalf. . .

The thirty-month "wind-up" period prior to March 31, 1982, when the jurisdiction of the United States Courts ended in Panama, was apparently a hectic one in the courts. Frank Violanti, then the U.S. Attorney in Panama, testified as follows:

> There was a large number of cases pending, admiralty cases. Counting them all, I think Judge Sear, at one time, had over seven hundred (700) cases. And, there was quite a bit of concern about disposing all of those cases.... Now, even Judge Sear would put a lot of pressure on us to move the cases, for all parties to be able to come in with authority to settle their cases. They didn't want much delay occasioned by the inability of an attorney to be able to contact his principal and get authority. They were able to come into these conferences....settlement conferences with the authority to settle the cases. . .

The record in this case discloses that a steady stream of letters, cables, and telephone calls flowed between Henry Newell and the New York and New Jersey representatives of Golden Panagia. From at least as early as 1980, the possibility of settlement was discussed in many of these communications . . .

From the Government's perspective, there could be no question but that Henry Newell had authority to represent Golden Panagia. Violanti's testimony makes this clear:

> The Plaintiff here cloaked Mr. Newell with all the authority to settle right from the very onset. In fact, in the pleadings it spells out that he had the authority to ... I mean, that he presented his complaint based upon facts supplied to him by the company, he appeared at pre-trial conferences, he appeared at settlement conferences. What more could you expect from our standpoint to believe, that he didn't have any authority?
> Violanti Dep. at 32.

On this record, and in the almost unique circumstances of this case, we have difficulty understanding what further "authority" Newell should, or could, have had for purposes of settling Golden Panagia's claims. As a practical matter, it appears that Newell would not have been able to negotiate effectively, if at all, on Golden Panagia's behalf if his every proposal and counter-proposal had to be processed through some anonymous foreign master. And in any event it is clear that Golden Panagia was following and participating in the developing settlement, which in fact took approximately the form Newell predicted.

If Newell had authority to sign the Consent Judgment on Golden Panagia's behalf, then he also had authority to receive the settlement check, made out to him, on Golden Panagia's behalf. When Newell -- along with the U.S. Attorney and the district court -- signed the consent Judgment, Golden Panagia's original claim was, at the stroke of a pen, compromised by more than $100,000. If Newell had no authority to make such a settlement, then he stole that $100,000 from Golden Panagia just as surely as he stole the remaining $195,000. But it seems hard to imagine that Newell's participation in the settlement agreement and the Consent Judgment could be attacked. They only appear suspect now because, in retrospect, Newell appears to be a deadbeat. At the time, there was nothing to put the Government on notice that Newell was anything other than a model of lawyerly respectability.[2]

On Golden Panagia's theory, the Government should presumably have refused to deal with Newell without further documentation of his authority. Then (assuming, *arguendo*, that a settlement could have been reached under such circumstances) the Government should presumably have made direct contact with Newell's client -- in effect, "going behind his back" -- to see whether it should really

---

[2] See Violanti Dep. at 36: Mr. Newell had a very good reputation. He was friends of the Judges, had been a member of the New Orleans Bar. There was no indication whatsoever that Mr. Newell would ever do anything of the nature in which he's done in this case. In fact, I think one of the members of your law firm came down and indicated similar surprise, I think Norman Sullivan when he came down.

pay over a settlement check made out, in the court-approved fashion, to Newell. As the Government observes, this scenario would entail, at the very least, a serious breach of professional ethics by the Government.

B. *Negligence, Real and Imagined*

... The district court concluded that in this case "apparent authority" was sufficient to bind a party to its attorney's exercise of authority, that the Government's duty of due care extended only to foreseeable risks, and that Newell's theft of the settlement funds was unforeseeable.

Apparently conceding the bulk of the district court's legal conclusions, Golden Panagia chooses to quarrel with the court's findings of fact. Golden Panagia first attacks as clearly erroneous the court's finding that no special circumstances existed at the time of the settlement to put any government official on notice that Newell might convert the funds to this own use. *Au contraire,* exclaims Golden Panagia: "[N]ot only was the criminal act foreseeable, it is admitted *it was foreseen*." Appellant's Brief at 33. Golden Panagia relies for this point on the deposition of Lawrence F. Ledebur, the Justice Department official who approved the check disbursement procedure. But when Ledebur's deposition is actually examined, it turns out to contain only a vague, pale, and wholly innocuous rendition of the picture Golden Panagia paints:

> Q. When Mr. Violanti approached you with this particular method of settling cases, did you perceive any dangers or risks in settling the cases in that manner?
>
> A. No. No more than usual. As I say, this was not unique to the Canal Zone.
>
> Q. Well, I understand you say no more than usual, but do you perceive any particular problem in settling cases in that manner?
>
> A. Certainly. If the attorney is dishonest, he can steal money from his client.
>
> Q. Did you perceive that as a risk prior to Mr. Violanti's approaching you with the request of resolving the cases in that manner?
>
> A. I don't know what you mean by perceive it as a risk. I was being aware of human frailty. Since I am human and frail myself, I was aware that there was such a thing as dishonest attorneys in the world, of course. And I was so aware prior to being approached by Mr. Violanti.... I could add I suppose there have been dishonest clients as well in the history of the law as well as dishonest attorneys.
>
> Ledebur Dep. at 25-26.

Golden Panagia also challenges the district court's conclusion that "The United States had no reason to foresee that *Newell* would steal the settlement funds" (emphasis added) as a misapplication of the law: "For a criminal act to be foreseeable, there is no requirement in any jurisdiction that the plaintiff know the name of the criminal who may commit the crime." Appellant's Brief at 33. But here again, it appears that Golden Panagia has gotten the story backward. Ledebur testified that the Justice Department officials in Washington had considered, and rejected as insufficient, the *general* risk posed by dishonest attorneys:

> Q. Was there ever any consideration given to not resolving the cases in that manner to avoid that particular risk of dealing with the dishonest attorney who would convert the funds?
> A. Other than I suppose since I approved it means that I didn't -- considered and rejected as sufficient grounds for not approving it what you suggest. Yes.
> Ledebur Dep. at 26.

Meanwhile, in Panama, Violanti had *specific* evidence that Newell did not pose such a risk: "Mr. Newell had a very good reputation. He was friends of the Judges, had been a member of the New Orleans Bar." Violanti Dep. at 36. There was no "requirement" that the Government know that Newell would commit a crime. The Government's affirmative evidence that he would *not* commit a crime was rather in the nature of a bonus, or added data, in the analysis. It tended to confirm that the Government's general supposition was valid in one specific case. As it turned out, of course, both Golden Panagia and the Government were spectacularly wrong about Henry Newell....

IV. A PANEGYRIC, BUT NOT A PANACEA

This is one of those unfortunate cases in which neither party has really done anything wrong. The real culprit, Henry Newell, is not before this court.[3] Golden Panagia is rightfully aggrieved, but for it to recover damages from the Government under our adversary system of justice it must prove that those damages are fairly traceable to some fault on the Government's part. Under a negligence theory an actor is held accountable only on the basis of the knowledge he could, or should,

---

[3] Consistent with its theory that there was no valid settlement, and that the stolen funds still belongs to the Government, Golden Panagia has declined to bring suit against Newell. Counsel for Golden Panagia informed this court at oral argument that Newell is now, in any event, dead. A Higher Court thus has jurisdiction over Henry Newell, and we are confident that any sins he may have committed will be dealt with appropriately there. See *Matthew* 24:41-46 (explaining Final Judgment procedures).

have had at the time he acted; fault in this context is measured from the perspective of the actor and the then foreseeable future. While in retrospect it probably would have been wiser for the Government not to make out a settlement check payable directly to Henry Newell, we cannot say that, in the circumstances, the Government's conduct or procedures rose to the level of negligence. Thus we can offer Golden Panagia only a panegyric, not a panacea.

We AFFIRM the decisions of the district court in both of the cases on appeal.

AFFIRMED.

UNITED STATES v. TURNBULL
United States Court of Appeals, Ninth Circuit
888 F.2d 636 (1989)

ROBERT R. BEEZER, Circuit Judge:

Larry Turnbull appeals the district court's judgment of conviction against him for failure to pay income taxes. We affirm in part and vacate in part.

I

The United States asserted its authority over Turnbull in matters temporal by charging him with failing to render unto Caesar that which was due, in willful violation of the Internal Revenue Code. 26 U.S.C. § 7201 (1982).

At Turnbull's initial appearance before the magistrate in Fairbanks, his arraignment was continued for a week. Turnbull then filed pleadings in the district court stating that he did not waive his right to counsel, but that his religious beliefs precluded him from using the services of any member of the bar. Turnbull stated his belief that the teachings of Jesus require him to avoid associating with lawyers. Turnbull requested that lay persons who shared his beliefs be appointed as his co-counsels. At his arraignment, Turnbull appeared without counsel and stood mute when asked to plead. The court entered a plea of not guilty on his behalf.

On March 16, Turnbull withdrew his motion asking for lay counsel. Magistrate Roberts held a hearing on March 29 regarding Turnbull's representation. Turnbull stated that he waived none of his rights, and contested the jurisdiction of the court. He repeated his religious objection to the services of a lawyer. The court examined him as to his level of understanding of the proceedings, and explained the advantages of trained counsel at some length. The court told Turnbull that it could not appoint lay counsel under the rules of the court. Since Turnbull declined to waive his right to counsel, but was unwilling to be represented by anyone the court could appoint, the magistrate appointed Federal Public Defender Michael Karnavas as Turnbull's "standby counsel," who would be available to Turnbull should he desire assistance, and who would be able to take over the defense should Turnbull be unable to continue it himself.

Between this decision and the trial date of May 3, 1988, Turnbull filed voluminous motions to dismiss, raising typical tax protestor arguments. All of these were denied. On May 3, Judge Fitzgerald inquired further into the counsel situation before allowing the trial to begin. Pursuant to Ninth Circuit law, the court was not willing to let Turnbull represent himself, even with standby counsel present, without a knowing and voluntary waiver of the right to counsel on the record. The court described the charges to Turnbull, again emphasizing the numerous benefits of the full assistance of counsel. Turnbull stated that he did not understand the charges, and again declined to waive his right to counsel. Judge Fitzgerald asked standby counsel Karnavas to sit at counsel table and conduct the defense.

No allegation is made that Karnavas was unprepared to conduct an adequate defense, or that he provided ineffective assistance. He did the best he could in the nightmarish position of representing a client who objected to his very presence on religious grounds, and refused to cooperate with him in any way. Karnavas cross-examined witnesses, made relevant objections, and made opening and closing statements. He did not put on any defense witnesses. The court offered numerous opportunities to Turnbull to participate in his own defense, but he refused each one because he said that Karnavas' presence prevented him from participating in the trial in any way.

The jury convicted Turnbull of all the charges, and he was sentenced to one year of imprisonment, probation, costs of prosecution, and special assessments. Turnbull timely appeals. Fed.R.Crim.P. 4(b). We have jurisdiction over this final judgment, 28 U.S.C. § 1291 (1982). We review the questions of law raised by this appeal de novo.

II

Turnbull claims, *inter alia*, that the district court's appointment of Karnavas, and its failure to appoint lay counsel, violated his sixth amendment right to the effective assistance of counsel and his first amendment right to the free exercise of religion. . . .

A defendant has a constitutional right to represent himself. . . . This right, however, is not absolute. Our recognition of the powerful advantage of competent counsel mandates extreme care in allowing pro se representation. A waiver of the right to counsel must be knowing and voluntary. [citation omitted] *United States v. Balough* sets forth the facts that the district court must establish on the record before it may accept a waiver. [citation omitted] Here, Turnbull's statement that he did not understand the charges made a waiver impossible, even if he had in fact attempted one. If a defendant does not knowingly and voluntarily waive counsel, and does not retain acceptable counsel, the court must appoint counsel.

The district court therefore had no alternative to appointing counsel. The magistrate initially attempted something of a compromise by appointing Karnavas as standby counsel. Absent a knowing and voluntary waiver, the appointment of advisory counsel is not sufficient to meet sixth amendment requirements. . . . The elevation of Karnavas to full-fledged trial counsel before trial cured that error, however.

Turnbull suggests that the court should have appointed lay counsel. He argues that "counsel" does not necessarily mean "lawyer." Turnbull withdrew his motion asking for lay counsel, but did raise the issue orally before the magistrate. He did not ask Judge Fitzgerald for lay counsel. As the status of his request is unclear, we will dispose of the matter on the merits.

"Counsel" means "attorney". . . . The District of Alaska Rules of Court permit only licensed attorneys to be admitted to the district court bar. D.Alaska R.Ct. 3 (1988).

The district court did not violate the sixth amendment by appointing counsel to conduct the defense of a person who did not voluntarily and knowingly waive his right to an attorney.

The federal courts may not improperly burden the free exercise of religion. To show a free exercise burden that is unconstitutional, however, a claimant must do more than merely show that the government action in some way affected his religion. . . . Our interpretation of Supreme Court precedent is most succinctly set forth in *Graham v. Commissioner* [citation omitted].

> To show a free exercise violation, the religious adherent . . . has the obligation to prove that a governmental [action] burdens the adherent's practice of his or her religion by pressuring him or her to commit an act forbidden by the religion or by preventing him or her from engaging in conduct or having a religions experience which the faith mandates. [Citations omitted]. This interference must be more than an inconvenience, the burden must be substantial and an interference with a tenet or belief that is central to religions doctrine. . .

Even assuming Turnbull meets this difficult test, to find a burden on the free exercise of religion to exist does not end the analysis. "[T]he government must accommodate the religious beliefs unless there is a compelling state objective for [the burdensome practice] in the particular case." The Supreme Court and this circuit have found a variety of legitimate state objectives to be compelling interests that override free exercise claims.

The case that is most persuasive comes from the Eastern District of Pennsylvania. *Africa v. Anderson*, 542 F.Supp. 224 (E.D. Pa. 1982). In *Africa*, the court had to decide what must be done to ensure adequate representation of a defendant who rejects the legal system entirely. Consuewella Africa was a member of the MOVE organization. She was tried on various charges in state court arising out of the confrontation between MOVE and the city of Philadelphia. Africa wished to proceed pro se. The court's. . . inquiry showed her to be disruptive, contemptuous, and entirely unable to represent herself adequately. The court appointed counsel.

Africa sued in federal court, contending that the state court's actions had unconstitutionally burdened the free exercise of her religion. Africa sincerely believed that the teachings of John Africa required her to represent herself. . . The court discussed the conflict between the first and sixth amendments. . . After weighing the respective interests, it found the state's interest in the protection of the constitutional rights of the accused to outweigh Africa's free exercise claim.

Turnbull's refusal to waive counsel, coupled with his apparent religious aversion to counsel, put the court in a more difficult position than did Africa's simpler demand for self-representation. The court did all it could do under the circumstances to ensure a fair trial. We hold that the state's compelling interest in a fair and orderly trial outweighs Turnbull's objection to counsel.

CONCLUSION

Turnbull's sixth amendment rights were not violated. His right to the free exercise of his religion was burdened, but the burden was excused by a compelling state interest. The conviction is affirmed, but the special assessments are vacated.

AFFIRMED in part, VACATED in part.

CHAPTER III

ALCOHOL, DRUGS, GAMBLING, VICE, PROFANITY, LEWDNESS, OBSCENITY, INDOLENCE, SLOTH, VAGRANCY AND OTHER ASSORTED PREVALENT EVILS

Now of all the laws, by which the Kingdoms of the Earth are governed, no Law so near this Law of Nature and the Divine Pattern, as the Law of England; a System of Laws, so Comprehensive, so Wise, so favourable to the Subject, and yet so strongly guarding the Prerogatives of the Prince, that no Nation upon Earth does enjoy the like.

- Fortesque[1]

It has now been said that the law of the land in countries under the Common Law of England is a "rubbish-heap which has been accumulating for hundred of years, and . . . is . . . based upon feudal doctrines which no one (except professors in law schools) understands" -- and rather with the implication that even the professors do not thoroughly understand them or all understand them the same way.

- Riddel, J.[2]

---

[1] The Right Honorable John Lord Fortescue, *Reports of Special Cases in all the Courts of Westminster Hall*; From preface, p. ii (1748).
[2] From *Miller v. Tipling*, 43 Ontario Law Reports 88 (1918).

WADDEL v. THE STATE OF GEORGIA
Supreme Court of Georgia
27 Ga. 262 (1859)

JOSEPH H. LUMPKIN, J.

The defendant having been convicted of vagrancy in the county of Marion, applied in the Court below for a new trial, on the ground that the verdict was contrary to the evidence. And the motion being refused, he brings up his case by writ of error to this Court.

I was never more impressed with the folly of sticking to forms, than when reading the presentment of the grand jury in this case. Jacob is accused of having with force and arms &c., doing what? Knocking some one down? No, but with force and arms, doing nothing; strolling about in idleness. He is not indicted for being a *know*-nothing,[1] but a *do*-nothing. The offence itself is somewhat anomalous. Every other in the Code charges the defendant with doing something. This for doing nothing.

Is the offence sufficiently sustained by the proof? The grand jury presented Jacob, and the traverse jury convicted him upon the testimony, notwithstanding Jacob was seen ploughing a potato patch, and doing some other small jobs, within the last two years. His fancy seems to have been mostly to walk the highways. The case is not a very strong one, still there was proof enough to warrant a conviction. And the jury are peculiarly the judges of the proof.

So Jacob will have to go to work; and not only work, but to *hard work*. So says the Code. We fear this will go *hard* with Jacob at first. It will be a great change in his habits. Might not the law, in this humanitarian age, have condemned the vagrant the first year, to work only; and the second year to *hard* work? Ought not a portion of the vagrant's *hard* earnings to be appropriated to his family, provided he have one?

I am quite satisfied that a large portion of the population of our towns could be convicted upon stronger proof than this. It is time, perhaps, to give them a scare; to admonish them of the old adage, that a bird that can sing, and won't sing, must be *made* to sing. That able-bodied man must not cumber the ground, living on the sweat of the other men's toil. "Why stand ye here all the day idle?"[2] is a question which the master of the vineyard propounds, and which the Penal Code will have answered.

Judgment affirmed.

---

1 [Ed. Note: The "Know-Nothings" were members of a secret political organization (anti-Catholic and anti-immigrant) in America from 1843-1861.]

2 [Ed. Note: *Matthew* 20:6]

KROBRE v. HEED
Justice Court of California, Tuolumne County
Case No. 606 (1851)

R. C. BARRY, J.P.

This was a suit between two Gamboleers E. Krobre the gamboleer who sooed Sam Heed the gamboleer to recover 3000 dolers wun at Keards. After much swarin one way and another the lawyers H. P. Barber and Leeander Quint argooed the caze which after a long while they got through with I discided that Barber was right whereupon Quint said please your honor I never can get justice in your coort putting out his finger and thum i told him the likes of him in my country often lost their fingers stealing corn or chickens and that if I had anything to say he never shood have justice here i ordered him to hold his tung and shetup when he went out of coort he began to grumble again i ordered John Luney the constable to arrest him and bring him into coort before me which he done I then fined him $25 for contempt of Court.

Cost of Court $10 which was pade.

September 10, 1851
John Luney, Constable.

UNITED STATES v. SENTOVICH
United States Court of Appeals, Eleventh Circuit
677 F.2d 834 (1982)

FRANK M. JOHNSON, JR., Circuit Judge

The ubiquitous DEA Agent Paul Markonni once again sticks his nose into the drug trade. This time he is on the scent of appellant Mitchell Sentovich's drug courier activities. We now learn that among Markonni's many talents is an olfactory sense we in the past attributed only to canines. Sentovich argues that he should have been able to test, at a magistrate's hearing on issuance of a search warrant, whether Markonni really is the human bloodhound he claims to be. Sentovich's claims, however, have more bark than bite. In fact, they have not a dog's chance of success. Zeke, Rocky, Bodger and Nebuchadnezzar,[1] and the drug dogs of the southeast had best beware. Markonni's sensitive proboscis may soon put them in the dog pound.

I.

An anonymous telephone caller told a Florida Sheriff's department that three males carrying seven suitcases full of marijuana would leave the Fort

---

[1] The court understands that Bodger and Nebuchadnezzar are in training.

Myers airport at seven the next morning. The next day local police, proving they had their noses to the grindstone, telephoned Atlanta police detective James Burkhalter and informed him that they had dogged Sentovich and two other men, Mark Diefenthaler and Randall Alander, at the airport. The men had purchased tickets for flights from Fort Myers to Montana, via Atlanta. Police located a cart with luggage to be put on the flight to Atlanta. Not having Drug Enforcement Agency Agent Paul Markonni about, they had to fall back on a mere canine, Rocky, with 50-60 hours training in marijuana detection, who sniffed the bags on the cart as well as other bags nearby. Rocky alerted strongly to two bags belonging to Diefenthaler. Police detained Diefenthaler. Alander, without being asked to do so, left the plane and proceeded to a security lounge. Before the plane left, police found and seized seven pieces of luggage, including two carry-on bags, belonging to the two men. Sentovich, showing what a dog-eat-dog world this is, abandoned the men to their fate and flew on to Atlanta with his two suitcases and shoulder-type bag.

Burkhalter informed the Drug Enforcement Agency of the information he had received. Agent Paul Markonni had the airline on whose flight Sentovich had arrived in Atlanta nose around and locate Sentovich's bags. Markonni, who stated in an affidavit that he had smelled marijuana more than 100 times over the past eleven years, applied his proboscis to the three bags and alerted to two of them because of the odor of marijuana. Not willing to have Sentovich depart from under his very nose, Markonni told Burkhalter of his discovery. Burkhalter stopped Sentovich as he was boarding a flight to Montana and asked him to consent to a search. Sentovich initially consented but, after talking to an attorney, changed his mind and refused to allow a search.

Markonni doggedly went to obtain a search warrant for the two bags that smelled of marijuana. He presented to a magistrate an affidavit containing the information obtained from Florida police and stating that he had detected the nose-tickling odor of marijuana emanating from the luggage. The magistrate issued the warrant after refusing to have the bags taken to the courthouse to be smelled by him or by another neutral party and after refusing to allow counsel for Sentovich to cross-examine Markonni. The counsel asked to be allowed to be present when the bags were opened. Markonni advised that counsel could be present but that he would not allow counsel to ride with him to the airport and would open the bags immediately. Markonni returned to the airport. Before defense counsel arrived, he opened the two bags in which he had detected the odor and found marijuana in them. Sentovich was convicted of possession of marijuana with intent to distribute, in violation of 21 U.S.C.A. § 841(1)(1).

II.

Sentovich argues that he should have been able to cross-examine Markonni before a search warrant was issued. Unless some compelling reason requires an ex parte hearing, he asserts that a police officer will be able to obtain a warrant too dog-cheaply unless the hearing on whether to issue a search warrant is adversarial. The Supreme Court has ruled otherwise. "To mandate an evidentiary hearing [with respect to a request for a search warrant], the challenger's attack must be more than conclusory and must be supported by more than a mere desire to cross-examine. There must be allegations of deliberate falsehood or of reckless disregard for the truth, and those allegations must be accompanied by an offer of proof. . . . Allegations of negligence or innocent mistake are insufficient." *Franks v. Delaware* [citation omitted].

Sentovich asserts that cross-examination would have provided an opportunity to test Markonni's ability to discern the odor marijuana. Neither on appeal nor below does he allege that Markonni deliberately lied or recklessly disregarded the truth in stating that he nosed out marijuana. Without a claim of such doggery, the magistrate was on the nose in finding that no adversarial hearing was necessary.

Sentovich next asserts that the magistrate should have ordered the bags to be brought to the court or that Markonni should have awaited the arrival of Sentovich's counsel before opening the bags. Because of the absence of third-party confirmation, he argues that important evidence was destroyed. Sentovich suggests several remedies: exclusion of the alleged odor of the luggage from a determination of whether probable cause for the warrant existed, suppression of the evidence of the marijuana discovered in the bags, or dismissal of the indictment.

We find no error by the magistrate or misconduct by the government. We address first Sentovich's arguments concerning the need to exclude the evidence from a finding of probable cause for a warrant and concerning the suppression of the evidence of marijuana. He raised neither argument in his motion to suppress. A party not raising an argument below waives his right to raise it on appeal absent plain error. . .

Indeed, reaching the merits, we find no error at all. The magistrate need not have required a neutral party to smell the luggage. As we noted above, *Franks* supplies the standard for determining when an evidentiary hearing is necessary. Since there was no allegation of deliberate falsehood or reckless disregard of the truth by Markonni, here was no reason for the magistrate to hold a hearing allowing third-party confirmation of Markonni's sense of smell.

There was also no misconduct by Markonni in failing to delay opening the luggage until Sentovich's counsel arrived at the airport. Police with a search warrant simply need not await the arrival of counsel before executing that warrant. Moreover, the inability of counsel to smell marijuana would have no bearing on the validity of the warrant. Even if Markonni was wrong in thinking that he smelled marijuana, his misstatement would invalidate the warrant only if it was intentional or made in deliberate disregard of the truth. . . We note again that Sentovich never alleges any malodorous motive or activity by

Markonni that was intentional or in reckless disregard of the truth.[2]

Sentovich did seek dismissal of the indictment against him because of the alleged destruction of the evidence of the odor of the marijuana. At the very least, Sentovich must make some showing of the materiality of the evidence the government suppressed. . . The standard for determining materiality varies somewhat with the situation at issue. [citation omitted] Here, however, we need not inquire into the exact applicable standard. Whatever the standard may be, Sentovich has not met it. The odor of the marijuana--as opposed to the marijuana itself--was of no relevance to Sentovich's conviction.

Markonni emerges with his nose unbloodied and his tail wagging. Sentovich's claims are without merit. Having also reviewed the evidence, we find it sufficient for his conviction. The judgment of the district court is AFFIRMED.

EPPLE v. STATE OF TEXAS
Court of Criminal Appeals of Texas
112 Tex. Crim. 612; 18 S.W.2d 625 (1928)

ALBERT B. MARTIN, J.

Offense, the unlawful transportation of intoxicating liquor; punishment, three years in the penitentiary.

An officer searched appellant's car without a search warrant. In it he found inside the upholstering of the seat eight pints of corn whisky. The claim is made that, both a search warrant and probable cause being absent, the officer's testimony was inadmissible, and the conviction without warrant of law. These various contentions are sufficiently answered by the following quotation from the searching officer's testimony: "I said, 'I want to look through it,' and he said, 'Help yourself, if you find anything, you are welcome to it.' He also said 'Go ahead, help yourself, if you find anything, you are welcome to it.'" The appellant having consented to the search, he is in no position to complain. . . [citation omitted]

---

[2] Sentovich also alleges that there was insufficient evidence of the reliability of the dog smelling the bags at Fort Myers for the dog's reaction to be used as a basis for the search warrant. His argument is that a mere statement that the dog had been trained in drug detection was not enough without an accompanying statement that the dog had proved reliable in the past and that an experienced handler was with the dog. Since we believe Markonni's statement concerning his detection of an odor of marijuana was sufficient alone for a finding of probable cause, the adequacy of the proof of the reliability of the dog is not essential to our holding. We believe, in any event, that his argument is without merit. The case on which Sentovich relies, *United States v. Klein,* [citation omitted] does state that statements that a dog had had training and had proved reliable in the past were sufficient indicia of the dog's reliability. The court did not, however, state that the handler had to be trained or that training alone was insufficient to show reliability. Two other circuits have held that training of a dog alone is sufficient proof of reliability. . . .

The contention is made that the court erred in overruling appellant's second application for a continuance. Appellant's bill presenting this matter is qualified to show that this case had been continued at the preceding December term of court on account of the absence of the same witness, which is made the basis of appellant's second application presented in March 12, 1928.

It appears that an application was made for a subpoena for this witness after its continuance in December, to wit, on February 25, 1928, and that, in response to a telegram sent on the day the case was called for trial, appellant was informed that no subpoena had reached Fort Worth, where the witness was alleged to reside. No excuse is shown either for the long lapse of time in applying for subpoena or appellant's lack of diligence in failing to ascertain prior to the time of trial that witness had not been served. It is further averred that the witness then resided in Fort Worth, not a great distance from Young county, where the case was tried; yet no affidavit from this witness was attached to appellant's motion for new trial, but instead the affidavit of the son of the witness shows to be attached, which contradicts that which appellant was proposing to prove by the absent witness. There being no diligence shown, the court's action was correct. . .

Under another well-known rule the court was justified in overruling appellant's motion for new trial presenting this matter. When the facts stated in the application are considered in connection with the evidence adduced on the trial, and do not appear probably true, there is no error in overruling the motion for new trial. . .

The main fact which appellant proposed to prove by this absent witness was that there was no whisky in the car in question when appellant and witness left it to go in a restaurant, and that, on coming out of the restaurant a short while thereafter and just before the search, witness saw an unknown stranger in the car, who suddenly left; that he did not know where he went and had never seen him before. The appellant's theory seems to have been that this stranger had in some way found a mysteriously hidden receptacle in the upholstering of his car and played him the mean trick of filling it with whisky. Like a cuckoo bird, this unfeathered follower of Bacchus surreptitiously slipped a whole settin' of eggs into appellant's nest, after which he was apparently swallowed up by space, leaving his troublesome brood to be hatched by another.

We believe in Santa Claus all right, but we confess the increasingly frequent appearance of this same stranger in whisky cases inclines us to relegate him to the mythical realm of Dido and Aeneas. This ubiquitous disciple of John Barleycorn seems to have a peculiar habit of hovering around places just prior to their raid and search by officers, and then as mysteriously evaporating as the mists of an April morning. Unlike the roaring lion seeking whom he may devour, this omnipresent individual moves with the silent tread of a fairy and the swiftness of the lightning stroke, and over practically the entire state there have come complaints from his victims.

In the light of the entire record and under the above authorities we do not feel authorized to say the trial court abused his discretion in refusing to continue that appellant might make proof of the presence of this evaporative personage, whoever he may be.

Finding no errors in the record, the judgment is affirmed.

CATLING v. BOWLING
King's Bench, Easter Term, 26 George II
96 E.R. 810; 1 Sayer 80 (1753)

SIR WILLIAM LEE, Chief Justice

Upon a motion for leave to bring a book into court, for the conversion of which an action of Trover was brought, it appeared; that the book, entitled *Memoirs of a Woman of Pleasure*, had been lent by a bookseller to some young ladies at a boarding school; that the defendant's wife, who was mistress of the school, took it from them and sent it to the bookseller, with a request that it might not be again sent to the young ladies; and that the book being afterwards found in the possession of one of the young ladies, the defendant's wife took it from her and kept it.

A rule was made to shew cause, why, upon bringing the book into court, the proceedings should not be stayed; and it is probable, that the plaintiff thereupon agreed to drop his action; for the court never heard any more of the rule.

PACETTI v. THE STATE OF GEORGIA
Supreme Court of Georgia
82 Ga. 297; 7 S.E. 867 (1888)

LOGAN E. BLECKLEY, C.J.

A social, genial gentleman, fond of company and a glass, by occupation a cigar-maker, who keeps his sleeping apartment with the doors "blanketed" in a fit condition for privately gaming therein, and who invites his friends at night to refresh themselves with beer, but has in the room, besides barrel and bottles, a table suitable for gaming, together with eleven packs of cards and two boxes of "chips," one containing eighty chips and the other three hundred, and a memorandum book with names and numbers entered in it, and whose guests, or some of them, retire hurriedly under the bed on being surprised by a visit from the police at one o'clock in the morning, may or may not be guilty of the offence of keeping a gaming-house. A verdict of guilty based on these and other inculpatory facts, such as the rattle of chips and money, and some expressions about seven dollars and twelve dollars heard by the police on approaching the premises, is warranted by the evidence, and is not contrary to law.

Judgment affirmed.

HAWKEYE DISTILLING COMPANY v. NEW YORK STATE LIQUOR AUTHORITY

New York Supreme Court, Special Term
118 Misc. 2d 505; 460 N.Y.S. 2d 696 (1983)

RICHARD W. WALLACH, Justice

This is a CPLR Art. 78 application by the Hawkeye Distilling Co. for a judgment annulling a determination of respondent New York State Liquor Authority ("SLA") denying to Hawkeye brand label registration for its alcoholic beverage known as M*A*S*H vodka. The determination is annulled and the court grants judgment in favor of petitioner.

Doubtless to bask in the afterglow left by the 4077th Mobile Army Surgical Hospital as it strikes its tents and steals away from the Korean and golden TV Hills, petitioner Hawkeye Distilling Co. obtained a license from Twentieth Century-Fox Film Corp. to use the name and logos of the popular television series, M*A*S*H in marketing its "M*A*S*H Vodka". To get the full benefit of the "tie-in" with the show, the distiller devised a rather special marketing technique: it packages its clearly labelled domestic vodka in the form of an intra-venous ("IV") feeding device. Sold together with the liquor is a metal contrivance permitting hookup of the bottle in the inverted position above the patient's head so familiar to experienced viewers of General Hospital and Marcus Welby, M.D.

The liquid can be drunk by placing the tube in the imbiber's mouth. Presumably the gaiety of many a suburban rumpus room will be enhanced as the harried commuter drags himself inside the door of his home after a hard day at the office to obtain the dramatic resuscitation available from an oral "transfusion" of the vodka.

The whimsical features of the promotion, however, were entirely lost upon respondent SLA when petitioner applied to register its Hawkeye brand for sale in New York State. The SLA found that "the proposed label and bottling is misleading, deceptive, offensive to the commonly and generally accepted standards of fitness and good taste, is not dignified ... approval would not be conducive to proper regulation and control...."

The decision of the authority cannot be upheld on the ground that the label of the product is misleading ... The court has inspected the bottle produced in open court and finds that it unmistakably labels the contents as 80-proof vodka manufactured in Skokie, Illinois. No rational person could believe that a serious medicinal application of the product was intended, certainly no more so than a buyer who might be induced to purchase an alcoholic beverage known as "Dr. Funk" or "MD 20/20" (both of which are distributed in New York) in the supposed belief that a medically or ophthalmologically beneficial result might ensue. Once it appears that neither the bottle nor its label are misleading, the Authority's writ runs no farther, certainly not so far as to empower it to reject a bottle (as opposed to a label) simply on the ground that it offends good taste.

Although the problem has not arisen in this form before in New York, a New Jersey decision under a similar regulatory scheme points to the correct result. In *Boller Beverages, Inc. v. Davis*, [citation omitted] the director of the New Jersey alcoholic beverage control authority had refused to sanction the sale of "Georgia Moon Corn Whiskey" in what appeared to be an ordinary home canning Mason jar. This determination rested in part upon lack of good taste. The court held that in the absence of any legislative mandate empowering the director to approve of bottling as such, his ruling could not be sustained simply as a matter of aesthetics. Although some jurisdictions empower their liquor authorities to regulate bottling [citation omitted], New York (like New Jersey) is pointedly not one of them.

It further appears that 39 other states, including some who are the exclusive purveyors, have approved the product for distribution (which surely says something, either praiseworthy or deplorable, about the good taste of this product). Be that as it may, this is a case for application of the maxim: *"de gustibus non disputandum"* [There is no disputing over personal tastes.] One of the prized qualities of Vodka is its tastelessness. Insofar as good taste may be relevant at all, it is worth recalling that the last public official who held the undisputed title of "Arbiter Elegantiae" (supreme judge of taste) was Gaius Petronius. He worked for the Emperor Nero. Both came to a bad end.

It follows that the decision of the SLA is found to be arbitrary and capricious, and that if the ruling is defended as discretionary, such discretion was exercised in an area where the authority has no jurisdiction to act. Its determination must be annulled ...

Let petitioner settle a judgment in its favor accordingly.

LEWIS v. THE STATE
Court of Appeals of Georgia
3 Ga. App. 322; 59 S.E. 829 (1907)

BENJAMIN HARVEY HILL, C. J.

Enoch Lewis was convicted in the city court of Americus, on an accusation charging him with vagrancy. The accusation contains in one count three classes of vagrancy, as defined by the 1st, 2d, and 3d sections of the act of 1905 (Ga. Laws, 1905, p. 109). The evidence in the case is applicable to only the 1st and 3d classes of vagrants as described by the act:

1st. "Persons wandering or strolling about in idleness, who are able to work, and have no property to support them."

3d. "All persons able to work, having no property to support them, and who have no visible or known means of a fair, honest, and reputable livelihood."

The act of 1905 is the re-enactment of what is known as the "Calvin Act of 1903" with an unimportant amendment (Acts of 1903, p. 46). This act enlarges somewhat the meaning of the term "vagrant." It declares that "visible or known means of a fair, honest, and reputable livelihood" shall be construed to mean "reasonably continuous employment at some lawful occupation for reasonable compensation. . ."

Now what would be "reasonably continuous employment" is difficult to determine. Keeping in mind the mischief to be remedied and the purpose of the law, we think any work or labor which is sufficient to furnish the means of livelihood to the laborer, if he has no family, as in this case, and to prevent him from wandering about in idleness, would be "reasonably continuous employment" as defined by the statute. The public is not concerned in the length of labor or the proceeds of labor. Its only object is to protect itself from the idler and the results of idleness. The solicitous inquiry of society, which the penal statute requires to be answered, is that of the Master of the vineyard, "Why stand ye here all the day idle?"

The only question made by this record is, does the evidence prove the charge of vagrancy? The accusation was filed September 5, 1907, and the proof of the labor performed by the accused during the year prior to the date of the accusation may be summarized as follows: During January and February, he helped build a house, and composted the ground of a neighboring farmer. In March and April he worked for 12 or 14 days as a carpenter, for which he was paid $1 a day. In May he hoed cotton and cut oats for another farmer. In June and July he cut 14 cords of wood and got out stock for a sawmill, for which he was paid from $10 to $15. The evidence does not show that he was paid for all his work, but it does show that he was paid at the rate of $5 per month for the eight months just prior to his arrest. . . .

. . . In this case the accused was without family, and his wants were probably few. He probably did not live in much luxury, but he lived without begging, and had a pig and a gun, and lived in a house. The witnesses declare that he was an ardent disciple of Isaac Walton, and was constantly seen going towards the river with his fishing pole on his shoulder, but that he was never seen with any fish.

We are sure that the evidence is entirely insufficient to establish the charge of vagrancy. Doubtless on much stronger evidence a large portion of the population of our towns and cities could be declared vagrants. The community where this defendant was convicted must be exceptionally industrious, or has a very high standard of labor. The evidence shows that the defendant did some considerable work during every month prior to his arrest, and that his only relaxation from too constant toil in working crops, cutting and cording wood, and building houses was in "plying his finest art, to lure from dark haunts, beneath the tangled roots of pendant trees," the alert and wary denizens of the river. Surely it will not be said that while thus engaged he was idling. If he was not successful, all the greater proof of his patient and hopeful labor. The individual members of this court know that fishing is far from idleness, and the court is unwilling to give its judicial approval to a verdict which even remotely so indicates.

Judgment reversed.

IN RE GILBERT COLT
Assize Court of Northumberland County
Northumberland Assize Rolls, 40 Henry III (1256)

ANONYMOUS, Judge

Gilbert Colt, a servant of the parson of Brombury, while driving a certain wagon with a large container of wine, as a result of excessive intoxication fell beneath this same wagon and was crushed under the wheel of this same wagon. No one is suspected in this incident. Verdict: misadventure. Value of the wine, oxen, and wagon: 8 marks, 2 shillings, for which the sheriff will be answerable. Also, John of Kestern and Gilbert of Worton falsely assessed the value of the aforesaid deodand; accordingly, they are to be fined.

COMMONWEALTH OF PENNSYLVANIA v. ROBIN
Supreme Court of Pennsylvania
421 Pa. 70; 218 A.2d 546 (1966)

MICHAEL A. MUSMANNO, Justice (dissenting).

[The Commonwealth of Pennsylvania brought an action in equity to restrain defendant Robin, a bookseller and publisher, from selling and offering for sale the book *Tropic of Cancer* by Henry Miller. The injunction was granted and the defendant appealed. The Pennsylvania Supreme Court (per Cohen, J.) held that the decision of the United States Supreme Court in *Grove Press, Inc. v. Richard E. Gersten*, 378 U.S. 577, 84 S. Ct. 1902, 12 L. Ed. 2d. 1035 (1964), (ruling that it was impermissible for the State of Florida to enjoin the sale of *Tropic of Cancer*, pursuant to its obscenity statute) controlled, and that the circulation of the book could *not* be enjoined.]

The decision of the Majority of the Court in this case has dealt a staggering blow to the forces of morality, decency and human dignity in the Commonwealth of Pennsylvania. If, by this decision, a thousand rattlesnakes had been let loose, they could not do as much damage to the well-being of the people of this state as the unleashing of all the scorpions and vermin of immorality swarming out of that volume of degeneracy called *The Tropic of Cancer*. Policemen, hunters, constables and foresters could easily and quickly kill a thousand rattlesnakes but the lice, lizards, maggots and gangrenous roaches scurrying out from beneath the covers of *The Tropic of Cancer* will enter into the playground, the study desks, the cloistered confines of children and immature minds to eat away moral resistance and wreak damage and harm which may blight countless lives for years and decades to come.

From time immemorial civilization has condemned obscenity because the wise men of the ages have seen its eroding effects on the moral fiber of a people; history is replete with the decadence and final collapse of mighty nations because of their descent into licentiousness and sloth. . .

What is obscenity? Rivers of ink have flowed in an attempted definition of this word, and, more often than not, the greater the attempt at specificity, the more ambiguous has been the resulting language. The fact of the matter is that there is nothing complicated or puzzling about the word *obscenity*. It is a word as simple as *cat*. No person with reasonable intelligence and a modicum of human decency and dignity has any trouble in determining what is obscene. The determination does not require any long study in the laboratory, no working out of a mathematical formula. One sees at a glance whether a given exhibit or situation is obscene or not. . . In the case of *Roth v. United States*, the Supreme Court. . . defined obscenity as follows:

> "[W]hether to the average person, applying con-
> temporary community standards, the dominant
> theme of the material taken as a whole appeals to
> prurient interest * * * and if it goes substan-
> tially beyond customary limits of candor in
> description or representation of such matters."

To say that *Cancer* has no social importance is like saying that a gorilla at a lawn party picnic does not contribute to the happiness of the occasion. *Cancer* is a definite sociological evil. It is not to be described negatively. It is a positive menace to the well-being of the community in which it contaminates the air it displaces. It condemns, outrages, and ridicules the most fundamental rules of good society, namely, honesty, morality and obedience to law. It encourages anti-Semitism and racial conflict. It incites to disorder. . .

Who is the author of this monstrous work, as described by the witnesses in Court? Henry Miller, who identifies himself in the book as a thief, an adulterer, and a "hopeless lecher." He is irreverent, profane and blasphemous. He lauds harlots and glorifies a sinful career. . . .

. . . Henry Miller himself proclaims the degenerate character of his work in the introduction where he says:

> "This then? This is not a book. This is libel,
> slander, defamation of character. This is not a
> book in the ordinary sense of the word. No, this
> is a prolonged insult, a gob of spit in the fact of
> Art, a kick in the pants to God, Man, Destiny,

> Time, Love, Beauty * * * what you will. I am
> going to sing for you, a little off key, perhaps,
> but I will sing. I will sing while you croak, I will
> dance over your dirty corpse."

A *favorable* review of *Cancer* describes it in the following language:

> "* * * Lice, bedbugs, cockroaches, and tape-
> worms crawl across its pages; they are spattered
> with spittle, pus, vomit, scum, and excrement;
> blood, bile, semen, and sewers flow through
> them. Women, most of them prostitutes, throng
> *Tropic of Cancer*. Miller and his pals lust after
> them daily, and perform feats of satyriasis; but
> in their thoughts and talk a woman is seldom a
> 'woman'" — she is a name for a portion of her
> anatomy. . .

The defendants argued that under the *Roth* case only hard-core pornography comes within the ban of obscenity, and this would exclude *Cancer*. The
defendant would have reason to say that *Cancer* is not hard-core pornography;
it is, in fact, *rotten*-core pornography. No decomposed apple falling apart
because of its rotten core could be more nauseating as an edible than *Cancer* is
sickening as food for the ordinary mind. *Cancer* is dirt for dirt's sake, or, more
appropriately, as Justice Frankfurter put it, dirt for money's sake.

Then the defendants say that *Cancer* is entitled to immunity under the
First Amendment because court decisions have declared that only worthless
trash may be proscribed as obscene. To say that *Cancer* is worthless trash is to
pay it a compliment. *Cancer* is the sweepings of the Augean stables, the
stagnant bile of the slimiest mudscow, the putrescent corruption of the most
noisome dump pile, the dreggiest filth in the deepest morass of putrefaction.

Falling back from position to position, arguing merit where none exists
and claiming immunity which no law upholds, the defendants maintain that
even if *Cancer* can be regarded filthy, obscene and rotten, it nevertheless
qualifies for legal guardianship, if it possesses the slightest literary value. In
effect, they say that if a fresh maple leaf should fall into a sewer, the sewage
could then be run into a swimming pool to refresh and engladden the bathers
disporting therein. The law is not so foolish.

And then, standing at the very last ditch, the apologists for *Cancer*
glibly assert that there is no proof anywhere that *Cancer* or any work of that
character has any bearing on human conduct. Of course, scientific research,
sociological study and juvenile and criminal court records, as well as the
realities of life are all to the contrary. . . .

Rape represents the most depraved animalistic aberration in the whole catalogue of offenses against society. For a youth or grown-up man to cast away the last modicum of social restraint and bestially inflict injury and irreparable harm on an innocent girl or woman means that the attacker has been prodded into primitive violence by a force of extraordinary excitation long continued. . .

A tide of printed filth is driving across the land at such height and volume as to cause wholesome-thinking people to wonder and worry whether it may not impair the very foundations of the basic morality upon which our nation and our Constitution were founded. In bookstores, railroad stations, air terminals, drug stores, everywhere that print is displayed and pictures revealed, there stand pyramids of smut, pornography, and obscenity.

Language which would be too raw and grating for the dives of opium-smoking debauchees degrades and defaces the paper which carries it. Magazines with pictures and sketches that would disgrace oriental harems are sold to children as if they were innocuous bags of popcorn. Exotic rites that would raise the blush of shame to the faces of the most primitive tribes are described with nonchalance in high-priced books, medium-priced books, and low-priced books. Themes which should be the subject only for clinical studies in the hospitals for the criminal insane are turned into scarifying stories which inflict untold harm to the youths into whose hands they fall.

Acts of degeneracy and unnatural conduct are being portrayed in contemporary literature as if they were normal and accepted practice in civilized life. Adultery and every other type of illegal and sinful conduct is being depicted glamorously, inviting emulation. The healthful, romantic, and poetic relationship between man and woman is being treated in the basest and grossest of terms.

It used to be that pornographic literature, to the extent that it existed, was trafficked in clandestinely. The secrecy and the furtiveness with which it was sold and circulated was an indication that the public looked upon it as something improper and not in consonance with the morals of the community. But now the most salacious books, the most degrading publications are sold openly practically everywhere. It is difficult to think of a mart where print appears that one's eyes and spirits will not be assailed by pornography of the vilest character. And it is impossible to believe that over a sufficient period of time, this situation can do other than deleteriously affect the moral standards of the nation.

So far as youth and immature minds are concerned, pornographic literature can do as much harm as narcotics. Of course, no one dares to defend illicit traffic in narcotics but a thousand tongues will wag to protect filthy books and magazines. Pornography is big business. It is conservatively estimated that the traffic in pornography in the United States amounts yearly to several billion dollars. Naturally the tycoons who can light cigars with hundred dollar bills as they ride in their luxurious yachts which cruise over rivers of printed filth will resist every effort to curb their de luxe and malodorous voyages.

And so, the false cry of censorship is heard in the land. But there is no censorship involved in banning pornography. The Supreme Court of the United States declared emphatically in the *Roth* case, as already stated, that "implicit in the history of the First Amendment is the rejection of obscenity as utterly without redeeming social importance."

There can be no more false notion than the one that the First Amendment protects everything that may be uttered orally or in print. We have laws which prohibit false advertising of food and drugs. If law will protect people from poison which may enter their systems through the throat, why may law not protect children from poison which may enter their minds, and do far more harm than any extra grain of aspirin? The constant fare of dirty books, to the exclusion of good literature, will eventually produce a sick mind. The mind governs the body and if the mind becomes sick, the body will become sick. . . .

The contention that anything printed is protected by the Constitution is arrant nonsense. It is the most bizarre notion imaginable that a printing press constitutionalizes every paper that passes between and beneath its rollers. Filth does not lose its stench or its bubonic characteristics because it is formed into letters of the alphabet. If everything that is printed or written is presumed to be good and incapable of evil, then correspondence on conspiracy to overthrow the government, ransom notes or even counterfeit money could not become the basis for prosecution of those who engage in its dissemination or use.

World War II which filled the universe with graves, cripples, devastation and ruin, began with a *book*! Hitler's *Mein Kampf* fired Germany with a bellicose spirit, a hatred for minority and helpless peoples, and whipped the nation into a global conflict which almost drove civilization to the very brink of destruction, where indeed it even teeters today. . .

The preface to *Cancer* characterizes its worthlessness when it tells the reader:

> "Let us try to look at it with the eyes of a Patagonian for whom *all that is sacred and taboo in our world is meaningless.*"

Cancer is not a book. It is a cesspool, an open sewer, a pit of putrefaction, a slimy gathering of all that is rotten in the debris of human depravity. And in the center of all this waste and stench, besmearing himself with its foulest defilement, splashes, leaps, crawls and wallows a bifurcated specimen that responds to the name of Henry Miller. One wonders how the human species could have produced so lecherous, blasphemous, disgusting and amoral a human being as Henry Miller. One wonders why he is received in polite society.

I would prefer to have as a visitor in my home the most impecunious tramp that ever walked railroad ties, a tramp whose raggedy clothes are held together by faith and a safety pin, a tramp who, throughout his entire life, always moved at a lazy pace, running only to avoid work, a tramp who rides the rods of freight cars with the aplomb of a railroad president in his private train, a tramp who knows as much about Emily Post's etiquette as a chattering chimpanzee, and who couldn't care less; I would prefer to invite that lazy, bewhiskered cavalier of the road to my residence for a short visit, than even to see on the highway that hobo of the mind, that licentious nomad called Henry Miller, whose literary clothes are plastered with filth, whose language is dirtier than any broken sewer that pollutes and contaminates a whole community; — Henry Miller who shuns a bath of clean words, as the devil avoids holy water, who reduces human beings to animals, home standards to the pigsty, and dwells in a land of his own fit only for lice, bedbugs, cockroaches and tapeworms.

So far as American standards are concerned, I would regard Henry Miller as Moral Public Enemy No. 1, doing more damage to the ethic foundations of our Republic than any criminal, whose picture appears in the lobby of post offices under the heading: "Wanted by the Police!" Those criminals have warred on society but Henry Miller's works, with those of his brother pornographic writers, unless curbed by the law, may eventually undermine the moral foundations of our nation because they are aimed at the youths of today who eventually will be the citizens of tomorrow.

Cancer is not a book. It is malignancy itself. It is a cancer on the literary body of America. I wonder that it can remain stationary on the bookshelf. One would expect it to generate self-locomotion just as one sees a moldy, maggoty rock move because of the creepy, crawling creatures underneath it.

Henry Miller is not the only foul-minded pornographic writer. There are others whose gangrenous productions raise a stench that would make polecats smell like new-mown hay in comparison. *Cancer* was published by the Grove Press whose printing presses must by now be corroded with the festering mildew emanating from the accounts of human depravity, abnormal relations and Satanic perversion which have passed over its purulent type. Recently it advertised *Cancer* as a "classic!" . . .

In view of these fundamental rules in the interpretation of judicial decisions, it is obvious that the Supreme Court of the United States, in the *Gerstein* case, left the door open as wide as the horizon for the State courts to determine for themselves whether so loathsome a beast as *Cancer* should enter into the ark of the First Amendment protection. But this court refused to see the door; instead, it looked out the narrow window of a restricted interpretation and declared that the *Gerstein* case locked our hands, fettered our minds, bound our conscience, gagged our expression and compelled us, with blindfolded eyes to follow a path that has no guidelines, no traveled surface and skirts the precipice of chaotic license. I refuse to go along. I prefer to follow the broad clean highway of decent literature, inspirational books, wholesomely entertaining stories, uplifting essays, enlightening histories and novels which one can read as easily as riding comfortably in a gondola — books which do not require one to don hipboots to slosh through muck, mire and filth which would make the pornographers of the early ages seem like a board of censors in comparison.

The Majority has missed a great opportunity to ring the Liberty Bell again for high moral standards. This was a case where the Court did not have to balance between literary excellence and moral turpitude in a book. It did not have to consider what the public might lose in being deprived of a work with some social value as against obscenity, because *Cancer* has no social worth whatever, it has no literary merit, and no information value. It is a scabious toad croaking obscene phrases in a pestiferous swamp of filth and degradation.

And then, the Majority Opinion speaks of *Gerstein* as if it were the last unchangeable word to be spoken on the subject of obscenity in literature. I refuse to accept the thought that once a decision is rendered on any particular subject, this means that the last bell has rung, the last whistle has blown, the last nail has been driven, the last rivet has been hammered, the last bus has departed, and all that is left to do is wait until Judgment Day. Particularly on the subject here involved is there is no such fatalism as would appear in the short ambit of the short Majority Opinion. . . .

The Majority seems to overlook the fundamental observation that the long-honored standards of American decency are part of our national heritage. The patriots of the Revolutionary War fought just as bravely, and the colonial statesmen who built our structure of government, labored just as earnestly and valiantly, for moral cleanliness as they did to destroy political tyranny.

I regret that the action of the Supreme Court of Pennsylvania, the oldest Supreme Court in the nation, should result, not in *Cancer's* being consigned to the garbage can malodorously yawning to receive it, but, instead, in *Cancer's* being authorized unquestioned entry into the Public Library in Philadelphia within ringing distance of Independence Hall where the Liberty Bell rang out joyously the proclamation of the freedom, independence and *dignity of man*.

I would recoil in dismay if I attempted to visualize the reaction of the founding fathers if they could see this, one of the foulest books that ever disgraced printer's type, now taking a place on the library shelves with the Bible, *Pilgrim's Progress*, Shakespeare's *Works*, Plutarch's *Lives*, Homer's *Iliad*, Sir Thomas More's *Utopia*, Cervantes' *Don Quixote*, Thomas Paine's *Common Sense*, and the other immortal books that inspired the brilliant architects, the brave leaders, the kneeling prayers, and the heroic soldiers who fashioned the United States of America.

From Pittsburgh to Philadelphia, from Dan to Beersheeba, and from the ramparts of the Bible to Samuel Eliot Morison's *Oxford History of the American People*, I dissent!

TWILLEY v. THE STATE OF GEORGIA
Court of Appeals of Georgia
9 Ga. App. 435; 71 S.E. 587 (1911)

BENJAMIN HARVEY HILL, C. J.

The accused was indicted with three others for the offense of gaming, the indictment charging that they "did play and bet for money and drinks of liquor, a thing of value, at a game played with cards, contrary to the laws of said State, the good order, peace and dignity thereof." . . .

. . . The evidence , substantially stated, is as follows: The accused and three others named in the indictment were caught by the marshal of the town of Sparta while playing a game of cards on the "headboard of a grave in the Catholic cemetery." Neither money nor whisky was seen, but the marshal testified that he "smelt whisky strong," and an empty bottle was lying on the ground, and two of the players were apparently under the influence of whisky.

After they had been caught and arrested, two of the players, not the accused, stated that they were "just playing for drinks," and the marshal and another witness testified that "a drink of whisky was a thing of great value in Hancock county." . . . The only evidence against the accused, except the circumstance that he was playing with the others, was the statement made by him, some time after the arrest, to the mayor, that he would like the mayor, as his friend, to have the thing "squashed," and that on the day when they were caught playing, one of the players came by his shop, stated to him that he had a bottle of whisky, and proposed that they go to the Catholic cemetery and play cards for drinks. This statement, while not amounting to a confession, was incriminatory, and, considered in connection with the other strongly suspicious circumstances, may be regarded as of sufficient probative weight to show the corpus delicti, and that the accused was a *particeps criminis* [participant in a crime.]

We can not say, as a matter of law, that the circumstances were not sufficient for that purpose. For four men to leave their business in the daytime and go to a cemetery and play cards on the headboard of a grave would seem to indicate that there was something more in the way of temptation than the mere pleasure of playing an innocent game of cards, and in view of the indicia of the presence of intoxicants, and the evidence that a beverage of this character was hard to get in Hancock county and was very valuable, it would seem to be not unreasonable to infer that the "drinks" furnished the inducement for the playing of the game, and it is difficult to believe, in view of the evidence as to the great value of whisky in Hancock county, that the generosity of one of the players would have furnished without price the tempting stake. It is so natural for men who play cards, and for those who drink, to play for drinks, that this court is constrained to the conclusion that the verdict of the jury was not wholly unauthorized. Apparently the law against gaming, as well as against the sale of liquor, is most vigorously enforced in Hancock county, and in the town of Sparta, when the citizens of the town are compelled to resort to a cemetery to play cards for drinks, and when, even in that secluded spot, they don't have a ghost of a chance.

. . . The evidence, however, was entirely circumstantial. Even the incriminatory statement only inferentially indicates guilt. In such case it is well settled, by the repeated rulings of the Supreme Court, that it is the duty of the trial judge, even in the absence of a request, to charge the jury the law defining the probative value of circumstantial evidence, as laid down in section 1010 of the Penal Code (1910).

The writer confesses his inability to see any practical difference between the universal rule of "reasonable doubt," applicable in all criminal cases, and the special rule of "reasonable hypothesis," applicable to cases of circumstantial evidence. Whether dependent upon direct or circumstantial evidence, a conviction is unauthorized unless the jury believe that guilt is proved beyond a reasonable doubt; and so long as there is a reasonable hypothesis of innocence, a reasonable doubt of guilt exists. And where a jury is instructed that a verdict of guilty can not be legally found unless the evidence proves guilt beyond a reasonable doubt, this would seem to be tantamount to telling the jury that they could not legally convict unless the evidence excluded "every other reasonable hypothesis save that of the guilt of the accused."

But the law has made a difference between "reasonable doubt" and "reasonable hypothesis," and the Supreme Court has many times declared that, when a conviction is based alone on circumstantial evidence, it is reversible error for the trial judge to fail to instruct the jury that the evidence must exclude every reasonable hypothesis save that of guilt, although he has clearly charged that a conviction would be unauthorized unless the evidence proved the guilt of the accused beyond a reasonable doubt.

Judgment reversed.

THE CENTRAL RAILROAD AND BANKING CO. v. PHINAZEE
Supreme Court of Georgia
93 Ga. 488; 21 S.E. 66 (1893)

LOGAN E. BLECKLEY, Chief Justice.

There is no less scepticism in law than in theology. This court is called upon again and again for a fresh revelation on some legal truth which has already been revealed. After the cases of *Macon and Augusta R. R. Co. v. Mayes*, [citation omitted] *Singleton v. Southwestern R.R. Co.*, [citation omitted] and *Chattanooga, Rome and Columbus R. R. Co. v. Liddell*, [citation omitted] it would seem that there could be no reasonable doubt of the liability of a chartered railroad company permitting another company to run trains over its railway, and thus to use its franchise, to respond for any damage occasioned by negligence, whether its own or that of its lessee or licensee. Obviously the principle of those cases extends to an injury sustained by a passenger in consequence of a derailment of a train caused by negligence in failing to have and maintain a safe track. . . .

. . . A common carrier, who by negligence, injures a passenger, cannot shun, in whole or in part, liability to make compensation for the injury because the passenger was intoxicated, unless his being intoxicated contributed either to produce or aggravate the injury, and surely the carrier cannot complain that he failed in diligence to protect himself against the consequences of the carrier's negligence, if the exercise of diligence up to the measure of that which a prudent sober man could and would have exercised, under like circumstances, would not have been available. There is no rule of law which requires a passenger to preserve his capacity to act at all times as a prudent man would act. If an occasion arises by reason of the carrier's negligence when a prudent sober man could not, by the exercise of all ordinary diligence, protect himself, it would be of no consequence that a passenger injured by such negligence had by voluntary drunkenness incapacitated himself for the exercise of ordinary diligence. The loss of capacity to do that which, if done, would be unavailing, could not rationally count for an excuse to the carrier, or be chargeable to the passenger as a reason why he should not have compensation for his injuries. Morally it might be a grievous fault in him, but legally it could have no significance, inasmuch as the result of the carrier's negligence would have been the same with the presence of the capacity as it was in its absence. . . .

Judgment affirmed.

THE COCA-COLA COMPANY v. THE KOKE COMPANY OF AMERICA
United States Supreme Court
254 U.S. 143; 41 S.Ct. 113; 65 L.Ed. 189 (1920)

OLIVER WENDELL HOLMES, Justice.
This is a bill in equity brought by the Coca-Cola Company to prevent the infringement of its trade-mark Coca-Cola and unfair competition with it in its business of making and selling the beverage for which the trade-mark is used. The District Court gave the plaintiff a decree. . . . This was reversed by the Circuit Court of Appeals. . . . Subsequently a writ of certiorari was granted by this Court. . . .

It appears that after the plaintiff's predecessors in title had used the mark for some years it was registered under the Act of Congress of March 3, 1881, . . . Both the Courts below agree that subject to the one question to be considered the plaintiff has a right to equitable relief. Whatever may have been its original weakness, the mark for years has acquired a secondary significance and has indicated the plaintiff's product alone.

It is found that defendant's mixture is made and sold in imitation of the plaintiff's and that the word Koke was chosen for the purpose of reaping the benefit of the advertising done by the plaintiff and of selling the imitation as and for the plaintiff's goods. The only obstacle found by the Circuit Court of Appeals in the way of continuing the injunction granted below was its opinion that the trade-mark in itself and the advertisements accompanying it made such fraudulent representations to the public that the plaintiff had lost its claim to any help from the Court. . . .

Of course a man is not to be protected in the use of a device the very purpose and effect of which is to swindle the public. But the defects of a plaintiff do not offer a very broad ground for allowing another to swindle him. The defense relied on here should be scrutinized with a critical eye.

The main point is this: Before 1900 the beginning of the good will was more or less helped by the presence of cocaine, a drug that, like alcohol or caffeine or opium, may be described as a deadly poison or as a valuable item of the pharmacopoeia according to the rhetorical purposes in view. The amount seems to have been very small, but it may have been enough to begin a bad habit, and after the Food and Drug Act of June 30, 1906, c 3815, 34 Stat. 768, if not earlier, long before this suit was brought, it was eliminated from the plaintiff's compound.

Coca leaves still are used, to be sure, but after they have been subjected to a drastic process that removes from them every characteristic substance except a little tannin and still less chlorophyl. The cola nut, at best, on its side furnishes but a very small portion of the caffeine, which now is the only element that has appreciable effect. That comes mainly from other sources. It is argued that the continued use of the name imports a representation that has ceased to be true and that the representation is reinforced by a picture of coca leaves and cola nuts upon the label and by advertisements, which however were many years before this suit was brought, that the drink is an "ideal nerve tonic and stimulant," &c., and that thus the very thing sought to be protected is used as a fraud.

The argument does not satisfy us. We are dealing here with a popular drink not with a medicine, and although what has been said might suggest that its attraction lay in producing the expectation of a toxic effect the facts point to a different conclusion. Since 1900 the sales have increased at a very great rate corresponding to a like increase in advertising. The name now characterizes a beverage to be had at almost any soda fountain. It means a single thing coming from a single source, and well known to the community. It hardly would be too much to say that the drink characterizes the name as much as the name the drink. In other words Coca-Cola probably means to most persons the plaintiff's familiar product to be had everywhere rather than a compound of particular substances. . . . The coca leaves and whatever of cola nut is employed may be used to justify the continuance of the name or they may affect the flavor as the plaintiff contends, but before this suit was brought the plaintiff had advertised to the public that it must not expect and would not find cocaine, and had eliminated everything tending to suggest cocaine effects except the name and the picture of the leaves and nuts, which probably conveyed little or nothing to most who saw it. It appears to us that it would be going too far to deny the plaintiff relief against a palpable fraud because possibly here and there an ignorant person might call for the drink with the hope for incipient cocaine intoxication. . .

Decree reversed.

SEPMEIER v. TALLAHASSEE DEMOCRAT, INC.
District Court of Appeal of Florida, First District
461 So. 2d 193 (1984)

E. EARLE ZEHMER, Judge.

This is an appeal from a final order dismissing with prejudice a complaint alleging libel and service mark infringement. The trial court found the allegedly libelous statements privileged expressions of pure opinion. It also found no basis for a service mark infringement action. We affirm in part and reverse in part.

On May 20, 1983, *The Tallahassee Democrat* newspaper (Democrat) published a column[1] by Mary Ann Lindly, one of its regular columnists. The column was headlined "Leathergrams: Agony without the Ecstasy" and dealt, in part, with the novelty message delivery service, Leathergram.

---

[1] The column is reprinted below in its entirety:

Leathergrams: Agony without the Ecstasy

Streaking turned out to be, as one headline writer of the era predicted, "just another passing fanny."

Some say streaking started on the Florida State University Campus, a post-sexual-revolution springtime rite. Others say it originated at the University of Maryland but never caught on because it gets too cold there.

Wherever it started, streaking was hot for a while during March 1974. Spectators would gather almost nightly on Landis Green to witness the sensation that was putting FSU on the map-before the football team did. With the anticipation of those who look for leprechauns in the grass, they hoped to glimpse these Panlike figures whisk across the Green.

CHAPTER III: ALCOHOL, DRUGS & GAMBLING

The next day, the Democrat published a letter to the editor [2] which it captioned "Customer offended." The letter expressed the author's "unfortunate pleasure" in watching a Leathergram performance and urged businesses not to allow such entertainment during business hours.

What they got instead was a bunch of naked college men-with more courage than assets-climbing flagpoles, drinking beer and just hanging around. Then-Sheriff Raymond Hamlim was about the only one to take streaking very seriously, and except for the one fellow with an Indian headdress and maracas, the whole business lost its charm when it lost its spontaneity.

But at least streaking was free.

Today's exhibitionist equivalent is the Leathergram, and it will run you about $50 a shot.

I would like to reveal that I, for one, don't find these shows very sexy. No, let me go further. I find them excruciating.

Even Gov. Bob Graham was (almost) rendered speechless a while back when a lithe woman in Spandex, a dog collar and black boots roared on stage at Capital Press Club skits at the civic center. I was sitting close to one of Graham's bodyguards, who lurched forward when she lashed her whip. Alas, it never got any better than that.

Recently an editor was working her last day at the Democrat when the Machogram version of the Leathergram zoomed into the newsroom to bid her farewell. This pale, thin male in a cowboy outfit put his ghetto blaster on the floor by her desk, turned up the music and began to gyrate. While the bored hordes looked on, he shed everything but some very red bikini briefs.

Admittedly, it is worth a lot to hear a woman alternately shriek, "Oh, no. Oh, no" and "I don't believe this." And, yes, it worth something to be able to say for months on end: "You should've seen the look on her face."

But it is not worth $50.

For one thing, the show itself is interminable. Long after your grin muscles are aching with lactic-acid buildup, long after the wisecracks have waned and the puns begun to pale, these O-gram people dance on.

Removing his outfit piece by piece, the Machogram man in question revealed an underfed frame that did American manhood no great honor. And while I cannot speak for the male reaction to the Leathergram lady, the one I saw was no Nastassia Kinski.

But maybe that's what keeps the Leathergram business in business: The sanctity of sex is never in jeopardy. A business executive could go home at night and say to his wife, "Hi, dear. Guess what? A woman wearing whips and black boots came to the office today." And her response would be, "That's nice. Did you pick up the laundry on your way home?"

[2] The letter is reprinted below in its entirety:

Customer Offended

Last week I took my teen-age son for a hair cut at a local styling salon. We had the unfortunate pleasure of having to sit though [sic] a "leathergram."

This letter is not being written to hurt the business or to degrade a young person who thinks she needs to make a living in this manner.

I am writing to local business owners and managers. As a paying customer, my request is simple. Please do not allow this type of entertainment during business hours. Or at least tell your clients about the upcoming event.

While the "act" was going on, I took a good look at the people around me. A 65-year old woman became teary-eyed and her mouth began to quiver. It was as if she could hardly believe what she saw. Also a little boy, about 3 years old, told his mother he did not like the lady dancing and didn't want to watch. For them and for people like them, I write my letter.

To be invited to a private home or to a business before or after hours for such entertainment, at least gives an individual a choice. Business owners and managers, think about your customers. They are the ones who keep you in business.

ELLEN DAVIS

Fantasy Dancers, Inc., the corporation offering the Leathergram service, and its officers, Faye and Charles Sepmeier, filed suit on July 12, 1983, against the Democrat, its publisher, three of its editors, and Lindley. The complaint alleged the defendants libeled the plaintiffs by publication of the May 20, 1983, column and the May 21, 1983, letter to the editor. The complaint also alleged the use of the word Leathergram in the column unlawfully infringed upon Fantasy Dancers, Inc.'s registered service mark.

The Democrat filed a motion to dismiss the complaint. Following a hearing, the trial court issued a final order dismissing the complaint with prejudice.

Whether statements are privileged expressions of pure opinion or unprivileged mixed expressions of opinion is a question of law properly resolved by the trial court. . . . A privileged expression of pure opinion "occurs when the defendant makes a comment or opinion based on facts which are set forth in the article or which are otherwise known or available to the reader or listener as a member of the public." . . .

The plaintiffs contend that the article published by defendants is defamatory because it implies that the plaintiff Faye Sepmeier, the only messenger for

Leathergram, performs a striptease act, nude or nearly nude, incident to delivering Leathergram messages. This fact is false, they say, because the messenger is fully clothed at all times. They take exception to the trial court's legal conclusion that the article, taken as a whole, is an expression of pure opinion and, thus, privileged.

In *Smith v. Taylor County Publishing Co., Inc.,* [citation omitted] . . . the court held the newspaper column there involved was not merely an expression of pure opinion. In reaching that conclusion, the court reaffirmed the following rule:

> Although pure expression of opinion is constitutionally protected, mixed expression of opinion is not. Pure expression of opinion exists when an article expressing an opinion is published and sets forth, in the article, the facts on which the opinion is based or when the parties to the communication are aware of the facts or assume their existence and the opinion is clearly based on those facts. Mixed expression of opinion exists when a published statement containing an opinion is made and is not based on facts set forth in the article, or assumed facts and, therefore, implies the existence of some other undisclosed facts on which the opinion is based. . .

A statement that a person is clothed or is nude obviously constitutes a statement of fact, not opinion. A statement that a person removes his or her clothing to reveal the naked body in whole or in part is a statement of fact, not opinion. The article does not state that the Leathergram messenger is fully clothed; rather, it implies the contrary. The reference to a "lithe woman in Spandex, a dog collar, and black boots" is not the equivalent of a statement that the messenger is at all times fully clothed. Spandex is a fabric, not a garment, and it may be used in making garments to cover the entire body or virtually none of the body, depending on design and intent. Hence, the meaning of the quoted description must be determined in context with the immediately following paragraphs of the article described in the "Machogram version of the Leathergram" as a male messenger who, while gyrating to music, "shed everything but some very red bikini briefs." We can only conclude that the article equates Machogram and Leathergram as being essentially the same type presentation:

> Removing his outfit piece by piece, the Machogram man in question revealed an underfed frame that did American manhood no great honor. And while I cannot speak for the male reaction to the Leathergram lady, the one I saw was no Nastassia Kinski. [3]

The article concludes with a reference to the appearance at the office of "a woman wearing whips and black boots," statement also implying that the Leathergram messenger is, at best, scantily clothed. Moreover, the reference at the beginning of the article to "streaking," described as "a bunch of naked college men," with the comparison that "today's exhibitionist equivalent is the Leathergram," further reinforces an obvious implication of fact that the Leathergram messenger is nude or nearly so. Read in totality, the article strongly implies, as a predicate to the opinions expressed, the material fact that the Leathergram messenger wears little, if any, clothing in the performance of her act.

Appellees have argued that all material facts upon which the columnist's opinion is based "are explicitly stated" in two sentences concerning the Leathergram episode with Governor Graham:

> Even Gov. Bob Graham was (almost) rendered speechless a while back when a lithe woman in Spandex, a dog collar and black boots roared on stage at Capital Press Club skits at the civic center. I was sitting close to one of Graham's

---

[3] The purpose of this reference is not entirely clear. Nastassia Kinski is a movie star of some reknown and has starred in at least one "R" rated movie described in a recent cable television guide as involving nude scenes.

> body guards, who lurched forward when she
> lashed her whip.

We respectfully disagree with this limited conception of the facts material to the opinion expressed because it fails to conform to the test from *Smith* that "the court must consider all the words used, not merely a particular phrase or sentence. . ."

We have no quarrel with the right of this columnist to compare the Leathergram with "streaking" and Machogram for the purpose of expressing a personal opinion that the messenger presentations described are not worth the cost of fifty dollars and are as socially unacceptable, if not downright reprehensible, as "streaking." If the essential facts forming the predicate for this comparison and opinion had been fully, fairly and truthfully stated, the comparison would constitute a privileged expression of pure opinion. But such was not the case here.

This columnist compared "streaking" (described as "pure nakedness"), Machogram (a striptease down to near nakedness-"red bikini"), and Leathergram (unstated state of nakedness-" a lithe woman in Spandex, dog collar and black boots") and thereby made the Leathergram messenger's state of dress a material fact underlying the comparison being drawn as a basis for the pure opinion being expressed. Having done so, the article did not explain that there was any material difference between the dress of the Leathergram messenger and Machogram messengers or "streakers," but necessarily left the Leathergram messenger's state of dress to implication from the descriptions being compared.

It necessarily follows that the article constituted mixed expression of opinion under the rule in *Smith* that "mixed expression of opinion exists when a published statement containing an opinion is made and is not based on facts set forth in the article," but "implies the existence of some other undisclosed facts on which the opinion is based" [citation omitted]. We venture no opinion on whether plaintiffs should ultimately prevail in this action before a jury; we conclude only that plaintiff should have a chance to convince them.

It is difficult to understand the plaintiff's argument concerning the May 21, 1983, letter to the editor. The plaintiffs do not contend on appeal that the letter or its caption is defamatory. They argue instead that publication of the letter the day after publication of the column was somehow defamatory. We disagree and reject this argument for the obvious reason that publication of nondefamatory statements does not provide the basis for a defamation cause of action. . . .

That portion of the judgment dismissing the cause of action for defamation based on the publication of the letter to the editor and the cause of action for service mark infringement is affirmed. The dismissal of the defamation action based on libelous statements in the published column is reversed, and the case is remanded for further proceedings thereon.

AFFIRMED in part and REVERSED in part.

AN ACTE CONCERYNING PUNYSSHEMENT OF
BEGGERS & VACABUNDS
Statutes of The Realm of England
22 HENRY VIII, Chap. 12 (1530)

WHERE in all places throughe out this Realme of Englande, Vacabundes & Beggers have of longe tyme increased & dayly do increase in great & excessyve nombres by the occasyon of ydelnes, mother & rote of all vyces, wherby hathe insurged & spronge & dayly insurgethe & spryngeth contynuall theftes murders & other haynous offences & great enormytes to the high displeasure of God the inquyetation & damage of the Kyngs People & to the marvaylous disturbance of the Comon Weale of this Realme.

And whereas many & sondry goode lawes, streyte statuts & orden*ncs have ben before this tyme devysed & made as well by the Kyng our Soverign Lorde as also by divers his most noble pregenytours Kyngs of Englande for the most necessary & due reformacion of the permysses, yet that notwythstondyng the sayde nombers of vacabundes & beggers be not sene in any pertie to be nynysshed, but rather dayly augmentyd & encreased into greate routes & companyes as evydently & manyfestly yt dothe & maye appere;

Be it therfore enacted by the Kyng oure Sovereign Lorde & by the Lordes Spuall & Temporall & the C mons in this present perliament assembled & by aucterhoryte of the same; That the Justices of the Peace of all & synguler the Shires of England wythin the lymytts of theyr Commyssions & all other Justyces of Peace Mayres Sheryffs Baylyffs & other Offycers of all & every Cytie Borough Ryddyngs or Franches wythin the Realme of England wythin the lymytes of theyre aucterhorytes, shall from tyme to tyme as often as nede shall requyre by theyre discresions devyde themselfes wythin the sayde Shires Cites Boroughes Ryddyngs or Frauncheses. . .

. . . & so beyng devyded shall make dylygent serche & inquyre of all aged poore & impotent persones whiche lyve or of necessyte be compelled to lyve by Almes of the charyte of the people that be or shalbe hereafter abydyng wythyn. . .

. . . wythin the lymytts of theyre dyvysion & after & upon suche serche made the sayde Justics of Peace Mayres Shireffs Baylyffs & other officers that ys to saye, every of them wythin theire lymytts of theire aucterhorytes wherunto they be devyded shall have power & aucterhoryte by theyre dyscrecions to enable to begge wythin suche Hundrede Rape Wapentake Cytie Towne Parysshe or other lymytts as they shall apoynte of the sayde impotent persones whiche they shall fynde & thynke most convenient wythyn the lymytts of theyre dyvision to lyve of the charyte & almes of the People & gyve in commaundement to every suche aged & ympotent begger by them enabled that none of them shall begge wythout other lymytts to them so apoynted & shall also regester & wryte the names of every suche ympotent begger (by them apoynted) in a bill or rolle indented the one parte therof to remayn wyth them selfe & the other parte by them to be certefyed before the Justices of Peace att the next Sessions.

And yf any suche impotent person so authorysed to begge, do begge in any other place than wythin suche lymytts that he shalbe assigned unto, that then the Justics of Peace Mayres Shireffs Baylyffs Constables & all other the Kyngs Offycers & Mynysters shall by theyre dyscrescions punysshe all suche persones by imprysonament in the Stockes by the space of ii dayes & ii nyghtes, gyvyng them but onely breade & water, & after that, cause every suche person to be sworne to retourne ageyn wythout delaye to the Hundrede Rape Wapentake Cytie Boroughe Towne Parysshe or Franches where they be aucterhorysed to begge in.

AND YT YS ENACTED That no suche ympotent person (as ys above sayde) after the Feast of the Natyvyte of Seynt John the Baptyst next comyng shall begge wythin any parte of this Realme, excepte he be authorized by wrytyng under Seale as ys above sayde. And yf any suche ympotent person after the sayde Feast of Seynt John, be vagrant & goo abeggyng havyng no such letter under seale as ys above specefyed, that [than[1]] the Constables & all other ynhabytaunts wythin such Towne or Paryshe where suche person shall begge, shall cause every suche begger to be taken & brought to the next Justyce of Peace or Highe Constable of the Hundrede; and therupon the sayde Justyce of Peace or Highe Constable shall commaunde the sayde Constables & other inhabytaunts of the Towne or Parysshe whiche shall bryng before hym any suche begger, that they shall strype hym naked from the myddel upwarde & cause hym to be whypped wythyn the Towne where he was taken or wythin some other towne where the same Justice or Highe Constable shall apoynte if it shall seme to the discretion of the sayde Justice of Peace or Highe Constable that yt be convenyent so to pynysshe suche begger to hym brought:

And yf not, then to commaunde suche begger to be sette in the Stocks in the same Tone or Paryshe where he was taken by the space of iv dayes & iii nights there to have onely breade & water; and therupon the sayde Justyce or Highe Constable afore whom suche beggar shalbe brought, shall lymytt to hym a place to begge in, & gyve to hym a letter under seale in forme above remembred & swere hym to departe & repayre thither ymedyatly after his punysshement to hym executed.

AND be yt farther enacted by the aucterhortye aforsayde that yf any person or persones beyng hole & myghtie in body & able to laboure, at any tyme after the sayde feast of Seynt John be taken in beggyng in any parte of this Realme, or yf any Man or Woman beyng hole & myghty in body & able to laboure navyng no Lande [Master[2]] nor usyng any lawful marchaundyse crafte or mystery, wherby he myght gette his lyvyng after the same feast, be vagarant & can gyve none rekenyng howe he dothe lefully gett his lyvyng, that than yt shalbe lefull to the Constables & all other the Kyngs Offycers Mynysters & Subjects of every Towne Paryshe & Hamlet to arest the sayde Vacabounds &

---

[1] then O.
[2] Maister O.

ydell persons & them bryng to any of the Justics of Peace of the same Shyre or Libtie, or els to the Highe Constable of the Hundrede Rape or Wapentake wythin whyche suche persones shalbe taken; and yf he be taken wythin any Cyte or Towen Corporate, than to be brought before the Mayre, Shereffs or Baylyffs of every suche Towne Corporate;

AND that every suche Justyce of Peace Highe Constable, Mayres, Shereffs & Bayleffs by their dyscretions shall cause every suche ydell person so to hym brought to be had to the next market Towne or other place, where the sayde Justics of Peace, Highe Constable, Mayres, Baylyffs or other Officers shall thynke most convenyent by his or there discretions & there to be tyed to the end of a Carte naked and be beten wyth Whyppes thoroughe oute the same Market Towne or other place tyll his Body be blody by reason of suche whyppyng; and after suche punysshement & whyppng had, the person so punysshed by the dyscretion of the Justice of Peace, Highe Constable, Mayre Sheryffs, Baylyffs & other Officers, afore whom suche person shalbe brought, shalbe enyoyned upon his othe to retourne forthewyth wythout delaye in the nexte & streyght waye to the place where he was borne, or where he last dwelled before the same punysshement by the space of iij yeres & there put hym selfe to laboure, lyke as a trewe man oweth to doo; and after that done every suche person so punysshed & ordered shall have a letter sealed wyth the Seale of the Hundrede Rape Wapentake, Cyte, Boroughe, Towne, Libtie, or Fraunches, wherin he shalbe punysshed wytnessyng, that he hath bene punysshed accordyng to this estatute & conteynyng the daye and place of his punysshement & the place wherunto he ys lymytted to goo & by what tyme he is lymytted to come thither, wythin whiche tyme he may lawfully begge by the waye, shewyng the same letter, & otherwyse not:

And yf he do not accomplysshe the order to hym apoynted by the sayde letter, than to be eftsones taken & whypped & so as often as any defaute shall be founde in hym cont*ry to the order of this Estatute, in every place to be taken & whypped tyll he be repayred where he was borne or where he last dwelled by the space of three yere and there put his body to laboure for his lyvyng or otherwyse trewly gett his lyvyng wythout beggyng as long as he ys able so to doo; & yf the person so whypped be an ydell person & no common begger [than[1]] after suche whippyng he shall be kepte in the Stocks till he hathe founde suertie to goo to servyce or ells to laboure after the dyscretion of the sayde Justice of Peace, Mayres, Shireffs, Baylyffs, Highe Constables or other suche Offycers afore whome any suche ydell person beyng no comen begger shalbe brought, yf by the dyscretion of the same Justice of Peace, Mayer, Shyreff, Bayly, High Constable, or ther suche hedde offycer, yt be so thought convenyent & that the partie so punysshed be able to fynde surety or ells to be ordered & sworne to repayer to the place where he was borne or where he last dwelled by the space of three yeres & to have lyke letter & such further punysshement yf he efstones offende this Estatue as ys above apoynted to & for the comen strong and able beggers, and so from tyme to tyme to be ordered & punysshed tyll he put his body to laboure or otherwyse gette his lyvyng trewly accordyng to the Lawe:

...AND BE YT ENACTED by the aucterhoryte aforsayde that Scolers of the Universities of Oxford & Cambrydge that goo about beggyng, not beyng aucterhorysed under the Seale of the sayde Universities, by the Commyssary Chaunceloure or Vichauncelloure of the same; & all & syngular Shypmen pertendyng losses of theyre shyppes & goodes of the see goyng about the contrey beggyng wythout suffcyent aucterthoryte wytnessyng the same, shall be punysshed & ordered in maner & fourme as ys above rehersed of stronge beggers; AND that all Proctours & Pardoners goyng about in any contrey or contrayes without suffycyent authoryte, & all ydell personnes goyng aboute in any contreys or abydyng in any Cytie Boroughe or Towne, some of them usyng dyvers & subtyle craftye & unlawfull games & playes & some of them feynyng themselfes to have knowledge in Physke, Physnamye, Palmestrye, or other craftye scyences wherby they beare the people in hande, that they can tell theire destenyes deceases & fortunes & suche other lyke fantasticall ymagenacions to the greate deceypte of the Kyngs Subjects, shall upon examynacion had before two Justices of Peace wherof the one shalbe of the Quoz yf he by provable Wytnes be founde giltie of any suche deceytes be punysshed by whyppng at two dayes together, after the maner before rehersed: And yf he efstones offend in the sayde Offence or any lyke Offence, then to be scourged two dayes & the thirde day to be put upon the pyllory from ix of the Clocke tyll xi before none of the same daye, & to have one of his eares cutte of; and yf he offende the thyrde tyme to have lyke pynysshement whyppyng, stondyng on the Pillary & to have his other eare cutte off, & that Justics of Peace have lyke authoryte in every libertie & fraunches wythin theyre Shires where they be Justics of peace for the execution of this acte in every parte therof, as they shall have wythout the Libertie or Franchyse...

... AND FURTHERMORE be yt enacted, that yf any person or persones at eny tyme herafter gyve any herborowe monye or lodgyng to any beggers beyng stronge & able in theyre bodyes to worke whyche order them selfes cont'ry to the fourme of this estatute, that every suche person so doyng beyng suffycyently proved or presented afore any Justice of Peace shall make suche fyne to the Kyng, as by the dyscretion of the sayd Justices of Peace at theyre generall Sessions shalbe assessed;

...AND yt ys enacted yf any person or persons so beyng delyvered out of pryson at any tyme after the sayde feast do begge not havyng the sayde letter sealed in fourme above sayde, or begge cont'ry to the tenoure of the same letter, That [than[1]] he shalbe taken, ordered & whipped in every behalfe lyke as ys above apoynted for stronge beggers & that to be done & executed by suche as be above lymytted to do the same upon strong beggers, & in suche wyse & upon suche peyne as ys afore lymytted for none execution of the punysshement of stronge beggers...

REDD v. THE STATE OF GEORGIA
Court of Appeals of Georgia
7 Ga. App. 575; 67 S.E. 709 (1910)

ARTHUR GRAY POWELL, J.

The defendants were prosecuted under the Penal Code of 1895, §390, which provides, among other things, that "any person who shall be guilty of open lewdness, or any notorious act of public indecency, tending to debauch the morals," shall be punished as for a misdemeanor. The charge is that the defendants were guilty of a notorious act of public indecency, tending to debauch the morals, in that they, in a public place, adjacent to a highway and in the presence of a lady and several children, caused a bull and cow to copulate.

The proof was that these two men, having been entrusted with a cow that was in heat, for the purpose of taking her to the bull which was confined in a pasture adjacent to the public road, put the cow in the pasture, and tied her to the fence next to the road, and called the bull to her there. The copulation between the animals thus took place publicly, though there was a branch and a thicket about a hundred feet away in which the act could have been done privately. About thirty feet away, and just across the road, were a woman and several children. The defendants denied seeing these persons, but the proof was against them as to that.

There was ample evidence to sustain the proposition that the defendants wilfully, or at least in reckless disregard of the sensibilities of the woman and the children, put the bull to the cow in their presence. The road seems to have been a much frequented highway, for several persons passed in vehicles while the act complained of was in progress. . .

It is true, too, that it is contrary to the genius of our law, as well as repugnant to the popular notions of juridic justice, that punishable offenses should be left undefined. Intuitively the courts find themselves seeking for and declaring, by construction, limitations in the way of definition, where the legislature has spoken loosely. In the case of *McJunkins v. State*, [citation omitted] it was said: "The term 'public indecency' has no fixed legal meaning -- is vague and indefinite, and can not in itself imply a definite offense. . . ."

The reticence of the court to violate the chastity of their reports with narratives of indecent acts may account for the fact that we are able to find so few reported cases of public indecency not involving exposure of the person. For example in *Brigman v. State*, a conviction for public indecency was sustained, but the printed report contains no account of the specific act by which the defendant violated the statute. . . . Indeed, in the old and frequently referred to case of Sir Charles Sedley, which was tried during the reign of Charles II (see 1 Siderf. 168), the offense of public indecency alleged against the prisoner was not only that he stood naked on a balcony in a public part of London, but also that he threw down certain "offensive liquor" among the people passing along the highway. . . .

After careful reflection upon the matter, we have reached the conclusion that our statute, based as it is upon the common law, is broad enough to cover all notorious public and indecent conduct, tending to debauch the public morals, even though it be unattended by any exposure of the human body. If this is not so, then our law, broadly as it has been drawn, is not adequate to protect the public in this State from many acts shockingly obscene and tending to lower the moral standards. . . .

Can it be said that it would not be a notorious act of public indecency if, in a theater or other similar place, one should exhibit trained animals, say monkeys dressed as men and women, and cause them to go through the act of sexual intercourse in the presence of the audience? Can it be doubted that this would tend to debauch the public morals? Yet it would involve no exposure of the human body. Cases even worse than this, -- cases so extreme that even the duty of speaking plainly, imposed upon us by the nature of the question here involved, would not excuse the indelicacy of mentioning them, -- and yet involving no exposure of the person, may be imagined. . .

However, we should keep in mind that the word "indecency," as used in the statute, has not so broad a meaning as it has in popular speech. An act may be unconventional, may be such as to give offense to the finer sensibilities, may relate to acts which would bring a blush (real or feigned) to the cheeks of the prudish, and yet not be indecent. To determine whether an act is indecent within the purview of the statute, the time, the place, the circumstances, and the motives of the actors must be considered. . .

We believe in this case that these defendants, even though they were possessed of less than normal moral sensibilities, knew that it was indecent for them to put the bull to the cow in plain view of the highway and in the presence of this lady and her children, some of them little girls, when the necessary performance could have been accomplished privately with but little trouble and inconvenience.

As was said by Chief Justice Perkins in the case of *Ardery v. State*, [citation omitted] "Immediately after the fall of Adam, there seems to have sprung up in his mind an idea that there was such a thing as decency and such a thing as indecency; that there was a distinction between them; and since that time the ideas of decency and indecency have been instinctive in, and, indeed, parts of, humanity." As tending to preserve chastity, society has erected as one of its inviolable decencies that sexual intercourse, lawful or unlawful, and all things directly suggestive of it, shall be kept private, and has established that it is a shameful and an indecent thing for a person of one sex, especially of the male sex, intentionally, publicly, and unnecessarily to bring before the gaze or hearing of a person of the opposite sex the act of sexual intercourse, or things closely associated with it. Anything which tends to break down this standard of decency tends to promote unchastity, and thereby to debauch the public morals.

If one man may, without violating the law, deliberately cause his beasts to copulate on the highway and in the very presence of one woman rightfully there, another may lawfully bring his beasts for the same purpose to the school grounds where children are assembled, or to the church yard while the congregation is there. Can such things be allowed without offending the common instincts of decency in the strictest sense of the word, or without tending to impair the present standard of morals recognized as proper between the sexes?

It is true, as suggested by distinguished counsel for the plaintiffs in error, that according to the construction here announced, the patriarch Jacob, standing at the public watering place and holding the striped rods before Laban's bulls, rams, and he-goats when they leaped, in order that the young might be marked with stripes, would have been guilty of public indecency. Perhaps so. But as able counsel for the State has replied, it will not do to measure modern morals according to the standards of ancient and biblical times. King Solomon with his thousand wives would not be tolerated in Georgia; and King David, he the man after God's own heart, could hardly justify his whole life according to the provisions of the Penal Code of this State.

Our standards of morals have advanced since then, and our standards of decency have advanced accordingly. The time, -- the prevailing state of public morality at the particular period, -- more largely than any other one thing, determine what the decencies and indecencies of that particular day and generation shall be. Many things regarded (by law as well as by secular opinion) a hundred years ago as being indecent are not so regarded now; and on the other hand, the present age has developed decencies and indecencies unknown to or unobserved by our forefathers.

We conclude that according to the prevailing social standards in this State, and according to the notions of decency and indecency now commonly recognized among our people, the act of the defendants was a notorious act of public indecency, tending to debauch the morals. This, of course, is based on the assumption that the defendants had the intention of obtruding the spectacle upon the gaze of those present, or that they acted so wantonly or recklessly in the matter as to raise the legal imputation of such an intention. The act of the animals was not the thing that was indecent. The indecent thing was the conduct of the defendants in intentionally or wantonly displaying this act to the woman and the children. A moment's thought will develop this distinction. A lady of refined sensibilities, who, though in mixed company, should casually come upon animals in the sexual act, might feel a sense of shame, her refined tastes might be offended; yet it would be to attribute a mock modesty to her to say that her sense of decency was outraged. Yet, if some man were to catch the animals so engaged, and bring them before her and say, either by spoken language or by conduct capable of conveying an equivalent meaning, "Look at this," her sense of decency would be offended -- not by the act of the animals, but by the act of the man.

Judgment affirmed.

THE CITY OF CLINTON v. SMITH
Supreme Court of Mississippi
493 So. 2d 331 (1986)

JAMES L. ROBERTSON, Justice

At issue today is whether the people of the City of Clinton, Mississippi, have taken steps legally adequate to ban the sale of beer in their community. In a June 1985 referendum election, 52.5 percent of those casting ballots voted "No," that the sale of beer should be made illegal. The Circuit Court of Hinds County subsequently voided the election by reason of "irregularities" found to have existed in "the calling for a beer sales referendum . . . and in the subsequent voting upon that issue". In substantial part, we affirm.

The controversy surrounding the sale of beer in the City of Clinton, Mississippi has raged for some time. It appears to have been augmented by a recent annexation which brought within the City's jurisdiction a number of business establishments which theretofore had offered canned and bottled beer for sale under relatively lenient restrictions.

The sale of beer was a regular subject of discussion between the Clinton's Mayor and Board of Aldermen for the latter part of 1984. An ad hoc committee studied the controversy. Its work appears to have given impetus to efforts to call a citywide referendum on the issue. A moratorium was approved by the Mayor and Board regarding enforcement of the old ordinance and that moratorium was extended well into 1985. . . .

. . . On April 2, 1985, [the] city clerk, reported to the Mayor and Board that a combination of. . . purging of 30 names from the registration and poll books plus the addition of 126 registered voters to the petitions brought the number of registered voters signing the petition up to the required 20 percent. . . .

The special election was held June 4, 1985, and in due course thereafter the Elections Commissions for the City of Clinton certified to the Mayor and Board the following results:

FOR THE SALE OF BEER 2115
AGAINST THE SALE OF BEER 2337

. . . [T]he Mayor and Board then approved an order prohibiting the sale of beer of an alcoholic content of not more than four percent (4%) by weight in the City of Clinton, Mississippi, effective July 18, 1985.

On June 28, 1985, C.E. Smith filed with the Circuit Court of the First Judicial District of Hinds County, Mississippi, his bill of exceptions, thus timely perfecting his appeal. . . . On July 16, 1985, the Circuit Court found that

> Irregularities exist in the calling for a beer sales referendum for the City of Clinton and in the subsequent voting upon that issue.

The court thereupon voided the referendum election and the petition calling for same. . . .

III.

Our law is not and must never be regarded as an end in and of itself but as a means to positive societal ends. One of those ends is the tolerant accommodation of the conflicting values, beliefs, fears and self-interests of a pluralistic people. We seek to structure and administer our law that we be enabled better to live and let live. This being so, rather than deliver an arid legal opinion, we regard it as appropriate that we have in mind that ambiguous slice of life implicated in today's controversy.

This case is but the latest in our people's seemingly unending struggle over the sale and consumption of alcoholic beverages. Few issues have so tested our fidelity to law, nor presented greater tensions within our law's capacity to accommodate the will of the majority with respect for the privacy, integrity and
sensibilities of the individual. We have expended untold quantities of time, energy, oratory and money battling the bottle, and as this case makes clear the end is not in sight.

The lessons of three thousand years of the history of Western civilization are at least two: (1) that strong drink will be consumed by our people in varying quantities regardless of what the law may provide and (2) that such consumption will, as it always has, disturb us and our neighbors in forms ranging from inconvenience to tragedy, which from time to time will motivate some to employ the law to ban it.

The spirit besieged today has long been with us. In Xenophon's *Anabasis* penned in 398 B.C. we find these words:

> They had beer to drink, very strong when not
> mixed with water, but agreeable to those accus-
> tomed to it.

Beer has had its poetic defenders over the centuries. We recall John Still, bishop of Bath and Wells, fellow of Christ's College in the late Sixteenth Century, for his lusty appreciation of "jolly good ale and old" in his poem *In Praise of Ale*. Of the power of malt, A.E. Housman perceived that

> Many a peer of England brews livelier liquor
> than the Muse, and malt does more than Milton
> can to justify God's ways to man.

Ben Jonson regarded beer an inferior drink. It has always cost less than other alcoholic beverages, and for this reason has enjoyed widespread popularity among working class people and the poor. College students throughout the

Western world -- from the tables down at Mory's to Heidelberg's Inn of the Three Golden Apples, from the Warehouse to the Crossroads to the End Zone -- have had a special affection for beer, the encounter with which is almost a required rite of passage to young adulthood. It has emboldened many a student to olympian sophomoric heights, never to be forgotten nor, 'tis hoped, repeated. This in mind, as well that the scene of today's controversy is a college town, we recall Richard Hovey's tolerant reminder

> that God is not censorious when his children
> have their fling.

More soberly, Thomas Jefferson, almost as famous as a connoisseur of fine wines as he was a political leader and theorist, wrote of beer in 1815:

> I wish to scc this beverage become common
> instead of whiskey which kills one-third of our
> citizens and ruins their families.

Not even beer always produces harmless endings, as the legal reports of this state and nation, reflecting as they do only the tip of the iceberg, are replete with cases of persons who have imbibed excessively and inflicted serious personal injury, wrongful death, and engaged in destructive and seemingly senseless criminal activity including murder, manslaughter, aggravated assault, and threats of bodily harm to others. We put our heads in the sand if we ignore the darker side of beer.

The struggle to ban beer and other forms of booze suggests further reflections. Barroom settings and the availability of a choice of physiological aids have provided credible vehicles our poets, playwrights and philosophers have used to penetrate our souls. W.H. Auden begins *The Age of Anxiety* with four wartime lonelies in a New York bar and by the time Malin watches the sun rise from behind the East River has produced a powerful and prophetic declaration of hope, grounded in the sacrifice of the Christ. Eugene O'Neill employs a like setting as *The Iceman Cometh* teaches that the "lie of the pipe dream . . . [is] what gives life," and confronts the inevitability of death as have few others. Albert Camus chooses an Amsterdam bar in *The Fall* from which his fallen lawyer, Jean Baptiste Clamence, teaches us that genuine and unreserved personal penitence is the sole valid prerequisite to "the right to judge others".

In more popular mediums, the prime time television series, *Cheers* and Billy Joel's recent song, "Piano Man," employ the barroom genre to make us laugh, cry and understand life. Without these and so many others, we would be the poorer. Yet we are poorer for the hardship, misery, crime and tragedy occasionally the proximate result of excessive consumption of alcoholic beverages. Our experience with strong drink is as rich with complexity and ambiguity as it is inevitable.

CHAPTER III: ALCOHOL, DRUGS & GAMBLING

Our law is the witness and external deposit of the values and culture of our society. Seldom has our law attempted to regulate an area of our lives where our values have been so in conflict. The best known expression of that value conflict in this state is the 1952 Whiskey Speech of former Circuit Judge Noah S. Sweat, Jr., of Corinth. That speech blends the sober with the delightful and bears recitation in its entirety.

My Friends:

I had not intended to discuss this controversial subject at this particular time. However, I want you to know that I do not shun controversy. On the contrary, I will take a stand on any issue at any time, regardless of how fraught with controversy it might be. You have asked me how I feel about whiskey. All right, here is how I feel about whiskey . . .

If when you say whiskey you mean the devil's brew, the poison scourge, the bloody monster, that defiles innocence, dethrones reason, destroys the home, creates misery and poverty, yea, literally takes the bread from the mouths of little children; if you mean the evil drink that topples the Christian man and woman from the pinnacle of righteous, gracious living into the bottomless pit of degradation, and despair, and shame, and helplessness, and hopelessness, then certainly I am against it.

But,

If when you say whiskey you mean the oil of conversation, the philosophic wine, the ale that is consumed when good fellows get together, that puts a song in their hearts and laughter on their lips, and the warm glow of contentment in their eyes; if you mean Christmas cheer; if you mean the stimulating drink that puts the spring into the old gentleman's step on a frosty, crispy morning; if you mean the drink which enables a man to magnify his joy, and his happiness, and to forget, if only for a little while, life's great tragedies, and heartaches, and sorrows; if you mean that drink, the sale of which pours into our treasuries untold millions of dollars, which are used to provide tender care for our little crippled children, our blind, or deaf, our dumb, our pitiful aged and infirm; to build highways and hospitals and schools, then certainly I am for it.

This is my stand. I will not retreat from it. I will not compromise. [1]

Informed by these thoughts, we proceed to our institutional responsibility: the right interpretation and application of our law regarding beer sales referendum elections. . . .

V.

Our law regulates our conduct. It modifies our behavior. It accommodates our conflicting interests. When we employ law to these ends in an area of life, as here so rich in historical conflict, ambiguity, passion and divergent perceptions of the right, its seviceability is severely tested. Ofttimes the most we may hope to achieve is a regime of procedural fairness.

Our legislature had procedural fairness among its foremost goals as it in 1950 enacted what has become Miss. Code Ann. § 67-3-9 (1972). The legal structure within which this controversy must be adjudged has been provided in that legislative enactment. Legality of the sale of beer in a municipality of over 2,500 population may be determined in an election. Before the governing body of any such municipality has authority to call any such election, it must receive petitions "containing the names of twenty per centum (20%) of the duly qualified voters of such city asking for such election". Miss. Code Ann. § 67-3-9 (1972).

If such petitions are received, the election "shall be ordered," provided there has been no such election within the preceding five years and providing further that thirty days' public notice of the election shall be given. The statute further mandates that the municipality's governing body shall enact such ordinance as may be appropriate to implement the will of the citizenry as expressed in the election. . . .

---

[1] Judge Sweat's Whiskey Speech, together with an account of its origins, appear in M. Hughes, *Judge Sweat And "The Original Whiskey Speech,"* The Jurist (Vol. I, No. 2, Spring, 1986) at pp. 16-17.

Specially at issue is the authority of the Board to consider the 126 names submitted on March 26, 1985, and certified by the clerk as being those of registered voters. In the context of the facts of the case at bar, we consider that the Board handled the matter correctly. . . .

AFFIRMED IN PART; REVERSED AND REMANDED IN PART. . . .

ARMIS E. HAWKINS, Presiding Justice, specially concurring:

I concur in the result.

For my part I would have preferred that Part III be omitted from the opinion.

UNITED STATES v. ONE BOOK CALLED "ULYSSES"
United States District Court, S.D. New York
5 F. Supp. 182 (1933)

JOHN MUNRO WOOLSEY, District Judge.

The motion for a decree dismissing the libel herein is granted, and, consequently, of course, the government's motion for a decree of forfeiture and destruction is denied. Accordingly a decree dismissing the libel without costs may be entered herein.

I. The practice followed in this case is in accordance with the suggestion made by me in the case of United States v. One Book Entitled "Contraception" (D.C.) 51 F.2d 525, and is as follows:

After issue was joined by the filing of the claimant's answer to the libel for forfeiture against *Ulysses*, a stipulation was made between the United States Attorney's office and the attorneys for the claimant providing:

1. That the book *Ulysses* should be deemed to have been annexed to and to have become part of the libel just as if it had been incorporated in its entirety therein.
2. That the parties waived their right to a trial by jury.
3. That each party agreed to move for decree in its favor.
4. That on such cross-motions the court might decide all the questions of law and fact involved and render a general finding thereon.

5. That on the decision of such motions the decree of the court might be entered as if it were a decree after trial.

It seems to me that a procedure of this kind is highly appropriate in libels such as this for the confiscation of books. It is an especially advantageous procedure in the instant case because, on account of the length of *Ulysses* and the difficulty of reading it, a jury trial would have been an extremely unsatisfactory, if not an almost impossible method of dealing with it.

II. I have read *Ulysses* once in its entirety and I have read those passages of which the government particularly complains several times. In fact, for many weeks, my spare time has been devoted to the consideration of the decision which my duty would require me to make in this matter.

Ulysses is not an easy book to read or to understand. But there has been much written about it, and in order properly to approach the consideration of it is advisable to read a number of other books which have now become its satellites. The study of *Ulysses* is, therefore, a heavy task.

III. The reputation of *Ulysses* in the literary world, however, warranted my taking such time as was necessary to enable me to satisfy myself as to the intent with which the book was written, for, of course, in any case where a book is claimed to be obscene it must first be determined, whether the intent with which it was written was what is called, according to the usual phrase, pornographic, that is, written for the purpose of exploiting obscenity.

If the conclusion is that the book is pornographic, that is the end of the inquiry and forfeiture must follow.

But in *Ulysses*, in spite of its unusual frankness, I do not detect anywhere the leer of the sensualist. I hold, therefore, that it is not pornographic.

IV. In writing *Ulysses*, Joyce sought to make a serious experiment in a new, if not wholly novel, literary genre. He takes persons of the lower middle class living in Dublin in 1904 and seeks, not only to describe what they did on a certain day in June of that year as they went about the city bent on their usual occupations, but also to tell what many of them thought about the while.

Joyce has attempted--it seems to me, with astonishing success--to show how the screen of consciousness with its ever-shifting kaleidoscopic impressions carries, as it were on a plastic palimpsest, not only what is in the focus of each man's observation of the actual things about him, but also in a penumbral zone residue of past impressions, some recent and some drawn up by association from the domain of the subconscious. He shows how each of these impressions affects the life and behavior of the character which he is describing.

CHAPTER III: ALCOHOL, DRUGS & GAMBLING

What he seeks to get is not unlike the result of a double or, if that is possible, a multiple exposure on a cinema film, which would give a clear foreground with a background visible but somewhat blurred and out of focus in varying degrees.

To convey by words an effect which obviously lends itself more appropriately to a graphic technique, accounts, it seems to me, for much of the obscurity which meets a reader of *Ulysses*. And it also explains another aspect of the book, which I have further to consider, namely, Joyce's sincerity and his honest effort to show exactly how the minds of his characters operate.

If Joyce did not attempt to be honest in developing the technique which he has adopted in *Ulysses*, the result which would be psychologically misleading and thus unfaithful to his chosen technique. Such an attitude would be artistically inexcusable.

It is because Joyce has been loyal to his technique and has not funked its necessary implications, but has honestly attempted to tell fully what his characters think about, that he has been the subject of so many attacks and that his purpose has been so often misunderstood and misrepresented. For his attempt sincerely and honestly to realize his objective has required him incidentally to use certain words which are generally considered dirty words and has let at times to what many think is a too poignant preoccupation with sex in the thoughts of his characters.

The words which are criticized are dirty old Saxon words known to almost all men and, I venture, to many women, and are such words as would be naturally and habitually used, I believe, by the types of folk whose life, physical and mental, Joyce is seeking to describe. In respect of the recurrent emergency of the theme of sex in the minds of his characters, it must always be remembered that his locale was Celtic and his season spring.

Whether or not one enjoys such a technique as Joyce uses is a matter of taste on which disagreement or argument is futile, but to subject that technique to the standards of some other technique seems to me to be little short of absurd.

Accordingly, I hold that *Ulysses* is a sincere and honest book, and I think that the criticisms of it are entirely disposed of by its rationale.

V. Furthermore, *Ulysses* is an amazing tour de force when one considers the success which has been in the main achieved with such a difficult objective as Joyce set for himself. As I have stated, "Ulysses" is not an easy book to read. It is brilliant and dull, intelligible and obscure, by turns. In many places it seems to me to be disgusting, but although it contains, as I have mentioned above, many words usually considered dirty, I have not found anything that I consider to be dirt for dirt's sake. Each word of the book contributes like a bit of mosaic to the detail of the picture which Joyce is seeking to construct for his readers.

If one does not wish to associate with such folk as Joyce describes, that is one's own choice. In order to avoid indirect contact with them one may not wish to read *Ulysses*; that is quite understandable. But when such a great artist in words, as Joyce undoubtedly is, seeks to draw a true picture of the lower middle class in a European city, ought it to be impossible for the American public legally to see that picture?

To answer this question it is not sufficient merely to find, as I have found above, that Joyce did not write *Ulysses* with what is commonly called pornographic intent, I must endeavor to apply a more objective standard to his book in order to determine its effect in the result, irrespective of the intent with which it was written.

VI. The statute under which the libel is filed only denounces, in so far as we are here concerned, the importation into the United States from any foreign country of "any obscene book." Section 305 of the Tariff Act of 1930, title 19 United States Code, § 1305 (19 USCA § 1305). It does not marshal against books the spectrum of condemnatory adjectives found, commonly, in laws dealing with matters of this kind. I am, therefore, only required to determine whether *Ulysses* is obscene within the legal definition of that word.

The meaning of the word "obscene" as legally defined by the courts is: Tending to stir the sex impulses or to lead to sexually impure and lustful thoughts.. . .

Whether a particular book would tend to excite such impulses and thoughts must be tested by the court's opinion as to its effect on a person with average sex instincts--what the French would call *l' homme moyen sensuel* [the person of average sensuality] --who plays, in this branch of legal inquiry, the same role of hypothetical reagent as does the "reasonable man" in the law of torts and "the man learned in the art" on questions of invention in patent law.

The risk involved in the use of such a reagent arises from the inherent tendency of the trier of facts, however fair he may intend to be, to make his reagent too much subservient to his own idiosyncrasies. Here, I have attempted to avoid this, if possible, and to make my reagent herein more objective than he might otherwise be, by adopting the following course:

After I had made my decision in regard to the aspect of *Ulysses*, now under consideration, I checked my impressions with two friends of mine who in my opinion answered to the above-stated requirement for my reagent. These literary assessors--as I might properly describe them--were called on separately, and neither knew that I was consulting the other. They are men whose opinion on literature and on life I value most highly. They had both read *Ulysses*, and, of course, were wholly unconnected with this cause. Without letting either of my assessors know what my decision was, I gave to each of them the legal definition of obscene and asked each whether in his opinion *Ulysses* was obscene within that definition.

I was interested to find that they both agreed with my opinion: That reading *Ulysses* in its entirety, as a book must be read on such a test as this, did not tend to excite sexual impulses or lustful thoughts, but that its net effect on them was only that of a somewhat tragic and very powerful commentary on the inner lives of men and women.

It is only with the normal person that the law is concerned. Such a test as I have described, therefore, is the only proper test of obscenity in the case of a book like *Ulysses* which is a sincere and serious attempt to devise a new literary method for the observation and description of mankind. I am quite aware that owing to some of its scenes *Ulysses* is a rather strong draught to ask some sensitive, though normal, persons to take. But my considered opinion, after long reflection, is that, whilst in many places the effect of *Ulysses* on the reader undoubtedly is somewhat emetic, nowhere does it tend to be an aphrodisiac.

Ulysses may, therefore, be admitted into the United States.

METRO. GOV'T OF NASHVILLE v. MARTIN
Supreme Court of Tennessee
584 S.W.2d 643 (1979)

JOSEPH W. HENRY, Chief Justice.

The Metropolitan Beer Permit Board of Nashville and Davidson County suspended the beer permit of Classic Cat II, pursuant to two citations. The Davidson County Circuit Court, pursuant to statutory writs of certiorari and a *de novo* hearing as provided in [Tenn. Code, Sec. 57-209] reversed. . . .

II
The Second Citation

The second citation was properly certified by the Beer Board and is included in the record. It charges the permittee with allowing "an[y] intoxicated person to loiter on or about the premises," on April *14*, 1978.

All the proof was directed to activities occurring on April *16*, 1978; however, counsel makes no issue of this discrepancy. Therefore, we do not treat it as being of critical significance. It is but another of many instances of sloppy Beer Board procedure.

The proof presented to the Beer Board was meager and marginal. If there were no other proof in the record we unhesitatingly would affirm the Trial Judge and hold that the Beer Board acted arbitrarily; however, upon the *de novo* hearing before the Trial Judge additional proof was presented which placed the matter in an entirely different light. . .

. . . Before the Trial Court the Beer Board presented the deposition of the "loitering drunk" and his cohort and companion. This proof was not presented to the Beer Board.

He is a member of the regular army stationed at Fort Campbell. He and his companion, another soldier, arrived in Nashville in the early afternoon of April 16, 1978 and took a room at a local motel.

About mid-afternoon they wended their way to the Classic Cat II, where they stayed several hours imbibing seven and sevens,[1] "[m]aybe 10 to 15." Thereafter, they left, bought a bottle of Seagrams V.O. and settled down to some serious drinking--"drinking out of the bottle."

Around 9:30 or 10:00 p.m. they returned to the Classic Cat and the seven and sevens. While he denies that his first 10-15 drinks caused him to be "smashed," he admits that after his interlude with Seagrams V.O. and after topping that off with more seven and sevens, he was drunk.

He says that every time he drinks "hard liquor" he gets drunk or tries to. He admits that he was in Nashville to get "bombed," and that he went to the Classic Cat to get drunk and "watch the women." Of course, he denies that he has a drinking problem; he says he just likes to drink.

They apparently remained at the Classic Cat for some two or three hours on their second visit.

When we analyze this soldier's actions in terms of his stated intention "to get bombed," the conclusion is inevitable that success crowned his efforts. While he lolled, loafed, and loitered about the Classic Cat satisfying his lickerish craving for liquor by lapping up lavish libations, he fell from his chair, clutching his drink in his hand, into the waiting hands of vice squad officer McElhaney, who helped him up and took him to jail.

We subject his conduct to the most liberal standard that has come to the attention of the author of this opinion.

> *Not drunk is he who from the floor*
> *Can rise alone and still drink more;*
> *But drunk is he, who prostrate lies,*
> *Without the power to drink or rise.*[2]

This soldier fails the test. He was drunk--openly, visibly, notoriously, gloriously and uproariously drunk.

The Classic Cat II violated one of the great commandments by which "beer joints" must live. In summary and in short, in paraphrase and in idiom, the law "don't allow no [drunken] hanging around" beer establishments.

---

[1] Seagrams and 7-up.
[2] Thomas L. Peacock, *The Misfortunes of Elphin* (1827). Translated from the Welsh.

We do not deal with an isolated case of a drunk who came in from the cold and was drunk on arrival, or with a customer who consumed beer and became intoxicated as a result of that consumption under circumstances where the management reasonably could not be expected to realize that the customer had reached the point of intoxication. We deal purely and simply with permitting a drunk to "hang around" a beer joint under circumstances that were known, or should have been known to the permittee, or her employees.

We find no reported cases wherein the courts have attempted to define the offense of drunken loitering about premises where beer was sold. However, *Hopper v. State*, [citation omitted] deals with an analogous prohibition against permitting minors to loiter about such premises. There, this Court quoted with approval the definition of "loitering" as contained in a decision of the Connecticut Supreme Court:

> To be slow in moving; to delay; to linger; to be
> dilatory; to spend time idly; to saunter; to lag
> behind. . .

See also *McCoy v. State*, [citation omitted] where the Court approved a definition from Black's Law Dictionary:

> To be dilatory, to be slow in movement, to stand
> around, to spend time idly, to saunter, to delay,
> to idle, to linger, to lag behind. . .

We approve these definitions; they accord with the common understanding of the term "loiter" or "loitering."

Appellants' assignment . . . is sustained and the action of the Beer Board in suspending Classic Cat II's license for a period of thirty (30) days is upheld. . .

. . . Affirmed in part; reversed in part; remanded.

LANGSTON v. THE STATE OF GEORGIA
Court of Appeals of Georgia
10 Ga. App. 82; 72 S.E. 532 (1911)

BENJAMIN HARVEY HILL, C.J.

The facts of this case present another of the daily occurring instances showing the monstrous and measureless evil of intoxicating liquors. This hydra-headed and remorseless monster, with ceaseless and tireless energy, wastes the substance of the poor, manufactures burdensome taxes for the public, monopolizes the valuable time of the courts, fills jails, penitentiaries, and asylums, ruins homes, destroys manhood, terrorizes helpless women and innocent children, baffles the church, and mocks the law, and, answering its inexorable demands, "each new morn new widows mourn, new orphans cry, new wrongs strike Heaven in the face."

These are the products of a curse not imposed by the decree of God, but self-inflicted by the voluntary conduct of man, its weak and wicked victim. Judges of criminal courts, speaking from official experience, have grown weary in calling attention to the drink habit as the principal cause of crime, and nothing that the writer could say would add to this manifest truth. But I can not refrain from saying that, after five years' observation of the cases that have been before this court, three fourths of the crimes are due directly or indirectly to the excessive use of intoxicants, and that, if the church and the State and public sentiment could unitedly make Georgia sober, the prisons would be vacant, the chain gangs empty, the cities, towns, and country would be filled with prosperous people and happy homes. The grand English premier did not exaggerate when he declared that "greater calamities have been inflicted on mankind by intemperance than by the three great historic scourges, war, pestilence, and famine," and that this evil is "the measure of a nation's discredit and disgrace."

We have been led to say this much because of the sad tragedy disclosed by the horrible facts of this record. A husband, "beastly drunk," goes to his home at night, finds his sick wife in bed, and, with brutal curses and violent threats to kill, drives her into the night and from home. The accused, their 19-year old son, resents this cruel treatment of his mother, and reproaches the father for his brutal language and cruel conduct. The father, frenzied with liquor, immediately turns on his son, curses him, knocks him down with a chair, cuts him with a knife, and threatens to kill him. The son (as he contended, in self-defense, but, as found by the jury, under the excitement of passion aroused by these attacks) picks up a rock from the floor, where it was placed to prop open the door, hurls it at his father, hits him on the head, and from the wound thus inflicted death ensues on the following day.

A careful review of the evidence convinces us that it largely preponderates in favor of the plea of self-defense. Yet we can not say that the verdict of voluntary manslaughter is not supported by some slight evidence, and to this standard of mental conviction we must come before we would be authorized to set aside the verdict on the general grounds. . . .

We do not hesitate to state that if it were our province, or we had the right to weigh the evidence and decide the issue of fact, we would grant another trial, because the evidence in favor of the plea of self-defense is so strong, and that in support of voluntary manslaughter, or any other offense, is so weak. . .

The evidence showed that the decedent was a man of great violence when under the influence of liquor, and that he was much larger and stronger than the accused. It is contended by learned counsel that the trial judge, without request, should have instructed the jury "as to the law touching the violent character of the deceased and the great disparity in his size and that of the accused." We have no clear opinion or exact knowledge as to what would be the law on this subject that the judge was called upon to charge, and we have received no assistance from learned counsel on this point. We are therefore inclined to think that the jury, especially where a mutual combat or struggle was shown, could be safely relied upon to deal with these questions without the aid of any rule of law. The violent character of one party, and the relative strength and size of two parties engaged in a mutual combat, or where an assault and struggle took place, so forcibly and necessarily illustrate the issue of guilt or innocence that he would be a profoundly stupid juror who would not give these questions full weight and significance, even without any suggestion from the court as to his right to do so.

We repeat that we affirm the judgment because we find no legal error in the trial, and there is some slight evidence to support the verdict. We doubt not that the learned trial judge, if he has not already imposed a merciful sentence, will do so, and will humanely temper justice with a large and generous clemency.

Judgment affirmed.

IN RE T. SMITH AND FELIPE VEGA
Justice Court of California, Tuolumne County
Case No. 60 (1850)

R. C. Barry, J.P.

This was a gambling scrape in which T. Smith the monte deeler, shot and wounded Felipe Vega. After heering the witnesses on both sides, I adjudged Smith guilty of the shooting and fined him 10 dolars and Vega guilty of attempting to steele 5 ounces. I therefore fined him 100 dolars, and costs of coort.

Costs of Coort 3 ounces.

Sept. 4, 1850
U. H. Brown, Constable

STATE OF ALASKA v. STAGNO
Court of Appeals of Alaska
739 P.2d 198 (1987)

ROBERT G. COATS, Judge

The issue presented in this case is whether a court may revoke the driver's license and forfeit the vehicle of a person convicted of driving while intoxicated on public property in an airboat. The trial judge, Judge H.E. Crutchfield, ruled that he had no authority to revoke a driver's license or forfeit the vehicle under these circumstances.

Frank Stagno spent the evening of August 23, 1985, airboating on the Chena and Tanana rivers with two friends. Stagno was operating a fifteen-foot 1985 Air Gator airboat, powered by a 455 cubic inch Buick engine. The three men headed back to Fairbanks around midnight or 1:00 a.m. on August 24, 1985. They beached their airboats and went to a local bar where they drank alcoholic beverages. Stagno's friends each bet him $200 that he could not take them, via airboat, from their present location to a nearby topless bar. The destination was about three-quarters of a mile away, over land. Stagno apparently accepted the bet, because the three men boarded Stagno's airboat, and headed for the next bar.

Herbert Sobey, who had driven from Anchorage to Fairbanks on business, caught sight of the "vehicle" in his rearview mirror. Sobey thought that it was an airplane about to crash into the bed of his truck and kill him. Sobey eventually realized that it was an airboat moving on land. He reported the incident to the night personnel at his motel, who then called the Alaska State Troopers.

Meanwhile, Stagno was contacted by airport security police. They told him to return the boat to the water since it was a traffic hazard. As Stagno was complying, he was stopped by a state trooper who ultimately arrested him for driving while intoxicated (DWI). Stagno's Intoximeter reading was .197. Following a jury trial, Stagno was convicted of DWI. It was his third such conviction in ten years.

At sentencing on May 30, 1986, the state pointed out that Stagno was subject to the mandatory minimum penalties for DWI: thirty days in jail, a $1,000 fine, and alcohol rehabilitation counseling. Stagno did not challenge this assertion, and the court imposed sentence accordingly.

The state also argued that Judge Crutchfield was required to revoke Stagno's driver's license and was authorized to forfeit the airboat. Judge Crutchfield concluded that he did not have the authority to take either of those actions.

The state petitioned for review. Stagno also urged us to resolve this question in order to help clarify the status of his driver's license with the division of motor vehicles. We accepted review. . .

[Alaska Statute, Section 181 provides as follows:] (a) Conviction of any of the following offenses is grounds for the immediate revocation of a driver's license:. . . (5) driving a motor vehicle while intoxicated;. . . (c) A court convicting a person of an offense described in (a)(5) of this section *arising out of the operation of a motor vehicle for which a driver's license is required* shall revoke that person's driver's license. . . .

The state argues that the statute requires everyone who drives a motor vehicle on public property to have a driver's license. . .

Judge Crutchfield concluded that current [Alaska Statute, Section 10] seemed to emphasize that a person had to have a license "for the type and class of vehicle driven" rather than requiring every person who drove a motor vehicle on a highway to have a driver's license. Judge Crutchfield also pointed out that [Alaska Statute, Section 41] authorizes the Commissioner of Public Safety to "provide by regulation for the classification of drivers' licenses." The regulations established by the Commissioner do not provide for a driver's license for an airboat. In other words, there are driver's license provisions for certain types of vehicles, and no such provisions for other types of vehicles, such as airboats. This supports Judge Crutchfield's conclusion.

Reading all the statutes in context, we conclude that an airboat is not "a motor vehicle of a type for which a driver's license is required" and that the present offense does not arise "out of the operation of a motor vehicle for which a driver's license is required." It follows that [Alaska Statute, Section 181] and [Alaska Statute, Section 30] which provide for mandatory revocation of a driver's license if the person is convicted of DWI for operating a motor vehicle for which a driver's license is required, do not apply to Stagno. Neither does [Alaska Statute, Section 36] which authorizes forfeiture of a motor vehicle "of a type for which a driver's license is required."

The judgment of the district court is AFFIRMED and the case is REMANDED to the district court for further proceedings.

EX PARTE TOWNSEND
Court of Criminal Appeals of Texas
64 Tex. Crim. 350; 144 S.W. 628 (1912)

A. J. HARPER, J.

On October 27, 1911, an information was filed by the county attorney in the county court of Orange County against the relator, W.H. Townsend, charging him with the offense of pursuing the occupation of selling non-intoxicating malt liquors without paying the tax and procuring the license, as is provided for in chapter 19, p. 51, Acts of the Thirty-First Legislature.

The relator was arrested upon said charge, and made application to the county judge of Orange County for a writ of habeas corpus. The writ being refused, the relator made application to this court, and the application was granted by this court. The relator was released on bond, and the case in now before this court on said habeas corpus hearing. . .

. . . The facts show that the relator was on the date charged by the information engaged in the grocery business in the city of Orange, and, in connection with said business, he was engaged in the occupation and was selling cold drinks, including ginger ale, ginger pop, soda water, and a malt drink known as "Hiawatha," without having paid the occupation tax required therefor by law, and without having obtained the license required therefor. It is further agreed in so far as this case is concerned, that "Hiawatha" is a non-intoxicating malt liquor manufactured by the Houston Ice & Brewing Company, of Harris county, Tex.; that the commissioner's court of Orange County has regularly levied a tax of $1,000 on the occupation of selling nonintoxicating malt liquors;. . . The relator does not hold a retail liquor dealer's or malt dealer's license, and, in fact, holds no license of any kind to sell either intoxicating or nonintoxicating liquors. . .

". . .The relator vigorously attacks the validity of the law on two grounds: (1) Because the amount of the tax imposed is prohibitory and prevents the citizens of the state from engaging in a lawful business; and (2) that the act has the effect to make the tax on the pursuit of the business named in it unequal and not uniform. . .

Alcohol is the intoxicating element in all spirituous, vinous, malt, and other intoxicating liquors. Joyce on Int. Liq. § 17. We think it well established that under the police power the Legislature may regulate, if it so desires, the sale of all beverages which contain any degree of alcohol. It is the alcohol which makes the liquor dangerous, and it is the presence of alcohol which gives rise to the exercise of police power. If the alcohol is present in any quantity, the power to regulate springs into life. Whether the liquor contains enough alcohol to warrant regulation is a question wholly within the sound discretion of the Legislature. It would be within the province of the court to inquire if the beverage necessarily contains alcohol or some other inherently injurious ingredient. If it does, it is a subject of police regulation. But the court has no right to usurp the legislative prerogative, and, after finding that the Legislature has the power, attempt to dictate to it when and where it shall exercise that power. Whether it has the power is for the court to say. Whether it shall exercise that power is for the Legislature. . .

. . .Intoxicating liquor is any liquor is any liquor containing alcohol which can be drunk as a beverage in such quantity as will produce intoxication. Of such liquors as these the Legislature has provided a system of taxation and regulation. . . [B]ut the Legislature evidently, for some good reason, deemed it wise to deal with another class of liquors which, though denominated by name, and which were in fact non-intoxicating, yet containing alcohol in various proportions. It must be borne in mind that a liquor is not intoxicating unless it will make a person drunk who drinks it, and it is extremely difficult to draw the line on a 'drunk.' There are various stages, such as 'quarter drunk,' 'half drunk,' and 'dead drunk.' There are the stages of being vivacious, foxey, tipsy, and on a 'high lonesome,' and it is about as difficult to determine when a young lady gets to be an old maid as it is to tell when a man has taken enough alcoholic stimulant to pass the line between a 'jolly sober' and a 'gentlemanly drunk.'

Mr. Justice Dibrell, in the case of *Railway Co. v. Robinson*, [citation omitted] has laboriously and learnedly attempted to define the vague term 'drunk,' but he practically gives up the question in despair. His discussion, in connection with this case, however, is interesting and instructive. The Legislatures of different states have undertaken in some instances to prescribe what per cent of alcohol in a liquor will constitute it intoxicating, and it is commonly understood that ordinarily a liquor which contains less than 2 per cent of alcohol will not produce intoxication, though there is no fixed rule in regard to this matter.

Whatever the per cent is, say for convenience, 2 per cent, then an alcoholic liquor which contains 1-3/4 per cent would not be intoxicating, yet can it be said that an alcoholic liquor which lacks only one-fourth of 1 per cent of alcohol to make it actually intoxicating is a beverage that can safely be sold promiscuously at cold drink stands and soda fountains to unsuspecting persons who do not knowingly drink intoxicants or alcoholic beverages, and to boys and children of tender years, who may thus be injured in health, or may thus innocently cultivate an appetite for stronger drinks. The Legislature could well assume that the taste and effect of such alcoholic stimulants, especially with children, would be extremely injurious to the health and morals, and that it was necessary to deal with this class of drinks in some way.

It is a matter of common knowledge, and of which this court will take notice, that the text-books which the children of Texas study in the public schools teach and impress the idea that alcoholic stimulants are injurious to the health and morals, and even the temperate use of such is discouraged. The Thirtieth Legislature, in prescribing a course of study in the public schools among other things, required that the children should be instructed in physiology and hygiene, including the effects of alcoholic stimulants and narcotics on the human system. Three textbooks have been selected by the text-book board which are now in use in all the public schools of Texas, which deal in no uncertain terms with the injurious and pernicious effects of alcoholic stimulants. We call attention to some of the lessons set out in the *First Book of Physiology and Hygiene*, by Krohn; it being one of the official text-books adopted. On pages 66 to 68, under the title 'Alcohol,' we find the following:

"Alcohol is as clear and colorless as water; but as a drink it is just the opposite of water. If you have had your throat or chest rubbed with alcohol when you had a cold, you know how strong it smells. If you have seen it used in an alcohol lamp you know how quickly it flames up when it is lighted, and how soon it is all burned out. That is just what alcohol does inside the body; it burns. It burns and destroys the parts of the body. It does not quench thirst. It makes the mouth dry and the throat drier, and the person who drinks it more thirsty still.

"Alcohol Not a Food. — Is alcohol a food? No, it does not nourish the body; it does not give it more strength; it does not make it warmer. It might seem for a few moments to warm it; but the feeling would not last long, and in a few moments the body would feel colder than before. It might for a few moments make us feel brighter and more lively. Why would it? It would be only like the whip used on a tired horse. It would excite us, but it would not help us.

Afterward we should be duller and slower than before. What do we call a drink that excites, but does not nourish us?

"Athletes Drink No Alcohol — No young man who is being trained in athletics ever touches alcohol. His trainer would not allow him to do so; for there would be no use in helping a man to build a splendid body, if the man were all the time taking something to tear it down. The athlete must have food to give him strength and quickness. He would stand no chance of winning in a contest if he should take drinks made of alcohol. If an athlete drinks alcohol — if he "breaks training," as it is called — his comrades look down upon him. Why do they? Because he was so weak as to give up the thing he set out to do just for the pleasure of a taste.

"Alcohol and Habit — Most alcoholic drinks are not pleasant when first tasted. Some burn the mouth and throat. A man has to learn to like them. And what a silly thing to do — to try to like a thing that is harmful. But the young man thinks it "looks big" to drink with other men. He is afraid of being laughed at, and not thought manly if he refuses. If he only knew how much more manly it would be to refuse! Not only would he save his own health; he might help his companions by setting a good example. Most men begin by taking just a little once in a while. But very few men who once begin to drink find it easy to stop. That is the other queer thing about alcohol; it starts a craving for more. Then the man will take stronger liquors and take them oftener, until he has so broken down his health that he is weak-minded as well as weak-bodied. Then he cannot stop. The drunkard cannot reason; he cannot do what he makes up his mind to do; for he has whipped and abused his body, instead of feeding it, until is has broken down. Can such a man be a useful citizen?"

These strictures apply to alcoholic drinks, and not alone to intoxicating liquors; and, while the above language is made simple for children to understand, the truth of the deductions are too well known to deny, and, if the indictment is true, it would seem clear that the Legislature has the right to deal with all alcoholic drinks under the police power of the state.

While the law under consideration only applies to non-intoxicating malt liquors, and while the agreed statement of facts in the record shows that Hiawatha, one of the beverages which realtor was selling, is a non-intoxicating malt liquor, it seems that it is not without a judicial history in this state, and, as we shall presently show, it may not always be as harmless as this record would indicate. As we have heretobefore shown, all 'malt liquor' contains alcohol, and, as this beverage therefore contains alcohol, we are not surprised at the effect it seems to have had on some persons who imbibe it too freely. The inoffensive sounding, though illustrious, name would not indicate a dangerous character, but we are reminded that --

> "Strong of arm was Hiawatha;
> He could shoot an arrow upwards,
> Shoot them with such strength and swiftness

That the tenth had left the bow string
Ere the first to earth had fallen!"

And we are persuaded that this namesake has on occasion manifested a good deal of 'strength'; and, while its arrows might not be as effective as the other Hiawatha's, we are not at all surprised to know that, when they have struck home, the recipients were at least 'half shot,' if not more seriously wounded. . .

. . . Accordingly, it is held that the law in question is not violative of any provision of the state Constitution, and is but an exercise of the police power inherent in sovereignty, and relator is remanded.

CRIPPEN v. MINT SALES CO.
Supreme Court of Mississippi
139 Miss. 87; 103 So. 503 (1925)

JOHN BURT HOLDEN, J.

The appellee, Mint Sales company, sued out an injunction against the appellant, Crippen, sheriff of Leflore County to restrain him from interfering with the operation of certain vending machines, commonly known as slot machines, in Leflore County. . .

The controversy presented for our decision is whether or not the vending machine involved in this case is such a device as is prohibited by chapter 339, Laws of 1942, or whether the machine comes within the exception specified in the act and is deemed lawful and legalized by the language in the latter part of the statute. . . .

In order to first understand the statute invoked, we shall here set out chapter 339, Laws of 1924, which is as follows:

> "It shall be unlawful for any person or persons, firms, copartnership or corporations, to operate any cane rack, knife rack, artful dodger, punch board, roll down, merchandise wheel, or slot machine, or similar devices. . . . Provided, however, that this act shall not apply to automatic vending machines which indicated in advance what the purchaser is to receive on each operation of the machine."

It will be observed the act makes it unlawful for any person to operate any "slot machine, or similar device." Then it provides further "that this act shall not apply to automatic vending machines which indicate in advance what the purchaser is to receive on each operation of the machine. . ."

. . . The appellee contends the machine is lawful because the player can see in advance what he will get on each operation of the machine, and is therefore not a gambling device; but that whether it be a gambling device or not, the statute specifically authorizes the operation of the machine involved in this case.

There is an agreed statement of facts in the record as to what the machine is and how operated. We here quote the agreed statement of facts, which is as follows:

> "It is hereby agreed between counsel for complainant and defendant that, by placing a nickel or a trade check in the slot and pulling the lever, it is possible for this mint machine to pay off as many as 2, 4, 8, 12, 16 and 20 trade checks, and it will pay off, in addition to a package of mints from each operation of said mint machine either 2 trade checks, 4 trade checks, 8 trade checks, 12 trade checks, 16 trade checks, or 20 trade checks, all of said trade checks being good for 5 cents worth of merchandise in the store in which the machine is located and that the number of checks which the party playing the machine will receive on each play are indicated in the window in advance of each operation of the machine, and that on each operation a package of mints is indicated and will be paid whether operated by a trade check or a coin."

. . . It is our conclusion that the vending machine here involved is a gambling device, "a slot machine or similar device." It is plain to us that the element of chance involved is in the second operation of the machine, which may give to the player a large return or a small one for his money. . .

. . . The provision of the statute that the act shall not apply to automatic vending machines which indicate in advance what the purchaser is to receive "on each operation" of the machine, does not apply to the kind of machine here in question, because it does not indicate in advance what the purchaser, in the whole purchase, is to receive "on each operation of the machine."

It is true the player can see in advance what he will get on the first operation, but not on the second. Each play by the player at the machine may consist of many operations by pulling the lever, but the player engages in the element of chance as to what the indicator will show on the second or next operation because he does not then know what it will indicate on the second pull when he pulls the lever the first time. Therefore, taking the play as a whole, the machine does not indicate in advance what the player will get on each and all operations of the machine, and it is not the kind of vending machine that the Legislature intended to exempt in the statute. . .

. . . In view of these conclusions we think it is unlawful to operate the machine, and the decree of the chancellor should be reversed, and the bill dismissed.

GEORGE H. ETHRIDGE, Jr., J. (dissenting).

I am impelled to dissent in this case, not because of the importance of the subject-matter in controversy, for the subject-matter is a very trivial affair in my view, a veritable "tempest in a teapot," a "much ado about nothing," a pee-wee lawsuit. However the principle of the decision is more important and, as I see it, is a plain refusal to construe the law as written by its plain language, but in effect, though not in name, a reformation of the statute.

I want to say at the outset that what I say in this opinion is not intended as a reflection on the judges who disagree with me. I have lived too long in the polemical atmosphere of the law not to know that wise men differ honestly--that what appears to one man to be a certainty, by another is regarded as its exact opposite.

The concluding provision of chapter 339, Laws of 1924: "Provided, however, that this act shall not apply to automatic vending machines which indicate in advance what the purchaser is to receive on each operation of the machine," --means to except from the statute a machine which indicates what the purchaser is to receive in advance each time he places a coin in the aperture. It does not mean and could not mean that the machine must indicate in advance all of the operations of the machine, because no person knows how many times any operator might operate it. It would be as impossible for human intelligence to know this, not knowing how many times a player was going to play, as the habit of the Eastern despots in ancient times to dream a dream and forget, and demand of the soothsayer that he tell him the dream first and then what it meant. Nothing short of divine revelation could foretell those things.

As used in the statute the word "each" refers to the several operations and not the aggregate operations. All that is required or could be required logically would be for the player to see before placing his coin in the aperture what he would get for his coin on that particular operation, and that is exactly what the machine here involved does. If the player will only get mints for his money, that is indicated. If he would get mints plus a trade check, that is indicated before he puts his money in. In no case is there the slightest element of chance in his getting anything other than what is indicated by the machines. He knows precisely what he is going to get before he places his money and there is not any possibility of his being deceived thereby. As to how such a machine could be construed to be a gambling appliance is beyond my compre-hension. . . .

. . . Whether the Legislature acted wisely or unwisely in passing this statute and in making the exception is no concern whatever of the courts. The Legislature is intrusted with all the law-making power of the state--it is the exclusive custodian of that power. People have the right through their lawful representatives to make any law they desire so long as it is not prohibited by the state and federal Constitutions. It is the very essence of free government that the separation of the powers of government should be maintained. The court is limited in its powers to disregard statutes to the question as to whether or not they are constitutional. It has no kind of power to control the Legislature in shaping the public policy of the state. It cannot review or set aside the law because it may be unwise, unjust, or oppressive, or for any other consideration of that nature. The court's inquiry is solely as to whether the statute is constitutional, and if constitutional it must be enforced. The Legislature clearly had power to enact the law. At common law it is not an offense to gamble, even if this machine should be classed as a gambling machine, which it is not.

The Legislature has power to prohibit gambling or to permit it, and if it does a foolish thing or an unwise thing, the remedy is not in the courts but at the ballot box. . . .

. . . Courts of equity have jurisdiction to reform a contract, but have no jurisdiction to reform a statute, as a rose would smell as sweet by any other name, so the essence of the proceeding to reform is not changed by calling it construction or interpretation.

Independent of jurisdiction it would be a dangerous undertaking for the court, if it had the power to undertake the job of correcting legislative mistakes and follies, for there is much in the statutes of the past dozen years evidencing midget-minded statesmen and much of folly. Still I am not disposed to be hard on the Legislature. Taken as a whole it does good work and eliminates many unwise measures. There are men in the Legislature who could fill any station in the government with credit, and the majority would class as "average and better." But there are usually some 35 per cent. to 40 per cent. of the membership whose only excuse for being sent to the Legislature is to keep them out of the race for constables and justices of the peace. These men have votes and have to be reckoned with by the wise ones in shaping the legislation of the session. If you antagonize their bills they strike back. They are strong on midget legislation and when they introduce a bill to place jay birds under peace bonds, or to muzzle seed ticks, or to prohibit vending machines in stores, the wise ones will vote with them for the sake of more important measures coming on. None of these pigmy statesmen go after large questions and undertake their solution, they attack small tasks. They are strong on moral questions or something that sounds well which they can take back home to their people for home consumption in future politics. They go around with a spiritual microscope searching for the germs of evils in trifles, while utterly ignoring the mountains of iniquity which stand out in plain view in the nearby landscape.

Instead of making war on the beasts and birds of prey that menaced society they hunt for earth worms. Conscious of their inability to deal with large matters they make a record from trifles garbed in high sounding phrases.

The importance of recognizing the right of the people to have the laws made by the law-making department, even though sometimes that department may act unwisely, is too essential to the perpetuity of free institutions to permit the court, being in a separate department of the government with separate powers, to cross the proper limits for the purpose of undertaking to change the logical results expressed in legislation.

Those who hold judicial power and exercise the function of judging men's rights under the law should perform their duty unshrinkingly and unmindful of public opinion of popular clamor. However, when this public opinion is crystallized into law, the courts should recognize it and give effect to it, but so long as it is not crystallized into law it should have no influence in administering the law. It is the very essence of liberty and justice that rights be measured and enforced by certain standards and uniforms rules.

A judge must adhere to the law. He cannot rightfully make law or change law. The law should be a rule of conduct for all from the highest to the lowest. It should not be perverted even to attain a good temporary purpose. It will always happen that some wrong will be found to exist under any general rule. The human race is not perfect. They cannot declare any general rule that may not sometimes shield wrong. As long as some men are wiser than others, and as long as selfishness and greed shape the affairs of men, particular cases will arise making a departure from fixed principles seemingly desirable. It will be found, however, that adhering to the fixed principle is better, and that less injustice will result from that course in the long run. Mistakes in statutes can be corrected by the appropriate department of the government before very great mischief results, and the Legislature should be looked to to make the change and not the courts.

PASCHAL v. THE STATE OF GEORGIA
Supreme Court of Georgia
84 Ga. 326; 10 S.E. 821 (1889)

LOGAN E. BLECKLEY, Chief Justice.

[The defendant, Paschal, was convicted of selling whiskey in violation of a county ordinance. Paschal appealed alleging that the finding was not warranted by the evidence.]

. . . A witness testified that a few days before or after Christmas, 1888, Paschal came to him at his shop in Fort Valley, Houston county, and told him that he (Paschal) wanted to get witness's buggy to go out to a grocery in Macon county for some whiskey, and if witness would let him have the buggy, he would bring him (witness) a bottle of whiskey; that there was to be free whiskey at the grocery that day. Witness let him have the buggy, and on his return Paschal delivered to witness a bottle of whiskey containing perhaps a quart. The witness added that he did not expect Paschal to bring the whiskey, and would have let him have the buggy without the agreement to do so if Paschal has so applied for it. It seems to us that this transaction amounted to a hiring of the buggy and paying for the same in whiskey, and that the county judge was well warranted in taking that view of it.

There was no evidence, not even by any statement made at the trial by the accused, that there was free whiskey in Macon County; but if there had been, it is not free in Houston County to the owner of the buggy, for he paid for the bottle which he received by giving the use of his buggy to go after it. It is altogether probable that the accused took care to get some for himself in addition to that which he disposed of to the witness as compensation for this use of the buggy. That the witness expected him to break his contract, or that he would have loaned him the buggy without making terms, could not vary the actual transaction as it took place.

The contract proposed was actually made and performed, and we see not why it did not amount to a sale by the one party and a purchase by the other. Very probably the suggestion that there was free liquor that day in Macon County was a mere pretext; for had it been true, there is no explanation of the failure to prove its truth or to make some attempt in that direction. Free liquor in one county for use in another is rare enough to require proof. Not even a county court can notice such a fact judicially as matter of public history. . .

Judgment affirmed.

PFEFFER v. DEPARTMENT OF PUBLIC SAFETY
Court of Appeals of Georgia
136 Ga. App. 448; 221 S.E.2d 658 (1975)

H. SOL CLARK, Judge

"Not drunk is he who from the floor
Can rise alone and still drink more;
But drunk is he, who prostrate lies,
Without the power to drink or rise." [1]

That fabled folklore favorite for testing inebriation contrasts with our modern mechanical method of an intoximeter machine, the use of which is here involved.

---

[1] Bartlett's Familiar Quotations (13th Ed.) page 449.
[Ed. Note: See also *Metro Gov't of Nashville v. Martin*, supra, fn. 2.]

Appellant has taken this appeal form the superior court judgement affirming the suspension of his motor vehicle operator's license for failure to comply with the Implied Consent Law. (Ga.L. 1968, pp.448, 452, Code. Ann. § 68-1625.1).

The evidence at the agency's hearing consisted of the testimony of the arresting officer, the state trooper who administered the breath analyzer test, and the appellant.

The officer stated that while on patrol he observed appellant's car weaving down the highway. Upon stopping the automobile he observed the driver had a strong odor of alcohol and showed other signs of intoxication. He then placed the driver under arrest "and told him that under the Georgia Implied Consent Law he was required to take either a blood test or a breath test, failure to do so would result in the suspension of his driver's license for six months." The state trooper who was in charge of the test testified that appellant put the nozzle to his mouth but did not follow instructions to "breathe deeply and blow into the bag real hard."

The testimony of the two officers was that despite repeated requests, there was no effort by the appellant to co-operate. The operator of the breathilizer added that "He [appellant] didn't expand his jaws to attempt to blow the machine up, he just put it to his mouth and pulled it down and made the statement that he had taken this test before and that we couldn't write him up for DUI once he put it to his mouth."

Appellant testified that his throat was bothering him which impeded his efforts to comply with the requests. This evidence was supported by a physician's statement that he had been treating appellant for swollen lymph glands and that the patient had been advised to breathe through his nose as much as possible to alleviate throat irritation. Appellant also contradicted the officer's testimony as to being informed that he could take a blood test.

The findings of fact by the Hearing Officer of the Agency were adverse to appellant. Among these were that appellant had been advised of the Implied Consent Law by the arresting officer and that appellant had refused "a blood or breath test by refusing to blow air into the machine." The driver's license was suspended for six months. The Superior Court of Houston County[2] entered an order with findings of fact and conclusions of law affirming the agency's decision.

Both here and in the trial court appellant argued that the agency decision was legally erroneous on the basis of *Burson v. Collier*, [citation omitted] and *Department of Public Safety v. Orr*, [citation omitted]. The trial court was correct in holding that the instant case is not controlled by those decisions. In

[2] Pronounced "How-stun," this County was named for a Savannah lawyer, John Houstoun (1744-1796), twice Georgia Governor (1778 and 1784). "Houstoun" was the nineteenth century spelling of today's "Houston."

both of those decisions the driver was afflicted with emphysema. The effect of that serious respiratory disease was shown in the *Orr* case where the motorist could not inflate the bag although he made two efforts to do so. While a sore throat or swollen lymph glands may cause pain when the driver complies with instructions for intoximeter tests, that is not the type of inability which prevents the accused motorist from being able to inflate the bag.

The Implied Consent Law requires a meaningful submission to the test as otherwise the purpose of the law would be frustrated. . .

We concur with the trial court's judgment that "The findings of fact made by the Department of Public Safety are neither clearly erroneous, in view of the entire record, nor characterized by an arbitrary and capricious abuse of discretion such as would warrant this court substituting its judgment for that of the Department of Public Safety as to the weight of the evidence on those factual issues. . ."

Judgment affirmed.

CATT v. STATE OF ARKANSAS
Supreme Court of Arkansas
691 S.W.2d 120 (1985)

GEORGE ROSE SMITH, Justice

This appeal is from a judgment in two drug prosecutions that were consolidated for trial. The appellants are Kilkenny and Gallico Catt, twin brothers who sought to use their remarkable resemblance to avoid justice. That effort failed, for each was found guilty of a drug offense. They jointly present the same arguments for reversal: First, the evidence is insufficient to show which brother committed which offense. Second, the jury's finding that each of the offenses is a lesser included offense of the other is an impossibility on its face. Our jurisdiction is under Rule 29(1)(c).

We state the facts chronologically. In 1983 an undercover narcotics officer, Les Javert, arranged to buy cocaine from an Irish immigrant he had come to know as Kilkenny Catt. Upon completion of that "buy" the officer arranged with Catt for a second purchase, which took place three days later. Charges were not filed immediately, however, because the police hoped that other contacts with Catt might lead to his supplier. Unfortunately, the officer's "cover" as a narcotics agent was "blown" as a result of the publicity created a few weeks later when the officer's home was damaged by a tornado while he was in bed. Another complication arose when the State Crime Laboratory's analysis of the purchased drugs showed that Catt had delivered cocaine in the first transaction, but in the second he had delivered ordinary sugar instead of cocaine. The prosecuting attorney accordingly charged Kilkenny only with the unlawful sale of cocaine in the first transaction.

Counsel for Catt filed a motion to suppress Officer Javert's identification, for unreliability. At that time no one connected with the case except Kilkenny knew that he had a twin brother. At the suppression hearing the officer positively identified the accused person in the courtroom as the man he had bought cocaine from. In response to a leading question on cross examination the officer declared: "Of course I'm sure that's the man I dealt with. If that's not Kilkenny Catt, he looks enough like him to be his twin brother." The officer testified that in both transactions he noticed the same scratch on the seller's cheek. Before the hearing, however, the scratch had healed completely.

After the officer's identification had been nailed down, so to speak, Kilkenny disclosed the existence of his brother Gallico and said in an unsworn statement that Gallico had been the seller in both instances. The prosecutor, caught by surprise, responded by charging Gallico with having agreed to sell cocaine in the second transaction and having substituted sugar, a fraud made a class B felony in 1981. Ark. Stat. Ann. § 82-2619(a)(5)(ii) and (b)(2)(i) (Supp.1983). On motion of the defense, perhaps in the hope of confusing the issues, the two cases were consolidated for trial. Before the trial Officer Javert was seriously injured in line of duty. The court ruled him to be unavailable, and his testimony at the suppression hearing was admitted in evidence at the trial under Uniform Evidence Rule 804(b)(1).

At trial each brother testified that he himself had not committed either offense and did not know whether or not his brother had done so. The State had succeeded in identifying the twins by name, by comparing their fingerprints when they were admitted to this country with those taken when each was booked. At trial their identities were kept straight by I.D. tags securely fastened to their wrists. Nevertheless, the positive fingerprint identification had not come to light until after Officer Javert's pretrial testimony; so neither the judge nor the jury could know with certainty which twin, with the scratched cheek, had committed the two crimes or which had been identified at the suppression hearing.

The prosecutor, in the hope of getting one conviction for sure, prevailed upon the judge to submit to the jury not only the actual charge filed against each twin but also the charge against the other twin as a lesser offense included within the principal charge. The jury, with that sure sense of justice that typifies the jury system, convicted both defendants. One snag: Kilkenny, charged with selling cocaine, was convicted of selling the counterfeit, and Gallico just the reverse. Identical five-year sentences were imposed.

Learned counsel first argues that neither verdict is supported by substantial evidence, because the State's inability to identify either twin with certainty as the seller compelled the jury to resort to speculation and conjecture, perhaps even to guesswork. It is further insisted that since the scratched cheek proves by the State's own evidence that the same twin committed both crimes, the verdicts finding each to be guilty involve a manifest impossibility.

At first blush these arguments have a certain plausibility, so much so that they might appeal strongly to minds untrained in the fine points of the law. Nevertheless, our careful study of the case convinces us that the arguments have no substance. Officer Javert had testified that the man in the courtroom at the suppression hearing had committed both crimes and that he looked enough like Kilkenny to be his twin brother. Only the twins know which was actually in the courtroom that day. Can they hide behind their guilty knowledge? We cannot better answer that question than by quoting the eloquent language of Chief Justice Harris, speaking for a unanimous court: "No!" *Commercial Printing Co. v. Lee*, 262 Ark. 87; 553 S.W.2d 270 (1977).

Our reasoning is simple. The law has long been settled that in a consolidated trial like this one the jury may properly return inconsistent verdicts, because if the cases had been separately tried the two different juries might have reached opposite conclusions on the same testimony. *Brown v. Parker*, 217 Ark. 700; 233 S.W.2d 64 (1950); *Leech v. Missouri Pac. R.R.*, 189 Ark. 161; 71 S.W.2d 467 (1934). In the case at bar obviously one jury might take Officer Javert's statement to mean that the man in the courtroom was Kilkenny; the witness so identified him. On the other hand, a different jury might take the statement to refer to Gallico, because the man in the courtroom looked enough like Kilkenny to be, and therefore in fact was, Kilkenny's twin brother. We have no alternative except to hold that each verdict is supported by Officer Javert's unshaken identification of the culprit, no matter who he was.

Learned counsel's second argument is that both verdicts cannot be upheld, because if offense A is less than and included in offense B, then logically offense B cannot be less than and included in offense A. A reference is made (we hope not with unseemly jocularity) to the classic Greek fable of the two serpents that began to swallow each other tail first and eventually succeeded, disappearing altogether. This argument has a superficial appearance of logic, but we hold that the Criminal Code dictates a different conclusion.

First, it is clear that when an accused is charged with selling cocaine, he may be convicted of having agreed to sell that drug and having substituted sugar. The Criminal Code has three separate tests for determining whether one crime is included within another. One test is that the lesser differs from the greater only in that a less serious risk of injury to the same person suffices to establish the commission of the lesser. Ark. Stat. Ann § 41-105(2)(c)(Repl.1977). That test fits this case like a rubber glove. Cocaine presents a serious risk to the purchaser, but sugar is harmless to the average person. It is argued that sugar may be dangerous to a diabetic, but there is not one scintilla of proof that the officer is diabetic. We cannot spend our valuable time in exploring hypothetical questions. On this record Kilkenny, though charged with selling cocaine, was properly convicted of having sold a counterfeit substitute.

Gallico's appeal presents a more challenging issue. The legislature, however, in its wisdom has provided another test of lesser inclusivity. That is, an offense is included if it is established by proof of less than all the elements required to establish the offense charged. § 41-105(2)(a). Here the information charged that Gallico "agreed to sell cocaine and actually delivered *sugar instead of cocaine*." That is precisely what he was convicted of. It is inescapable that each offense is included within the other.

We are firmly convinced by our study of the record and briefs that the appellants received a fair trial and that substantial justice was achieved by the jury.

Affirmed. [1]

---

[1] [Ed. Note: The Honorable George Rose Smith (Associate Justice, Arkansas Supreme Court, 1949-1987) *was* the author of this "opinion," which was dated April 1, 1985 (April Fool's Day), an actual opinion day for the court that year. The work was published in the official reports at 691 S.W. 2d 120 (through a misunderstanding, *not* deception) where it resides in perpetuity and "is doubtless the only fictional opinion in the National Reporter System." Hon. George Rose Smith, "A Critique of Judicial Humor," 43 *Ark. Law Rev.* 1, 23-25 (1990).]

CHAPTER IV

BUSINESS, TRADE, COMMERCE, CONTRACTS, PROPERTY, PROFESSIONS, CORPORATIONS, REGULATION, TAXATION AND RELATED MERCANTILE MATTERS.

The true law, everywhere and at all times, delighteth in the payment of just debts. Blessed is the man that pays. The practice of paying promptly, and to the last cent, tends to the cultivation of one of the most excellent traits of human character. If debtors were guided by their own true interest, on an enlarged scale, they would be even more clamorous to pay than creditors are to receive. Tender would be more frequent than calls for money. Debt is the source of much unhappiness. The best possible thing to be done with a debt is to pay it. . .

- Logan E. Bleckley, J.[1]

---

[1] From *Robert v. N.& A. F. Tift*, 60 Ga. 566 (1878).

CHAPTER IV: BUSINESS, TRADE & COMMERCE

HARRELL v. HANNUM & COLEMAN
Supreme Court of Georgia
56 Ga. 508 (1876)

LOGAN E. BLECKLEY, Judge.

This case presents a contest over cattle and turpentine. The herdsman makes a stand against the aggressions of the manufacturer. The man whose vocation it is to turn the herbage into beef rises up against the man who seeks to convert the trees into turpentine. The disputed element is fire. Fire is the friend and ally of him who seeks after turpentine, but the mortal enemy of him who rejoices in the possession of many cattle. The one ranges the forest with his brands of burning; the other, in alarm, cries fire! and clamors for its extinction by a court of equity. And equity, it seems, finds this a difficult business. The fire department of the court is very indifferent. It is wanting in hooks and ladders, engines and other appliances, and has no water works. How equity is to put out fire, or to prevent it from spreading, is more than we know, without some thoughtful consideration. The complainant, however, is in court with application for aid by the writ of injunction; and that is a writ which has arrested many things, and may possibly arrest fire itself. Let us see.

Looking first to the mere power of the court to meddle in the matter, equity cannot interfere to save property, even in cases of conflagration, without he who applies for its aid shows that he has an interest in what is to be burned.

The right alleged must be one which the law recognizes as property. The complainant has made an effort to comply with this indispensable condition by averring that he has, in the woods in question, the right of common pasture for his cattle, which are numerous, and which have been accustomed to range in those woods heretofore. The position of the bill is, not that the burning is a nuisance because the cattle will go there, to their injury, and cannot be prevented from browsing on the impoverished burned patches, so long as the lands are left unenclosed, but that it is the complainant's right for them to be there in the woods and enjoy pasture. This is substantially what is alleged on the subject of his title; and we are constrained to say that it is wholly insufficient.

He does not set forth any contract, prescription or other lawful basis for the right he claims. He presents no state of facts showing it to be a right in him to pasture his cattle there, which would not have equal validity in favor of all mankind. For ought that we can see in his bill, all the inhabitants of Georgia, at least, might claim with him a similar and co-equal privilege. This vastness of extent as to the number of beneficiaries might hold as the navigable rivers, etc., but not, we apprehend, as to common of pasture upon lands, which are all private property. For the right to be in anybody it is essential that it should not be in particular. . .

. . . It will be already clear that in our judgment a court of equity cannot visit the scene of the fire at the complainant's instance. He is, legally speaking, a mere spectator of whatever destruction may happen to the grass in that region, unless he shall choose to change his forum and try penalty instead of injunction.

Judgment affirmed.

IN RE W. T. BULL
Justice Court of California, Tuolumne County
Case No. 859 (1851)

R. C. BARRY, J. P.

W. T. Bull in this caze is charged of attempting to murther R. F. Cole by shooting at him with a riffle loded with powder and ball wilst working in his clame. I examined a large number of witnesses, each contradicting the other flatly. After much patient hearing and taking time to think over it I concluded that R. F. Cole had jumped 1/2 of W. T. Bull's clame and that he was only defending his justs & rites which he probably was only doing. Therefore after long studdy and thinking it just and proper I ordered Cole to restore to Bull the part of the clame and to pay Bull $500 for the dammage he has done to it in so jumping it. Cost of Court $40.

Sonora, Oct. 31, 1851
John Luney, Constable

THE OGLETHORPE MANUFACTURING COMPANY v. VANWINKLE
Georgia Supreme Court
54 Ga. 569 (1875)

LOGAN E. BLECKLEY, Judge.

In this case no appeal is made to our knowledge of law, but we are invited to exercise our skill upon a couple of facts—one, whether a house was built according to contract, and the other, whether the work was paid for. We have exerted such skill as we possess, touching the mysteries of building and paying, and the result is, that we are unable to make a better verdict for the plaintiff in error than the jury made, and so the judgment of the court below must stand affirmed.

Judgment affirmed.

MRS. AGNES GARNER v. JOSEPH BURNSTEIN
Louisiana Court of Appeals
1 La.App. 19 (1924)

WESTERFIELD, J.

Plaintiff purchased a hat from the defendant, who conducts a millinery establishment in this city, for the sum of $20.00. The hat was to be paid for on delivery or, as it is termed commercially, C.O.D. The hat was delivered as agreed upon by the porter employed by defendant and according to the positive testimony of plaintiff and a lady friend of hers, whom she was visiting, was paid for by handing the porter two ten-dollar bills. The porter returned to defendant's place of business and upon being asked for the money stated that no money had been paid him, and that he was induced to leave the hat by plaintiff stating that she had called at the hat shop of defendant earlier in the day and paid for the hat. Whereupon the porter was told to return to plaintiff's residence and get the hat or the money.

The porter returned and finding plaintiff absent persuaded the servant to give him the hat and returned same to his employer. Upon plaintiff returning home and discovering her hat was gone she immediately repaired to the hat shop and demanded the hat, which the defendant refused to surrender unless she paid him the price. This plaintiff refused to do upon the ground that she had already paid for it. Thereupon plaintiff entered suit against defendant for $270.00; twenty dollars of which sum she claims to have paid defendant and $250.00 as consequential and punitive damages.

The first question for our consideration is whether the porter of defendant was paid for the hat and we have no difficulty in concluding that he was. Plaintiff is corroborated in this regard by another lady and both swear positively and circumstantially that the hat was paid for with two ten-dollar bills given the porter of defendant. Payment to defendant's agent was payment to him and whether he got the money or not plaintiff should have had her hat. His refusal to give her the hat renders him liable to pay any damages which might be reasonably contemplated as resulting from his refusal to do so. . .

The damages claimed here are, so far as we can consider them (punitive damages not being allowable at all) said to be due to mental anguish caused by disappointment due to the fact that the hat was bought to be worn with a certain dress to a dinner party on the very evening it was to be delivered. Plaintiff went to the party, though she alleges in her petition that she was unable to do so because of the lack of a proper hat, but says she was unable to wear the dress for which the hat was bought, causing her deep humiliation, disappointment and distress.

We are not inclined to treat her alleged state of mind on this occasion jocosely. It is said "The apparel oft proclaims the man".[1] It more often proclaims the woman. Nature seems to have intended that the male should be more pulchritudinous. Witness the majestic beauty of the male lion as compared with the plainness of its mate and the beauteous plumage of the mallard drake as compared with the drab appearance of the duck. But man, at least modern man, has decreed otherwise and countless industries and hosts of individuals are devoted to the production of clothing, jewelry, feathers, powders and, we regret to say, paints designed exclusively for the ornamentation of the female form in an effort to "paint the lily". No Rubens or Van Dyke ever studied the colors of their masterpieces with greater care than the modern woman studies the color scheme of her costume, for the laws of modern convention, though subject to frequent change, are inexorable.

---

[1] [Ed. Note: Shakespeare, Hamlet, Act I, Scene 3.]

Therefore, when the plaintiff in this case tells us that the yellow hat bought of defendant and that yellow hat alone was suitable for her new dress which she had bought for the dinner party and that not having the hat she was compelled to wear an inappropriate costume, to her great embarrassment, mortification and, yes mental anguish, we believe her. The only question is, could the defendant reasonably contemplate the result of his refusal to surrender the hat? He might be charged with knowledge of the intricate rules of feminine attire; indeed, his business in largely based upon the rigidity of these rules, and he must be held to be familiar with them, but he could not know the condition of the plaintiff's wardrobe, and since the record does not disclose that he was advised of the dinner dance and the special purpose for which the hat was intended, he cannot be charged with such knowledge, for it might well be, so far as defendant knew anything to the contrary, that plaintiff possessed a number of hats suitable for the occasion.

In the case of *Lewis v. Holmes*, [citation omitted] the defendant was held liable for damages caused by the disappointment of a bride in not having her trousseau properly made in time for the wedding and for social functions incident thereto. Holmes made the dresses, but they were four inches too short and the bride could not wear them without embarrassment and mortification, thus preventing her from being properly attired at social functions given in her honor. But in the instant case we are not dealing with bridal robes, which in themselves impart a warning of their importance, but with a hat in itself suggestive of none of the consequences which have resulted here.

We conclude, therefore, that the judgment appealed from must be amended by reducing the amount awarded plaintiff to twenty dollars, and it is so ordered.

COMPANIA MARTIARTU v. ROYAL EXCHANGE ASSURANCE CORPORATION
The House of Lords
40 T.L.R. 669 [June 27, 1924]

EARL OF BIRKENHEAD

[This was an appeal from an order of the Court of the Kings Bench, Court of Appeal reversing a judgment of the trial court.]

My Lords: In my opinion this case is a particularly clear one. A Spanish company brought an action against underwriters for the loss by perils insured against of the steamer Arnus. They allege that the vessel sank through the entry of water by reason of a collision with floating wreckage. Underwriters retorted that she sank, on the contrary, because she was scuttled in the interests, and with the privity of, the owners.

The case was tried at first instance by Mr. Justice Bailhache, who found in favour of the owners. The learned Judge did not reach this conclusion without "the gravest anxiety;" and he had apparently formed the view that his decision, being based almost entirely upon facts, was not open to review. Indeed, he spoke of it with some degree of sanguineness as practically "unappealable." Unhappily the learned Judge had made an error which would not be lacking in humour if it had not been so costly to the parties.

The second officer of the vessel was one Felipi Ybarra, of whom the learned Judge observes: "He gave his evidence on commission, and repeated it here, and I was impressed with his demeanour and his frankness." This impression was somewhat surprising, having regard to the fact that Felipi Ybarra gave no evidence before the learned Judge at all, and enjoyed therefore small opportunity of exhibiting either his demeanour or his frankness. The learned Judge having thus founded himself upon a faulty recollection of the facts, the whole matter is plainly open to review. I have no doubt that the Court of Appeal was right and that the learned Judge was wrong.

The facts may be very shortly stated. On April 26, 1921, at 9:30 p.m. the steamship Arnus left the Spanish port Vivero bound for Rotterdam and carrying a cargo of iron ore. The appellant company, the owners, a Spanish corporation, purchased the vessel in May, 1920, for £160,000. On the night she put out to sea she was worth less than £14,000, but was happily insured for a total sum of £174,000 on policies which expired in less than a month. If, therefore, the vessel was to be lost at all during the pendency of the policy, this voyage afforded the last opportunity.

I find it necessary in the first place to state the conclusion that this vessel was wilfully scuttled by the chief engineer and the captain, with the almost certain complicity of many other persons on board. If the owners were not privy to this fraud they can evidently support a claim for a barratrous loss. But of course, if they themselves were accomplices in the fraud, the case is not one of barratry. Every Judge who has hitherto applied his mind to the case has reached the conclusion that if the ship was scuttled the owners directed the scuttling. I agree with this view.

We were much pressed by counsel with the gravity of this conclusion. It is very grave. We were told of the respectability and responsibility of those involved in this accusation; and we were reminded with reiteration that an onus, carrying with it a criminal charge, must be discharged by those who undertake it with meticulous completeness.

The case must, of course, be proved. So must every other case. But some offences admit of much more direct proof than others. It was no doubt for this reason that the principle of circumstantial evidence was admitted into our law. Those who contrive crimes do not as a rule summon witnesses. There are certain crimes which are specially easy to conceal and therefore specially difficult to discover. In fact many would be entirely undiscoverable unless the law permitted inferences to be drawn. The question in such cases is always whether the facts of the case, taken as a whole, render the general inference proper to be drawn from those facts so irresistible that the matter though not established by direct evidence, has escaped from the atmosphere of reasonable doubt. I cannot doubt that this is such a case.

The plaintiff company carried on its affairs in a pleasant family atmosphere. Its managing director was Juan de Longaray. He, his two brothers, and his ten step-children held the bulk of the 4,800 shares of 500 pesetas each issued by the company. On the night when the Arnus commenced her last voyage of all the only assets of the company were the ship and the sum of about £400. And there were outstanding liabilities in respect of loans amounting to 936,986 pesetas. The company was insolvent; there was not the slightest prospect of paying its creditors; if such indeed was its purpose.

The intimate family atmosphere which was so striking a feature of the company is not altogether lost when we pass to consider the vessel. She was commanded by Thomas Enciendo. The captain was in a position somewhat singular in that he had no shares in the company. The first mate was Jose Ybarra. The second was Felipe Ybarra. Both these men were nephews and also step-sons of Longaray, the managing director. The chief engineer was one Gomcza, who held 80 shares in the company. Each of the Ybarras was the owner of 72. The enterprise had all the elements of co-adventureship.

The voyage, and the loss of the ship which followed, presented remarkable incidents. The course from Vivero to Rotterdam would, in normal circumstances, be laid by a competent navigator so as to pass clear of the dangers of Ushant. A course, in fact, was set which, if prolonged, would have taken the vessel ashore inside Armen Rock; a course altogether unexplained; out of the track of ships passing from Finisterre to Ushant; but presenting the advantage to anyone who had by good fortune foreseen the casualty, that it would bring the vessel nearer the fishing fleet south of Penmarch. This fleet, in fact, by a happy coincidence, picked up the crew when in their boats.

On the night of April 27, in fine weather; with a smooth sea; little or no wind blowing; the vessel sank in deep water. The vessel did not actually founder for five hours after the crew had prudently taken to their boats. No attempt was made to attract attention or secure assistance by wireless or by rockets. To complete a singular chapter of maritime misfortune, we are assured that all the ship's logs and papers perished in an attempt which failed to launch the first boat. No evidence whatever was offered at the hearing of any casualty to which the sinking of the ship could be attributed except the influx of sea water. The second mate indeed says that he saw some wreckage. But his evidence is valueless because he evidently had not formed the view that the Arnus was struck by it. Other evidence there was none.

I find myself, as I have already indicated, in complete agreement with all the Judges who have reached the conclusion that the vessel was scuttled. Mr. Justice Bailhache alone has taken a different view. It becomes necessary, therefore, to ask what motive influenced those on board, and particularly the captain and the engineer, in so scuttling her. The captain in particular had no pecuniary interest in adopting a course so little likely to advance his professional reputation.

It is not suggested that they had any quarrel with, or cherished any spite against, the owners. They were comparatively small men; with a relatively small interest in the venture. The owners, on the other hand, had a gigantic interest in the scuttling. The loss of the vessel at that particular moment meant indeed the difference to the company between solvency and insolvency. When once the fact of deliberate scuttling is established, the probability which remains to be balanced is as to whether such scuttling took place with or without the privity of the owners. Their counsel pressed upon us the terms in which the minutes of the meetings were couched in the period immediately preceding the loss. I find this argument particularly uncon-vincing. If a man who has an immense pecuniary interest in casting away his ship has decided to commit this fraud, I should not expect any hint of it to be contained in his papers. On the contrary, unless besides being a rogue he was also a fool, I should expect his papers carefully to convey the impression that he was engaged in arranging for the further employment of his vessel.

Applying the general test which I have already indicated, I am satisfied that the respondents have discharged the task which this case imposed upon them. In other words, they have proved facts from which there springs an irresistible inference that the owners were accomplices in the fraudulent destruction of the vessel. There would have been ample evidence to place before a jury upon this issue; and I have no doubt as to the conclusion which a jury would have reached.

The appeal therefore, in my judgment fails, and I move your Lordships in this sense.

IN RE JAMES TOVER
Justice Court of California, Tuolumne County
Case No. 500. (1851)

R. C. BARRY, J.P.

This was a caze in which James Tover had jumped a peece of grund that the Wideawake company claimed as part of thear clame. Upon hearing the evidence of all the witnesses on boath sides, and taking the caze under avisement I came to the following conclusion that boath parties is in falt. I therefore decree that the ground be equally divided, and one haf be returned to James Tover and one half to the Wideawake Company and that each pay one haf of the Costs of Coort share and share alik.

Costs of Coort 6 ounces, and that each stand committed until each of them pays there amount.

Sonora, Aug 14, 1851
U. H. Brown, Constable.

GRIMALDI v. LOCAL NO. 9, JOURNEYMEN BARBERS, HAIRDRESSERS AND COSMETOLOGISTS INTERNATIONAL UNION
Supreme Court of Pennsylvania
397 Pa.1; 153 A.2d 214 (1959)

MICHAEL A. MUSMANNO, Justice.

Louis J. Grimaldi is the owner of, and the only barber in, a barber shop located at 1438 South 58th Street, Philadelphia. Thus, he has no employees, and at the same time he has no employer. He is a one-man operation, solely and exclusively. He opens his shop when he pleases, he closes it when it suits his will to do so. He has no labor trouble because he employs no labor. He has no dispute with an employer because, obviously, he has no employer. He is as much a one-man operation as a man on a unicycle. He has as much undisputed control over his barber shop as Robinson Crusoe had over his island on the Thursday before Friday arrived.

Although, as mentioned, Grimaldi has no labor problem within the confines of his domain, on July 31, 1956 a major trouble was deposited on his doorstep and a haunting threat began to walk his sidewalk, none of which dire visitations he provoked, and certainly did not desire. On that evening there assembled outside his shop several men wearing sandwich slings calling upon Grimaldi to join Local No. 9, Journeymen Barbers, Hairdressers and Cosmetologists International Union (hereinafter to be referred to as Local No. 9). T h i s union is made up of barbers, hairdressers and cosmetologists who are employees in barber and beauty shops owned by others. Grimaldi is not qualified for membership in this union because he is not an employee. As already stated, and as will be repeated, he is a one-man institution. He works for no one else. He toils only for himself. He cuts hair, shaves faces, administers shampoos, applies lotions and does all that is traditionally expected of a barber. As absolute owner of his place of business, and as master of himself and his work, he would be entirely out of place in a union composed of men who are employees in shops in which they do not have the slightest proprietary interest.

At meetings of Local No. 9, the discussions naturally revolve around such subjects as wages to be asked of employers, working conditions to be requested of employers, vacations to be sought of employers. Grimaldi could not participate in such discussions because it would be grotesque for him to ask himself how much salary he should pay himself, how much vacation he should allow himself, and what working conditions he should demand of himself.

Nevertheless, on July 31, 1956, pickets appeared in front of Grimaldi's place of business with signs urging prospective customers to stay away. The picketing was effective. Many patrons turned on their heels when they read the signs; men with supplies refused to cross the picket line; deliveries of towels ceased. Stagnation was immediate and decisive. With customers frightened away, supplies cut off, and laundry service severed, it could only be a matter of days until Grimaldi's business would expire like an undersea diver whose oxygen line has knotted. He appealed to the courts. He petitioned the Court of Common Pleas of Philadelphia County to restrain and enjoin Local No. 9, with its officers and members, from picketing his shop, from interfering with his business, and from intimidating or attempting to intimidate him to join Local No. 9.

After a hearing . . . a preliminary injunction issued. . . [and] a final decree [was entered] which granted the plaintiff the full relief prayed for. . . .

The decree must be affirmed. The picketing attempted by Local No. 9 is a flagrant violation of the law and cannot be supported. The picketing of a one-man establishment is an invasion of an American's freedom to determine his own economic destiny when he stands alone in an enterprise of his own. Labor unions have the right to picket for organizational purposes, that is, to persuade non-union employees of an establishment to join a union. Such peaceful picketing is constitutionally protected and cannot be enjoined. . . . But the picketing in this case was not for organizational purposes and could not be for that purpose. There are no non-union employees in Grimaldi's shop. On what basis then, can there be lawful picketing for organizing employees? What is to be organized? Who are to be united?

Local No. 9, through its secretary Vincent Pace, of whom more will be said later, inflicted upon Grimaldi an harassment and intimidation which violated his rights and prerogatives as a United States citizen. Because he refused to join something he did not need and which could not help him he was threatened with economic extinction - - and then the means to so extinguish him were put into motion. . . .

In the early part of January, 1956, Vince Pace, accompanied by three other men of Local 9, called on Louis Grimaldi in his barber shop and endeavored unsuccessfully to persuade him to join the union. . . . Then, on April 16, 1956 Vincent Pace, accompanied by five members of Local 9, met with Louis Grimaldi and five other self-employed barbers who were members of a social and educational organization known as the Pennsylvania League of Master Barbers. At this meeting Pace endeavored to induce the self-employed barbers to dissolve the Pennsylvania League of Master Barbers and to join up with Local No. 9. When Grimaldi and his companions stated they were not receptive to this idea, Pace became very abusive. He called the officers of the Pennsylvania League of Master Barbers opprobrious names and used language which was profane, vicious and obscene. He then outrightly threatened the organization and its members, declaring that if the self-employed barbers did not join his local, he would bestow upon them the "kiss of death." His threats were all garbed in a vileness of speech that offends the very paper on which it is printed.

Grimaldi and his companions refused to be intimidated and returned to their respective barber shops. On the morning of July 31, 1956, when Grimaldi arrived at his establishment to open it for business he found two of Pace's men sitting at the curb in a "cream colored Cadillac." They informed him that it was his "turn to join." Grimaldi replied, "Look, fellows, how many times must you be told that I can't join your union? You know my position. I can't join your union," and went into his shop to prepare for the day's work.

Several minutes later one of the Cadillac-borne men knocked at Grimaldi's door and informed him: "Well, we called up the office and we were told to picket your shop." Grimaldi replied, "Gentlemen, there's a big, wide sidewalk. Go ahead."

A few minutes later police arrived in response to a call made by the operator of a beauty shop in the vicinity. Still later the police captain of the district appeared, and when Grimaldi asked him "What can you do about this?" the police captain answered: "I can't do anything about it. The only thing I can do here is to see that nothing happens."

The pickets then, as Grimaldi was to testify later, "walked around the shop, you know, back and forth, back and forth, back and forth." And as they walked back and forth, Grimaldi's customers walked away.

The lower court found that this picketing was coercive and illegal and therefore enjoinable. Local 9, through its attorneys, argue that the court's injunction was illegal under the Labor Anti-Injunction Act of June 2, 1937, P.L. 1198, 43 P.S. § 206a et seq., as amended, which provides that no court shall have jurisdiction to issue an injunction "in any case involving or growing out of a labor dispute." . . . But the Act has no application here. The Act specifically states that:

> "A case shall be held to involve or to grow out of
> a labor dispute when the case involves *persons*
> who are engaged in a single industry, trade, craft
> or occupation, or have direct or indirect interests
> therein, or who are *employees* of the same em-
> ployer, or who are *members,* of the same or an
> affiliated organization of employers or employ-
> ees * * *."

It will be noted that the statute uses the plural throughout. It speaks of "persons," of "employees," and of "members." But there are no persons, employees or members in Grimaldi's shop. . .

In defining a labor dispute the Act says:

> "(c) The term 'labor dispute' includes any contro-
> versy concerning terms or *conditions of employ-
> ment*, or concerning the association or representa-
> tion of persons in negotiating, fixing, maintain-
> ing, changing, or seeking to *arrange terms or
> conditions of employment* or concerning employ-
> ment relations or *any other controversy arising
> out of the respective interests of employer and*

employee, regardless of whether or not the disputants stand in the proximate relation of employer and employee, and regardless of whether or not the *employees* are on strike with the employer."

. . . Here again we find the plural "employees." There was no controversy over conditions of employment and there was no discord arising out of "respective interests of employer and employee." Nor could there be, since there was no employer or employee at Grimaldi's shop. Moreover, the Local did not claim, and does not now claim, that Grimaldi was charging unfair prices or that he was working improper hours, or that he was undermining in any way the working conditions of journeymen barbers--those employed in other shops. . .

Grimaldi's industrial status is entirely different from that of the journeymen barbers who belong to Local 9. Grimaldi, as a one-man, self-employed barber, lives in an economic world entirely different from the one inhabited by the journeyman barber. The journeyman barber receives wages from his employer, he is saddled with no financial burden so far as the shop is concerned, he pays no rent, buys no equipment, he suffers no personal loss in the event of fire or other disaster. The self-employed barber, on the other hand, carries the whole responsibility of the shop on his back, he owns or rents the place in which he conducts his business, he purchases the equipment, he pays all expenses in maintaining the shop and keeping it clean. If there is a fire, he personally suffers what is lost. Of course, all profits of the business are his, as all losses are borne by him.

Grimaldi's position in Philadelphia is not unique. There are some 2,600 barber shops in Philadelphia. Of this number, 1,700 are one-man shops, leaving only 900 which are manned by multiple barbers. Why should 1,700 legitimately-owned and legitimately-operated institutions be required to conform to the standards of practically only one-half that number? While, of course, no one can or would object to the multiple-operated barber shop, there are many people who prefer being barbered in a one-man shop, and there is no reason in the law, no custom in society, and no argument in the armory of common sense which militates against the enjoyment of that one-man service.

The profession of barbering is an old and honored one. There was a time when the barber was, in a measure also a surgeon. His functions included the dressing of wounds, blood-letting, and other surgical operations. While the barber of today, of course, no longer practices surgery in any form (intentionally!), he is still an indispensable and highly desirable factor in the pattern of today's civilization. And if the barber prefers to practice alone, no one may compel him to abandon his independence, while there is a public willing to avail itself of his specialized attention.

The one-man business in America contributes greatly to the well-being of the nation and its people. It is not necessary to point out that much of the magnificent industrial and commercial structure which is America's greatest

269

wealth today originated in one-man operations which pioneered, invented and dared to go forward alone in the development of ideas for the improvement of man's comforts and conveniences, as well as in protecting his physical and economic health.

Labor organizations are not concerned with one-man enterprises, except to encourage the proprietors in their endeavors, hoping that they will eventually achieve that success and expansion which will make it possible for them to employ workers, thereby increasing the prosperity and general well-being of the whole county. But until that happens, labor organizations allow these one-man affairs to proceed unhampered, unannoyed, and unpicketed. To picket a one-man job is like sticking pins into a hen that is sitting on eggs, concentrating on the important job of hatching vital forces which will contribute to the preservation of the human race. Labor organizations thus do not enter into the industrial barnyard until the new chickens are hatched and new workers are in being.

The purpose of labor organizations is to offer protection to multiple employees through collective bargaining, which is the backbone of the labor movement. It is the *e pluribus unum* of the industrial state. Where two or more workers are employed by the same employer, the way is open for them to form an organization for the purpose of discussing and negotiating with the employer on the subjects of wages and working conditions. Without collective bargaining, employees could be at the mercy of an employer who refuses to be guided by fundamental concepts in humanity and fair dealing.

But collective bargaining cannot possibly be used against an individual who has neither employees nor employer. The very word *collective* excludes the solitary individual. A man cannot collect with himself. And if an attempt is made to use collective bargaining against an individual who does not come within the purport of collectiveness, damage is done to the very cause of collective bargaining. The blade which is used to strike down the innocent, becomes stained and blunted with injustice, thereby diminishing its capabilities for protecting those who are dependent on it for the protection of their inalienable rights.

The extraordinary tactics of Local 9 in this case cannot possibly help the cause of organized labor and could well draw the censure of labor leaders who are concerned about advancing the wholesome collective cause of labor and not in supporting ruffianism as displayed by Vincent Pace and his associates. Labor has come a long way since the era when the workman was practically looked upon as the serf of his master. The treatment of workmen in those years wrote a black page in the industrial history of mankind. Fortunately, that melancholy era is behind us. Legislation throughout the world and particularly in America has elevated the wage earner to a dignity which commands respect and consideration.

Wage earners who are welded together into a labor organization form an entity of responsibility and accountability which the law recognizes as a force for good in the economic and social society of the State. But Vincent Pace attempted to use Local 9 as a personal slingshot for the attainment of an objective which no labor organization ever heretofore attempted in Pennsylvania, so far as recorded litigation is concerned. The action of Local 9 detracts from labor's record and, if unrestrained, could in itself write a page of oppressiveness of which no labor organization would be proud.

If Local 9 were to be allowed to picket as it attempted to picket here, it would mean that no individual could perform any work of his own without the possibility of molestation. Even a member of Local 9 itself could be harassed by the shadows of marching sandwich men if he mowed the lawn in his own back yard, or built a little wall around his garden, or dug a pond for his children to play in, or helped his wife to paper the walls in the kitchen.

Moreover, if what Local 9 contended for would become law, it would mean that even a member of Local 9 when he retires would not be permitted to add to a pension or to social security payments. He could not knock together, with hammer and saw, a few little wood novelties to sell to passers-by; he could not fashion with his hands some odd toys, souvenirs and knickknacks to vend to tourists in the little retreat to which he had withdrawn to spend the twilight days of his life; he would not be permitted to open a little store or to plant a garden in which to grow roses to bestow, for a consideration, on those who are distant from flower shops; he would be prohibited from roasting peanuts and selling them in little bags to those on the way to a sandlot baseball game. To picket a peanut vendor would be the ultimate in abuse of the weapon of picketing, but in principle it would be no different from what Local 9 endeavored to do against Grimaldi.

The picketing of a one-man business has dire and sinister possibilities. If Local 9 may drive a one-man barber shop out of business, why may not a hypothetical Local 999 do the same to a one-man lawyer's office? It could happen that the lawyers in large law offices would form a union and then demand that the country lawyer in his little office, or the city lawyer practicing by himself, join Local 999 or be humiliated and stripped of the emoluments of his profession by the placarding of his office with signs that he is unfair to other lawyers. Doctors in large hospitals could form a union and picket the country doctor, demanding that he make calls only at certain hours and charge only certain minimum fees, or run the risk of having no patients at all because of the omnipresent threat of picketing. If the one-man barber may be picketed, so may the one-man engineer, the one-man architect, the one-man artist, and the one-man author. And if that should happen, then liberty in America would be known only as the name of a statue. . .

God gave man hands to use for self-protection and for the obtaining of food, shelter, raiment, and happiness for himself and for those dependent upon him. No one may deprive him of the benefits those hands may bring him when they are occupied in his own behalf. Those hands may be used to acquire property, the ownership of which will be protected by the Constitution of Pennsylvania, P.S. which declares:

> "All men * * * have certain inherent and indefea-
> sible rights, among which are those of enjoying

the defending life and liberty, of acquiring, possessing and protecting property and reputation, and of pursuing their own happiness." (Art.1, Sec.1)

In the exercise of that constitutional right, one may acquire for himself a barber's chair, a carpenter's bench, or a bricklayer's trowel, and so long as he uses these implements himself and in a manner which does not adversely affect the economic rights of others, no one may dictate the method or the hours in which he may utilize them.

Local 9 was given every opportunity to present its case fully in the lower Court and we are satisfied that the Findings of Fact and Conclusion of Law are justified by the record. We therefore, affirm the decree entered in the Court of Common Pleas, and place the cost on the appellants.

HALL v. MOORING
Court of Appeals of Georgia
12 Ga.App. 74; 76 S.E. 759 (1912)

JAMES ROBERT POTTLE, J.

This was a contest between two members of the gentler sex. The plaintiff was a practitioner of the art or science of osteopathy, and the defendant either needed, or thought she did (which is the same thing), the services of the plaintiff. Several visits were made at $3.10 per visit, the ten cents being added for streetcar fare, and the whole bill amounted to $27.90. The defendant says she paid all she really owed, and that the plaintiff charged her for a number of social calls, during the course of which the defendant was importuned to continue the treatment. The defendant says that she declined to do so, and that the services rendered by the doctor gave her no relief, and were so unsatisfactory that she was forced to resort to a physician of the allopathic school, who administered pills and mixtures in the good old-fashioned way.

On the issues of fact the plaintiff outswore the defendant, or at least the jury in the justice's court thought she did, and the judge of the superior court refused to interfere. This is the end of the law so far as this branch of the case is concerned.

It would never do to hold that a doctor is entitled to recover only where he cures the patient. If we did, the members of this learned profession might hesitate to respond in extreme cases where the chances were against them. So far as we are concerned the doctors may continue to bury their mistakes and recover for their services as they have always done. If we were dealing with lawyers, the rule might be different, but sufficient unto the day is the evil thereof.

The defendant says she ought not to pay the extra ten cents per visit, because the doctor usually walked. However, the plaintiff testified that the charge was usual and reasonable. If so, she had a right to walk and save the ten cents.

It appears from the record that the trial waxed warm, and, during the testimony of the defendant, the plaintiff became excited and exclaimed, "liar, liar, liar;" and while the defendant's counsel was endeavoring to persuade the jury to accept his client's theory of the case, the plaintiff did, at intervals, "yell out in court that the defendant was a liar and had lied." Complaint is made that this conduct of the plaintiff humiliated and embarrassed the defendant and prejudiced the jury against her, and that the verdict ought to be set aside because the magistrate failed to punish the plaintiff for contempt.

Doubtless the conduct of the plaintiff overawed the chivalrous young justice and embarrassed him quite as much as it did the defendant, and we are not disposed to criticize too harshly his exhibition of judicial timidity. At any rate the failure of the magistrate to punish the contumelious plaintiff must be allowed to rest upon his judicial conscience. If we had any means of knowing that the plaintiff's conduct terrorized the jury and coerced the verdict in her favor, we would, in the interest of a fair and impartial trial, direct another hearing. But the jury doubtless felt secure under the protection of the bailiff and the sacred precincts of the court-room; and if they had returned a verdict adverse to the plaintiff, there was, no doubt, some rear door through which they might have dispersed and thus have escaped violence at the hands of a litigant outraged at the injustice which had been meted out to her. Viewing the matter from this safe distance, we are inclined to think that the unseemly conduct of the plaintiff would more likely have prejudiced her own cause than it did the defendant's. . . .

Judgment affirmed.

CHEMICAL SPECIALTIES MANUFACTURERS ASSOCIATION INC. v. CLARK
United States Court of Appeals, Fifth Circuit
482 F.2d 325 (1973)

PER CURIAM, [JOHN R. BROWN, HOMER THORNBERRY, LEWIS R. MORGAN, JJ.]:

On March 30, 1971, the Board of County Commissioners of Dade County, Florida adopted an ordinance amending its Municipal Code by adding Section 24-44. That ordinance, as now modified, required that every product within the definition of "detergent" or "synthetic detergent" must bear a label showing the ingredients of the product, listed in descending order of their presence by weight. CSMA consists of manufacturers and marketers of products falling within the scope of the ordinance. Their basic premise is that Congress preempted this field of regulation through the 1966 Amendments to the Federal Hazardous Substances Act (FHSA), 15 U.S.C.A. § 1261. Thus, they seek a declaratory judgment that the Dade County ordinance is invalid. . . Finding no conflict between the Dade County ordinance and FHSA the trial Judge upheld the ordinance. We reverse.

Reading the plain words of the 1966 Amendment to FHSA in light of their legislative history, [citation omitted] and the obvious desirability of a uniform Federal standard, we hold that the Dade County regulation must give way to the supremacy of Federal law. . .

Reversed and remanded.

JOHN R. BROWN, Chief Judge (concurring):

As soap, now displaced by latter day detergents is the grist of Madison Avenue, I add these few comments in the style of that street to indicate my full agreement with the opinion of the court and to keep the legal waters clear and phosphate-free.

As *Proctor* of this dispute between the representative of many manufacturers of household detergents and the Board of Commissioners of Metropolitan Dade County, Florida, who have promulgated regulations which seek to control the labeling of such products sold within their jurisdiction (largely to discourage use which pollutes their waters), the Court holds that congress has specifically preempted regulatory action by Dade County. Clearly, the decision represents a *Gamble* since we risk a *Cascade* of criticism from an increasing *Tide* of ecology-minded citizens. Yet, a contrary decision would most likely have precipitated a *Niagara* of complaints from an industry which justifiably seeks uniformity in the laws with which it must comply. Inspired by the legendary valor of *Ajax*, who withstood Hector's lance, we have *Boldly* chosen the course of uniformity in reversing the lower Court's decision upholding Dade County local labeling laws. And, having done so, we are *Cheered* by the thought that striking down the regulation by the local jurisdiction does not create a void which is detrimental to consumers, but rather merely acknowledges that federal legislation has preempted this field with adequate labeling rules.

Congress, of course, has the *Cold Power* to preempt. Of the three situations discussed by the Court, the first (direct conflict) is easy, for it is *Crystal Clear* that the state law must yield. The third, in which the ordinance may *supplement* the federal law and thereby extend or increase the degree of regulation, is more troublesome. For where Congress has chosen to fashion a regulatory scheme that is only the *Head and Shoulders,* but has not opted to regulate every aspect of the area, the states have implied power to flesh out the body. It is where Congress fails to clearly signify, with an appropriate preemption clause, its intent to fully occupy the area regulated that the problem arises. With some *Joy*, the Court finds there is such a clause.

Concerning the precautionary labeling aspect, this is *SOS* to consumers. If we *Dash* to the heart of the question, it is apparent, as the Court points out, that the 1966 Amendments to FHSA indicate an explicit congressional purpose to preempt state regulation of the labeling of these substances. Undoubtedly, this unequivocal congressional *Salvo* was directed at such already existing regulations as those of the Fire Department of New York City relating to pressurized containers. . .

Indeed, Congress intended to wield its *Arm and Hammer* to *Wisk* away such local regulations and further, to preclude the growing *Trend* toward this proliferation of individual community supervision. Its purpose was at least two-fold: (i) to put day-to-day responsibility in the hands of local government, but (ii) at the same time to impose detailed identical standards to eliminate confusion or overlapping.

With this clear expression of congressional intent to create some form of preemption, the only thing remaining was whether the meaning of the term "precautionary labeling" is sufficiently broad to embrace the words of the Dade County ordinance, *Vel* non. In making this determination, the Court is furnished with a *Lever* by our *Brothers* of the Second Circuit. [citation omitted] And so we hold. This is all that need be said. It is as plain as *Mr. Clean* the proper *Action* is that the Dade County Ordinance must be superseded, as *All* comes out in the wash.

WEBSTER v. BLUE SHIP TEA ROOM, INC.
Supreme Judicial Court of Massachusetts
347 Mass. 421; 198 N.E.2d 309 (1964)

PAUL CASHMAN REARDON, Justice.

This is a case which by its nature evokes earnest study not only of the law but also of the culinary traditions of the Commonwealth which bear so heavily upon its outcome. It is an action to recover damages for personal injuries sustained by reason of a breach of implied warranty of food served by the defendant in its restaurant. An auditor, whose findings of fact were not to be final, found for the plaintiff. On a retrial in the Superior Court before a judge and jury, in which the plaintiff testified, the jury returned a verdict for her. . . .

The jury could have found the following facts: On Saturday, April 25, 1959, about 1 P.M., the plaintiff, accompanied by her sister and her aunt, entered the Blue Ship Tea Room operated by the defendant. The group was seated at a table and supplied with menus.

This restaurant, which the plaintiff characterized as "quaint," was located in Boston "on the third floor of an old building on T Wharf which overlooks the ocean."

The plaintiff, who had been born and brought up in New England (a fact of some consequence), ordered clam chowder and crabmeat salad. Within a few minutes she received tidings to the effect that "there was no more clam chowder," whereupon she ordered a cup of fish chowder. Presently, there was set before her "a small bowl of fish chowder." She had previously enjoyed a breakfast about 9 A.M. which had given her no difficulty. "The fish chowder contained haddock, potatoes, milk, water and seasoning. The chowder was milky in color and not clear. The haddock and potatoes were in chunks" (also a fact of consequence). "She agitated it a little with the spoon and observed that it was a fairly full bowl * * *. It was hot when she got it, but she did not tip it with her spoon because it was hot * * * but stirred it in an up and under motion. She denied that she did this because she was looking for something, but it was rather because she wanted an even distribution of fish and potatoes." "She started to eat it, alternating between the chowder and crackers which were on the table with * * * [some] rolls. She ate about 3 or 4 spoonfuls then stopped. She looked at the spoonfuls as she was eating. She saw equal parts of liquid, potato and fish as she spooned it into her mouth. She did not see anything unusual about it. After 3 or 4 spoonfuls she was aware that something had lodged in her throat because she couldn't swallow and couldn't clear her throat by gulping and she could feel it." This misadventure led to two esophagoscopies at the Massachusetts General Hospital, in the second of which, on April 27, 1959, a fish bone was found and removed. The sequence of events produced injury to the plaintiff which was not insubstantial.

We must decide whether a fish bone lurking in a fish chowder, about the ingredients of which there is no other complaint, constitutes a breach of implied warranty under applicable provisions of the Uniform Commercial Code, the annotations to which are not helpful on this point. As the judge put it in his charge, "Was the fish chowder fit to be eaten and wholesome? * * * [N]obody is claiming that the fish itself wasn't wholesome. * * * But the bone of contention here--I don't mean that for a pun--but was this fish bone a foreign substance that made the fish chowder unwholesome or not fit to be eaten?"

The plaintiff has vigorously reminded us of the high standards imposed by this court where the sale of food is involved . . . and has made reference to cases involving stones in beans . . . trichinae in pork . . . and to certain other cases, here and elsewhere, serving to bolster her contention of breach of warranty.

The defendant asserts that here was a native New Englander eating fish chowder in a "quaint" Boston dining place where she had been before; that "[f]ish chowder, as it is served and enjoyed by New Englanders, is a hearty dish, originally designed to satisfy the appetites of our seamen and fishermen"; that "[t]his court knows well that we are not talking of some insipid broth as is customarily served to convalescents." We are asked to rule in such fashion that no chef is forced "to reduce the pieces of fish in the chowder to minuscule size in an effort to ascertain if they contained any pieces of bone." "In so ruling," we are told (in the defendant's brief), "the court will not only uphold its reputation for legal knowledge and acumen, but will, as loyal sons of Massachusetts, save our world-renowned fish chowder from degenerating into an insipid broth containing the mere essence of its former stature as a culinary masterpiece." Notwithstanding these passionate entreaties we are bound to examine with detachment the nature of fish chowder and what might happen to it under varying interpretations of the Uniform Commercial Code.

Chowder is an ancient dish preexisting even "the appetites of our seamen and fishermen." It was perhaps the common ancestor of the "more refined cream soups, purées, and bisques." Berolzheimer, *The American Woman's Cook Book* (Publisher's Guild Inc., New York, 1941) p. 176. The word "chowder" comes from the French "chaudière," meaning a "cauldron" or "pot." "In the fishing villages of Britany * * * 'faire la chaudière' means to supply a cauldron in which is cooked a mess of fish and biscuit with some savory condiments, a hodge-podge contributed by the fishermen themselves, each of whom in return receives his share of the prepared dish. The Breton fishermen probably carried the custom to Newfoundland, long famous for its chowder, whence it has spread to Nova Scotia, New Brunswick, and New England." *A New English Dictionary* (Macmillan and Co., 1893) p. 386.

Our literature over the years abounds in references not only to the delights of chowder but also to its manufacture. A namesake of the plaintiff, Daniel Webster, had a recipe for fish chowder which has survived into a number of modern cookbooks[1] and in which the removal of fish bones is not mentioned at all. One old time recipe recited in the New English Dictionary study defines chowder as "A dish made of fresh fish (esp. cod) or clams, stewed with slices of pork or bacon, onions, and biscuit. 'Cider and champagne are sometimes added.'" Hawthorne, in *The House of the Seven Gables* (Allyn and Bacon, Boston, 1957) p. 8, speaks of "[a] codfish of sixty pounds, caught in the bay, [which] had been dissolved into the rich liquid of a chowder." A chowder variant, cod "Muddle," was made in Plymouth in the 1890s by taking "a three or four pound codfish, head added. Season with salt and pepper and boil in just enough water to keep from burning. When cooked, add milk and piece of butter."[2] The recitation of these ancient formulae suffices to indicate that in the construction of chowders in these parts in other years, worries about fish bones played no role whatsoever.

---

[1] "Take a cod of ten pounds, well cleaned, leaving on the skin. Cut into pieces one and a half pounds thick, preserving the head whole. Take one and a half pounds of clear, fat salt pork, cut in thin slices. Do the same with twelve potatoes. Take the largest pot you have. Fry out the pork first, then take out the pieces of pork, leaving in the drippings. Add to that three parts of water, a layer of fish, so as to cover the bottom of the pot; next a layer of potatoes, then two tablespoons of salt, 1 teaspoon of pepper, then the pork, another layer of fish, and the remainder of the potatoes. Fill the pot with water to cover the ingredients. Put over a good fire. Let the chowder boil twenty-five minutes. When this is done have a quart of boiling milk ready, and ten hard crackers split and dipped in cold water. Add milk and crackers. Let the whole boil five minutes. The chowder is then ready to be first-rate if you have followed the directions. An onion may be added if you like the flavor." "This chowder," he adds, "is suitable for a large fishing party." Wolcott, *The Yankee Cook Book* (Coward-McCann, Inc., New York City, 1939) p. 9.

[2] Atwood, *Recipes for Cooking Fish* (Avery & Doten, Plymouth, 1896) p. 8.

This broad outlook on chowders has persisted in more modern cookbooks. "The chowder of today is much the same as the old chowder * * *." *The American Woman's Cook Book*, supra, p. 176. The all embracing Fannie Farmer states in a portion of her recipe, fish chowder is made with a "fish skinned, but head and tail left on. Cut off head and tail and remove fish from backbone. Cut fish in 2-inch pieces and set aside. Put head, tail, and backbone broken in pieces, in stewpan; add 2 cups cold water and bring slowly to boiling point * * *." The liquor thus produced from the bones is added to the balance of the chowder. Farmer, *The Boston Cooking School Cook Book* (Little Brown Co., 1937) p. 166.

Thus, we consider a dish which for many long years, if well made, has been made generally as outlined above. It is not too much to say that a person sitting down in New England to consume a good New England fish chowder embarks on a gustatory adventure which may entail the removal of some fish bones from his bowl as he proceeds. We are not inclined to tamper with age old recipes by any amendment reflecting the plaintiff's view of the effect of the Uniform Commercial Code upon them. We are aware of the heavy body of case law involving foreign substances in food, but we sense a strong distinction between them and those relative to unwholesomeness of the food itself, e.g., tainted mackerel [citation omitted], and a fish bone in a fish chowder. Certain Massachusetts cooks might cavil at the ingredients contained in the chowder in this case in that it lacked the heartening lift of salt pork. In any event, we consider that the joys of life in New England include the ready availability of fresh fish chowder. We should be prepared to cope with the hazards of fish bones, the occasional presence of which in chowders is, it seems to us, to be anticipated, and which, in the light of a hallowed tradition, do not impair their fitness or merchantability. While we are buoyed up in this conclusion by Shapiro v. Hotel Statler Corp., [citation omitted], in which the bone which afflicted the plaintiff appeared in "Hotbarquette of Seafood Mornay," we know that the United States District Court of Southern California, situated as are we upon a coast, might be expected to share our views.

We are most impressed, however, by Allen v. Grafton, [citation omitted] where in Ohio, the Midwest, in a case where the plaintiff was injured by a piece of oyster shell in an order of fried oysters, Mr. Justice Taft (now Chief Justice) in a majority opinion held that "the possible presence of a piece of oyster shell in or attached to an oyster is so well known to anyone who eats oysters that we can say as a matter of law that one who eats oysters can reasonably anticipate and guard against eating such a piece of shell * * *." [citation omitted]

Thus, while we sympathize with the plaintiff who has suffered a peculiarly New England injury, the order must be

Exceptions sustained.

Judgment for the defendant.

CHAPTER IV: BUSINESS, TRADE & COMMERCE

GASPARI v. MUHLENBERG TOWNSHIP BOARD OF ADJUSTMENT
Supreme Court of Pennsylvania
391 Pa. 7; 139 A.2d 544 (1958)

MICHAEL A. MUSMANNO, Justice.

Prior to recent years, commercially grown mushrooms obtained most of their substance, but fortunately, not their flavor, from horse manure. . . .

> "* * * The Mushroom is a plant but it is not a plant
> like a green plant which needs only sun, light,
> water, carbon dioxide from the air; the mushroom
> would never be able to grow. The mushroom
> must be fed more like an animal is fed because it
> cannot make its own food. It must be fed special.
> The compost is that kind of material. The tradi-
> tional method was horse manure."

With the advent of the motor age which brought in its train the disbanding of the cavalry by the United States Army, the abandonment in most cities of mounted police, the emancipation of brewery wagon Percherons, and the general substitution of gasoline as fuel for vehicles theretofore horse-drawn, it was only natural that considerably less horse manure was produced. As a consequence, the mushroom industry faced a crisis. Thus do many seemingly unrelated subjects bear heavily upon the fact of one another.

However, science came to the rescue with the invention or development of an artificial manure which has become known as synthetic compost. This object of man's fertile ingenuity seems to fulfill all the requirements of alimentation and agricultural growth associated with horse manure, that is, insofar as mushrooms are concerned, and it has, therefore, practically supplanted the earthier product. In fact, one of the plaintiffs here, Anthony Gaspari, testified that he would not use horse manure if he could get it for nothing.

Arthur Gaspari and his two brothers, Pietro and Gino, own 17 acres of land south of Frush Valley Road in Muhlenberg Township, Berks County. Since 1929 the Gaspari land has been utilized for the growing of mushrooms for sale. Beginning with 1933 the Gasparis have also engaged in the sale of mushroom supplies as mushroom paper, mushroom wire, baskets, manure baskets, wash tubs of all sizes, ground tubs, electric cords, insecticides and fungicides, thermometers and different types of hoses and spraying nozzles.

From 1936 to 1951 the Gasparis produced for sale mushroom spawn. (Mushroom spawn is the medium from which mushrooms grow.)

In 1948 the shadow of a manure famine began to fall over the Gaspari land. It seems that not only was horse manure gradually disappearing, because of the increased elimination of the producers, but what manure was available had considerably decreased in quality. While the scarcity, of course, was explained, no witness testified as to why the manure had deteriorated in tone to such an extent that the mushrooms depending on it for sustenance failed to achieve the stature of marketability.

Thus it was that in 1949 the Gasparis turned to science for manure. They succeeded beyond their most effluvial aspirations. They succeeded in producing a synthetic manure of such fertility and salubrity that, as already indicated, the plaintiff A. Gaspari would not today exchange his synthetic manure for horse manure if he could get horse manure gratis. But trouble of another odor was brewing for A. Gaspari and his brothers.

On August 26, 1955, the Building Inspector of Muhlenberg Township ordered the Gasparis to cease and desist in the production of synthetic manure and to dispose in 20 days of "all stock of manure not required for your own immediate use." The Gasparis appealed to the Board of Adjustment. . . . The matter was then heard in the Court of Common Pleas of Berks County which affirmed the decision of the Board of Adjustment. The appeal to this Court followed. The Gaspari property is located in an area known as "F" Farm District, according to an ordinance of the Township of Muhlenberg enacted June 8, 1943. Articles 2 and 3 of this ordinance permit:

> ". . . Farming in all its branches, including the
> erection or alteration of the usual accessory farm
> buildings, incident to agriculture and animal hus-
> bandry."

It is the legal position of Muhlenberg Township that the production of synthetic compost is not farming but manufacturing and that, therefore, being prohibited by ordinance, the order of the lower Court should be affirmed. The Gasparis argue, on the other hand, that the lower Court's order should be reversed on the grounds that the production of the artificial compost is an agricultural activity and therefore comes within the ambit of the authorized "farming in all its branches. . ."

What are the ingredients which go into the making of compost and what is the process whereby those ingredients become compost? The ingredients are simply hay and crushed corn cobs which are mixed and aerated, and treated with cyanamid, potash and gypsum. The completed operation usually takes 15 days, during which time the accumulations are moved approximately every three days. The lower Court says in its opinion:

> " If the component parts of the synthetic compost
> were mixed and then used as a medium for the
> growing of mushrooms, the growing medium
> would be ineffective. The ingredients must be
> thoroughly mixed, water must be applied together
> with a prescribed chemical, and the resulting

mass periodically turned mechanically so that a
bacteriological change may take place. After the
change has taken place, the end product is a
synthetic manure of compost which is an effective
growing medium."

After this exposition it arrives at the conclusion that synthetic manure is
achieved via a manufacturing process. It calls upon the language in our decision
of Commonwealth v. Weiland Packing Co. [citation omitted]:

"* * * the process of manufacture brings about the
production of some new article by the application of skill and labor to the original substance or material out of which such new product
emerges. . ."

But here, it is not a question as to whether one is or is not producing a new
article. The tomato which finally hangs on the plant is quite a new article when
compared to the tiny seed which went into the ground. The oak tree is certainly
a new article when compared to the acorn from which it sprang. The newness must
come about through the application of skill and labor, entirely or mostly apart from
what is done by Nature herself. . . . production of concrete is manufacturing. The
metamorphosis of sand, gravel and cement into pavement is exclusively a
mechanical process under the domination and control of man. The production of
synthetic compost is something entirely different.

It was not necessary for the Court of Common Pleas to consider, nor is it
necessary for us, whether the production of synthetic compost was a valid
extension of a non-conforming use because the activity never entered into the
category of a non-conforming use, coming, as it did, well within the ambit of
"farming in all its branches."

Reversed.

WELLS v. MAYOR & ALDERMEN OF SAVANNAH
Supreme Court of Georgia
87 Ga. 397; 13 S.E. 442 (1891)

LOGAN E. BLECKLEY, Chief Justice

[The plaintiff, held certain real estate in Savannah, Georgia, under a
purchase agreement with the city. The terms of purchase being the payment of an
annual ground rent forever, or, at the election of the plaintiff, his heirs, executors,
administrators or assigns, the payment in full of the stipulated purchase money at
any time. The lower court held that the real estate was property taxable by the
municipal government as the property of the purchaser or his successor in the
title.]

Some cases task the anxious diligence of a court not by their difficulty but their simplicity. This is one of them. Because the case seemed too plain for controversy, we have had some apprehension that we might decide it incorrectly. Impressed always by the ability and learning, the wise research and earnest advocacy of the distinguished counsel for the plaintiffs, we have experienced a vague dread that we might stumble over legal obstacles which, if they exist, a treacherous darkness conceals. In order to examine the ground thoroughly, we have held up the case for months, read authorities cited and not cited, perused books before unknown to us, deliberated, meditated, considered and reconsidered. But to the last hour we have discovered nothing debatable in the controlling question raised for our decision, fringed though it certainly is with technical niceties of great delicacy and much interest. To which side the artificial logic of these niceties would incline the scale is immaterial, for the solid practical subject of taxation must be dealt with on broader principles.

The value of property consists in its use, and he who owns the use forever, though it be on condition subsequent, is the true owner of the property for the time being. This holds equally of a city lot or of all the land in the world. Where taxation is *ad valorem,* values are the ultimate objects of taxation, and they to whom the values belong should pay the taxes. . . .

There was no error, either of practice or decision, in denying the injunction. Whatever the expectation of purchasers, or the unbroken practice of the city hitherto may have been, the mandate of the constitution of 1877 is to tax all property, save that expressly exempted by the legislature under constitutional authority, if any is taxed. That this mandate may have heretofore been disregarded, is no reason why it should not be obeyed now.

Judgment affirmed.

CROFT & SCULLY CO. v. M/V SKULPTOR VUCHETICH
United States Court of Appeals, Fifth Circuit
664 F.2d 1277 (1982)

JOHN R. BROWN, Circuit Judge:
Appellant Croft & Scully Co. appeals from a decision by the District Court limiting to $500 its recovery in an incident where the parties stipulated negligence. Finding that the District Court applied an incorrect standard in determining what constitutes a "package" for purposes of the Carriage of Goods by Sea Act (COGSA), 46 U.S.C.A. § 1300 *et seq.*, we reverse and remand. 508 F.Supp. 670.

Things Go Better With Coke

Croft & Scully contracted to ship 1755 cases of soft drinks from Houston, Texas to the middle eastern country of Kuwait. Apparently Kuwaitis would like to be Peppers, too. Croft & Scully arranged to ship the soft drinks on board M/ V SKULPTOR VUCHETICH, which would arrive in Houston on December 8, 1977. Baltic Shipping Co., owner of SKULPTOR, dispatched a 20-foot steel container to Croft & Scully's supplied in Wharton, Texas. Employees of the supplier loaded the 1755 cases, each containing 4 "6-packs" or 24 cans, into the container, closed and sealed it--a real Teem effort. The supplier then trucked the container to Goodpasture's yard, near the Houston Ship Channel, which Baltic had selected as a convenient storage facility pending arrival of SKULPTOR.

During the Refreshing Pause between arrival of the container and arrival of SKULPTOR, the vessel's agent prepared a Bill of Lading[1] and hired Shippers Stevedoring, Inc., to load the soft drink container on board SKULPTOR.

Pepsi Cola Hits the Spot--On the Pavement

As one of the Stevedore's employees was lifting the container, with the use of a forklift, he negligently dropped it.[2] By our calculations, 42,120 cans of soft drinks crashed to the ground, never a thirst to quench. In the Crush, the cans were damaged. The stevedore, no doubt, was in no mood to have a Coke and a smile.

Dr. Pepper at 10, 2 and § 1304

Croft & Scully sued Goodpasture, Shippers Stevedoring, and SKULPTOR and her owners to pick up the Tab for its damages. The District Court dismissed the
suit as to Goodpasture because it had no agency relationship with Shippers Stevedoring. Relying upon a so-called Himalaya Clause in the Bill of Lading, it granted the remaining defendants' motion for summary judgment and, finding that the container constituted a "package" within the meaning of § 4(5) of COGSA[3], limited Shippers Stevedoring's liability to $500. Croft & Scully appeals. Things Go Better on appeal, and we reverse and remand.

---

[1] The Bill of Lading described the container's contents as follows: "20' CONTAINER STC*: 1755 CASES DELAWARE PUNCH."

*In maritimese STC stands for "said to contain".

[2] The parties stipulated to the stevedore's negligence.

[3]§ 1304(5) states: Neither the carrier nor the ship shall in any event be or become liable for any loss or damage to or in connection with the transportation of goods in an amount exceeding $500 per package. . . or, in case of goods not shipped in packages, per customary freight unit. . . unless the nature and value of such goods have been declared by the shipper before shipment and inserted in the bill of lading. This declaration, if embodied in the bill of lading, shall be prima facie evidence, but shall not be conclusive on the carrier. . .

A Peek at the Himalaya Clause

Croft & Scully asserts that the Himalaya Clause limiting recovery to $500 violates public policy. That claim fails to make the grade, given our decision in *Brown & Root v. M/V PEISANDER*, 648 F.2d 415, --A.M.C.--(5th Cir. 1981), upholding such a clause. Indeed, the conflict which we surmounted there does not even arise in this case. Clause 17 of the Bill of Lading makes clear provision for an increased valuation at a higher freight rate.[4] A more unequivocal declaration, in fact, one could not find. As Croft & Scully could have availed itself of extra loss or damage protection but chose not to, the District Court correctly ruled that the Himalaya Clause applied.

Don't Judge The Package By Its Appearance

Even if liability is limited to $500 per package, Croft & Scully argues, the cardboard cases of soft drinks rather than the 20-foot container should constitute the relevant "package." Shippers Stevedoring responds with equal fervor that the container is the "package". Their argument, we think, given the recent decision in *Allstate Insurance Co., v. Inversiones Navieras Imparca,* 646 F.2d 169, --A.M.C.--(5th Cir. 1981), holds no water, carbonated or otherwise.

We begin by pointing out that COGSA does not apply by its own force and effect, since the incident occurred in the yard and not on the vessel. Rather, the Bill of Lading incorporates COGSA. Thus, its provisions are merely terms of the contract of carriage which, like any other contractual terms, call out for judicial interpretation in case of dispute...

The District Court further observed that the Fifth Circuit had not established a test to determine what constitutes a "package" under COGSA. Since the date of its order, this Court has formulated such a test in whose good hands the parties--and the District Court--must rest.

Allstate involved the loss of 341 cartons of stereo equipment. The shipper loaded the cartons inside a container, sealed it, and had its agent deliver it to the carrier. The carrier issued a Bill of Lading which described the contents both in number and in kind. When the container arrived in Venezuela, it was as empty as

---

[4] Clause 17

In case of any loss or damage to or in connection with goods exceeding in actual value $500.00... per package, or, in case of goods not shipped in packages, per customary freight unit, the value of the goods shall be deemed to be $500.00 per package or per unit, on which basis the freight is adjusted, and the carrier's liability, if any, shall be determined on the basis of $500.00 per package... *unless the nature of the goods and valuation higher that $500 shall have been declared in writing by the shipper upon delivery to the Carrier and inserted in this bill of lading* and extra freight paid if required and in such cases... the Carrier's liability, if any, shall not exceed the declared value... The limitations of liability and other provisions contained in this article shall inure not only to the benefit of the carrier, its agents, servants and employees, *but also to the benefit of any independent contractor* performing services *including stevedoring* in connection with goods hereunder. (emphasis added)

a can of soda on a hot summer day. The shipper sought recovery for its full damages, but the carrier, relying on COGSA, sought shelter in the $500 limitation. Although the District Court concluded that the container was the COGSA package, the winds of judicial change Schwepped away the $500 shelter and exposed the carrier to full liability. . . .

We find nothing in the Bill of Lading to indicate that the contracting parties intended some special meaning of the term "package." Since Croft & Scully included information about the contents of the container and their number, *Allstate* governs. Therefore, the District Court erred in granting summary judgment on the "package" issue.

Customary Freight Unit

Even if the container was not a COGSA "package," Shippers Stevedoring contends, the Court should uphold the $500 award because the container was a "customary freight unit" within the ambit of § 4(5) of COGSA, and thus the Himalaya Clause still applies. At the outset, we reject Croft & Scully's argument that Shippers Stevedoring waived this point in the trial below. The District Court, of course, never considered the issue, given its conclusion that the container was a "package," but in the light of our decision that *Allstate* supercedes the District's Court's finding, we must necessarily address this claim. . .

> . . . [T]he phrase 'per customary freight unit' in this context in the light of its legislative history, refers to the *unit of quantity, weight or measurement* of the cargo customarily used as the basis for the calculation of the freight rate to be charged. Generally, in marine contracts, the word 'freight' is used to denote remuneration or reward for carriage of goods by ship, rather than the goods themselves. . .

. . . From these cases, we deduce that "customary freight unit" is a question of fact that will vary from contract to contract. Of particular importance in this as in any contractual dispute, then, is the parties' intent, as expressed in the Bill of Lading, applicable tariff, and perhaps elsewhere . . .

Although Croft & Scully admitted that the freight charge was $2200, calculated on a "flat container rate," we do not know how the parties arrived at that rate. Does it depend upon the contents, weight, value, custom of the trade, applicable tariffs, if any, or other factors? The District Court must consider these questions on remand. If it finds that the container was a "customary freight unit," then the Court should reinstate the $500 limitation of liability. If not, then it should hold further proceedings to determine the amount of damages. We, of course, express no opinion concerning the outcome.

Recap

We affirm the District Court's dismissal of Goodpasture and its conclusion that the Himalaya Clause applies. We reverse its grant of summary judgment for Shippers Stevedoring and its finding that the steel container was a COGSA package. As the District Judge never reached the important factual question whether the container of soft drink cartons was a "customary freight unit," we remand for further inquiry into the facts and for consideration of the parties' intent, factors that will guide the trial Court in determining the meaning of that COGSA clause.

AFFIRMED IN PART, REVERSED IN PART AND REMANDED.

LEMY v. WATSON
Supreme Court of Judicature, King's Bench Division
[1915] 3 K.B. 731

RUFUS DANIEL ISAACS, LORD READING, C. J.

The respondents were summoned for having unlawfully sold goods to which they had applied a false trade description, namely, sardines, and they were convicted after a long hearing before Sir John Dickinson, the Chief Magistrate. They appealed to the Court of quarter session, and in the result the Court of quarter sessions . . . quashed the conviction and thus allowed the appeal. . .

The case made by the appellant, who represents a French trade society, is that a sardine is a small pilchard which is prepared in oil, packed in a tin in a way with which we are all familiar, and then sold in the tin as a tin containing sardines. The appellant says that the respondents have used a fish known as a brisling, which is the Norwegian name for a sprat or something like a sprat, which is prepared in oil in a similar fashion to the preparation of sardines in France, packed in tins, and sent over to this country and sold under the trade description of "Norwegian sardines." The appellant contends that the respondents have no right to apply the term "sardine" to their goods, and that they commit an offence by so doing.

The respondents have contended before us, not that they are entitled to use the term "sardine" simpliciter, but that they are entitled to use the term "sardine" if accompanied by the local prefix, that is "Norwegian," their contention being that the expression "Norwegian sardines" is a conventional description of the goods which they have been selling under that description, that this conventional description was in use and was applied before the passing of the Merchandise Act, 1887. I understand the whole of the judgment, after the consideration that I have given to it, to mean this, that these Norwegian brisling or sprats, prepared in oil and packed in tins, could not properly be described under the statute of 1887 as Norwegian sardines. They were not sardines in fact because they were not the small pilchard which is the sardine proper, and even with the prefix "Norwegian" it was false in fact to say that these fish so prepared were Norwegian sardines. It is true they were Norwegian, but they were not sardines. That is what I understand the finding to be when it says that the description was false in fact. . .

It follows in my judgment, from what I have said, that, not only from the way in which the case is stated but also from the way in which the case has been argued and presented before us, the conclusion to which Sir John Dickinson arrived was the right conclusion and that the Court of quarter sessions was wrong, and for these reasons I think this appeal must be allowed and the conviction restored.

SIR CHARLES JOHN DARLING J. [Concurring]

I have come to the same conclusion, though I admit that my opinion has wavered a good deal during the argument, not always in favour of the counsel addressing the Court.

The question really is, as it seems to me, whether it is legitimate to offer for sale under the name of Norwegian sardines sprats caught and prepared in Norway in a manner which makes them look like what are commonly sold as sardines. . .

There are many erroneous terms consecrated by common use. One which has been mentioned in the course of the argument, a glaring instance, is the term "Bombay ducks" as applied to an Indian fish, and it is agreed that if anybody ordered Bombay ducks and somebody supplied him with ducks from Bombay the contract to supply Bombay ducks would not be fulfilled. Another obvious instance is eau de Cologne. Whatever eau de Cologne may be, as to which I know nothing, it certainly is not water from the Rhine. If eau de Cologne were ordered and you simply supplied a gallon of water from Cologne that would not fulfill the contract.

Another instance where anybody would understand what was meant is if you speak of Roman pearls. They are not pearls with which any oyster has had anything to do, nor do I know that they are Roman. They indicate something which is probably neither Roman nor a pearl, just as it was said by a well-known historian[1] that the Holy Roman Empire had for its chief characteristic that it was neither holy nor Roman nor an empire. One other instance occurs to me of a term consecrated, or if I may say so, by common user which does not indicate the true fact, and that is when people speak as they commonly do of the judicial ermine, meaning merely any white fur when worn by a judge.

These expressions have become conventional terms, and are, I think, instances of a trade description lawfully and generally applied; and I come to the conclusion that they are generally applied for the reason that their use is not limited to the particular persons who produce the article and those who buy it for the purpose of retailing it to the public. . . .

---

[1] [Ed. Note: Voltaire, *Essai sur les Moeurs et l'Esprit des Nations.*]

Therefore, seeing that there is no excuse for the selling of these things as Norwegian sardines, unless the excuse can be found in s. 18 of the Act of 1887, I think that the decision of the Court of quarter sessions, which proceeded upon a wholly different interpretation of the statute from that which I have indicated, was wrong and should be reversed. . .

BETHUNE v. HUGHES, MARSHALL, &C.
Supreme Court of Georgia
28 Ga. 560 (1859)

JOSEPH H. LUMPKIN, J.

[This was an application in Habeas Corpus by Bethune, plaintiff in error, to be discharged from an alleged illegal imprisonment to which he was subjected, under, and by virtue of, a warrant issued by the city council of Columbus, for a violation of one of the market ordinances of said city. After argument, the court below refused to discharge petitioner, who, thereupon, excepted, and assigned error.]

The only question which we propose to consider and decide is: Did the mayor and council of the city of Columbus have the power to pass an ordinance making it penal, to sell such articles as are usually vended at a public city market, at any other place (within certain hours) than at the market?

By the 3d section of the Act 1858, it is declared that "the mayor and council of the city of Columbus shall have the power to establish and keep up one or more public markets in said city for the sale of poultry, eggs, butter, milk, fresh meats and vegetables of any kind and all other such articles as are usually vended at the city public market, and shall govern the same as such mayor and council shall deem necessary and proper; and may prescribe and enforce fines and penalties for a violation of market laws and regulations; *Provided, however*, That said mayor and council may grant private licenses for the sale of marketable articles, or any of them, at a place or places in said city, other than the public market upon such terms, regulations and control as the said mayor and council may adopt. . . "

It will be seen that the Act contains only a broad grant "to *establish* and *keep up* a market" or markets at one or more public places in the city. It confers no power to prohibit the sale of marketable articles elsewhere than at the market place.

Now it is laid down expressly in Grant on Corporations [citation omitted] and in *Mayor of Macelsfield vs. Chapman* [citation omitted], that the grant of a market does not of itself imply the power to exclude all persons from selling elsewhere marketable articles within market hours. And we find no power contravening this. Mr. Grant adds, that "it may be taken for law that the King himself could not, at the present day, convey the right to enforce so great a restriction upon trade."-(*Ibid.*) Perhaps Parliament, in its omnipotence, might. Whether our Republican Legislature has this power, it is unnecessary to decide. It is enough to know that they have not undertaken to exercise it in the present case.

And they will hesitate long before they will knowingly compel decent poor women and boys to attend at the market place, to mingle with the rabble that often assemble there in order to sell a few pounds of butter, or a few vegetables-before they will coerce poor men who bring in poultry and eggs on their load of wood to wait for hours before they can return to their labors, remaining around the market exposed to the weather; or, indeed, before they will restrict any person, in this land of liberty, from selling his cotton, corn, wheat, beef, pork, chickens, or anything else, when he pleases, where he pleases, and to whomsoever he pleases. . . .

Again, it is insisted, that as the power is given not only to *establish*, but to *keep up* a market; and as this can not be done but by prohibiting sales elsewhere, the power to do this is necessarily included in the grant, as indispensable to its exercise. Even this result would not justify the assumption or power not delegated. The most that could be said would be that the grant would prove unavailable. But it is not true in point of fact. And here lies the fundamental error of this whole doctrine.

A market may be established in such a way as to induce most persons who vend articles to go there for that purpose. It possesses inherent advantages over other places. Property sold in market is attended with certain incidents which do not attach to private sales. Besides, stalls and other conveniences might be furnished without expense to the producer. Even bounties and premiums may be awarded, so as to encourage both the quantity and good quality of the articles vended at the market. Individuals are compelled to hold out inducements to secure trade; why should not communities be required to do the same? Private persons coax trade to their doors; whereas, municipal corporations force it to their market places by penal enactments, levying a tax at the same time upon the producer, to supply their treasury with revenue. Let the burden fall, where it ought to fall, upon the consumer. In short, let anything and everything be done, rather than restrict commerce, rather than force and imprison tradespeople, to coerce them to submit to all kinds of discomfort and inconvenience, not to say loss, to gratify the selfishness, or avarice, or convenience of a favored few; to be taxed to support the pomp and parade of a few municipal lords.

The best feeling formerly subsisted in our country towns between the consumer and the producer; they were mutually respectful and friendly; the country people frequently contracting with the citizen consumer for weekly or even winter or summer, or yearly supplies of certain edibles. Weights and measures were satisfactory, and prices remunerating. The wives, daughters and boys of the small farmer were treated with the civility due to their sex and condition. But how changed under these anti-free-trade regulations. No wonder that irritation has taken the place of good feeling!

A convention of the people, called by the people, I would most respect-fully suggest is imperiously needed to impose additional restraints upon the powers of the Legislature, now more unlimited, in the opinion of some of our ablest jurists, than those of the British Parliament. Our honest, simple-hearted ancestors supposed that when they had guaranteed trial by jury, freedom of the press and of religious worship, no more was needed. Our State Constitution contains fewer safeguards, perhaps than any other in the Union. The new States are far ahead of this, and most of the old States, in this respect. But times have changed. And well as our system has worked in days past, a Bill of Rights is *demanded*. The great fundamental principles of human rights should be put beyond the reach and control even of constitutional change by the Legislature. Let the sovereign people convene, and say to the law-making power: thus far shalt thou go and no further.

Excessive legislation-the vice of all free governments-is, perhaps, the fault of the State. Through haste, inadvertence, and other causes, case legislation and class legislation is to be found frequently upon our statute book. Something should be done to arrest this evil. The dearest rights of the people are jeopardized.

A peaceable citizen, who discharges punctually all his public duties, and respects scrupulously the rights of others, should be left free and untrammeled as the air he breathes, in the pursuit of business and happiness. Fetters are equally galling, whether imposed by one man or by a community; and I am not ashamed to confess that the best sympathies of my heart are, and always will be, interested for one who is, or may be, incarcerated, because, in the proud consciousness of a freeman, he claims the right to offer for sale, at any hour of the day, on the highway, or in the streets, as interest or inclination may prompt him, any commodity he may possess, the traffic in which is not forbidden by the laws of the land.

Judgment reversed.

VANN v. IONTA
Municipal Court of City of New York, Borough of Queens
157 Misc. 461; 284 N.Y.S. 278 (1935)

NICHOLAS M. PETTE, Justice.

Plaintiff sues the owner of a combined barbershop and beauty parlor at Neposit, Rockaway, on the theory of respondeat superior, for injuries sustained when his left hand was cut while he was being shaved by a barber employee of the defendant. It is alleged that Jimmie, the employee, was negligent in the use of the razor as follows: Plaintiff, who is a business man in the neighborhood, sat in Jimmie's chair to be shaved. He testified that Jimmie had shaved him twice before without trouble, but that this time Jimmie "started to fool around" and began "wisecracking and tickling" him. Plaintiff claims that he told Jimmie to stop, that he was very ticklish, but Jimmie persisted. He says that Jimmie made wisecracks and "poked him in the ribs" at the same time, causing plaintiff, as he says, to be in a "continuous state of laughter, uncontrolled." About the time plaintiff had been shaved over once, he claims that Jimmie again tickled him, and that this time he (plaintiff) jumped up, his hand caught the razor, and a severe cut resulted, requiring fourteen surgical sutures.

Jimmie testified that he has been a barber for ten years and had been working for defendant about two years. He admits talking to the customer, but denies that he poked or tickled him. When plaintiff came in this time, they got to talking "about things" and the customer started laughing. Jimmie says that he does not recall the object of conversation, but that he went right on with his task and got through shaving once over; but that as he was about to wipe the razor on the tissue paper which was resting upon the customer's chest, the razor "must have tickled him," so that plaintiff jumped up and grabbed the razor.

The question is one of negligence on two theories: (1) In the operation or handling of the razor by the employee, and (2) in employing a helper with "an unusual propensity for fooling around with customers."

With respect to the first ground of negligence, I am inclined to find for defendant for the reason that the facts seem to support the view that this was an unavoidable accident, as to which there can be no recovery. I do not believe that this barber of ten years' experience, with razor in hand, intentionally poked and tickled the plaintiff with the other hand. My observation of the witnesses rather impresses me that owing to plaintiff's easily excitable ticklishness, when the back of the razor struck his stomach or chest, he instinctively caught hold of the razor, thereby unfortunately sustaining the injuries.

The second theory of negligence requires a determination of what constitutes an "unusual propensity" on the part of a barber "for fooling around with customers." This very theory presupposes that barbers *usually* have a tendency to "fool around with customers."

In order to ascertain what conduct is to be classified as unusual on the part of a barber, we are first to see what is usual. There is no testimony either way, and the court is called upon to fix the usual rule of conduct substantially by resorting to judicial notice. There being no reported precedent, we are free to inquire into what is the common practice, as one of first impression. Considerable significance is to be attached to the fact that no similar case appears to have reached the courts heretofore, that is, at least the higher courts, so that there might be a record thereof.

The presiding judge may have personal knowledge of the adaptability of some barbers to jest and humor so as to entertain their patrons, but that would not permit the taking of judicial notice. The custom must be so widespread that it can be said that the tribunals will take cognizance thereof without special proof, and accept it as an established fact. What, then, is a barber's habit of "fooling around" with customers. The answer may have equal application to ladies' beauty parlors, which are closely related to the barbershop in primary and ultimate purpose.

A passage in Jimmie's testimony is a guide to an examination of the subject. He was asked by the court whether he was not "usurping the functions of a comedian," that is, whether he was "pulling an Eddie Cantor" on plaintiff, by "wisecracking," to which he, wistfully enough, replied: "Well, when a customer comes in he doesn't like to sit in the chair and be still, he wants you to talk to him."

So that, while admitting the talking, Jimmie tenders the proposition that barbering and talking go hand in hand, and that although the conversation evokes laughter, there can be no negligence based on the fact alone. Let us therefore see whether talking, and what quality and quantity, are really integral with tonsorial manipulations. My reading of reference books upon the barber's antecedents reveals him as a gentleman extraordinary, a factotum of no mean attainments, and a useful adjunct to civilization itself.

The barber's art is rooted in antiquity, and its field is rich in fascinating lore and history revolving about the art's versatility since early days and its reduction from a profession to a calling of more humble character. In biblical times he was shaving both the face and beard, presumably because there were no cosmetics or hair tonics in those days. The prophet Ezekiel, 5:1, commanded, apparently in keeping with the times: "And thou son of man, take thee a . . . barber's razor, and cause it to pass upon thine head and upon thy beard." (Holy Bible, King James Version, Oxford Ed.) Of course, the departure in modern times from the command to shave the head is indicative of a wisdom that has grown with the years.

The barber appears to have been introduced in Rome about the year 454 of that city,[1] antedating the Christian era. It was about that time that the barber first began to earn his reputation for versatility that was to attach to his calling down through the years. Indeed, he appears to have been the first medium for the dissemination of news of public or private interest. Historically, therefore, he is viewed as the original "newspaper," besides his other activities presently to be observed. Barbers are alluded to by Horace as "the most accurately informed in all the minute history both of families and of the state." The Encyclopedia Americana records that in Rome "as elsewhere, when once introduced, they became men of great notoriety, and their shops were the resort of all the loungers and newsmongers in the city."

The Italian lexicon published in 1865 advises that the index of publicity was whether a subject had been discussed in a barbershop. If it had, it was public enough, that it had then reached the dignity of public property. Indeed, the authors give what then appeared to be the classical definition of a "barber" as "the twin brother of the surgeon, the cousin of the physician, the vicar of the confessor and the substitute for the secretary," adding that whosoever desired to hear any news, all he had to do was to go to a barbershop. The book does not tell us if any fee or honorarium was exacted for the service, but it seems that the events were narrated

---

[1] [Ed. Note: 300 B.C.]

merely as an incident to the profession, the barber acting as the gatherer of information coming to him from patrons of all sorts.

That the news-gathering branch of the art was only a small part of the promiscuous duties imposed upon the barber by the community, and that the nature of his services may have aided the artist, with the passing of time, to become a loquacious and jesting fellow, is manifest upon further inquiry. The Encyclopedia Americana states that in bygone days the barber was also an elementary physician and surgeon. "The art of surgery and the art of shaving went hand in hand;" that the barbers dressed wounds; did blood-letting and other surgical operations. The title of "barber-surgeons" was generally applied to them and they were even incorporated as such by King Edward IV in 1461, being at the time the only persons who practiced surgery. The present barber's pole had its origin in those days, when the spiral bands or "fillets" around the pole were intended to indicate the bandage twisted around the arms previous to letting out blood. The basin which formerly hung from the pole designated the receptacle to receive blood, which (we learn otherwise) was drawn by making incisions or by applying leeches to the affected parts.

The new International Encyclopedia sustains the foregoing information, adding that the blood-letting barber-surgeon, was honored as a professional man, and Chambers' Encyclopedia recites that the barber was also "celebrated for his garrulity, and general obliging qualities, such being required by those who place them selves in his hands;" that the barbershops of Athens and Rome were great meeting places for idlers and gossipers; and that in provincial towns they continue to serve such purposes up to the present time. The Encyclopedia Britannica supplements that "in addition to its attraction as a focus of news, a lute, viol or some such musical instrument was always kept for the entertainment of the waiting customers." We know that to be a fact in our own rural communities, and the custom would seem to be a salutary one, because the music no doubt serves to relieve the nervous tension of the intrepid patron or "patient" about to assume the attitude of the "customer in the chair" by placing himself in the physical control of the artist.

Common observation furnished proof that the barber is truly a philosophic person, of amiable and tractable disposition, ready to be accommodating, and always dispensing vocal wares with varying degrees of humor and intelligence, while the razor follows the facial contours and maybe, the course of least resistance, depending upon when it was last sharpened. That barbers talk cannot be disputed. Some talk more, some less, some humorously, some not, but talk they do. It is traditional and hereditary with them. The subjects are varied and the train of thought develops in endless chain, tempered only by the customer's assertion of his right to be free from enforced restraint as soon as the operations are over.

The artist's sources of information are manifold, and with the next customer he puts to use what he has learned from the last one, thereby keeping in circulation all sorts of topics, although he may have a personal inclination for literature, art, music, or the sciences; and it naturally follows that he becomes well-versed in the affairs of the world, past, present, and the speculative future. From his ranks there have risen men who have infiltrated themselves in our social structure with commendable success. I sometimes suspect that great structure with commendable success. I sometimes suspect that great oratorical, silver tongues of history may have begun their undying orating upon the willing or unwilling ears of the customer in the chair.

That the barber's qualifications are more or less generally understood as above stated appears to be reflected by that jovial character Figaro in Beaumarchais' comedy "The Barber of Seville," immortalized by Rossini. The opera is one of the wittiest of all dramas and the central hero, Figaro, the barber, is described as "a marvelous half autobiographic combination of gaiety and philosophy, disillusioned shrewdness, deep reflection and lambent wit; his dialogue, throughout, sparkles with overflowing wit, unexpected turns of phase, words of double intent, topsy-turvy application of proverbial wisdom and often quite superfluous jests." *Ency. Amer*. Figaro's many occupations, conjoined as they are with the principal one of shaving, appear to be typical of the barber's versatility of the times (1775), and of the requirements of the public.

That the barber's activities were multi-various indeed in medieval days and even in comparatively modern times is to be seen by a study of that famous character: (1) He gaily proclaims that he was the factotum of the whole city, and that as such everybody should make way for him to pass. (2) He announces that no profession compares with that of such a barber as he, for besides his services with scissors and razor, he is confidential adviser to all sorts of people, cavaliers and ladies alike. (3) He reveals himself as a perambulating matrimonial agency, by boasting that without him not a girl in Seville could find a husband. To him, he says, comes the little widow who would like to be married again, and it is all so easy, for what with his comb and razor by day, and his guitar at night, he is admitted everywhere. (4) Why, in the very house where Rosina, the old doctor's ward, lives is not he (Figaro) barber, coiffeur, surgeon, herbalist, druggist, vet and confidential man, in general? (5) He administers a purgative to a lawyer ill of indigestion (6) He prepares wigs for ladies. (7) He shaves and cuts the hair of the officers of a whole regiment. (8) Acts as the go-between to the loving count and the gracious Rosina, and by his original stratagems, arranges for their meeting and marriage against the imprecations of her guardian, the old doctor, who himself was conspiring to marry the girl and her money. That Figaro acquits himself nobly in all his missions demonstrates that the recent barber's predecessor was a genial and astute fellow with courageous directness, witty lies, proverbial shrewdness, and a somewhat charmed life.

Our own knowledge of the contemporary barber shows that he has lost none of the finesse of his ancestral prototype down through the ages. Indeed, he cannot escape from following in the footsteps of those that have gone before, for the very reason that his clients of yesteryear are the same to-day. There, in the barber's chair, the statesman, the executive, the professor, the tradesman, the peasant, the candlestick maker, the husband and the lover alike, each in turn trends his way to receive the benefits that nimble fingers may administer to his facial contours. That at the same time the artist pours upon his ears friendly words of general interest, humor, or a philosophical discourse, is but an attribute incidental to the manipulations themselves. It goes without saying that fingering one all over the face is a strictly personal and privileged transaction. Therefore, being a student of human nature by force of his profession, the barber deals strictly with the customer in the chair, the individual whose fastidious or peculiar traits he must minister to.

His sources of information being varied and recurrent, he becomes a storehouse of human knowledge, and dispenses it by applying his strategy and his inborn philosophy to meet the exigencies of the occasion. One cannot imagine a silent barber. Nor does he use his silver tongue without cause. While oftentimes prompted by the customers themselves, whose talkative disposition varies, it would seem that nature has predisposed the barber to overcome the difficulty of making a customer feel at ease, by so mixing the elements in him that his vocal chords and his mannerisms might be employed, softly but surely, to assuage the customer's inherent fears, and lull him into a sense of confidence that deprives his constricted situation of any of the terrors of the dentist's chair, or the awe which the witness chair inspires. Nor is the position of such a customer akin to that of the witness in the chair to whom a recent editorial referred as "the most miserable of all creatures," what with being the complacent friend of the side he espouses, the subjective instrument of the court's majesty, the football of the cross-examining attorney, the focus of the jury's inquisitorial powers, and the object of plaintiff's or defendant's fervent prayers.

Happily, to the customer in the barber's chair, such ordeals are spared. In that chair all traces of the man's condition in life are temporarily subjugated to the barber's physical control to which the customer readily submits unscathed by the experience, for the purpose of facial embellishment, common to all mankind. So situated, the customer in the chair furnished a vivid example of the truth of the great Lincoln's motto that "all men are created equal." It being his innate design to render his patient impervious to the risk attendant upon the use of the razor, the barber approaches the man before him tenderly but warily, and by the use of his faculties at once renders the personal encounter a friendly one, whether by propounding a question or by making a statement. A polite "good morning" from either side is enough incentive to start the ball rolling. From then on, with the customer's limited locomotion, there may ensue a conversation which, according to the given position of the razor, may assume the qualities of a suppressed duet in various forms, for the barber's chair is not a place where one may repose, in the words of Bryant, "like one who wraps the drapery of his couch about him and lies down to pleasant dreams." Courageous indeed is the man who ventures forth in a reclining position in the barber's chair, for well may he recall, before he engages in conversation, the words of Dante upon entering Inferno, "Abandon all hope all ye who enter here," since we all know that the razor has a facile way of cutting flesh more so than the beard. And while the customer may appear to be resting, whether his eyes be open or shut, yet must he be on the qui vive,[1] although in docile mien, to answer the artist, if need be, by word of mouth, by grimace, by grunt, or by wiggling his toe, whichever he is permitted to do at the moment, having regard to the proximity of that ominous instrument to the throat and with an eye upon the barber's countenance, to see if he is still friendly.

And if you do not answer, you may ipso facto be treated as a cranky customer, which may so reflect upon the smooth cutting qualities of the razor as to produce a shave half pulled and half scraped, so that the face may smart for days. If you speak at an inopportune moment, you may flirt with injury, or at least with a mouthful of soap that will be far from appetizing. If you seek a compromise by winking, maybe intending thereby to tell the barber to shut up, the wink may have the opposite effect, for the barber may think that the customer is encouraging him in his discourse. If you move a foot, you may break a mirror and thus incur the proverbial seven years' hard luck, and if you shift your position the barber reprimands you, humorously but firmly, because he loses his equipoise, or the razor may refuse to cut at all, if the hand that guides it is not attuned to the barber's thoughts, which find articulation through his silver tongue.

Grave problems may be pervading the customer's mind, and he may be meditating upon his next step the moment he is released from restraint, again to breathe in the free air; but those things do not coincide with the barber's thoughts, for he is a high-class salesman, not by forceful or high-pressure methods, but by a more subtle, persuasive process, which develops as the soapy nebula begins to accumulate around and about the facial orifices. It is then that the artist begins to approach the subject nearest to his heart and furthest from the average customer's mind, by trying to induce the customer to have his map or pate smeared with one or more of the dozens of familiar lotions of dubious value which daily seem to change in color and aroma, though not in substance or price, nor even in efficacy, as many of us perceive by a look in retrospective contemplation, to the remains of a once luxuriant shock, that has either thinned and grayed or disappeared altogether.

Bearing upon the development of the art from remote days, I learn from the December issue of the *Reader's Digest* that in a barbershop in Rockefeller Center there is on display a collection of pictures showing various types and combinations of beards and moustaches in all ages and places, and ancient razors and tools, which may almost be regarded as a mirror of the progress of civilization itself.

In the light of the foregoing views, I hold to the opinion that the barber's business is fraught with a degree of inevitable risk, obvious and known to both the artist and the customer, and to which the patron is voluntarily exposed, as a necessary incident of the manipulations which must be performed to produce the

---

[1] [Ed. Note: In French, "Qui vive?" means "Who lives?" or "Who goes there?" To be "On the qui vive" means, "to be on the alert"]

ultimate result. The barber is traditionally a man's friend, and though adventurous within the sphere of his field, he may and usually is trusted to do his job with the least possible harm. More than that, from time immemorial he has accomplished his duty with dignity, tempered with humor and good fellowship. That is far from negligence. That injury sometimes results must be attributed, as here, to a fortuitous occurrence rather than to fault.

Prompted by the recognized fact that we do not know a good thing until we have to do without it, I venture to say that if the barber's courtesy, jocular ways, and pleasant disposition were suddenly to stop, there would be considerable hesitation to sit in his chair, which would not be unlike the sensation one must experience in facing the fatuous "life's darkest moment." The world need have no qualms about the barber's mission on earth, for he and his traits, recognized since biblical times, have successfully withstood the ravages of the centuries and fraught that appears will outlive many people and many customs in the far-flung corners of the world before his craft shall perish, if ever.

Basing my finding upon the barber's historical background, I am unable to discern any "unusual propensity for fooling around with customers," on the part of the defendant's employee. He appears to have proceeded about his work by talking while shaving, in a manner quite in keeping with the usages of the art in vogue since the dark days of ages past.

Plaintiff at most shows a pure accident. No extra precautions appear to be likely to have prevented it. The barber was engaged in the performance of a lawful act by lawful means. There is no evidence, nor in the nature of things was it probable that by the exercise of the utmost degree of care Jimmie could have foreseen that plaintiff would impulsively grab hold of the razor. Plaintiff certainly had knowledge of the peril he incurred in the attitude of a customer being shaved. A different situation might arise if plaintiff's hand had been resting about his breast or stomach and had been cut by the razor that would ordinarily have no business in that region of the patron's anatomy. In the aspect of the facts most favorable to plaintiff, therefore, he comes clearly within the rule that no recovery may be had where the accident occurs under circumstances indicating that it was unavoidable, even though due to want of provision that one would act in a certain manner upon a given stimulus or occurrence. The *causa causans* [cause that causes, the immediate cause] was not negligence on Jimmie's part, but plaintiff's act in grasping the razor, which act Jimmie is not shown to have had reasonable cause to anticipate even by the exercise of ordinary prudence. [citation omitted]

Of course, the result here reached does not give Jimmie or his kindred artists a free rein in the discharge of their duties. They will undoubtedly be held to strict accountability in law if an accident is due to their negligence, whether it be founded upon a state of extreme or unreasonable garrulity or gesticulation, or both, or otherwise. This particular accident was regrettable enough, and in the nature of things a similar misfortune will not happen again in many a moon.

Therefore, since liability must be measured only in terms of law, I direct judgment for defendant on the merits.

SWINDLE v. MUNFORD
Supreme Court of Georgia
59 Ga. 337 (1877)

LOGAN E. BLECKLEY, Judge.

The note sued upon was dated January 1, 1862, and due one day thereafter. It was for $154.75. The consideration, as proved at the trial, was merchandise purchased in 1860 and 1861 -- not payable in Confederate money nor rated at Confederate prices. Barber's table was put in evidence, according to which the difference between Confederate money and gold, at the date of the note, was twenty cents on the dollar. The jury returned a verdict in favor of the plaintiff for twenty dollars, and interest.

The plaintiff moved for a new trial, alleging that the verdict was contrary to evidence, to law, and to the charge of the court. A new trial was granted, the order granting it being headed: "At Chambers, December 3, 1876"... whereupon defendent except[ed] . . . [T]he bill of exceptions proceeds to specify the following: That the verdict was not contrary to law, nor to evidence, nor to the charge of the court, and that "the order shows said new trial was improperly and illegally granted."

If a verdict can shock the moral sense, this does it. Twenty dollars on a note for $154.75, and not a cent ever paid! Doubtless the explanation is, that the note was given during the war. The war destroyed many things, but justice was not killed out. It went through, and is still alive. Private debts are extinguished, not by arms, but by payment, or discharge in bankruptcy, or voluntary release. Debtors cannot fight out of their just obligations to creditors.

The brief of counsel asserts that the new trial was granted on Sunday. If it was, this objection should have been openly specified in the bill of exceptions, and not concealed under a generality that affords of it no hint whatever. We cannot permit a judgment to be ambushed in this court in any such way.

Judgment affirmed.

FERGUSON v. NATIONAL BROADCASTING CO., INC.
United States Court of Appeals, Fifth Circuit
584 F.2d 111 (1978)

IRVING L. GOLDBERG, Circuit Judge:

This is an action for copyright infringement. The sole issue raised on appeal is whether the trial court correctly granted defendant's motion for summary judgment.

In 1953 plaintiff composed and copyrighted a musical composition entitled "Jeannie Michele." The unpublished composition was never performed in this country; nor was it sold, offered for sale, or circulated to the general public. In fact, plaintiff distributed only six copies of the composition. A copy was sent to Guy Lombardo, Mills Publishing Company, Dinah Shore, Broadcast Music Incorporated, Jerri Greene, and Don Cherry. None of these potential publishers showed any interest in "Jeannie Michele," and each copy was returned to the plaintiff.

Plaintiff alleges that the first sixteen and last eight measures of "Jeannie Michele" are used in the theme song of a television program aired in 1973 called "A Time to Love." She filed a copyright infringement complaint against both NBC, the network which aired the show, and John Williams,[1] the musician who composed the allegedly infringing theme song. The district court dismissed Williams from the action for lack of personal jurisdiction.

The remaining defendant, NBC, moved for summary judgment. In support of its motion, it submitted the affidavit of Williams which stated that Williams had never heard of the plaintiff or her composition. NBC also submitted affidavits of experts in musicology which stated that the only similarity between the two composition was a recurring three note sequence found also in the works of Johann Sebastian Bach. The plaintiff's affidavits did not countervail these statements made in support of the defendant's motion for summary judgment. The district court granted summary judgment for the defendant, and the plaintiff appeals.

In order to establish a copyright infringement, a plaintiff must prove (1) his ownership of the copyright and (2) "copying" by the defendant or person who composed the defendant's work. . . .

Here the defendant, for purposes of its motion for summary judgment, assumed that plaintiff owned a valid copyright in "Jeannie Michele." Its summary judgment affidavits attacked the second element of plaintiff's cause of action — the alleged "copying" by Williams. Since there is seldom direct evidence of "copying," the plaintiff generally proves this element by showing that the person who composed the defendant's work had access to the copyrighted work and that the defendant's work is substantially similar to the plaintiff's. . .

. . . If the two works are so strikingly similar as to preclude the possibility of independent creation, "copying" may be proved without a showing on access. . .

. . . Here, the plaintiff showed that she had sent a copy of her composition to four individuals and two companies. Each copy was returned, and Williams, in his affidavit, stated that he had no contact with any of the individuals or with Mills Publishing, one of the two companies. Although he admitted having had

---

[1] Williams is an accomplished musician. He has composed, arranged, and directed the music for more than thirty motion pictures including Jaws, Earthquake, Poseidon Adventure, and Fiddler on the Roof. In 1972 he received the Academy Award for his musical arrangements in Fiddler on the Roof.

some contacts with Broadcast Music Incorporated (BMI), the other company, he stated that these contacts were not related to either the plaintiff or her composition. Furthermore, Williams stated he had never heard of plaintiff or her composition prior to this copyright infringement action. Plaintiff adduced no evidence contradicting Williams' statements.

Even without proof of access, plaintiff could still make out her case if she showed that the two works were not just substantially similar, but were so strikingly similar as to preclude the possibility of independent creation. . . . Here however, plaintiff presented no evidence of similarity aside from the two compositions. She merely asserted that parts of her composition were "used in" the defendant's work and that it is unlikely that Williams could have composed the defendant's work without having had access to "Jeannie Michele." Such conclusions are not probative evidence in a summary judgment proceeding. . . .

In contrast, defendant submitted affidavits by experts analyzing the two compositions and showing that the only similarity between them is a recurring three note sequence found also in the works of Johann Sebastian Bach. The evidence presented clearly does not raise a question of fact as to whether the two compositions were so strikingly similar as to preclude the possibility of independent creation. . .

In this case we find that the defendant properly supported its motion for summary judgment. It showed that there was no genuine issue of fact on either access or striking similarity. The plaintiff offered no probative evidence in rebuttal. In such a case the Federal Rules of Civil Procedure provide that summary judgment is proper. . . .

We wish to add that we are sensitive to the plaintive note in the plaintiff's complaint. Notwithstanding the result of this opinion, a court must feel great sympathy for the symphonic trials of our creative pleader. We know it is slight consolation that in this case the plaintiff's song has finally come out in a judicial record. But even indulging every permissible inference in favor of the plaintiff's affidavit to support what she must establish under the law, what the affidavit purports still falls far short of musicological Bach-like proportions.

In truth the plaintiff fails to establish mimicry. A few notes do not a song make. Jeannie Michele simply did not, in this case, negotiate the obstacles in Tin Pan Alley. Of course, a copyright plaintiff need not establish a measure for measure, but her proof must have some musical measurability. The evidence here shows that Jeannie Michele had precursors and predecessors and access was negated. It is not enough to place two works back to back, if both track their ancestries back to Bach.

For these reasons we hold that the district court correctly granted the defendant's motion for summary judgment.

AFFIRMED.

HUGHES v. STATE BOARD OF MEDICAL EXAMINERS
Supreme Court of Georgia
162 Ga. 246; 134 S.E. 42 (1926)

HIRAM WARNER HILL, J.

The State Board of Medical Examiners caused to be served upon Talbert W. Hughes, a physician who had been licensed to practice medicine in this State, a notice preferring certain charges against him, a copy of which charges it was alleged was served upon Hughes personally by the deputy sheriff of Fulton County, Georgia, on January 21, 1924, as provided by the act of 1913 (Acts 1931, P. 101), as amended by the act of 1918 (Acts 1918, p. 173).

The charges preferred were: (1) conviction of crime involving moral turpitude; (2) causing the publication and circulation of an advertisement relative to diseases of the sexual organs, and the proposed curing of the same. . .

. . . [At] the hearing before the State Board of Medical Examiners. . .[Dr. Hughes] was found guilty on both charges. From this judgment of the board he filed his appeal to the superior court. . .

[Hughes] attack[s] the constitutionality of the acts of 1913 and 1918, which latter act is amendatory of the act of 1913, on the ground that they deny . . . [him] due process of law under both the State and Federal constitutions. . .

Section 14 of the act of 1918 (Acts 1918, pp. 173, 193), is as follows:

"Be it further enacted, that said board may refuse to grant a license to practice medicine in this State, or may cause a licentiate's name to be removed from the records in the office of any clerk of court in this state, on the following grounds, to wit: The employment of fraud or deception in applying for license or in passing the examination provided for in this act; conviction of crime involving moral turpitude. . . habitual intemperance in the use of ardent spirits, narcotics, or stimulants to such an extent as to incapacitate him for the performance of professional duties; the procuring or aiding or abetting in procuring a criminal abortion; the obtaining of a fee on representation that a manifestly incurable disease can be permanently cured; causing the publication and circulation of an advertisement of any medicine by means whereby the monthly periods of women can be regulated, or the menses if suppressed can be re-established; causing the publication and circulation of an advertisement relative to any disease of the sexual organs. . . ."

We are of the opinion that the act in question does not deny to . . . [Hughes] the equal protection of the laws, and that the classification made in the act is not arbitrary, but is a reasonable one made for the protection of the citizens of the State.

The question of the regulation of the professional conduct of doctors and of their fees is not of recent origin. "The oldest code of laws in the world" of which we are aware, promulgated by Hammurabi, King of Babylon, B.C. 2285-2242, published by T. & T. Clark, Edinburgh, 1905, and which was discovered on a buried monument, or block of black diorite, nearly eight feet high, by an archaeologist in 1902 in Babylonia, and which has been translated and published, contains the following:

> 215. If a doctor has treated a gentleman for a severe wound with a bronze lancet and has cured the man, or has opened an abscess of the eye for a gentleman with a bronze lancet and has cured the eye of the gentleman, he shall take ten shekels of sliver. (A shekel of silver is equivalent to about 62½ cents.)

> 216. If he [the patient] be the son of a poor man, he shall take five shekels of silver.

> 217. If he be a gentleman's servant, the master of the servant shall give two shekels of silver to the doctor.

> 218. If the doctor has treated a gentleman for a severe wound with a lancet of bronze and has caused the gentleman to die, or has opened an abscess of the eye for a gentleman with the bronze lancet and has caused the loss of the gentleman's eye, one shall cut off his hands.

> 219. If a doctor has treated the severe wound of a slave of a poor man with a bronze lancet and has caused his death, he shall render slave for slave.

> 220. If he has opened his abscess with a bronze lancet and has made him lose his eye, he shall pay money, half his price.

> 221. If a doctor has cured the shattered limb of a gentleman, or has cured the diseased bowel, the patient shall give five shekels of silver to the doctor.

> 222. If it is the son of a poor man, he shall give three shekels of silver.

> 223. If a gentleman's servant, the master of the slave shall given two shekels of silver to the doctor.

From what has been said above and the authorities cited, we are of the opinion that the grounds of the demurrer are without merit, and the court did not err in overruling the same.

Judgment affirmed.

CHAPTER IV: BUSINESS, TRADE & COMMERCE

PARADINE v. JANE
Court of King's Bench, Michaelmas Term
[1558-1774] All E.R. Rep. 172; 82 E.R. 897; Aleyn 26, Sty. 47 (1647)

LORD BACON AND HENRY ROLLE, J J.

[Plaintiff Paradine sued for rent due for lands let to the defendant, Jane. The plaintiff declared upon a lease rendering rent quarterly, and for rent in arrears for three years ending Lady Day[1], 1646. The defendant pleaded that a German prince, Prince Rupert, an alien born enemy to the King and kingdom, had invaded the realm with an army of men, and with the same force had entered upon the lands let by the plaintiff to the defendant and had expelled him therefrom, and held him out of possession from July, 1642, until Lady Day, 1646, whereby he could not take the profits. To this plea the plaintiff demurred.]

The plea was resolved insufficient on the following grounds: first, because the defendant had not answered to one quarter's rent; secondly, he had not averred that the army were all aliens, which shall not be intended, and then he has his remedy against them; and BACON J., cited Y.B. 33 Hen. 6 fo. 1, pl. 3, where the gaoler in bar of an escape pleaded that alien enemies broke [into] the prison, etc., and an exception was taken to it, for that he ought to show of what country they were, i.e., Scots.

Thirdly, it was resolved that the matter of the plea was insufficient, for although the whole army had been alien enemies, yet the defendant ought to pay the rent. This difference was taken, that where the law creates a duty or charge, and the party is disabled from performing it without any default in him, and has not remedy over, there the law will excuse him. As in the case of waste, if a house be destroyed by tempest or by enemies, the lessee is excused. [citation omitted]. . .

. . . But when the party by his own contract creates a duty or charge upon himself he is bound to make it good, if he may, notwithstanding any accident by inevitable necessity because he might have provided against it by his contract. Therefore, if the lease covenants to repair a house, although it is burnt by lightning or thrown down by enemies [citation omitted] . . . yet he ought to repair it; [citation omitted].

The rent is a duty created by the parties upon the reservation, and had there been a covenant to pay it there would have been no question but the lessee must have made it good, notwithstanding the interruption by enemies, for the law would not protect him beyond his own agreement, no more than in the case of reparations.

This reservation, then, being a covenant in law and whereupon an action of the covenant has been maintained (as ROLLE, J., has said) it is all one as if there had been an actual covenant. Another reason was added, that as the lessee is to have the advantage of casual profits, so he must run the hazard of casual losses and not lay the whole burden of them upon his lessor. . .

Judgment for plaintiff.

---

1 [Ed. Note: March 25.]

UNITED STATES v. VEN-FUEL, INC.
United States Court of Appeals, Fifth Circuit
602 F.2d 747 (1979)

JOHN R. BROWN, Chief Judge:

> *This case presents a vicious duel,*
> *Between the U.S. of A. and defendant Ven-Fuel.*
> *Seeking a license for oil importation,*
> *Ven-Fuel submitted its application.*
> *It failed to attach a relevant letter,*
> *And none can deny, it should have known better.*
> *Yet the only issue this case is about,*
> *Is whether a crime was committed beyond reasonable doubt.*
> *Ven-Fuel was convicted of fraudulent acts,*
> *By the Trial Court's finding of adequate facts.*
> *We think it likely that fraud took place,*
> *But materiality was not shown in this case.*
> *So while the Government will no doubt be annoyed,*
> *We declare the conviction null and void.*

The Procedural Background Is Easily Stated . . .

The appellant, Ven-Fuel, Inc., was charged with 15 violations of 18 U.S.C.A. § 542, which prohibits the importation of merchandise by means of a false statement of practice. Counts II through VIII alleged that Ven-fuel introduced seven shipments of residual fuel oil[1] into the United States while operating under an import license obtained by false statements to the Office of Oil and Gas, Department of the Interior (OOG). Counts IX through XV charged that in connection with these same seven shipments, Ven-Fuel deprived the United States of lawful duties. Count I alleged that Ven-Fuel conspired with Jack Gusler, then Vice-President of Ven-Fuel, and with "unnamed and diverse other persons to the Grand Jury unknown" to commit the substantive offenses alleged in Counts II through XV.

At the completion of the second trial, the Court entered its findings of fact and conclusions of law. Ven-Fuel was found guilty of Counts II through VIII and was acquitted on Counts IX through XV.

Ven-Fuel now appeals its convictions (Counts II through VIII) on a variety of grounds. Since we believe that Ven-Fuel's alleged fraudulent statements are immaterial as a matter of law, we reverse the conviction without reaching Ven-Fuel's other challenges.

---

[1] Residual fuel oil has unique characteristics and requires special methods of receipt, storage, and transportation.

But The Facts Are Far More Complicated.

On March 14, 1973, Ven-Fuel applied to OOG for an allocation and license to import one million barrels of residual fuel oil into District I. According to Department of Interior regulations, Ven-Fuel was required to demonstrate (1) that it was already in the business of selling residual fuel oil, and (2) that it had "a throughput agreement with a deepwater terminal operator under which agreement the person has delivered to the terminal residual fuel oil to be used as fuel which he owned when it was so delivered."

. . . The government contends that Ven-Fuel violated 18 U.S.C.A. § 542 in that Ven-Fuel falsely represented that it had a throughput agreement with Southland Oil Company, a deepwater terminal operator located in Savannah, Georgia.[2] Ven-Fuel did not reveal to OOG that its agreement with Southland was to go into effect only if Ven-Fuel succeeded in reaching a contract with Savannah Electric and Power Company (SEPCO) for the sale of residual fuel oil.

At the time Ven-Fuel applied for its license, SEPCO and Ven-Fuel had not even come close to reaching an agreement. Indeed, Ven-Fuel and SEPCO never reached an agreement (and the Southland/Ven-Fuel "agreement" thereby became a nullity).

After obtaining the import license from OOG, Ven-Fuel entered into an agreement with Jacksonville Electric Authority for the sale of the oil authorized by the license. Ven-Fuel proceeded to make seven shipments of oil to Jacksonville Electric Authority through the Port of Jacksonville. Jacksonville Electric had the necessary unloading and storage facilities to receive and store the oil. Ven-Fuel did not have, or even claim to have had, a throughput terminal in Jacksonville. . .

The crucial letter for purposes of this case is the one Ven-Fuel did not disclose to OOG. That letter, dated March 22, 1973 [the March 22 letter], made clear the conditional nature of the throughput agreement and specifically limited Ven-Fuel's liability to Southland. . .

Based on Ven-Fuel's failure to disclose the March 22 letter, the Trial Court found Ven-Fuel guilty of a fraudulent practice.

Applying The Law Is Even Worse . . .

Ven-Fuel was convicted under 18 U.S.C.A. § 542, which provides in pertinent part:

> Whoever enters or introduces, or attempts to enter
> or introduce, into the commerce of the United
> States any imported merchandise by means of any

---

[2] To qualify as a "deepwater terminal operator," the storage company was required to have special loading and storage capabilities set forth in the regulations.

> fraudulent or false invoice, declaration, affidavit, letter, paper, or by means of any false statement, written or verbal, or by means of any false or fraudulent practice or appliance, or makes any false statement in any declaration without reasonable cause to believe the truth of such statement, . . . Shall be fined for each offense not more than $5,000 or imprisoned not more than two years, or both.

Section 542 does not on its face require that false or fraudulent statements relating to the entry or attempted entry of merchandise be material. However, we believe that for the statute to make sense, materiality must be read into it. . . .

On the surface, it would appear that fraudulent statements with respect to the existence of a throughput agreement may be highly material, since the existence of a throughput agreement is the sole requirement for obtaining an import license. Under this reasoning, Ven-Fuel's failure to disclose the March 22 letter would constitute a material fraudulent misstatement, since . . . the March 22 letter clearly revealed the contingent nature of the throughput agreement.

However, we reject this superficial approach. Instead, we hold that even though a throughput agreement is required to obtain an import license, fraudulent statements relating to the quality of this throughput agreement are immaterial as a matter of law to the importation of residual fuel oil. Indeed, the license itself explicitly stated that the residual fuel allocated was "for entry for consumption or withdrawal from warehouse for consumption . . . *at any port of entry* [in District I]" . . . Absent a logical nexus between the throughput agreement requirement and the actual importation of fuel, we cannot say that misstatements regarding the quality of the throughput agreement are material for purposes of 18 U.S.C.A. § 542.

But For The Reasons Stated We Must Reverse

Since we fail to see how a misrepresentation regarding the quality of this throughput agreement is material to the importation of residual fuel oil, we must reverse the conviction.

REVERSED.

APPEAL OF UNIVERSITY OF PITTSBURGH
Supreme Court of Pennsylvania
407 Pa. 416; 180 A.2d 760 (1962)

BENJAMIN R. JONES, Justice.

Is the residence of the chancellor of the University of Pittsburgh, owned by the university and located approximately 2½ miles from the university campus, exempt from local taxation? The court below held that it was tax exempt. The propriety of that ruling is now before us. . . .

In our review, the residence of the chancellor fully meets the standard required under both the Constitution and the Act of 1933, supra, to qualify for a tax exempt status.

Order affirmed.

MICHAEL A. MUSMANNO, Justice (dissenting).

Every adult person in the Commonwealth carries on his back an invisible sack into which the government periodically drops an ever-increasing burden of taxes. If any person somehow manages to keep his sack closed and empty and the tax-man passes him by, this does not mean that the tax which the escaping person does not pay is lost to the government. The tax-man places the weight of that uncollected tax into other sacks so that the other persons in that given area or classification are required to carry heavier loads than otherwise would be theirs. For that reason, if for no other reason, every citizen is interested in seeing to it that there is not lifted to his shoulders a millstone which belongs to someone else.

While taxation applies to all persons uniformly, an appreciation of the obligations owed by society to certain non-profit entities causes government to exempt schools, churches, hospitals and charitable institutions from tax levies. The exemptions, however, must be bona fide and they must be strictly applied because, as already stated, what is not paid by one entity or person will be exacted from other persons or entities. Thus, the law proclaims that not everyone in the vicinity of institutions enjoying a rain bath of tax immunity is entitled to that same immunity merely because he stands close enough to feel the splash and the coolness of the exempting waters.

The question involved in the appeal before us is whether the Chancellor of the University of Pittsburgh is relieved from paying taxes on the house in which he lives. If this dwelling is his domicile and he uses it only as his home, he is obliged to pay taxes on it like everybody else pays taxes on his home. If, on the other hand, his house is in effect an adjunct of the University of Pittsburgh, the property falls within the same tax exemption allowed the University. The County Court of Allegheny County, after a hearing on the subject, decided that the Chancellor's home is really a facility of the University of Pittsburgh and therefore enjoys the same prerogatives as the University insofar as governmental fiscal obligations are concerned. The Majority of this Court has affirmed that finding.

I do not agree. . . . In the case of Ogontz School Tax Exemption, [citation omitted] we said: "A claimant for exemption *must bring himself clearly within the exempting statute.*" (Emphasis supplied).

Did the Chancellor bring himself clearly within the exempting statute? The Majority Opinion does not go into the facts of the case and is wholly satisfied to accept the findings of the Court below. My study of the record convinces me that the evidence submitted at the hearing did not place the Chancellor's residence within the curtilage of the exempting statute.

The residence in controversy is a large, three-story brick Georgian style house with 15 rooms and 4½ baths, located at 1129 Beechwood Boulevard, Pittsburgh. It reposes amidst extensive lawns which cover approximately an acre of ground. The household consists of the Chancellor, his wife, four children and a nursemaid.

When the present Chancellor, Dr. Edward H. Litchfield, was invited by the Trustees of the University, in 1955, to accept the post of Chancellor, he was informed that he would live in a comfortable, three-story modern residence at 651 Morewood Avenue, where the previous Chancellor had lived. Dr. Litchfield did not like this house. He inspected many dwellings and finally selected the one on Beechwood Boulevard as the one he preferred and the University purchased it for $75,000. He moved into the property in 1956. . . .

The domicile of a university head, in order to be declared tax-exempt on the basis that it is part of the university, should have some geographical, cultural and pedagogical kinship with the university itself. The present Chancellor's home is located two and one-half miles from the University campus and is physically isolated from the University by many business establishments, public thorough-fares, public buildings and innumerable other residences. Given this distance and professional detachment, the Chancellor in his home cannot exercise directional, supervisional or disciplinarian control over students and faculty at the University. The Morewood home, although still not on the University campus, was located only one mile from the main campus grounds.

Applying the unmistakeable intent of the Statutory Construction Act, as heretofore quoted, the University had the evidentiary burden at the hearing in the Court below to prove that the Beechwood domicile formed an integral part of the whole University educational plan. It did not meet this burden. There was no evidence that the Chancellor carried on university administrative functions in this house, there was no evidence of any routine of meetings with students and faculty members in the house, there was no evidence that classes of any kind were ever conducted in the house.

But the University counsel argue that the Chancellor needs this large residence because of the many official receptions, entertainment events and meetings which come within the sphere of his official functions. Dr. Litchfield himself testified that during the year 1960, 2,200 people called at his home. When I first saw this statement in the record I visualized this long parade of 2,200 persons coming to the Chancellor's home to talk with him and discuss with him the many educational problems of the University and I must admit I sensed an instinctive sympathy for the Chancellor who had to devote so much time and energy in handling so many individual problems. However, when I examined the nature of the events which brought so extraordinarily large a number of callers to the Chancellor's home, I found that 775 of them came to dance! The exhibit submitted by the University in this connection shows that on October 7, 1960, there was held at the Chancellor's home a Dance for University Faculties and that 775 persons attended.

I recognize that entertainment and even dances are part of the inevitable social life of any modern educational institution, but it should not be the responsibility of the president of a university of college to provide the facilities for such events. Dr. Litchfield has himself stated that he preferred to use his home only as a home and there is no reason why, insofar as the record in this case is concerned, he may not do so. The head of a large university is entitled to peace and quiet in his home and is not required to endure the moanings and groaning of saxophones with the earsplitting assaults of piercing trumpets and detonating drums producing the cacophony for gyrating dancers performing the contortions and non-cerebral terpsichorean monstrosity known as "the twist."

While modern education is imparted in an atmosphere quite different from that which prevailed within the classic shades of Plato's Academy and Artistotle's Lyceum, the large majority of students still look upon education as something serious and solemn and a preparation for the awesome responsibilities of life. The Chancellor or President symbolizes that dignified dedication and he should not have to supply the quarters for the off-campus entertainment of students.

Of course, it is self-evident that distinguished visitors will come to so large and justly renowned a university as the University of Pittsburgh, and there should be a place within the University, and worthy of the University, to receive these personages and provide for their needs and comfort. The University of Pittsburgh apparently has such a place and it is known as Bruce Hall in the Schenley Apartments. Dr. Litchfield testified that Bruce Hall is --

> "used primarily as a group facility for visiting people on the campus who come and stay there overnight, who sometimes have breakfast and sometimes luncheons and dinners and who frequently bring staffs with them and have their own meetings there in the library in conjunction with their sleeping quarters. Examples of this are the Prime Minister of Turkey and his staff used this as a guest facility; the Director of the Iranian Plan Organization and his immediate entourage used it for sleeping, for part of their meals and for meetings. . ."

When the Chief Justice of the United States, the Honorable Earl Warren, spoke at the University commencement exercises, the reception for him was held at Bruce Hall.

The infrequent and sporadic official receptions which have taken place in the Litchfield residence cannot, in point of numerousness and intensity of scholastic application, be compared with the beehive activities unceasingly buzzing in the home of the President of Rutgers College, as above indicated.

According to the list submitted by the University of Pittsburgh at the hearing in the Court below, the Chancellor's home was used for non-residential functions on only eighteen occasions during the whole year of 1959, the tax year here involved. . . .

I do not believe that the taxpayers of Allegheny County should be required to make up the taxes which would otherwise be applied to the Chancellor's home merely because of five events (in one year) which, if not accommodatable at Bruce Hall, could have been held elsewhere. In the case of Ogontz School Tax Exemption Case, 361 Pa. 284; 65 A.2d 150, this Court said:

> "Every wage earner and every property owner feels the burden of taxation growing constantly heavier. Millions of American income producers are now forced to pay each year in the form of direct and indirect taxes nearly half of their income for the support of national, state and local governments. The heavier the burden of taxation becomes the more exigent is the demand for its equitable distribution. . . ."

I have great admiration for the University of Pittsburgh, which is one of the truly great universities of the world. Its graduates have, in various parts of the country and even in distant foreign climes added lustre in the fields of science, the professions and the arts, to the fame of the venerable and pre-Revolutionary-War city of Pittsburgh, whose name the University proudly bears. In athletic prowess the University teams have quickened the pulse of the populations of Western Pennsylvania and parts of West Virginia and Ohio which look upon this University as their own. It is with infinite regret, therefore, that I see this magnificent institution being brought into litigation over so insignificant a sum as is involved in the taxes on the Chancellor's home -- I say insignificant, in comparison to the gigantic sums spent by the University in a year in the operation of an establishment which is a small city in itself. With a student enrollment of approximately 13,000, and a faculty and administrative staff of approximately 2,000, the University, as one of its publications points out, "has become a complex institution of schools and divisions offering undergraduate, graduate, and professional eduation, performing scores of public services, supporting a vast research program, and administering a great Health Center. It is large and highly diversified."

The University spends twenty million dollars a year, five million more than the amount expended by Thomas Jefferson in purchasing one-half of the United States. In view of such leviathan expenditures, why should it be concerned over a small tax item, the payment of which would not only not add significantly to its budget but would serve as a demonstration of its appreciation of the benefits it receives from the entire Commonwealth? The payment of those taxes would also serve as a demonstration, in a tangible way, of its recognition of the democratic idealism involved in taxation. . . .

In addition, although taxation is a burden, it is also a badge of honor. Although heavy, it is, like the staff which holds upright the Flag of our country, something every true American regards as a privilege to carry.

I subscribe wholeheartedly to what was stated by Justice (later Chief Justice) Maxey in the case of Y.M.C.A. of Germantown v. Philadelphia, [citation omitted].

> "Taxes are not penalties, but are contributions which all inhabitants are expected to make (and may be compelled to make) for the support of the manifold activities of government. Every inhabitant and every parcel of property receives governmental protection. Such protection costs money. When any inhabitant fails to contriute his share of the costs of this protection, some other inhabitant must contribute more than his fair share of that cost. . ."

BONDARCHUK v. BARBER
Court of Chancery of New Jersey
135 N.J.Eq. 334; 38 A.2d 872 (1944)

WILFRED H. JAYNE, Vice Chancellor.

Mrs. Barber is the kind of a wife who stands by her husband in all the troubles he would not have had if he had not married her. Her husband, the defendant, contractually obligated himself to convey to the complainant a parcel of land in the City of Trenton. He desires to fulfill his undertaking. She is inexorable in her refusal to unite with him in the conveyance. The complainant seeks a decree constraining Mr. Barber to specifically perform. Mrs. Barber is not a party to the cause. She did not execute the instrument embracing the option to convey. . . . She appeared, however, at the final hearing to express her immutable resolution to retain her inchoate dower and the personal reasons for her persistent adherence to that determination.

Although the option clause of the lease does not specify the estate to be conveyed, it is reasonably construed to obligate the defendant to convey the premises in fee simple and without encumbrance. . . . Obviously, a deed executed by the defendant alone is not in compliance with the undertaking. . . .

Except in cases of noticeable collusion, deception, or imposture, a decree of specific performance against a husband so circumstanced has been uniformly denied. It has been the policy of the law to permit a wife to exercise her own volition in the disposition of her dower interest in the lands of her husband, for said Chancellor Williamson (1855):

> "If the court decrees a specific performance according to the terms of the contract, the husband must procure his wife to sign the deed in some way, *per fas aut nefas*, [by fair means or foul] [citation omitted] or else take the consequences of disobedience to the order of the court. . . . It is plain to be seen that this mode of alienation might be adopted by an improvident and oppressive man to strip a prudent wife of all the reliance for her future support. Her refusal to sign a deed would be easily overcome by her husband entering into a contract that she shall join him in a conveyance; and then a decree of this court is looked to as the instrument of her oppression. She may have firmness enough to resist his unreasonable demand and entreaties, but yield to the persuasion of a decree of this court, which threatens her continued refusal with the incarceration of her husband".

The rule in this state is indubitable that in a suit for specific performance, a husband will not be decreed to procure his wife to join in the execution of a deed for the purpose of releasing her inchoate right of dower, if she is unwilling to do so. . . .

Adverting to the evidence, it is not intimated, much less substantiated, that the wife of the defendant ever manifested by word or conduct any willingness to relinquish her dower interest in the property in the consummation of a conveyance to the complainant. . . .

Mrs. Barber was not present when the lease was prepared and executed. Indeed, it is not distinctly evident that she was aware of the infused option until the complainant sought to exercise it. Although the defendant makes no point of it, he nevertheless assured me with apparent sincerity that he always entertained the notion that he had afforded the complainant "the first refusal," so called, in the event he desired to sell the demised premises. If he harbored that impression, it is fallacious to infer that he forewarned his wife of the obligatory covenant to convey.

Despite the earnest endeavors of counsel for the complainant to elicit some evidence that the refusal of the wife to release her inchoate right of dower was induced by the defendant, the fact that she resisted all his reasonable persuasions is sustained by his testimony and corroborated by hers. When interrogated upon this point, the defendant with perspiration flowing down his face, and in a state of exasperation, exclaimed: "My God, I wish she would sign today, now! It makes me sick! I don't like court!" I believe him. The vehemence and spontaneity of his interjection exemplified the philosophic quotation: "When a man has no design but to speak plain truth, he may say a great deal in a very narrow compass."

Incidentally, the evidence discloses that the complainant knew that the defendant was a married man at the time of the execution of the instrument containing the agreement to convey the premises. Whether that circumstance renders the equitable remedy with indemnity or abatement unavailable to this complainant need not be decided. It is a subject concerning which there is a noticeable diversity of opinion in other jurisdictions. ...

Conformable to the established rule that has endured imperishable in our jurisprudence for so long a period, I must deny a decree for specific performance against the defendant with either an abatement of the purchase price or indemnity against the inchoate dower of the defendant's wife. ...

The bill will be dismissed without prejudice to the prosecution of any action at law which the complainant may be advised to institute.

ROBERT v. N. & A. F. TIFT
Supreme Court of Georgia
60 Ga. 566 (1878)

LOGAN E. BLECKLEY, Judge.

[The Plaintiff, Robert, as trustee, filed a suit in equity to protect the assets of the trust estate from being made subject to a debt owed to defendant N. & A. F. Tift for farming supplies sold to the trustee, N. & A. F. Tift cross-complained for the principal amount of the debt. The Chancellor appointed a receiver and ordered that two-thirds of the annual net income of the trust estate be applied to the debt until full repayment was had. Plaintiff appealed.]

A married woman entitled to receive interest annually, may look to the actual produce of the fund, and it may be to her advantage to do so, for the fund may, under good and fortunate management, produce more than the equivalent of legal interest. Here, it seems, the trustee carried on a trust farm with the approbation of Mrs. Robert, and supplies were procured for her support, and for conducting the farming operations. In this way, a considerable debt was incurred. Equity could give its sanction to the arrangement, and has done so. Honest creditors ought to be protected as far as possible. The Code declares that their rights should be favored--Section 1945.

The true law, everywhere and at all times, delighteth in the payment of just debts. Blessed is the man that pays. The practice of paying promptly, and to the last cent, tends to the cultivation of one of the most excellent traits of human character. If debtors were guided by their own true interest, on an enlarged scale, they would be even more clamorous to pay than creditors are to receive. Tender would be more frequent than calls for money. Debt is the source of much unhappiness. The best possible thing to be done with a debt is to pay it.

Of course, where means are wanting, there must need be postponement until they can be had. Here the court took a moderate and discreet method, and endeavored to do something for the relief of the creditors, without wholly depriving Mrs. Robert of an income. It was competent, and, so far as we can see, it was wise and just, to place the farm in the hands of a receiver, and decree that a part of the future net income, year after year, be applied to the claims of creditors. In this way there can be a gradual working out: and the sooner a complete deliverance is realized the better will it be for all parties.

The management of the trustee has proved unfortunate. Perhaps that of the receiver will turn out better. At all events, it can be tried for a time, and when shown to be unprofitable can be discounted. . . In view of the broad discretion of chancery in superintending trusts, ratifying contracts, and shaping remedies adapted to the exigencies of each case, we are unable to pronounce that any error was committed on the trial or in rendering the decree. . .

. . . Judgment affirmed.

ANDERSON GREENWOOD AND COMPANY v. NATIONAL LABOR RELATIONS BOARD
United States Court of Appeals, Fifth Circuit
604 F.2d 322 (1979)

IRVING L. GOLDBERG, Circuit Judge:
The National Labor Relations Board ("NLRB") appeals from an order of the district court requiring it to provide appellee Anderson Greenwood & Co. with certain statements of witnesses taken during the NLRB's investigation of a challenged representation election. Since the date of the trial court's order, we have decided *Clements Wire & Mfg. Co., Inc. v. NLRB,* 589 F.2d 894 (5th Cir. 1979). Clements Wire requires us to reverse the judgment of the trial court.

The facts are not in dispute. After a representation petition was filed by the International Association of Machinists and Aerospace Workers, AFL-CIO ("the Union") seeking certification as a collective bargaining unit for certain employees of appellee, the NLRB duly conducted a representation election. The election was extremely close,[1] and both sides filed timely objections to it. The

---

[1] Of the 325 ballots cast, there were 156 for the Union and 156 against the Union; twelve ballots were challenged and one was treated as void.

NLRB conducted an investigation into the election, during which it interviewed a number of individuals and secured affidavits and statements from some of them. On the basis of this investigation, the Regional Director of the NLRB issued a report ordering that an evidentiary hearing be conducted on certain issues raised by the investigation.

On January 6, 1978, ten days prior to the scheduled hearing, appellee filed with the Regional Director a request under the Freedom of Information Act ("FOIA"), 5 U.S.C. § 552, seeking copies of all affidavits and written statements of employees of appellee or others taken by or submitted to the regional office of the NLRB in the course of the investigation into the election, as well as other documents acquired by the regional office in the course of the investigation. The Regional Director denied the request in its entirety, relying on Exemptions 7(A), (C), and (D) of the FOIA, 5 U.S.C. § 552(b)(7)(A), (C), and (D). Appellee appealed this denial to the NLRB's General Counsel, who denied appellee all requested documents except campaign letters written by appellee. The General Counsel relied on FOIA Exemptions 5 and 7(A).

On January 12, 1978, appellee filed a complaint in United States District Court for the Southern District of Texas seeking an order compelling the NLRB to provide the requested documents prior to any hearing on the election objections. The district court, relying on our opinion in *Robbins Tire and Rubber Co. v N.L.R.B.*, 563 F.2d 724 (5th Cir. 1977), found that the documents were not exempt from disclosure under the FOIA, and entered final judgment ordering the NLRB to provide appellee with any affidavits or written statements acquired in its investigation. The NLRB obtained a stay of execution of the judgment and brought this appeal.

> Our decision in Robbins Tire,
> Interpreting Congresses' reported desires,
> Exposed workers to their bosses' ire.
> The High Court, avoiding this sticky quagmire,
> And fearing employers would threaten to fire,
> Sent our holding to the funeral pyre.[2]
> Then along came Clements Wire,[3]
> Soon after its venerable sire.
> To elections, Wire extended Tire,
> Leaving app'llees arguments higher and drier.
> Now to colors our focus must shift,

---

[2] *N.L.R.B. v. Robbins Tire and Rubber Co.* 437 U.S. 214, 98 S.Ct. 2311, 57 L.Ed.2d 159 (1978) held that the witness statements there sought were exempt from disclosure under Exemption 7(A) because disclosure would interfere with the N.L.R.B.'s pending unfair labor practice proceeding.

[3] *Clements Wire & Mfg. Co. Inc. v. N.L.R.B.* 589 F.2d 894 (5th Cir. 1979). Clements Wire extended Robbins Tire to representation election hearings. . . .

To Green wood and stores that are Red.[4]
We hope this attempt at a rhyme, perhaps two,
Has not left this audience feeling too blue.

Since *Clements Wire* directly controls our decision here, we reverse.

REVERSED.

FENTON v. QUABOAG COUNTRY CLUB, INC.
Supreme Judicial Court of Massachusetts
353 Mass. 534; 233 N.E.2d 216 (1968)

PAUL CASHMAN REARDON, Justice

[Owners of house adjacent to defendant's golf course sought an injunction designed to terminate the operation of one of the holes in the nine-hole course and damages for injuries to themselves and their property. The case was referred to a master who filed a report which was confirmed by the Superior Court. The injunction was granted and plaintiffs were awarded damages. Defendant appealed.]

This appeal has to do with the game of golf and in particular with the abilities of certain golfers in the county of Hampden whose alleged transgressions gave rise to a suit. The plaintiffs, husband and wife, state in their bill that they are the owners of a home in Monson adjoining a golf course operated by the defendant, and after the recitation of a series of grievances seek an injunction designed to terminate the operation of one of the holes in the defendant's nine-hole course, together with damages for injuries to person and property.

The defendant's answer makes certain admissions and acknowledges the existence of a problem. It further states "that cooperation in the problem the * * * [plaintiffs] have been one way and although the * * * [plaintiffs] may have had no knowledge of the game of golf when they purchased the property they have certainly, over the years, become somewhat familiar with the game, but rather than be cooperative and understanding of the interest of the Quaboag Country Club, Inc. * * * have maintained an inexorable position of antagonism towards the Club and its members, and when suggestions were made to them which were anything less than the complete surrender of the use of the ninth fairway to all intentions and purposes, the * * * [plaintiffs] continued to be dissatisfied."

A master to whom the case was referred filed a report which illuminates the deep antagonisms which spring to life when home and family are threatened by devotees of the great outdoors. We refer to his findings.

---

[4] *Red Food Stores v. N.L.R.B.*, 604 F.2d 324, No. 78 3546 (5th Cir.), also decided today, presents a very similar issue to this case.

In 1952 the plaintiffs, John F. and Miriam E. Fenton, "not familiar with the details of the game of golf," bought their house, garage and land from one Lussier and his wife. The east side of the premises fronted on the Monson-Palmer Road. Otherwise the property was bounded on all sides by land owned by the defendant. The Lussiers had purchased the land from the defendant in 1944 and had, as one may gather from the report, coexisted happily with the golf club, a state of affairs no doubt enhanced by the fact that during their tenure Lussier and his family had sold soft drinks and sandwiches to golfers on the course and thus found no fault when errant golf balls descended upon their property.

The club itself had a lengthy history. It opened in 1900 as a six-hole course, and in 1922 expanded to nine holes. "Adjoining the westerly boundary of the * * * [plaintiffs'] land is the * * * [defendant's] ninth fairway. It has occupied this location since before 1927, and even prior to that," as far back as 1900, "the east side of the now ninth fairway * * * [was] the east side of a fairway."

Into this picture, fraught with potential trouble which only a golfer could fully appreciate, came the plaintiffs "not familiar with the details of the game of golf." Any deficiency in their knowledge was soon remedied as they immediately came under the assault of balls "hit onto and over their property." "Except for a few isolated occasions, these balls were not intentionally directed" at the Fenton estate. However, the master has provided us with some chilling statistics which cast grave doubt on the proficiency of the golfers of Hampden County, at least those who were playing the defendant's course. From 1952 an annual average number of 250 balls "were left" on the land of the plaintiffs, save for the year 1960 when a grand total of 320 such deposits were made. Over the years sixteen panes of glass in the plaintiffs' house were broken, for six of which fractures the plaintiffs have received reimbursement. The cost of such replacements apparently defied inflation and remained constant throughout the years at $3.85 for each new pane.

Affairs worsened in 1961 when the defendant added a sand trap "to the northwest corner of the ninth green." Since golfers intent on achieving the green drove from the tee in a southerly direction, they were faced with alternatives. They might aim somewhat to the west and face the sand trap, or they might veer more to the east and face the Fentons. The master inclined to the belief that they were prone to make the latter choice although, as he found, this was not without hazard, for the plaintiff John F. Fenton collected "all the balls he found on his land and sold them periodically."

Continued unbridled hooking and slicing caused further aggravation. Some years back the Fentons were possessed of a German Shepherd dog which developed apprehension at the approach of golfers to the point that they were forced to dispense with his companionship. In his place they acquired a Doberman evidently made of sterner stuff. The dog is still with them notwithstanding that he has been struck by a flying golf ball. On one occasion the male plaintiff himself stopped an airborne ball supposedly directed to the ninth green but winging its way off course. At another time a Fenton family steak cookout was interrupted by a misdirected ball which came to rest "just under the grill." There were additional serious evidences of mutual annoyance. In an episode "after dark, a ball was driven from the * * * [defendant's] fairway directly against the * * * [plaintiffs'] house." In another, a battered ball bearing the greeting "Hi, Johnnie" descended upon the plaintiffs' close. Hostile incidents occurred. One player venturing on the plaintiffs' property to retrieve a ball swung his club first at the Fentons' dog, then raised it at John Fenton, following which, according to the master's report, he "withdrew."

It need not be emphasized that from the year 1952 the plaintiffs were not silent in their suffering, and there was some talk about a fence. After the commencement of this suit the defendant constructed on its land a fence twenty-four feet high and three feet in from part of the boundary lines on the northern and western sides of the plaintiffs' land. The master states that while this fence has substantially, it has not entirely, abated the problem caused by the rain of golf balls. We are told that the erection of the fence in 1965 was followed by the flight of some eighty-one balls in that year onto the plaintiffs' territory. This somewhat minimized invasion the master terms "a continuing nuisance and trespass."

For all these depredations he assessed damages at $38.50 for those broken panes as yet unreimbursed, and $2,250 "for loss in the fair market value of * * * [the] property" because of the trespasses as well as because the fence "seriously diminishes the value of the property aesthetically." He also found damages at $2,600 for disturbance of the plaintiffs' "peace and comfort" for the thirteen years prior to the erection of the unaesthetic fence. He placed a value on the loss of the plaintiffs' peace and comfort since the fence went up at $50.

Following confirmation of the master's report the court entered a final decree enjoining the defendant from so operating its course "as to damage the property of the Plaintiffs, or to cause golf balls to be cast upon or propelled upon or against the property of Plaintiffs." The failure to employ the technical language peculiar to the game of golf in the decree in no sense muddies its meaning. The damages assessed by the master were awarded in the interlocutory and final decrees.

We have the case on appeals from the decrees.

1. We have no doubts about the propriety of the injunction. The plaintiffs are clearly entitled to an abatement of the trespasses. *Stevens v. Rockport Granite Co.*, [citation omitted] We paraphrase the apt expression of Chief Justice Rugg in the *Stevens* case: "The pertinent inquiry is whether the noise [the invasion of golf balls] materially interferes with the physical comfort of existence, not according to exceptionally refined, uncommon, or luxurious habits of living [e.g. golf addiction], but according to the simple tastes and unaffected notions generally prevailing among plain people [nongolfers]. The standard is what ordinary people [again those who eschew golf], acting reasonably, have a right to demand in the way of health and comfort under all the circumstances."

Were it not that this court cannot assume the function of a Robert Trent Jones we should make a judicial suggestion that the defendant's burden under the injunction will be considerably eased by shifting the location of the trap to the northeasterly corner of the green on the assumption, and on this the record is silent, that none exists there now.

2. On the damages awarded, the plaintiffs are entitled to the sum of $38.50 for the cost of replacing the glass, and also for the sum of $2,650 awarded them for their distress and discomfort over fourteen years. The master took testimony on the effect on the plaintiffs of their discomfort which was sufficient to enable him to make the award which he did. *Stevens v. Rockport Granite Co.*, [citation omitted].

3. There was error, however, in the award of damages based on the loss in the fair market value of the property due to what the master found to be a continuing trespass. This was a trespass of such a nature that it might be terminated by appropriate action, which is what the injunction in fact seeks to do. As such the true measure of the damages is the loss in rental value of the property while injury continues. [citation omitted]. In the assessment of damages the defendant's erection of the fence on its own property can play no part. The interlocutory and final decrees are reversed. The case is remanded to the Superior Court for further proceedings consistent with this opinion.

So ordered.

BENNETT v. ZONING BOARD OF ADJUSTMENT
Supreme Court of Pennsylvania
396 Pa. 57; 151 A.2d 439 (1959)

MICHAEL A. MUSMANNO, Justice.

One passing by plane over the area along the Roosevelt Boulevard in North Philadelphia, where it intersects with Hartel Street, might gain the impression he was looking upon a reproduction of the historical scene of Conestoga Wagons poised for their dash into the newly-opened Oklahoma Territory. A closer inspection would reveal, however, that the assumed pioneer wagons are in fact auto-trailers with protruding tongues ready to lick up the highway behind automobiles, to which they are babblingly attached for transportation of household goods, furniture and other rattling cargo.

These trailers are rented and sold by Roger J. Bennett who operates a gasoline service station at this point (7800 Roosevelt Boulevard). The trailers differ in size, weight and construction, ranging in weight from 500 to over 1,000 pounds, varying in length from 5 feet to 14 feet, and differing in type -- being two and four-wheeled vehicles, open and roofed.

The people living in the area, which is zoned partly "B" and "C" Residential, object to the presence of the seried ranks of trailers with their accompanying dollies. They complain that the traffic turmoil caused by the

319

attachment of these vehicles to these mother cars, their maneuvering into position and taking to the highways, all create noises, smells, and a general hubbub which are inimical to the health, welfare, and safety of the community.

In an appropriate proceeding, following a duly constituted hearing, the Zoning Board of Adjustment of Philadelphia agreed with the protestants and ruled that Bennett's use of his land (a three-quarter acre plot) in the clamorous manner indicated constituted a violation of the Philadelphia Zoning Ordinance. Bennett appealed from this decision to the Court of Common Pleas No. 7 of Philadelphia County which affirmed the action of the Zoning Board, and he then appealed to this Court.

Mr. Bennett contends here, as he maintained before the Zoning Board and the Court of Common Pleas, that the trailer business which he conducts is an activity inextricably part of his gasoline service business. But even his operation of a gasoline service station in the tranquil and attractive residential district on Roosevelt Boulevard is already a departure from what is ordinarily allowed in that area. It was only because the Court of Common Pleas No. 2 of Philadelphia (March Term, 1956) specially allowed him to use his property for a gasoline service station that he can be in business there at all. Being, then, already in enjoyment of one exception to the zoning regulations he seeks a full accordion expansion of that exception to the point where he may engage in a business wholly apart from what is permitted him by the non-conforming use.

Bennett is authorized to conduct at 7800 Roosevelt Boulevard the business of a gasoline service station. A gasoline service station is intended for the convenience of motoring wayfarers whose gasoline and oil gauges inform them of the immediate need of fuel and lubrication. It is in the nature of a roadside restaurant for hungry cars, it is an oasis on the Sahara of a long journey. It is not a hotel, it is not a *general* repair shop, it is not a warehouse where one may obtain permanent accessories and Siamese attachable dump carts, wagons, vans and freight trailers.

It is argued by Mr. Bennett that many gasoline service stations sell tires, batteries, cigarettes, bottled soda, cleaning fluids and insecticides. On the foundation of this assumed permitted extension of the purpose of a gasoline station he builds his asserted right to deal in auto-trailers. To begin with there is no established legalized right for a gasoline service station to sell the articles mentioned, although certainly it would be unreasonable for a community to object to occasional sales of soda to quench the thirst of a dusty motorist, cigarettes to satisfy a nicotine-famished traveler, and a tire to help the driver who encountered an aggressive nail on the road. But it is equally certain that if the service station proprietor sold cigarettes, tires, and refreshments in large and continuing quantities, a protest would be acceptable for adjudication in the courts.

It was testified in behalf of the appellant that some 118 gasoline service stations in Philadelphia rented trailers. Photographs introduced before the Zoning Board showed that at some of those stations one or more (not exceeding four) parking trailers were noted. But on April 8, 1959, as many as 89 trailers were parked on Bennett's premises and on April 14th the number had increased to 91. And then, even if a trailer or two encumbered the ground around 118 gasoline service stations, this number would represent but a small fraction of 5,000, the estimated number of gasoline stations in Philadelphia. Furthermore, no evidence was adduced to show what the trailers were doing at the 118 service stations. If they were being rented, the rentals could have fallen within the protection of permissible non-conforming uses, variances, or proper uses within zoning classification. And there was the possibility also that they were being rented in outright violation of law. This would not justify Bennett doing the same thing. The man who sells dynamite without authority cannot justify his violation of the law by arguing that a neighbor also sells the dangerous article without authority and without a record of recent travels. . . .

The appellant has not attempted to camouflage his flouting of the zoning restrictions. In the Philadelphia Telephone Directory (yellow classified section), he carries a quarter-page advertisement in which he proclaims that: "Our Business is Trailers." The advertisement is enlivened with the sketch of a man riding a trailer, clinging to a large box while about him are clustered lamps, brooms, and trunks. Then, there are other sketches of furniture vans and wheel boat trailers. The advertisement calls upon the reader to "Buy--sell--rent--Trailer Hitches--Couplings--Overload Springs--Dollies--Refrigerator Hand Trucks--Auto Tow-bars--Tarpaulins." One studies the stirring appeal in vain for the slightest suggestion that at 7800 Roosevelt Boulevard one may buy gasoline to keep his car rolling after he has hooked it up to a lumbering furniture van or a trailing, swaying motor boat.

The appellant argues that there is an "affinity" between selling gasoline and the rental-sale of auto-trailers. This may be true but there is also an affinity between the sale of gasoline and the sale of new and used cars. Still, no one would argue that a gasoline service station could clutter up its lot with dilapidated and worn-out cars and sell them to its customers who stop to get a tank full of gas. Affinity does not mean synonymous. The sale of shoestrings is an affinity to the selling of shoes but no sidewalk peddler of shoestrings would be allowed on that basis to open up a shoe shop and dispense all types of footgear.

The appellant says that zoning regulations may not be applied to resist a natural operation of economic laws. But natural economic laws must still wear the harness of state and municipal regulation where health, safety, and morals are concerned. Otherwise a bicycle vendor could easily persuade himself that he has the right to take orders for Cadillacs.

It is not enough that the trailer business have an affinity to the gasoline selling business or that it be "subordinate to the main use." It must also be "customarily incidental" to the main use. . . .

Order affirmed; each party to bear own costs.

MYGATT v. GOETCHINS
Supreme Court of Georgia
20 Ga. 350 (1856)

JOSEPH H. LUMPKIN, J.

[Plaintiff landowner filed a bill in equity against the owner of an adjacent parcel of property seeking to enjoin the construction of a "steam manufactory (to be propelled by an engine of fifty-horse power), for the manufacture of sash and blinds. . ." The bill alleged that "if said steam manufactory is erected as proposed, it will result in very great damage, annoyance and inconvenience, as well as prove a great nuisance to complainants and all the neighbors, and to the public at large; that the character of defendant's business would not admit of the employment of an experienced engineer to manage the engine used, and there would be constant danger of explosion; that the smoke and soot arising from such fuel as is ordinarily used in the furnace attached to such engine, will be scattered all over the premises of complainants, without the possibility of preventing it and the sparks emitted, as well as the constant burning of fuel, and the fact that manufactories of the kind are filled with combustible matter, will render the property of complainants more liable to be destroyed by fire; that the continued noise made by letting off steam from the boilers, and by blowing the whistle attached to the engine and by the rolling, changing and working of the machinery, and will be, in cases of sickness, an insufferable nuisance; that complainants, on account of the facts aforesaid, would, if said manufactory is erected, have to pay larger rates to insure their property aforesaid, and the same would be much depreciated in value; that the erection of said manufactory would tend greatly to disturb the congregation which worships in said Methodist Church, and to frighten horses tied in front of said church during service, and also to disturb the exercises of said public school--thus becoming a public nuisance. . . ." The bill was granted and the injunction issued. Defendant appealed.]

. . .Taking the bill and answer, the contemplated structure, prima facie, will not be a nuisance. It will neither work hurt, discomfort or damage. The only sense it will offend, is that of hearing. And we know of no sound, however discordant, that may not, by habit, be converted into a lullaby, except the braying of an ass or the tongue of a scold. . . .

All persons purchase town lots in view of the possible purposes to which they may be appropriated. And if it be true, that the risk from exposure will increase the insurance on contiguous lots, it can not be denied that it will be more than counterbalanced by the enhanced value of property produced by the prosperity of the city, occasioned by the establishments. It is suicidal to oppose them. There is too much that is fanciful and conjectural in the evils and dangers which are menaced. But be this as it may, as well attempt to stop up the mouth of Vesuvius as to arrest the application of steam to machinery to this day.

[Affirmed]

CHAPTER IV: BUSINESS, TRADE & COMMERCE

OIL & GAS FUTURES, INC. OF TEXAS v. ANDRUS
United States Court of Appeals, Fifth Circuit
610 F.2d 287 (1980)

PER CURIAM: IRVING L. GOLDBERG; PAUL H. RONEY; and GERALD BARD TJOFLAT, JJ.

In this appeal we are asked to determine whether ".82" is the equivalent of "82%." Having successfully completed grammar school, we are able to answer in the affirmative.

This dispute has its origins in a sealed competitive bidding process for an oil and gas lease to develop an offshore tract off the coast of Louisiana. Pursuant to section 8(a) of the Outer Continental Shelf Lands Act, 43 U.S.C.A. § 1337(a) (West 1964), the appellant, the Secretary of the Interior, invited bids for the lease. The notice of sale stipulated that "[a]ll royalty bids must be expressed in a percent to a maximum of five decimal places." *See* 39 Fed.Reg. 31670 (1974). Furthermore, the notice stated that only bids offering a royalty of "12-50 percent or more" would be considered. *See Id.*

Under a heading entitled "Percent Royalty Bid Expressed to Maximum of 5 Decimals," the appellee, Oil and Gas Futures, Inc. of Texas [Oil and Gas Futures], offered a royalty of "73.45689%" in its bid. A competitor, Texas Gas Exploration Corporation [Texas Gas], presented a royalty expressed as ".82165" in its bid. After examining the materials that Texas Gas submitted with its bid, and taking into account the fact that royalty bids were required to exceed 12.50%, the Secretary construed this latter bid to be an offer of a royalty of 82.165% and awarded the lease of Texas Gas. In the district court below, Oil and Gas Futures successfully argued that the secretary's construction of Texas Gas' royalty bid was arbitrary and capricious, and an abuse of discretion. Accordingly, Oil and Gas Futures was awarded judgment in its favor. We reverse.

We find it quite incredible that not only was this suit ever brought, but that the appellee convinced the district court that the Secretary abused his discretion by construing ".82165" to be the equivalent of "82.165%." We are in complete accord with the appellant's characterization of this quibble:

> [B]ooks intended for scholars in and below the eighth grade do deal with just this question. On page 87 of their treatise entitled *Growth in Arithmetic* (Revised Edition, Grade Eight) (World Book Co., Yonkers-On Hudson: 1956), John R. Clark and Rolland R. Smith ask the pertinent question: "Do you know how to change a per cent to a decimal?" Assuming a negative response, the authors set forth certain examples of equivalency:

6 per cent means 6 hundredths; so 6% - .06
7½ per cent means 7 1/2 hundredths;
    7½% = .07 1/2 or .075
3¼ per cent means 3 1/4 hundredths;
    3 ¼% = .03 1/4 or .0325

After inviting the students to study these equivalencies carefully, the authors announce this principle:

> To change a per cent to a decimal, omit the per
> cent sign and move the decimal point two places
> to the left.

The authors then ask their readers to "Study these examples and see if you can make up a rule for changing decimals to per cents." The examples given are:

.06 = 6%
.075 = 7.5% = 7½%
.0325 = 3.25% = 3 ¼%
.125 = 12 ½% = 12.5%

And then the authors set forth this principle:

> To change a decimal to a per cent, move the
> decimal point two places to the right, and write the
> percent sign after the number.

And so, with this rule in mind, any eighth grader can tell that .82165 = 82.165% (the decimal has been moved two places to the right, and a per cent sign placed after the number). . .

In view of the appellant's proper use of this higher mathematics and the fact that all bids were required to be in excess of 12.50%, the Secretary's decision cannot in any conceivable way be characterized as arbitrary and capricious or as an abuse of discretion. As a result, the judgment of the district court is reversed with instructions to enter judgment in the appellant's favor.

REVERSED

AN ACTE CONCERNING HATTS AND CAPPS
Statutes of The Realm of England
3 Henry VIII, Ch. 15 (1511)

WHERE BY the workers and makers of Cappes and Hattes within this Realme of England have dailly occupied and sett on work in making of cappes and hattes of the Kyngs naturall Subjethis that is to sey Men Women Maydens and Children borne wythin this Realme of England to the great relief and comfort of poore [Prisoners[1]] within this Realme to the nombre of thre score thowsand persones and above in carding spynnyng stitchyng knyttyng thikkyng dressyng dyeng sheryng and pressyng wyth other certen feates concernyng the workyng and makyng of cappes and hattes made and wrought wythin the Citie of London and in dyverse and many other Cities Boroughes and Townes within this Realme wherby the Kings Subjects here naturally borne have had their poore lyving tyme out of mynde, Till of late yeres past that so great haboundaunce of cappes and hattes redy wrought and made have been and daily be brought from the perties of beyond the See into this Realme, and here have been and daylly bee uttred and sold to the great perfite occupieng encreace and relyef of Straungiers of other Realmes which had and have the workyng and makyng of the same cappes and hattes, and to the great Idelnesse enpoverysshyng and utter undoing of great multitude of the Kyngis naturall subjectis borne wythin this said Realme;

By reason wherof the Kyngs Subjects borne wythin this Realme have not their poore leving nor be not occupied nor sett on worke in making of cappes and hattes as they were wont to be;

By occasyon wherof they fall to Idelnesse & other inconvenients to beggery & manyfold skynes to the great impoverysshement of the commons of this Realme;

In consideracion of the premisses be yt ordeigned enacted and establysshed by the Kyng or Souveraigne Lord the Lorde spuall and temporall and the Commons in this present perliament assembled and by the auctorite of the same, that from the furst day of May next c myng ther be no cappes nor hatts made and redy wrought in any partie beyond the See bought by any of the Kinges Subjects borne undre the Kingis obbeysaunce except Lordes or Knyghts uppon peyne of Forfeiture for every suche cappe or hatte so by theym or any of theim bought xl s. the oon moyte of the same forfeyture to be to the King our Soveraigne Lord, and thother moyte to hym or theym that wyll sue for the same by accion of dett or otherwise; In whiche accon the pertie defendaunt shalnot be admytted to wage his Law nor perteccon nor essoyne to be allowed in the same accion. Ferthermore be it enacted by the said auctorite that no Capper nor Hatter nor other persone selle not putt to sale any cappe or hatte that shalbe made within this Realme after the Fest of Midsomer next c myng but that it be sufficently wrought and of a sufficent colour in every point after the goodnesse and fynesse of the woll wherof they shalbe made uppon peyne of forfeyture of every cappe or hatte so sold vj s. viij d.

And that the Capper nor none other persone shalnot take by hym self or any other persone to his use for any Cappe made of the fynest Leemynster woll above iij s. iiij d.;

Nor for any Cappe made of the seconde sort of the same Leemynster wolle above ij s. vj d. nor for any cappe made of the third sort of Leemynster wolle above xx d. nor for any cappe made of the fourth sorte of the same Leemynster wolle above xij d.;

---

[1] So also the original Act reads.

And that no Capper Hatter nor any other persone shall not take by hymself or any other persone to his use for any Cappe made of the fynest Cotteswold woll above ij s.; Nor for any cappe made of the seconde sorte of the same Cotteswold woll above xvj d.

And that all other cappes and hattes of other woll to be sold at suche price as the bier and seller may resounably agree.

The cappe made of the seid fynest Leemynster woll to be marked in the lynyng of the same cappe with a tre L.; The cappe made of the seconde sorte of the same Leemynster woll to be marked with this mark Lr; The cappe made of the fynest Cotteswold woll to be marked with a tre C. in the lynyng therof; And the seconde cappe of the seconde sorte of Cotteswold woll to be marked wyth this marke Cr.; And the Hatter Capper nor other persone by hym self nor any other persone to his use shall take of any of the Kyngs Subjects for any hatte of the best makyng not engreyned more than ij s.;

And yf any Capper Hatter or other persone take more money for any cappe or hatte contrary to this athe, he is to forfayte for every cappe and hatte for which he shall take more than is aforerehersed xl. s. The moite thereof to be to the Kyng our Soveraigne Lord, and the other moite to the pertie grevid or any other persone that woll sue accion for the same forfaiture by Writt Byll or Pleynte at the Commen Lawe or after custome of Citie or Towne wher it shall fortune suche forfaiture to bee by like percesse as is used in the accions of Debt in Court wher it shalbe pursued. And that the Defendaunt in that behalf be not admytted to wage his Lawe nor that any perteccion or essoyne be to hym allowed.

And that all and singular Estatutes hertofore made concernyng hattes or cappes be fromhensforth repelled and adnulled by vertue of this present parliament.

COLCORD v. CARR
Supreme Court of Georgia
77 Ga. 105; 3 S.E. 617 (1886)

LOGAN E. BLECKLEY, Chief Justice.

[Plaintiff Carr brought an action for trespass against defendants Colcord and Bacon, alleging that they had entered onto a parcel of land leased by him and upon which he manufactured turpentine, and that the defendants had cut down and removed the existing timber, thereby destroying plaintiff's turpentine business. The defendants alleged that the plaintiff had granted them an express license to harvest the timber.

At trial, the evidence disclosed that the owners of the land had sold the timber to the defendants, and that their agent had approached plaintiff seeking permission to have it cut. The plaintiff agreed to permit the cutting as soon as the "scrape" was removed from the trees. A letter from the plaintiff to the agent confirmed this agreement, which, in turn, was communicated orally to the defendants.

The plaintiff admitted writing the letter but testified that he later notified the defendants orally that they could not cut the timber until after he had got the "stuff" off; that the "scrape" had been removed before the cutting began, but the "stuff" had not; and that he had notified the defendants to stop. The plaintiff prevailed and was awarded $140 damages.]

. . . An executory license to cut trees after the "scrape" has been taken off, is modified by notice not to cut till the "stuff" has been removed. . . Where the original license was by letter to a third person, and by oral communication from that person to the licensee, a subsequent modification by parol would be effective.

It is very apparent that this whole controversy has grown out of not paying sufficient attention to the difference between "scrape" and "stuff." It was the intention, the deliberate purpose of the plaintiff, I have no doubt, to allow the cutting of those trees as soon as the "scrape" had been removed; but he afterwards changed his mind, and concluded that he would take the "stuff" off as well as the "scrape;" and he made known to the defendants, or their agents and servants, that he had undergone this important change of purpose; and they were warned that they must wait until the "stuff" was removed.

They would not wait; the "scrape" was off, and they went forward and cut the trees, and injured or destroyed the "stuff," and that caused damage to the plaintiff, and he sued accordingly. It seems to me that if the defendants could ever have been brought to comprehend in its full force the difference between "scrape" and "stuff," they would have submitted to the verdict without bringing this case here for review. But when people get into a confused state of mind on the distinction between one thing and another, there is no limit to the rage for litigation in which they may possibly indulge.

Whoever can comprehend the distinction between "scrape" and "stuff," can understand that a license to cut trees after the "scrape" has been taken off is not the same thing as a license to cut after the "stuff" has been removed.

If there had been no modification of the original license, there would have been no trespass, for it is certain that the trees were not cut until after the "scrape" was taken off. But there is clear evidence that before the cutting was begun, the plaintiff below gave warning that it must not be done until the "stuff" was removed. It is equally clear that the "stuff" had not been removed when the trees were cut.

The question then is, whether the license could be modified by giving this warning or notice. And why not? The license was executory, and a mere gratuity. Nothing was paid or promised for it. The plaintiff was under no obligation by contract, or otherwise, to grant it, and when he did grant it, he could, while it was still executory, revoke or modify it at pleasure. The evidence shows that he gave timely notice of the change of terms upon which his permission was accorded. If the defendants were unwilling to accept the terms ultimately announced, they ought to have declined to cut the trees at all until his lease, which was prior in date to their own, had expired. Had they waited until then, they might have kept clear of all complication with "stuff" and "scrape."

Judgment affirmed.

HORWOOD v. MILLAR'S TIMBER AND TRADING COMPANY, LTD.

King's Bench, Court of Appeal

[1916-1917] All E.R. Rep. 847; [1917] 1 K.B. 305 (1917)

SIR THOMAS EDWARD SCRUTTON, L. J.

[Appeal from a decision of the court below whereby it was declared that a contract contained in a certain deed dated July 1, 1913, and made between one Bunyan and the plaintiff, was bad as being contrary to public policy.]

I am of the same opinion, and desire, in view of the importance to the public of the subject-matter of this case, to express my opinion in my own words. The only thing that has made me hesitate as to whether I should do so is that I am doubtful whether I can express my judgment in language of sufficiently judicial moderation in view of the facts of this case. Any judge who has heard criminal business in the city of London knows that one of the great evils of London at present is the system by which money-lenders lend money to clerks who have small salaries in offices in London, and, under the terror of telling their employers that they have lent such money, drive clerks to crime and inflict any amount of evil on their families.

When sitting as a judge of the king's Bench Division in what is called their Saturday jurisdiction, when gentlemen bearing royal and noble names pass before one as plaintiffs lending money at very high rates of interest, I have seen a good deal of the ways of money-lenders, but it had not entered into my wildest imagination that any of them could have concocted a document of the nature of that which we have before us in this case, and I am glad that at last the Court has an opportunity of pronouncing an opinion upon it -- to which from my experience of money-lenders I do not suppose they will pay any attention whatever.

The case arises in this way: There is a Mr. Bunyan who is a clerk at a small salary in a London office; his salary is under £3 a week. He was in monetary difficulties; he was owing money to three money-lenders and to a solicitor. His only other debts were under £5 to two tradesmen.

Mr. Horwood, the plaintiff, who describes himself as a builder, but who appears to be a registered money-lender, lent him money undertaking to pay off or compound with his creditors, and he lent him a sum of £42, which included £4 to himself, some £7 or £8 expenses of the loan, some £20 to pay off the money-lenders, and some £5 or £6 to pay off what I may call the legitimate debts. His loan was repayable by instalments of £2 a month including £30 for interest, but the whole sum to become payable immediately default was made in any instalment or any breach of the covenants to which I am about to refer; and he took as security the document that we have to consider.

The document bound the debtor never to change his residence without the consent of the money-lender; it bound him never to change his employment without the consent of the money-lender; it bound him not to consent to a reduction of his salary without the consent of the money-lender; it bound him not to part with any of his property without the consent of the money-lender; it bound him to incur no obligations on credit without the consent of the money-lender, and to incur no obligation, legal or moral, without the consent of the money-lender, and it appears to me that it is not using overstrained or poetical language to say that it made this unfortunate man the slave of the money-lender.

Now the question comes before us because what might have been expected to happen did happen. The clerk made default in respect of one of the £2 instalments. Thereupon the money-lender gave notice to his employer and now sues his employer for salary due to the clerk after the notice of assignment. The judge in the city of London Court took the view that it was not an absolute assignment. The Divisional Court differed from that view, but took the view which jumps to the eyes on looking at the document that it was contrary to public policy. The money-lender now appeals to this Court against that decision. Now what test has the Court to apply?. . .

Now I look at this agreement from this point of view: is there no more than is necessary for the protection of the money-lender? It seems to me that there is far more than is necessary for the protection of the money-lender in whose interests it is imposed. Is it reasonable in the interests of the public? I can conceive nothing more dangerous to the interests of the public than that a system of money-lending like this to small people in offices where they have great temptations, and great opportunities to be dishonest if money pressure is put upon them, should be allowed to exist for a single minute, and, looking at the agreement as a whole, it seems to me to be quite clear that it goes far beyond what is reasonable for the purpose for which it is imposed. . .

THE WESTERN RAILROAD v. THORNTON & ACEE
Supreme Court of Georgia
60 Ga. 300 (1878)

LOGAN E. BLECKLEY, Judge.

It may be doubted whether the personal baggage of a traveler can be reached or affected by garnishment. If the wearing apparel which his trunk contains is protected, the trunk containing it, and which is necessary for taking due care of it while his journey is in progress, and until his return to his abode, ought, it would seem, to be equally protected. The trunk is a part of his baggage proper, as well as its contents. For the time being, it is but an adjunct or incident, the apparel and other articles of necessity within it being the principal. Should not the rule apply, that the incident follows the principal?. . .

. . . The rind and pulp of an orange, or the envelope of a letter and the letter itself, are not much more closely connected than a passenger's trunk and its contents, when the trunk is in the care of the carrier, and the key in the passenger's pocket. To delay or detain baggage by the use of the garnishment, would, or might, work great inconvenience to the traveling public; which, in these times, is almost identical with the public at large. If a debtor's baggage could be stopped, that of his family being frequently mingled with it, all would be stopped together. The family, when at a distance from home, might thus be brought into perplexity and distress of a kind which all women and children, if not all men too, should be spared.

To catch up baggage for debt is the next thing to taking the person of the debtor. The traveler had almost as well be put in jail for an hour or two, as to have his trunk or valise locked up at the railroad station. Perhaps he would rather go to jail for a little while if he could have the company of his baggage, than be free on condition of parting with it. To separate him from that which is the object of his chief care and solicitude through the whole course of his wanderings, is hard upon him indeed. Between passenger and baggage there is a relation beyond that of mere ownership. When baggage is lost, it is not simple privation; it is bereavement. . .

. . . Judgment reversed.

PRODUCTOS CARNIC, S.A. v. CENTRAL AMERICAN BEEF AND SEAFOOD TRADING COMPANY
United States Court of Appeals, Fifth Circuit
621 F.2d 683 (1980)

JOHN R. BROWN, Circuit Judge:

Insurrection, armed conflict, battles in the streets, terrorist attacks, riots, war, revolution, and the overthrow of a dictator permeate this appeal. General Anastasio Somoza was forced to resign as President of Nicaragua on July 17, 1979. The new government promptly nationalized a great portion of the vast holdings of Somoza and his family, including a small Nicaraguan meat processing company--already close to bankruptcy--Productos Carnic, S.A. (Carnic).

During the two months before Somoza's downfall, Carnic exported approximately 862,000 pounds of frozen boneless meat to the United States. The meat was airlifted to neighboring San Salvador, where Central American Beef & Seafood Trading Co. (CABS) took possession, shipped the beef to Miami, and placed it into cold storage. The Nicaraguans, through the nationalized Carnic and its court-appointed receiver in bankruptcy, seek to recover the beef or its value from CABS. To do so, complex issues of commercial and international law will have to be decided.

The District Court sought to preserve the *status quo* pending a full resolution of those issues by enjoining movement of the beef. CABS appeals the preliminary injunction. With slight modification, we affirm.

CHAPTER IV: BUSINESS, TRADE & COMMERCE

No Bones About It

Our review of the District Court's preliminary injunction is limited to determining whether there was an abuse of discretion. ... Those cases recognize, however, that the movant carries the burden of persuading the District Court that the four-part test for an injunction has been met: (1) the movant has a substantial likelihood of eventual success on the merits; (2) irreparable injury will be suffered unless the injunction issues; (3) the threatened injury to the movant outweighs the damage which the injunction may cause the opponent; and (4) the injunction would not be adverse to the public interest.

Appellant's Beef

CABS principally argues that Carnic will not prevail on the merits. CABS claims it is a *bona fide* purchaser of the beef and upon sale will owe the proceeds, less a set amount, to the Somozas as the pre-revolution owners who were not compensated when Nicaragua nationalized Carnic. It is true that confiscation is normally contrary to our public policy and such acts by foreign governments will not be enforced against property within our jurisdiction. ...

But Carnic produced some evidence that General Somoza's ouster was actively supported by the United States and his holdings in Carnic and other companies were obtained by corrupt practices in violation of Nicaraguan law. Moveover, at this point of the litigation Somoza has not even submitted to the jurisdiction of the Court and is not a party. CABS produced no evidence rebutting that produced by Carnic. . .

. . . We find that Carnic met its burden of showing a substantial likelihood of success on the merits. This is especially so because the Somozas have not appeared to directly assert their interests. And we certainly cannot say that Carnic has *no* likelihood of prevailing on the merits. As long as this factor is present to some degree, it is not even necessary that a *substantial* likelihood of success on the merits will justify temporary injunctive relief. ...

What's At Steak

Adequate and essentially uncontradicted evidence supports the District Court's determination that without an injunction a meaningful decision on the merits would be impossible. ... The District Court found that General Somoza controls CABS and "intends to transfer the subject beef and/or its proceeds out of the jurisdiction of this Court, with the result that any judgment ultimately obtained against CABS Trading would be unenforceable. . . "

The District Court's finding is supported by evidence that CABS once attempted to transfer the beef to a fictitious trading company, that CABS may have altered documents while the beef was in San Salvador, and that the Carnic bank account in Ft. Lauderdale, Florida, was closed and over $300,000 withdrawn at the instruction of General Somoza. By showing that CABS intended to frustrate any judgment on the merits, the Judge was entitled to conclude that Carnic undoubt-edly had shown potential irreparable injury. . .

Ground For Modification

The time expended by this appeal prompts us to direct a slight modifica-tion of the injunction. The District Court quite properly encouraged the parties to sell the beef and deposit the proceeds with the Court. The parties now indicate that the District Court renewed its encouragement during the pendency of this appeal. Why this obviously prudent course was rejected or not actively supported is beyond discernment. We think it best for reasons of judicial economy and common sense to direct a modification of the injunction at this time. The frozen beef may already have very slightly deteriorated. Thus the parties' rights may be slightly impaired should the beef remain unsold a great deal longer. . . .
Further, the public interest favors economic efficiency and the avoidance of useless expense. Holding the beef over a long period senselessly uses up storage space and charges of $7,000 per month. The coup de grâce of litigation caused by revolution usually comes *long* after that of the revolution. . . .

We therefore direct that the prudent course for the District Court is to require the sale of the beef and deposit of the proceeds in an interest-bearing account under direction of the District Court. . .

AFFIRMED and MODIFIED.

MORRIS v. THE STATE OF GEORGIA
Supreme Court of Georgia
117 Ga. 1; 43 S.E. 368 (1902)

JOHN S. CANDLER, J.

The accused was tried in the city court of Mount Vernon, upon an accusation charging that on the 17th day of July, 1902, in the county of Montgomery, he did "unlawfully and with force and arms engage in the practice of dentistry for fee, without registering in said county as required by law, and without legal authority from the Board of Dental Examiners of said State to practice dentistry on the 15th day of December, 1897, and not coming within the class of persons exempt from the provisions of the act approved December 15th, 1897, and the said Ralph Morris not being then and there a regularly licensed physician or surgeon."

We will remark, in passing, that we have in the past had frequent occasion to doubt the appropriateness of the indiscriminate and almost universal use, in indictments and accusations, of the time-worn phrase, "with force and arms." We can not, for example, see the necessity of charging force and arms in indictments and accusations for perjury, forgery, vagrancy, and similar crimes involving the employment of no physical force. Suffering humanity, however, will attest the peculiar aptness of the phrase in cases like the present; and from this we should learn well the lesson that, amid the kaleidoscopic changes wrought by twentieth century progress and advancement, it behooves us to be careful lest we slip too far from the moorings of our fathers, or desecrate with too ruthless a hand the ancient landmarks of the English law.

The case was tried by the judge below, without a jury, and the accused was found guilty. The evidence for the State showed that the accused had practiced dentistry in Montgomery county during the year 1902. That for the accused, and his statement, were to the effect that he had practiced dentistry in that county since April 1, 1897. At the conclusion of the evidence, and after both sides had announced closed, counsel for the accused moved orally to dismiss the accusations, on the grounds that the act on which the accusation was founded was unconstitutional, . . .

. . . After a careful reading of the act approved December 15, 1897 (Acts 1897, p. 119), upon which it seems to be conceded, the accusation in the present case was founded, we conclude that it is not, for any of the reasons assigned in the bill of exceptions, unconstitutional. . . .

Judgment affirmed.

STATE OF OREGON v. HUNTER
Supreme Court of Oregon
300 P.2d 455; 208 Or. 282 (1956)

WALTER L. TOOZE, J.

Defendant, Jerry Hunter, a person of the feminine sex, was charged by complaint filed in the district court for Clackamas county, with the crime of "participating in wrestling competition and exhibition," in violation of the provisions of ORS 463.130. The complaint, omitting formal parts, charged as follows:

> "Jerry Hunter is accused by W.L. Bradshaw, District Attorney, by this Complaint of the Crime of Person of Female Sex Participating in Wrestling Competition and Exhibition committed as follows: The said Jerry Hunter on the 25th day of October A.D., 1955, in the County of Clackamas and State of Oregon, then and there being a person not of the male sex, to wit: of the female sex, did then and there unlawfully and wilfully participate in a wrestling competition and wrestling exhibition, said act of defendant being contrary to the statute in such cases made and provided, and against the peace and dignity of the State of Oregon."

To this complaint defendant filed a demurrer based upon the following grounds: . . .

> "That this Court has no jurisdiction over the subject
> of the complaint in that the statute on which said
> complaint is founded is unconstitutional."

The demurrer was overruled by the district court. . . .

ORS 463.010 to 463.990, inclusive, provides for the creation of boxing and wrestling commissions, for registration of boxers and wrestlers, authorizes certain prize fights and wrestling exhibitions, with certain regulations pertaining to the same, invests the commissions created with certain powers, including the rule-making power, provides for licensing, for penalties, and, in general, assumes to cover the entire field involved in boxing and wrestling exhibitions. ORS 463.130 provides as follows:

> "Wrestling competitions; females barred; licensing; fees (1) The commissioners may license referees, professional wrestlers, the managers of wrestlers and seconds, and collect such fees as they deem just and reasonable. Wrestling competitions shall be held only under license of the commission. *No person other than a person of the male sex shall participate in or be licensed to participate in any wrestling competition or wrestling exhibition. . .*"

The principal question for decision is whether the foregoing ban against women wrestlers constitutes an unreasonable exercise of the police power of the state and violates Art. XIV, § 1, of the U.S. Constitution and Art. 1, § 20, of the Oregon Constitution. Is the classification contained in the statute arbitrary and unconsti-tutional, or is it based upon a reasonable distinction having a fair and substantial relation to the object of the legislation and, therefore, is constitutional?

. . .Class legislation is permissible if it designates a class that is reasonable and natural and treats all within the class upon the basis of equality. We take judicial notice of the physical differences between men and women. These differences have been recognized in many legislative acts, particularly in the field of labor and industry, and most of such acts have been upheld as a proper exercise of the police power in the interests of the public health, safety, morals, and welfare. . . .

. . .Moreover, there is no inherent right to engage in public exhibitions of boxing and wrestling. Both sports have long been licensed and regulated by penal statute and, in some cases, absolutely prohibited. It is axiomatic that the Fourteenth Amendment to the U.S. Constitution does not protect those liberties which civilized states regard as properly subject to regulation by penal law. Neither does Art. 1, § 20, of the Oregon Constitution. . .

. . .In addition to the protection of the public health, morals, safety, and welfare, what other considerations might have entered the legislative mind in enacting the statute in question? We believe that we are justified in taking judicial notice of the fact that the membership of the legislative assembly which enacted this statute was predominately masculine. That fact is important in determining what the legislature might have had in mind with respect to this particular statute, in addition to its concern for the public weal.

It seems to us that its purpose, although somewhat selfish in nature, stands out in the statute like a sore thumb. Obviously it intended that there should be at least one island on the sea of life reserved for man that would be impregnable to the assault of woman. It had watched her emerge from long tresses and demure ways to bobbed hair and almost complete sophistication; from a creature needing and depending upon the protection and chivalry of man to one asserting complete independence. She had already invaded practically every activity formerly considered suitable and appropriate for men only. In the field of sports she had taken up, among other games, baseball, basketball, golf, bowling, hockey, long distance swimming, and racing, in all of which she had become more or less proficient, and in some had excelled.

In the business and industrial fields as an employe or as an executive, in the professions, in politics, as well as in almost every other line of human endeavor, she had matched her wits and prowess with those of mere men, and, we are frank to concede, in many instances had outdone him. In these circumstances, is it any wonder that the legislative assembly took advantage of the police power of the state in its decision to halt this ever-increasing feminine encroachment upon what for ages had been considered strictly as manly arts and privileges?

Was the Act an unjust and unconstitutional discrimination against woman? Have her civil or political rights been unconstitutionally denied her? Under the circumstances, we think not. . . .

The judgment is affirmed.

MARSHALL v. BAHNSEN
Court of Appeals of Georgia
1 Ga.App. 485; 57 S.E. 1006 (1908)

ARTHUR GRAY POWELL, J.

Bahnsen, a veterinary surgeon, residing at Americus, at the request of Dunn, the plaintiff in error's intestate, went to Bronwood, a distance of some thirty miles, and made an "examination for soundness" of two cars of mules, fifty-four head. There was no express contract, and Bahnsen sued for the service at the rate of $5 per head. Dunn denied the reasonableness of the charge made, and tendered $25 as being sufficient.

Less than a day's time was consumed in making the examination; however, it is fair to the plaintiff to say that the evidence showed that he was very expert in his line of work, and was able to make an examination and to form an intelligent opinion with a rapidity much greater than could be approached by a novice. There was evidence that $5 per head was the usual and reasonable charge for such services; but also evidence that this charge was excessive. The jury found for the plaintiff the full amount sued for.

$270 does seem to be a right heavy charge for a few hours work by what the folks colloquially call a "horse doctor," and what is styled with greater gentility of "veterinary surgeon;" but the law very wisely considers that juries know, very much better than judges, especially appellate judges, do, what is reasonable and just pay not only for "horse doctors," but also for all other classes of professional men. In such matters their finding, when approved by the trial judge, is final, and not reviewable upon the facts. . .

Judgment affirmed.

CONWAY, INC. V. ROSS
Supreme Court of Alaska
627 P.2d 1029 (1981)

JOHN H. DIMOND, Senior Justice.

Cleopatra Ross entered into an employment contract on September 20, 1976, with Conway, Inc., which does business in Ketchikan as the Shamrock Bar. By the terms of the contract, Ross was to appear as the Shamrock's "feature topless stripper" for nine weeks, from September 22 to November 23, 1976. During the third week of this employment, Conway fired Ross at the request of the Ketchikan district attorney because Ross allegedly had engaged in an act of prostitution during the contract period. Shortly after this, Ross filed suit against Conway in the district court, claiming that Conway's termination of her employment was a breach of their contract.

A trial was held and the district court found that Ross had engaged in one act of prostitution. It concluded, however, that this conduct was not prohibited by the contract and did not justify the termination of her employment. It therefore held that Conway had breached the parties' contract when it fired Ross. The court entered a judgment for Ross, awarding her $1,975.52 as damages for loss of income for the remainder of the contract period. . . .

Conway appealed to the superior court, which affirmed the judgment. Conway then brought this appeal, ...

We first consider the argument that the district court erred in holding that Conway breached its contract with Ross when it fired her. . . .Conway does not suggest that Ross violated any of the express contract provisions. Conway argues, instead, that Ross breached the implied term of every employment contract that the employee will do nothing which could tend to injure the employer's business interests. . . . The question thus becomes whether Conway's business could have been injured if it had continued to employ Ross after learning of her act of prostitution.

Ross's prostitution was unrelated to Conway's business. She did not solicit any of the Shamrock's customers. Her single act of prostitution involved a gentleman
she met apart from the Shamrock Bar. Ross's encounter with this gentleman occurred at her own premises and during the hours she was not working for Conway. In short, there was nothing to connect Ross's act of prostitution with her employment at the Shamrock Bar.

Conway argues that its liquor license could have been jeopardized if it had not discharged Ross when the district attorney request it to do so. 15 AAC 20.010 sets forth the only grounds upon which the Alcoholic Beverage Control Board can suspend or revoke a license. . . .

. . . At trial, Ross was asked whether she believed Conway could fire her if she engaged in prostitution while in Ketchikan. In response she testified, "That's understood for every contract." The dissent argues that this, coupled with the fact that Conway fired Ross after her act of prostitution, indicates that refraining from acts of prostitution was an impled term of the parties' contract.

We disagree. At most, Ross' testimony suggests what her understanding was of the contract. One party's understanding may be incorrect, and it does not bind the parties or the court. . .

We note that only the Alcoholic Beverage Control Board can suspend or revoke liquor licenses. . . If Conway had refused to discharge Ross, the district attorney could not have suspended or revoked Conway's license, nor could he have compelled the board to do so. Thus, refusing to act upon the district attorney's request could not in itself have jeopardized Conway's license.

Employing an individual who has engaged in one act of prostitution is not specified as grounds for suspending or revoking a license. . . .Ross's liaison was consummated entirely apart from her employment at the Shamrock Bar. She did not solicit any of the bar's patrons and any of her activities related to prostitution occurred away from the bar's premises. . . .

The complete separation of Ross's prostitution-related activities from her employment with Conway prevented these activities from injuring Conway's business interests. . . .

Conway's possible fear of reprisals from the authorities if it did not act upon the district attorney's request would similarly not provide cause for firing Ross because no action could be taken against Conway as long as its business activities complied with the law. The situation brought about by the district attorney's request may have been a difficult one for Conway, but Conway could hardly have expected to operate a topless bar without encountering some difficulties similar to this. We agree with the district court that Conway did not have good cause to fire Ross and we therefore affirm its judgment in Ross' favor. . . .

JAY A. RABINOWITZ, Chief Justice, dissenting.

The majority correctly perceives that Cleopatra Ross has been wronged in this case; however, I cannot agree with the majority's conclusion. If Cleopatra Ross has a remedy, it is not against Conway, Inc., d/b/a/ the Shamrock.

It is not seriously disputed that Cleopatra did engage in an act of prostitution with one A. Otto Lincoln.[1] The district court made this finding of fact, with which the superior court agreed, and the majority does not take issue.[2]

My conclusion that Cleopatra Ross cannot recover is not, however, based on the moral reprehensibility of her conduct. Indeed, assuming the application of a moral litmus, she places a distant second to the Shamrock. The Shamrock is a local tavern in Ketchikan, of the genre that constantly treads the fine line between mere poor taste and outright illegality.[3] With such establishments, license revocation never falls below the level of a distinct possibility, and this fact was apparent to Conway, Inc., d/b/a/ the Shamrock.

The superior court noted that the local police maintained a "close scrutiny" of the tavern; and its position was evidently precarious enough that an admonishing telephone call from the district attorney triggered this litigation. However, the Shamrock's affinity for the green was such that it never allowed such considerations to interfere with its pursuit of profits. And yet the Shamrock's attitude towards its "girls" was somewhat schizophrenic. On the one hand, it clearly wanted to hold out to its customers, the pleasurable prospect of following in A. Otto's footsteps, and thus such regulations as: "Girls are expected to mix

---

[1] Cleopatra Ross does argue that this particular finding by the district court was not supported by the evidence, in that her testimony was presented in person, whereas that of A. Otto Lincoln was submitted by deposition. I cannot agree. The district court was faced with little more than two conflicting bare assertions of fact, and his conclusion was supported by substantial evidence. It is not likely that A. Otto was mistaken about Cleopatra Ross's identity; in the community of Ketchikan, it is unlikely that one would find more than one exotic dancer with (according to A. Otto's deposition) "a diamond ring in her nose, which is quite unusual." Nor can I accept the suggestion that A. Otto was, as Ms. Ross contended in her testimony at trial, lying to retaliate for her refusal to kiss him in "Howard's Charcoal Broiler." A. Otto's deposition incriminated himself as well as Ms. Ross; and the lone attempt of her attorney (who was present when A. Otto's deposition was taken) to discredit the witness was unsuccessful, as the only prior crime to which A. Otto would admit was a "[p]olitical crime. I . . . was involved against the Russian Communists, and when they were within the border of the country [apparently Rumania] I volunteered fighting against the Russians. Boys that got Congressional Medals of Honor here, I was convicted as an ordinary political criminal."

[2] Not only was this finding of an act of prostitution supported by substantial evidence in the record, it appears it was also somewhat unfulfilling, according to A. Otto's description of his $150 fling: "[T]he basic purpose that I was there . . . was to go to bed with her which [I] did. It wasn't all that difficult because the bed, I don't suppose it was ever made and the color TV was constantly playing which I didn't like at all. It made everything look like such commercialized entertainment."

[3] At trial, Mr. Conway, the owner of Conway, Inc., admitted that he permitted his employees to solicit drinks for a commission in violation of former AW 04.10.040(b). . . .

with all the customers, not to sit all together at one table;" "Keep your boy friends out of the club;" and "Girls must dance topless for one song out of each three songset."

On the other hand, it is also clear that the Shamrock intended its customers' reaches to exceed their grasps, and thus: "No leaving the bar with men" and "No men will be allowed in the living quarters." As the superior court noted, "As best I can interpret it, the dancers are required to tease but are not expected to connect."

Thus, I share with the majority some sympathy for Cleopatra Ross's position here; the Shamrock's objections to her exploitation of her body for financial gain ring a trifle hollow, in light of its own clear intent to do the same.[4] However, I am convinced that a proper application of the principles of contract law leads to the conclusion that the discharge was justifiable, in that Ms. Ross had violated a condition of the employment contract.

Resolution of the issue must start with an assessment of the contract itself. The document appears to be a form contract put out by "Danny Zezzo's Dancers A-La Carte,"[5] with a copy of the Shamrock's rules and regulations attached. It contains no express provision prohibiting prostitution. However, "contractors can 'express' their intentions otherwise than by the use of specific words." 3A A. Corbin, *Contracts* § 631 (1960).

Here, I think that both parties evinced an understanding that the contract would be terminable if Cleopatra Ross engaged in prostitution. The Shamrock did so by its actions in terminating her employment; Ms. Ross did so even more explicitly, at trial, where she testified that it was her understanding that, if she engaged in prostitution in Ketchikan, Mr. Conway could terminate the contract.

---

[4] Indeed, in light of the parallel aims of the Shamrock and Ms. Ross, it might also be said that the Shamrock is asking us to find an implied condition to Ms. Ross's part not to compete, which, being subject to a rule of strict construction as a covenant in restraint of trade, should not lightly be implied. *See* 6A A. Corbin, Contracts § 1392 (1962). However, the parties do not raise this argument.

[5] Although it took a while to establish this point, it appears that Danny Zezzo was Cleopatra Ross's agent:

Q. And, Miss Ross, could you identify the signature on that contract?
A. Yes. In the left-hand corner, there's the agent that I work for.
Q. And what is his name?
A. Danny Zezzo.
Q. Excuse me, what's that name?
A. Danny Zezzo.
Q. Danny Zezzo?
A. Um-hm.
Q. And whose agent is he?
A. He's my agent.
Q. I see. All right. Please continue.

Even if resort must be made to a "constructive" condition (*i.e.*, one implied in law) as the majority assumes, I must disagree with the majority's conclusion, although not with its analysis: "The question thus becomes whether Conway's business could have been injured if it had continued to employ Ross after learning of her act of prostitution." I would be inclined to answer this question as the majority has, were we considering solely the conduct of Cleopatra Ross herself; but here, her conduct must be coupled with that of the district attorney who, although the record contains no evidence that he attempted to convict this latter-day Queen of the Nile through proper channels (perhaps due to A. Otto's somewhat casual attitude toward court attendance),[6] took it upon himself to rid Ketchikan of Ms. Ross by applying pressure on the hapless Conway, Inc., d/b/a/ the Shamrock.

This venerable institution was, like virtually all the characters in this drama, caught in a compromising position. Conway, the owner, admitted at trial that the Shamrock consistently violated at least one law, former AS 04.10.040(b) and a parallel provision in the Ketchikan Municipal Code; indeed, the violation is explicitly required as part of the contract in the record. This would have constituted grounds for action by the Alcohol Beverage Control Board and perhaps independently by the district attorney, and thus I think Conway's fear of reprisals was not unjustified.

Even assuming the majority is correct in concluding that the district attorney's attempts to get the ABCB to revoke the Shamrock's license would ultimately have proven groundless, the Shamrock would have been put through considerable expense and effort in defending its rights to retain its license and Cleopatra's right to remain free of unwarranted intrusions by the district attorney into her contractual relations with the Shamrock. Especially since the case law indicates that a tendency to injure, rather than actual injury to, the employer's business is all that need be shown, I must conclude that the Shamrock has demonstrated that Cleopatra Ross has violated the constructive covenant noted above,[7] and discharge was therefore justified. . .

---

[6] At the original trial of this matter, the district court judge refused to admit A. Otto's deposition because A. Otto, although subpoenaed on the day of his deposition (the day preceding trial), was not present at the trial itself. The superior court overturned this ruling in a prior decision, which we summarily upheld.

[7] See also 3A A. Corbin, Contracts § 681 (1960): "To a candid observer, it would seem that such conduct as drunkenness, sexual immorality, or persistent lying, would justify the discharge of a minister of the gospel, a Y.M.C.A. secretary, or the superintendent at a home for children. The employer in such cases could reasonably expect that the value of the promised performance would be gravely affected." Although Cleopatra Ross does not fit any of these categories precisely, I think that the value of her promised performance would be gravely affected, and thus the same principle applies.

CHAPTER IV: BUSINESS, TRADE & COMMERCE

CARSON v. FEARS
Supreme Court of Georgia
91 Ga. 482; 17 S.E 342 (1892)

SAMUEL E. LUMPKIN, Justice.

The Chief Justice asked the writer, one day, when we were considering whether or not certain acts of a corporation were valid, "Did anybody imagine, when you were an infant in caps, that you would ever be called upon to pass judicially upon the law of *ultra vires*?" At that time such a thing might have seemed quite improbable, but it was hardly less so than that in the year of grace 1893 I would participate in deciding a case begun on the 26th day of July, 1860, when I was in my first term at school; and yet both these things have come to pass. I *have dealt*, judicially, with the law of *ultra vires*, and I am now attempting to write an opinion in a case which was actually in court when I was a little child.

This case is certainly a venerable piece of litigation. It began nearly one third of a century ago, has already lived the average time allotted to the life of man, has been upon the docket of the superior court during the terms of many judges, including one who afterwards served a term upon the Supreme Bench of this State, and is now of counsel for the plaintiff in error, and surviving earthquakes, famines, wars and political revolutions, it still lives and flourishes. Neither one of the two original parties to the action is now in life, and as it goes back to the court where it originated, for another trial, we are not at liberty to predict that another generation of litigants will not participate in it before it reaches a final determination.

On the day above specified, James J. Carson brought an action in the statutory form upon two promissory notes against Riley S. Fear. Years afterwards, the case proceeded in the name of the plaintiff's administrator against the administrator of the defendant. At one time a judgment was rendered against this defendant, but for reasons not now material, it was afterwards set aside.

At the March term, 1884, the plaintiff filed an amendment to his declaration; and at the March term, 1889, he filed still another amendment, which was an amplification and enlargement of the first. By these amendments the plaintiff alleged that the only property of Riley S. Fears, the original defendant, from which the payment of the notes sued upon could be realized, was a tract of land which the administrator of Riley S. Fears had permitted the children of the latter to recover from him in a fraudulent action brought for the purpose of defeating the plaintiff in the collection of his claim against the estate; that this action had no just or valid foundation, but was the result of a fraudulent and collusive arrangement and conspiracy between the administrator and these other parties for the purpose stated; that immediately after recovering the land from the administrator, the children of Riley S. Fears sold it, in different parcels to Charles Giles, Crockett Giles and James Crawford, who bought with notice of plaintiff's claim against the estate of Riley S. Fears. . .

Assuming the right of the plaintiff to make new parties and bring in equitable rights by amendment, we are satisfied that a good cause of action was stated against the children of Riley S. Fears. After long years of litigation and fruitless endeavors to collect his debt, with the details of which we have not encumbered the foregoing statement of facts, the plaintiff now shows to the court that the administrator and the children of his intestate have fraudulently attempted to put beyond his reach the only property out of which his claim against the estate can be collected, and have, *prima facie*, succeeded in doing so. . .

Judgment reversed.

PEERLESS INS. CO. v. TEXAS COMMERCE BANK
United States Court of Appeals, Fifth Circuit
791 F.2d 1177 (1986)

IRVING L. GOLDBERG, Circuit Judge:

This diversity case involves the question whether § 3-419 of the Uniform Commercial Code displaced the common law action for money had and received under Texas law. It arises, one could say, from Vincent J. Menier's desire for more cream in his coffee. While Joe Dimaggio confidently extolled the virtues of "Mr. Coffee" coffee makers, which are manufactured by appellant North American Systems, Inc., Menier, the Vice President of North American's Fairfield Filter Division, pilfered and filched checks through the financial filter of forged endorsements. Menier personally endorsed and deposited checks payable to the Fairfield Filter Division in his personal bank accounts at the Fist National Bank of New Braunfels, Texas, whose successor-in-interest is appellee Texas Commerce Bank.

Appellant Peerless Insurance company had insured North American against losses of up to $500,000 caused by fraudulent or dishonest acts by North American's employees. On March 1, 1983, North American submitted to Peerless a proof of loss that showed, according to its investigation, that Menier had misappropriated at least $1,275,880.12 of North American's funds from December 27, 1978, through December 8, 1982. Peerless paid North American under a reservation of rights and has become subrogated to all of North American's rights against Texas Commerce. Peerless and North American then sued Texas Commerce to recover the lost funds. . .

The Uniform Commercial Code, as adopted by Texas, states: "An instrument is converted when ... it is paid on a forged indorsement." Tex.Bus. & Com.Code ann. § 3.419(a)(3)(Vernon 1968). When a bank accepts for deposit a check whose endorsement is forged, the person to whom the proceeds of the check rightfully belong may sue the bank in tort for conversion.

Section 3.419(c) altered the common law by providing that a bank is not liable "in conversion or otherwise" if it has acted "in good faith and in accordance with the reasonable commercial standards" applicable to the banking industry. A defendant may also assert, as did appellee here, the two year statute of limitations applicable to conversion.

The common law also provides a plaintiff pained by such pecuniary perfidy an action in contract -- with a four year statute of limitations, which has not expired in this case -- for money had and received. This venerable equitable doctrine holds that:

> "a collecting bank which accepts a check on an-
> other bank on a forged indorsement acquires no
> title thereto, and holds the proceeds thereof, when
> collected from the drawee bank, for the rightful
> owner, who may recover from the collecting bank
> as for money had and received, even though such
> bank has fully paid over and accounted for the
> same to the forger without knowledge or suspi-
> cion of the forgery. . " [citation omitted.]

The question therefore becomes whether the particular provisions of the U.C.C. have *displaced* the common law action for money had and received. . .

CONCLUSION

When he decided to forsake the placid world of coffee filters for the feast or famine of fakes and forgeries, probably nothing was farther from Vincent Menier's mind that the question of whether the Uniform Commercial Code laid to rest the common law action for money had and received. The question is, however, close to our minds now, and we decide that the U.C.C. did not displace this common law action. Accordingly, the judgment of the district court against Peerless and North American for failure to state a claim is reversed, and the case is remanded for further proceedings not inconsistent with this opinion.

REVERSED AND REMANDED.

GUNN v. WADES
Supreme Court of Georgia
62 Ga. 21 (1878)

LOGAN E. BLECKLEY, JUSTICE.

A decree foreclosing a mortgage upon land was rendered in the circuit court of the United States. The land was sold under the decree, and purchased by one of the parties to the present suit. After the decree was rendered the mortgagor conveyed the land to the other party to the present suit. The title derived through a judicial sale under the decree, and the title derived through a private sale by the mortgagor are thus brought into direct collision, and the question is, which must give way?

The whole attack is upon the decree of foreclosure. The effort is to overthrow that as fraudulent and void, or as rendered without jurisdiction. The precise point made is, that the mortgage did not in fact belong to the complainant in the federal court, who was a citizen of New York, but to Gunn, who was a citizen of Georgia, of which state the mortgagor and defendant in the bill was also a citizen. Now, this precise question of title to the mortgage was adjudicated by the federal court as a necessary part of the decree of foreclosure. There was a judicial determination that the mortgagor was the debtor of the complainant, and that the debt was secured by the mortgage, and that the condition of the mortgage had been broken.

There is no suggestion that the mortgagor was not duly served with subpoena in the foreclosure proceeding. He was before the court with full opportunity to question the jurisdiction, or make any other defense that he thought proper to present. The decree went against him; and by him all who hold, or may hold, under him thereafter were represented. In him they fell. He, their head, was condemned, and they in him were condemned also. He was the Adam of their race. They are lost.

Judgment reversed.

AN ACTE FOR FOULDINGE OF CLOTHES IN NORTH WALES
Statutes of the Realm of England
33 HENRY VIII, Ch. 3 (1541)

WHERE a certen Kynde and Sorte of Welshe Clothes called Whytes Russetts and Kenetts, made and wroughte in North Wales and Orchester Hundred adjoinynge to North Wales, of longe tyme have byne and be ([1]) craftely and harde rolled together that the buyer therof cannot perceyve nor discearne the untrue makinge and breadeth therof, to the great hurte deceipte and ympoverisinge of the

Kings true and lovinge Subjects; For remedy whereof be it enacted ordeyned and established by the Kinge our Soveraigne Lorde his Lordes spuall [spiritual] and temporall and the Commons in this present Parliament assembled and by auctoritie of the same, that all and everie the saide Clothes from and after the Feast of the Natyvitie of Saincte John Baptiste next c mynge that shalbe brought to any c mon marketts or fayres to be uttered and soulde shalbe foulded either in pleights or cuttell, as the Clothes of all other Countries of this Realme c monlye have byne used and bene used; to thintent that the buyers thereof may playnly see and perceave the bredeth and goodnes of suche Clothe and Clothes that he shall buy;

And that everie peece of the saide Clothes whiche after the saide Feast shalbe brought to any markett or fayre to be uttered and soulde cont*rie to the forme abovesaide shalbe forfeyted, that ys to saye, the Moytie or one halfe thereof to the use of our saide Soveraigne Lorde the Kinge, and thother Moytie therof to any of the Kings Subjects whiche will sue for the same in any of the Kings Courts of Recorde by Action of Debte Bill Playnte Information or otherwise, wherein the Defendaunte shall not be admytted to wage his lawe nor any protection nor essoyne or any delatorye plee admytted or allowed.

DILBERTO v. HARRIS
Georgia Supreme Court
95 Ga. 571; 23 S.E. 112 (1894)

THOMAS J. SIMMONS, J.

The proprietor of a barber-shop kept for public patronage is liable to a customer for the value of his hat, which was deposited on a hat-rack in the shop and which, while the customer was being shaved, disappeared from the shop and was thus lost, such proprietor being, under these facts, a bailee for hire as to the customer's hat.

Judgment affirmed.

LOGAN E. BLECKLEY, C. J., dissenting.

. . . The suit was on an account of "one black derby hat of the value of $5." Plaintiff testified, that he entered defendant's barber-shop to be shaved, and gave his coat and hat to a little boy who placed them on the rack with coats and hats of other men being shaved. After being shaved, plaintiff discovered that his hat had been taken and another like it but of different size left in its place. . . .

---

[1] so in O.

. . . It hath never happened from the earliest times to the present, that barbers, who are an ancient order of small craftsmen serving their customers for a small fee, and entertaining them the while with the small gossip of the town or village, have been held responsible for a mistake made by one customer whereby he taketh the hat of another from the common rack or hanging place appointed for all customers to hang their hats, this rack or place being in the same room in which customers sit to be shaved. The reason is, that there is no complete bailment of the hat; the barber hath no exclusive custody thereof, and the fee for shaving is too small to compensate him for keeping a servant to watch it. He himself could not watch it and at the same time shave the owner. Moreover, the value of an ordinary gentleman's hat is so much in proportion to the fee for shaving, that to make the barber an insurer against such mistakes of his customers would be unreasonable. The loss of one hat would absorb his earning for a whole day, perhaps for many days. The barber is a craftsman laboring for wages, not a capitalist conducting a business of trade or trust. . .

CHAPTER V

PASSION, ROMANCE, LOVE, LUST, LICENTIOUSNESS, FORNICATION, MARRIAGE, INTRIGUE, INDIFFERENCE, DISENCHANTMENT, DISGRACE, DISSOLUTION AND DIVORCE.

I like to think that the work of a judge is an art. . . After all, why isn't it in the nature of an art? It is a bit of craftsmanship, isn't it? It is what a poet does, it is what a sculptor does. He has some vague purposes and he has an indefinite number of what you might call frames of preference which among he must choose; for choose he has to, and he does.

> - Learned Hand [1]

Law, say the gardeners, is the sun,
Law is the one
All gardeners obey
Tomorrow, yesterday, today.

Law is the wisdom of the old
The impotent grandfathers feebly scold;
The grandchildren put out a treble tongue,
Law is the senses of the young. . .

> - W. H. Auden [2]

---

[1] Remarks at Proceedings of a Special Session of the United States Court of Appeals for the Second Circuit in Commemoration of Judge Learned Hand's Completion of Fifty Years of Federal Service, quoted in H. Shanks, *The Art and Craft of Judging: The Decisions of Judge Learned Hand,* at flyleaf (1968).

[2] From "Law like Love" reprinted in *The Norton Anthology of Poetry,* p. 532-533 (1970).

CHAPTER V: PASSION, ROMANCE, & LOVE

ARCHER v. ARCHER
Court of Appeals of Tennessee
31 Tenn.App. 657; 219 S.W.2d 919 (1947)

WINFIELD B. HALE, Judge

This is an alienation of affections suit which has shaken Raccoon Valley in Union County from center to circumference. It was brought by Lillie Archer, the former wife of Esker Archer, against Daisy Kiser (Archer), who, it is alleged, supplanted plaintiff in the affections of said Esker, and succeeded her as his wife some three weeks after Lillie and Esker were divorced. Upon a trial by a jury of the selection of the parties, under evidence to which there were no objections and a charge to which there were no exceptions, the plaintiff was awarded a judgment of five hundred dollars as the value of the affections so alienated, which apparently is not badly out of line in view of the matters hereinafter mentioned. This verdict was approved by the trial judge and the defendant below appeals and assigns errors.

The only assignment of error briefed and relied upon is that there was no evidence authorizing a submission of the case to the jury; that the proof showed conclusively there was no affection of Esker for his wife Lillie when the acts complained of occurred; and that the defendant below was not the pursuer, but rather the pursued. Certain other assignments were attempted to be made, but they are neither briefed nor supported by the record and will not be noticed further.

The evidence (in narrative form), when taken in the light most favorable to the verdict. . . reveals that Esker and Lillie Archer were married in 1919, and remained on intermittently friendly terms for several years, or, at least, until seven children were born to them. In 1935 she filed a bill for divorce, charging cruel and inhuman treatment, and adultery with one Lucy Sturgeon. They became reconciled and the divorce suit was withdrawn. Thereafter, on account of ill health, for a part of the time at least, Lillie refused to have marital relations with him and would "throw up" other women to him. This led to another separation in March, 1942, when Esker and his sixteen year old son moved to another place and "batched" there for about three months. Again their difficulties were patched up, and they resumed cohabitation, living together until the final separation in the fall of 1944.

Apparently, this parting of the ways was due to the advent into Raccoon Valley of the defendant below, Mrs. Daisy Kiser. She was a widow, fifty-one years of age, and the mother of twelve children, the youngest of whom was eight years of age. She apparently was of some little property, being the owner of one of the few automobiles in Raccoon Valley, which she used liberally for the benefit of her neighbors especially Esker, toward whom she pursued a good-neighbor policy which was extremely distasteful and obnoxious to his wife.

As to her personality and pulchritude there is no evidence except from a statement attributed to Esker soon after the Widow Kiser came to the Valley. Esker and Ben Shipley were working in a field near the highway when Mrs. Kiser came along in her car and called Esker to her. Then, to quote Shipley, "* * * the said Esker Archer did go down to the road where she was at. And on that occasion he [Esker] said. . .'that Kiser woman would be plumb pretty if she had a new set of teeth.'" Soon afterward, when she was in Knoxville having dental work done, she accidentally ran into Esker and brought him back home.

Following this there developed a relationship which the jury found culminated in Esker's leaving home in October, 1944, and instituting a divorce suit against Lillie. She filed an answer and cross bill, obtaining a divorce in February, 1945. It is apparent that the relations of Esker and the Widow Kiser were contributing factors to the divorce suit. They were married some three weeks after the obtention of the divorce. This suit followed, with the result noted.

The record shows that Mrs. Kiser (now Archer) would go by Esker's home, honk her car horn, call him to her, and take him riding. On one trip she took him to Knoxville and left a note for him at a doctor's office. At other times he drove the car for her, once taking her to a pie supper at the Raccoon school, after which they returned to her home, being joined there by some of the artists who had "made music" at the pie supper. Evidently a good time was had by all. On other occasions she would walk along a path by his home. She performed acts of neighborly kindness by taking him and his beans to market. He, in turn, would put brake fluid in her car, as well as act as chauffeur for her, and so on. She took him to dinner once because he loved fish. At another time she fed him and his son. At still another time, after Esker's separation from his wife, the plaintiff below, the Widow Kiser went to the house where he was staying, but said she did so to have him fix a flashlight. She would also park her car in front of his house, and Esker would, on occasion , ask her to go to the store for him. She contends these things were done innocently, but the jury found to the contrary. The evidence contained disputes as to material facts, and also as to the conclusions to be drawn from the whole evidence. We are concluded by the verdict, approved as it is by the trial judge. . . .

We think the evidence adopted by the jury authorized the inference that the defendant below did by feminine wiles and guile incite and welcome the attentions of this husband. The consistent and persistent manner in which she managed to get in his company, the trips they took his visits to her home, and their marriage within three weeks after his divorce all lead to the conclusion that she was the pursuer, although it was done with a degree of subtlety worthy of any daughter of Eve. This brings the case within the rule announced in Wilson v. Bryant [citation omitted], to-wit:

> "The weight of authority is that in alienation suits
> the plaintiff must establish that the defendant is
> the enticer - the active or aggressive party. If it
> develops that the plaintiff's spouse was merely
> bent on the gratification of lust, and was not
> particular in the choice of a guilty partner,

> plaintiff's case is not made out. Likewise we
> think plaintiff's case would fail if it should appear
> that for any other reason the plaintiff's spouse was
> the pursuer rather than the pursued. . . ."

It is true that Esker Archer had in the past shown himself to have a roving eye and an errant disposition. He and his wife Lillie had many trials and vicissitudes. He had affection enough for her, and she for him, to bring about reconciliations, and they were living together when the defendant below appeared on the scene and, as the jury found, began her campaign for Esker's affections. Her actions, in part, were known to the plaintiff below, and the family jars then became a vicious circle of cause and effect, leading finally to the divorce court. Esker's affections, such as they were, were transferred from his wife to Mrs. Kiser.

The fact that the jury allowed only five hundred dollars indicates a rather low opinion as to the value of the husband's affections. They were worth but little, but such as they were belonged to the wife. The judgment below is affirmed with interest and costs.

Affirmed.

KMICZ v. KMICZ
County Court of Luzerne County, Pennsylvania
50 Pa.C.C. 588 (1920)

HENRY A. FULLER, P.J.

> Libel in divorce by husband against wife.
> Answer by wife.
> Issue on cruel and barbarous treatment.
> Trial by judge without jury.
> She his second.
> He her second.
> Her dowry to him five ready-made children.
> His contribution to her the same number.
> None added since.
> She, without a vestige of feminine loveliness.
> He without a mark of masculine attraction.
> From start to finish a perfectly inexplicable and
>   hopeless connubial absurdity.
> One averred ground of divorce, her cruel and
>   barbarous treatment.
> Another, indignities to his person.
> Only proved specific instance of former his nose
>   broken by her use of a stove lifter.

Only proved specific instance of latter her unladylike
        behavior in the privacy of nuptial privilege.
Nose possibly broken in self-defense as testified.
Unladylike behavior possibly incited by his own lack
        of good manners.
No course of bad treatment on one side more than on the other.
Blame balanced as six and half a dozen.
Mutually mean.
He mean enough to seek divorce.
She mean enough to resist.
Parties too much alike ever to have been joined in marriage.
Also too much alike to be separated by divorce.
Having made their own bed must lie down in it.
Lying out of it, no standing in court.
Decree refused with allowance to respondent of $25.00
        for counsel fees to be paid by the libelant.

PAVLICIC v. VOGTSBERGER
Supreme Court of Pennsylvania
390 Pa. 502; 136 A.2d 127 (1957)

MICHAEL A. MUSMANNO, Justice.

George J. Pavlicic has sued Sara Jane Mills [1] for the recovery of gifts which he presented to her in anticipation of a marriage which never saw the bridal veil. At the time of the engagement George Pavlicic was thrice the age of Sara Jane. In the controversy which has followed, Pavlicic says that it was Sara Jane who asked him for his hand, whereas Sara Jane maintains that Pavlicic, following immemorial custom, offered marriage to her. We are satisfied from a study of the record that it was Sara Jane who took the initiative in proposing matrimony -- and, as it will develop, the proposal was more consonant with an approach to the bargaining counter than to the wedding altar.

George Pavlicic testified that when Sara Jane broached the subject of holy wedlock, he demurred on the ground that he was too old for her. She replied that the difference in their ages was inconsequential so long as he was "good to her." Furthermore, she said that she no longer was interested in "young fellows" -- she had already been married to a young man and their matrimonial bark had split on the rocks of divorce. Hence, she preferred an older man. George qualified. He was 75. Sara Jane was 26.

---

[1] The defendant was married twice and her name appears in various spellings in the record. For convenience in this discussion, she will be referred to as Sara Jane. For similar convenience the plaintiff George J. Pavlicic will be referred to as George.

CHAPTER V: PASSION, ROMANCE, & LOVE

The May-December romance began on a very practical footing in April, 1949, when Sara Jane borrowed from George the sum of $5,000 with which to buy a house, giving him a mortgage on the premises. In three and one-half years she had paid back only $449 on the mortgage. On the night of November 21, 1952, she visited George at his home and advanced the not illogical proposition that since they were to be married, there was no point in their having debts one against the other and that, therefore, he should wipe out the mortgage he held on her home. George said to her: "If you marry me, I will take the mortgage off." She said: "Yes," and so he promised to satisfy the mortgage the next day. To make certain that there would be no slip between the promise and the deed, Sara Jane remained at George's home that night; and on the following morning drove him in her automobile to the office of the attorney who was to make, and did make arrangements for the satisfaction of the mortgage.

Being enriched to the extent of $4,551 by this transaction, Sara Jane expatiated on another rational thesis, namely, that since they were going to be married and they would be riding around together she should have a better car than the dilapidated Kaiser she was driving. She struck home with her argument by pointing out that in a new car he would not fall out, for it appears this was an actual possibility when he rode in her worn-out Kaiser. Thus, without any tarrying, she drove George from the Recorder of Deed's Office, where she and the mortgage had been satisfied, to several automobile marts and finally wound up at a Ford agency. Here she selected a 1953 Ford which she said would meet her needs and keep him inside the car. George made a down payment of $70 and on the following day he gave her $800 more, the latter taken from his safety deposit box. Still later he handed her a check for $1,350, obtained from a building and loan association -- and Sara Jane had her new car.

Less than a year later, Sara Jane complained that her feet got wet in the Ford and she proposed the purchase of an Oldsmobile. She explained that by trading in the Ford, which she characterized as a "lemon," she would need only $1,700 to acquire the Oldsmobile. George was not averse to transportation which would keep his future wife's feet dry, but he said that since they were to be man and wife, and he apparently was paying for all the bills, it might be more businesslike if title to the car were placed in his name. This suggestion, according to George's testimony at the trial, made Sara Jane "mad" and he practically apologized for being so bold and inconsiderate as to ask title to an automobile which he was buying with his own money. Accordingly he withdrew his suggestion, said: "All right," and made out a check in Sara Jane's name for $1,700. And thus Sara Jane got her new Oldsmobile.

In January, 1953, in the enthusiastic spirit of an anxious swain, George presented Sara Jane with a $140 wrist watch. Sara Jane selected the watch.

In February, 1953, Sara Jane represented to George that they would both make a better appearance if she had an engagement and wedding ring. George took her to a jewelry store and she made a selection consistent with discretion. George paid $800.

Sara Jane then asked George to take care of the repairing of a ring she had received from her mother. It was a mere matter of adding a diamond. George paid the bill.

Even before George's bank book became Sara Jane's favorite literature she had prevailed upon him to advance substantial sums to her. In June, 1952, she told George she needed $800 to cover her house with insulbrick. George gave her $800 to cover her house with insulbrick.

It is not to be said, however, that Sara Jane was completely lacking in affectionate ante-nuptial reciprocity. In June, 1953, she bought George a wedding ring for him to wear. She conferred upon him at the same time a couple of woolen shirts. There is no way of learning how much the ring and shirts cost because she did not take George into her confidence or into the store where she purchased the items.

George testified that when he wore the wedding ring people laughed and asked him when he was to be married. He replied: "Pretty soon." He tried to live up to the prediction and asked Sara Jane for the wedding date. She said she could not name the month. In view of what was to develop, she could have added with truth that she could not name the year either.

In October, 1953, Sara Jane expounded to George the economic wisdom of purchasing a business which would earn for them a livelihood in his old and her young age. She suggested the saloon business. George agreed it was a good idea. She contacted a saloon-selling agent and George accompanied her to various saloons which the agent wished to sell. George was impressed with one saloon called the "Melody Bar," but the price was above him. Sara Jane then said that if he would give her $5,000 she would buy a cheap saloon outside of Pittsburgh. George gave her $5,000. And Sara Jane disappeared -- with the $5,000.

The next time she was heard from, she was in Greensburg operating Ruby's Bar -- with George's $5,000. From Ruby's Bar she proceeded to the nuptial bower where she married Edward Dale Mills. Although she had many times assured George she would marry him because she liked the idea of an old man, the man she then actually married was scarcely a contendor for Methuselah's record. He was only 26 -- two years younger than Sara Jane.

When George emerged from the mists and fogs of his disappointment and disillusionment he brought an action in equity praying that the satisfaction of the mortgage on Sara Jane's property be stricken from the record, that she be ordered to return the gifts which had not been consumed, and pay back the moneys which she had gotten from him under a false promise to marry. Sara Jane filed an Answer and the case came on for trial before Judge Marshall of the Allegheny County Court of Common Pleas. Judge Marshall granted all the plaintiff's prayers and entered a decree from which the defendant has appealed to this Court.

The defendant urges upon us the proposition that the Act of June 22, 1935, P. L. 450, 48 P.S. § 171, popularly known as the "Heart Balm Act," outlaws the plaintiff's action. This is the first time that the Act of 1935 has come before this Court for interpretation and ruling. Although the Act contains several sections, the heart of it lies in the first sentence, namely "All causes of action for breach of contract to marry are hereby abolished."

There is nothing in that statement or in any of the provisions of the Act which touches contracts subsidiary to the actual marriage compact. The Act in no way discharges obligations based upon a fulfillment of the marriage contract. It in no way alters the law of conditional gifts. A gift given by a man to a woman on condition that she embark on the sea of matrimony with him is no different from a gift based on the condition that the donee sail on any other sea. If, after receiving the provisional gift, the donee refuses to leave the harbor, -- if the anchor of contractual performance sticks in the sands of irresolution and procrastination -- the gift must be restored to the donor. *A fortiori* would this be true when the donee not only refuses to sail with the donor, but, on the contrary, walks up the gangplank of another ship arm in arm with the donor's rival.

The title to the gifts which Sara Jane received, predicated on the assurance of marriage with George, never left George and could not leave him until the marital knot was tied. It would appear from all the evidence that the knot was fully formed and loosely awaiting the ultimate pull which would take title in the gifts from George to Sara Jane, but the final tug never occurred and the knot fell apart, with the gifts legally falling back into the domain of the brideless George.

The appellant in her argument before this Court would want to make of the Act of June 22, 1935, a device to perpetuate one of the very vices the Act was designed to prevent. The Act was passed to avert the perpetration of fraud by adventurers and adventuresses in the realm of heartland. To allow Sara Jane to retain the money and property which she got from George by dangling before him the grapes of matrimony which she never intended to let him pluck would be to place a premium on trickery, cunning, and duplicitous dealing. It would be to make a mockery of the law enacted by the Legislature in that very field of happy and unhappy hunting.

The Act of 1935 aimed at exaggerated and fictional claims of mortification and anguish purportedly attendant upon a breach of promise to marry. The legislation was made necessary because of the widespread abuse of the vehicle of a breach of promise suit to compel overly-apprehensive and naive defendants into making settlements in order to avoid the embarrassing and lurid notoriety which accompanied litigation of that character. The legislation was intended to ward off injustices and incongruities which often occurred when by the mere filing of breach of promise suits innocent defendants became unregenerate scoundrels and tarnished plaintiffs became paragons of lofty sensibility and moral impeccability. It was not unusual in threatened breach of promise suits that the defendant preferred to buy his peace through a monetary settlement rather than be vindicated by a trial which might leave his good name in shreds.

There is no doubt that in the history of romance a nation could be populated with the lovers and sweethearts (young and old) who have experienced genuine pain and agony because of the defection of their opposites who promised marriage and then absconded. Perhaps there should be a way to compensate these disillusioned souls, but it had been demonstrated that the action of breach of promise had been so misemployed, had given rise to such monumental deceptions, and had encouraged blackmail on such a scale, that the Legislature of Pennsylvania, acting in behalf of all the people, concluded that the evil of abuse exceeded to such an extent the occasional legitimate benefit conferred by a breach of promise suit that good government dictated its abolition.

Thus the law of 1935 prohibited, but prohibited only the suing for damages based on contused feelings, sentimental bruises, wounded pride, untoward embarrassment, social humiliation, and all types of mental and emotional suffering presumably arising from a broken marital promise. The Act did not in any way ban actions resulting from a tangible loss due to the breach of a legal contract. It could never be supposed that the Act of 1935 intended to throw a cloak of immunity over a 26-year old woman who lays a snare for a 75-year old man and continues to bait him for four or five years so that she can obtain valuable gifts and money from him under a false promise of marriage.

George Pavlicic is not asking for damages because of a broken heart or a mortified spirit. He is asking for the return of things which he bestowed with an attached condition precedent, a condition which was never met. In demanding the return of his gifts, George cannot be charged with Indian giving. Although he has reached the Indian summer of his life and now at 80 years of age might, in the usual course of human affairs, be regarded as beyond the marrying age, everyone has the inalienable right under his own constitution as well as that of the United States to marry when he pleases, if and when he finds the woman who will marry him. George Pavlicic believed that he had found that woman in Sara Jane. He testified that he asked her at least 30 times if she would marry him and on each occasion she answered in the affirmative. There is nothing in the law which required him to ask 31 times. But even so, he probably would have continued asking her had she not taken his last $5,000 and decamped to another city. Moreover he had to accept 30 offers of marriage as the limit since she now had married someone else. Of course, mere multiplicity of proposals does not make for certainty of acceptance. The testimony, however, is to the effect that on the occasion of each proposal by George, Sara Jane accepted -- accepted not only the proposal but the gift which invariably accompanied it.

The Act of 1935 in no way alters of modified the law on ante-nuptial conditional gifts as expounded in 28 C.J. 651, and quoted by us with approval . . .

> " A gift to a person to whom the donor is engaged
> to be married, made in contemplation of marriage,
> although absolute in form, is conditional; and
> upon breach of the marriage engagement by the
> donee the property may be recovered by the
> donor. . ."

As already stated, the Act of 1935 provides that "All causes of action for breach of contract to marry are hereby abolished." This language is as clear as the noonday sun. The appellant would darken it with the eclipse of artificial reasoning. The appellant would want us to read into the statute the provision that "All causes of action *for the recovery of property* based on breach of contract to marry are abolished." The appellant would want the statute to be read "All actions *resulting from* a breach of contract are abolished." But we cannot so read or so interpret the statute. The abolition is confined to actions *for* breach of contract to marry, that is, the actual fracture of the wedding contract.

It thus follows that a breach of any contract which is not the actual contract for marriage itself, no matter how closely associated with the proposed marriage, is actionable.

. . . we come to the conclusion that the final decree entered by Judge Marshall is eminently just and in accordance with established principles of law and equity. It is accordingly

Decree affirmed at appellant's costs.

MORRIS v. MORRIS
Supreme Court of Georgia
202 Ga. 431; 43 S.E.2d 639 (1947)

T. S. CANDLER, Justice.

[On May 27, 1946, John Harvey Morris brought suit against his wife, Martha Elizabeth Morris, for divorce upon the ground of cruel treatment. In substance, the petition as finally amended alleged: The plaintiff and the defendant were married in 1911, and separated about May 24, 1946. The plaintiff was 76 and the defendant much younger. During the entire period of their married life, the defendant was possessed of an "uncontrollable temper and would, without cause, go into a rage and curse and abuse petitioner, and curse their son, in the presence of their son's two small children." Her cursing was so vile, and so continuous, that the plaintiff was unable to get sufficient sleep, and as a result therefrom his health and nervous system had become so impaired that he was unable properly to carry on his work as a cabinet maker. During the first year the plaintiff and the defendant were married, she began nagging him and this continued to the date of their separation, but from day to day and year to year grew worse until it reached the point of being unbearable to a person of his advanced years. The defendant's misconduct consisted of wilful, wanton, and deliberate acts of cruelty, which she inflicted upon the plaintiff for the purpose of causing him to suffer mental pain and anguish, and which did actually impair and injure his health and physical well-being. None of the acts complained of has been condoned.]

The kind of cruel treatment which is a ground for divorce in this State "is the wilful infliction of pain, bodily or mental, upon the complaining party, such as reasonably justifies an apprehension of danger to life, limb, or health. . . "

"Mental anguish, wounded feelings, constantly aggravated by repeated insults and neglect, are as bad as actual bruises of the person; and that which produces the one is not more cruel than that which causes the other." [citation omitted.] Cruel treatment, or cruelty in the broad and unrestricted sense which it is used in our statute (Code, §§ 30-103, 30-104), is any act intended to torment, vex, or afflict, or which actually afflicts or torments without necessity, or any act of inhumanity, wrong or oppression, or injustice, considered collectively or singly. . . .

Under the allegations of the petition as amended, we are of the opinion that the petition alleged such acts of cruel treatment as, under our law, will authorize a divorce. In *Wilkinson v. Wilkinson*, [citation omitted] this court, quoting trial Judge Meldrim, said: "From the days of Socrates and Xantippe, men and women have known what is meant by nagging, although philology can not define it or legal chemistry resolve it into its elements. Humor can not soften or wit divert it. Prayers avail nothing, and threats are idle. Soft words but increase its velocity, and harsh ones its violence. Darkness has for it no terrors, and the long hours of the night draw no drapery of the couch around it. The chamber where love and peace should dwell becomes an inferno, driving the poor man to the saloon, the rich one to the club, and both to the arms of the harlot. It takes the sparkle out of the wine of life, and turns at night into ashes, the fruits of the labor of the day." And to this he might well have added the words of Solomon, that "It is better to dwell in the corner of the housetop, than with a brawling woman and in a wide house." Proverbs, 25:25. . . .

It is alleged in the petition that during the first year the plaintiff and the defendant were married she began to curse and abuse him, and that this continued until the date of their separation, but from day to day and year to year grew worse until it reached the point of being unbearable to a person of the plaintiff's advanced years. . . . There are certain things which when wilfully done amount to cruelty on account of the very fact that they are repeated from time to time. It is the constant repetition which makes them unbearable. As was said by Mr. Justice Grice in *Alford v. Alford*, [citation omitted] "One or two petty fault-findings may be to a degree annoying, but it is the persistency of the fretting that causes the real vexation. It is the accumulation of the instances, the never-ending borings, the sum total of the repeated irritations; no one smarting, but the continued scraping of the surface already made raw and sore and inflamed by the previous annoying and provoking conduct. One briar prick, while not a pleasant sensation, may cause no serious pain, but a thousand of them may be harassing."

One or even several drops of water falling on the surface of a block of granite will make no perceptible change, but a constant dripping over a period of many years will mark its effect. At some time there is placed the straw that breaks the camel's back. There is nothing in the record to negative the idea that the unpleasant experience of the very last day this couple spent together may have been that straw. That last cursing may have been the one which convinced the plaintiff that others in the future, like those so often in the past, would be unbearable. In such a situation the husband's living with his wife did not amount to such condonation as canceled the prior elements of cruel treatment. We think that the facts alleged present a very clear picture of one whose patience at long last became exhausted. . . .

Judgment affirmed.

KOISTINEN v. AMERICAN EXPORT LINES, INC.
City Court of City of New York, New York County
194 Misc. 942; 83 N.Y.S.2d 297 (1948)

FRANK A. CARLIN, Justice.

The plaintiff, a seaman, rated as a fireman and watertender, on the S.S. John N. Robins, was injured while on shore leave in the port of Split, Yugoslavia, on February 3rd, 1946; he went ashore about noon; in the exercise of a seaman's wonted privilege he resorted to a tavern where he drank one glass of wine like to our familiar port; thereafter in the course of a walk about town he visited another liquid dispensary where he quaffed two glasses of a similar vintage; there he met a woman whose blandishments, prevailing over his better sense, lured him to her room for purposes not particularly platonic; while there "consideration like an angel came and whipped the offending Adam out of him;" the woman scorned was unappeased by his contrition and vociferously remonstrated unless her unregarded charms were requited by an accretion of "dinner" (phonetically put)[1]; the court erroneously interpreted the word as showing that the woman had a carnivorous frenzy which could only be soothed by the succulent sirloin provided at the plaintiff's expense; but it was explained to denote a pecuniary not a gastronomic dun; she then essayed to relieve his pockets of their monetary content but without the success of the Lady that's known as Lou in Service's Spell of the Yukon where the man from the creeks, unlike plaintiff, was not on his toes to repel the peculation; completely thwarted the woman locked plaintiff in her room whereupon he proceeded to kick the door while he clamored for exit; not thus persuasive, he went to the window which was about six to eight feet above ground and while there contemplating departure he was quickened to resolution by the sudden appearance of a man who formidably loomed at the lintels; thus, tossed between the horns of a most dire dilemma to wit, the man in the doorway and the window, the plaintiff eyeing the one with the duller point, elected the latter means of egress undoubtedly at the time laboring under the supposition that he was about to be as roughly used as the other man in a badger game; parenthetically it may be observed

---

[1] [Ed. Note: "Dinar" is the Yugoslavian unit of currency.]

that it is a matter of speculation for contemporary commentators as well as for discussion by the delegates to U.N. how the refinements of that pastime came to penetrate the ferruginous arras of Yugoslavia especially as the diversion is reputed to be of strictly capitalistic American origin. So the plaintiff thus confronted leaped from the window and sustained injuries which hospitalized him in Yugoslavia and the United States; during the extensive period of his incapacitation his wages and hospital bills were paid by defendant; the only question confronting the court is his claim for maintenance over a period of thirty-six days.

The defendant resists the claim on the foregoing facts contending that it is founded in immorality; it further defends against the claim on the ground that during all the times involved in this action the United States and not the defendant was the owner of the ship and, therefore, was exclusively liable in the event plaintiff had a claim. It appears that defendant managed and operated the ship under the usual General Agency Agreement with the government; it further appears that plaintiff, when he signed the shipping articles and subsequently, neither knew nor was told that he was working for the United States; the only intimation of defendant's General Agency Agreement with the government was contained on the front page of the shipping articles which was not displayed nor explained to the plaintiff when he signed as crew member; according to the testimony of the master a facsimile of the front page of the articles was posted on the bulletin board in the crew's mess; this plaintiff denies; presupposing that such was the fact it is hard to conceive how such publication would have been enlightening to plaintiff who testified he could neither read nor write English; the difficulty in following his testimony given in broken English without the aid of an interpreter corroborated his ignorance of our language; so that presupposing that the record of the government's ownership was posted on the bulletin board it could hardly come to the knowledge of plaintiff unless he was actually so informed; the master on his testimony established that he neither read nor was asked to read to plaintiff the shipping articles and that he did not reveal to plaintiff that, as a member of the crew, he was an employee of the United States; the master further testified that the crew was procured from the Maritime Union in New York which supplied seamen on defendant's call; that defendant paid the crew; that any disputes regarding its wages were taken up by the master with the representative of the union who in turn would discuss it with defendant; that all the ship's business was reported by the master to the defendant.

Without presently passing upon whether the circumstances under which plaintiff met with his injuries entitle him to recover maintenance suffice it to observe that the defendant cannot defeat the right to recovery merely by establishing that it managed and operated the ship under a General Agency Agreement with the government as owner [citation omitted]; as appears from the facts of the instant case the plaintiff was not apprized of defendant's status as agent for the government, as principal, therefore, plaintiff without knowledge or disclosure of the agency agreement cannot be deprived thereby of his rights as a seaman against the defendant, as agent of an undisclosed principal. [citation omitted].

CHAPTER V: PASSION, ROMANCE, & LOVE

From the foregoing authorities the court concludes that defendant may not defeat plaintiff's cause of action merely on the ground that it was not the owner of the ship. This brings us to a consideration of the peculiar circumstances under which plaintiff met with his injuries; do they militate against the recovery of maintenance from the defendant? No authority with an analogous state of facts was cited by either side; the defendant contends that as the plaintiff did not accompany the woman to her room for heavenly contemplation his leap from the window was tainted with his original immoral intent and, therefore, he is not entitled to sue for maintenance.

While it is true that there was a gross degree of culpability in the original purpose of the plaintiff for which he went to the woman's room it cannot be consistently argued that plaintiff, having abandoned that purpose before consummation and having sought to conserve his safety as well as the life of a good sailor, was acting in continuance of the initial immoral intent; in the court's opinion the proximate cause of plaintiff's leap from the window was not his original intent but was the concurrence of the locked door from which he sought egress and the subsequent looming threat of the man with the menacing mien; the expedition of plaintiff's violent fear outran the pauser, reason, causing him in the exercise of an erroneous judgement to jump rather than drop to the ground which undoubtedly would have been a safer means in view of the comparatively short space he had to negotiate for escape. Under the circumstances the window was the only solution presented to plaintiff in his emergency; at least he cannot be condemned for so conjecturing despite his starting on the wrong moral foot in the first instance; again the ticklish situation which confronted plaintiff immediately before his leap was not a reasonably foreseeable consequence of his original intention.

It may be argued that the foregoing pronouncement is *obiter dicta* [incidental remarks] but the court holds that it is consistent with the law enunciated by more respectable authority; as heretofore intimated no case cited in the briefs of either side squares analogously in its facts with those presented to the court in this case; though of novel impression it does not fall without well defined principles found in the decisions. In Ellis v. American Hawaiian S.S. Co., [citation omitted] a seaman on shore leave was not found to be definitely intoxicated from the consumption of three bottles of beer and his diving into a swimming pool was not construed as willful or gross misconduct; nor does the court find in the present case that the drinking of three glasses of wine rendered plaintiff intoxicated; nor did his jump from the window denote inebriation; to hold otherwise would argue strongly against his ability to choose the means of escape and would indict him for an error of judgment which is not the law against one who chooses in an emergency one means of safety when another might have been more conducive to that end. [citation omitted]. Peculiarly the plaintiff chose the only means of escape even though it resulted in his injuries; had he elected to go out the door with the threatening man, there barring the way, his injuries reasonably might have been more dire and serious than those sustained by his jump from the window; at least he's still alive.

In the Anna Howard Shaw case, [citation omitted] the seaman is held to be entitled to maintenance unless his injury resulted from some wilful misbehavior or deliberate act of indiscretion; gross negligence according to the rule of this case would deprive the seaman of maintenance. As appears from the foregoing it may be argued that plaintiff's immoral indiscretion first put him in the woman's room but it did not impel him to jump from the window; that was occasioned by the barred door with the man thereat menacingly looming; nor did the Anna Howard Shaw case hold that the seaman on shore leave was so intoxicated as to constitute wilful misbehavior prejudicial to his right to maintenance and cure. Quoting from the Anna Howard Shaw case, supra:. . . "A seaman, injured in the service of his ship, is entitled to maintenance at its expense. * * * Only some wilful misbehavior or deliberate act of indiscretion suffices to deprive' him of maintenance, the 'traditional instances' being 'venereal disease and injuries received as a result of intoxication'. . ." In other words the courts have been liberal in their attitude toward seamen who receive injuries on shore leave through their notorious penchants not stemming from intoxication or deliberate acts of indiscretion; neither is established in the present case under the facts adduced. The plaintiff in the court's opinion is entitled to recover. The question remaining is how much; cases have been cited which have variously held a range for maintenance between $2.50 to $4.00 a day; this court in the case of Proctor v. Sword Line, Inc., [citation omitted] held that $5.20 a day was a reasonable allowance for maintenance; considering the costs of living and lodging under the standards prevailing in the recent times involved in this claim which differ no whit from those obtaining now, the court adheres to its prior determination that $5.20 a day is a fair and reasonable allowance for maintenance. . .

Judgment for plaintiff against defendant for $187.20 for thirty-six days of maintenance at $5.20 a day.

WHITE v. BIRMINGHAM POST CO.
Supreme Court of Alabama
233 Ala. 547; 172 So. 649 (1937)

THOMAS E. KNIGHT, Justice.

Action to recover damages for an alleged libel brought by the appellant against the appellee.

From adverse rulings by the trial court, in sustaining the demurrers of the defendant to the several counts of the complaint, the plaintiff suffered a nonsuit. . .

The publication complained of, and which appeared in the Birmingham Post, in its issue of July 13, 1935, is as follows:

CHAPTER V: PASSION, ROMANCE, & LOVE

"Arabian Sheik Asks Friend Here
to Buy Him an American Girl for Harem.

"Roebuck man urged to look for 'Chief Wife' in Birmingham.

"The pleasure, privilege and honor of being chief-wife in an Arab sheik's harem awaits some Birmingham or Alabama maiden, it was revealed today.

"The Hon. Fareed J. Iman, member of an old aristocratic Arabian family, has asked a friend in Birmingham to find him a wife. And the lucky girl would be chief-wife in his four-wife harem."

"Sheik Iman's American friend is Lytle White of Roebuck, who made the Arabian's acquaintance, while touring in Asia-Minor in the summer of 1930.

"Mr. White spent two weeks in the home of the Arabian in Jerusalem and also visited with the latter's relatives. Ever since that time the two have corresponded regularly.

"In a recent letter, Mr. Iman, who is 29 years old and fears he may reach 30 before he obtains a chief-wife to his taste, has asked his Birmingham friend to help him out. And in accordance with Arabian customs, he is ready to purchase a suitable girl from her parents.

"Arab sheiks feel, explained Mr. White, who has made a study of Arabian customs, that they must obtain a wife by the time they become 30 years of age or they won't visit them. And not to have visitors would be the greatest affront to Arabian hospitality, he explains.

"Mr. Iman, according to Mr. White, is the descendant of an influential line of Arab rulers. A relative is the present mayor of Jerusalem.

"Describing his Arab friend, Mr. White says, 'he is a man of unusual personal charm, is cultured and has advanced beyond his people in moral and aesthetic living. He is Orthodox Moslem, believing in a harem of four wives, as provided by Moslem law.'

"Sheik Iman hopes to obtain a 'beautiful and competent' wife in America. As his chief wife, she will supervise his harem and household and will raise 'many marketable daughters and hearty sons.'

"She will have the benefit of the traditional Arabian protective treatment of women but she can't be seen by those who are not members of her household, being required to wear a veil when outside.

"Sheik Iman is by the occupation an archaeologist and tourist contractor, Mr. White said. He is opposed to all intoxicants and tobacco because 'he cannot afford to defile his body which to him is a divine instrument.' He speaks correct English but with an Oriental accent, Mr. White said, having been educated in an American school near his home.

"Besides Mr. Iman's occupation, he is greatly interested in astrology and geology.

"And although Mr. White will not take the responsibility of selecting Sheik Iman's 'Chief Wife,' he will be glad to make contact with the Arabian for those interested. Mr. White can be reached by telephone at 9-1817 or by mail at Roebuck Springs.

"Is there a Birmingham miss, 'Beautiful and competent,' who would like a life-time job in foreign service? Sheik Fareed J. Iman, 29 years old Arabian aristocrat and archaeologist living in Jerusalem, is looking for just such young American woman to head his harem as 'Chief-Wife,' he has notified his friend, Lytle White of Birmingham."

When the suit was filed, the complaint consisted of one count, but thereafter a number of other counts were added, each predicated upon the publication set out above. In some of the counts the plaintiff, by use of an innuendo, undertook to explain the published words, and to show that, with such meaning given to them as set out in the innuendo, they constituted a libel upon him.

The court sustained demurrers to the original count, and to each of the added counts. . .

If the publication in question was in fact libelous, the court committed error in sustaining the defendant's demurrers.

In 17 Ruling Case Law, p. 286, § 26, the rule on this subject is expressed by the author in the following language: "It is well settled that, to constitute libel, it is not necessary that written statements should contain an imputation of an offense that may be punished as a crime. It is sufficient if the language tends to injure the reputation of the party, or to throw *contumely* or to *reflect shame* or *disgrace* upon him. As a general rule written words exposing the person to whom they refer to *hatred*, ridicule, contempt, shame or disgrace are libelous per se. (Italics supplied.)

In the case of Marion v. Davis, [citation omitted] this court, in an exhaustive opinion by Mr. Justice Brown, said:

> "The right to the enjoyment of a private reputation, unassailed by malicious slander, is of ancient origin, and is necessary to human society. A good reputation is an element of personal security, and is protected by the Constitution equally with the right to the enjoyment of life, liberty, and property. . ."

In cases of libel, if the language used exposes the plaintiff to *public ridicule or contempt*, though it does not embody an accusation of crime, the law presumes damage to the reputation, and pronounces it actionable per se. * * *

In determining their actionable character, they [the words printed] are to be taken in their natural meaning, and according to the sense in which they appear to have been used and the idea they are adapted to convey to those who heard them. . .

The publication is not to be measured by its effect when subjected to the critical analysis of a trained legal mind, but must be construed and determined by its natural and probable effect upon the mind of the average lay reader. . .

The published words may be actionable in themselves, or per se; or they may be actionable only on allegation and proof of special damage or per quod. . .

With these statements of law governing the case, we will now consider the language of the offending publication, to determine whether or not it was of such character as to make it libelous per se, or libelous per quod.

The plain import of this published statement was: That a certain named Arab wanted an American woman to be his chief wife in his harem in some far-off country; that the Arabian was ready to purchase from her parents a suitable girl for his chief wife; that the Arab's harem, to be complete, must contain four wives; that Mr. White, the plaintiff, was friend of this Arab, had visited his home in Jerusalem, and held himself out as being ready and willing to make contact with this Arabian with any one who might be interested in accepting his offer to become one of his wives.

The very idea of a harem is repulsive to our American conception of morality and virtue. The purchase of a girl from her parents here in America, to be carried to some distant country, to complete an Arab's harem of four wives, is abhorrent to our American institutions and our conceptions of morality. And to falsely and maliciously publish to the world that one stood ready to aid and abet in the consummation of such a scheme is nothing short of a libel actionable per se. . .

Revised and remanded.

RITTER v. RITTER
Supreme Court of Pennsylvania
31 Pa. 396 (1858)

GEORGE W. WOODWARD, J.

[The plaintiff (wife) and defendant (husband) were married about the 19th April 1856; and on the 14th June 1856, the husband executed a promissory note for $1050.00, on which the suit was brought--The trial court found for the wife upholding the enforceabiity of the note.]

The general question in this case is, whether a married woman can, in her own name, by her mother as next friend, maintain an action of debt against her husband on a contract made during coverture.

The parties were married in February 1856, the contract in suit was made between them 14th June 1856, and this suit was brought 18th February 1857.

Both the court below, who sustained the action, and the counsel who argued in support of it here, rest it entirely on the Married Woman's Act of Assembly of 11th April 1848, and the subsequent and supplemental acts. From the birth of the common law down to the Act of 1848, it is admitted such an action would not lie; but, says the learned counsel, "we start with the Act of 1848 in a new era; with fresh necessities; with *rights* created by the act itself, requiring new remedies, and turning the old common law doctrines, decisions, fictions and absurdities, into fossil remains, dead as mummies, and, what is commendable, without mourners."

This is a spirited defence of an anomalous action, and it is worthy of consideration how far it is sound. We have not been in the habit of considering the Act of 1848 as inaugurating a new era. The marriage relation, as old as the human race, and the basis of the family, which is itself the basis of society and civil states, had always been sedulously guarded and cherished by the common law.

One of the favourite maxims of the common law is, that marriage makes the man and woman one person in law, and of course it excludes the possibility of a civil suit between them. Now this characteristic of the contract may be considered a fiction, an absurdity, a fossil, or whatever else the necessities of the new era may denominate it, but it is in exact accordance with the revealed will of God, was designed for the protection of the woman, and leads to that identification of sympathies and interests, which secures to families and neighbourhoods the blessings of harmony and good order.

It is doubtless competent for the legislative power to change and modify the qualities of the marriage relation, perhaps to abolish it altogether; but if the history of the human race teaches any lesson whatever, it is, that concubinage is the alternative of marriage. In just so far as you impair the one, you encourage the other. In just so far as you sever the material interests of husband and wife, you destroy the sympathies which constitute the oneness of the relation, and degrade the divine institution to mere concubinage.

Nothing could so complete that severance and degradation, as to throw open litigation to the parties. The maddest advocate for woman's rights, and for the abolition on earth of all divine institutions, could wish for no more decisive blow from the courts than this. The flames which litigation would kindle on the domestic hearth would consume in an instant the conjugal bond, and bring on a new era indeed -- an era of universal discord, of unchastity, of bastardy, of dissoluteness, of violence, cruelty, and murders.

But will the courts expose this fundamental relation to the consequences of unbridled litigation? Never. If it is to be done, it must be by the legislature, and then by no indirection, or inferential consequence, but by direct, plain, unmistakable English.

CHAPTER V: PASSION, ROMANCE, & LOVE

We are asked to deduce the legislative intention to confer a right of action, from the provisions of our several Acts of Assembly; but it is a sufficient answer that no one of those acts expresses that intention. If the legislature meant that such actions as the present should be sustained, they had command of a very copious language in which to express their will. They have not done it and until they do, we will not infer it. When it is done, the consequences must rest with those who do it.

The object of the Act of 1848 was to protect the wife's separate property from the creditors of the husband. This was accomplished before the act, by means of marriage settlements; but occasional instances of hardship occurred, which magnified by that prurient philanthropy that begins its work where the wise and good leave off, and demolishes what they build up, led a too susceptible legislature into declaring not only that the wife's property should be exempt from seizure by the husband's creditors, but that it should continue to be her property "as fully after her marriage as before," and should be "owned, used, and enjoyed by such married woman as her own separate property."

It was this language that led Judge Rogers to declare, in Cummings' Appeal, 1 *Jones 275*, that a married woman must hereafter be considered a *feme sole* [single woman] in regard to any estate of whatever name or sort, owned by her before marriage. To that extent, the Act of 1838 tends, undoubtedly, to the destruction of the marriage relation. Marriage makes her a *feme covert* [married woman], suspends her civil existence, is a gift of her personal estate in possession to the husband, and of her power to reduce her choses in action into possession, and entitles him to the custody of her person and the enjoyment of her earnings.

The act makes her a *feme sole* in respect to her property, and confers rights utterly inconsistent with the duties of the marriage relation; for whilst she uses and enjoys her own estate as a *feme sole*, it is impossible that she can be fulfilling all the duties of a *feme covert*. It is, that far, a permanent severance of the material interests of the relation. . .

But to emancipate her from the conjugal vow, even to the extent of her separate estate, wise or unwise as it may have been, was not to confer on her a right of action against her husband. It is said she could not own, use, and enjoy her property, without the right of action, and hence it is argued that the legislature of 1848 meant to confer all the means which were essential to the end in view.

For the reasons already hinted at, we are not inclined to admit such reasoning in a case where the highest interests of society would be endangered thereby. . .

The judgment is reversed, and a *venire de novo* [new trial] awarded.

KEYES v. KEYES
Superior Court of New York City, Equity Term
6 Misc. 355; 26 N.Y.S. 910 (1893)

DAVID McADAM, J.

The defendant, by fraudulently misrepresenting himself as an honest, industrious man, induced the plaintiff, a confiding young woman, to become his wife. If the misrepresentation had been as to the defendant's social position, rank, fortune, manners, or the like, they would have furnished no ground for declaring the marriage void. Fabrications and exaggerations of this kind, while not commendable, are so common as to be tolerated by the law on grounds of public policy. Persons intending to act upon such representations must verify them at their peril, for, though they enter into the inducements to marriage, they are not considered as going to the essentials of the relation, on the theory that the parties take each other for better or worse. Indeed, in some cases, marriage likens itself to the veritable mouse trap, which is "easier to get into than out."

In this case the defendant represented himself as an honest, industrious man, and appearances favored him, when in truth he was a professional thief, whose picture has a place in the rogues' gallery, and he is now "doing time" in the Clinton prison for crime. It was an unholy alliance, begotten in fraud, and the plaintiff is the victim. What fraud, in kind and amount, should be deemed sufficient to annul a marriage, has led to a fruitful amount of discussion and contrariety of opinion. The statue provides that a marriage may be annulled, where the consent of one of the parties was obtained by force, duress, or fraud, (Code, § 1743, subd. 4,) any one being sufficient. This provision was intended to protect the party imposed upon and to punish the one guilty of the wrong.

The difficulty in inducing courts to act upon this provision is the stupefying fear that dissolution may lead to carelessness and blind credulity on the part of those contemplating marriage. But "love is blind," always has been, and will be. Nothing born of the law will prevent indiscreet and unsuitable marriages. The average individual judges and acts on appearances, on his own likes and dislikes; and if he or she exercises his or her best judgment, and is deceived by the arts and wiles of an unscrupulous, designing person, there should be no unwillingness, in a proper case, to afford relief to the injured, when it can be done without injury to any one except the guilty. There can be no consent to a contract unless it be voluntary. If it be induced by misrepresentation, duress, or constraint, the guilty party will be allowed to obtain no benefit from it. . .

In all these matters, much is left to the good sense and judgment of the court or jury, if there be one. . .

In the present instance the plaintiff found, after marriage, that a professional thief had, by fraud, been substituted for the honest, industrious man she was led to believe she had married. While the cases are dissimilar, the result in either is substantially the same. Companionship, with its reciprocal duties, is the basis of marriage, and no respectable young woman should be obliged to divide the life companionship of a husband between herself and the penal institutions of the state. No conception of married life or reciprocal duties would tolerate such a thing. There could be nothing more degrading in its influence. Such a husband is not a fit subject for the household, nor one to be looked up to for advice and guidance. Men may have vices at the time of their marriage, and, if these are dropped at or before the time of their vows, they should not be resurrected, and made the basis of domestic strife, but where they are continued after marriage they may give rise to serious matrimonial difficulties. In Wier v. Still, [citation omitted] a widow induced to marry a "jail bird" by means of false representations as to his respectability was refused relief on the ground of her folly and credulity. Bigelow, in his work on Fraud, [citation omitted] cites the above case "as especially applicable to a widow."

And in Moot v. Moot, [citation omitted] the court, in granting a decree of nullity, was influenced by the fact that the plaintiff was a "school girl,"-- distinctions obviously founded more on the judicial policy or discretion of the courts than upon strict legal principles. . .

As the plaintiff's age is between that of the school girl and the widow, there would seem to be a discretionary choice of alternatives left for the court to determine which rule it will adopt to satisfy the requirements of this controversy. If the defendant had reformed after marriage, and become exemplary in conduct, the court might have required the plaintiff to overlook the past, and screen it from the world with the mantle of charity, but he had not chosen the pathway of the penitent, and is, in consequence, again under state surveillance, in its penitentiary at Clinton. Consortium and conjugal society have scarcely risen to the dignity of memories. The consequence is not a temporary sorrow, which may be buried under the oblivion of recurring time, or forgotten in the solitude of despair, but an ever-present affront and reproach that "will not down."

The fraud perpetrated upon the plaintiff goes to the substance and essence of the contract, and while this may be regarded as an exceptional case, resting on its own peculiar merits, yet, if the statute authorizing a decree of nullity for fraud does not reach such a case, it is difficult to imagine one it is capable of comprehending. There are, fortunately, no children to bear the obloquy of the marriage; and unless a premium is to be placed on fraud, and the guilty taken under the protecting aegis of the law, there is no reason founded on principle or policy why the plaintiff should not have that justice which the decree prayed for will afford. The application must be granted.

MAIN v. MAIN
Supreme Court of Iowa
168 Iowa 353; 150 N.W. 590 (1915)

SILAS M. WEAVER, J.

The petition filed July 3, 1912, shows that the parties were married on November 16, 1911, and charges that defendant is a person of "very high and violent temper," which she does not try to control; that without cause she curses and swears at plaintiff, and applies to him vile names and epithets; that she possesses a revolver, and has repeatedly threatened to shoot and kill him, and that when, thus cast out, he took his team and started to find refuge at his farm in the country, defendant took another horse, pursued and overtook plaintiff, again threatening to kill him, and that, seeing her reach for her revolver, he submitted to her demand and drove back to the home "to avoid further trouble and to protect his person." On this showing he asks an absolute divorce.

Defendant appeared to the action, and before answer moved for temporary alimony and suit money, and by agreement of counsel the application was allowed in the sum of $250, and the same was duly paid. Answering the petition defendant denied all its allegations of abuse and ill treatment, and further alleged that in June, 1912, the plaintiff willfully and without cause deserted her, and has ever since absented himself from her, refusing to live with her, though she has often requested him to return to the bosom of his family.

Defendant further alleges that plaintiff is the owner of much valuable property, and worth at least $100,000, while she herself is without means to defend the action or for her support. She therefore asks that the petition be dismissed, and that she have judgment against plaintiff for alimony and support so long as he continues to live apart from her, and that she have general relief.

Replying to the answer, plaintiff denies the same, and alleges that, while he has property to the amount of about $100,000, he is indebted to the extent of $30,000.

The trial court denied the divorce, and on November 1, 1912, entered a decree dismissing the petition, reserving the defendant's claim for alimony and support for further consideration, and from this decree plaintiff appealed April 29, 1913.

The court subsequently awarded defendant the use of the homestead, except a specified room or office therein set apart for the storage of plaintiff's personal effects, and requiring plaintiff to pay her $50 per month as alimony and support.

The appeal presents two questions for our consideration — the merits of the plaintiff's demand for a divorce, and the merits of the defendant's claim for support money and attorney's fees.

I. A reading of the testimony satisfies us that the trial court did not err is dismissing the petition. At the time of the trial plaintiff was 66, and the defendant

42, years of age. Defendant had been twice married, once widowed and once divorced. Plaintiff had been twice married and twice divorced — each time at the suit of his wife. He had subsequently been defendant in an action for breach of promise, and had sought the graces of other women with a fervor not altogether Platonic.

The parties did not drift into love unconsciously, as sometimes happens with younger and less experienced couples. Both knew from the start exactly what they wanted. She wanted a husband with money — or money with a husband. He wanted a wife to adorn his house and insure that conjugal felicity of which fate and the divorce court had repeatedly deprived him. With an ardor, the warmth of which was in no manner diminished by the frosts of age, he pressed his suit for defendant's favor for a period of a year and a half, though it is but fair to say the speed of his wooing was held in check by the pendency of the damage suit above referred to which had been brought against him by another member of the sex which has been the bane of his strenuous life. He visited defendant frequently and had ample opportunity to ascertain her virtues, faults, and peculiarities — so far at least as these things are ever visible to a suitor before marriage. In short, they had ample opportunity to become well acquainted with each other and form a fair judgment whether marriage was desirable. Considering their worldly experience and matrimonial trials, it is not credible that either believed the other an angel, and in this respect it is quite clear that neither was mistaken.

Counsel for plaintiff tell us that defendant is an adventuress who came to Colfax, where plaintiff resided, for the express purpose of "trapping him into a marriage in order that she might secure a portion of his money," and that their subsequent union was thus brought about with an ulterior view to her financial advantage. In support of this claim a woman testifying for plaintiff states that shortly before the marriage she said to defendant, "No woman of our age would marry an old man of 70 unless she married him for money," and that defendant responded, "You are darned right they don't. If there wasn't some money back of old John Main I wouldn't marry him," and that to this remark she added the further information that she came to Colfax at the suggestion of friends who told her she might there trap a rich old widower, and that she did come and "set her trap" for plaintiff and "caught him." Waiving the improbability that a wise trapper such as defendant is said to be would be bragging of her catch to another woman before the trap was sprung, and accepting the truth of her story, it is very far from affording ground for a divorce. It may show a lack of affection and lay bare the sordid motive which prompts marriages of the kind we have here to deal with, but it is otherwise irrelevant to the issue.

The desire for a home and the comforts of wealth has been the controlling influence of many marriages, especially of those who have passed the bloom of youth, and it is not at all inconsistent with a faithful observance of all the duties and proprieties of the married state. Strategy and management in securing an eligible matrimonial partner is not the exclusive privilege of the man, and the game law of the state provides no closed season against the kind of "trapping" of which appellant complains.

That this marriage has proven an unhappy one is perfectly clear, and that neither has treated the other with the consideration and kindness which ought to mark the conduct of husband and wife we have no doubt; but the charges of extreme cruelty endangering life are by no means sustained. We shall not take the time to embody in the opinion the testimony bearing upon that question. The squabbles and quarrels between the parties, as related by them upon the witness stand, are, as a rule, trivial to the verge of the ridiculous. The threat or assault which plaintiff seems to think most serious, and the only one which is specifically charged in the petition, dwindles in his testimony to the charge that when plaintiff took to his carriage and sought to escape to his farm he was pursued and overtaken by the defendant, who insisted in very ungentle terms that he return home, and that upon his refusal to do so she threatened to kill him, and began feeling under her skirt in a manner which convinced him she had a revolver in her stocking, whereupon he turned his horses toward town and drove back at top speed, closely pursued by defendant, breathing threatenings and slaughter.

Defendant's story of this episode is of a very different character, and, if she tells the truth, plaintiff was never in the slightest danger of bodily injury. We do not undertake to say which is the more credible. Assuming that the parties are of equal veracity or inveracity — which is the charitable view — there is a manifest lack of that preponderance of evidence for the plaintiff which justifies the court in dissolving the marriage contract. Certain it is that plaintiff has failed to make good the one material allegation of his petition that his life is or will be endangered at the hands of his wife.

The profane and abusive language which plaintiff claims was heaped upon him by the defendant is quite generally denied by her, though enough perhaps is admitted to add an unsavory spice to their domestic discussions whenever these became animated. It must be said, however, that in vigorousness of diatribe plaintiff was himself at least a good second, and if we may judge from their own statements neither is made of that delicate moral fiber which character- izes those whom hard words can kill. While marriage is a civil contract, it is one against the obligation of which the common-law plea of failure of consideration is of no avail. The grounds of divorce are purely statutory, and of these, as we have already said, none has been established.

It is further objected that the allowance made is excessive. The amount to be granted in such cases is largely within the sound discretion of the trial court, and will not be disturbed in the absence of apparent abuse of such discretion. We see nothing unreasonable in the allowance made to the wife. The plaintiff has seen fit to withdraw from the home upon what we have found insufficient grounds, and he is in duty bound to contribute a reasonable amount for his wife's support. Fifty dollars per month is not an extravagant sum upon which to live and maintain a home. If he can do better by returning to his home, living peaceably with his wife, and supplying her reasonable needs, as married men and heads of families ordinarily do, there is no law to prevent him from pursuing that course, and when the family relations has been restored the court has undoubted power to set aside the order to which he now objects. The attorney's fees taxed are liberal, but, we think, not excessive, and we cannot attempt to interfere with it.

We discover no grounds for disturbing the decree or order appealed from, and they are affirmed.

DEEMER, C.J. and EVANS, LADD, and GAYNOR, J.J., concurring.

YOEMANS v. YOEMANS
Supreme Court of Georgia
77 Ga. 124; 3 S.E. 354 (1887)

LOGAN E. BLECKLEY, Chief Justice

. . . The wife petitioned for alimony, addressing her petition to the judge exercising jurisdiction in chancery. It was not stated expressly whether the alimony wanted was temporary or permanent, or both. No *subpoena* was prayed for, and none was annexed to the petition, and there is no entry of service, or even of the filing of the petition in the clerk's office.

The judge passed an order at chambers, requiring the husband to show cause, at a specified time, why an order should not be granted as prayed for; and the order prayed for was "to pay your petitioner $25.00 per month for the support of herself and child and an order for the expense of this litigation and counsel fees, as allowed by statute."

The husband answered, and the judge at chambers ordered that he pay to his wife eighteen dollars down and eighteen dollars on the fourth of each month thereafter until further order of the court, for her support and maintenance. To this order the husband excepted on the ground, amongst others, that the judge had no authority to pass it.

We think that he had no jurisdiction of the subject-matter at chambers, because there was no pending suit of any kind for alimony. If there had been, then on three days' notice, he might have heard it, whether commenced by bill or petition, and granted temporary alimony in terms of the order which he passed. Code, § 1747. This section of the Code certainly contemplates that after the judge has acted, the main case may proceed to a hearing before a jury, but how can this take place when there is no case in court? For there to be "a proceeding by bill or petition on the equity side of the court," there must be prayer for process or *subpoena*, filing of the bill or petition, and process or *subpoena* issued or else waived. This puts the "proceeding" "in court," and then the judge can deal with it, but not before, or at the utmost, not before the filing.

It looks too military for a judge to sit in his chambers and there call before him the heads of families and order them peremptorily to do thus and so in the way of furnishing support to their wives and children, though living apart from them, until a suit of some sort has been instituted in some court, either of law or equity. We think the statute does not contemplate anything so anomalous in a time of peace, and we cannot construe it as a war measure. . .

. . . Judgment reversed.

PAYNEL v. THE KING
King's Bench
Y.B. 30 Edward I; 1 Rot. Parl. 146 (1302)

At another time, namely, at the Parliament of our Lord the King at Westminster, in the 28th year of his reign, William Paynel and Margaret, his wife, made supplication to our Lord the King by means of a certain request, that our Lord the King would deign to bestow upon them a third part of Torpell Manor with its appurtenances, as the dowry of Margaret which rightfully belonged to her from the freeholdings that were in the possession of John de Camoys, her first husband, etc.

Nicholas de Warrick, who was prosecuting for our Lord the King, said that the aforesaid Margaret ought not to have the dowry in this case, nor should any request for a dowry in this case be heard or admitted, because a long time before the death of this said John, who was once her husband etc., she voluntarily and freely left her husband, and went to live in adultery with the aforementioned William, who is her husband now, while the aforesaid John was still alive, nor were she and John reconciled before John's death. Wherefore, in accordance with the terms of the statute of our Lord the King now published, concerning women who remove themselves from their husbands and live with their lovers in adultery, and who have not been reconciled to them, of their own free will and without the compulsion of the Church, before the death of their husbands, the request of the aforementioned Margaret must be completely denied. And he sought a judgement for the King etc.

Concerning this, the aforementioned William and Margaret exhibited a certain document made in the name of the aforesaid John of Camoys, the first husband etc. in these words:

"To all the faithful in Christ to whom the present document may come, John de Camoys, son and heir of Sir Ralph de Camoys, sends greetings in the Lord. Know ye that of my own free will I have divorced my wife, Margaret de Camoys, daughter and heir of Sir John de Gatesden, and have entrusted her to the care of Sir William Paynel, Knight; Also, that I have given, granted, remitted and quitclaimed to this same Sir William, all goods and chattels which Margaret posses, or in the future could possess, and also whatever goods or chattels I have, with their appurtenances, from the aforesaid Margaret. So that neither I, nor anyone else acting in my name, may have the ability or cause in the future to exact a payment from the aforesaid Margaret or to assert title to Margaret's goods or chattels, with their appurtenances, in perpetuity, I desire and grant, and confirm by the present document, that the aforesaid Margaret may reside and remain with the aforesaid Sir William at William's pleasure. In evidence of which I have affixed my seal to this present document. Witnesses: Thomas de Repeston, John de Farringdon, William de Icombe, Henry Brown, Steven Chambers, Walter Blount, Gilbert de Batecombe, Robert de Forest, and others."

And they said, that this same Margaret took up residence with William in accordance with the terms stated in the said document, and with the consent and permission of this said John, then Margaret's husband, while John was still alive, and after John had divorced her and entrusted her to his care, just as our Lord the King and his Court could find it expressly stated by the words of this same document, and did not take up residence with this same William in the manner of a lover, in adultery. And they sought a judgement concerning this. And then William and Margaret were told to be at the next Parliament, to hear the judgement upon their case etc.

Afterwards, at the next Parliament following, namely, at the Parliament of our Lord the King at Lincoln in the Octaves of the Feast of Saint Hilary, in the 29th year of his reign, the aforesaid William came, and Margaret was represented by her attorney, and made an urgent request for the aforesaid dowry of Margaret. And a day was set for them at the next Parliament following.

Afterwards, at the next Parliament of our Lord the King following namely at Westminster, in the Octaves of the Feast of Saint John the Baptist, in the 30th year of his reign, the aforesaid William came, and the aforesaid Margaret was likewise represented by a certain Walter Blount, appointed Margaret's attorney before John Abel by means of a brief of our Lord the King. And they requested the aforesaid dowry of Margaret in the aforesaid terms etc.

Concerning this, when the response made earlier on behalf of our Lord the King was read aloud before our Lord the King and His Council in full Parliament, and when in addition the purport of the aforesaid document that had previously been submitted by William and Margaret had been heard and an appraisal had been made of it; and when the aforesaid statute made by our Lord the King and his council and put forward on behalf of the King, and in which it is expressly stated that if a wife should abandon her husband of her own free will and should go away and should take up residence with her lover in adultery, she shall forever lose her right to request that dowry of hers, which might fall to her from the holdings of her husband, if she should be convicted of this, unless her husband, of his own free will and without the compulsion of the Church, should be reconciled to her and permit her to cohabit with him, had likewise been read and heard, and an appraisal had been made of it; William and Margaret then said that they were prepared to prove in the presence of the nation that Margaret was not residing with William as her lover in adultery, while the aforesaid John, her first husband, was alive, etc. . . nor did they say anything else.

Since William and Margaret were not able to show that Margaret had not left and gone to live with this same William while the aforesaid John, her first husband, was alive, completely abandoning her husband, that is to say, the aforesaid John: and of her own free will; as is manifestly obvious, since during the lifetime of this same John, Margaret never appealed to establish any claims, either acting on her own behalf or through somebody else, in any matter or in any way, nor should she now make a claim; on the contrary, by proclaiming that her first choice had been undertaken voluntarily, and by persisting in the affection she had conceived for William while the aforesaid John was living, she permitted herself to marry that same William after the death of this same John;

And since William and Margaret do not say or show anything by which the Court can be assured that the aforementioned John, her first husband, was reconciled to her during his own lifetime in any way; And it is expressly apparent from the aforesaid document submitted by William and Margaret, that in the lifetime of the said John, Margaret was granted leave by means of her divorce and transferal to remain with the said William in perpetuity; Nor is it necessary to conduct a national Inquest in the King's Court concerning these facts which a side is not able to show are otherwise, and which are manifestly apparent to the Court, nor on these matters which are set forth and conceded in the pleading by a side;

But it is more likely and rather to be presumed, and in the King's Court and in any other Court whatsoever it is more to be believed, that from the time when the Wife of any man, while her husband is alive, takes up with any other man of her own free will, in no way appealing for some other status or denying it, that she lives in adultery rather than in some other, proper or legitimate estate, and especially when there follows afterwards such a solid declaration of the wife's freely--considered wishes, that a marriage between them follows soon after the death of the husband; and it is not fitting for the King's Court to conduct a national inquest concerning a case of adultery;

It is the opinion of the Court that it is not necessary to procede to any national inquest in the face of such great and such obvious evidence, presumptions, proofs and admissions of the aforementioned William and Margaret, in the terms in which the said William and Margaret allege it to be necessary; On the contrary, it is the opinion of the Court that the aforesaid Margaret, by the terms of the aforesaid statute, ought not to be allowed to request her aforesaid dowry, or to be heard, for the aforesaid reasons.

Accordingly, it is the decision of the Court that the aforesaid William and Margaret should receive nothing on account of their aforesaid request, but should be fined for making a false claim etc. . . . FINED.

STATE OF TENNESSEE v. SILVA
Supreme Court of Tennessee
477 S.W.2d 517 (1972)

EBBY L. JENKINS, Special Judge.

The defendant below, Gene Silva, was convicted in the Criminal Court of Williamson County in a non-jury trial of violating T.C.A. §37-270, by contributing to the delinquency of a minor and was sentenced to six months in the county jail or workhouse and was fined $50.00.

The indictment under which he was convicted charged that the defendant, Gene Silva, on the 8th day of January, 1970, unlawfully did contribute to or encourage the delinquency of a certain child, to-wit: one Diane Fowler, then and there under the age of eighteen years, by aiding or abetting or encouraging the said child in the commission of an act of delinquency, to-wit: "The said Gene Silva attempted to persuade the said Diane Fowler to check into a motel room with him, they not being married."

. . . The defendant below, a twenty-nine year old married man in the bloom of youth, with two children, prior to and at the time of the inception of his troubles, was the solicitor for a so-called charitable organization known as Mission Workers Organization.

In the conduct of his business, he employed one Diane Fowler, fifteen years of age, who according to the record, shook or rattled a tambourine around the streets and in front of business houses mostly during the long holidays before Christmas when the average person is in a giving mood.

On the day and date in question, the defendant picked up Diane, she being out of school on account of snow, and drove to a combination motel-restaurant near Franklin, parked in front of said place, and was seen by a witness who said "they were hugging and kissing, and that sort of thing." The defendant had earlier overpaid Diane to the extent of about ten dollars, it appearing in the record that Diane was to receive one-third of what she collected, and we think it can be more or less assumed that the defendant, Gene Silva, in the operation of this so-called charitable business and in the red-tape of the administration thereof took his fair share of the offerings, and thus, charity in this instance began at home. Anyway, it is apparent from the record that the solicitors were to benefit more financially and otherwise than the needy children that they were allegedly collecting for.

Be that as it may, on said date, the defendant, after picking up Miss Fowler, attended to some business in Nashville and drove to the Roberson Motel in Williamson County, and parked in front of its restaurant, it being a combination motel and restaurant, and after "hugging and kissing" for some thirty minutes, borrowed ten dollars from her and entered the motel, rented a room and purchased two cokes to go.

As heretofore stated, while the two of them were parked in front of the motel, they were observed by the principal of the Franklin Junior High School, who was apparently out of school on account of snow. It could be said that he was of a suspicious nature, but nevertheless this conduct aroused his suspicion, as it should, and he called the sheriff whose deputy and a highway patrolman arrived and asked Miss Fowler if anything was wrong, and she replied that there was not. During this time, Gene Silva, who was on the inside in the act of renting a room, saw the officers, and according to witnesses, became nervous, left his change, went to his automobile and drove off, and was apprehended by the officers some ways off who arrested him and placed him in jail. He called his wife from jail and she, at that time, took a dim view of the situation.

On the trial of the case, the State, of necessity, used Diane Fowler as a State's witness and she was, to say the least, not sympathetic with the State's case, and we have some misgivings about her conduct in front of the motel as well as her testimony. She testified that she told the defendant three times that "she wasn't going in there" and ". . . you know, I didn't know what to say or do, I just sat there." She testified that the defendant made her no proposition, but the trial judge was justified in taking her testimony with a grain of salt. As a matter of fact, the learned judge disbelieved both Gene Silva and Miss Fowler, and for good cause.

Of course, it is fundamental that when the State calls a party as a witness it vouches for his or her credibility but it is also fundamental that while the State cannot directly impeach its own witness unless caught by surprise or the witness is shown to be a hostile witness, it is not bound by said witness' testimony but can offer other testimony on facts and circumstances that are in conflict with the testimony of the witness and then it is for the Court and jury to sift the evidence and weigh it and decide who is telling the truth. . .

. . . We approve the language contained in 58 Am.Jur. 707:

> *"Contradictory Evidence.*--The rule that a party cannot directly impeach his own witness cannot be taken as meaning that a party is bound by what his witness says, even though he does not deny or contradict his witness' statements at the time. Although he may not impeach the general reputation of the witness for truth and veracity, he may, by other witnesses, prove that the facts are otherwise than as stated, and it is no objection to any relevant evidence of material facts on which he relies to sustain his case that it may operate to contradict, and thus discredit, his own witness. There is no rule which prevents a party from showing his witness to have been mistaken as to a particular fact by means of other witnesses. . ."

CHAPTER V: PASSION, ROMANCE, & LOVE

. . . If the law were otherwise, the State would be in a precarious position in offering any witness because the State, in the prosecution of criminal cases, must offer such proof as it has and to say that the State is bound by the testimony of a witness without considering all the other facts and circumstances would be to impose an unfair and sometimes impossible burden on the State.

This defendant was not convicted on the testimony of Miss Fowler alone, but also on the testimony of the school principal, the testimony of officers and other witnesses, and also by surrounding facts and circumstances. Incidentally, in this time when people close their eyes to open crimes, we need more citizens of prying proclivities and urgent speech, and we commend the school principal for his conduct in this case.

When this defendant parked in front of the combination motel-restaurant and began hugging and kissing this fifteen-year-old girl in wide open daylight and where witnesses could observe him, he was sorely tempted and the passion that possessed him had conquered his reason and swayed his judgment, and in this blinded state he went to the motel clerk and rented a room, and bought two cokes. At that time, his mind and thoughts were far from his hearthstone, and his testimony that he was renting this room for himself and his wife, who was then many snowy miles away from him, is too thin to believe, for it is apparent from the record that the signs point toward his guilty intentions, and his conduct in front of the motel was not that of the true and faithful husband and father, for at the moment he had forgotten the wife of his bosom when temptation beset him. It is not clear whether Diane tempted him or he tempted her, or whether they just tempted each other.

Be that as it may, this ridiculous excuse of renting a room for himself and his wife is unbelievable. It must be remembered that at the time the defendant was renting the room, his wife was in Nashville at home with the children, unaware of his so-called plans to take her out for the night, and that to accomplish his stated purposed he would have had to drive home and tell his wife of his plans; she would have had to ready herself for the occasion, obtain a baby sitter, and they then would have driven back to the Roberson Motel, covering a total distance of more than thirty miles in rough winter weather, consuming at least three hours in time. Human experience teaches us that by this time his ardor would have subsided and his blood run cold.

However, he was apparently either a good father and husband, or a good salesman, for by trial time his wife had either forgiven him of his indiscretions or believed in his innocence for she gave aid and comfort to him in that she swore that at times they did go to a motel room to find surcease from the workaday world of taking care of two children. We must say this is not the usual way of married life as we have observed it, but she rose to his defense as good wives often do when "we are in trouble."

The Court does not condemn her for coming to the aid of her beleaguered husband, the defendant, but takes a rather clouded view of this angle of the defense because we think it is rather unusual that a man would be "hugging and kissing" another woman, borrow money from her, and enter a motel and rent a room for himself and his wife. When passion rules, concern for the woman at hand is the usual pattern, and it is not suddenly and without temptation or provocation transferred from one to the other, especially when the other is many miles distant and it is cold and snowy outside. The learned trial judge had a right to disbelieve this testimony.

We, therefore, reverse the action of the Court of Criminal Appeals and sustain the judgment entered by the Criminal Court of Williamson County. However, since it appears that the defendant works regularly, and from the record, at trial time, had the confidence, love and affection of his wife, we would suggest to the Court below that it modify its judgment and put the defendant on probation so that he can continue to make a living for his family. We believe that the ends of justice will be met if the case is handled in this manner. . .

. . . In making this suggestion, we believe the State has had its day in court. We know the defendant has had more time in court than he wants. To place him on probation would not be too merciful. He has suffered the humiliation of a trial for a would-be sin of the flesh, and had to seek refuge behind the petticoats of an angry wife who publicly forgave him, but whatever is done by the courts cannot restore the peace and harmony of that happy marriage, for if the pattern of wifely conduct runs true to form, he will throughout his natural life be reminded of the time she saved him from jail. When the members of this Court have passed to their respective rewards, whether upwards or downwards, the defendant will in all probability still be reminded of this unfortunate incident for it is a woman's right never to forget. She may think that she has forgiven him, and when she reminds him of his waywardness, she will not be fussing, only "telling him."

And if perchance the defendant should ever rise to high office, such as Justice of the Peace, a Deacon in the church, or a member of an appellate court, he will until death brings him blessed relief hear "if it hadn't been for me, you'd been a jail bird." Six months in jail would be a small price to pay for his sudden heat of passion, for he will all his married life remain suspect in her eyes, and as the shadows of life lengthen and his hair grows grey and he has more children and then grandchildren, he could hear the ever-present theme of "remember when I saved you from jail!" Jail in his declining years could be a sanctuary from an ever-remembering and never-forgiving wife. The prisoner of Chillon could become a kindred spirit.

A convict stays in jail for a stated time, is released, and aside from the stigma of prison, he is free, but a convict husband must forever bear the shackles of guilt, and no matter how hard he works, how much he accomplishes, how much he does for his partner in marriage, or how high he rises in the esteem of his fellows, he will remain a convict to her, and he will only escape temporarily each day while at work making a living.

This defendant has in the eyes of the law done wrong, but not enough in this instance to be jailed, and the least the trial judge can do is to relieve him of his temporary sentence, and remember that he is forever and eternally on probation

380

to this wife, who will be his wife, his warden and parole officer all wrapped up in one. What a sad fate for any poor mortal to face. Whenever he is late from work and not home "on the dot," he can envision his wife wrinkling her brow in a gathering storm and nursing her wrath to keep it warm. This problem was recognized long ago, in Proverbs XX:19, where it is said, "it is better to dwell in a corner of the housetop than with a brawling woman in a wide house."

In his twilight years, after a life of toil, failure or success, when he is entitled to dream dreams and see visions, remember parts of a pleasant past and contemplate a place among the Blessed when he passes from this green earth to a better land, and after he no longer remembers the name of Diane, much less her shape, form or figure, his musings will no doubt be interrupted by the shrill voice of his wife, warden and probation officer, "What are you thinking about--that woman the sheriff caught you with down in Franklin?"

We do not have the power to restore the defendant's matrimonial tranquility, would that we could; all we can do is make the suggestion of probation to the trial judge with the hope that he understands life and can foresee the bleak and lacerated future of the defendant.

The action of the Court of Criminal Appeals is reversed and the judgment of the trial court is sustained with the suggestion that a petition for probation be entertained as set out herein. . .

JACKSON v. THE STATE OF GEORGIA
Supreme Court of Georgia
91 Ga. 322; 18 S.E. 132 (1892)

LOGAN E. BLECKLEY, Chief Justice

As defined by the code, §4357, an assault is an attempt to commit a violent injury on the person of another. Where a rape is intended, the injury contemplated can be inflicted only by actual contact of the sexual organs of the man with those of the woman. In order for an assault with intent to rape to be committed, is it necessary that the persons of the two should be in such proximity as that the organs of the male shall be within what may be termed, "striking distance" of the organs of the female? Or, is the virile member to be treated as a gun which is harmless until brought within "carrying distance" of the target? We think not.

It seems to us that where rape is intended, and the would-be ravisher, with the purpose of presently executing his intention, enters the bedroom of the woman when she is asleep, and mounts upon her bed, thus bringing himself near enough to seize at will her person or some part of it, the attempt to commit a violent injury upon her is complete. Certainly, when matters have proceeded thus far, she would be in imminent danger of being ravished. Nothing but a change of intention on the part of her assailant, the interference of some third person, or her own resistance, would be likely to shield her. No actual touching of the woman's person is necessary to complete the assault. There need be nothing more than the intention to accomplish sexual intercourse presently by force, and the active prosecution of that intention until a situation of immediate, present danger to the woman is produced.

If, in the case before us, the accused, under the excitement of lust and with the intention of gratifying it by force, entered the bedroom of the girl near midnight and got upon the bed in which she was sleeping, within reach of her person, for the purpose of ravishing her, he committed an assault upon her, even if he did not actually touch her except casually and incidentally whilst she was in the act of leaping out of bed to escape from him, or even if he did not touch her at all, he being prevented from consummating his design by her outcry and by the intervention of her father who occupied the adjoining room. Under the evidence in the record, the acts done by the accused, if they were accompanied with an intention to ravish, were quite sufficient to constitute an assault. . . .

We confess to a serious doubt upon our own minds as to whether the accused really intended to commit rape. Two facts strongly indicate the contrary; one of these being that he knew the father of the girl occupied an adjoining room and was near enough at hand to protect her; and the other being that, instead of seizing her while asleep, he paused upon the bed and called her by name. Why he should have done this, if his mind was made up to violate her person, we are at some loss to understand or even to conjecture.

But the workings of a criminal mind, especially while under the dominion of brutal passion, are often mysterious. A bad man who has procured his own consent to commit a great outrage will frequently take great risks and prosecute his criminal enterprise in the most foolish manner. Desperation and folly are close relatives, and are found not seldom in each other's company. Guilt is shrewd only when it is timid; when it becomes bold and reckless, it is in no mood to consult discretion or to heed the dictates of prudence. The jury had a right to interpret the prisoner's conduct in light of this trait of vicious human nature, and so doing, there was no violation of sound logic in reaching the conclusion at which they arrived. . . . Our conclusion is that the evidence was sufficient, though barely sufficient, to uphold the verdict; and that in denying a new trial no error was committed.

Judgment affirmed.

TAMI v. PIKOWITZ.
Court of Chancery of New Jersey.
138 N.J.Eq. 410; 48 A.2d 221 (1946)

WILFRED H. JAYNE, Vice Chancellor.
In several of its aspects this cause is an unfashionable one to be introduced to a court of equity for determination. Basically it pertains to the title and possession of a Plymouth automobile which, in the existing industrial conditions,

is alleged to be a rare and unique article of personalty. . . . In retaining jurisdiction I have preferred to recognize the suit as one prosecuted to nullify a bill of sale alleged to have been procured fraudulently and without consideration.

The controversy recoils from the indiscretions of the parties. In its broad factual appearance, the indecorous acts of the complaint are manifestly surpassed by the dishonorable perfidy of the defendant. The story can be readily summarized.

The parties were employed at the establishment of a war industry, where their acquaintance and ensuing associations originated. Both were married persons, but in the initial period of their companionship neither thought it prudent or necessary to divulge that incidental fact to the other.

While the defendant is noticeably lacking in the physical comeliness of an Adonis, nevertheless the complainant's interest in him, like Aphrodite's, gradually ascended to an altitude of infatuation. When released from work, they frequently convened at a neighboring tavern, where they enjoyed, and she paid for, the refreshments. She bestowed upon him many gifts, such as a wrist watch, a wallet (he conserved his earnings), gloves, neckties, and sun glasses. Indeed, he smoothly persuaded her to loan him $200. Up to this point he rejoiced in playing the role of a subsidized escort. He subsequently permitted her to contemplate the dissolution of their former marriages and their future alliance in matrimony.

On December 13, 1945, she purchased the automobile at the price of $1,000. She did not have a license to operate a motor vehicle, but the vendor had promised to instruct her. The defendant forthwith expressed to the complainant his ardent desire to visit his relatives in Pennsylvania, and he implored her to permit him to have the use of the car for the accomplishment of that journey but, according to the testimony of the complainant, he shrewdly informed her that if, perchance, the vehicle should be involved in some accident, she, by virtue of her ownership of it, might incur some personal pecuniary liability. He accordingly recommended that it would be entirely feasible and extremely precautious for her to transfer temporarily the apparent ownership of the vehicle to him. She did so on December 20, 1945, whereupon the defendant departed for Pennsylvania.

During his absence, his wife either fortuitously or designedly met the complainant. The interview inspired the complainant to make an unexpected personal visit at the address in Pennsylvania where the defendant had assured her he intended to sojourn. The defendant was not at that address. The complainant was informed that the defendant could be reached at a designated residence in a near-by village in the company of one "Amelia." It may be inferred that Amelia was no more pleased to meet the complainant than the latter was pleased to meet Amelia.

The circumstances of that occasion caused the curtain of implicit faith to drop from the complainant's eyes, and she discovered that the pretended fidelity of the defendant was merely a deceptive shadow. "Now sighs steal out and tears begin to flow," said Pope.

The defendant returned to Middlesex County, New Jersey, early in January 1945. The complainant immediately requested him to surrender the automobile and its title to her. He refused. She intimated her intention to consult an attorney. He threatened that should she do so, he would impart to her husband full knowledge of their associations. He then retired as a gigolo to become a cad. But let me continue.

Upon the institution of the present cause, the defendant filed an answer in which he averred that "the complainant meretriciously had sexual relations with this defendant on many occasions since the month of October 1945," and that the complainant gave him the automobile "in consideration of the meretricious relation existing between the complainant and this defendant."

Furthermore, the defendant at the final hearing, and in the presence of the complainant's husband, related brazenly and without a blush of humility, his sexual performances with the complainant, and he sought to multiply the number of such occurrences as if he were endeavoring to establish as adequate quantum meruit. Thus again the defendant retrogrades; this time to the level of venality.

The words of Justice Kalisch, expressive of the sentiment of the Court of Errors and Appeals in Letts v Letts, 79 N.J.Eq. 630, 635, 82 A. 845, 848, Ann.Cas.1913.A, 1236 reverberate: "I doubt if there can be found in the history of the divorce court anywhere such a *rara avis* [rare bird], a male co-respondent, who had voluntarily come forward in aid of an injured husband suing for a divorce; who had sunk his manhood, his morals, and his honor so low as to go voluntarily upon the witness stand and with brazen impunity proclaimed his triumph over his victim, to irretrievably disgrace and ruin her. The experience of mankind has been to the contrary; and therefore when a case arises which is contrary to this experience, it is such an aberration from the normal trend of human action that it requires convincing proof to confirm it."

The complainant denied that her associations with the defendant had included any sexual indulgences. I can attribute some measure of credibility to her testimony, but I do not hesitate to declare that I cannot repose any credulence whatever in that of the defendant. The defendant claims the automobile as a remunerative reward for her "meretricious" servitude. His counsel confronts the complainant with the maxim "He who comes into equity must come with clean hands." It is the defendant himself who has sought to soil and besmear the hands of the complainant. The maxim has its limitation. It does not banish all sinful suitors from a court of equity. The iniquitous conduct must be related proximately to the act of the defendant which is the subject matter of the cause of action; it must be evil practice of wrongful conduct in the particular transaction in respect to which the complainant seeks redress. . . .

It must be realized that the doctrine of unclean hands has its logical justification only in considerations of good conscience and natural justice. There are cases in which a court of equity in fulfillment of the reasons and objects of its creation and existence may in furtherance of natural justice aid the one who comparatively is the most innocent. . . . The complainant's benevolence and the defendant's malevolence do not escape attention. In the posture of the proof in this case I shall not permit the defendant to profit from the feminine weaknesses of the complainant. The defendant acknowledges that he never contributed a penny to the purchase price of the automobile. When first interviewed by an attorney of the complainant, he suggested a compromise by which he might purchase the vehicle by means of installment payments. He has since chosen to darken some corner in which to hide his loot. Indeed, it required some coercion from the bench to induce the defendant to disclose where he was concealing the automobile.

I am unable to accept the doctrine of unclean hands as a positive defense to the complainant's cause of action. I have, however, paused to consider whether there was an absolute, unconditional, and unqualified gift under the rigid rules of the common law. I think not. Notwithstanding the unwholesome motives of the complainant, I conclude that she intended the transfer to be essentially a bailment. The transfer on her part was undoubtedly conditionally and deceitfully procured by means of an imposition upon her enchantment.

Neither my judgment derived from an observation of the witnesses nor my conception of equity and natural justice permits me to absolve the defendant. The decisions of our courts are intended to be expressive or explanatory of the rules that are to govern the relations and conduct of individuals in our social organization. There must be an organic connection between the community sentiment and opinion upon such subjects as manhood, integrity, honor, and fairness, and the laws and decisions of our courts. It would seem to me to be a barbarian rule of human conduct that would enable this defendant to succeed in his deliberate brigandage and attempted extortion.

I shall advise a decree for the complainant.

KENDRICK v. McCRARY
Supreme Court of Georgia
11 Ga. 603 (1852)

JOSEPH H. LUMPKIN, J.

This was an action of trespass on the case, instituted in the Superior Court of Stewart County, by Isaac McCrary against John B. Kendrick, for the seduction of plaintiff's daughter. The Jury returned a verdict for $1,049; and a new trial is asked, on the grounds that the daughter was twenty-one years old at the time the injury occurred, and there was no contract of service between her and her father; that the service rendered was voluntary. And it is contended that the father could not sue for, and recover damages, for the loss of that which he had no legal right to claim; that the measure of damages was the actual loss sustained; and that the right of action belonged to the daughter and not to the father. . .

In the case before us, the daughter lived in her father's house at the time of the seduction, under his control, and in the performance of actual services. . .

This action was originally given to the *master*, to enable him to recover damages for the loss of service occasioned by the seduction of his *servant*. He was restricted in his recovery to the actual damages sustained. The loss of service is still the legal foundation of the action; and the father cannot maintain the action without averring in his declaration and proving on the trial, that from the consequences of the seduction, his daughter is less able to perform the duties of servant; but the proof upon both of these points need be very slight. It matters not how small the service she rendered, though it may have consisted in milking his cows, or even pouring out his tea, he is entitled to his action. . .

The second exception is equally as untenable as the first. It assumes that the only consequential injury to the father, of which he has a right to complain, consists in the loss of the services of his daughter, and the expenses he may incur during her confinement. This certainly is not so. If it were so, and pregnancy did not result from the seduction, the father would have no action.

All the authorities show that the relation of master and servant, between the parent and the child, is but a figment of the law, to open to him the door for the redress of his injuries. It is the substream on which the action is built; the actual damage which he has sustained, in many, if not in most cases, exists only in the humanity of the law, which seeks to vindicate his outraged feelings. He comes into the Court as a master, he goes before the Jury as a father.

Never, so help me God, while I have the honor to occupy a seat upon this bench, will I consent to control the Jury, in the amount of compensation which they may see fit to render a father for the dishonor and disgrace thus cast upon his family; for this atrocious invasion of his household peace. There is nothing like it, since the entrance of Sin and Death into this lower world. Money cannot redress a parent who is wronged beyond the possibility of redress; it cannot minister to a mind thus diseased. Give to such a plaintiff, all that figures can number, it is as the small dust of the balance. Say to the father, there is $1,049, embrace your innocent daughter, for the last time, and let her henceforth become an object for the hand of scorn to point its finger at! What mockery! And yet this is the identical case we are considering.

It has been truly said, that more instructive lessons are taught in Courts of Justice, than the Church is able to inculcate. Morals come in the cold abstract from the pulpit; but men smart under them practically, when Juries are the preachers. In cases of deliberate seduction, there should be no limitation to verdicts because there is none to the magnitude of the injury.

The judgment of the Circuit Court is affirmed.

CHAPTER V: PASSION, ROMANCE, & LOVE

REGINA v. COLLINS
Court of Appeal of England, Criminal Division
[1972] 3 W.L.R. 243, [1972] 2 All E.R. 1105, 56 Cr.App.R. 554 (1972)

EDMUND DAVIES, L.J.

This is about as extraordinary a case as my brethren and I have ever heard either on the Bench or while at the Bar. Stephen William George Collins was convicted on 29th October 1971 at Essex Assizes of burglary with intent to commit rape and he was sentenced to 21 months' imprisonment. He is a 19 year old youth, and he appeals against that conviction by the certificate of the trial judge. The terms in which that certificate is expressed reveals that the judge was clearly troubled about the case and the conviction.

Let me relate the facts. Were they put into a novel or portrayed on the stage, they would be regarded as being so improbable as to be unworthy of serious consideration and as verging at times on farce. At about two o'clock in the early morning of Saturday, 24th July 1971, a young lady of 18 went to bed at her mother's home in Colchester. She had spent the evening with her boyfriend. She had taken a certain amount of drink, and it may be that this fact affords some explanation of her inability to answer satisfactorily certain crucial questions put to her. She had the habit of sleeping without wearing night apparel in a bed which is very near the lattice-type window of her room. At one stage of her evidence she seemed to be saying that the bed was close up against the window which, in accordance with her practice, was wide open. In the photographs which we have before us, however, there appears to be a gap of some sort between the two, but the bed was clearly quite near the window.

At about 3:30 or 4:00 a.m. she awoke and she then saw in the moonlight a vague form crouched in the open window. She was unable to remember, and this is important, whether the form was on the outside of the window sill or on that part of the sill which was inside the room, and for reasons which will later become clear, that seemingly narrow point is of crucial importance. The young lady then realised several things: first of all that the form in the window was that of a male; secondly that he was a naked male; and thirdly that he was a naked male with an erect penis. She also saw in the moonlight that his hair was blond. She thereupon leapt to the conclusion that her boyfriend, with whom for some time she had been on terms of regular and frequent sexual intimacy, was paying her an ardent nocturnal visit.

She promptly sat up in bed, and the man descended from the sill and joined her in bed and they had full sexual intercourse. But there was something about him which made her think that things were not as they usually were between her and her boyfriend. The length of his hair, his voice as they had exchanged what was described as "love talk," and other features led her to the conclusion that somehow there was something different. So she turned on the bed-side light, saw that her companion was not her boyfriend and slapped the face of the intruder, who was none other than the appellant. He said to her, "Give me a good time tonight," and got hold of her arm, but she bit him and told him to go. She then went into the bathroom and he promptly vanished.

The complainant said that she would not have agreed to intercourse if she had known that the person entering her room was not her boyfriend. But there was no suggestion of any force having been used on her, and the intercourse which took place was undoubtedly effected with no resistance on her part.

The appellant was seen by the police at about 10:30 a.m. later that same morning. According to the police, the conversation which took place then elicited these points: He was very lustful the previous night. He had taken a lot of drink, and we may here note that drink (which to him is a very real problem) had brought this young man into trouble several times before, but never for an offense of this kind. He went on to say that he knew the complainant because he had worked around her house. On this occasion, desiring sexual intercourse — and according to the police evidence he had added that he was determined to have a girl, by force if necessary, although that part of the police evidence he challenged — he went on to say that he walked around the house, saw a light in an upstairs bedroom, and he knew that this was the girls' bedroom. He found a step ladder, leaned it against the wall and climbed up and looked into the bedroom. What he could see inside through the wide open window was a girl who was naked and asleep. So he descended the ladder and stripped off all his clothes, with the exception of his socks, because apparently he took the view that if the girl's mother entered the bedroom it would be easier to effect a rapid escape if he had his socks on than if he was in his bare feet. This is a matter about which we are not called on to express any view, and would in any event find ourselves unable to express one. Having undressed, he then climbed the ladder and pulled himself up on to the window sill. His version of the matter is that he was pulling himself in when she awoke. She then got up and knelt on the bed, she put her arms around his neck and body, and she seemed to pull him into the bed. He went on:

> "* * * I was rather dazed, because I didn't think she would want to know me. We kissed and cuddled for about ten or fifteen minutes and then I had it away with her but found it hard because I had had so much to drink."

The police officer said to the appellant:

> "It appears that it was your intention to have intercourse with this girl by force if necessary and it was only pure coincidence that this girl was under the impression that you were her boyfriend and apparently that is why she consented to allowing you to have sexual intercourse with her."

It was alleged that he then said:

> "Yes, I feel awful about this. It is the worst day of
> my life, but I know it could have been worse."

Thereupon the officer said to him — and the appellant challenges this — "What do you mean, you know it could have been worse?" to which he is alleged to have replied:

> "Well, my trouble is drink and I got very frustrated.
> As I've told you I only wanted to have it away
> with a girl and I'm only glad I haven't really hurt
> her."

Then he made a statement under caution, in the course of which he said:

> "When I stripped off and got up the ladder I made
> my mind up that I was going to try and have it
> away with this girl. I feel terrible about this now,
> but I had too much to drink. I am sorry for what
> I have done."

In the course of his testimony, the appellant said that he would not have gone into the room if the girl had not knelt on the bed and beckoned him into the room. He said that if she had objected immediately to his being there or to his having intercourse he would not have persisted. While he was keen on having sexual intercourse that night, it was only if he could find someone who was willing. He strongly denied having told the police that he would, if necessary, have pushed over some girl for the purpose of having intercourse.

There was a submission of no case to answer on the ground that the evidence did not support the charge, particularly that ingredient of it which had reference to entry into the house "as a trespasser." But the submission was overruled, and, as we have already related, he gave evidence.

Now, one feature of the case which remained at the conclusion of the evidence in great obscurity is where exactly the appellant was at the moment when, according to him, the girl manifested that she was welcoming him. Was he kneeling on the sill outside the window or was he already inside the room, having climbed through the window frame, and kneeling on the inner sill? It was a crucial matter, for there were certainly three ingredients that it was incumbent on the Crown to establish. Under Section 9 of the Theft Act of 1968, which renders a person guilty of burglary if he enters any building or part of a building as a trespasser and with the intention of committing rape, the entry of the appellant into the building must first be proved. Well, there is no doubt about that, for it is common ground that he did enter this girl's bedroom. Secondly, it must be proved that he entered as a trespasser. We will develop this point a little later. Thirdly it must be proved that he entered as a trespasser with intent at the time of entry to commit rape therein.

The second ingredient of the offence — the entry must be as a trespasser — is one which has not, to the best of our knowledge, been previously canvassed in the courts. Views as to its ambit have naturally been canvassed by the textbook writers, and it is perhaps not wholly irrelevant to recall that those who were advising the Home Secretary before the Theft Bill was presented to Parliament had it in mind to get rid of some of the frequently absurd technical rules which had been built up in relation to the old requirement in burglary of a "breaking and entering." The cases are legion as to what this did or did not amount to, and happily it is not now necessary for us to consider them. But it was in order to get rid of those technical rules that a new test was introduced, namely that the entry must be "as a trespasser."

What does that involve? According to the learned editors of Archbold [1]

> "Any intentional, reckless or negligent entry into a building will, it would appear, constitute a trespass if the building is in the possession of another person who does not consent to the entry. Nor will it make any difference that the entry was the result of a reasonable mistake on the part of the defendant, so far as trespass is concerned."

If that be right, then it would be no defence for this man to say (and even were he believed in saying), "Well, I honestly thought that this girl was welcoming me into the room and I therefore entered, fully believing that I had her consent to go in." If Archbold is right, he would nevertheless be a trespasser, since the apparent consent of the girl was unreal, she being mistaken as to who was at her window. We disagree. We hold that, for the purpose of Section 9 of the Theft Act 1968, a person entering a building is not guilty of trespass if he enters without knowledge that he is trespassing or at least without acting recklessly as to whether or not he is unlawfully entering. . . .

Having so held, the pivotal point of this appeal is whether the Crown established that the appellant at the moment that he entered the bedroom knew perfectly well that he was not welcome there or, being reckless whether he was welcome or not, was nevertheless determined to enter. That in turn involves consideration as to where he was at the time that the complainant indicated that she was welcoming him into her bedroom. If, to take an example that was put in the course of argument, her bed had not been near the window but was on the other

---

side of the bedroom, and he (being determined to have her sexually even against her will) climbed through the window and crossed the bedroom to reach her bed, then the offence charged would have been established. But in this case, as we have related, the layout of the room was different, and it became a point of nicety which had to be conclusively established by the Crown as to where he was when the girl made welcoming signs, as she unquestionably at some stage did.

How did the learned judge deal with this matter? We have to say regretfully that there was a flaw in his treatment of it. . .

. . . Unfortunately the trial judge regarded the matter as though the second ingredient in the burglary charged was whether there had been an intentional or reckless entry, and when he came to develop this topic in his summing-up that error was unfortunately perpetuated. The trial judge told the jury:

> "He had no right to be in that house, as you know, certainly from the point of view of [the girl's mother], but if you are satisfied about entry, did he enter intentionally or recklessly? What the Prosecution says about that is, you do not really have to consider recklessness because when you consider his own evidence he intended to enter that house, and if you accept the evidence I have just pointed out to you, he, in fact, did so. So, at least, you may think, it was intentional. At the least, you may think it was reckless because as he told you he did not know whether the girl would accept him."

We are compelled to say that we do not think the trial judge by these observations made it sufficiently clear to the jury the nature of the second test about which they had to be satisfied before the appellant could be convicted of the offence charged.

There was no doubt that his entry into the bedroom was "intentional." But what the appellant had said was, "She knelt on the bed, she put her arms around me and then I went in." If the jury thought he might be truthful in that assertion, they would need to consider whether or not, although entirely surprised by such a reception being accorded to him, this young man might not have been entitled reasonably to regard her action as amounting to an invitation to him to enter. If she in fact appeared to be welcoming him, the Crown do not suggest that he should have realized or even suspected that she was so behaving because, despite the moonlight, she thought he was someone else. Unless the jury were entirely satisfied that the appellant made an effective and substantial entry into the bedroom without the complainant doing or saying anything to cause him to believe that she was consenting to his entering it, he ought not to be convicted of the offence charged.

The point is a narrow one, as narrow maybe as the window sill which is crucial to this case. But this is a criminal charge of gravity and, even though one may suspect that his *intention* was to commit the offence charged, unless the facts show with clarity that he in fact committed it he ought not to remain convicted.

Some question arose whether or not the appellant can be regarded as a trespasser *ab initio* [from the beginning]. But we are entirely in agreement with the view expressed in Archbold that the common law doctrine of trespass *ab initio* has no application to burglary under the Theft Act 1968. One further matter that was canvassed ought perhaps to be mentioned. The point was raised that, the complainant not being the tenant or occupier of the dwelling-house and her mother being apparently in occupation, this girl herself could not in any event have extended an effective invitation to enter, so that even if she had expressly and with full knowledge of all material facts invited the appellant in, he would nevertheless be a trespasser. Whatever be the position in the law of tort, to regard such a proposition as acceptable in the criminal law would be unthinkable.

We have to say that this appeal must be allowed on the basis that the jury were never invited to consider the vital question whether this young man did enter the premises as a trespasser, that is to say knowing perfectly well that he had no invitation to enter or reckless of whether or not his entry was with permission. . . .

Appeal allowed. Conviction quashed.

BRASWELL v. SUBER
Supreme Court of Georgia
61 Ga. 398 (1878)

LOGAN E. BLECKLEY, Justice.

[Suber brought ejection against Braswell for a tract of land in Sumter county. His title rested upon a deed made by Braswell to him on December 4th, 1875. Defendant sought to show that this deed was executed to secure the payment of a debt, admitting at the same time that the debt had not been paid, but insisting that as the defendant's wife had not consented to the making of the conveyance, no title passed and no recovery could be had thereon. The court excluded the testimony and defendant appealed.]

A wife may secure her creditors with her own property, in her own way, without the consent of her husband. And a husband has an equal privilege. He may invite the co-operation of his wife under the act of 1871, (Code, § 1969) if he choses, but he is free to dispense with it, notwithstanding that act, if such is his pleasure.

CHAPTER V: PASSION, ROMANCE, & LOVE

The wife has been much advanced by the general tenor of legislation of late years, in respect to her own property. She has acquired a pretty independent position as to title, control and disposition, but this relates to her property, not to his. The law has not yet raised her to the station of superintendent of her husband's contracts, and probably never will. He is bound to support her and the children she bears to him, and in order to fulfil this obligation, he ought to have as much freedom in the management of his business affairs with the world as unmarried men are allowed to exercise.

In taking a wife a man does not put himself under an overseer. He is not a subordinate in his own family, but the head of it. The law assigns him this position, not for his own advantage alone, but as much for the real good of his wife and children, and somewhat for the general interest of society. A husband left free to lead and govern in his own family is the most useful husband to all who may be concerned in the results of his conduct. That exceptions to this rule may be pointed out, is no objection to, or disproof of the rule itself.

Human institutions are all more or less imperfect, and their complete efficiency in practical working cannot be expected in every instance. It is enough if they produce beneficence to the great mass, and in the great majority of cases. A subjugated husband is a less pleasing and less energetic member of society, than one who keeps his true place, yet knows how to temper authority with affection. The law does not discourage conjugal consultations, or free and voluntary co-operation in all transactions which affect, or may affect, the welfare of the family. Perhaps, the true spirit and genius of the law favors nothing more than harmony of will and conduct on the part of the husband and wife. But the law does not undertake to secure this delightful harmony by coercion, but leaves it to issue spontaneously from the holy relation of matrimony.

In the conduct of his business, the husband may ask his wife's consent; but if he acts without it, especially in the virtuous and praiseworthy matter of securing or paying an honest debt, the law will excuse him, and let him be bound by what he does alone. If he wants her consent, he must procure it in time, and not wait until he has bound himself without it. For him to become anxious about her advice, not when he makes a conveyance, but when he finds himself unwilling to abide by it as made on his own responsibility some months or years ago, is to turn to her too late. The law permits him to neglect taking her counsel, but does not require him to neglect it. Being a husband, he is the free head of a family, and as such needs no license to bind himself by his contracts - not even the license of his true and lawful wife.

Judgment affirmed.

FRAMBACH v. DUNIHUE
District Court of Appeal of Florida, Fifth District
419 So. 2d 1115 (1982)

FRANK D. UPCHURCH, Jr., Judge.

The Frambachs appeal from a judgment awarding Dunihue an undivided one-half interest in their property. Two pieces of property were titled in the Frambach's names. In parcel A the court imposed a resulting trust. In parcel B, the court determined that Dunihue was entitled to a one-half interest as an "equitable lien and equitable interest." By this appeal, the Frambachs question only the court's ruling as to parcel B on which their home was located.

The history of this case is an amazing account of human relationships. Why people who for many years had demonstrated an incredible ability to solve their disputes would ultimately end up in litigation is mystifying.

Dunihue was a widower with seven children to raise ranging in age from three to eleven. The Frambachs lived nearby with their four children. Contact between the parties started when Mrs. Frambach, a devoted churchwoman, asked if she could take the Dunihue children to church. She later became a babysitter and took care of the Dunihue children sometimes at their home and sometimes at hers for which she was paid $25.00 per week.

This arrangement continued for a few months. In September, 1960, the Frambachs and the Dunihues waited out a hurricane in the Frambachs' home. The Frambachs' house was small (a bedroom, living room and kitchen, 600 square feet in all) and had no inside plumbing. As fate would have it, the relationships which developed as the storm howled proved so interesting and the two families so congenial that the Frambachs and Dunihues decided to see if the two families could live together.

Dunihue set out to enlarge the house. A bedroom and bath were added and various improvements were made. As the years passed, Mrs. Frambach had another child and for a time, until the Dunihue children began to move out, fifteen people (three adults and twelve children) lived in the house. Mrs. Frambach ran the household, did the cooking, and saw that the children cleaned, helped with the washing, and did such chores as were required and within their capabilities.

Both Dunihue and the Frambachs were employed. Dunihue on several occasions obtained employment for Mr. Frambach and their earnings were not substantially different, although Dunihue had the larger income. The Frambachs and Dunihue each had a bank account into which they deposited their respective earnings. Mrs. Frambach wrote checks on both accounts and decided in large measure which account would be used to pay a particular bill. Dunihue's characterization of the arrangement was probably the most appropriate, that it was just one family and whatever money was available was used wherever it was most needed. Very often the three shopped together for clothes, furniture, and automobiles.

Improvements in the home continued to be made. Dunihue's contributions to these improvements undoubtedly were the most valuable although everyone assisted. At the time of this litigation, the value of the home had appreciated to approximately $65,000. The court received considerable testimony of Dunihue's contributions to the improvements, but very little evidence was adduced as to the value of the services received by Dunihue and his family.

This arrangement lasted for nineteen years until the last of the Dunihue children were grown and gone. The relationship was suddenly terminated when Mrs. Frambach called Dunihue at work and told him to come get his things and get out. He was given thirty minutes to comply. The reason for the sudden end to the friendship was not clear.

After being ejected from the Frambachs' home, Dunihue brought suit to impose an equitable lien on the property. Dunihue claimed that the Frambachs had promised him a place to live for the rest of his life in exchange for his work. He further alleged that he had relied on this promise and that the Frambachs will be unjustly enriched at his expense if he is not compensated for his work. The Frambachs denied that they had made any such promise to Dunihue claiming that without the improvements it would have been impossible to house that many people.

The trial court determined that the two families had operated as a single family. While emphasizing that he was not making such an inference, the judge opined that the association of the parties was almost as close as though there had been a single wife and two husbands. The court then found that the pooling of assets and commingling of everything into a common pot was to assure Dunihue that he would have a home as long as he lived and that it would award Dunihue as equitable lien in the home. Regarding the amount of the lien, the court stated the following:

> They did start out with a thousand-dollar equity, the [Frambachs]. But in effect because of the way they treated everything through the years, they really are just as though this was a divorce. And we are dividing up the property between a wife that had two husbands, so to speak. That's why I think the only fair thing to do is to make them tenants in common right down the middle. So that's my judgment.

As a general rule, a court of equity may give restitution to a plaintiff and prevent the unjust enrichment of a defendant by imposing a constructive trust or by imposing an equitable lien upon the property in favor of the plaintiff. Restatement of Restitution §§ 160-161 (1937). However, where the plaintiff makes improvements upon the land of another under circumstances which entitle him to restitution, he is entitled only to an equitable lien upon the land and he cannot charge the owner of the land as constructive trustee and compel the owner to transfer the land to him. Restatement of Restitution § 161. Comment a. Neither a constructive trust nor a resulting trust arises in favor of a person who pays no part of the purchase price even though he pays for improvements on the property. [citation omitted] The person does not become, in whole or in part, a beneficial owner of the property although he may be entitled to reimbursement.

In the present case, the court, in effect, determined that the Frambachs held an undivided one-half interest in the property in trust for Dunihue. However, there was no evidence of a promise or agreement to deed a portion of the Frambachs' property to Dunihue in return for the improvements. Nor has Dunihue alleged that he actually paid a part of the purchase price. In these circumstances, Dunihue was not entitled to have a constructive trust imposed on the property. We therefore reverse the award to Dunihue of a tenancy in common and remand the cause for further consideration.

Upon remand, the trial court should determine the value of the respective contribution of Dunihue and the Frambachs. This can be accomplished by calculating the fair market value of the improvements attributable to Dunihue and the fair market value of the services rendered by the Frambachs to him during the nineteen years the parties lived together. In the alternative, the court could determine the cost to Dunihue for his labor, services and material in making the improvements as compared to the cost to the Frambachs of providing services to Dunihue. We suspect that, under either measure, the contributions of the parties will be equal. However, if the court finds that Dunihue's contributions exceed the value of the benefits received by him from the Frambachs, an equitable lien in this amount should be imposed to prevent the unjust enrichment of the Frambachs.

REVERSED and REMANDED.

JONES v. THE STATE
Supreme Court of Georgia
90 Ga. 616; 16 S.E. 380 (1892)

SAMUEL E. LUMPKIN, Justice

Sexual intercourse resulting from seduction must necessarily be committed and accomplished with the consent of the female. This is an essential and indispensable element of this particular crime. Rape being the carnal knowledge of a female forcibly and against her will, necessarily implies the entire absence of consent on her part. It follows, plainly enough and without argument, that a rape cannot be made the basis of a prosecution for seduction. The two offences are so totally different, they cannot be confused, nor can one of them be any possibility, legal or otherwise, be substituted for the other. . . .

CHAPTER V: PASSION, ROMANCE, & LOVE

While this is manifestly true, it can scarcely be doubted that no modest girl or woman, upon the occasion of her first carnal contact with a man, will readily submit to the intercourse without some reluctance and some show of resistance. The extent to which this resistance will go depends largely, we presume, upon the nature, education, surroundings and previous associations of the female. We imagine it would be very difficult indeed to find a virgin of any age who would boldly and without shame or hesitation indulge for the first time in the sexual act; and while she may consent to it, it is perfectly natural to expect a greater or less degree of reluctance on her part. Indeed, it is easy to imagine that a woman may yield herself to the sexual embraces of a man when the act is absolutely repulsive to her, and offends, in the highest measure, her every sense of delicacy. The coyness, shyness and modesty which actuate a virtuous woman on such an occasion naturally find expression in the manifestation of some degree of unwillingness, or of an endeavor, feeble though it may be, to shield herself from that to which she is averse, but to which she really consents only for the sake of the man she loves and trusts. It would be mere mawkishness to affect ignorance of these well-known traits of female character.

It is our duty to deal plainly and fairly with the questions made in this case, and this is impossible unless we recognize the existence of those principles of human nature, which are universally understood, and which are applicable to the facts presented. Pursuing this course, it is safe to say that females possessing any degree of modesty shrink from the first act of sexual intercourse. This, we apprehend, is true even of those having passionate natures, but Byron wrote:

> *"But who, alas! can love and then be wise?*
> *Not that remorse did not oppose temptation,*
> *A little still she strove, and much repented,*
> *And whispering, 'I will ne' er consent' --*
> *consented."*

And in the famous speech of the great Erskine, in *Howard v. Bingham*, he drew a picture of a "charming woman, endeavoring to conceal sensations which modesty forbids the sex, however enamoured, too openly to reveal, -- wishing beyond adequate expression what she must not even attempt to express, and *seemingly* resisting what she burns to enjoy."

That a woman exhibits hesitation, reluctance and a slight degree of physical resistance does not, by any means, make the intercourse, when accomplished, rape. .... The evidence in this case shows beyond doubt that Miss Smith, on the occasion when she first had sexual intercourse with the accused, really consented to the act, and that he did not then, nor at any other time, have carnal knowledge of her by force. On cross-examination she did use some expressions tending to show a want of consent on her part, and from which it is sought to draw the inference that the connection was had by force and violence and against her

397

will; but the only fair and reasonable conclusion from her testimony is that she yielded to the wishes of the accused, and this is doubtless the truth of the case. . .

The little resistance she made was the outcome of her maidenly modesty, and was of the kind we have endeavored to describe. She exhibited in testifying the same sort of hesitation to confess her disgrace she had shown in consenting to the act by which it was accomplished. . . .

The evidence adduced on the trial of this case shows that Miss Smith was a modest, gentle, tenderhearted and confiding young girl; that from her childhood she had learned to love and trust the accused with all the fondness of her heart, and that he repaid her tender confidence and implicit faith by blasting and ruining her young life. The sad and simple story contained in her evidence, of the cruel wrong inflicted upon her, by its own eloquent pathos, will convince the mind of any candid reader that she yielded her virtue, under the persuasions and promises of the accused, for the sake of her love, and that the slight resistance she offered when the criminal intercourse first occurred was but the last despairing and feeble effort of a maiden's inborn modesty to save herself from disgrace and shame. The following brief extract from her testimony presents the case with painful and touching clearness:

"I just yielded to him by loving him; I told him if he would marry me, I would yield to him; he told me he would, and I yielded to him by my love."

While there is not evidence, in so many words, that persuasion as well as promises of marriage was used to accomplish the seduction, the circumstances detailed are ample to warrant the inference that persuasion, even to importunity, was resorted to in order to gain consent. The accused, with utter selfishness, ruined this unfortunate young woman and left her to her fate. Doubtless remorse has already overtaken him. Be this as it may, it was but just that the strong hand of the law should be laid upon him; and in the light of this record, we sanction the verdict of the jury and the judgment of the court, which for the time being, at least, makes the way of this transgressor hard.

Judgment affirmed.

CHAPTER VI

CLEVER SCHEMES, BIZARRE CLAIMS, RIDICULOUS CONTENTIONS, NOVEL DEMANDS, STRANGE LAWSUITS AND GOOD OLD-FASHIONED FRAUD AND DECEIT

Judicial humor is a dreadful thing. In the first place, the jokes are usually bad; I have seldom heard a judge utter a good one. There seems to be something about the judicial ermine which puts its wearer in the same general class with the ordinary radio comedian. He just is not funny. In the second place, the bench is not an appropriate place for unseemly levity. The litigant has vital interests at stake. His entire future, or even his life, may be trembling in the balance, and the robed buffoon who makes merry at his expense should be choked with his own wig.

- William Prosser[1]

There is assuredly some differences of opinion among appellate judges about the basic problem whether humor can be proper in a judicial opinion. When we asked the presiding judges of sixty appellate courts for citations to judicial humor, about ten percent of the forty-odd who responded said that humor is never used in the courts. We cannot quarrel with that firm position, for that was our own view until we had worked for more than a year, off and on, in the preparation of this critique. In the event, humor is used occasionally by the great majority of our appellate courts. . . Laying aside the cases in which humor should never be used, we now share Cardozo's belief that an opinion may not be the worse for being lightened by a smile.

- Hon. George Rose Smith[2]

---

[1] William Prosser, *The Judicial Humorist*, p. viii (1952).
[2] Hon. George Rose Smith "A Critique of Judicial Humor", 43 *Ark. Law Rev.* 1, 25-26 (1990).

CHAPTER VI: SCHEMES, CLAIMS, & CONTENTIONS

UNITED STATES ex. rel. MAYO v. SATAN AND HIS STAFF
United States District Court, W. D. Pennsylvania.
54 F.R.D. 282 (1971)

GERALD J. WEBER, District Judge.

Plaintiff, alleging jurisdiction under 18 U.S.C. § 241, 28 U.S.C. § 1343, and 42 U.S.C. § 1983 prays for leave to file a complaint for violation of his civil rights in forma pauperis. He alleges that Satan has on numerous occasions caused plaintiff misery and unwarranted threats, against the will of plaintiff, that Satan has placed deliberate obstacles in his path and has caused plaintiff's downfall. Plaintiff alleges that by reason of these acts Satan has deprived him of his constitutional rights.

We feel that the application to file and proceed in forma pauperis must be denied. Even if plaintiff's complaint reveals a prima facie recital of the infringement of the civil rights of a citizen of the United States, the Court has serious doubts that the complaint reveals a cause of action upon which relief can be granted by the court. We question whether plaintiff may obtain personal jurisdiction over the defendant in this judicial district. The complaint contains no allegation of residence in this district. While the official reports disclose no case where this defendant has appeared as defendant there is an unofficial account of a trial in New Hampshire where this defendant filed an action of mortgage foreclosure as plaintiff.[1] The defendant in that action was represented by the preeminent advocate of that day, and raised the defense that the plaintiff was a foreign prince with no standing to sue in an American Court. This defense was overcome by overwhelming evidence to the contrary. Whether or not this would raise an estoppel in the present case we are unable to determine at this time.

If such action were to be allowed we would also face the question of whether it may be maintained as a class action. It appears to meet the requirements of Fed.R. of Civ.P. 23 that the class is so numerous that joinder of all members is impracticable, there are questions of law and fact common to the class, and the claims of the representative party is typical of the claims of the class. We cannot now determine if the representative party will fairly protect the interests of the class.

We note that the plaintiff has failed to include with his complaint the required form of instructions for the United States Marshal for directions as to service of process.

For the foregoing reasons we must exercise our discretion to refuse the prayer of plaintiff to proceed in forma pauperis.

It is ordered that the complaint be given a miscellaneous docket number and leave to proceed in forma pauperis be denied.

---

[1] [Ed. Note: See "The Devil and Daniel Webster" by Stephen Vincent Benét.]

SEARIGHT v. STATE OF NEW JERSEY
United States District Court, D. New Jersey.
412 F. Supp. 413 (1976)

VINCENT P. BIUNNO, District Judge.

The complaint says that in October, 1962, Searight was taken to the Eye, Ear and Speech Clinic in Newark, while in custody, and that the State of New Jersey there unlawfully injected him in the left eye with a radium electric beam. As a result, he claims that someone now talks to him on the inside of his brain. He asks money damages of $12 million.

The State has moved to dismiss for failure to state a claim, F.R.Civ.P. 12(b)(6), on the ground that it appears from the face of the complaint that the claim, if otherwise valid, is barred by the statute of limitations.

Ordinarily, that bar is a matter to be pleaded as a separate defense, but when the essential facts appear on the face of the pleading, it may be raised by motion as a matter of law as though by demurrer.

The incident is said to have happened in October, 1962, and the complaint was filed in February, 1976. Absent an Act of Congress (there is none), the *lex loci* [law of the place] governs. . . . The applicable New Jersey statute allows 2 years after the cause of action accrues to file suit. N.J.S.A. 2A:14--2. Thus, suit was filed here more than 13 years after the statute had run out.

There is clear ground for dismissal. Yet, because Searight sues pro se, the court ordinarily would direct that judgment of dismissal not be entered within a period of perhaps a month, during which he would be allowed leave to file an amended complaint that surmounts the bar, if he can.

But in this case, the court observes that for other considerations, equally obvious, it lacks jurisdiction to entertain the claim, and so may also dismiss for that reason, F.R.Civ.P. 12(h)(3).

Searight is a citizen of New Jersey, suing his own State; thus, there is no diversity jurisdiction under 28 U.S.C. § 1332, and no suggestion of a federal question appears under 28 U.S.C. § 1331. At the founding of the nation, there was no question that a citizen of New Jersey could not sue that State anywhere because of the doctrine of sovereign immunity. In Chisholm v. Georgia, 2 Dall. 419, 1 L.Ed. 440 (1793), it was ruled that a State could be sued in the courts of the United States by a citizen of another State or of a foreign country. At the first meeting of Congress after that decision, Amendment XI was proposed, almost unanimously, and thereafter adopted. . . .

May the claim be viewed as coming within the civil rights law, 42 U.S.C. § 1983, etc.? Aside from the bar of the statute of limitations, it is clear that it may not. Ordinary tort claims, though cast in terms of civil rights claims, but which do not rise to constitutional levels, are not within the jurisdiction of the district courts. . . .

The allegations, of course, are of facts which, if they exist, are not yet known to man. Just as Mr. Houdini has so far failed to establish communication from the spirit world (See E.L. Doctorow, *"Ragtime,"* pp. 166-169, Random House, 1974), so the decades of scientific experiments and statistical analysis have failed to establish the existence of "extrasensory perception" (ESP). But, taking the facts as pleaded, and assuming them to be true, they show a case of presumably unlicensed radio communication, a matter which comes within the sole jurisdiction of the Federal Communications Commission, 47 U.S.C. § 151, et seq. And even aside from that, Searight could have blocked the broadcast to the antenna in his brain simply by grounding it. See, for example, Ghirardi, *"Modern Radio Servicing,"* First Edition, p. 572, ff. (Radio & Technical Publishing Co., New York, 1935). Just as delivery trucks for oil and gasoline are "grounded" against the accumulation of charges of static electricity, so on the same principle Searight might have pinned to the back of a trouser leg a short chain of paper clips so that the end would touch the ground and prevent anyone from talking to him inside his brain.

But these interesting aspects need not be decided here. It is enough that the bar of the statute of limitations clearly appears from the face of the complaint and independently thereof, that the court lacks jurisdiction. The complaint will be dismissed with prejudice.

McDONALD v. JOHN P. SCRIPPS NEWSPAPER
California Court of Appeal, Second Appellate District
210 Cal. App. 3d 100; 257 Cal. Rptr. 473 (1989)

ARTHUR GILBERT, J.

Question--When should an attorney say "no" to a client? Answer--When asked to file a lawsuit like this one.

Master Gavin L. McDonald did not win the Ventura County Spelling Bee. Therefore, through his guardian ad litem,[1] he sued. Gavin alleges that contest officials improperly allowed the winner of the spelling bee to compete. Gavin claimed that had the officials not violated contest rules, the winner "would not have had the opportunity" to defeat him. The trial court wisely sustained a demurrer to the complaint without leave to amend.

We affirm because two things are missing here--causation and common sense. Gavin lost the spelling bee because he spelled a word wrong. Gavin contends that the winner of the spelling bee should not have been allowed to compete in the contest. Gavin, however, cannot show that but for the contest official's allowing the winner to compete, he would have won the spelling bee.

---

[1] We do not hold Gavin responsible.

In our puzzlement as to how this case even found its way into court, we are reminded of the words of a romantic poet.

> *"The [law] is too much with us; late and soon,*
> *Getting and spending, we lay waste our powers:*
> *Little we see in Nature that is ours;*
> *We have given our hearts away, a sordid boon!"*

(Wordsworth, "The World Is Too Much With Us" (1807), with apologies to William Wordsworth, who we feel, if he were here, would approve.)

FACTS

Gavin was a contestant in the 1987 Scripps Howard National Spelling Bee, sponsored in Ventura County by the newspaper, the Ventura County Star-Free Press. The contest is open to all students through the eighth grade who are under the age of 16. Gavin won competitions at the classroom and school-wide levels. This earned him the chance to compete against other skilled spellers in the county-wide spelling bee. The best speller in the county wins a trip to Washington D.C. and a place in the national finals. The winner of the national finals is declared the national champion speller.

Gavin came in second in the county spelling bee. Being adjudged the second best orthographer in Ventura County is an impressive accomplishment, but pique overcame self-esteem. The spelling contest became a legal contest.

We search in vain through the complaint to find a legal theory to support this metamorphosis. Gavin alleges that two other boys, Stephen Chen and Victor Wang, both of whom attended a different school, also competed in the spelling contest. Stephen had originally lost his school-wide competition to Victor. Stephen was asked to spell the word "horsy." He spelled it "h-o-r-s-e-y." The spelling was ruled incorrect. Victor spelled the same word "h-o-r-s-y." He then spelled another word correctly, and was declared the winner.

Contest officials, who we trust were not copy editors for the newspaper sponsoring the contest, later discovered that there are two proper spelling of the word "horsy," and that Stephen's spelling was correct after all.[2]

Contest officials asked Stephen and Victor to again compete between themselves in order to declare one winner. Victor, having everything to lose by agreeing to this plan, refused. Contest officials decided to allow both Victor and Stephen to advance to the county-wide spelling bee, where Gavin lost to Stephen.

---

[2] [H]orsey also horsy 1: relating to, resembling, or suggestive of a horse 2: addicted to or having to do with horses or horse racing or characteristic of the manners, dress, or tastes of horsemen." (Webster's Third New Internat. Dict. (1961) p. 1093.)

CHAPTER VI: SCHEMES, CLAIMS, & CONTENTIONS

Taking Vince Lombardi's aphorism to heart, "Winning isn't everything, it's the only thing," Gavin filed suit against the Ventura County Star-Free Press and the Scripps Howard National Spelling Bee alleging breach of contract, breach of implied covenant of good faith and fair dealing, and intentional and negligent infliction of emotional distress.

In his complaint, Gavin asserts that contest officials violated spelling bee rules by allowing Stephen Chen to compete at the county level. He suggests that had Stephen not progressed to the county-wide competition, he, Gavin would have won. For this leap of faith he seeks compensatory and punitive damages.

The trial court sustained Scripp's demurrer without leave to amend because the complaint fails to state a cause of action. The action was dismissed, and Gavin appeals.

DISCUSSION

Gavin asserts that he has set forth the necessary elements of a cause of action for breach of contract, and that these elements are: "(1) The contract; (2) Plaintiff's performance; (3) Defendant's breach; (4) Damage to plaintiff. 4 Witkin, California Procedure, Pleading, § 464 (3rd Ed. 1985)."

Gavin's recitation of the law is correct, but his complaint wins no prize. He omitted a single word in the fourth element of an action for breach of contract, which should read "damage to plaintiff therefrom." (Witkin, Cal. Procedure (3d ed. 1985) Pleading, § 464, p. 504, italics added.) Not surprisingly, the outcome of this case depends on that word. A fundamental rule of law is that "whether the action be in tort or contract compensatory damages cannot be recovered unless there is a causal connection between the act or omission complained of and the injury sustained." . . .

The erudite trial judge stated Gavin's shortcoming incisively. "I see a gigantic causation problem...." Relying on the most important resource a judge has, he said, "common sense tells me that this lawsuit is nonsense."

Even if Gavin and Scripps had formed a contract which Scripps breached by allowing Stephen Chen to compete at the county level in violation of contest rules, nothing would change. Gavin cannot show that he was injured by the breach. Gavin lost the spelling bee because he misspelled a word, and it is irrelevant that he was defeated by a contestant who "had no right to advance in the contest."

Gavin argues that had the officials "not violated the rules of the contest, Chen would not have advanced, and would not have had the opportunity to defeat" Gavin. Of course, it is impossible for Gavin to show that he would have spelled the word correctly if Stephen were not his competitor. Gavin concedes as much when he argues that he would not have been damaged if defeated by someone who had properly advanced in the contest. That is precisely the point.

Gavin cannot show that anything would have been different had Stephen not competed against him. Nor can he show that another competitor would have also misspelled that or another word, thus allowing Gavin another opportunity to win. "It is fundamental that damages which are speculative, remote, imaginary, contingent, or merely possible cannot serve as a legal basis for recovery.". . .

Gavin offers to amend the complaint by incorporating certain rules of the spelling bee which purportedly show that the decision to allow Stephen to advance in the competition was procedurally irregular. This offer to amend reflects a misunderstanding of the trial court's ruling. The fatal defect in the complaint is that Gavin cannot show that but for Stephen Chen's presence in the spelling bee, Gavin would have won.

"The general rule is that it is an abuse of discretion to sustain a demurrer without leave to amend unless the complaint shows that it is incapable of amendment. [Citation.] But it is also true that where the nature of plaintiff's claim is clear, but under substantive law no liability exists, leave to amend should be denied, for no amendment could change the result." . . .

The third cause of action, states that plaintiff has suffered humiliation, indignity, mortification, worry, grief, anxiety, fright, mental anguish, and emotional distress, not to mention loss of respect and standing in the community. These terms more appropriately express how attorneys who draft complaints like this should feel.

A judge whose prescience is exceeded only by his eloquence said that "...Courts of Justice do not pretend to furnish cures for all the miseries of human life. They redress or punish gross violations of duty, but they go no farther; they cannot make men virtuous: and, as the happiness of the world depends upon its virtue, there may be much unhappiness in it which human laws cannot undertake to remove." (Evans v. Evans (1790) Consistory Court of London.) Unfortunately, as evidenced by this lawsuit, this cogent insight, although as relevant today as it was nearly 200 years ago, does not always make an impression on today's practitioner.

In Shapiro v. Queens County Jockey Club [citation omitted] plaintiff's horse was the only horse to run the full six furlongs in the sixth race at Aqueduct Race Track after racing officials declared a false start. A half hour later the sixth race was run again, and plaintiff's horse came in fifth out of a total of six.

The Shapiro court held that plaintiff had no cause of action against the race track. Plaintiff could not support the theory that his horse would have won the second time around if all the other horses had also run the six furlongs after the false start. Plaintiff was not content to merely chalk up his loss to a bad break caused by the vicissitudes of life. The lesson to be learned is that all of us, like high-strung horses at the starting gate, are subject to life's false starts. The courts cannot erase the world's imperfections.

The Georgia Supreme Court in Georgia High School Ass'n v. Waddell [citation omitted], decided it was without authority to review the decision of a football referee regarding the outcome of the game. The court stated that the referee's decision did not present a justiciable controversy. Nor does the decision of the spelling bee officials present a justiciable controversy here.

Our decision at least keeps plaintiff's bucket of water from being added to the tidal wave of litigation that has engulfed our courts.[3]

Sanctions--A close call

Causation has been counsel's nemesis. Its absence makes Gavin's quest for "justice" an illusory one. The lack of causation in the complaint is the cause for dismissal of the complaint. Counsel could not show us or the trial court how an amendment could cure the complaint. The lesson should have been learned at the trial court. As the law disregards trifles (Civ. Code. § 3533), so, too, one should not trifle with the Court of Appeal. The filing of an appeal here, for a case so trivial, and so lacking in merit, makes it a likely candidate for sanctions.

To counsel's credit, we are convinced that he did not prosecute this appeal for an improper motive or to delay the effect of an adverse judgment. He, therefore, at least avoids two criteria set forth in In re Marriage of Flaherty [citation omitted]. This case, however, lacks merit, and we cannot conceive of a reasonable attorney who would disagree with this appraisal.

Falling within a criterion of Flaherty, however, does not in and of itself compel sanctions. The Flaherty court warned that "any definition must be read so as to avoid a serious chilling effect on the assertion of litigants' rights on appeal....An appeal that is simply without merit is not by definition frivolous and should not incur sanctions. Counsel should not be deterred from filing such appeals out of a fear of reprisals." . . .

It is creative and energetic counsel who from time to time challenge existing law and question past policies. This insures that the law be a living and dynamic force. Although noble aims were not advanced here, we are mindful of the caution in Flaherty that the borderline between appeals that are frivolous and those that simply have no merit is vague, and that punishment should be used sparingly "to deter only the most egregious conduct." . . . We therefore decline to impose sanctions, but we hope this opinion will serve as a warning notice for counsel to be discerning when drawing the line between making new law or wasting everyone's time.

---

[3] Judge Irving Kaufman of the Second Circuit Court of Appeals, in a speech, has spoken of the alarming tidal wave of litigation in this country that shows no signs of abatement. (Cherna v. Cherna (Fla Dist. Ct. App. 1983) 427 So.2d 395, 396, fn.2.)

Advice to Gavin and An Aphorism or Two

Gavin has much to be proud of. He participated in a spelling bee that challenged the powers of memory and concentration. He met the challenge well but lost out to another contestant. Gavin took first in his school and can be justifiably proud of his performance.

It is this lawsuit that is trivial, not his achievement. Our courts try to give redress for real harms; they cannot offer palliatives for imagined injuries.

Vince Lombardi may have had a point, but so did Grantland Rice--It is "not that you won or lost--but how you played the game".

As for the judgment of the trial court, we'll spell it out. A-F-I-R-M-E-D [sic]. Appellant is to pay respondent's costs on appeal.

KENT © NORMAN v. REAGAN
United States District Court, D. Oregon.
95 F.R.D. 476 (1982)

JAMES A. REDDEN, District Judge

In this action, Kent © Norman [1] seeks redress of grievances. I previously dismissed the action as frivolous, see Bell v. Hood, 327 U.S. 678, 682-3, 66 S.Ct. 773, 776, 90 L.Ed. 939 (1946). A panel of the Ninth Circuit disagreed and reversed. A brief summary of the contents of this file may be helpful in understanding my present decision to dismiss this case for lack of prosecution.

There are numerous defendants and claims. The first defendant appears to be Ronald Reagan, who, in terms of the plaintiff's "amendment complaint," has caused the plaintiff great vexation:

> Plaintiff alleges that defendant Reagan has acted with deliberate, reckless, and nefarious disregard of his constitutional rights, in this, to wit:
>
> 1) Defendant caused "civil death" without legislation.
>
> 2) Defendant allowed plaintiff to suffer irrepairable [sic] harm and neglect.
>
> 3) Defendant has acted with redundance and malicious conduct in neglecting plaintiff.

---

[1] The plaintiff's name apparently includes the copyright sign.

4) Defendant allowed numerous abuses of plaintiff's person, property, and liberty while governor of California and president.

5) Defendant Reagan has deprived plaintiff of his right to vote and caused, either directly or indirectly, arrests upon false, incorrect, or misleading information.

6) Plaintiff has no adequate remedy at law to redress these wrongs without due course of process.

There are also a number of parking tickets in the file. The plaintiff apparently demands a jury trial in federal court for the parking fines assessed by Multnomah County. The plaintiff also seeks an order requiring the Interstate Commerce Commission to investigate White Line Fevers From Mars, which is succinctly referred to elsewhere in the file as "W.L.F.F.M." This defendant is not, despite the name, of genuine extraterrestrial origin, but is apparently a fruit company which shipped marijuana and cocaine in "fruit boxes" for Mother's Day. The plaintiff's trucking license was suspended by the Interstate Commerce Commission as a result of some incident involving the plaintiff's transportation of White Line Fevers' fruit boxes. Plaintiff also seeks Supplemental Security Income (SSI) payments, apparently as a result of this incident, and punitive damages against Reagan and the Secretary of the Treasury for withholding of the SSI payments.

There are also certain other claims which the court is at a loss to characterize, and can only describe. There is included in the file a process receipt which bears the "Received" stamp of the Supreme Court of the United States. On this form are the notations, apparently written by the plaintiff, "Taxes due" and "D.C. Circuit was green" as well as "Rule 8... Why did you return my appeal form? Why isn't the '1840' W. 7th mailbox still next to the 1830 one?" and "something suspicious about that mailbox." There are also other notations on the form.

There is also the following "claim":

> The birds today
> Are singing loudly,
> The day is fresh
> With the sounds
> Upon the wind
> The crickets.
> The blackbirds
> The woodpeckers

Beauty in every
Spark of life
Just So their sounds
Are appreciated
Their sounds are beauty
The ants are silent
But always searching
The birds noise a song
and the fade of the automobile tires
Chirp. A shadow from
a passing monarch butterfly
Breathless in Colorado.

Kent © Norman
1981

It is possible, of course, that this is not intended as a claim at all, but as a literary artifact. However it may be that, liberally construed, the references to the birds, crickets, ants, and butterfly could constitute a Bivens claim. See Bivens v. Six Unknown-Named Agents, 403 U.S. 388, 91 S.Ct. 1999, 29 L.Ed.2d 619 (1971); U.S. ex rel. Mayo v. Satan and His Staff, 54 F.R.D. 282 (W.D. Penn. 1971).

At any rate, following the Ninth Circuit's remand the marshals attempted to serve the President and the other defendants. The plaintiff, however, seems to have lost touch with the court, or lost interest, or both. Since the receipt of the remand in the district court on March 1, 1982, he has taken no action on the case. Mail addressed to him is returned. The discovery deadline and Pre-trial Order deadline have passed, without any response to the court's notifications to the plaintiff. Perhaps the plaintiff has elected to pursue his remedies in some more convenient forum. I therefore DISMISS this action for want of prosecution.

HALL v. HALL
High Court of Chancery
21 E.R. 447; Dick. 710 (1788)

[EDWARD THURLOW, Chancellor]
Reprisal was said by Lord Thurlow, C., to be a common drawback.[1]

---

[1] [Ed. Note: This is the entire opinion.]

HAYNES v. ANNANDALE GOLF CLUB
Supreme Court of California
4 C.2d 28; 47 P.2d 470 (1935)

JOHN W. PRESTON, Justice

This action is by a golfer against his club for declaratory relief. He wishes to resign as a member of the club and be allowed to go in peace, after paying all obligations levied against him and turning in his certificate of membership properly indorsed. Doubtless this is the only case in history where a golf club has failed to heed the plaintiff cry of one of its flock. And the court below indorsed its action by refusing to say that plaintiff was entitled to any balm at all. The judgment of the court was that he was "stymied" and must so remain forever and aye unless perchance the board of directors might experience a change of heart and vote him a furlough. Hence this appeal upon an agreed statement of facts.

We must review the action in a manner becoming the importance of the issue and the prominence of the litigants. Plaintiff fails to appreciate the implied compliment to him in defendant's desire to retain him as a member. But the record pointedly suggests that plaintiff in the "twilight dim" is bridging this chasm "dark and grim" for some "forlorn" or "shipwrecked" brother who may follow after him. Defendant insists that unless and until it changes its mind and consents to plaintiff's release, and follows it by a suitable entry in its book of life, plaintiff must gracefully submit and continue to "roll in the fiery gulf." However, when we consult the statute under which defendant is organized, we are forced to hold that it requires defendant to provide a way of escape for members, imposing only such restrictions upon the right of resignations as may be just and reasonable.

Defendant was organized in 1916 as a nonprofit corporation under title 22, part 4, division 1 of the Civil Code (section 653t et seq.). Later in the same year plaintiff became a regular member of defendant corporation and continued as such until September 18, 1931, on which date he paid all dues and assessments against him, indorsed his certificate of membership in blank, and tendered it, along with his written resignation, to the club. Defendant, acting through its board of directors, declined to release him, relying upon a bylaw which reads: "The resignation of any member shall be made in writing addressed to the Board of Directors. No resignation of a member shall be effective until accepted by the Board of Directors, nor shall the same be accepted while such member is in anywise indebted to the Club nor until he has assigned and delivered his certificate of membership. Until the transfer of the certificate of membership on the books of the corporation, or until the date of the expulsion of a member, the record owner of each membership shall be and remain liable for all dues, fees or other charges which have accrued or which may thereafter accrue.

... Paragraphs 4 and 5 of section 598 state that the by-laws of a nonprofit corporation, such as respondent club, may contain provisions for "the admission, election, appointment, withdrawal, suspension and expulsion of members" and for "the transfer, forfeiture and termination of membership. * * *" Section 602 in part provides: "Memberships may be terminated in the manner provided in the articles or by-laws."

By paying the dues and turning in his certificate, plaintiff did every substantial thing required by the by-law. For defendant to hold him as a perpetual member on its mere fancy or caprice would be obnoxious to the spirit as well as to the clear meaning of the statute. The contention that an assignment of a new candidate for membership is required by the by-law is clearly untenable. An indorsement of the certificate and delivery thereof to the club satisfies the provision of the by-law on that subject.

So much of said by-law as allows defendant to deny the right of resignation on the ground that it has merely withheld its consent or has declined to make the necessary book entries is invalid because unreasonable and arbitrary.

The judgment is reversed and the cause remanded for proceedings not inconsistent with this holding.

THE BILL AYENST CONJURACONS & WICHECRAFTES AND SORCERY AND ENCHANTMENTS
Statutes of the Realm of England
33 Henry VIII, Ch. 8 (1541)

WHERE dyvers and sundrie persones unlawfully have devised and practised Invocacons and conjuracons of Sprites, pretendyng by suche meanes to understande and get Knowlege for their owne lucre in what place treasure of golde and Silver shulde or mought be founde or had in the earthe or other secrete places, and also have used and occupied wichecraftes inchauntemen's and sorceries to the distruccon of their neighbours persones and goodes, And for execucon of their saide falce devyses and practises have made or caused to be made dyvers Images and pictures of men women childrene Angelles or develles beastes or fowles, and also have made Crownes Septures Swordes rynges glasses and other thinges, and gyving faithe & credit to suche fantasticall practises have dygged up and pulled downe an infinite nombre of Crosses w'in this Realme, and taken upon them to declare and tell where thinges lost or stollen shulde be bec me; whiche thinges cannot be used and exercised but to the great Offence of Godes lawe, hurt and damage of the Kinges Subjectes, and loss of the sowles of suche Offenders, to the greate dishono' of God, Infamy and disquyetnes of the Realme:

FOR REFORMACON wherof be it enacted by the Kyng oure Soveraigne Lorde w' thassent of the Lordes spirituall and temporall and the Comons in this present Parliament assembled and by auctoritie of the same, that yf any persone or persones, after the first day of May next comyng, use devise practise or exercise, or cause to be used devysed practised or exercised, any Invocacons or conjuracons of Sprites wichecraftes enchauntmentes or sorceries, to thentent to get or fynde money or treasure, or to waste consume or destroy any persone in his bodie membres or goodes, or to pervoke any persone to unlawfull love, or for any other unlawfull intente or purpose, or by occacon or color of suche thinges or any of them, or for dispite of Cryste, or for lucre of money, dygge up or pull downe any Crosse or Crosses, or by suche Invocacons or conjuracons of Sprites wichecraftes enchauntementes or sorcerie or any of them take upon them to tell or declare where goodes stollen or lost shall become, That then all and every suche Offence and Offences, frome the saide first day of May next comyng, shalbe demyde accepted and adjuged Felonye; And that all and every persone and persones offendyng as is abovesaide their Councellors Abettors and Procuros and every of them from the saide first day of Maye shalbe demyde accepted and adjuged a Felon and Felones; And thoffender and Offenders contrarie to this Acte, being therof lawfullie convicte before suche as shall have power and auctoritie to here and determyn felonyes, shall have and suffre suche paynes of deathe losse and forfaytures of their landes tenants goodes and Catalles as in cases of felonie by the course of the Common lawes of this Realme, And also shall lose pivilege of Clergie and Sayntuarie.

ORESTE LODI, REVERSIONER v. ORESTE LODI, BENEFICIARY
Court of Appeal of California, Third Appellate District
173 Cal. App. 3d 628; 219 Cal. Rptr. 117 (1985)

RICHARD M. SIMMS, III, Associate Justice.

This case started when plaintiff Oreste Lodi sued himself in the Shasta County Superior Court.

In a complaint styled "Action to Quiet Title Equity," plaintiff named himself, under the title "Oreste Lodi, Beneficiary," as defendant. The pleading alleges that defendant Lodi is the beneficiary of a charitable trust, the estate of which would revert to plaintiff Lodi, as "Reversioner," upon notice. Plaintiff attached as Exhibit A to his complaint, a copy of his 1923 New York birth certificate, which he asserts is the "certificate of power of appointment and conveyance" transferring reversioner's estate to the charitable trust. Plaintiff Lodi goes on to allege that for 61 years (i.e., since plaintiff/defendant was born), defendant has controlled the estate, that plaintiff has notified defendant of the termination of the trust by a written "Revocation of all Power" (which apparently seeks to revoke his birth certificate), but that defendant "intentionally persist [sic] to control said estate . . . " Plaintiff requested an order that he is absolutely entitled to possession of the estate, and terminating all claims against the estate by any and all persons "claiming" under defendant.[1]

---

[1] The purpose of plaintiff's action is not entirely clear. However, we note plaintiff caused a complimentary copy of his complaint to be served upon the Internal Revenue Service. It may be that plaintiff hoped to obtain a state court judgment that, he thought, would be of advantage to him under the Internal Revenue Code.

The complaint was duly served by plaintiff Lodi, as "Reversioner," upon himself as defendant/beneficiary. When defendant/beneficiary Lodi failed to answer, plaintiff/reversioner Lodi had a clerk's default entered and thereafter requested entry of a default judgment. At the hearing on the entry of a default judgment, the superior court denied the request to enter judgment and dismissed the complaint.[2]

In this court, appellant and respondent are the same person.[3] Each party has filed a brief.

The only question presented is whether the trial court properly dismissed the complaint even though no party sought dismissal or objected to entry of judgment as requested.

As is obvious, the complaint states no cognizable claim for relief. Plaintiff's birth certificate did not create a charitable trust; consequently, there was no trust which could be terminated by notice. In the arena of pleadings, the one at issue here is a slam-dunk frivolous complaint.

We conclude the trial court was empowered to strike or dismiss the complaint by section 436 of the Code of Civil Procedure[4] which provides in pertinent part: "The court may, upon a motion . . . or at any time in its discretion, and upon terms it deems proper . . . [¶] (b) Strike out all or any part of any pleading not drawn or filed in conformity with the laws of the state, a court rule, or an order of the court."

Section 425.10 provides in pertinent part: "A complaint . . . shall contain . . . the following: [¶] A statement of the facts constituting the cause of action, in ordinary and concise language."

Discussing the notion of a "cause of action," Witkin writes: "California follows the 'primary right theory' of Pomeroy: 'Every judicial action must therefore involve the following elements: a primary right possessed by the plaintiff, and a corresponding primary duty devolving upon the defendant, a delict or wrong done by the defendant which consisted in a breach of such primary right and duty; a remedial right in favor of the plaintiff, and a remedial duty resting on the defendant springing from this delict, and finally the remedy or relief itself . . . Of these elements, the primary right and duty and the delict or wrong combined constitute the cause of action . . . [T]he existence of a legal right in an abstract form is never alleged by the plaintiff; but, instead thereof, the facts from which that right arises are set forth, and the right itself is inferred therefrom. The cause of action, as it appears in the complaint when properly pleaded, will therefore always be the facts from which the plaintiff's primary right and the defendant's corre-

---

[2] The minute order indicates that the court also suggested to plaintiff/reversioner/defendant/beneficiary that he seek the assistance of legal counsel.

[3] Plaintiff/reversioner filed a notice of appeal from the order of dismissal. No judgment was entered. However, in the interest of judicial economy, we treat the notice of appeal as one from the judgment. (Cal. Rules of Court, rule 2(c).)

[4] All further statutory references are to this code.

sponding primary duty have arisen, together with the facts which constitute the defendant's delict or act of wrong.' " (4 Witkin, Cal.Procedure (3d ed. 1985) Pleading, § 23, pp. 66-67, quoting Pomeroy, Code Remedies (5th ed.) p. 528, emphasis in original.)

Here, plaintiff's complaint fails to state facts showing a primary right by plaintiff or a primary duty devolving on defendant or a wrong done by defendant. The complaint therefore fails to state facts constituting a cause of action as required by section 425.10. Consequently, the complaint was not drawn in conformity with the laws of this state and was thus properly subject to the court's own motion to strike under section 436, subdivision (b).

We need not consider whether the court's power under this statute should be exercised where plaintiff seeks leave to amend. Here, so far as the record before us shows, plaintiff made no such request nor is any prospect of saving the pleading by amendment apparent. The trial court therefore properly struck and dismissed the complaint on its own motion. (§ 436, subd. (b).)

In the circumstances, this result cannot be unfair to Mr. Lodi. Although it is true that, as plaintiff and appellant, he loses, it is equally true, as defendant and respondent, he wins! It is hard to imagine a more even-handed application of justice. Truly, it would appear that Oreste Lodi is that rare litigant who is assured of both victory and defeat regardless of which side triumphs.

We have considered whether respondent/defendant/beneficiary should be awarded costs of suit on appeal, which he could thereafter recover from himself. However, we believe the equities are better served by requiring each party to bear his own costs on appeal.

The appeal is dismissed. Each party shall bear his own costs.

IN RE EMMANUEL BARRETTA
Justice Court of California, Tuolomne County
Case No. 998 (1851)

R. C. BARRY, Justice Peace

Having investigated the caze where in Emmanuel Barretta has been charged by an old woman Maria Toja with having abstracted a box of munney which was burried in the ground, jointly belonging to her self and daughter, and carrying it or its contents away from her dwelling and appropriating it the same to his owne use and beniffit the supposed amount being over too hundred dolars but faleing to prove positively that it contaned more than 20 dolars and proven by testimony of his owne acknowledgement the caze being so at varriance with the common dictates of hoomanity and having been done under verry paneful surcumstances at the time when the yung woman was about to close her existance the day before she died and her aged muther at the same time lying upon a bead of sickness unable to rise or to get a morsel of food for herself and he at the time presenting his self as an Angel of Releaf to the poor and destitute sick when 20 poor dolars might have releaved the emejate needsessities of the poor infeabled sick and destitute old woman far from hoam and frends calls imperitively for a severe rebuk and rep remand for sutch inhuman and unpresedented conduct as also the needsesity of binding him over to the Court of Sessions in the sum of $500.00.

Costs of Court $40.

Sonora City, Nov. 10, 1851
John Luney, Constable

CLEGG v. HARDWARE MUTUAL CASUALTY COMPANY
United States Court of Appeals, Fifth Circuit.
264 F.2d 152 (1959)

JOHN R. BROWN, Circuit Judge.

The jury found for the defendant. The plaintiff, Clegg, appealing here, asserts that this resulted from the unexpected use by the Judge of a jury verdict in the form of three questions. In proof of it, plaintiff points out that the Insurer's defense contented itself with testimony of a single witness, the truck driver, who virtually swore the defendant into liability, and the cross examination of plaintiff's witnesses, several of whom were psychiatrists. The Insurer refutes both the claim of error and the asserted cause of the adverse verdict. On the latter, it says that the jury rejected the plaintiff's thesis because it was patently unacceptable to thinking jurors. The Insurer describes the claim as bizarre. If it is not that, it is an understatement to call it anything less than unique.

The Insurer's truck, southbound on Airline Highway near Norco, Louisiana, suddenly swerved onto its right shoulder to avoid hitting school children alighting from a northbound school bus. The truck hit and smashed several cars and ran into gasoline pumps of a roadside filling station causing fire and widespread destruction. Clegg, of Baton Rouge, was standing nearby. He was not physically injured. He was not touched in any way by anything. What happened to him, he said, was that on seeing this holocaust and the need for someone to rush in to help rescue victims, he suddenly became overwhelmed by fear and realized for the first time in his life that he was not the omnipotent, fearless man his psyche had envisioned him to be. His post-accident awareness that this event had destroyed his self-deceptive image of himself precipitated great emotional and psychic tensions manifesting themselves as psychosomatic headaches, pain in legs and neck, a loss of general interest, a disposition to withdraw from social and family contacts, and the like.

CHAPTER VI: SCHEMES, CLAIMS, & CONTENTIONS

As it might have appeared to the jury of lay persons, the medical theory was that the accident had made Clegg see himself as he really was, not as Clegg had thought himself to be. In short, the accident had destroyed the myth. No longer was he the brave invincible man. Now, as any other, he was a mere human, with defects and limitations and a faint heart. It was, so the Insurer argued with plausibility to the jury, the strange case of a defendant being asked to pay for having helped Clegg by bringing him back to reality — helping him, as it were, to leave Mount Olympus to rejoin the other mortals in Baton Rouge.

To this elusive excursion into the id of Clegg, there were added many irrefutable earth-bound events that made it sound all the more strange. At the time of the accident, Clegg was a TV advertising salesman. Within a short space of time, he had changed employment. He became president of a company, in which he was apparently personally interested, at a salary over twice as high as he had previously earned. He bought and sold several pieces of real estate, had made $25,000 in one trade, and had purchased and moved into a new $40,000 home. Within nine months of the accident he had successfully undertaken a campaign to become elected a city Councilman of Baton Rouge. The psychiatrists, acknowledging these external facts, then reasoned that this was a part of his struggle by which to recapture his lost self esteem, and that while these things were most assuredly being accomplished, it was being done at further damage to Clegg.

We have mentioned this briefly not to disparage the claim or intimate its insufficiency or sufficiency as a matter of law. The jury verdict has relieved us of the necessity of passing judgment on the inherent merits. The District Court submitted it as one under the Louisiana doctrine allowing recovery for emotional damages even though unaccompanied by physical injury. . . .

The medical thesis was advanced with great earnestness by two psychiatrists, both of whom were apparently well regarded in the medical community. So for our purposes here we may assume that on a proper showing of facts, or medical facts, or accepted medical theory as fact, the law may accommodate Blackstone and Freud to allow recovery for real psychic or psychosomatic harm. Rather, we have dwelt at some length on this phase of the case because it was, after all, a medical theory which we may assume arguendo the jury could have credited but was not compelled to. More important, it is against this background that the very narrow claim of error and harmful effect must be judged.

The Court gave a long and detailed general charge covering sixteen pages of the record. It covered the usual matters such as credibility, fact-finding function of the jury, principles of negligence law, due care, proximate cause, elements of damages, and was generally indistinguishable from the many general charges which Louisiana Federal Judges on their common law oasis in the midst of a civil law system, have to give in these direct action cases. No exception was taken to any substantive instruction on the governing principles of law.

Toward the end of the charge, the Court stated that the jury should return its verdict by answers to the three questions stated in a form of verdict to be furnished inquiring whether (1) the truck driver was negligent, (2) such negligence was the proximate cause of damage and (3) the dollar amount of damages.[1] The charge carefully instructed the jury as to the legal principles to be followed in answering the questions. Not a single exception was taken to these instructions. Nor was there any exception that the charge did not adequately inform the jury how the questions were to be handled either mechanically or in the application of the legal principles so thoroughly elaborated.

The sole claim[2] made is that the Court should not have used the three special questions and that, on the contrary, the Court should have used the traditional general verdict form which impliedly carries two[3] questions.

Of course this able and widely-experienced advocate is too well informed to suggest that a Federal Court in a damage suit must give a general charge. His brief recognizes, as it must, that we and others have many times pointed out that whether the verdict is to be one on a general charge or by special questions, or a blend of both under F.R.Civ.P. 49, 28 U.S.C.A., is a matter left to the sound discretion of the Trial Court. . . .

---

[1] The form of the verdict with the answers given by the jury was as follows:

		Jury Answer
(1)	Was the driver of the [insured] truck guilty of negligence? If your answer to number one is the affirmative, answer question number two:	Yes
(2)	Was the negligence of the driver of the * * * truck the proximate cause of damage to the plaintiff? If your answer to question number two is the affirmative, answer number three:	No
(3)	What amount do you find to be just and adequate compensation for the damages sustained by the plaintiff?	[Not answered]

[2] "Mr. Brumfield [plaintiff's counsel]:

"May it please Your Honor, I object to the form which you submitted this case to the jury, particularly the method of using interrogatories for the jury to answer. It is plaintiff's position that the case should have been submitted to the jury and they were advised that they could bring in a general verdict either for the plaintiff or for the defendant without answering specific interrogatories."

[3] On the usual form a general verdict divides itself up along these lines:

We the jury:

[1] Find for the . . . .
　　　　　　　　(Plaintiff or Defendant)
　　　　　　　　　　AND
[2] Find damages in the sum of $. . . . .
　　　　. . . . .
　　　　　　　Foreman

On the hearing of the motion for new trial, in response to the inquiries from the Court on how the three questions could have adversely affected plaintiff, counsel stated that had intended use of them been known in advance, "we would have had an opportunity to maybe suggest or present counterproposals in those interrogatories for the Court to submit." But except for the deficiency or error in question 2, note 1, supra, . . . neither on brief nor argument before us, does the plaintiff ever point out what the added questions might have been or how these would have been restated or modified.

As the matter goes to the assurance of a trial of substantial fairness, not technical perfection, the nature and time of the indication which the Court should give counsel, and the showing of harm from any supposed dereliction must be measured likewise in the same light of substantial justice. F.R.Civ.P. 61. If done here, the plaintiff can show no real error or harm.

In this analysis, it is unnecessary to try to catalogue this charge and verdict as a general one, a special issue verdict under Rule 49(a), a general one with special questions under 49(b), or an adaptation of both under 49(a) which provides that the Court "* * * may use such other method of submitting the issues and requiring the written findings thereon as it deems most appropriate." It is immaterial because a consideration of this whole record, the charge as a whole, and the arguments of counsel themselves comprising thirty-two pages of the record, reflects that at this stage of the trial, Court and counsel were concerned with three matters and three matters only. First, there was the negligence of the truck driver. This was scarcely debated since it seemed self-evident, as the jury later found, that he was.

The real controversy raged over the question whether Clegg had really suffered any damage at all. The plaintiff said he was worse off and that this episode had triggered this psychic mechanism. The Insurer, just as stoutly, claimed that Clegg was better, not worse, off, and that it was simply absurd to say that a truck owner should be held responsible for any such farfetched consequences. This was the issue, then, of proximate cause.

Finally, there was the question of the money award to compensate for the damages if any were found. From Clegg's standpoint, this ranged from some nineteen hundred dollars covering numerous small items of medical, psychiatric, hospital bills, and car rental to a demand for seventy-five thousand to two-hundred fifty thousand dollars for mental pain and anguish. To the Insurer the amount was zero.

These were the precise questions, in that very order, which counsel argued vehemently. These were the precise questions, in that very order, which the Court asked the jury to answer. Indeed, to read the arguments now, it is almost as though each had been advised specifically that these very questions would be put. Moreover, these are the very precise questions which the jury would have to answer under the same general principles stated to them had the verdict form been the traditional one, see note 3, supra.

... To resolve this elusive and abstruse medico-psychic debate was, as plaintiff's counsel put it, "the function of the jury." To this the District Court responded "Well, they functioned." And since no error is found and the verdict is binding on all, including this Court, we may conclude that the Court below had the prerogative to say that "They functioned right."

Affirmed.

BROWN v. SCHEOPH
Justice Court of California, Tuolomne County
Case No. 39 (1850)

R. C. BARRY, Justice Peace

This was a case in which John Brown brought sute to recover from E. Scheoph one goold watch, and 2 goold wrings of the valee of about 250 dolars. After hearing the evidence in the caze I adjeudged that Brown was trying to swindle Mr. Scheoph. I therefore dismissed the case and found 50 dolars which not having I caused him to be taken to jail until he paid.

Costs of Court $40, 20 of which Mr. Scheoph pade.

May 31, 1850
U. H. Brown, acting Constable.

THE PEOPLE OF CALIFORNIA v. GLEGHORN
California Court of Appeal, Second Appellate District
193 Cal. App. 3d 196; 238 Cal. Rptr. 82 (1987)

May a person who enters the habitat of another at 3 o'clock in the morning for the announced purpose of killing him, and who commences to beat the startled sleeper's bed with a stick and set fires under him be entitled to use deadly force in self defense after the intended victim shoots him in the back with an arrow? Upon the basis of these bizarre facts, we hold that he may not, and instead, must suffer the slings and arrows of outrageous fortune (with apologies to William Shakespeare and Hamlet, Act III, sc. 1).

Kelsey Dru Gleghorn appeals his conviction by jury of one count of simple assault (Pen. Code, § 240) and one count of battery with the infliction of serious bodily injury (Pen. Code, § 243, subd.(d)). He contends the trial court erred in denying his motion for mistrial based on his allegation of inconsistent verdicts and insufficient evidence to support the conviction on count II and erred in instructing the jury pursuant to CALJIC 5.42. We find no error and affirm the judgment.

CHAPTER VI: SCHEMES, CLAIMS, & CONTENTIONS

FACTS

This case is a parable of the dangers of weaponry in the hands of unreasonable powers who become unduly provoked over minor irritations. Melody Downes shared her house with several persons, including appellant. She rented her garage to Michael Fairall for $150 per month. She believed he was to give her a stereo as part of the rent. He believed her intent was only to borrow it. He asked for the return of the stereo; she said she sold it.

Fairall, a man of obvious sensitivity, smashed all the windows of her automobile, slashed the tires, and dented the body. Not quite mollified, he kicked in her locked door, scattered her belongings in the bedroom, and broke an aquarium freeing her snake. (It was scotched, not killed. See Macbeth, W. Shakespeare.)

Ms. Downes advised appellant of Fairall's behavior, he apparently took umbrage. On the fateful night in question, Fairall, having quaffed a few went to the garage he called home and then to bed, a mattress laid upon a lofty perch in the rafters. He was rudely awakened by a pounding on the garage door accompanied by appellant's request that he come out so that appellant might kill him. Fairall wisely advised him that they could exchange pleasantries in the morning.

Undeterred, appellant opened the garage door, entered with stick in hand and began beating on the rafters, yelling for Fairall to come down. In the darkness, Fairall claimed he could see sparks where the board hit the rafters. Appellant said that if Fairall did not come down, he would burn him out. No sooner said than done, appellant set a small fire to some of Fairall's clothes.

Fairall, who happened to have secreted a bow and quiver of arrows in the rafters to prevent its theft, loosed one but did not see where it landed.[1] Fairall, abandoning his weapons, swung down from the rafters and was immediately hit from behind. He yelled for someone to bring a hose and attempted to extinguish the fire with his hands.

Meanwhile, appellant, in an ill humor from the gash in his back caused by the arrow, continued to beat him, causing a two-inch-wide vertical break in Fairall's lower jaw, tearing his lips, knocking out 6 to 10 teeth, mangling two fingers, and lacerating his arm, stomach and back. Fairall also suffered burns on the palms of his hands.

Fairall testified under a grant of immunity given concerning the vandalism of the car.

---

[1] I shot an arrow into the air, it fell to earth, I knew not where. (The Arrow and the Song, Henry Wadsworth Longfellow.) In this case, appellant learned where it had landed — in his back.

DISCUSSION

1. Verdicts Not Inconsistent.

The jury returned verdicts of guilty of simple assault as a lesser included offense of assault by means of force likely to incur great bodily injury (Pen. Code, § 245, subd. (a)(1)) on count I and of battery with the infliction of serious bodily injury on count II. Appellant moved for a new trial (Pen. Code, § 1181) on grounds that the verdicts were contrary to the law or evidence. He contends that since the jury found his acts prior to being shot constituted only simple assault, Fairall was not justified in replying with deadly force. Since the victim responded with deadly force, he continues he could not be convicted of battery with the infliction of serious bodily injury.

Not every assault gives rise to the right to kill in self-defense. Penal Code section 197 explains when homicide is justifiable, i.e., "2. When committed in defense of habitation, property, or person, against one who manifestly intends or endeavors, by violence or surprise, to commit a felony, or against one who manifestly intends and endeavors, in a violent, riotous or tumultuous manner, to enter the habitation of another for the purpose of offering violence to any person therein; or, [¶]3.. . . when there is reasonable ground to apprehend a design to commit a felony or to do some great bodily injury and imminent danger of such design being accomplished . . . " However, to repel a slight assault, the person assaulted is not authorized to resort to unduly violent measures. [citation omitted]

Generally, if one makes a felonious assault upon another, or has created appearances justifying the other to launch a deadly counter attack in self-defense, the original assailant cannot slay his adversary in self-defense unless he has first, in good faith, declined further combat, and has fairly notified him that he has abandoned the affray. [citation omitted] However, when the victim of simple assault responds in a sudden and deadly counter assault the original aggressor need not attempt to withdraw and may use reasonably necessary force in self-defence. [citation omitted]

Appellant contends that, since he initially committed only a simple assault, he was legally justified as a matter of law in standing his ground even though he was the initial attacker, and in utilizing lethal force against Fairall. He asserts that the jury did not follow special instruction number, 5 which stated: "Where the original aggressor is not guilty of a deadly attack but of a simple assault or trespass, the person assaulted has no right to use deadly or other excessive force. [¶] And, where the counter assault is so sudden and perilous that no opportunity be given to decline further to fight and he cannot retreat with safety, he is justified in slaying in self-defense."

We disagree both with appellant's conclusion that there is no evidence to support the verdict on count II and that the verdict on count II is, as a matter of law, inconsistent with the jury's verdict on count I. . .

The right of self-defense is based upon the appearance of imminent peril to the person attacked. [citation omitted] The right to defend one's person or home with deadly force depends upon the circumstances as they reasonably appeared to that person. [citation omitted] That right cannot depend upon the appellant's supposedly non-felonious secret intent. [citation omitted] Similarly, justification does not depend upon the existence of actual danger but rather upon appearances, i.e., if a reasonable person would be placed in fear for his or her safety, and defendant acted out of that fear. [citation omitted]

Moreover, even though a person is mistaken in judgment as to the actual necessity for use of extreme measures, if he was misled through no fault of carelessness on his part and defends himself correctly according to what he supposed the facts to be, his act is justifiable. [citation omitted.] These are usually questions of fact for the jury to resolve. [citation omitted.] It is beyond the province of this court to reweigh the evidence. [citation omitted.] We will not reverse a jury's verdict simply because the evidence might support a contrary conclusion so long as the circumstances reasonably justify the findings. [citation omitted.]

Here, the jury could reasonably infer from the evidence that: (1) Fairall acted reasonably upon the appearances that his life was in danger of (2) even if Fairall acted unreasonably in shooting appellant with the arrow and appellant was justified in responding with deadly force, appellant continued to beat his attacker long after the attacker was disabled. If a person attacked defends himself so successfully that his attacker is rendered incapable of inflicting injury, or for any other reason the danger no longer exists, there is no justification for further retaliation.

The evidence supports a finding that Fairall did not threaten or take any action against appellant after Fairall descended from the loft. On the other hand, if the jury found, as it could have, that Fairall was justified in reasonably fearing for his life on the appearances of appellant's actions, appellant never obtained the right of self-defense in the first place. We find no error. . .

The judgment is affirmed.

ELLIS v. NEWBROUGH
Supreme Court of New Mexico
6 N.M. 181; 27 P. 490 (1891)

ALFRED A. FREEMAN, J.

This is a most extraordinary proceeding. So far as we have been enabled to extend our researches, it is without a precedent. It comes to us by appeal from a judgment of the district court for Dona Ana county, refusing to set aside a verdict of a jury in favor of the appellee. It is an action of trespass on the case.

The declaration sets out substantially the following cause of action, viz.: That, at the time of the committing of the grievances that the plaintiff complains of the defendants were engaged "in organizing and establishing a community called 'Faithists;'" and, being so engaged, the defendants heretofore, to-wit, about the years 1881, 1883, and 1884, wrongfully and corruptly contriving and intending to deceive and injure the plaintiff, issued and published certain false, fraudulent, and deceitful writings, falsely and fraudulently and deceitfully pretending in said writings to describe the true nature and objects of said community, and to set forth the true state of facts in connection with said enterprise, and thereby to induce the plaintiff to believe that said objects and purposes of the defendants, and said facts in connection with said enterprise, were far different from what they really were, and from what said defendants really intended they should be.

The declaration then proceeds to set out what it is alleged the defendants held out the enterprise to be, viz.: That the property of the community was to be held in common, — no one individual to have any separate title and property; that said community was to be conducted on principles of brotherly love, without master or leader to exercise control over the members; that all the members were to enjoy equally a permanent place in the community, with no authority on the part of any member or members to exclude another; that said community was laid on principles of sound morality and purity of life; that the plaintiff, misled by these pretenses, was induced to become a member of the community;

> "that he did then and there enter into said commu-
> nity with defendants; * * * did consecrate his life,
> his labor, and all his worldly effects and pros-
> pects, together with those of his two children,
> placing all good faith and confidence in said
> community; whereas, in truth and in fact, said
> defendants knew at the time of making said false
> statements and pretenses that the property of the
> said community home would not be held in com-
> mon by the members of said community, but that
> the title thereto was then and would in future be
> vested by deed in one individual, to-wit, the
> defendant Andrew M. Howland; and whereas, in
> truth and in fact, defendants well knew, before
> and at the time of making said false statements
> and misrepresentations, that said community
> would not be conducted on principles of equality
> and kindness, without a master."

The declaration then proceeds to charge defendant Newbrough with acts of tyranny, also with living a life of immorality, etc.; that, by reason of the false representations aforesaid, the plaintiff was induced to become a member of the community; and that he remained a member of such community from October, 1884, until April, 1886, both he and his two children working for the improvement of the home;

> " and the plaintiff saith that the defendants refused, and still refuse, to pay plaintiff for his said work and labor, or any part thereof; by reason whereof plaintiff saith that he has sustained great damage in loss of time and labor and opportunity and in the education of his children, and that he has suffered great anguish of mind in consequence of the dishonor and humiliation brought upon himself and his children by reason of his connection in said community; to the damage of the plaintiff in the sum of $10,000."

To this unique and weird complaint a demurrer was interposed. The second and fourth grounds of the demurrer are as follows:

> "(2) Because there are no sufficient facts alleged in plaintiff's said declaration to charge these defendants, or either of them, with any liability to plaintiff in his said declaration complained of."

> "(4) Because the said declaration is duplicitous, in this: that plaintiff in his said declaration has attempted to plead more than one, and various and distinct and different, causes of action in one and the same count."

We think the court erred in overruling this demurrer. The most that can be gathered from the declaration is that the defendants had conceived some Utopian scheme for the amelioration of all the ills, both temporal and spiritual, to which human flesh and soul are heir; had located their new Arcadia near the shores of the Rio Grande, in the county of Dona Ana, in the valley of the Mesilla; had christened this new-found Vale of Tempe the "Land of Shalam;" had sent forth their siren notes, which, sweeter and more seductive than the music that led the intrepid Odysseus to the Isle of Calypso, reached the ears of the plaintiff at his far-off home in Georgia, and induced him to "consecrate his life and labors, and all his worldly effects." etc., to this new gospel of Oahspe. This much is gathered from the pleadings.

The evidence adduced in support of the plaintiff's demand is as startling as the declaration is unique. What the declaration leaves as uncertain, the proof makes incomprehensible. If the court below had been invested with spiritual jurisdiction, it might have been enabled, through an inspired interpreter, to submit to a mortal jury the precise character of plaintiff's demand. We think an examination of the record before us will amply support these conclusions.

The first and principal witness offered by plaintiff was himself. He sets out in full the nature of his grievance. He admits, on page 59 of the record, that he made no sacrifice of property to become a member of the new organization, but that he "threw up a situation" in which he could make a good living. What induced him to make this sacrifice is set out in his testimony.

First in order came some specimen of the literature published by the society, community, order, church, or "Faithists," as they were pleased to call themselves. Over the objections of the defendants, two books were allowed to go to the jury. The first and larger volume is entitled as follows:

> "Oahspe: A New Bible in the words of Jehovah and his Angel Embassadors. A sacred history of the dominions of the higher and lower heavens on the earth for the past twenty-four thousand years, together with a synopsis of the cosmogony of the universe; the creation of planets; the creation of man; the unseen worlds; the labor and glory of gods and goddesses in the etherean heavens. With the new commandments of Jehovah to man of the present day. With revelations from the second resurrection, formed in words in the thirty-third year of the Kosmon era."

In the preface of the book it is said of it that "it blows nobody's horn; it makes no leader." It is further stated: "When a book gives us information of things we know not of, it should also give us a method of proving that information true. This book covers that ground."

The inspired author of this new revelation was doubtless somewhat familiar with the writings of his early predecessors. He had read of the jealousies that had arisen between Paul and Barnabas, so that he takes occasion in his preface to assure his disciples that these gospels are not intended to establish the fame of any one, — "it blows nobody's horn." And again having seen innumerable sects spring up as a result of a misconstruction, or rather of a diversified construction, of the earlier gospels, we are furnished with the consoling assurance that this book presents the "method of proving that information to be true."

With this comfortable and comforting assurance, the witness opens this volume of light, and bids us satisfy the hungry longing of our restless spirits by feasting our eyes on its simple truths. This new gospel, in order to prepare our minds for the acceptance and enjoyment of its simple truths, proceeds to dispel the mists of superstition that for nearly 2,000 years have obscured our spiritual vision.

It gives a plain and unvarnished story of the origin of the Christian Bible. It is this: That once upon a time the world was ruled by a triune composed of Brahma and Budha and one Looeamong; that the devil, entering into the presence of Looeamong, tempted him by showing him the great power of Buddha and Brahma, and induced him (Looeamong) to take upon himself the name Kriste, so that it came to pass that the followers of Kriste were called Kristeyans; that Looeamong or Kriste, through his commanding generals, Gabriel, captured the opposing gods, together with their entire command of 7,600,000 angels, and cast them into hell, where there were already more than 10,000,000, who were in chaos and madness.

This Kriste afterwards assembled a number of his men to adopt a Code. At this meeting it is said there were produced "two thousand two hundred and thirty-one books and legendary tales of gods and saviors and great men," etc. This council was in session for four years and seven months, "and at the end of that time there had been selected and combined much that was good and great, and worded so as to be well remembered of mortals." Plaintiff's Exhibit A, p.733, verse 55.

The council, or "convention," as it would now be termed, having adopted a platform, — that is, agreed upon a Bible, — then proceeded to ballot for a god. "As yet no god had been selected by the council, and so they balloted in order to determine that matter." Plaintiff's Exhibit A, p.733, verse 36. On that first ballot the record informs us there were 37 candidates, naming them. The list includes such well-known personages as Vulcan, Jupiter, Minerva. Kriste stood twenty-second on this ballot. "Besides these, there were twenty-two other gods and goddesses who received a small number of votes each." Plaintiff's Exhibit A, p.733, verse 37. The names of these candidates are not given, and therefore there is nothing in the record to support the contention of the counsel that this list includes the names of Bob Ingersoll and Phoebe Coussins.

The record tells us that at the end of seven days' balloting "the number of gods was reduced to twenty-seven." And so the convention or council remained in session "for one year and five months, the balloting lasted, and at the end of that time the ballot rested nearly equal on five gods, namely, Jove, Kriste, Mars, Crite, and Siva;" and thus the balloting stood for seven weeks. At this point Hataus, who was the chief spokesman for Kriste, proposed to leave the matter of a selection to the angels. The convention, worn out with speech-making and balloting, readily accepted this plan.

Kriste, who, under his former name of Looeamong, still retained command of the angels, (for he had prudently declined to surrender one position until he had been elected to the other,) together with his hosts, gave a sign in fire of a cross smeared with blood; whereupon he was declared elected, and on motion his selection was made unanimous. Plaintiff's Exhibit A, p.733. We think this part of the exhibit ought to have been excluded from the jury, because it is an attack in a collateral way on the title of this man Looeamong, who is not a party to this proceeding, showing that he had not only packed the convention (council) with his friends, but had surrounded the place of meeting with his hosts, "a thousand angels deep on every side;" thus violating that principle of our laws which forbids the use of troops at the polls.

After thus endeavoring to demonstrate that Christianity had its origins in fraud, and thus to prepare the minds of its disciples for the new gospel, the *Oahspe* proceeds to unfold the beauties and the simplicity of the new faith. Passing over many interesting features contained in this exhibit, such as the birth of Confucius, the rise and fall of Mohammedanism, the discovery of America by Columbus, etc., the record brings us to the discovery and settlement of the Land of Shalam, which forms the subject of this controversy. As already seen, the record shows that a tract of land in the county of Dona Ana was selected. This was bought and paid for by the appellant Howland, and conveyed in trust for the use of the society.

Among other conditions attached to the trust, one was to the effect that "no meat nor fish nor butter nor eggs nor cheese, nor any animal food save honey, shall ever be used upon any part of the premises, except that milk may be given to children under five years old." Transcript of Record, p.167. It is admitted that this, among many other conditions of the trust, was violated; so that on the 13th day of March, 1886, the trustees, among whom was the appellee, made a reconveyance of the property to the said Howland.

There are many other interesting features presented by this record. Much proof was taken as to the conduct of the society or community which was incorporated under the name and style of the "First Church of the Tae." Record, p.180. They organized also a general cooperative system; established what they called the "Faithist Country Store," (Record, p.87,) — an institution, as we are advised, that did well as long as it kept on hand a good stock of faith. There was an outer and an inner council, and contributions were received, to be devoted to the care and education of orphan children.

It was charged in the declaration that the members did not practice that degree of morality which was set forth in their circular, and proof was introduced with a view to show the questionable relations existing between one of the promoters of the scheme and one Miss Vandewater, alias Miss Sweet; but as the plaintiff remained on the premises 18 months, and as he assigned no such reason for leaving, (page 88,) and as he made no demand at the time for compensation for work and labor done, nor for his injured sense of morality, we think this is an after-thought.

This society of Faithists, while communistic in theory, agrarian in habits, and vegetarian in diet, was not altogether void of sentimentality nor indifferent to the Muses. One of the fair members of the society, inspired by the poetic surroundings of this fair Land of Shalam, composed some beautiful lines that are incorporated into the record on page 62. The are as follows:

CHAPTER VI: SCHEMES, CLAIMS, & CONTENTIONS

> *"For all things are held in common,*
> *Hooray! Hooray!*
> *Thus everything belongs to all,*
> *And peace abounds in Shalam;*
> *Away, away, away out west in Shalam!"*

The authoress of these beautiful and touching lines is Nellie Jones, a member of the society. She is not made a party to this action, however, and therefore no judgment can be rendered against her. The lines were, by direction of one of appellants, Dr. Newbrough, sung to the air of Dixie. We cannot give our assent, however, to the views of the able counsel for the appellee that causing these lines to be sung to the air or "tune of Dixie" was of itself such an act of disloyalty as to entitle the plaintiff to a verdict.

The writer of this opinion, like the appellee, is himself a native of the land of Dixie, that

> *"Fair land of flowers,*
> *And flowery land of the fair."*

— And, as he reads these lines of Nellie Jones, memory carries him back to the days of his boyhood, and to the land of the "magnolia and the mocking bird."

O, glorious Land of Shalam! O, beautiful Church of Tae! When the appellants, the appellee, Ada Sweet, and Nellie Jones, aforesaid, formed their inner circle, and like the morning stars sang together, it matters not whether they kept step to the martial strains of Dixie, or declined their voices to the softer melody of Little Annie Rooney, the appellee became forever estopped from setting up a claim for work and labor done; nor can he be heard to say that "he has suffered great anguish of mind in consequence of the dishonor and humiliation brought on himself and children by reason of his connection with said defendants' community." His joining in the exercises aforesaid constitutes a clear case of estoppel in Tae.

There is another reason, however, why this act of disloyalty on the part of the appellants should not prejudice them; and that is that the plaintiff himself joined in the chorus when the "tune of Dixie" was sung. On page 109 of the record appears the following, the plaintiff himself being upon the witness stand: "Question. You all sang this with a good deal of lustiness? Answer. No, sir; we sang it to the tune of Dixie. Q. All joined in the chorus? A. Yes, sir; all that could."

Pretermitting any expression of opinion as to whether it would, under the circumstances, be competent to allege and prove in this court that the ode to Shalam had been sung to the tune of Dixie, it is in proof, as we have seen, that the parties were *in pari delicto*, and therefore neither can avail himself to the other's wrong.

It is insisted, however, that the appellee was deceived by the appellants; that they did not carry out the purposes set forth in their circular and manifestos; and that they did not live up to the doctrines contained in their Bible. The plaintiff admits that he had read their books thoroughly before he joined them. He belonged to the inner circle; was one of the trustees; joined in the worship; sang in the choir; and listened to the soul-enrapturing voice of Nellie Jones.

Moreover, he had entered into the Holy Covenant. That covenant is found in chapter 5 of the Book of Jehovah's Kingdom on Earth. Plaintiff's Exhibit A, p.833. The twenty-fourth verse of the covenant is as follows:

> "I covenant unto Thee, Jehovah, that, since all things are thine, I will not own nor possess, exclusively unto myself, anything under the sun, which may be intrusted to me, which any other person or persons may covet or desire, or stand in need of."

Under the terms of this covenant, he cannot maintain his suit, for the defendants insist, and the proof is clear, that they "covet or desire or stand in need of" the $10,000 for which the plaintiff sues. This is a complete answer to so much of plaintiff's cause of action as is laid in assumpsit, just as his participation in the church exercises, music, etc., was an estoppel to his right to set up "anguish of mind" and ruined reputation and other matters founded in tort.

It is insisted, however, that the appellee has a right to recover for a deceit practiced upon him; that he was misled by the *Oahspe* and other writings of the society. On the contrary, the defendants maintain that the appellee is a man who can read, and who has ordinary intelligence, and this the appellee admits. This admission precludes any inquiry as to whether appellee's connection with the Faithists, their inner and outer circles, their music and other mystic ceremonies, their general warehouse and co-operative store, and other communistic theories and practices, gave evidence of such imbecility as would entitle him to maintain this suit.

Admitting, therefore, that the appellee was a man of ordinary intelligence, we find nothing in the exhibits which in our opinion was calculated to mislead him. True, the *Oahspe*, like other inspired writings, such as the *Koran*, Bunyan's *Pilgrim's Progress*, and other works of like character, deals largely in figures and tropes and allegories. But, read in the light of modern sciences, they are beautiful in their very simplicity. We would be glad to embody the whole of plaintiff's Exhibit A, but must confine ourself to such citations as will, in our opinion, be sufficient to sustain this view.

A careful examination of appellee's Exhibit A, the *New Bible of Oahspe*, leads us to the inevitable conclusion that its splendid exhibitions of word painting were not confined to the Mesilla valley, although it is in proof, and, indeed, is not denied, that a much larger volume might be written, and yet not exhaust the subject of that valley's many attractions. But, while there are many descriptive features in the record that unquestionably apply to the section in controversy, there are others that bear on their face a very different application.

CHAPTER VI: SCHEMES, CLAIMS, & CONTENTIONS

As a specimen of the former, we cite the following, found on page 370 of the Exhibit A:

> "Next south lay the kingdom of Himalawo-
> woaganapapa, rich in legends of the people who
> lived here before the flood; a kingdom of seventy
> cities and six great canals, coursing east and west,
> and north and south, from the Ghiee mountain in
> the east, to the West mountain, the Yublahahcola-
> esavaganawakka, the place of the king of bears,
> the EEughehabakax, (grizzly.) And to the south,
> to the middle kingdom, on the deserts of
> Geogiathhaganeganewohwoh, where the rivers
> empty not into the sea, but sink into the sand, the
> Sonogallakaxhax, creating prickly Thuazhoo-
> gallakhoomma, shaped like a pear."

As an illustration of that portion of the exhibit which, in our opinion, was not designed as a description of the Land of Shalam, we cite the following, found on the same page of the exhibit:

> "In the high north lay the kingdom of Olegalla, the
> land of giants, the place of yellow rocks and high
> spouting waters. Olegalla it was who gave away
> his kingdom, the great city of Powafuchs-
> wowitchahavagganeabba, with the four and twenty
> tributary cities spread along the valley of
> Anemoosagoochakakfuela. Gave his kingdom to
> his queen, Minneganewashaka, with the yellow
> hair, long hanging down."

This unquestionably refers to Chicago.

The author, after giving a general description of many lands and cities, leads his "deciples" to some high point, most probably Sierra Blanca, (from whose snow-covered summit the summer breezes fall like a gentle cascade over the valley of the Pecos,) and spreads out before them a vast system of irrigation.

The following is taken from the record, and will be found commencing on page 369 of appellee's Exhibit A: "Beside the canals mentioned, there were seven other great canals, named after the kings who built them, and they extended across the plains in many directions, but chiefly east and west." Speaking of the vast canals that formed a net-work of the beautiful valley, the record says:

> "Betwixt the great kings and their great capitals
> were a thousand canals, crossing the country in
> every way, from east to west and from north to
> south, so that the seas of the north were connected
> with the seas of the south. In kanoos the people
> traveled, and carried the productions of the land in
> every way."

We are of the opinion that a proper cause of action was not set out in the declaration, and that there was no evidence to sustain the verdict of the jury awarding the plaintiff $1,500. . .

UNITED STATES v. BATSON
United States Court of Appeals, Fifth Circuit
782 F.2d 1307 (1986)

IRVING L. GOLDBERG, Circuit Judge:

> *Some farmers from Gaines had a plan.*
> *It amounted to quite a big scam.*
> *But the payments for cotton*
> *began to smell rotten.*
> *Twas a mugging of poor Uncle Sam.*
> *The ASCS and its crew*
> *uncovered this fraudulent stew.*
> *After quite a few hearings,*
> *the end is now nearing --*
> *It awaits our judicial review.*

The United States initiated these seven suits in 1979 to enforce administrative determinations of the Agricultural Stabilization and Conservation Service (ASCS), which ordered appellants to refund over-payments of cotton subsidies obtained in 1972 and 1973 through a scheme or device to defeat the purpose of the Upland Cotton Price Support Program, 7 U.S.C. § 1444(e), or to evade the program payment limitation.

The scheme first came to the attention of the ASCS when audit reports revealed that program payments to recipients in Gaines County, Texas, were five times that of comparable cotton producing regions.

The scam involved millions of dollars, and the facts underlying the cases are set . . . Suffice it to say here that by combining the operation of two farms whose yield and payment rates under the program differed significantly, the appellants created a synergistic union in which the combined or "reconstituted" farm received payments several times greater than the sum of the payments that each farm would have received separately. . . .

. . . After hearings at the county, state, and national level, the ASCS determined that appellants had knowingly engaged in a scheme or device to defeat the purpose of the Upland Cotton Program or to evade the program limitation. When appellants refused to refund the amounts for which they had been held liable, the United States filed twelve suits in 1979 to enforce the administrative determinations. . .

. . . The appellants responded that the administrative proceedings were riddled with violations of due process. Alleged violations included inordinate delay in the administrative process, bias and prejudgment on the part of hearing officers, and the lack of an opportunity to call, confront, and cross-examine witnesses. Some appellants also claimed that, as "operators," they could not be held liable under a regulation that only required refunds from "producers." Others claimed that they never actually received any payments.

The district court [citation omitted] rejected each of defendants' claims, entered summary judgment in favor of the United States, and assessed an award in the amount of the subsidy overpayments as determined by the agency, plus interest from the dates of the final agency determinations. . .

. . . We affirm the judgment of the district court, but we reverse as to its award of interest. . .

III. INTEREST

The district court awarded interest on the refunds from the date of the ASCS's final determinations. The United States claims, on the basis of the general policy underlying awards of prejudgment interest, that interest should run from the date of the program payments. . .

The basic interest statute under federal law, 28 U.S.C. § 1961, provides:

> Interest shall be allowed on any money judgment in
> a civil case recovered in a district court .... Such
> interest shall be calculated from the date of the entry
> of the judgment, at the rate allowed by State law.

The district court, in awarding interest from the date of the final administrative judgment, apparently relied on this statute, although an argument could be made that the statute only authorized an award of interest from the date of judgment in the district court. Regardless of the merits of this argument, we believe the district court erred in denying interest from the dates the subsidies were paid. . .

. . . As the common law recognizes in analogous situations, the only way the wronged party can be made whole is to award him interest from the time he should have received the money. The United States has been wrongfully deprived of these funds since 1973. To deny the government prejudgment interest would grant appellants a windfall equal to the value of the use of the funds since that time. Accordingly, we reverse the district court's award of interest and remand with instructions to enter an award of interest of 6% from the date the subsidies were paid.

IV. CONCLUSION

With thought and comment most candid,
affirmance shall now be commanded.
But the court below missed
the prejudgment interest:
The cases are therefore remanded

AFFIRMED IN PART, REVERSED IN PART AND REMANDED.

AN ACTE CONCERNYNG EGYPSYANS [1]
Statutes of The Realm of England
22 Henry VIII, Ch. 10 (1530)

FOR AS MOUCH as afore this tyme dyverse and many outlandysshe People callynge themselfes Egyptians usyng no crafte nor faithe of marchaundyse have commen into this Realme, and gone from Shire to Shire and Place to Place in greate company and use greate subtyll and crafty meanes to decyve the people, beryng them in hande, that they by Palmestre coulde telle menne and womens fortunes, and so many tymes by crafte and subtyltie have deceyved the people of theyr money, and also hath commytted many and haynous felonyes and robberies to the greate hurte and deceyte of the people that they have comyn amonge;

Be it therefore, by the Kynge or Sovereign Lorde the Lordes Spirituall and Temporall and by the Commons in thys presente parliament assembled, and by the authorytie of the same, ordenyned establysshed and enacted that from hensforth no such persones be suffred to come within this the Kynges Realme, And yf they do [than[2]] they and every of them so doynge shall forfayte to the Kynge our Sovereign Lorde all theyr goodes and catalls and then to be comaunded to avoyde the Realme wythin xv. dayes next after the comaundement upon payne of imprisonament;

And it shalbe laufull to every Sheryff Justice of Peace and Eschetour to sease to the use of our Sovereign Lorde his Heyres and Successours all suche Goodes as they or any of them shall have, and therof to accompte to our said Sovereign Lord in his Exchequer;

And yf it shall happen any suche Straunger hereafter to comytte wythin this Realme any murder robbery or other felonye and therof be indicted and

---

[1] [Ed. Note: i.e., Gypsies.]
[2] then O.

arayned, and to plede not giltie or any other plee triable by the contrie, that then thenqueste that shall passe betwene the Kyng and any suche partie shall be all together of Englysshemen, albeit that the partie so indicted pray [mediatem[3]] lingue[4] according to the Statute of Anno viii Henrici VI or any other Statute therof made.

PROVYDED alwaye that the Egyptians nowe beynge in thys Realme have monycyon to departe within xvi dayes after proclamacyon of thys estatute amonge them shalbe made, upon payne of imprisonament and forfeyture of theyr goodes and catells, and yf they then so departe that then they shall not forfayte theyr goods nor any parte therof; thys presente Estatute not wythstondyng;

[5]PROVYDED alwaye that every such persone or persones which canne perve by ii credable persones before the same partie that seaseth such money goodes or catalls of the same Egyptians, that any parte of the same goodes money or catalls were craftely or felonously taken or stolne from hym, shalbe incontynent restored unto the same goodes money or catalls wherof he maketh suche perve before the same partie that so seaseth the same money goodes or catalles upon payne to forfayte to the same partie that make such prove the double value of the same by accyon of Dette Bill, or otherwyse in any of the Kynges Courtes to be sued, upon which accyon and sute he shall not be admytted to wage hyse Lawe, nor any perteccion or essonyne to be alowed; any thyng in the athe to the cont[a]ry not wythstondyng.

PROVYDED always and be it farther enathed that yf any Justice of Peace, Sheryff or Eschetour which by authorytie of this Athe have power to take or sease any goodes or catels of any Egyptians, at any tyme hereafter do sease or take the goodes or cattels of any suche Egyptians, that then every such Justice Sheryff or Eschetour doyng the same shall have kepe and retayne to his owen use the moyte of all suche goodes so by hym seased, and of the other moytie so by hym seased or taken shall make answere and accompte to the Kyng in his Escheker accordyng to the tenour of this present acte; any thynge in the same Acte conteyned to the cont[a]ry herof notwithstondying; and that upon any accounte hereafter to be made for the said other moytie of the same goodes, the accountant shall paye no manner of fees or other charges for his accounte or discharge to be hadd in the Kynges Eschequer nor els where.

---

[3] medietat O.

[4] [Ed. Note: i.e., medietatem linguae (moiety of tongue); the right of a foreigner to trial by a jury consisting of six native Englishmen and six of the defendant's own countrymen.]

[5] The two Provisoes following are contained in two Schedules attached to the Original Acte.

UNITED STATES v. CARMICHAEL
United States Court of Appeals, Fifth Circuit
497 F.2d 36 (1974)

JOHN R. BROWN, Chief Judge:

Appellant, Ms. Jean Carmichael, was convicted on two counts of violating 18 U.S.C.A § 1343 and one count of violating 18 U.S.C.A. § 2314. The sum and substance of these violations was that appellant devised a scheme to defraud Ms. Laura Harris, Ms. Vonna McNiff, and Mr. Heywood Allen out of a total of $17,500.00 by means of false and fraudulent pretenses. The appellant's sole contention appeal is that there was insufficient evidence to support the verdict as to these three counts. Viewing the evidence in a light more favorable to the verdict, . . . we find more than sufficient evidence to support the jury's findings. We therefore affirm.

The Set-Up

The saga of the parting of Ms. McNiff, Ms. Harris, Mr. Allen and their money began one night in May of 1971. Ms. McNiff and Ms. Harris, while on vacation in Miami, Florida from Atlanta, Georgia, requested their friend Mr. Allen to squire them to a local exclusive private club to dine. While at the club, Mr. Allen saw the appellant who was an acquaintance of his and took the opportunity to introduce the three women.

The appellant immediately impressed Ms. Harris and Ms. McNiff as being a person of great charm, generosity, wealth, and social position. She dressed elegantly, engaged Mr. Allen in a conversation concerning the Cadillac she was planning on purchasing and insisted that she and her escort pay for everyone's dinner. Later that evening she invited everyone to her sumptuous home and proceeded to dazzle them with her expensive and varied wardrobe. She made it a point to display her two full-length mink coats, one of which she said was given her by a prominent politician. She was, she stated, on very good terms with the politician's prestigious family.

During the early months of her friendship with Ms. McNiff and Ms. Harris, the appellant clearly attempted to perpetuate the illusion of wealth and grandeur she had already created. For example, the appellant on one occasion off-handedly remarked to the two women that she wished she could take them to her house in Jamaica but unfortunately she had recently sold it. On another occasion she paid for the two women's memberships and dinners plus $100.00 life membership for herself at a cystic fibrosis fund raising affair. Still another time she was observed paying the expenses of herself, her two daughters, her son-in-law, her grandchild, and two of her friends during an ocean cruise to the Bahamas.

If there ever lingered doubt in the minds of Ms. McNiff and Ms. Harris as to the appellant's solvency, it was dispelled after they attended the wedding the appellant provided for her daughter. The appellant had 5,000 yellow long-stemmed roses flown in from California at what she indicated was a "great expense". She also provided at least one orchestra and several bars for some 600 guests and held a reception and dinner at an exclusive Miami club following the wedding.

At one time during the affair, the appellant indicated to the two women that she may have spent as much as $30,000.00 on the wedding although at trial she confessed that $8,000.00 was a more reasonable estimate and that the roses were donated by her ex-husband, a wholesale florist in California. Although it is not necessary to conclude that the appellant calculated such events solely to mislead Ms. McNiff and Ms. Harris, it is certain the fact finder could hold that she grossly exaggerated her expenditures and her financial ability and that she took every advantage to create a false impression of wealth.

The Sting

Some time in early June of 1972, the appellant telephoned Ms. McNiff, who had returned to Atlanta, long distance from Miami. The appellant was distraught. When asked to reveal the source of her distress, she confessed it was financial. She owned, she alleged, a large tract of land in Ohio which could be sold for a $2,000,000.00 profit as a shopping center development if only she could raise $90,000.00 with which to pay off back taxes and attorneys' fees. She stated that one of her bankers would lend her $50,000.00 and a mortgage on her home would yield $20,000.00. The rest of her wealth, however, was tied up in various investments and thus unliquid. She desperately needed several thousand dollars, and would be able to repay whoever lent her that amount within two weeks since the shopping center deal was about to be closed.

Based on over a year of observing the appellant act as a woman of means, Ms. McNiff wired her $7,500.00, the majority of her life's savings. Unfortunately, the appellant owned no property in Ohio. In fact she stated at trial, she needed the money to repay several other of her friends who had also lent her various sums and to encourage her ex-husband to put the title of their sumptuous home in her name.

Two weeks later, on the date the loan was to be repaid, Ms. McNiff and Ms. Harris flew to Florida and met the appellant. By then, however, a curious thing had happened--the appellant needed more money. Without stating why Ms. McNiff's $7,500.00 was insufficient, she reiterated her plea for more money based on the apocryphal Ohio land scheme. To induce Ms. Harris to make her a loan, the appellant produced a stock receipt for $130,000.00 worth of IBM stock which she indicated was in the hands of her broker being sold and could be used as collateral.

The stock receipt was indeed genuine but unfortunately belonged to a friend of the appellant's, Mr. Robert Connally, who had only temporarily lent the appellant the certificates for business reasons. As a further inducement, the appellant also stated that if Ms. Harris would lend her $7,500.00 both she and Ms.

McNiff would receive their principal plus a $1,500.00 profit within two more weeks. Ms. Harris agreed to the loan.

Encouraged by her success, the appellant then made the incredibly audacious suggestion that Ms. Harris telephone their mutual friend, Mr. Heywood Allen, and ask him for a loan of $10,000.00. To soften the blow, the appellant suggested Ms. Harris tell Mr. Allen that the money was to be used in a profitable business venture, that he would be repaid in two weeks with 10% interest, and that the borrower (who was to remain anonymous) had $130,000.00 worth of IBM as collateral.

Based on these representations plus his friendship of long-standing with Ms. Harris, Mr. Allen consented to the loan. He asked Ms. Harris, however, to personally sign a note for the full amount. After making arrangements with her bank and obtaining Mr. Allen's check, Ms. Harris wired the $17,500.00 to the appellant in Miami. Several days later, after being pressed by Ms. Harris, the appellant signed unsecured notes to Ms. Harris, Ms. McNiff and Mr. Allen covering their loans.

No Blood In The Turnip

As was predictable, the months that followed the making of the loans were filled with a series of unsuccessful attempts by Ms. Harris, Ms. McNiff, and Mr. Allen to collect their money and a series of ingenious and sometimes belligerent explanations by the appellant as to why she was unable to repay them. On the day the money was due, for example, when Ms. Harris called to arrange repayment, the appellant stated she had just lost $40,000.00 in the stock market and could not be bothered thinking about repaying such an insignificant sum as $17,500.00. When contacted several days later, the appellant was unable to repay the loan because her fictitious Ohio property had been flooded. On another occasion, the appellant stated her husband was suing her for a large sum of money as a result of their divorce and every dollar she had was tied up in court--perhaps the most accurate and truthful of all her excuses.

Each time she was contacted concerning repayment, she assured the women they would be repaid shortly because she was anticipating some external source of funds. In July, the source was to be appellant's married friend Bob. In September, she expected funds from her father's estate in California. On several occasions she promised she would stop in Atlanta on her way to or from settling her father's estate in California and deliver the money. Of course she never did. Meanwhile, however, she continued to live a profligate life, indulging in several ocean cruises with her daughters as was her wont.

Sometime in late August Ms. Harris' already aroused suspicions that she would never be repaid were heightened. Increasingly curious as to why her seemingly wealthy friend was unable to repay such a modest amount, Ms. Harris contacted appellant's attorney and in response to her questioning he related that to the best of his knowledge appellant neither owned any property in Ohio nor $130,000.00 worth of IBM stock. He also stated that "there were judgments against [the appellant] and unless [Ms. Harris] wanted to stand in line behind a quarter of a million dollars he didn't think there was much of a chance of [her] getting [her] money in a civil suit."

After several more fruitless telephone calls to the appellant, both Ms. McNiff and Ms. Harris flew to Miami to attempt to register their unsecured notes. In attempting to register their notes, they discovered there was in fact a $250,000.00 judgment on record against the appellant which sufficiently deterred them from taking further legal action.

Sometime in November of 1972, after a particularly threatening phone call from Ms. Harris, the appellant did forward Ms. McNiff a check for $500.00 in Ms. Harris' name with a note stating she was on her way to California to raise more money. After one last attempt to obtain payment on November 17, Ms. Harris ceased contact with the appellant and sought help from the FBI.

What Ms. McNiff, Ms. Harris, and Mr. Allen did not know either at the time they made the loans or during the attempted collection process was that in January of 1971, the appellant had asked for and obtained a $25,000.00 loan from another friend, Mr. Robert Connally, on the strength of his appraisal of her illusionary wealth and the representation that she was about to realize a $2,000,000.00 profit on property she held in Ohio if she could pay off back taxes. Over a two year period, she only repaid $5,000.00 despite constant urgings by Mr. Connally.

Sufficiency of the Evidence

The essence of a violation of 18 U.S.C.A §§ 2214 and 1343 is the act of devising a scheme or artifice to defraud by means of fraudulent or false pretenses. It is such a scheme we assume, that appellant contends is unsupported by substantial evidence when in her brief she states that "[t]he evidence in this case conclusively shows a loan and not a theft. . .

We think that there was more than sufficient evidence to support the jury's verdict. Such a scheme could be supported by the jury's belief that appellant lied in inducing Ms. McNiff and Ms. Harris to lend her money on the basis of a non-existent property in Ohio. It could further be supported by the jury's belief that appellant offered as collateral $130,000.00 worth of stock she did not own and that appellant had in January of 1971, tricked her friend Robert Connally out of $25,000.00 by using the same bogus tales of a get-rich-quick land scheme as an inducement for the loan.

Appellant's gross exaggerations of financial solvency, and her numerous evasions and half-truths concerning her ability to repay the loans all contribute to supporting the jury's verdict of guilt. That the jury chose not to believe appellant's testimony that Ms. McNiff and Ms. Harris volunteered to lend her their life's savings because they knew she was having financial problems, is well within their province as the ultimate triers of fact and can certainly not be said to be erroneous. . . .

Affirmed.

TRUSTEES OF COLUMBIA UNIVERSITY v. JACOBSEN
Superior Court of New Jersey, Appellate Division
53 N.J. Super. 574; 148 A.2d 63 (1959)

SIDNEY GOLDMANN, S.J.A.D.

Defendant appeals from a summary judgment of the Superior Court, Law Division, dismissing his counterclaim with prejudice and denying his counter-motion for summary judgement. The judgment also denied his motion for self-disqualification of the trial judge.

I.

Columbia brought suit in the district court against defendant and his parents on two notes made by him and signed by them as co-makers, representing the balance of tuition he owed the University. The principal due amounted to $1,049.50, but plaintiff sued for only $1,000, waiving any demand for judgment in excess of the jurisdictional limit of the court.

Defendant then sought to file an answer and counterclaim demanding, among other things, money damages in the sum of $7,016. The counterclaim was in 50 counts which severally alleged that plaintiff had represented that it would teach defendant wisdom, truth, character, enlightenment, understanding, justice, liberty, honesty, courage, beauty and similar virtues and qualities; that it would develop the whole man, maturity, well-roundedness, objective thinking and the like; and that because it had failed to do so it was guilty of misrepresentation, to defendant's pecuniary damage. . .

Following oral argument the Law Division judge refused to disqualify himself and concluded that the statements attributed by defendant to plaintiff did not constitute a false representation. The judgment under appeal was then entered.

II.

Following a successful freshman year at Dartmouth defendant entered Columbia in the fall of 1951. He continued there until the end of his senior year in the spring of 1954, but was not graduated because of poor scholastic standing. Plaintiff admits the many quotations from college catalogues and brochures, inscriptions over University buildings and addresses by University officers cited in the schedules annexed to the counterclaim. The sole question is whether these statements constitute actionable misrepresentations.

Plaintiff's motion was brought under two heads: (1) to dismiss the counterclaim under R.R. 4:12-2 for failure to state a claim upon which relief can be granted, and (2) for summary judgment under R.R. 4:58 on the ground that there was no genuine issue as to any material fact. . . The motion was directed to the entire counterclaim. There was no responsive pleading. Although the remedy of summary judgment is admittedly drastic and cautiously granted, it is so well established as scarcely to require citation that the remedy should not be withheld where, as here, there is no genuine issue of material fact. . .

CHAPTER VI: SCHEMES, CLAIMS, & CONTENTIONS

The attempt of the counterclaim, inartistically drawn as it is, was to state a cause of action in deceit. The necessary elements of that action are by now hornbook law; a false representation, knowledge or belief on the part of the person making the representation that it is false, an intention that the other party act thereon, reasonable reliance by such party in so doing, and resultant damage to him. . . .

We are in complete agreement with the trial court that the counterclaim fails to establish the very first element, false representation, basic to any action in deceit. Plaintiff stands by every quotation relied on by defendant. Only by reading into them the imagined meanings he attributes to them can one conclude — and the conclusion would be a most tenuous, insubstantial one — that Columbia University represented it could teach wisdom, truth, justice, beauty, spirituality and all other qualities set out in the 50 counts of the counterclaim.

A sampling from the quotations cited by defendant will suffice as illustration. Defendant quotes from a Columbia College brochure stating that

" * * * Columbia College provides a liberal arts education. * * * A liberal arts course. * * * has extremely positive values of its own. Chief among these, perhaps, is something which has been a principal aim of Columbia College from the beginning: It develops the whole man. * * * [Columbia's] aim remains constant: to foster in its students a desire to learn, a habit of critical judgment, and a deep-rooted sense of personal and social responsibility. * * * [I]ts liberal arts course pursues this aim in five ways. (1) It brings you into firsthand contact with the major intellectual ideas that have helped to shape human thinking and the course of human events. (2) It gives you a broader acquaintance with the rest of the world. (3) It guides you toward an understanding of people and their motivations. (4) It leads you to a comprehending knowledge of the scientific world. (5) It helps you acquire facility in the art of communication. * * *"

He then cites the motto of Columbia College and Columbia University: *"In lumine tuo videbimus lumen"* ("In your light we shall see light"), and the inscription over the college chapel: "Wisdom dwelleth in the heart of him that hath understanding." He also refers to an address of the president of Columbia University at its bicentennial convocation:

"There can never have been a time in the history of the world when men had greater need of wisdom. * * * I mean an understanding of man's relationship to his fellow men and to the universe. * * * To this task of educational leadership in a troubled time and in an uncertain world, Columbia, like other great centers of learning in free societies, unhesitatingly dedicates itself. * * *"

We have thoroughly combed all the statements upon which defendant relies in his counterclaim, as well as the exhibits he handed up to the trial judge, including one of 59 pages setting out his account of the circumstances leading up to the present action. They add up to nothing more than a fairly complete exposition of Columbia's objectives, desires and hopes, together with factual statements as to the nature of some of the courses included in its curricula. As plaintiff correctly observes, what defendant is seeking to do is to assign to the quoted excerpts a construction and interpretation peculiarly subjective to him and completely unwarranted by the plain sense and meaning of the language used. To defendant a college is not "Mark Hopkins at one end of a log and the student at the other," but his dream of a universal scholar *cum* philosopher *cum* humanitarian at one end of the school bench and defendant at the other.

At the heart of defendant's counterclaim is a single complaint. He concedes that:

> " I have really only one charge against Columbia:
> that it does not teach Wisdom as it claims to do.
> From this charge ensues an endless number of
> charges, of which I have selected fifty at random.
> I am prepared to show that each of these fifty
> claims in turn is false, though the central issue is
> that of Columbia's pretense of teaching Wisdom."

We agree with the trial judge that wisdom is not a subject which can be taught and that no rational person would accept such a claim made by any man or institution. We find nothing in the record to establish that Columbia represented, expressly or even by way of impression, that it could or would teach wisdom or the several qualities which defendant insists are "synonyms for or aspects of the same Quality." The matter is perhaps best summed up in the supporting affidavit of the Dean of Columbia College, where he said that "All any college can do through its teachers, libraries, laboratories and other facilities is to endeavor to teach the student the known facts, acquaint him with the nature of those matters which are unknown, and thereby assist him in developing mentally, morally and physically. Wisdom is a hoped-for end product of education, experience and ability which many seek and many fail to attain."

Defendant's extended argument lacks the element of fraudulent representation indispensable to any action of deceit. We note, in passing, that he has cited no legal authority whatsoever for his position. Instead, he has submitted a dictionary definition of "wisdom" and quotations from such works as the *Bhagavad-Gita*, the *Mundaka Upanishad*, the *Analects of Confucius* and the *Koran*; excerpts from Euripides, Plato and Meander; and references to the *Bible*. Interesting though these may be, they do not support defendant's indictment of Columbia. If his pleadings, affidavit and exhibits demonstrate anything, it is indeed the validity of what Pope said in his Moral Essays:

> " A little learning is a dangerous thing; Drink deep,
> or taste not the Pierian spring. . . "

The papers make clear that through the years defendant's interest has shifted from civil engineering to social work, then to physics, and finally to English and creative writing. In college he became increasingly critical of his professors and his courses; in his last year he attended classes only when he chose and rejected the regimen of examinations and term papers. When his non-attendance at classes and his poor work in the senior year were called to his attention by the Columbia Dean of Students, he replied in a lengthy letter that "I want to learn, but I must do it in my own way. I realize my behavior is non-conforming, but in these times when there are so many forces that demand conformity I hope I will find Columbia willing to grant some freedom to a student who wants to be a literary artist." In short, he chose to judge Columbia's educational system by the shifting standards of his own fancy, and now seeks to place his failure at Columbia's door on the theory that it had deliberately misrepresented that it taught wisdom.

III.

In light of our conclusion that the defendant has failed to state a cause of action in deceit based on fraudulent representation, we need not deal with plaintiff's further contentions that (1) even assuming an unequivocal representation by Columbia that it would teach wisdom, this amounted to nothing more than a promise to do something in the future and therefore was not an actionable misrepresentation of fact; and (2) the counterclaim is defective for failure properly to plead the particulars of the alleged fraud.

IV.

In his motion to have the trial judge disqualify himself, defendant charged that the judge had rendered a premature judgment after hearing only plaintiff's side of the controversy; had needlessly added to defendant's difficulty in presenting his "unusual case"; wrongfully claimed to be entirely familiar with the matter; and was partial to Columbia and overlooked misconduct by its attorney. To these reasons he added a suspicion that the assignment judge who had accepted his counterclaim was transferred away from the case in order to have it tried by the Law Division judge in question. These charges were set in a frame of intemperate, if not scurrilous, accusations.

There was no premature judgment. What happened was that at the first hearing on the motion for summary judgment, Columbia's attorney proceeded to make his argument and the trial judge then asked defendant if he wanted to reply. Defendant said that if there was any possibility of the motion being granted, he would want leave to file a brief. The judge then remarked that on the basis of what counsel for plaintiff had said and the papers the court had read, there was a strong likelihood of the motion being granted; and because defendant was a layman appearing pro se, the court would adjourn the matter for two weeks to give him an opportunity to prepare a brief and file affidavits. The motion was finally decided on the adjournment date.

As for the other reasons advanced by defendant, we find nothing in the record which lends them even the shadow of support.

V.

In view of the entirely unjustified accusations made against the trial judge and the intemperate characterization (so admitted by defendant at the oral argument) of the proceedings below, defendant's appendix and brief will be suppressed and all copies withdrawn from the clerk's files.

The judgment is affirmed.

COLLATZ v. FOX WISCONSIN AMUSEMENT CORPORATION
Supreme Court of Wisconsin
239 Wisc. 156; 300 N.W. 162 (1941)

CHESTER A. FOWLER, Justice.

The plaintiff sues to recover from the defendant the value of a half interest in an automobile which the defendant offered as a prize in a contest participated in by the plaintiff the entire interest in which the defendant awarded to a person other than the plaintiff. Trial was had to the court and findings made by the circuit judge. There is no bill of exceptions, so the case is before us for determination upon the findings, and such allegations of the complaint are not denied by the answer.

From the allegations of the complaint not denied, it appears that the defendant publicly advertised that the fifteen persons who during a specified week most nearly guessed the number of beans in a jar publicly displayed during said week would be eligible to engage in a "Quiz Contest" held at defendant's theatre at a time specified "until all but one (1) of their number should be eliminated" and that the winner in the contest would be awarded a new Chevrolet automobile; that the plaintiff was one of the fifteen who most nearly guessed the number of beans in the jar; that he duly notified the defendant that he would enter said contest and was accepted by the defendant as a contestant therein, and participated in the contest.

The trial judge found that the plaintiff was one of nine participants in the contest; that the contestants drew numbers by lot and seated themselves on the stage of the theatre in the order they were to be quizzed and the plaintiff drew the first position; that the contestants were each asked a question in the order determined by the draw; that three contestants failed to answer correctly the first question put to them and thereby eliminated themselves; that two contestants failed to answer the second question put to them and thereby eliminated themselves; that two contestants failed to answer the third question put, and thereby eliminated themselves, thus leaving only the plaintiff and one other contestant in the contest; that the plaintiff failed to answer the fourth question put to him, and that the other remaining contestant failed to answer the fourth question put to him; that the manager of the defendant announced to the audience before commencement of the contest that the automobile would "be awarded to the person who is last to be eliminated" and to the contestants that they would be "given fifteen seconds to answer each question," and if they did not so answer they "automatically" eliminated themselves.

On the plaintiff and the other remaining contestant both failing to answer the fourth question, the manager peremptorily declared the contest ended, and the other contestant who was last asked the fourth question was declared the winner of the contest and was awarded the automobile. The judge found the value of the automobile to be $782; he also found as fact that "it was the intention of the defendant in conducting said contest that the award be given to the contestant who, by reason of his superior ability to answer questions of an intellectual nature, would by process of elimination survive all other contestants." As conclusion of law the judge concluded that the construction of the words "the person last to be eliminated" in the announced rules of the contest required by necessary implication that such person must "be the sole successful survivor of the contest." On these findings and the facts admitted by answer, the trial judge concluded that the plaintiff was entitled to recover one-half the value of the automobile and entered judgment accordingly.

The theory of the plaintiff is and that of the trial judge was that a contract relation existed between the plaintiff and the defendant and that the defendant breached its contract by not going on with the contest until one of the two contestants who survived to the fourth "round" answered the question put to him in some succeeding "round" and the other in the same round failed to answer his question. But if so, this breach did not entitle the plaintiff to the car or to a half interest in it. He did not win the contest; he did not win anything; he did not become entitled to anything. He suffered no damage because of the defendant's breach of the contract, for it can not be assumed nor is it susceptible of proof that had the contest proceeded to a proper finish he would have become the winner.

The defendant caused no injury to the plaintiff by awarding the car to the other contestant even though such other was not entitled to it as a prize. The defendant could give it away as and to whom it saw fit, and the plaintiff may not complain that it did not see fit to give it to him or to give him a half interest in it.

The judgment of the circuit court is reversed with directions to dismiss the complaint.

BRANHAM v. THE STATE OF GEORGIA
Supreme Court of Georgia
96 Ga. 307; 22 S.E. 957 (1895)

SAMUEL E. LUMPKIN, Justice.

[One who obtains a loan of money by representing that he has been employed by a named person of known solvency and credit and has thus earned a sum of money which that person will shortly pay to him, and by promising to repay the loan out of that sum when collected, all of these representations being utterly false, and they and the promise being deceitfully made for the purpose of obtaining credit with the lender and defrauding him out of the money loaned, is guilty of being a cheat and swindler under section 4587 of the code.]

Under the facts summarized [above] the accused was, under the provisions of section 4587 of the code, properly convicted of the offense of being a cheat and swindler. According to that section, if any person, by falsely representing his wealth, obtains a credit, and thus defrauds another person of anything of value, he shall be deemed guilty of this offense.

The word "wealth," as used in this section, does not import a great fortune or vast possessions, as is frequently implied from its ordinary use; but its real meaning is the possession or ownership of such means or property as would reasonably entitle one to expect and receive the credit he seeks to obtain. Indeed, this word is at last a mere relative term.

Among millionaires, a man worth only a hundred thousand dollars is poor indeed; while in some localities, a man worth five thousand dollars over and above all his liabilities would be considered a very wealthy citizen. In principle, and very properly, this section applies to one who, by falsely pretending and representing that he owns or has earned and will receive something of value which he neither owns nor is entitled to, thus defrauds another of his property, whether the amount involved by large or small. . . .

Judgment affirmed.

NICKERSON v. HODGES
Supreme Court of Louisiana
146 La. 735; 84 So. 37 (1920)

BEN C. DAWKINS, J.

Miss Carrie E. Nickerson brought this suit against H.R. Hayes, William or "Bud" Baker, John W. Smith, Mrs. Fannie Smith, Miss Minnie Smith, claiming $15,000 as damages alleged to have been caused in the form of financial outlay, loss in business, mental and physical suffering, humiliation, and injury to reputation and social standing, all growing out of an alleged malicious deception and conspiracy with respect to the finding of a supposed pot of gold.

CHAPTER VI: SCHEMES, CLAIMS, & CONTENTIONS

Subsequent to the filing of the petition, and before the trial, the said Miss Nickerson died, and her legal heirs, some 10 in number, were made parties plaintiff, and now prosecute this suit.

All of the defendants, save and except Miss Minnie Smith, William or "Bud" Baker, and H.R. Hayes, filed, in effect, a general denial, denying any knowledge of or connection with the matters out of which the alleged damages arose. These three defendants filed a joint answer, in which, after denying the injuries charged, or that there was any malicious or unlawful intent, admitted that they had fixed up an old copper bucket or pot, filled with dirt and rocks, and had buried it at a point where the said Miss Carrie Nickerson and her helpers would likely dig in search of an imaginary pot of gold; that she and her said associates had been, for several months, digging over the property of defendant, John W. Smith, on information obtained from a negro fortune teller in the city of Shreveport, and boarding at the home of the said Smith, father of the said Minnie Smith, without paying therefor, and generally acting in such a manner as to make themselves nuisances to the community; that the course adopted by these three defendants was for the purpose of convincing the explorers of their folly; that it was intended as a practical joke, and succeeded in accomplishing the purpose mentioned.

For some reason the case was allowed to remain on the docket of the lower court for more than three years before being tried, when it was finally submitted to a jury, and resulted in a verdict in favor of the defendants. After an unsuccessful motion for a new trial, the plaintiffs prosecuted this appeal.

Statement of Facts.

Miss Nickerson was a kinswoman of Burton and Lawson Deck, the exact degree of relationship not being fully shown by the record, and there had been, in the family, a tradition that these two gentlemen, who died many years ago, had prior to their deaths, buried a large amount of gold coin on the place now owned by the defendant, John W. Smith, or on another near by. She was employed by the California Perfume Company to solicit orders for their wares in the towns, villages, etc., in Webster and other parishes, and on the occasion of a visit to the city of Shreveport seems to have interviewed a negro fortune teller, who told her that her said relatives had buried the gold, and gave her what purported to be a map or plat showing its location on the property of Smith.

Thereafter, with the help of some three or four other persons, principally relatives, and one Bushong, she spent several months digging, at intervals, around the house and on the premises of Smith, who seems to have extended them a cordial welcome, and to have permitted them to dig almost without limit as to time and place, and in addition boarded the fortune hunters, while so engaged, without charge. We assume that this was due, perhaps, to the fact that he, too, had a slight hope that they might find something, and he was to receive a part thereof for his concessions.

At any rate, the diggers pursued their course with such persistence and at such lengths, digging around the roots of shade trees, the pillars of his house, etc., until finally, his daughter, the said Minnie Smith, William or "Bud" Baker, and H.R. Hayes conceived the idea of themselves providing a "pot of gold" for the explorers to find. Accordingly they obtained an old copper kettle or bucket, filled it with rocks and wet dirt, and buried it in an old chimney seat on the adjoining place, where the searchers had been or were intending to also prospect for the supposed treasure. Two lids or tops were placed on the pot, the first being fastened down with hay wire; then a note was written by Hayes, dated, according to some, July 1, 1884, and, as to others, 1784, directing whoever should find the pot not to open it for three days, and to notify all the heirs. This note was wrapped in tin, placed between the first and second lids, and the latter was also securely fastened down with hay wire. This took place some time toward the latter part of March, and according to these three defendants, was to have been an April fool; but plans miscarried somewhat, and the proper opportunity for the "find" did not present itself until April 14th.

On that day Miss Nickerson and her associates were searching and digging near the point where the pot had been buried, when one Grady Hayes, a brother of H.R. Hayes, following directions from the latter, and apparently helping the explorers to hunt for the gold, dug up the pot and gave the alarm. All of those in the vicinity, of course, rushed to the spot, those who were "in" on the secret being apparently as much excited as the rest, and after some discussion, it was decided to remove the lid.

When this was done, the note was discovered, and H.R. Hayes advised Miss Nickerson that he thought it proper that its directions should be carried out, and that the bank at Cotton Valley, a few miles distant, was the best place to deposit the "gold" for safe-keeping, until the delays could run and the heirs be notified, as requested. Following this suggestion, the pot was placed in a gunny sack, tied up, and taken to the bank for deposit. Defendant Gatling was the cashier of the bank, but refused to give a receipt for the deposit as a "pot of gold," because, as he insisted, he did not know what it contained.

As might have been supposed, it did not take long for the news to spread that Miss Nickerson and her associates in the search for fortune, had found a pot of gold, and the discussion and interest in the matter became so general that defendant A.J. Hodges, vice president of the bank, went over from his place of business in Cotton Valley to the bank, and he and Gatling, after talking the matter over, decided to examine the pot, so that, in event it did contain gold, proper precautions to guard the bank might be taken, pending the return of Miss Nickerson and the appearance of those who might claim the fortune.

These two undid the wire sufficiently to peep into the pot, and discovered that it apparently contained only dirt. They then replaced the lid and held their tongues until the reappearance of Miss Nickerson. However, the secret leaked out from other sources, that the whole matter was a joke, and this information too, became pretty well distributed.

CHAPTER VI: SCHEMES, CLAIMS, & CONTENTIONS

After depositing the pot in the bank, Miss Nickerson went to Minden, La. and induced Judge R.C. Drew to agree to accompany her to Cotton Valley on the following Monday (the deposit at the bank having been made on Saturday) for the purpose of seeing that the ceremonies surrounding the opening of the treasure were properly conducted. Judge Drew swears that he had heard in some way that the matter was a joke, and so informed Miss Nickerson, warning her not to place too much faith in the idea that she was about to come into a fortune, but that finally, because of his friendly relations with and kindly feeling toward her, he consented and did go, mainly to gratify her wishes in the premises. Some half a dozen other relatives of Burton and Lawson Deck were notified, and either accompanied or preceded Miss Nickerson to Cotton Valley.

With the stage thus set, the parties all appeared at the bank on Monday morning at about 11 o'clock, and among the number were H.R. Hayes, one of the defendants, who seems to have been one of the guiding spirits in the scheme, and one Bushong, the latter, we infer, from intimations thrown out by witnesses in the record, being at the time either an avowed or supposed suitor of Miss Nickerson's. Judge Drew, as the spokesman for the party, approached Gatling and informed him that it was desired that the pot be produced for the purpose of opening and examining the contents for the benefit of those thus assembled.

The testimony of the witnesses varies a little as to just when the storm began; some say, as soon as the sack was brought out. Miss Nickerson discovered that the string was tied near the top, instead of down low around the pot, and immediately commenced to shout that she had been robbed; others insist that she was calm until the package was opened and the mocking earth and stones met her view. Be that as it may, she flew into a rage, threw the lid of the pot at Gatling, and for some reason, not clearly explained, turned the force of her wrath upon Hayes to such an extent that he appealed for protection, and Bushong, with another, held her arms to prevent further violence.

Miss Nickerson was a maiden, nearing the age of 45 years, and some 20 years before had been an inmate of an insane asylum, to the knowledge of those who had thus deceived her. She was energetic and self-supporting in her chosen line of employment, as a soap drummer, until she met the colored fortune teller who gave her the "information" which she evidently firmly believed would ultimately enable her to find the fortune which the family tradition told her had been left hidden by her deceased relatives. The conspirators, no doubt, merely intended what they did as a practical joke, and had no willful intention of doing the lady any injury. However, the results were quite serious indeed, and the mental suffering and humiliation must have been quite unbearable, to say nothing of the disappointment and conviction, which she carried to her grave some two years later, that she had been robbed.

If Miss Nickerson were still living, we should be disposed to award her damages in a substantial sum, to compensate her for the wrong thus done; but as to the present plaintiffs, her legal heirs, we think that a judgment of $500 will reasonably serve the ends of justice. . .

... The evidence fails to connect any of the defendants with the conspiracy, so as to render them liable, save and except H.R. Hayes, William or "Bud" Baker, and Miss Minnie Smith; hence the judgment will be awarded against these only.

For the reasons assigned, the judgment appealed from is annulled and reversed, and it is now ordered and decreed that the plaintiffs do have and recover judgment against the defendants H.R. Hayes, William or "Bud" Baker, and Miss Minnie Smith in the full sum of $500, and as to the other defendants the demands are rejected; the defendants so cast to pay all costs.

JOHNSON v. HARRIGAN-PEACH
LAND DEVELOPMENT COMPANY
Supreme Court of Washington
79 Wash. 2d 745; 489 P.2d 923 (1971)

FRANK HALE, J.

Who would doubt that life could be beautiful in a mobile home on a freshwater canal at Golden Sands hard by the Strait of Juan de Fuca? There it was at Dungeness, north of Sequim, a flat, grassy meadow running down to the beach along the strait. Each mobile home would front on a continuously flowing freshwater canal, navigable for small boats; and there would be locks to let residents maneuver their small craft from fresh water out into Dungeness Bay and then return to the Golden Sands Yacht and Beach Club to which all who dwelt there could belong. There would be a swimming pool, too, and a strip of ocean beach set apart for everyone in Golden Sands to enjoy.

Mr. Ted. G. Peach, a real-estate broker and former owner of Peach's Used Cars at Sixth and Blanchard in Seattle, was mindful of these natural endowments when he helped Mr. Wayne C. Harrigan organize the Harrigan-Peach Land Development company. Mr. Peach had been in the automobile business for about 25 years, he said, but left it to go into real estate in 1962 or 1963, obtaining his broker's license in 1964. He had organized, he said, the Homes Harbor Yacht and Golf Club, and served as a real-estate salesman at Sun Land in Sequim for about 6 months.

Defendants distributed sales material printed in color which said:

> Fish from your own lot in a beautiful waterway
> stocked with Rainbow and Easter Brook Trout.
> Dig clams or trap the famous Dungeness crab.
> Nearby, rivers offer the best steelhead fishing in
> the Northwest, salmon fishing supreme is at your
> doorstep. Near Golden Sands the hunter will find

elk, deer, bear, cougar, and an abundance of pheasants, ducks, geese and brant. Without a doubt, this is the most unique, cleverly planned land development for mobile homes anywhere. It is so fantastic, words cannot justify its beauty. The clean clear fresh waterways, leisurely flowing into the straits of Juan de Fuca, are surrounded by the beautiful Olympic Mountains. Directly to the north you see Mt. Baker and the San Juan Islands, ocean liners are most always in view, cruising up and down the straits.

The brochures, distributed to prospective lot purchasers, promised--and included an application form for--a free introductory membership in the Golden Sands Yacht and Beach Club. On the membership application form were such caveats as "After 8:00 p.m. gentlemen will wear jackets in the dining room and cocktail lounge," and a warning that, during the day, dry bathing suits could be worn but wet bathing suits would be prohibited in the clubhouse at all times-- presumably to protect the furniture. . . .

Plaintiffs purchased lots in Golden Sands from defendant Harrigan-Peach Land Development Company. The court found that, aside from the more lyrical commentary concerning the beauties of nature, climate and scene, the buyers relied upon what the court described as personal warranties, representations and inducements made either by the corporation's officers, directors, incorporators or promoters, or with their knowledge and consent, or under such circumstances that the individual parties defendant knew or were charged with knowing of . . . included the following:

1. All underground power and water lines had been installed and were usable by each owner solely on payment of a hook-up charge;

2. A sanitary sewer treatment plant would be installed by December 31, 1966, with stubs for each lot at no expense to the lot purchasers except for a hook-up charge estimated at $250;

3. Each lot would be raised and graded to provide drainage and planted with grass by December 31, 1966;

4. A waterway would be constructed, flowing among the lots as shown on a map outlining Golden Sands division No. 1, . . .

5. Each lot owner would have access to the ocean beach. . .

6. Roads, described as Golden Sands Boulevard, Sealand Drive, Sands Place, and others shown on the map of division 1 as being acceptable to Clallam County, would be in and open by December 31, 1967; and

7. All work and development with respect to the "channels, water ways, boat accesses, road accesses ... would be done promptly in a first-class work-man like manner."

The court made specific findings that the defendants had failed and refused to install the promised underground power and water lines; defendants failed to raise the level of and plant grass on the lots, leaving them swampy; the waterways were only partially constructed, and there was no continuous flow of fresh water as promised; no pumping or other facility had been installed to provide a continuous flow of fresh water; no attempt had been made by defendants to install sanitary sewer service or a sanitary sewer treatment plant, and no provision had been made for building a sewage plant or sewage collection lines; defendants had not provided beach access for each property owner, nor means of navigating their small boats from the promised canals or channels to the ocean; and that defendants had not, as they had promised, oiled or blacktopped the roads within the division, and the same had not been accepted and would not be maintained by Clallam County. . .

. . . Apply[ing] plaintiffs' theory of damages, the court allowed them recovery for the proved difference in value and, upon payment of actual value, a conveyance of the lots they had purchased. . .

. . . The link to Wayne Harrigan and Theodore Peach holding them liable along with the corporation for plaintiffs' damages is, as the court's finding described it, that "representations, warranties and inducements" oral and written were made to the plaintiffs with knowledge they were false and with knowledge that plaintiff purchasers would and did rely on them. . .

. . . Incorporation does not in law shield the actor from the legal consequences of his own tort. Where individuals carry on a business or enterprise by means of a corporate structure but in such relationship to the corporation that it can be said as a matter of fact that the acts of the corporation are the acts of the individuals and vice versa, then the same conclusion should be reached as a matter of law, i. e., that the acts of the corporation are in law as well as fact the acts of the individuals and vice versa.

An officer of a corporation, consequently, is liable for a tort committed in the course and within the scope of his official duties to the corporation the same as any other agent or servant is liable for his torts . . . for an agent is not exonerated from the consequences of his torts by the fact that, in committing them, he acted for his principal.

Affirmed.

FOSTER v. THE STATE OF GEORGIA
Court of Appeals of Georgia:
8 Ga. App. 119; 68 S.E. 739 (1910)

ARTHUR GRAY POWELL, J.

The defendant was convicted of cheating and swindling. It seems from this record that there was in Gainesville a grass-widow named Mrs. Robertson, and that she had as an intimate acquaintance the defendant, Foster, who was a young married man, connected with some kind of a show. According to Mrs. Robertson's version of the transaction here involved, Foster told her that he represented a Cincinnati company which organized lodges and furnished counterfeit money to its members; that he could cause her to be initiated by her paying the sum of $100, and that she would receive $500 in counterfeit money; but that she would have to go to Jacksonville, Florida (where the company's agent would be on January 12-14), to be initiated and get the money.

It was understood between them that they were to leave Gainesville secretly; so, on the night of January 12th, she privately met him at the railroad station. Here she gave him $10 to purchase her ticket to Atlanta. He purchased it for $3.15 and offered her back the change, but she told him to keep it for her. In Atlanta she gave him $20 with which to buy her a mileage book, and he bought that for her, putting the book in his pocket after securing her transportation to Jacksonville from it. Arriving in Jacksonville next day, she gave him the $100 with which he was to get her the $500 in spurious currency. He didn't come back. She was left penniless, but borrowed enough money from a policeman to get back home. She returned from Jacksonville on the same day she arrived there.

The defendant's statement was, that the affair was purely a meretricious escapade; that he and the woman left secretly and went to Jacksonville merely on a pleasure trip of a libidinous nature; that she gave him her money to keep for her, because she had no safe means of keeping it herself; that on the day of their arrival in Jacksonville, after they had spent a while in the room they were jointly occupying, he went down to the bar, where he met a number of old acquaintances; that he there became involved in a fight in which he was severely cut and slashed with a knife, and he was sent to a hospital, where he was confined for some time; that Mrs. Robertson, taking fright at what had happened, left him and returned to Gainesville. No other witness testified.

What the truth of this affair is, we, of course, do not know. Our personal views on that subject are not material. The jury's finding has given credence to the woman's version, and we must accept that as conclusive of the facts.

But do the facts make a case of cheating and swindling in Hall county, in which Gainesville is located? The accusation was apparently based on § 670 of the Penal Code of 1895, which provides: "Any person using any deceitful means or artful practice, other than those which are mentioned in this code, by which an individual, or the public, is defrauded and cheated, shall be punished as for a misdemeanor."

In Scots and civil law, the word "stellionate" is used to denote all such crimes in which fraud is an ingredient as have no special names to distinguish them, and are not defined by any written law. This section may, therefore, be said to be the statute against stellionates. However, the elements essential to the maintenance of a prosecution under it are tolerably well defined by the decisions of the court. There must be a false pretense, device, trick, or contrivance fraudulently made or enacted by the defendant with intent to deceive the prosecutor or person injured, so successfully accomplished that the prosecutor or person injured is in fact deceived and thereby suffers loss or damage. . . .

But beyond all this, the prosecution should not lie for the offense of cheating and swindling, under the facts of this case. How was Mrs. Robertson swindled? We must eliminate all transactions occurring out of Hall county, except in so far as they illustrate and give legal point to what occurred there. Was Mrs. Robertson deceived in Hall county? Yes; she was deceived into believing that if she would go to Jacksonville, Florida, she could get $500 in spurious currency in return for $100. She makes no complaint of not getting all she expected to get out of the trip and in return for the money she expended in connection therewith, except that she did not get the counterfeit money.

The transaction in Jacksonville, whereby she was induced to turn the $100 over to Foster, must be eliminated; for that occurred in Florida. So the question resolves itself into this: Can the defendant be convicted of cheating and swindling because he falsely represented to the prosecutrix that the existing conditions were such that, if she would go to certain expense, she could buy a certain amount of counterfeit money, and she, believing him, incurred that expense and did not get the counterfeit money? The question must be answered in the negative. If the representation had proved true, she would have been in a worse fix than she was when it proved untrue. The very possession of the counterfeit money would have made her a felon. As it was, when she did not get it, she was simply left as a foolish woman with less money and more experience; and, in legal contemplation at least, even this is better than being a felon.

We are not to be understood as holding that cheating and swindling can not be predicated of an unlawful transaction. There are many transactions for which the State can prosecute where the parties, by reason of the uncleanness of their hands, would not be allowed to maintain a civil action. Thus, although the sale of liquor is a crime in this State, yet if the keeper of a "blind tiger" should represent to a prospective purchaser that a bottle contained corn whisky, and should sell it as a bottle of corn whisky, receiving therefor the purchaser's money, when in fact it contained water only, he could be held for cheating and swindling. Or, if in a similar case the prospective purchaser should palm off on the keeper of a "blind tiger," in the nighttime, a worthless slip of paper as a dollar bill, and receive in exchange therefor a quart of whisky, the person so deceiving the seller of the liquor could be convicted of cheating and swindling. However, it must be noticed in each of these illustrations that the person deceived parts with something of value.

It is true that in this State liquor can not be said to have any market value in the full sense of the words; yet it is a thing of value. . . . But in no sense is counterfeit money a thing of value. The very possession of it is criminal. It is a violation of law to make it, to own it, or use it. It is utterly without value.

Suppose that the defendant had said to the prosecutrix, "Your sworn enemy is in Jacksonville; if you will go there with me and pay me $100, I will show that enemy to you that you may poison him." Suppose the defendant's statement were a lie, could the transaction be treated as cheating and swindling? The privilege of poisoning one's enemy is not a thing of value.

This case is also to be distinguished from those cases in which the defendant, by imposing on the credulity of weakmindedness of the prosecutor, has caused him to pay money for something which could not be of value, but which the prosecutor was led to believe was in fact so. In such cases a prosecution for cheating and swindling may lie. But in this case the prosecutrix acted with her eyes open; she admitted that she knew that the money she was to get would not be good money.

Plainly, the conviction can not rest on the failure of the defendant to return the change out of the ten-dollar bill which he received from the prosecutrix at Gainesville to buy her railroad ticket to Atlanta. She asked him to keep that for her. If he failed to return it on demand, the criminality of the transaction might be investigated under an indictment for larceny after trust, but not under this accusation for cheating and swindling.

However consummate the defendant's knavery may appear, however pitiable is the plight of the prosecutrix, we are constrained to hold that the defendant's conviction must be set aside. And after all--

> *"When lovely woman stoops to folly*
> *And finds too late that men betray,*
> *What charm can soothe her melancholy?*
> *What art can wash her guilt away?"* [1]

Judgment reversed.

AN ACT AGAYNST WEARING OF COSTLY APPARELL
Statutes of the Realm of England
1 Henry VIII, Chap. 14 (1509)

FORASMUCHE as the greate and costly array and apparrell used wythin this Realme contrary to good Statutes therof made hathe be the Occasion of grete impoverisshing of divers of the Kings Sugieths and pervoked meny of them to

---

[1] [Ed. Note: From Oliver Goldsmith, *The Vicar of Wakefield*, Chap.29.]

robbe and to doo extorcon and other unlawfull Dedes to mayntenyne therby ther costeley arrey: In eschewyng wherof, Be it ordeyned by the Authoritie of this present Perliament that no persone of whate estate condicon or degre that he be use in his apparell eny Cloth of golde of Purpoure Coloure or Sylke of Purpoure Coloure but onely the Kyng the Qwene the Kyngs Moder the Kyngs Chylder the Kings Brethers and Susters, upon payne to forfett the seid Apparell wherwyth so ever yt be myxte, and for usying the same to forfaite xx pounde;

And that no man under the astate of a Duke use in eny apparell of his Body or uppon his Horses eny clothe of gold of tyssue uppon payne to forfeyt the same apparell wherwyth so ever yt be myxte and for usying the same to forfette xx marke; and that no man undre the degree of an Erle were in his apparrell any Sables uppon payne to forfeyt the same apparell. And that no manne undre the degree of Baron use in his Apparell of his body or of his Horses eny clothe of golde or clothe of Sylver or tynsyn Satten ne no other Sylke or Clothe myxte or broderd wyth Golde or Sylver uppon payne of forfeyture of the same apparrell, albeit that yt be myxte wyth eny other Sylke or clothe, and for usyng of the same to forfett x marke;

And that no Mane under the Degree of a Lorde or a Knyght of the Garter were any Wollen Clothe made oute of this Realme of Englonde Irelonde Wales Cales or the Marches of the same or Berwyk, upon payne to forfayte the seid Clothe and for usyng of the same to forfayte x pounde. And that no mane undre the degree of a Knyght of the Garter were in his goune or Cote or eny other hys apparell any Velvett of the Colour of Crymesyn or blewe uppon payne to forfett the same Gowne or Cote or other apparell and for usyng of the same to forfett xl Shyllyngs. . .

And that no manne undre the degree of a Knyght, excepte Esquyers for the Kyngs body hys Cuppe beres Carvours and Sewers havyng the ordynarie Fee for the same and all other Esquyers for the body havyng possession of Landes and Tenements or other Hereditaments in theyr handes or other to ther use to the yerely value of CCC marke and Lordes Sonnes and Heyres, Justices of the one Benche or the other, the Maister of the Rolles, and Barons of the Kyngs Eschequer and all other of the Kyngs Councell and Mayres of the Citie of London for the tyme beyng, use or were eny Velvett in theyr gowenes or Rydyng Cootes or Furres of Martron in theyr apparrell uppon payne to forfett to same Furre and apparell wherwyth so ever yt be myxte and for usyng of the same to forfett xl Shyllyngs;

Nor no persone other then be above named were Velvet in their Dubletts nor Satten nor Damaske in their gownes nor Cotes, excepte he be a Lordes Sone or a Gentilman havyng in his possession or other to his use Landes or Tenements or annuytyes at the leste for Terme of Lyffe to the yerely valewe of an hundreth pounde above all repryses, uppon payne to forfeyte the same apparell wherwyth so ever yt be myxte and for usyng of the same to forett xl Shillyngs; Nor no persone use or were Satten of Damaske in ther Dobletts nor Sylke or Chamlett in their Gowenes or Cootes nott havyng Landes or Tenements in hys possession or other to hys use Office or Fee for terme of Lyffe or Lyffs to the yerely value of xx^{ti}

Pounde, excepte he be a Yoman of the Crowne or of the Kyngs garde or gromes of the Kyngs Chambre or of the Qwenys having therfore the Kyngs Fee or the Qwenes uppon payne to forfett the same apparell wherwyth soever hyt be myxte, and for usyng of the same to forfett xl Shyllyngs;

And that no mane undre the degree of a Gentilman excepte Graduates of the Universities and excepte Yomen Gromes and pagys of the Kyngs Chambre and of oure Souveraigne Lady the Qwenes, and excepte suche Men as have Landes Tenants or Fees or Anuytyes to the yerely value of xx ^{ti} pounde for Terme of Lyffe or an hundrethe pounde in Goods use or were eny Furres, wherof ther ys no like kynde growyng in this lande of Englonde Wales or in any Lande under the Kyngs obeysaunce, upon payne to forfett the same Furres and for usying of the same to forfett xl Shelyngs;

And that no mane under the degree of a Knyght excepte spirituall Mene and Sergeauntes at the Lawe or graduates of Universities use any more Clothe in eny longe Gowne then foure broyde yerdes, and in a Rydyng Gowne or Cotte above thre yerdes uppon payne of forfeyture [of the same. [1]] And that noo serving mane undre the Degre of a Gentilman use or were eny Goune or Coote or suche lyke apparrell of more Clothe then too brode yerdes and an halfe in a shorte Gowne and thre brode yerdes in a longe Gowne, and that in the seid Gowne or Coote they were not manner Furre, uppon payne of Forfeyture of the sayd apparrell or the value thereof;

And that no servyng mane waytyng uppon his Maister under the degree of a Gentilman use or were eny garded Hose or eny clothe above the pryce of xx d. the yerde in hys Hose except yt be of his Maisters weryng Hose apon payne of forfeyture of iij s. iiij d. And that no mane undre the degree of a Knyght were any garded or pynshed Sherte or pynched [partelet[2]] of Lynnen clothe uppon payne of Forfeyture of the same Sherte or [Partelett[3]] and for usying of the same [to forfeyte[4]] x. shillyngs;

And that no servaunte of [Husbondy[5]] nor Sheparde nor comen Laborer nor serv^{a}nte wnto eny Artificer owte of Cytie or borowe nor husbondman havyng no goods of his owne above the value of x. pounde use or were any Clothe wherof the broode yerde passythe in pryce twoo shillyngs nor that eny of the seid serv^{a}nts of Husbondrye Sheppardes nor Laborers were eny hose above the pryce of x d. the yerde uppon payne of imprisonament in the Stokkys by thre days;

And that he that wyll sue for eny of the seid Forfetures of the seid apparell forfeyted by eny persone undre the degree of a Lorde or a Knyght of the Garter have the seid apparell so forfeyted by accone of detynue. And the Kyng oure

---

[1] thereof O.
[2] perlet O.
[3] ptlett O.
[4] O. omits.
[5] husbondrye O.

Souveraigne Lorde to have the oon halfe of the forfeyture of the seid Money so forfeyted, or the Lord of the Franchysse yf yt be recoverd or presented wythin a Fraunches or Lete, and the pertie that wyll sue have the other halfe;

. . . And that the Lorde Stuarde of the Kyngs House for the tyme beyng wythin the Verge and Justices of Assize and Justices of the Peace, Stewardes in letes or lawe-days and every of them have also power to inqwere and holde plee of every Defaulte of the permysses as well by examynacon of the pertie as after the course of the Comen Lawe, and to determyn the same aswell at the Kyngs sute as at the suet of the pertie. . .

GROVE v. CHARBONNEAU BUICK-PONTIAC, INC.
Supreme Court of North Dakota
240 N.W.2d 853 (1976)

PAUL M. SAND, Judge.

This is an appeal from the decision of the Stark County District Court awarding to Lloyd B. Grove damages equivalent to the value of the automobile which was offered by Charbonneau Buick-Pontiac, Inc. as a prize in a golf contest.

The Dickinson Elks Club conducted its annual Labor Day Golf Tournament on September 1 and 2, 1974. Posters were placed at various locations in the area announcing the tournament and the prizes to be awarded to the flight winners and runners-up. Included in the posters was an offer by Charbonneau of a 1974 automobile "to the first entry who shoots a hole-in-one on Hole No. 8." This offer was also placed on a sign on the automobile at the tournament. Grove testified that he learned of the tournament from a poster placed at the Williston golf course. He then registered for the tournament and paid his entry fee.

The Dickinson golf course at which the tournament was played has only 9 holes, but there are 18 separately located and marked tee areas so that by going around the 9-hole course twice the course can be played as an 18-hole golf course. The first nine tees are marked with blue markers and tee numbers. the second nine tees are marked with red markers and tee numbers. Because of this layout of the course, the tee area marked "8" and the tee area marked "17" are both played to the eight hole. The tee area marked "17" lies to one side of tee area "8" and is approximately 60 yards farther from the hole.

Grove scored his hole-in-one in hole No. 8 on the first day of the tournament while playing from the 17th tee in an 18-hole match. He had played from the 8th tee previously on the same match and had scored a 3 on the hole.

Grove claimed he had satisfied the requirements of the offer and was entitled to the prize. Charbonneau refused to award the prize, claiming that Grove had not scored his hole-in-one on the 8th hole, as required, but had scored it on the 17th hole.

The trial court found that Grove had performed all of the conditions set out in the offer by Charbonneau so that there was a completed contract which Charbonneau had unlawfully breached by failing to donate the car. The court awarded damages to Grove of $5,800.00, plus interest.

Charbonneau claims the evidence was insufficient to support the trial court's finding that Grove had properly accepted and performed in accordance with the offer made by Charbonneau so as to impose a contractual duty upon Charbonneau to deliver the automobile or in the alternative be liable for damages. He also claims the trial court applied the wrong rule of law and that the findings of fact are clearly erroneous.

The selected following definitions found in Section II of The Rules of Golf as approved by the United States Golf Association and the Royal and Ancient Golf Club of St. Andrews, Scotland, effective January 1, 1974, may be helpful:

"Flagstick

The 'flagstick' is a movable straight indicator provided by the Committee, with or without bunting or other material attached, centered in the hole to show its position. It shall be circular in cross-section."

"Hole

The 'hole' shall be 4¼ inches in diameter and at least 4 inches deep. If a lining be used, it shall be sunk at least 1 inch below the putting green surface unless the nature of the soil makes it impractical to do so; its outer diameter shall not exceed 4¼ inches."

"Putting Green

The 'putting green' is all ground of the hole being played which is specially prepared for putting or otherwise defined as such by the Committee. A ball is deemed to be on the putting green when any part of it touches the putting green."

"Teeing Ground

The 'teeing ground' is the starting place for the hole to be played. It is a rectangular area two club-lengths in depth, the front and the sides of which are defined by the outside limits of two markers. A ball is outside the teeing ground when all of it lies outside the stipulated area."

Similar and other definitions may also be found under the title Golf, page 559, of Volume 10 of the *Encyclopaedia Britannica*, copyrighted in 1973.

The offer made by Charbonneau Buick stated that a 1974 Pontiac Catalina would be awarded to the "first entry who shoots a hole-in-one on Hole No. 8." Grove claims that his performance was an acceptance of this offer and created a binding contract.

Rewards and prizes are governed by the general rules of contract. There must be a genuine offer and an acceptance. To collect a prize, the person must perform all of the requirements of the offer in accordance with the published terms in order to create a valid and binding contract under which he may be entitled to the promised award. . . .

. . . the offerer has a right to prescribe in his offer any conditions as to time, place, quantity, mode of acceptance, or other matters which it may please him to insert in and make a part thereof, and the acceptance, to conclude the agreement, must in every respect meet and correspond with the offer, neither falling short of, nor going beyond, the terms proposed, but exactly meeting them at all points and closing with them just as they stand, and, in the absence of such an acceptance, subsequent words or acts of the parties cannot create a contract. . . .

The acceptance or performance may not be a modification of the offer. . . Substantial compliance, however, is sufficient. . . .

The general rule of the law of contracts which provides that where an offer or promise for an act is made, the only acceptance of the offer that is necessary is the performance of the act, applies to prize-winning contests. . .

The offer under consideration was as follows:

> "As an added addition to this year's Labor Day Tournament, Charbonneau Buick-Pontiac will donate a 1974 Pontiac Catalina 4-door sedan with factory air to the first entry who shoots a hole-in-one on Hole No. 8."

There were also some other prizes offered by the sponsor of the tournament. The entry fee was $20.00. From the advertisements and publications of the tournament there appears to be no question that the game was to consist of 18 holes, rather than 9 or some other number.

The problem arises from the fact that the golf course used for the tournament was a 9-hole course upon which 18 holes were played by going around the course twice. If the course would have been an 18-hole course we do not believe a question would have arisen because each hole would have had its own designation from 1 through 18, but because a 9-hole course was converted to an 18-hole course each hole had an actual number and a hypothetical number.

Under this setting we are required to construe and interpret the language of the offer.

The North Dakota Legislature has enacted statutes designed to help in the interpretation of contracts and obligations.

Section 9-07-09, NDCC, states:

> "The words of a contract are to be understood in their ordinary and popular sense rather than according to their strict legal meaning, unless used by the parties in a technical sense, or unless a

special meaning is given to them by usage, in
which case the latter must be followed.". . .

The Rules of Golf, to which reference has been made earlier herein, do not address themselves to situations where a 9-hole course is converted to an 18-hole course and thus are of little or no help in the interpretation and construction of the language used in the offer. . .

None of the words used in the offer stand out as being technical words. The argument was made by Charbonneau that the offer provided for a hole-in-one on hole No. 8, not in hole No. 8. However, this in itself is not controlling.

Grove contends that the words of the offer, when used in their ordinary sense, mean that any time in the process of an official play in the tournament a ball is hit into the eighth hole in one stroke, from either tee No. 8 or tee No. 17, the conditions of the offer are satisfied. Charbonneau, however, contends that the language of the offer has a technical meaning under the rules of golf and that there cannot be a hole-in-one on hole No. 8 unless the ball, with a single stroke, is hit from tee area No. 8 and lands in hole No. 8. . .

We have examined the rules, but have not found any, nor has any rule been called to our attention, which applies or covers the dispute under consideration. Rule 1 under Section III was called to our attention. It provides:

"The Game of Golf consists in playing a ball from
the teeing ground into the hole by successive
strokes in accordance with the Rules."

Unfortunately, it is not of any significant assistance.

Rule 30, under Section II, defines a "stipulated round" as consisting "of playing the holes of the course in their correct sequence unless authorized by the Committee. The number of holes in a stipulated round is 18 unless a smaller number is authorized by the Committee ..." However, this rule does not cover or apply to the dispute.

Charbonneau further contends that the claim for the prize was not submitted to the committee for consideration. Again, the rules do not cover the situation under dispute. The committee, according to Rule 11 of Section III, decides those items set forth in the Rule which do not include awards or prizes. For that matter, the offer made no reference to any committee which would act in determining whether or not the conditions of the offer had been met. It should be noted the sponsors of the tournament in this case were not the ones that made the offer. The offer was made by Charbonneau who could have placed some conditions or qualifications in the offer as to who should resolve the dispute, etc., in the event one arose, but this was not done.

The principal or sole dispute, in reality, between Grove and Charbonneau relates to the interpretation or construction of the words and phrases used in the offer. There is no significant dispute as to what happened on the golf course.

If the language of a contract leaves an uncertainty as to its meaning, the Legislature has provided for another test to be applied by the court in Section 9-07-19, NDCC, which states:

> "In cases of uncertainty not removed by the preceding rules, the language of a contract should be interpreted most strongly against the party who caused the uncertainty to exist. The promisor is presumed to be such party, except in a contract between a public officer or body, as such, and a private party, and in such case it is presumed that all uncertainty was caused by the private party.". . .

Where a contract contains ambiguous terms which are in dispute it is the duty of the court to construe them. . .

We believe the rule on ambiguous contracts applies to this case, and therefore any language of this contract which is not clear and definite or in which an uncertainty exists as to its meaning must be interpreted most strongly against Charbonneau.

Our research disclosed only one case in which the court dealt with a hole-in-one question, but in a different setting. The Supreme Court of Nevada, in Las Vegas Hacienda v. Gibson, [citation omitted] had under consideration the question whether or not the offer and promise to pay an award to a person who, having paid fifty cents for an opportunity to make a hole-in-one, actually did make a hole-in-one, constituted wagering on the contention that a hole-in-one was a game of chance rather than a game of skill and that on such basis the offer or promise was invalid. . . The court concluded that the contract or offer was valid and enforceable. . .

The crucial or pivotal point in this case rests upon the meaning of the language "a hole-in-one on Hole No. 8," where the 9-hole golf course was converted to or used as an 18-hole course without adding any additional holes. Does this language, "on Hole No. 8," refer to the actual, physical designation of the hole, which is generally identified with the number on the flagstick, or does it refer to the hypothetical number given to the hole because of the sequence in which it is "played"? If it is the latter, the 8th hole could also become the 17th hole in the second round of an 18-hole game of golf where the course is played around twice to make an 18-hole course out of a 9-hole course. The term could also mean the 8th hole in sequence of play regardless of the actual physical identification of the hole; as an example, if a player were to start his game with or on hole No. 2 (actually so marked) the 8th hole in sequence would be the 9th hole (actually so marked). The 8th hole under this concept would change depending upon the actual numerical designation of the hole from which the player started.

Charbonneau claims that the hole-in-one was actually accomplished on hole No. 17 because the course was a 9-hole golf course which was converted into an 18-hole course by going around the course twice.

However, Charbonneaus' own testimony in this respect is not in support of his contention but rather tends to suggest a basis for the ambiguity.

> Q. [Anseth] In reality there is no such thing as hole number 17 at the Dickinson Golf Course.
>
> A. [Charbonneau] There is. Oh, I am sorry, no. . .
>
> Q. [Anseth] Is there, in reality, a hole on green--what is called a green number 8 that says hole number 17 on it?
>
> A. [Charbonneau] No; there isn't.
>
> Q. What would the marker of the hole say on green 8?
>
> A. On green 8?
>
> Q. Yes.
>
> A. It would remain as the flag would say, yes.
>
> Q. Hole number 8?
>
> A. There is only one flag, and that's 8.
>
> Q. It would be 8 on the flag?
>
> A. Right.

In this instance, Grove and his group of players started with (from) tee No. 4 or hole no. 4. "On Hole No. 8" would then correspond to either hole No. 11 or No. 2, depending upon the particular sequence in which the holes were played, if the term "on Hole No. 8" refers to and means the hole played in sequence, as distinguished from the actual numerical designation of the hole.

Grove, on the other hand, argues that "hole-in-one on Hole No. 8" simply means a hole-in-one on the actual numerical designated hole No. 8 from any legitimate tee, in this instance from either No. 8 or No. 17, each having hole No. 8 as the final destination for the ball.

The following testimony explains the sequence in which the holes, both actual and hypothetical were played.

> Q. [Kirby] And then you played holes 4, 5 through 9 on the first go around and you don't remember the color of the tees, but you were playing the first nine?
>
> A. [Grove] Yes.

Q.   And then when you had completed the play on hole number 9, you went to hole number 1, did you not?

A.   Yes. . .

Q.   And then you went to green--you were playing green number 4, but you went to a different tee this time; did you not?

A.   Yes.

Q.   And that tee was marked as hole number 13, was it not?

A.   I assume it would be, yes. . .

Q.   And you played through 14, 15, 16 and you finally got to the tee marked number 17, which is a two hundred and eighteen yard hole?

A.   Yes.

Q.   And there is where you swung your club once from the teeing area and your ball went in on the first stroke; isn't that correct?

A.   Yes.

The sequence in which the holes were played also suggests room for misunderstanding. Why were the holes not played in the following sequence: 4, 5, 6, 7, 8, 9, 10, 11, 12, 13, 14, 15, 16, 17, 18, 1, 2, 3; instead of: 4, 5, 6, 7, 8, 9, 1, 2, 3, 13, 14, 15, 16, 17, 18, 10, 11, 12? This tends to illustrate, however, why misunderstandings arise in converting a 9-hole course into an 18-hole course. The rules of golf to which reference has been made do not provide the manner or sequence in which the holes should be played where a 9-hole course is converted or used for an 18-hole course.

The record contained little or no evidence which would have a bearing on the interpretation and construction of the language in the offer.

In an effort to learn more about the term "on hole No. _____" or if it has a meaning peculiar to golfers, we resort to an article by John P. May, entitled "Hole-in-One Roundup" found in Golf Digest for March 1976. We found the following expressions for a hole-in-one:

"holed out a tee shot on . . . 165-yard third hole."

"Knocked one in on the 103-yard 13th hole."

"aced the 13-yard 13th hole."

"tee shot on the 190-yard 12th hole bounced into the hole."

"dunked his tee shot on the 110-yard fifth hole."

"tee shot . . . found the cup on the 80-yard first hole."

"Scored a hole-in-one on the 135-yard fourth hole."

"She dropped in her tee shot on the 119-yard ninth hole."

"put his tee shot into the hole."

"zonked the 9th."

In the same article the following interesting description of consecutive holes-in-one (apparently a 9-hole course converted and used as an 18-hole course) was found on the nine-hole . . . "Golf Club course in Frampton, Quebec, Aug. 24 by holding tee shots on the 220-yard eighth and the 155-yard ninth (the 17th and 18th holes of the day for him)."

We presume this article used golfer's language, but whether it did or not is not significant. However, we note specifically that in describing where the consecutive holes-in-one occurred the actual numerical designation for each hole instead of the hypothetical number was used, such as "on the eighth and ninth" with the hypothetical numbers 17th and 18th, in parenthesis. While our conclusion does not rest upon this article, we are satisfied that it clearly demonstrates the need for greater clarity and specificity where a 9-hole course is converted or used for an 18-hole course, instead of a regular course with 18 holes.

The offer does not contain any qualifications, restrictions, or limitations as to what is meant by the phrase "on hole No. 8." Neither does the award or offer make any statement restricting or qualifying that the hole-in-one on hole No. 8 may be accomplished only from tee No. 8. If Charbonneau had in mind to impose limitations, restrictions, or qualifications he could have made this in the offer so that a person with ordinary intelligence would have been fully apprised of the offer in every respect.

The distance from tee No. 17 to hole No. 8 was greater than the distance from tee No. 8 to hole No. 8. Thus an argument cannot be made that a player had an advantage playing from tee No. 17 to hole No. 8, as compared to playing from tee No. 8 to hole No. 8. Actually, it would be a disadvantage.

The record does not disclose that either Grove or any other party made inquiries of Charbonneau or that Charbonneau made any explanation as to what was intended by the offer, particularly on the phrase "on hole No. 8," prior to the event here in question. We are thus limited to the actual words themselves.

The offer was not limited to professionals but was open to golfers generally who paid the fee and entered the tournament. Second § 9-17-10, NDCC, has little application because technical words were not used. The offer must be construed by giving the meaning commonly ascribed to the words used. . . .

It has become quite obvious that the answer or solution to the overriding question which initially may have seemed relatively simple and easy, even suspiciously so, is now actually, upon closer examination and after further analysis, considerably more challenging, demanding and difficult.

This court in In re Estate of Johnson, [citation omitted] in substance said that when good arguments can be made for either of two contrary positions as to the meaning of a term in a document an ambiguity exists. It also stated that the question whether or not an ambiguity exists is a question of law for the court. The contending parties have made good arguments, if not convincing arguments, for their positions.

Taking into account all of the foregoing considerations, we are satisfied that the language in question, "hole-in-one on Hole No. 8," in the offer, under this setting[1] is ambiguous.

Having concluded as a matter of law that the offer in this setting is ambiguous, the rule of law providing that the ambiguous terms will be construed and interpreted most strongly against the party who caused the ambiguity applies. . . .

The record does not provide any evidence whether or not anyone directed or exercised any influence over Charbonneau as to the language employed in the offer. However, such evidence would not be of much assistance unless it were in such form and nature so that the general public would have benefited from it in forming the meaning of the offer. We assume that Charbonneau is responsible for the language employed.

We have no reason to suspect that anyone other than Charbonneau deliberately chose the ambiguous language. We are not suggesting that Charbonneau intended to trifle with the public, but if we do not apply the rule of law on ambiguous contracts, as set out earlier herein, to this situation we would permit promotors to trifle with the public, which we do not believe the law should permit, and in fact, does not permit.

If this rule of law were not applied it would permit the promoter who is so inclined, where there has been a performance, to keep adding requirements or conditions which were not stated in the offer. As an example, such as, "must use a certain club; the ball must be of a certain brand; the play must be accomplished by a person playing left-handed," to name only a few.

Both of the constructions and interpretations of the language in the offer as contended by the parties are reasonable and each has some strong convincing points, but that does not constitute legal grounds for not applying the rule of law as to how ambiguities in a contract are to be resolved in a situation or setting we have here.

The fact that another golfer, amateur or professional, may not have made a claim for the award under the same circumstances would not have any bearing on this question.

---

[1] "In this setting" as used in this opinion means a situation where a 9-hole golf course was converted into and used as an 18-hole course by merely giving the existing nine holes hypothetical numerical designation in addition to the actual designation rather than by physically adding more holes, and by adding an additional set of tees to correspond to the hypothetically numerical designations.

By interpreting and construing the ambiguous provisions of the offer most strongly against the party who caused them as set out in § 9-07-19, NDCC, and as announced in case law developed on this subject, we construe it to mean that an entrant in the golf tournament who had paid the fee and who during regular tournament play drives the ball in one stroke into hole No. 8 from either the 8th or 17th tee has made a hole-in-one on hole No. 8, and has met the conditions of the offer and is entitled to the award or the equivalent in money damages.

The judgment of the district court is affirmed.

DYCUS v. SILLERS
Supreme Court of Mississippi
557 So. 2d 486 (1990)

JAMES L. ROBERTSON, Justice, for the Court:

This is a case about a fishin' hole. It lies in western Bolivar County near the River, and at birth was named Beulah Crevasse, though many have long called it the Merigold Blue Hole. People who can get there without trespassing on land want to enter and fish. Landowners and their long time lessee hunting club want just as badly to keep the public out. The relative scarcity of good fishing spots, Landowners' bona fide needs for protection of their valuable timber and water resources, club members' desire for undisturbed aesthetic and sporting enjoyment of the blue hole they have long thought theirs, the violent life of Old Man River, notions of fish as *ferae naturae* [of a wild nature], and, as well, the human penchant for confusing want with right, desire and entitlement, and the familiar with the necessary--these and more form important background forces driving this civil warfare which we are charged to channel within the levees of the law.

II.

This is also a case about a people, the waters they fish, and a unique culture and lore. These form an ambiguous but real part of our life whose pulse is preserved in the product of our poets from the famous to the obscure.[1]

Many think fishing the most leisurely of leisure activities, the positive pursuit of the lazy. In describing his childhood in Yazoo County, Willie Morris recalls

> We did cane-pole fishing, both to save money and because it was lazier, for we seldom exerted ourselves on these trips to Wolf Lake or Five Mile.[2]

---

[1] More often than we dare or can admit, law's lame language cannot convey the realities and mood of the matter the judge must adjudge.

[2] W. Morris, *North Toward Home* 75 (1967).

It was a leisure to be consumed and cherished, a spot in the shade preferred, and whether the fish were biting was secondary.

> When the biting was good, we might bring home
> twenty or thirty white perch or bream or goggle-
> eye; when it was bad we would simply go to sleep
> in the boat.[3]

But there was always a Miss Julia Mortimer, the local school marm, revered in time but then the scourge of every young Willie Morris, Miss Julia who'd "get behind some barefooted boy and push," said Uncle Percy. "She put an end to good fishing."

> Outside the home, we boys was more used to
> sitting on the bridge fishing than lining the reci-
> tation bench. Now she wanted that changed,[5]

Uncle Curtis remembered of Miss Julia.

Fishing is a part of the very life and being of many in Mississippi, as with Eudora Welty's enigmatic Billy Floyd, of whom "it was said by the old ladies that he slept all morning for he fished all night,"[6] and who Jenny noticed when he walked down the street because "his wrist hung with a great long catfish."[7] Ellen Douglas' Estella, who had just given birth said "Baby or no baby, I got to go fishing after such a fine rain."[8] the same Estella in whose fishing style Douglas sees poetry, Estrella who

> addressed herself to the business of fishing with
> such delight and concentration .... she stood over
> the pool like a priestess at her altar, all expectation
> and willingness, holding the pole lightly as if her
> fingers could read the intentions of the fish vibrat-
> ing through line and pole.[9]

Then there is Walker Percy's Anna Castagna, Binx Bolling's mother, who "looks like the women you see fishing from highway bridges,"[10] who sits on the porch over-looking the water at Bayou des Allemands and

---

[3] Id.

[4] E. Welty, *Losing Battles* 235 (1970).

[5] Id. at 236.

[6] E. Welty, "At the Landing" in *Collected Stories* 243 (1980).

[7] Id. at 240.

[8] E. Douglas, "Hold On" in *Black Cloud White Cloud* 166 (1963).

[9] Id. at 171.

[10] W. Percy, *The Moviegoer* 148 (1961).

> casts in a big looping straight-arm swing, a clumsy yet practiced movement that ends with her wrist bent in a womanish angle. The reel sings and the lead sails far and wide with its gyrating shrimp and lands with hardly a splash in the light etherish water. Mother holds still for a second, listening intently as if she meant to learn what the fishes thought of it, and reels in slowly, twitching the rod from time to time.[11]

Many Mississippians, including our own Chief Justice Roy Noble Lee,

> feel that a person who has never . . . angled for bass or caught bream on a light line and rod, or taken catfish from a trotline and limb hook has never lived.[12]

Still, some of us are like Faulkner's Lucius Priest who at age 11, when Uncle Parsham asked, "Do you like to go fishing?," thought "I didn't really like it. I couldn't seem to learn to want--or maybe want to learn-- to be still that long," but quickly: "Yes, sir."[13] Lucius, being led to Mary's fishing hole,

> sat on the log, in a gentle whine of mosquitoes.... Then I even thought about putting one of Lycurgus's crickets on the hook, but the crickets were not always easy to catch.... [When nighttime finally fell Uncle Parsham returned,] "had a bite yet?" [Lucius finally confess,] "I ain't much of a fisherman" I said, "how do your hounds hunt?[14]

Binx Bolling was of Lucius' mind, though it is doubtful they had anything else in common. "You know I don't like to fish." Binx said to his mother.

> "that's true," she says after a while "You never did. You're just like your father..... He didn't like to fish."[15]

---

[11] Id.

[12] Strong v. Bostick 420 So.2d 1356, 1364 (Miss. 1982) quoted in Pharr v. State, 465 So.2d 294 at 298.

[13] W. Faulkner, *The Rivers* 248 (1962).

[14] Id. at 249.

[15] W. Percy, *The Moviegoer* 149 (1961).

And so of Preston Cunningham,[16] even though his unwitting son, Carroll, had had a pond dug for him beyond the yard "stocked with bass and perch."

But even for those who warm to it so much more than Lucius and Preston and Binx, and maybe even Binx' father, fishing is not the central motion of our outdoor life but is always second fiddle to the hunt. Not quite the afterthought, it is the interlude, the escape, relaxation, almost taken for granted until you can't fish, not nearly so ennobling or paradoxical as hunting the deer, with its ritual rite of passage of adolescence and loss of innocence as when the old half-Indian Sam Fathers "dipped his hands into the hot blood" and marked young Ike McCaslin's face teaching him humility and pride.[17]

Perhaps it is because the fish is less like us--and more plentiful and more familiar, it is not the centerpiece but the analogy, the simile, as Ike thought as the bear disappeared into the woods:

> It faded, sank bank into the wilderness without
> motion as he had watched a fish, a huge ole bass,
> sink back into the dark depths of its pool and
> vanish without even any movement of its fins.[18]

Or Eudora Welty's "[m]uscadine spread under the waters rippling their leaves like schools of fishes."[19] Will Barrett's "knee leapt like a fish."[20] Gary, Larry Brown's lonesome night hawk, found Connie "cold as a fish."[21] And from Beverly Lowry:

> Might have been pleasant. Looking at his white
> behind-the-ear skin. White as a cooked perch,
> Emma Blue wistfully thought after she had re-
> fused John Robert's offer of a ride to school.[22]

Fish furnish less pleasant images. Again, Welty, describing the house after the floodwaters had receded:

> "The slime, that's just as slick"! You know how a
> fish is, I expect." the postmaster was saying
> affably to both of them, ... "That's the way a house
> is, been under water."[23]

---

[16] B. Lowry, *Emma Blue* 34 (1978).

[17] W. Faulkner, *Go Down, Moses* 165, 350-51 (1942).

[18] Id. at 209.

[19] E. Welty, supra, note 6 at 251.

[20] W. Percy, *The Last Gentleman* 187 (1966).

[21] L. Brown, "Night Life" in *Facing the Music* 116 (1988).

[22] B. Lowry, *Emma Blue* 19 (1978)

[23] E. Welty, supra, note 6 at 248.

CHAPTER VI: SCHEMES, CLAIMS, & CONTENTIONS

Mississippi's game fish are of many stripes, their personalities as different as our people.   There are the bream, Nash Buckingham's matchless little marauders"[24], but the biggest, little bigger than the size of your hand,[25] to any objective observer "the sweetest eatin' there is."[26] There are the perch and crappie, but little poetry about these.

Then there is the large mouth bass, Buckingham's "leviathans,"[27] "placed in the waters of the South so that fishermen have a preordained reason for idleness and spending money."[28] Outdoorsman Jim McCafferty says of bass: "This savage fighter will attack the right crank bait with all the fury of a treed wildcat."[29] Fishing for white bass on the oxbow lakes in the Delta, McCafferty exaggerates only slightly when he talks of "his duels with bruising white bass tak[ing] on an image of a sheriff looking for the outlaws."[30] David Chapman Berry, who grew up in the Delta, encounters the bass and is moved to poetry:

> Stump in the pond, stump in my eye. My fly
> pops inches from the stump. Bass, all wrist,
> roiling deep in thought, wedge from the bottom
> of the headpan, and buckling the surface under
> the fly, blur through their tunnel of scales,
> shattering the mirrory surface, the fly engorged,
> the fly, the fly leading the bass by the lip.
>
> I break their heads with the butt of the Buck knife.
> They stiffen shimmering. Scaling rakes the silver
> off mirrors--my raw eye a dump of shimmers?
> I eat fish to keep my head stocked.
> Some fellows refinish mirrors,
> but I eat fish to restore ponds.
> Don't believe it that life's only a matter of how
> you look at it. Smell my hands.[31]

---

[24] N. Buckingham, "Jailbreak" in *Game Bag*, 165 (1943).

[25] E. Douglas supra, note 8 at 171.

[26] See J. Autry, "Fishing Day" in *Life After Mississippi* 3 (1989).

[27] N. Buckingham, "The Sally Hole" in *The Tattered Coat*, 55 (1939)

[28] G. Morris, "Fishing" in *Encyclopedia of Southern Culture*, 1221 (1989)

[29] J. McCafferty, "White Bass Basics", in *MS Outdoors* 8 March, 1983).

[30] Id. at 16.

[31] D. Berry, "Bass" in *An Anthology of Mississippi Writers* (Polk and Scafidel eds.) 502 (1979).

Finally, is the ubiquitous catfish, of the family *Ictaluridae*, the blue, the channel and the flathead, of whom legends transcend the fact-fiction dichotomy. A gargantuan catfish bumped into Marquette's canoe, almost prompting the French explorer to believe what the Indians had told him about the river's roaring demon.[32] Huckleberry Finn and Jim caught a catfish that was as big as a man and "weighed over two hundred pounds."[33] Hodding Carter claimed to have "gigged a catfish that measured almost five feet in length."[34] Though still regarded rough fish, channel catfish farming has become the nation's leading aquaculture industry with Mississippi producing an estimated 200,000,000 pounds of farm-raised catfish a year.

The fisherman's tackle and gear vary widely, from the cane pole used to fish for bream and catfish. The legendary Kentucky reel is still the favorite of the bass fisherman.[35] Brooks Haxton tells of jug fishing. "[Y]ou took gallon jugs. Empty Clorox bottles were the best."[36] Hodding Carter jugfished for catfish.

> In jug fishing--to explain to the uninitiated-- empty, gaudily-painted gallon jugs float downstream, each dangling a heavy cord and hook and smelly bait from its corked mouth. The fisherman's boat follows lazily. When the catfish strikes, under go jug and fish and both remain there until the fish's strength is gone. There both erupt into the air and the fisherman approaches to pull in his catch. Incidentally, you don't scale a catfish. You nail him against a tree or barn and--since he has no scales, but a heavy, tough skin--you skin him.[37]

> The Encyclopedia of Southern Culture suggests a correlation between the economic and social stature of fishermen, the game fish they pursue, and the method they prefer to use. At the bottom of the economic scale, the preferred fishing is catfish/ bream by cork or bobber fishing/bait casting, bass/spinner fishing is the choice of blue collar families, bass fly-rod fishing of white collar workers, and artificial fly fishing for native trout is the preserve of upper income professionals.[38]

---

[32] Young, "Catfish" in *Encyclopedia of Southern Culture*, 378 (1989)

[33] M. Twain, *Huckleberry Finn* 60 (1885).

[34] H. Carter, *Man and the River: The Mississippi* 30-31 (1970).

[35] See Henshaw, "Evolution of the Kentucky Reel" in *Outing Magazine*.

[36] B. Haxton, "To Be a Jug Fisherman" *Dead Reckoning*, 84 (1989). Haxton's powerful poem reminds us of other realities of jug fishing for catfish and for life.

[37] H. Carter, supra, note 34 at 30-31 (1970).

[38] G. Morris, "Fishing", in *Encyclopedia of Southern Culture*, 1221 (1989).

CHAPTER VI: SCHEMES, CLAIMS, & CONTENTIONS

The point is belied by Ellen douglas' ten year old Ralph Glover, hardly a child of poverty or disadvantage.

> "I brought my gig," Ralph said, as they all trudged across the levee toward the Yacht Club. "I'm going to gig one of those great big buffalo or a gar or something."[39]

Still few would deny Larry Brown's truth

> The rich have never seined minnows to impale upon hooks for pond bass. The rich do not camp out. The rich have never been inside a mobile home.[40]

Not every Mississippi fisherman experiences what Mabry Anderson calls "the hypnotic lure of the outdoors."[41] Consider the Yocono River, Faulkner's Yoknapatawpha River, starkly seen by James Sey in his "Grabbling in Yokna Bottom."[42]

> The hungry come in a dry time
> To muddy the water of this swamp river
> And take in nets what fish or eel
> Break surface to suck at this world's air
> But colder blood backs into the water's wood--
> Fills the silt rather than rise to light--
> And who would eat a cleaner meat
> Must grabble in the hollows of underwater stumps
>   and roots,
> Must cram his arm and hand beneath the scum
> And go by touch where eye cannot reach
> Must seize and bring to light
> What scale or slime is touched--
> Must in that instant--on touch--
> Without question or reckoning
> Grab up what wraps itself cold-blooded
> Around flesh or flails the water to froth,
> Or else feel the fish slip by,
> Or learn that the loggerhead's jaw is thunder-deaf,
> Or that the cottonmouth's fangs burn like heated needles
> Even under the water.

---

[39] E. Douglas, supra, note 8 at p. 168

[40] L. Brown, "The Rich" in *Facing the Music* 38 (1988).

[41] M. Anderson, Outdoor Observations 166 (1977).

[42] J. Seay, "Grabbling in Yokna Bottom" in *Let Not Your Hart* (1970.)

The well-fed do not wade this low river. Mississippi is "the only state with a season for..[grabblin']."[43] Others compelled to fish are left by law and society no choice but to fish in such undesirable places as the ramp at Ellen Douglas' Lake Okatukla leading to the Phillip Yacht Club.

> Even in this terrible heat, at noon on the hottest day of the year, breathing this foul, fishy air, there will always be a few people fishing off the terminal barges, bringing in a slimy catfish or a half-dead bream from the oil water, raising their long cane poles and casting out their bait over and over again with dreamlike deliberation, ...[44]

Of course, mention of Huck Finn's and Hodding Carter's catfish tales suggests another inexorable feature of fishing, what Nash Buckingham called "finwhoppers."

> The worst of us get fed up and bored with pure, unadulterated lying. But a certain amount of rod and reel spoofing is absolutely essential to salve conscience, offset temptation and lend color.[45]

Barry Hannah tells us of water liars of another dimension in his story about "Farte Cove off the Yazoo River ... where the old liars are still snapping and wheezing at one another."

> "MacIntire, a Presbyterian preacher, I seen him come out here with his son-and-law, anchor near the bridge, and pull up fifty or more white perch big as small pumpkins. You know what they was using for bait?"

> "What?" asked another geezer.

> "Nuthin. Caught on the bare hook. It was Gawd made them fish bite," said Sidney Farte, going at it good.

> "Naw. There be a season they bite a bare hook. Gawd didn't have to've done that," said another old guy, with a fringe of red hair and a racy Florida shirt.[46]

---

[43] J. Autry, "Grabblin'" in *Life After Mississippi* 10 (1989).

[44] E. Douglas, supra, note 8, 161-62 (1963).

[45] N. Buckingham, "Over the Brook Cedron," in *Ole Miss'* 111 (1937).

[46] B. Hannah, "Water Liars" in *Airships* 5 (1978).

CHAPTER VI: SCHEMES, CLAIMS, & CONTENTIONS

Like tales are told at the Coffee Shop off the square in Clanton, Mississippi, where the folks talk "local politics, football and bass fishing."[47]

Fishermen see a different world than the rest of us. According to Mabry Anderson, "Unless you are over forty years old and a bream fisherman, you probably think a cockroach is just a dirty black bug."[48] They humanize these unhuman-like piscators, often talking the fish into the boat.[49] Lawyer Frank Wynne, a witness at trial, describing the contours of the Merigold Blue Hole, how the waters back out when the River is falling, lapses and tells of "a good fishing place" back where the waters come out of the woods and over the road. "I'll tell you what, you can go in there and catch a nice bass," and through the cold record his smile and priorities are seen.

The waters as well compete for bragging rights. The night before on what Doc had called "the best river dragging he'd ever been on," William Wallace had said "There is nothing in the world as good as ... fish. The fish of the Pearl River."[50] But none is the source of more lore and awe than the Mississippi. David Cohn said in the Delta, folks "fear God and the Mississippi River."[51] Mabry Anderson said, "The Old Man just rolls on and on and wipes out most of man's mistakes each spring when it charges right out of its banks."[52]

> No man alive can bob about on its surface in a puny fourteen-foot boat when the gauge is showing fifty feet or more at Helena, Arkansas, without becoming a little more tolerant and just a little less sure of himself.[53]

Still some see a flood a blessing, some like Luke Wallin's Watersmith and his sons Jesse and Bean and Robert Elmer who fish the Mock Orange Slough.

> They waded in the muddy cool water up to their waists, ... On their first pass they got a bucketful of bluegills and a small catfish. They wiped the mud and sticks from the net to try again.

"Every time the river floods," Paw said, "it brings us all these here treasures."

"Sho' does," Bean said.

"I think it's fine," Paw went on. "I think it's right nice of the old river."[54]

---

[47] J. Grisham, *A Time To Kill* 23-24 (1989).

[48] M. Anderson, *Outdoor Observations* 132 (1977).

[49] E. Douglas supra, note 8 at 171; and Anderson, *Outdoor Observations* at 161, 163 (1977).

[50] E. Welty, "The Wide Net," in *Collected Stories* 181 (1980).

[51] D. Cohn, *Where I was Born and Raised* 43 (1948).

[52] M. Anderson, *Outdoor Observations* 41 (1977).

[53] M. Anderson, *Outdoor Observations* 41 (1977).

[54] L. Wallin, "The Redneck Poacher's Son" in *I Mississippi Writers: Reflections of Childhood and Youth: Fiction* 618 (D. Abbott ed., 1985).

This is a case about a fishin' hole, and the people who contest for it and care for it so variously, who are charged by the infinite to accept it in its ambivalence and antinomy. Such a fishin' hole is Lake Chatula in the far southwest corner of Ford County which

> in the spring ... hold[s] the distinction of being the largest body of water in Mississippi. But by late summer the rains were gone, and the sun would cook the shallow water until the lake would dehydrate. Its once ambitious shore lines would retreat ..., creating a depthless basin of reddish brown water.[55]

> ...was deep flashing--
> Tiny grid-like waves wire-touched water--
> No more, and comes what is left
> Of the gone depths duly arriving
> Into the weeds belly-up:
> one carp now knowing grass
> And also thorn-shucks and seeds
> Can outstay him:
>
> * * * * *
>
> A hundred acres of canceled water come down
> To death-mud shaking
> Its one pool stomach-pool holding the dead one diving up
> Busting his gut in weedsin scum-gruel glowing with belly-white
> Unhooked around him all grass in a bristling sail taking off back-
> blowing. Here in the dry hood I am watching
> Alone, in my tribal sweat my people gone my fish rolling
> Beneath me and I die
> Waiting will wait out
> The blank judgment given only
> In ruination's suck-holing acre
> wait and make the sound surrounding NO
> Laugh primally: be
> Like an open-gut flash an open under-
> water eye with the thumb
> pressure to brain the winter-wool head of me,
> Spinning my guts with my fish in the old place,
> Suffering its consequences, dying,
> Living up to it.[56]

---

[55] J. Grisham, supra, note 47 at 11.

[56] J. Dickey, "Remnant Water" in *The Central Motion: Poems. 1968-1979* at 108-109 (1983).

CHAPTER VI: SCHEMES, CLAIMS, & CONTENTIONS

Buelah Crevasse is but ninety-two acres of not yet canceled water, and to those who war so over it Dickey seems to say that, if you like it when it is beautiful and serene and full of life, you must accept it--love it--equally when it has been taken away by nature and become but a mudhole with a dead carp in it, or when it has been taken by man, by the social invention he calls law. Dickey had these in mind when he said of such waters

> [Y]ou have to accept the "gone depths" as well as the real depths that used to be there when the lake was whole, the dead fish as well as the live ones, the repulsive aspects of the scene as well as the beautiful ones that have disappeared: and if you are left with "ruination's suck-holing acre" it is your due: you know this and accept it, even with a kind of exultation, because the bond between you and the lake still exists no matter what, and you can therefore "laugh primally," maybe no better than the dead belly-up fish but still, like he, in the old place, where you both belong, and know it.

We are informed by these thoughts, knowing that law is about life, that law is not an end but a means to the end of a society in which all should want to live, with its paradox and ambiguity, its irony and contrariety even that the law has wrought. We proceed to our institutional responsibility: the right interpretation and application of our law regarding rights to these waters.

III.

Named Plaintiffs include the heirs of Walter Sillers, specifically his widow, Lena R. Sillers, who died in 1983 after suit was filed, Mary S. Skinner, Evelyn S. Person, Lilian S. Holleman, John L. Pearson, Evelyn P. Weems, Vernon W. Holleman, Sr., and Florence H. Schoefeld. Alice K. Jones, the widow of Roy Jones, is a named Plaintiff, as in the Merigold Hunting Club, Inc., a Mississippi corporation. These are the parties who have brought this action, and in the main we call them "Landowners".

Landowners' contestants--Defendants below and Appellants here--are fishermen. Walter Allen Ford grew up and lived but a few miles from Lake Beulah. He fishes commercially, the tools of this trade trot lines, nets and a small outboard motor boat. He fishes for "rough fish"--buffalo, catfish, gar. And so of the Dycusses and Charley Allen. They fish mainly at night.[57]

---

[57] Compare E. Welty, supra, note 6 at 243; . . .

At the center is the Merigold Blue Hole, formally though erroneously known as the Beulah Crevasse,[58] and a remarkably good fishing hole in western Bolivar County, about six miles below Rosedale, covering in the main some ninety-two acres, a map of which appears as Appendix A. To the north and west a chute 112 feet wide from treeline to treeline and 192 feet from top bank to top bank runs to the southern end of Lake Beulah, an oxbow lake some six to seven miles long. In the chute connecting crevasse and lake the water is ten feet deep six to eight months a year.

West of the southwestern end of the oxbow, and somewhat northwest of the Crevasse, a drain traverses some two miles of wooded lands, connecting Lake Beulah to the Mississippi River. A dam or plug lies across the drain, built to help maintain the water level in Lake Beulah. There is a washout around the dam and small boars may pass from the River to Lake Beulah and back again at some river stages. Water roughly four feet deep often runs down the drain or chute.

The Mississippi River substantially affects the waters of Lake Beulah and the Beulah Crevasse. It generates aquatic and, more specifically, piscatorial life. The River also affects human life through its influence on water levels. When the Arkansas City Gauge measures 22 feet, water flows from the River to Lake Beulah and into Crevasse, and when it reaches 31 feet the "water breaks the road on the south side of the Crevasse and flows south." Water flows in the opposite direction, from the Beulah Crevasse and Lake Beulah north to the Mississippi River even when the water level is quite low (i.e., 4.8 on the Arkansas City gauge). There is

---

[58] The linguist knows that a crevasse in life on the River refers to a breach in the top bank of the levee, not a lakelike body of water. When this happens "furious blue waters roar down the remains of the levee scouring deep holes in the earth." Daniel, *Deep'n As It Come: The 1927 Mississippi River Flood* 22 (1977).

Nash Buckingham's short story, "The Sally Hole" tells of one such:

> Between the levee and the house lay a twenty-acre lake, formed years ago when a lower barrier broke under the strain of an over-whelming freshet and dug out a deep, somnolent "Blue Hole." Buckingham, *Tattered Coat* 56 (1930). In his story of the Great Flood, Pete Daniel mocks a Corps of Engineers Colonel's dissertation on "*blew* holes." Almost any inhabitant of the flooded area could have told the Colonel that it was a b-l-u-e hole because the water usually turned blue, and that it was the hole, some fifty to a hundred feet in depth, which was left when a crevasse gouged out the earth. Daniel, *Deep'n As It Come: The 1927 Mississippi River Flood*, 148 (1977). For a broader perspective, see W.A. Percy, *Lanterns on the Levee* 244 (1941).

Our search of the judicial literature has yielded but a glancing reference to the formation of a blue hole. See *Drainage District No. 48 of Dunklin County v. Small*, 318 S.W.2d 497, 504 (Mo. 1958).

In this opinion we consciously misuse the word "crevasse", because the parties do, and by it refer to the body of water south of Lake Beulah left when the floodwaters receded in 1912. Indeed, the U.S. Army Corps. of Engineers labels it "Buelah Crevasse (1912))" in *Flood Control and Navigation Maps of the Mississippi River*, Map No. 24 (56th ed. 1988).

no continuous one direction flow between Lake Beulah, Beulah Crevasse or the Mississippi River. When the River rises, however, there is a southward current, and vice versa as the water recedes. There is no commercial navigation qua transportation in the area.

Even so, had it been ever thus few would doubt the public's right to enter the Beulah Crevasse by water and to fish.

But it was not always so. For one thing, in the days of Tom Sawyer and Huckleberry Finn, Lake Beulah was the River itself. The Napoleon Cutoff [59] of 1863 "straightened" the River to the west and left its old bed an oxbow that became and has remained Lake Beulah. Alluvial deposits imperceptibly created batture land south and west of the new lake where Beulah Crevasse now lies, but in those days there was no crevasse and at least as early as 1883 the land was in cultivation. Before April 16, 1912, Landowners' predecessors in title farmed this land, as by then it was protected from the River and Lake Beulah by a levee to the north and west.

The world changed on April 17, 1912, as the levee broke and the River roared through at 208,000 cubic feet per second in the eighth greatest flood in history (but still the flood 1927 has made us forget) scouring several blue holes out of the earth. When the waters receded some forty-five acres remained lakelike and covered with waters. The mighty Mississippi had destroyed much but had given birth to the Beulah Crevasse of 1912.

Still seventeen years lay before the advent of the wide chute, today joining Beulah Crevasse to Lake Beulah so completely that the Dycuses and Allen and Ford insist that there is but one body of water, Lake Beulah. After the River receded in 1912 two small waterways connected Beulah Crevasse to Lake Beulah. One lay near the present chute, and not all agree regarding its dimensions nor its utility as a waterway, though the map shows it less modest than human memory suggests. A second more easterly drain appears on a map made in June of 1912 but became silted and impassable within the next eight to ten years.

By far the most persuasive evidence of the capacities of these post-flood drains is the contour map prepared by W.J. Shackelford, Chief Engineer, Mississippi Levee District, dated June 20, 1912--sixty-four days after the levee broke. That map reflects the westerly drain (the present chute) being approximately 728 north-south feet in length, ranging in width from approximately 100 feet at either end narrowing to about 78 feet in its center.[60] Its depth from top bank to bottom is some fourteen to fifteen feet. The easterly drain appears about 416 feet long. It is around 130 feet wide at its opening to Lake Beulah, narrowing to some 78 feet wide near its center and opening again to some 104 feet at its entrance to the

---

[59] For a brief description of the avulsion known as the Napoleon Cutoff, see *Chicago Mill & Lumber Co. v. Tully*, 130 F.2d 268, 270 (9th Cir.1942).

[60] These dimensions are easily computed by measurement of the appropriate parts of the Shackelford map, multiplied by its scale.

Crevasse. Its top bank to bottom depth is about seven to eight feet. With all of this detail, the most critical facts are missing, as water levels are not shown on the Shackelford map. . . .

No one disputes that the waters of Lake Beulah are public and anyone who wishes may fish there to his or her heart's content, subject only to the State of Mississippi's game and fish regulations which are enforceable precisely because the waters of Lake Beulah are public.[61] By the same token, for close to half a century there has been a considerable dispute regarding public access to the Beulah Crevasse.

Record title to most of what is now the lake bed of the Crevasse was in the McLemore family in 1912. In 1937 Walter Sillers bought most of the area and later sold half to Roy Jones. To this day Sillers' and Jones' heirs own the property, the boundaries of which are reflected on the map appearing as Appendix B. Several remaining acres of the Crevasse to the west and near the chute are owned by the Anderson-Tully Company, which has apparently had its fill of litigation over the years, and, parting waters with the Sillers, was not involved in this action. The Merigold Hunting Club, Inc. leases the hunting, trapping, fishing, ingress and egress rights from the remaining plaintiffs. It appears this relationship has existed since 1912, at least with the Landowners' predecessors in title.

Over the years these parties have employed a variety of stratagems to exclude the general public from the Crevasse. They have placed pilings and wire fences across the chute linking the Crevasse to the lake. They have posted the entrance to the chute. They have had the Hunting Club's caretaker deputized, a common practice up and down the River, and have arrested and prosecuted numerous "trespassers." Indeed, a long time Bolivar County prosecuting attorney is a life member who said below that he had prosecuted between fifty and one hundred people for "trespassing" in the Crevasse.

Landowners find significance in Disclaimer No. 881 given by the State Land Commissioner, the import of which is that the State of Mississippi claims no interest in certain lands which include by legal description the Beulah Crevasse. Walter Sillers[62] sought and obtained this Disclaimer in 1938, a year after he bought the property. Of course, no one denies Landowners' record title to the bed of the Crevasse, only their right to exclude the public from fishing its waters. Disclaimer No. 881 makes no reference to such waters. That Landowners pay no taxes on the Crevasse is interesting but similarly unpersuasive.

The year 1950 saw litigation not wholly unlike today's. On September 13 of that year, in an action styled *Merigold Hunting Club, et al. v. Paul Avant, et al.*, Docket No. 5198, the Chancery Court of the First Judicial District of Bolivar

---

[61] *State Game and Fish Commission v. Louis Fritz Co.*, 187 Miss. 539, 565-66, 193 So. 9, 12 (1940); *Ex Parte Fritz*, 86 Miss. 210, 217-18, 38 So. 722, 723 1905).

[62] From 1916 until 1966, Sillers represented Bolivar County in the Mississippi House of Representatives. From 1944 until 1966, Sillers served as Speaker of the House.

County held that the hunting club was "the lawful owner of the exclusive right and privilege to hunt, fish and trap wild game and fish on said lands and waters thereon . . ." None of today's defendants--the Dycus family, Allen or Ford, nor the members of the general public, were parties to that action, which insofar as the record reflects, hardly quieted anything.

Today's chapter begins in the spring of 1983 when Jimmy and Roger Dycus were caught in the crevasse and arrested. On April 29, 1983, a Bolivar County jury found Jimmy and Roger not guilty of trespass charges. This served only to enhance the frustrations of Landowners and the Hunting Club who soon thereafter--on May 11, 1983, to be exact--brought the present action in the Chancery Court of the First Judicial District of Bolivar County to quiet and confirm the title they claim in and to the Beulah Crevasse, and by injunction to exclude all others from the waters of the Crevasse. The Dycus family, Charley Allen, Allen Ford and, as well, the world were named as defendants, the named parties among whom promptly counterclaimed and sought to enjoin the Landowners and the Hunting Club from interfering with their right of ingress and egress through the chute and into the Beulah Crevasse and to fish its waters, always afloat.

The Chancery Court heard the case on September 12, 1984, and in due course entered final judgment, with findings of fact and conclusions of law, favoring Landowners and the Hunting Club and denying Dycus' counterclaim. . .The Dycuses, Allen and Ford appeal and ask that the Court reverse and declare a public right of access to the waters of the crevasse. . . .

[Not] all waters nor all fish swimming therein are public, . . . "artificially created water courses, inlets, slips, marinas the lake, . . . [and, as well,] physical improvements or alterations thereto upon lands theretofore private under state law remain private," the salt content of the waters notwithstanding. . . .Easiest are the now familiar catfish ponds, wholly man-made, which dot the Delta and into which fingerlings are placed, fed, raised and harvested, at all times privately owned by reason of the law of property. Where a lake or pond is wholly man-made or "artificial", the record title holders own the waters and all life within them as their interests may appear, . . . whether the lake or pond has been built for commercial, drainage, recreational or aesthetic reasons. By the same token, our law protects from interference a record titleholder's interest in small, completely landlocked natural (spring fed) lakes. Were Beulah Crevasse entirely landlocked and had it been so since 1912, Landowners of right could exclude all others from access to the surface waters. . . [S]mall artificial man-made bodies of water upon lands theretofore private remain private, and as well small, naturally-created ponded bodies of water by human means made accessible from public waters.

We described above the contours and characteristics of Beulah Crevasse and the chute leading to Lake Beulah and suggested that if it had been ever thus there could be no doubt that access to the waters of the Crevasse was available to the public. We are not at liberty to so view the matter, as our law ascribes great consequence to how what now is came to be.

If the Crevasse and chute had been entirely made by man, title thereto and the right to exclude others from the surface waters would reside in the owners of record. . . .This would not be true if the Crevasse and chute of today had been created entirely by a natural though avulsive process, as we have noted above. An avulsion may leave undisturbed title to lands or minerals, and indeed state sovereignty, . . . but the public right to waters formed by an avulsion is as great as any other public waters.

. . .The legal principles before us, we must apply them to the facts. . . . Our focus turns to the Flood of 1912 and, more pointedly, the flood's wake. Had the Crevasse been completely landlocked once the floodwaters receded so that neither fish nor fisherman could by water enter from Lake Beulah or by water exist the Crevasse, and had things remained so until 1929, the case would be easy. Landowners would win. Conversely, had the Flood of 1912 washed away the levee and merely expanded Lake Beulah a mile or so to the south, covering the entire of the Crevasse as shown on the Shackelford map of June 1912 and, as well, what lay between the Crevasse and lake so completely that the first time observer of the map or water would regard them as one, and had things remained so thereafter, the case would be easy. Landowners would lose.

Thus our point of beginning becomes whether, once the waters receded in the summer of 1912, the Crevasse as the forces of nature had left it was legally a separate body of water, a point turning on whether the two chutes or drains leading from Lake Beulah to the Crevasse were at the time capable of supporting substantial navigation by commercial fishermen for the better part of the year. . . .

The Chancery Court made no finding on the point and the evidence is less than crystal clear. The dimensions of the two chutes as they appear on the Shackelford map, coupled with the fact that there was another major flood in 1913, though not so great as that of the year before, suggest quite likely the waters of the chutes were sufficient that the waters of the Crevasse were then public. But this only begins our inquiry as nature in its brutal neutrality may give and take away almost willy-nilly. . . . Except for the avulsion exclusion above noted, the law leaves title holders at nature's risk and the State of Mississippi is as much at risk as any private landowner.

What is critical--and outcome-determinative--is the state of the water-courses connecting the Crevasse and Lake Beulah immediately prior to the 1929 artificial enlargement of the chute and the Crevasse.

The Chancery Court made extensive findings of fact regarding (non)navigability of the chute. The problem is that these findings are not tied to any particular point in time, this in the face of the certain though imperceptible evolution of geophysical reality over the seventeen years from 1912 to 1929. In such a setting we hesitate to employ the familiar substantial evidence rule. . . . Instead, we review the evidence to see whether we may find with confidence the state of things immediately before 1929, or whether we should remand for further findings under the principles of law articulated above.

For one thing, the 1925 survey map published by the Mississippi River Commission makes clear that Shackleford's 1912 easterly drain has vanished, at least 500 feet of land separating the Crevasse from Lake Beulah. The 1925 map reflects the westerly drain, but narrowed considerably from what it once was. Assuming accuracy of the map's scale, the chute would not be more than ten to twenty feet wide. Its depth and water levels are not given.

Austin Smith's personal observations of the conditions existing in 1929 at the time of the dredging powerfully support a non-navigability conclusion. Smith's analysis of River gauge readings suggests that in the last years before 1929 the waters between the Crevasse and Lake Beulah communicated only when the River was at flood stage. Immediately prior to 1929, the Beulah Crevasse was a separate and distinct body of water from Lake Beulah, and the Court below found "the communication of the waters [since 1929] is the direct result of the manmade outlet between the Crevasse and Lake Beulah created by the Corps of Engineers dredging.[63]

We have indicated above that the Shackelford map calls into serious question the suggestion that the waters of the Crevasse and Lake Beulah did not communicate shortly after the Flood of 1912 and in the few years thereafter. However, the 1925 map together with the eye-witness testimony offered by Landowners and the Hunting Club leave us without doubt that in the days immediately pre-1929 the chute was non-navigable. Likewise, the evidence is clear that the navigability of the chute is directly attributable to the Corps of Engineers' 1929 dredging operation, an artificial source. We find the evidence essentially uncontradicted that, in the days just before 1929, there was so little water in the chute one could step across it. From this we derive the ultimate fact that, immediatley prior to the 1929 dredging operation, Lake Beulah and the Beulah Crevasse did not communicate and were separate bodies of water, and upon this rock today's appeal founds. . .

AFFIRMED.

ROY NOBLE LEE, Chief Justice, concurring:
. . . Finally, I have never attempted to edit the opinions of my colleagues on this Court. However, in my view, the first twelve pages of the majority opinion would best have been left unsaid, or relegated to a work of prose or fiction. The Bench and Bar have much law and many opinions to read and digest and should be permitted to choose when and where to read for pleasure.

---

[63] From this we might imply a finding that immediately pre-1929 the waters of the Crevasse and Lake Beulah did not communicate, and then apply the substantial evidence rule, [citation omitted] were it not that the findings of fact before us make it clear that the Court never focused on that moment as distinguished from the 1912-1929 period generally.

CHAPTER VII

SCOUNDRELS, CROOKS, OUTLAWS, RENEGADES, ROGUES, KNAVES AND OTHER MISCREANTS; THEIR CRIMES, GRAND AND PETTY; AND THE PROCESSES AND PROCEDURES RELATED THERETO

. . . Despite history, general observation, and daily chronicles which record countless examples of evidence to the contrary, the fable persists that every person, including the worst villains of mankind, standing on the brink of eternity, allow only pearls of veracity to fall from their lips. . . Napoleon Bonaparte, with a fertility which surpassed Baron Munchausen's, invented memorabilia which still confuses historians, as he made ready for his last Waterloo. Nor is it recorded that Herod, Nero, Caligula, Tamburlaine, Attila, Genghis Khan, Alaric the Goth, Mithridates, Ivan the Terrible, Stalin or any of the other infamous scoundrels down through the ages regaled their entourages with stories on the moral verities as they were ferried across the river Styx. . . Godless ruffians, feudists, bandits, gangsters, all bent on their greedy, rapacious and vengeful deeds, have no scruples about dying as they lived,--with hate, dishonesty, and deceit in their mouths. . .

- Michael A. Musmanno, J.[1]
[Criticizing rule that a dying declaration may be given same probative value as sworn testimony.]

In works of labour, or of skill,
I would be happy too;
For Satan finds some mischief still
For idle hands to do.

- Isaac Watts[2]

---

[1] From dissenting opinion in *Commonwealth Of Pennyslvania v. Brown*, 388 Pa. 613; 131 A. 2d 367 (1957).

[2] From *State of Missouri v. Knowles*, 739 S.W. 2d 753 (1987) (Anthony P. Nugent, Jr., P.J.)

CHAPTER VII: SCOUNDRELS, CROOKS & OUTLAWS

CRUMBLEY v. THE STATE OF GEORGIA
Supreme Court of Georgia
61 Ga. 582 (1878)

LOGAN E. BLECKLEY, Justice

[Crumbley was placed on trial for the offense of shooting at another. He pleaded not guilty. The evidence disclosed that on the evening of December 25, 1877, as the passenger train on the Central Railroad was approaching Station No. 16, the defendant was standing, with three companions, about twenty steps from the track, having with him his shotgun; that when the train came within hearing, the defendant fired off his gun, commenced reloading with a shell containing powder only and no shot, and as the train passed, he fired at the engineer, who simultaneously ducked and was not injured; and that no shot struck the engine.]

. . . There is no dispute that the gun was loaded with powder, and that the prisoner fired at the engineer, at the distance of about twenty steps. Grant that it was done only "to have a little fun out of the engineer," in the merry season of Christmas, it was an assault. The engineer was not one of the revellers, but was engaged in the earnest and responsible vocation of running a locomotive and train upon a railroad. He had a right to pass on his way without being shot at from the roadside. It is not pretended that he knew with what the gun was charged, or for what purpose it was presented at him and fired.

Those who shoot at their friends for amusement ought to warn them first that it is mere sport, and that there is no danger. Fun is rather too energetic, even for Christmas times, when it looks like a disposition to indulge in a little free and easy homicide. Shooting powder guns at a man as a practical joke is among the forbidden sports.

Judgment affirmed.

REX v. HALLOWAY [Case 1]
Nisi Prius, Hereford Assizes (Crown Side)
171 E.R. 1131; 1 Car. & P. 126 (1823)

SIR JOHN HULLOCK, B.

The indictment in this case charged the prisoner with stealing one brass furnace, at the Parish of Brilley, in the county of Hereford.

From the evidence, it appeared, that the prisoner had stolen the furnace at a place called Clowes, in the county of Radnor, and that he carried it a little way, and then broke it, bringing the fragments into the county of Hereford. It appeared that Clowes, and the place at which he broke the furnace, were both more than five hundred yards from the boundary of the county of Hereford.

[In this case]. . . though a prisoner may be indicted for a larceny in any county, into which he takes stolen property, the present indictment must fail, as he never had the "brass furnace" in Herefordshire, or within five hundred yards of its boundaries: he merely had there certain pieces of brass.

(a) By the statute 59 George II, Chapter 96, § 2, it is enacted, that in any indictment for felony committed on the boundary of two or more counties, or within five hundred yards of the boundary, it shall be sufficient to lay the offence in either.

(b) With regard to description of stolen property in an indictment, it is particularly necessary to be precise. Nothing is so common as for the clearest cases to fail from a misdescription of this kind. I need not mention the well known cases of a man, indicted for stealing a pair of stockings, being acquitted, because the stockings were proved to be odd ones; or of the person acquitted of stealing a duck, because in proof it turned out to be a drake.

I was present at the acquittal of a man for forgery, in altering a *levari facias* [instrument of levy] from the county court, because it as called in the indictment a writ; a *levari facias* from the county court not being a writ, but only a warrant from the sheriff to his officer. It is best, at least in one county, to call the thing stolen by the same name the witnesses will call it in their evidence.

When an animal is described in an indictment by its name only, without the epithet dead, it will be considered to be alive. An indictment for stealing a horse would be but ill supported by proof of stealing a dead horse. The nearest case that I recollect to have met with is Rough's case, in Mr. East's Pleas of the Crown, where the prisoner was indicted for stealing a pheasant of the value of forty shillings, of the goods and chattels of the prosecutor: the twelve Judges held, that, from the description, it must be taken to be a pheasant alive, and so *feræ naturæ*; [of a wild nature] and, to show it to be a felony, the indictment should state it to have been dead or reclaimed; and the stating it to be of the goods and chattels, did not supply the deficiency. Perhaps the most curious distinction between living and dead is, that the stealing the skin of a dog, like stealing any other skin from the furrier, is a larceny; whereas stealing the living dog, which is the skin and something more, is no larceny; dogs being considered in law of a base nature, and not subject to larceny.

In actions against lords of manors for taking away game, the declaration usually is, that the defendant, "with force and arms, seized, took, and carried away" so many "dead hares," &c. *Bird v. Dale* [citation omitted], and *Churchward v. Studdy* [citation omitted], are instances of this. It may be said, that, in actions for penalties, for having game in possession, it is not usual to state that the defendant had a dead hare in his possession, but merely a hare. I apprehend the reason is, that this being an action on a statute, it is considered sufficient to follow the words of it.

Verdict--Not Guilty.

CHAPTER VII: SCOUNDRELS, CROOKS & OUTLAWS

REX v. HALLOWAY [Case 2]
Nisi Prius, Hereford Assises (Crown Side)
171 E.R. 1131; 1 Car. & P. 126 (1823)

SIR JOHN HULLOCK, B.

The same prisoner was also indicted for stealing "two turkies." (See Note (b) to the preceding case.)

Verdict - Not Guilty

STATE OF MISSOURI v. KNOWLES
Court of Appeals of Missouri
739 S.W.2d 753 (1987)

ANTHONY P. NUGENT, JR., Presiding Judge.

> In works of labour, or of skill,
> I would be busy too;
> For Satan finds some mischief still
> For idle hands to do.
>   Isaac Watts

As Mark Twain might have put it, this is a tale about what gets into folks when they don't have enough to do.

Old Dave Baird, the prosecuting attorney up in Nodaway County, thought he had a case against Les Knowles for receiving stolen property, to-wit, a chain saw, so he ups and files on Les.

Now Les was a bit impecunious, so the judge appointed him a lawyer, old Dan Radke, the public defender from down around St. Joe. Now, Dan, he looks at that old information and decides to pick a nit or two, so he tells the judge that the information old Dave filed against Les is no good, that under the law it doesn't even charge Les with a crime. Dan says Dave charged that Les "kept" the stolen chain saw and that's not against the law. You don't commit that crime by "keeping" the chain saw, says Day; the law says you commit the crime of "receiving" if you "retain" the saw, and that's not what Dave charged Les with, and the judge should throw Dave out of court. And that's exactly what the judge did.

But old Dave was not having any of that. No, sir! That information is right out of the book. MACH-CR 24.10. Word for word! Yes, sir!

Bystanders could plainly see the fire in old Dave's eyes. He was not backing down. Sure. Dave could simply refile and start over with a new information by changing only one word. Strike "kept"; insert "retained." But that is not the point. Dave knows he is right.

And so he is.

So we'll just send the case back to Judge Kennish and tell the boys to get on with the prosecution. And here's why:

The prosecuting attorney filed an information charging defendant Leslie Paul Kowles with receiving stolen property in the following language:

> The Prosecuting Attorney for the County of Nodaway, State of Missouri, charges that the defendant, in violation of Section 570.080, RSMo., committed the class C felony of receiving stolen property, punishable upon conviction under Sections 558.011.1(3) and 560.11 TSMo., in that on or about the 31st day of December 1986, in the County of Nodaway, State of Missouri, the defendant with the purpose to deprive the owner of a chain saw, kept such property of a value of at least one hundred fifty dollars ($150), knowing or believing that it had been stolen.

The form of the information precisely follows the form for the offense of receiving stolen property set out in MISSOURI APPROVED CHARGES-CRIMINAL (MACH-CR No.24.10) promulgated by the Missouri Supreme Court.

On defendant's motion, the circuit court dismissed the case without prejudice, holding that those allegations "did not constitute a crime under Section 570.080, RSMo., in that the language of the 'First Amended Information does not properly reflect the language of the statutory provision under which the defendant has been charged."

Rather than simply filing a new information in a slightly modified form, the prosecuting attorney chose to go to the mat with defendant.

> The statute in question, § 570.080.1, provides as follows:

> A person commits the crime of receiving stolen property if for the purpose of depriving the owner of a lawful interest therein, he receives, retains or disposes of property of another knowing that it has been stolen, or believing that it has been stolen.

Rule 23.01(e) of the Supreme Court's Rules of Criminal Procedure provides as follows:

All indictments or informations which are substantially consistent with the forms of indictments or information which have been approved
by this Court shall be deemed to comply with the
requirements of this Rule 23.01(b).

In sub-part 2, Rule 23.01 provides that an indictment or information must plainly, concisely and definitely state the essential facts constituting the offense charged. The rules do not require that the charge be brought only in the language of the statute.

The only question presented here is whether an information meant to charge a defendant under the receiving statute is sufficient if it charges that he "kept" the property rather than charging that he "retained" it. The answer is quite simply, "Yes." That is the end of the case.

Accordingly, we reverse the judgment and order that the prosecution proceed on the first amended information.

All concur.

IN THE MATTER OF CHARLOTTE K.
Family Court, Richmond County, New York
102 Misc. 2d 848; 427 N.Y.S.2d 370 (1980)

DANIEL D. LEDDY, Jr., Judge

Is a girdle a burglar's tool or is that stretching the plain meaning of Penal Law Sec. 140.35? This elastic issue of first impression arises out of a charge that the respondent shoplifted certain items from Macy's Department Store by dropping them into her girdle.

Basically, Corporation Counsel argues that respondent used her girdle as a kangaroo does her pouch, thus adapting it beyond its maiden form.

The Law Guardian snaps back charging that with this artificial expansion of Sec. 140.35's meaning, the foundation of Corporation Counsel's argument plainly sags. The Law Guardian admits that respondent's tight security was an attempt to evade the store's own tight security. And yet, it was not a tool, instrument or other article adapted, designed or commonly used for committing or facilitating offenses involving larceny by physical taking. It was, instead an article of clothing, which, being worn under all, was after all, a place to hide all. It was no more a burglar's tool than a pocket, or maybe even a kangaroo's pouch.

The tools, instruments or other articles envisioned by Penal Law Sec. 140.35 are those used in taking an item and not in hiding it thereafter. They are the handy gadgets used to break in and pick up, and not the bags for carrying out. Such is the legislative intent of this section, as is evident from the Commission Staff Comments on the Revised Penal Law of 1965 Title I, Article 140, N. Sec. 140.35, which reads in relevant part:

> "The new section, by reference to instruments 'involving larceny' . . . expands the crime to include possession of numerous other *tools*, such as those used for breaking into motor vehicles, stealing from public telephone coin boxes, tampering with gas and electric meters, and the like." (Emphasis added.)

The Court has decided this issues mindful of the heavy burden that a contrary decision would place upon retail merchants. Thus is avoided the real bind of having customers check not only their packages, but their girdles too, at the department store's door.

The Court must also wonder whether such a contrary decision would not create a spate of unreasonable bulges that would let loose the floodgates of stop and frisk cases, with the result of putting the squeeze on court resources already overextended in this era of trim governmental budgets.

Accordingly, the instant allegation of possession of burglar's tools is dismissed.

BROWN V. THE STATE OF GEORGIA
Court of Appeals of Georgia
134 Ga.App. 771; 216 S.E. 2d 356 (1975)

RANDALL EVANS, Judge.--

The D. A. was ready
His case was red-hot.
Defendant was present,
His witness was not.

He prayed one day's delay
From His honor the judge.
But his plea was not granted
The Court would not budge.

So the jury was empaneled
All twelve good and true
But without his main witness
What could the twelve do?[1]

---

[1] This opinion is placed in rhyme because approximately one year ago, in Savannah at a very convivial celebration, the distinguished Judge Dunbar Harrison, Senior Judge of Chatham Superior Courts, arose and addressed those assembled, and demanded that if Judge Randall Evans, Jr. ever again was so presumptuous as to reverse one of his decisions, that the opinion be written in poetry. I readily admit I am unable to comply, because I am not a poet, and the language used, at best, is mere doggerel. I have done my best but my limited ability just did not permit the writing of a great poem. It was no easy task to write the opinion in rhyme.

CHAPTER VII: SCOUNDRELS, CROOKS & OUTLAWS

The jury went out
To consider his case
And then they returned
The defendant to face.

"What verdict, Mr. Foreman?"
the learned judge inquired.
"Guilty, your honor."
On Brown's face--no smile.

"Stand up" said the judge,
Then quickly announced
"Seven years at hard labor"
Thus his sentence pronounced.

"This trial was not fair,"
The defendant then sobbed.
"With my main witness absent
I've simply been robbed."

"I want a new trial--
State has not fairly won."
"New trial denied,"
Said Judge Dunbar Harrison.

"If you still say I"m wrong,"
The able judge did then say
"Why not appeal to Atlanta?
Let those Appeals Judges earn part of their pay."

"I will appeal, sir"--
Which he proceeded to do--
"They can't treat me worse
Than I've been treated by you."

So the case has reached us--
And now we must decide
Was the guilty verdict legal--
Or should we set it aside?

Justice and fairness
Must prevail at all times;
This is ably discussed
In a case without rhyme.

The law of this State
Does guard every right
Of those charged with crime
Fairness always in sight.

To continue civil cases
The judge holds all aces.
But it's a different ball-game
In criminal cases.

Was one day's delay
Too much to expect?
Could the State refuse it
With all due respect?

Did Justice applaud
Or shed bitter tears
When this news from Savannah
First fell on her ears?

We've considered this case
Through the night--through the day.
As Judge Harrison said,
"We must earn our poor pay."

This case was once tried--
But should now be rehearsed
And tried one more time.
This case is reversed!

Judgment reversed.

IN RE WILLEM DOF
Justice Court of California, Tuolume County
Coroners Report No. 1 (1850)

R. C. BARRY, Justice Peace and Coroner pro tem.

No. 1 -- Willem Dof who was murthered with Buck October 20th 1850, (one mile from ofice,) after heering the evedense do find that he was barberously murthered, and that there was found $13 on the boddy of deseased, which ammount I handed over to the Publick Administrator, J. M. Huntingdon. Nothing more found to be his -- no clue to his murtherers. Justice Fees $10.

CHAPTER VII: SCOUNDRELS, CROOKS & OUTLAWS

IN RE MICHAL BURCK
Justice Court of California, Tuolumne County
Coroners Report No. 2 (1850)

R. C. BARRY, Justice Peace and acting Coroner.

No. 2 -- Michal Burck, found murthered one mile from my ofice October 20 1850, after dilegent sarch I find no deffects upon diseased. I couldn't find any clu to who murthered him.

Justice Fees $10.

IN RE GEORGE WILLIAMS
Justice Court of California, Tuolumne County
Coroners Report No. 3 (1850)

R. C. BARRY, Justice Peace and acting Coroner.

No. 3 -- George Williams who cutt his throt with a razor October 22 1850. Having heerd the evidense it is evident it is a case of Felo de see. Said Williams had no property that I could find out.

Justice fees, $10.

IN RE DR. JAMES SAY
Justice Court of California, Tuolumne County
Coroners Report No. 4 (1850)

R. C. BARRY, Justice Peace and acting Coroner.

No. 4 -- October 28th 1850. It was roomered that Dr. James Say was poisoned but upon a "bost morteum" examination by Dr. Bradshaw found that he died of disease of the hart. I found no property excepting $50 which I used in burrying the boddy.

Justice fees, $10.

IN RE T. NEWLY
Justice Court of California, Tuolumne County
Coroners Report No. 5 (1850)

R. C. BARRY, Justice Peace and acting Coroner.

No. 5 -- T. Newley killed by Fuller who shot him with a gunn January 30 1851. I found no property on the diseased. After trying Fuller and finding him guilty he was committed by me, and sentensed by the Court to two years confinement. He broke jale and run off.

Justice fees $10.

IN RE WM. A. BOWEN
Justice Court of California, Tuolumne County
Coroners Report No. 10 (1850)

R. C. BARRY, Justice Peace and acting Coroner.
No. 10 -- Wm. A. Bowen was found murthered morning of April 2, 1851
-- back of Washington street, ner Holdens Garden, was cut to deth with a knife -
- No clue to the guilty party, or who perpredaded the murther.
Justice fees $10.

IN RE WILLIAM BROWN
Justice Court of California, Tuolumne County
Coroners Report No. 11 (1850)

R. C. BARRY, Justice Peace and acting Coroner.
Wm. Brown found hanging to a tree May 1. 1851 ner Wood's Creek,
supposed he suicided himself two miles from town, no testimony. No property
found to belong to him.
Justice fees $10.

IN RE ANONYMOUS
Justice Court of California, Tuolumne County
Coroners Report No. 14 (1850)

R. C. BARRY, Justice Peace and Acting Coroner.
No. 14 -- Unknown man June 11 1851 found dead on the trale to Sullivan's
creek, no wounds on the boddy. After hearing all the surcumstances I concluded
he died a natural deth. No property found on the boddy but a roll of blankets, a
knife and pistol.
Justice fees $10.

IN RE JAMES HILL
Justice Court of California, Tuolumne County
Coroners Report No. 18 (1850)

R. C. BARRY, Justice Peace and acting Coroner.
No. 18 -- Inquest on the body of Jas. Hill hung by the mob back of Lecocks,
June 29, 1851. No clue to the parties purpedrading the hanging.
Justice Fees $10.

CHAPTER VII: SCOUNDRELS, CROOKS & OUTLAWS

IN RE WILLIAM CLARK
Justice Court of California, Tuolumne County
Coroners Report No. 19 (1850)

R. C. BARRY, Justice Peace and acting Coroner.

No. 19 -- Inquest upon the boddy of William Clark, July 16, 1851, was found dead in his bead about a mile north of this office in a Tent under verry supposed suspicions surcomstances but was found on examination to have died suddenly a natural death by diseese of the hart and lungs. No property but an old Tent, and a few little cooking, and keeping fixtures. Appropriaded them burrying the body.

Justice Fees $10.

IN RE HUNGRY TOM
Justice Court of California, Tuolumne County
Coroners Report No. 20 (1850)

R. C. BARRY, Justice Peace and acting Coroner.

No. 20 -- Hungry Tom, or Tom Welsh found stabed to deth July 20, 1851, supposed to have been fighting. No property found on his boddy but a large knife.

Justice Fees $10.

IN RE JUAN MONTALDA
Justice Court of California, Tuolumne County
Coroners Report No. 21 (1850)

R. C. BARRY, Justice Peace and acting Coroner.

No. 21 -- Juan Montalda July 20, 1851, found killed with his guts cut out, and stabbed to deth under same surcomstances and place. No evidence produced on his boddy was $51 which I appropriated to burrying the bodies.

Justice Fees $10.

IN RE WILLIAM FORD
Justice Court of California, Tuolumne County
Coroners Report No. 22 (1850)

R. C. BARRY, Justice Peace and acting Coroner.

William Ford, deputy sheriff, July 28, was shot and killed by a young man called Stud Horse Bob. Was considered justifiable, no property found with him but had some means in the hands of Major Holden who administered arrested him and examined the case no falt found.

Justice Fees $10.

STATE OF MINNESOTA v. McGLYNN
Supreme Court of Minnesota
292 Minn. 405; 195 N.W.2d 583 (1972)

C. DONALD PETERSON, Justice.

Defendant, Michael J. McGlynn, appealing from his conviction of aggravated robbery, challenges the constitutional propriety of testimony against him by two of his accomplices, Franklin J. Antell and Mary Anderson, both of whom had pleaded guilty to the offense but had not been sentenced, and the sufficiency of non-accomplice testimony to corroborate the Antell-Anderson testimony.

Defendant was the mastermind of a blundered fur robbery on December 12, 1968. At about noon of that day, defendant borrowed a blue 1963 Oldsmobile from Herbert Wroge, a used-car salesman, on the pretense of taking it to his wife for approval. This automobile was later identified by others as the getaway vehicle. At about 2:30 p.m. defendant and Raymond Stanley Smith (an accomplice who did not testify as state's witness) approached Antell, who was walking with his girl friend, Gail Dubak, and asked whether he "wanted to go on a score." Although Antell initially refused, he reconsidered after defendant assured him that the "score was real easy."

Mrs. Dubak did not hear the conversation since, at Antell's suggestion, she had continued walking to a nearby store to wait for him. Shortly thereafter, Antell and Mrs. Dubak accompanied defendant and Smith to Mary Anderson's apartment, which Smith shared with Mrs. Anderson, a divorcee. The presence of these persons together at the apartment both before and after the robbery was, as hereafter noted, attested by other witnesses.

At the apartment Antell, at defendant's direction, shaved off his beard and mustache and put on dress clothes supplied by defendant. Defendant gave Mrs. Anderson a blond wig to wear in the robbery, a wig similar to that which defendant gave for safekeeping to his downstairs neighbor, Colleen Clark, a few days after the robbery. Defendant at the same time handed a loaded .22-caliber revolver to Antell and supplied Antell and Smith with nylon hosiery with which to bind the persons to be robbed and laundry bags in which to carry the stolen furs.

Smith, Antell, and Mrs. Anderson then proceeded to execute the robbery of the Gershkow Fur Company at 1013 West Broadway, Minneapolis. Smith and Mrs. Anderson, who had previously visited the Gershkow store pretending to look at furs, entered first. As Mrs. Anderson was trying on a fur jacket, Antell entered twirling a revolver on his finger, and at some point he shot his own finger, an injury later observed by others. After tying up Gershkow and his wife with the nylon hosiery, Antell and Smith filled the laundry bags with furs, but they had tied Gershkow so ineffectually that he immediately escaped after they had left the store. Gershkow observed the blue Oldsmobile getaway car and ran to it, grabbing the car door handle. This so startled the robbers that they rear-ended another automobile. They drove away, but Gershkow noted the license number and reported it to the police.

The errant trio returned to the Anderson apartment. Antell proceeded to place the laundry bags loaded with the stolen furs into a panel truck which defendant had stated would be parked there for that purpose. However, the truck proved to be an exterminator's van, and Smith ran back from the apartment to assist Antell in carrying the loot into the apartment.

Defendant came to the apartment later to pick up the furs. Mrs. Dubak and Kathleen LaFore, a babysitter for Mrs. Anderson's children, observed defendant moving laundry bags in the apartment, and Mrs. Dubak saw defendant leave the premises carrying two large white bags which "looked like they were full of something." These bags were like those defendant supplied to Antell and Smith prior to the robbery.

Antell did not deliver all of the stolen furs to defendant but hid one fur coat under the bed before defendant came. He later offered to sell the coat to one Tim Janzen who, having read of the Gershkow fur robbery, turned the fur coat over to the police. Defendant himself sold one of the furs to his neighbor, Colleen Clark, who likewise turned the coat over to the police. Mrs. Gershkow subsequently identified one of the fur coats for the police from hand embroidery she had done on the inside of the coat.

The contention of defendant that the testimony of an accomplice is not adequately corroborated unless the evidence "directly" implicates the defendant in the crime is without merit. As we held in State v. Sorg, [citation omitted] corroborative testimony of nonaccomplices or other evidence may include:

> "* * *[P]articipation in the preparation for the criminal act; opportunity and motive; proximity of the defendant to the place where the crime was committed under unusual circumstances; association with persons involved in the crime in such a way as to suggest joint participation; possession of an instrument or instruments probably used to commit the offense; and unexplained affluence or possession of the fruits of criminal conduct. . ."

. . . The testimony of those persons, nonaccomplices, whose names are stated in the above recital of the facts clearly meets the Sorg-Stave criteria, amply corroborating the clear testimony of defendant's accomplices in the crime.

Defendant's contention that the circumstances under which his accomplices testified denied his right to a fair trial and due process is likewise without merit. The essence of this contention is that the accomplices, having been convicted but not yet sentenced at the time of trial, would too zealously cooperate with the state in testimony against the defendant in the self-serving expectation of a reward of leniency in their own sentences. If the jury was not instinctively aware of this impeaching possibility, defendant's counsel actively stimulated the jurors' awareness by vigorous cross-examination of Antell and Mrs. Anderson concerning promises of leniency made to them by either the prosecuting authorities or the court with respect to a sentence not yet imposed [1]. . .

Affirmed.

IN RE INQUIRY RELATING TO ROME
Supreme Court of Kansas
218 Kan. 198; 542 P.2d 676 (1975)

PER CURIAM:

This is an original proceeding in discipline against the Honorable Richard J. Rome, Judge of the Magistrate Court of Reno County. The Commission on Judicial Qualifications found that respondent Judge Rome, in issuing a written memorandum decision in a criminal case before him, had violated Canon 3A(3) of the Code of Judicial Conduct, for which it recommended that he be publicly censured. Judge Rome rejected the commission's finding and recommendation and the matter is here for determination. . .

The rule which respondent is charged with violating is a part of the code of judicial conduct adopted by this court effective January 1, 1974. It provides:

CANON 3

"A Judge Should Perform the Duties of His Office Impartially and Diligently. . . ". . . His judicial duties include all the duties of his office prescribed by law. In the performance of these duties, the following standards apply:

"A. Adjudicative Responsibilities. . .

". . . (3) A judge should be patient, dignified, and courteous to litigants, jurors, witnesses, lawyers, and others with whom he deals in his official capacity. . . "

---

[1] Their denial, to be sure, did not necessarily exclude the likely hope of the leniency that was subsequently accorded them. Antell and Mrs. Anderson, who pleaded guilty to charges of aggravated robbery, were subsequently sentenced to 5-year terms and were immediately granted probation. Smith, on the other hand, who had pled guilty but had not testified against defendant, was sentenced to a term of 3 years without probation. The court undoubtedly accorded Antell and Mrs. Anderson leniency because of their cooperation with the prosecutor, but the greater severity of Smith's sentence may additionally be attributed to a greater degree of culpability in the crime with respect to Smith's participating with defendant in the solicitation of Antell. . .

CHAPTER VII: SCOUNDRELS, CROOKS & OUTLAWS

On January 30, 1974, a woman was arrested in the south part of Hutchinson and charged with agreeing to perform an act of sexual intercourse for hire. Her arrest derived from her unwitting solicitation of a Hutchinson police officer to engage her services. Thereafter the defendant made bond for her court appearance.

Trial to the court was had on February 26, 1974, in the tribunal presided over by respondent. Defendant was represented by a Hutchinson attorney, Kerry Granger. She was found guilty and given the maximum sentence -- six months confinement in the Kansas correctional institution for women and a fine of $1,000. The defendant then filed a notice of appeal to the district court. The appeal was subsequently dismissed with her consent and the case was remanded to the magistrate court.

There, on May 20, 1974, defendant appeared with her attorney and applied for probation. Respondent took the matter under advisement and on May 23, 1974, he placed the defendant on probation for a period of two years.

In addition to filing an order of probation and making routine notations in his docket respondent also filed in the case a written instrument entitled "Memorandum Decision." The writing, which constitutes the subject matter of this proceeding, states (name of defendant deleted):

> This is the saga of _____ _____ _____,
> Whose ancient profession brings her before us.
> On January 30, 1974,
> This lass agreed to work as a whore.
>
> Her great mistake, as was to unfold.
> Was the enticing of a cop named Harold.
> Unknown to _____, this officer, surnamed Harris,
> Was duty-bent on _____'s lot to embarrass.
>
> At the Brass Rail they met,
> And for twenty dollars the trick was all set.
> In separate cars they did pursue,
> To the sensuous apartment of _____ _____.
>
> Bound for her bed she spared not a minute,
> Followed by Harris with his heart not in it!
> As she prepared to repose there in her bay,
> She was arrested by Harris, to her great dismay!
>
> Off to the jailhouse poor _____ was taken,
> Printed and mugged, her confidence shaken.
> Formally charged by this great State,
> With offering to Harris to fornicate.

Her arraignment was formal, then back to jail,
And quick as a flash she was admitted to bail.
On February 26, 1974,.
The State of Kansas tried this young whore.

A prosecutor named Brown.
Represented the Crown.
_____ _____, her freedom in danger,
Was being defended by a chap named Granger.

Testimony was presented and arguments heard,
Poor _____ waited for the Judge's last word.
The finding was guilty, with no great alarm,
And _____ was sentenced to the Women's State Farm.

An appeal was taken, to a higher court _____ went,
The thousand dollar fine was added to imprisonment.
Trial was set in this higher court,
But the route of appeal _____ chose to abort.

And back to Judge Rome, came this lady of the night,
To plead for her freedom and end this great fight.
So under advisement _____'s freedom was taken,
And in the bastille this lady did waken.

The judge showed mercy and _____ was free,
But back to the street she could not flee.
The fine she'd pay while out on parole,
But not from men she used to cajole.

From her ancient profession she'd been busted,
And to society's rules she must be adjusted.
If from all of this a moral doth unfurl,
It is that Pimps do not protect the working girl!

Subsequent to its filing the memorandum decision was widely published by quotation in the local news media, as well as over the state. This publicity evoked complaint against Judge Rome from a feminist group in Hutchinson in the form of a letter to the editor of the Hutchinson newspaper, with copies to the bar association and judicial authorities. The burden of the complaint was that the defendant in the case had been held up to public ridicule by Judge Rome.

Publication of the protest letter evoked a citation by respondent of its three signers to appear in magistrate court and show cause why they should not be held in indirect contempt of court. The three engaged legal counsel and appeared as directed. There, in an overcrowded courtroom, after voicing his views on the prostitution problem in the city of Hutchinson, respondent dismissed the contempt charges. The whole matter eventually reached the commission on judicial qualifications and this proceeding ensued. . .

Is the evidence here of such character as to sustain the conclusion reached by the commission? As already indicated the evidence in the record consisted of exhibits stipulated to by the examiner and respondent, plus respondent's testimony and in a sense the facts may be said to be undisputed so there is little reason for deference to the commission's superior opportunity to resolve sharply conflicting factual disputes.

Respondent, who has served as city attorney, as deputy county attorney and county attorney in his home county, and is a respected member of the Kansas bar practicing law in Hutchinson, testified as to his concern about the problem of prostitution in a particular area of Hutchinson: Prostitutes or their pimps were openly accosting people on the streets or waiting for stoplights; some prostitution cases had been tried in police court; he gave the maximum sentence in the defendant's case; his concern was "to jolt the south end and, more particularly, the pimps" and the memorandum decision was used "to get that point across;" he had no intent to degrade or ridicule the defendant; neither she nor her parents made complaint to him about the memorandum; her case had been previously publicized by the news media; he believed that women have been treated unfairly under our sex laws; he did not believe a judge should be denied the privilege of writing an opinion in poetic form.

Respondent cites several cases in which the decision was written in poetic form and argues he should not be chastised for doing that. He has not been proceeded against, nor found derelict, for use of the poetic form. The complaint is that in his decision he held the defendant up to public ridicule or scorn.

Judges have long been enjoined from the use of humor at the expense of the litigants before them for reasons which should be apparent. Under the heading of "Ancient Precedents" in the canons of judicial ethics adopted in 1924 by the American Bar Association this appears:

> "Judges ought to be more learned than witty; more
> reverend than plausible; and more advised than
> confident. Above all things, integrity is their
> portion and proper virtue. . .Patience and gravity
> of hearing is an essential part of justice; and an
> over-speaking judge is no well-tuned cymbal. . ."
> -- Bacon's *Essay* 'of Judicature.'

In 1967 a long time member of the supreme court of Arkansas in advising new judges on opinion writing had more to say on the subject. We quote: ". . . Judicial humor is neither judicial nor humorous. A lawsuit is a serious matter to those concerned in it. For a judge to take advantage of his criticism-insulated, retaliation-proof position to display his wit is contemptible, like hitting a man when he's down." (Smith, "A Primer of Opinion Writing, For Four New Judges," 21 *Ark.L.Rev.* 197, 210.)[1]

Judges simply should not "wisecrack" at the expense of anyone connected with a judicial proceeding who is not in a position to reply. When judges do this the stage is set for an imbroglio like that which apparently occurred after respondent here cited the three objectors for contempt of court, and respect for the administration of justice suffers.

Nor should a judge do anything to exalt himself above anyone appearing as a litigant before him. Because of his unusual role a judge should be objective in his task and mindful that the damaging effect of his improprieties may be out of proportion to their actual seriousness. He is expected to act in an manner inspiring confidence that even-handed treatment is afforded to everyone coming into contact with the judicial system.

Our reading of this memorandum decision leads to the conclusion the defendant in the prostitution case was portrayed in a ludicrous or comical situation -- someone to be laughed at and her plight found amusing. She was referred to throughout in terms designed to evoke chuckles over her activities. Her own integrity as an individual, convicted of crime though she was, was disregarded. The fact that neither she nor her parents made complaint is scarcely persuasive that she was not held out as a subject for public amusement. Respondent may not have intended to ridicule her or hold her out to public scorn yet that appears to be the effect of that which was done. Publicity about the memorandum was obviously expected.

Our code of judicial conduct and its implementing rules deal with a wide range of problems of varying degrees of seriousness. This particular proceeding does not present one of the greatest magnitude. Neither venality nor criminality is present nor can it be said the memorandum decision was written with deliberate intent to harm anyone. Yet, everything considered, we believe a violation of the canon in question has been shown. A litigant was not afforded the kind of treatment mandated.

It is therefore ordered that respondent Richard J. Rome be and he is hereby censured by this court. . .

---

[1] [Editors Note: It should be observed that Hon. George Rose Smith, author of the 1967 Article cited above has revised his opinion of Judicial humor, stating, *inter alia:* "In judicial language, that part of the Primer disapproving judicial humor is hereby overruled, set aside, held for naught, and stomped on!" Hon. George Rose Smith, "A Critique of Judicial Humor", 43 *Ark. Law Rev.* 1, 25 (Footnote 60) (1990). Judge Smith states also that: "There is assuredly some difference of opinion among appellate judges about the basic problem whether humor can be proper in a judicial opinion. When we asked the presiding judges of sixty appellate courts for citations to judicial humor, about ten percent of the forty-odd who responded said that humor is never used in the courts. We cannot quarrel with that firm position, for that was our own view until we had worked for more than a year, off and on, in the preparation of this critique. In the event, humor is used occasionally by the great majority of our appellate courts. . . Laying aside the cases in which humor should never be used, we now share Cardozo's belief that an opinion may not be the worse for being lightened by a smile.] *Id.* at pp 25-26.

AN ACTE FOR POYSONYNG
Statutes of The Realm of England
22 Henry VIII, Chap. 9 (1530)

THE KYNGES ROYALL MAJESTIE callyng to hys moste blessed remembraunce that the makyng of good and holsome lawes and due execution of the same agaynste the offendours therof is the only cause that good obedyence and order hath ben preserved in this Realme, and his Highnes havyng moste tender zeale to the same emonge other thynges consyderyng that mannes lyfe abouve all thynges is chyefly to be favoured, and voluntary murders moste highly to be detested and abhorred and specyally of all kyndes of murders poysonynge, which in this Realme hytherto our Lorde be thanked hath ben moste rare and seldome commytted or practysed;

And nowe in the tyme of this presente parliament, that is to saye, in the xviii[th] daye of Februarye in the xxiii yere of his moste vithorious reygn, one Richarde Roose late of Rouchester in the Countie of Kente coke, otherwyse called Richard Coke, of his moste wyked and dampnable dysposicyon dyd cast a certeyne venym or poyson into a vessell replenysshed with yeste or barme stondyng in the Kechyn of the Reverende Father in God John Bysshopp of Rochester at his place in Lamehyth Marsshe, wyth whych Yeste or Barme and other thynges convenyent porrage or gruell was forthwyth made for his famylye there beyng, wherby nat only the nombre of xvii persons of his said famylie whych dyd eate of that porrage were mortally enfected and poysoned and one of them that is to say, Benett Curwen gentylman therof ys decessed, but also certeyne pore people which resorted to the sayde Bysshops place and were there charytably fedde wyth the remayne of the saide porrage and other vytayles, were in lyke wyse infethed, and one pore Woman of them that is to saye, Alyce Tryppytt wydowe is also therof nowe deceassed:

OUR SAYDE SOVEREIGN LORDE THE KYNGE of hys blessed dispocision inwardly abhorryng all such abhomynable offences because that in manner no persone can lyve in suretye out of daunger of death by that meane yf practyse therof shulde not be exchued, hath ordeyned and enacted by authorytie of thys presente parlyament that the sayde poysonyng be adjudged and demed as high treason,

And that the sayde Richarde [Rose[1]] for the sayd murder and poysonynge of the sayde two persones as is aforsayde by auctorite of thys presented parlyament shall stande and by attaynted of highe treason; And by cause that detestable offence nowe newly practysed and committed requyreth condig e punysshemente for the same;

It is ordeyned and enathed by authoritie of this presente parliament that the said Richarde Roose shalbe therfor boyled to deathe withoute havynge any advauntage of his clargie.

---

[1] Roose O.

And that from hensforth every wylfull murder of any persone or persones by any whatsoever persone or persones herafter to be commytted and done by meane or waye of poysonynyng shalbe reputed demed and juged in the lawe to be highe treson; And that all and every persone or persones which hereafter shalbe laufully indyted or appeled and attynted or condempned by order of the Lawe of suche treson for any manner poysonyng of any persone shall not be admytted to the benefyte of hys or theyre clargye, but shalbe imedyatly after suche atteynder or condempnacion comytted to execucion of deth by boylynge for the same.

And that the Justyce of peace in every shire cytie or towne corporate wythin this Realme where Justices of Peace bene, shall have full power and authorytie in their Sessions to inquyre from tyme to tyme aswell of suche traytorous murderers and murders, as of the counterfaytynge of Coyne of any outewarde Realme, suffered to ronne and goo wythin this Realme by the Kynges assente, and to make percesse therapon by Capias onely;

And that the Justices of Assise in every Shire of Englonde shall have power and authoritie to here and determyne in theyre Sessyons aswell such tresons comytted and done by waye of poysonynge as the counterfeatyng of any such coyne sufferd to ronne wythin thys Realme by the Kynges assente as ys aforesayd.

AND FURTHERMORE it is enathed by authoritie of thys present parliament that all landes & tenants and other heredytamenete of any persone and persones which hereafter shalbe codempned or atteynted of any treson for poysonyng as is aforesaide, shall eschete remayne and be to the lordes of the fees, as by the lawes of this Realme landers and tenants of felons or murderers atteynted have heretofore excheted; this presente Acte of Treson or any thynge therein conteyned nat withstondyng. . .

IN RE CONFESSION OF TWEEDHALL
Assize Court of Northumberland County
Northumberland Assize Roll, 7 Edward I (1279)

ANONYMOUS, Judge

Robert of Tweedhall took sanctuary in the church of Saint Andrew of Newcastle, and confessed to being a highwayman, and abjured the realm in the presence of the coroner. His property: one penny, for which the sheriff will be answerable. Robert of Stokesley, coroner, was guilty of incompetence; accordingly, he is to be fined.

CHAPTER VII: SCOUNDRELS, CROOKS & OUTLAWS

IN RE TWO POTS
Assize Court of Northumberland County
Northumberland Assize Roll, 7 Edward I (1279)

ANONYMOUS, Judge

The jurors report that two pots were found in a field outside of the village of Tholkestor, and many valuables were found in them, but they do not know what the valuables were nor whose treasure it was. And they say that Simon, son of Folentinus and Robert Brand were the finders of this same treasure 22 years ago. They say that after they found the treasure, their standard of living increased a great deal. The aforesaid Simon is present; accordingly, let him be kept under guard. Robert is not present; accordingly, let him be put under arrest.

NEAL v. THE STATE OF GEORGIA
Supreme Court of Georgia
64 Ga. 273 (1879)

LOGAN E. BLECKLEY, Justice.

[Neal and Jackson were placed upon trial for the murder of one Houston, alleged to have been committed on February 2, 1879. The jury found the defendants guilty. Defendants moved for a new trial on the following grounds: Because during the argument of defendants' counsel, the court permitted one of the jurors to leave the courthouse without any other juror trying the case being with him. It was shown that the juror, by permission of the court, left the other members of the panel, in the charge of a bailiff, for the purpose of responding to a call of nature; that he spoke to no one during his absence, the bailiff being all the time in close proximity to him; that the bailiff only spoke to him to caution him against speaking to any one. The motion was overruled, and defendants appealed.]

In Monroe v. The State, [citation omitted] it was laid down and the rule has been followed in many subsequent cases, that where there has been an improper separation of the jury during the trial, the prisoner, if found guilty, is entitled to the benefit of the presumption that the irregularity was hurtful to him, the onus being upon the state to show, beyond a reasonable doubt, that it did him no injury. But must we therefore hold that a like presumption arises out of a proper separation - proper in time, manner and circumstances? Surely not. And what can be more fit than for the court to send out a juror, attended by a bailiff, when he is under a stress of nature which civilized man regards as a summons to retire? A comparison of the various possible methods of meeting and dealing with such an exigency had better be left to silent meditation than discussed here with needless realism. It is enough if those who may become interested in the subject will form a mental picture of the situation, and contemplate it for themselves. It is inferable from the record that the absence of the juror was not for a longer time than was necessary, and he was under the immediate watch and guard of the bailiff all the while. The facts are altogether unlike those of any of the cases cited by the counsel for the plaintiff in error. . .

. . . The separation discussed in these authorities is improper separation, not a retirement rendered necessary by habits of decency, expressly authorized by the court, and guarded by a sworn officer. . .

Judgment affirmed.

PEOPLE OF THE STATE OF MICHIGAN v. LUNDY
Court of Appeals of Michigan
145 Mich. App. 847; 378 N.W.2d 622 (1985)

WILLIAM R. PETERSON, Judge:

Defendant pursuant to a plea bargain entered a guilty plea to two counts of breaking and entering an unoccupied dwelling, M.C.L. Sec. 750.110. . .and to a supplemental information charging him as a third felony offender,[1] M.C.L. Sec. 769.11. Subsequently the court imposed sentences from 4 to 20 years on the breaking and entering convictions and from 6 to 20 years on the habitual offender conviction, to be served concurrently.

We must remand for resentencing.

In imposing sentence, the trial judge rejected the recommendation of the probation officer as being too short. His reasoning was based on the assumption that the actual sentence served would be far less than the minimum sentence imposed because the defendant would be the beneficiary of a number of 90-day time cuts under the Prison Overcrowding Emergency Powers Act, 1980 P.A. 519; M.C.L. § 800.71 et seq.. . .

We take judicial notice of that with which the trial judge was familiar, namely that the act was being invoked at a rate of four times every 13 months and that the Department of Corrections had advised Michigan's judges that rate would continue into the indefinite future unless additional prison facilities were provided.

We also note that the Governor of Michigan has recently declined to invoke the act, that the Legislature is considering repeal of the act, and that the Legislature is also considering new prison construction.

---

[1] Defendant had four prior felony convictions in other states and, while on bond for the within and other offenses in St. Joseph County, committed a breaking and entering in Kent County, Michigan, for which he had been sentenced as an habitual offender (second) to a term of from 3 to 15 years, which sentence was not consecutive.

CHAPTER VII: SCOUNDRELS, CROOKS & OUTLAWS

Other panels of this Court have noted the impropriety of lengthening a sentence as a buffer against possible sentence time cuts resulting from application of the emergency powers act, holding it impermissible to impose a sentence based on speculation and conjecture that the 90-day time-cut provisions of the act would continue to be implemented in the future or be utilized with the same frequency and regularity as in the past. *People v. Fleming,* [citation omitted]. . .

The decisions, however, are not an expression of confidence in the likelihood of legislative action to provide adequate prison space. And so, though remanding for resentencing, we sympathize with the frustration of the trial judge who is ordered to create certainty amid chaos. Though the Court in *Fleming* said that "[t]he sentencing court does not operate in a vacuum without consideration or concern for the actual effect of the judgment of sentence," that vacuum wonderland is precisely where the sentencing judge functions today.

The realities of contemporary sentencing suggest a different version of the case of The Emperor's New Clothes.[2] Perhaps the tailors who crafted the marvelous garments that no one could see were not swindlers but were honest craftsmen, ordered to deliver a product for which the Emperor provided no materials and appropriated no funds. Judicial craftsmen are ordered by statute and the ideal of *People v. McFarlin* [citation omitted] to produce a sentence

> "tailored to the particular circumstances of the case and the offender in an effort to balance both society's need for protection and its interest in maximizing the offender's rehabilitative potential."

It is sophistry to insist that this is or can be accomplished when the sentenced offender is delivered to a corrections system that is in shambles and from which, entirely apart from the EPA 90-day time cuts, inmates are precipitately returned to the community under a variety of programs designed to empty a cell for the most recently sentenced offender and with minimal regard for public safety, let alone for the needs of the offender. Pity the tailors; pity the jailers.

But the power to define limits of punishment and to provide the means of implementing corrections programs rests with the Legislature; the courts may not circumvent the legislative plan, even when that plan may seem to be an evasion of legislative responsibility. In its ordering of financial priorities, the Legislature has chosen to allow reduction of reasonable sentences and the early release of felons rather than to provide the prisons and the programs necessary to implement its own Criminal Code. By this we must abide. On remand, the sentencing judge must impose the sentence that he would have imposed without regard to the Prison Overcrowding Emergency Powers Act. . . .

The matter is remanded . . . for resentencing in conformity therewith.

---

[2] *Rex Imp. v. Tailors,* xxxx Dansk, H.C. Andersen reporter.

WHEAT V. FRAKER
Court of Appeals of Georgia
107 Ga. App. 318; 130 S.E. 2d 251 (1963)

HOMER C. EBERHARDT, Judge.

[The plaintiff, Douglas Fraker, obtained a verdict against the defendant, Judd Wheat, in a suit for damages growing out of an automobile collision. The defendant then moved for a new trial on the ground that the wife of the foreman of the jury was first cousin to plaintiff's wife and second cousin to defendant's wife. The motion was denied and the defendant appealed.]

> "Foul, foul play," the defendant cried.
>   "That I by kinsman be not trammeled
> Let the issue again be tried
>   Before another jury impanelled.
>
> Remember how from John at Runnymede
>   The Charta was forced and wrested
> That no matter what the issue or the deed
>   By my peers it must be tried and tested.
>
> With juror mine adversary durst
>   Try the cause, whose wife is second
>   cousin to my wife
> And to plaintiff's wife a first.
>   A new trial, sire, I demand to settle strife."
>
> "No foul play do I find or see,"
>   The judge replied. "Foreman's wife to thine
> And to plaintiff's wife may kinsman be,
>   But to Doug and thee no kinship do I find.[1]
>
> Thus, it doth not appear
>   For any cause or reason told
> That the juror was not thy peer
>   The case to try and verdict mold.

---

[1] "The groom and bride each comes within
   The circle of the other's kin;
   But kin and kin are still no more
   Related than they were before."
Central R. & Bkg. Co. v. Roberts, 91
Ga. 513, 517, 18 S.E. 315, 316.

> Moreover, when kinships we sought to learn
>   It doth not appear that as best befits
> One who would a kinsman spurn
>   Thou revealed that cousin did on the panel sit.
>
> Thy day in court thou hast had,"
>   The judge asserted, "and law commands
> That, no error made, whether good or bad,
>   The issue tried and settled stands."

Judgment affirmed.

IN RE GILBERT OF NIDDESDALE
Assize Court of Northumberland County
Northumberland Assize Roll, 40 Henry III (1256)

ANONYMOUS, Judge

The jurors report that a certain Gilbert of Niddesdale, a stranger, struck up an acquaintance with a certain hermit, whose name is Semannus of Bottlesham, and they were walking together in a certain moor, when this same Gilbert laid hold of that hermit and beat him, wounded him, and left him for dead, and stole from him his clothes and one penny, and fled. As he was fleeing, he ran into Randolph of Beleford, a sergeant of our lord the King, who laid hold of him and charged him with being a criminal, and took him to Alnwick. The aforesaid hermit came to Alnwick, and said that that other had robbed him and beat him, as was stated above. This same Gilbert confessed to same in the presence of the aforesaid bailiff and the people of the village of Alnwick. So the aforesaid sergeant had the aforesaid hermit cut Gilbert's head off. When the sheriff and coroner are asked by what warrant they had had Gilbert decapitated, they say that such is the custom of the county, that as soon as anyone is caught red-handed he is to be decapitated forthwith, and the plaintiff will receive the property of the one who is to be decapitated in place of what had been stolen from him.

IN RE JOHN OF CRAUMFORD
Assize Court of Northumberland County
Northumberland Assize Roll, 40 Henry III (1256)

ANONYMOUS, Judge

John of Craumford fled to the church of Bamburgh and there confessed to highway robbery, and abjured the realm in the presence of William of Bamburgh, who was then coroner. He had no property. Witness has been borne that the entire town charged him with highway robbery and wanted to arrest him, but he escaped from their hands to the aforesaid church, as related above; accordingly the village is to be fined. The 12 jurors concealed this matter; accordingly they, too, are to be fined.

NELSON v. STATE OF INDIANA
Supreme Court of Indiana
465 N.E. 2d 1391 (1984)

DONALD H. HUNTER, Justice.

In petition for post-conviction relief,
The petitioner herein expounds his grief.
The record shows he does not lie;
With the Code[1] the court did not comply.

The problem is, as we herein perceive,
Petitioner was not told he could receive
A possible increased sentence by reason
Of criminal convictions in another season.

In previous cases this Court has found
We must remand upon this ground.
It is the rationale of such decision
That rights be given with much precision.

We give the trial court instructions attendant:
To vacate the guilty plea of this defendant,
And the not guilty plea to reinstate;
It is so ordered from this date.

BIGGS v. THE STATE OF GEORGIA
Supreme Court of Georgia
29 Ga. 723 (1860)

JOSEPH H. LUMPKIN, J.

[The defendant, Biggs, was indicted in the court below, for an assault with intent to commit murder. There was also a count for shooting at another, not in his own defense. The jury found the defendant guilty.]

... The 9th charge given by the presiding judge to the jury, was in these words: "That although the shooting at another, might, if it resulted in death, be justifiable homicide, yet if death did not ensue, it would be a crime, under the Act of 1856, unless it were done in self-defence."

---

[1] The record shows that the court did carefully inform petitioner of the specific constitutional rights that he waived by pleading guilty. However, he did not inform petitioner "of any possible increased sentence by reason of the fact of a prior conviction or convictions" as the statute required. Ind. Code § 35-4.1-1-3(d). . . . Later, at the sentencing hearing, the court did use the prior convictions as one of the aggravating factors to enhance the sentence.

Such we concede is the letter of the 3d section of the Act of 1856. It provides, that from and after its passage, that any person who shall be guilty of the offence of shooting at another, or at any slave or free person of color, except in his own defence, with a gun, pistol, or other instrument of the like kind, shall, on conviction, be punished by a fine not exceeding one thousand dollars, and imprisoned not less than twelve months, or confinement in the penitentiary at the discretion of the court. . .

By the Penal Code, it is justifiable homicide to kill another, not only in self-defence, but in the defence of one's habitation, property or family, against one who manifestly intends to commit a felony on either. Can it be believed that the legislature intended, that if a husband or father shoots at one who is attempting to commit a rape on his wife or daughter, and fails to kill him, he is liable to be convicted under this Act, and imprisoned in the penitentiary? Never, we apprehend. The effects of such a construction would be too monstrous.

We must deviate then from the letter of the law, seeing that if literally interpreted, it leads to such absurd consequences, upon the same principle that it was decided, after long debate, that the Bolognian law, which enacted that whoever drew blood in the streets should be punished with the utmost severity, did not extend to the surgeon who opened the vein of a person that fell down in the street in a fit.

If it be justifiable homicide to shoot down a burglar who forcibly invades your house, with intent to commit a felony, as it undoubtedly is, and yet if you fail to kill him, you subject yourself to the penalty of the Act of 1856, the title of the statute should be amended. It should be "An Act to encourage good shooting." And yet it would seem to be passed for the purpose of preventing shooting altogether, except in cases of self-defence. . .

His honor, the presiding judge, charged the jury, "that under no circumstances of aggravation, however gross and direct, would a man be justifiable in taking the life of another, who attempts the seduction of his wife."

This instruction brings up broadly the meaning of the 16th section of the 4th division of the Penal Code. After treating of the various grades of homicide, murder, manslaughter--voluntary and involuntary and justifiable--it is provided that "all other instances which stand upon the same footing of reason and justice as those enumerated shall be justifiable homicide."

What is the meaning of this section? It signifies something. And it is the duty of the courts to give it effect. It has been suggested, that to bring cases within this provision, they must be accompanied with force. But has the legislature so limited it? Is it not more reasonable to suppose, that it was their purpose to clothe the juries in criminal cases, in which they are made the judges of the law as well as the facts, with large discretionary powers over this class of offenses; and leave it with them to find whether the particular instance stands on the same footing of reason and justice as the cases of justifiable homicide specified in the Code?

Has an American jury every convicted a husband or father of murder or manslaughter, for killing the seducer of his wife or daughter? And with this exceedingly broad and comprehensive enactment standing on our statute book, is it just to juries to brand them with perjury for rendering such verdicts in this State? Is it not their right to determine whether in reason or justice, it is not justifiable in the sight of Heaven and earth, to slay the murderer of the peace and respectability of a family, as one who forcibly attacks habitation and property? What is the annihilation of houses or chattels by fire and faggot, compared with the destruction of female innocence; robbing woman of that priceless jewel, which leaves her a blasted ruin, with the mournful motto inscribed upon its frontals, "thy glory is departed?" Our sacked habitations may be rebuilt, but who shall repair this moral desolation? How many has it sent suddenly, with unbearable sorrow, to their graves?

In what has society a deeper concern than in the protection of female purity, and the marriage relation? The wife cannot surrender herself to another. It is treason against the conjugal rights. Dirty dollars will not compensate for a breach of the nuptial vow. And if the wife is too weak to save herself, is it not the privilege of the jury to say whether the strong arm of the husband may not interpose, to shield and defend her from pollution?. . .

Judgment reversed.

AN ACTE AGAYNST DISGUYSED PERSONS AND WEARING OF VISOURS
Statutes of The Realm of England
3 Henry VIII, Chap. 9 (1511)

FORASMOUCHE as lately wythin this realme dyvers persones have disgysed and appareld theym, and covert theyr fayces with Vysours and other thyngs in suche manner that they shoulde nott be knowen and divers of theym in a Companye togeder namyng them selfe Mummers have comyn to the dwellyng place of divers men of honoᵣ and other substanciall persones; and so deperted unknowen; Wheruppon Murthres felonye Rape & oder greate hurtes & inconveniences have afore tyme growen and hereafter be lyke to come by the colour therof, yf the seid disordre shulde contynue not reformed:

Wherfore be it ordeyned and enathed by the Kyng oure Souveraign Lorde, & by the Lordes spirituall & temporall & the Comens in this present perliament assembled and by the authoritie of the same, That yf eny persone herafter dysgyse or apparell them wyth Vysoures or other wyse uppon theyr faces, and so disgysed or apparelde as Mommers or persones unknowen by reasone of theyr apparrell associate or accompanye theym to geder or aparte and attempte to entre or entre into the house of eny persone or persones, or assawte or affraye make uppon eny persone in the Kings hye waye, or in eny other place in forme aforeseid disgysed,

That then the seid Mommers or disgysed persones and every of theym shalbe arreasted by eny of the Kings liege people as Suspectes or Vacabundes and be committed to the Kings gaole, Ther to be imprisoned by the space of thre monthes wythowte bayle or maymprys, and then to make fyne to the Kyng by the discrescion of the Justices by whome they shalbe delyverd owte of prisone.

And also it is ordined and enacted by the seid auctoritie that yf eny persone or persones sell or kepe eny Vysoures or Vysoure in his house or in eny other place wythin this realme after the feaste of Easter nexte comyng and after this acte perclaymed, That the seid persone that kepyth the seid Vysoure or Vysoures shall forfeyte to the King oure Souveraigne Lorde for every Vysoure xx^{ti} shillyngs; and ferther shall suffre imprisonament and make fyne after the discrescion of the Justices afore whome he ys therof convicted, by examynacon or by inquisicon after the course of comen lawe.

And that the Justices of the Peace in their sessions, and Justices of gaole delivery and all other the Kings Justices have auctoritie to enquere hiere & determeyn all the premisses as well by examinacon as by inquisicion after the course of the Comen lawe. And this acte to endure to the nexte perliament.

PEOPLE v. INJUN BILL
Justice Court of California, Tuolumne County
Case No. 736 (1851)

R. C. BARRY, Justice Peace

In this caze injun Bill was indited for arsonizing a remada belonging to one John Brown by which he has lost all his furniture, bedding tools rifle shot gun pistol &c. Sentenced injun Bill to pay $32 and pay for the remada and contents, in defalt to be committed to gaol 60 days and be flogged 3 times on his bear back.

Cost of Court $32 all which was pade by some one.

Oct. 7, 1851
U. H. Brown, Consatable.

DICKSON v. THE STATE OF GEORGIA
Supreme Court of Georgia
62 Ga. 583 (1879)

LOGAN E. BLECKLEY, J.

[On October 29, 1878, defendants Preston Dickson, Irwin Dickson and Sarah Dickson were arraigned before the county court of Hancock county, on the charge of simple larceny.

The affidavit upon which the warrant was based, was made by T. J. Warthen before the county judge, and simply alleged that "to the best of deponent's knowledge and belief, Sarah Dickson, Preston Dickson and Irwin Dickson, did commit the offense of simple larceny in said county, on or about the 6th day of October, 1878, and deponent makes this affidavit that a warrant may issue for *her* arrest."

The warrant, issued by the county judge, directed the proper officer "to arrest the body of Sarah Dickson, Preston Dickson and Irwin Dickson, charged by T. J. Warthen with the offense of simple larceny, in said county, on or about the 6th day of October 1878, against the laws of this state, and to bring *him* before me, or some other judicial officer, etc." The petitioners waived indictment and trial by jury.

The written accusation, in proper language, charged the three defendants with the larceny in said county, on or about the sixth of October, 1878, of 1,500 pounds of seed cotton, of the value of $35.00, the property of David Dickson. It referred to the warrant as the basis of the accusation.

At the conclusion of the testimony for the prosecution the petitioners moved that the warrant and accusation be quashed upon the grounds that: the affidavit prays for the arrest of "*her*" and the warrant directs the arresting officer to bring "*him*" before a judicial officer for investigation, hence defendants say that no valid accusation can stand based upon a warrant so defective.]

The ground of the motion is grammatical, and involves the gender and number of two pronouns. "Her" in the affidavit should have been "them" and "him" in the warrant should also have been "them." This is an unsightly literary blemish, but not a grave legal infirmity. In school the composition would not pass, but it may be tolerated in the court-house. The meaning is clear, though the verbal inaccuracy is glaring. We may regret that those who write affidavits and warrants guard their pronouns with so little vigilance, but we cannot hold, as matter of law, that their bad grammar vitiates the documents. . .

The evidence of guilt may not have been conclusive, but it was enough to warrant the conviction. There was no error in refusing to sanction the petition for certiorari.

Judgment affirmed.

ROBERT ALDERS CASE
King's Bench, Michaelmas Term, 16 James
81 E.R. 654; 2 Rolle 52 (1676)

ANONYMOUS, Judge

Where the viscount explicitly states the county in which he is viscount. . . Alders was outlawed for murder, and an erroneous motion was made, that the viscount should return "To my county court held in my dominion in the county of Northumberland," and does not say "Into my county court held in Northumberland," etc. and this was held by the Court to be an error, in accordance with the case in the 6th year of Henry IV [A. D. 1405] where one is returned "to my county court held at Somersett," and for this reason it was held to be erroneous, for one can be Viscount of Surrey and Sussex, and also of Huntington-shire and Cambridge-shire.

EBERHART v. THE STATE OF GEORGIA
Supreme Court of Georgia
47 Ga. 598 (1873)

H. K. MCCAY, J.

[Defendants Enoch F. Spann and Susan Eberhart were indicted for the murder of Sarah Spann, alleged to have been committed on May 4, 1872. The indictment contained additional counts against defendant Susan Eberhart, charging her as a principal in the second degree, and as an accessory before the fact. The jury returned a verdict of guilty.] . . .

It gives us great pain to be compelled by our sense of duty to the law and to the public, to affirm this judgment.

We have, however, no sympathy with that sickly sentimentality that springs into action whenever a criminal is at length about to suffer for crime. It may be a sin of a tender heart, but it is also a sign of one not under proper regulation. Society demands that crime shall be punished and criminals warned, and the false humanity that starts and shudders when the axe of justice is ready to strike, is a dangerous element for the peace of society. We have had too much of this mercy. It is not true mercy. It only looks to the criminal, but we must insist upon mercy to society, upon justice to the poor woman whose blood cries out against her murderers. That criminals go unpunished is a disgrace to our civilization, and we have reaped the fruits of it in the frequency in which bloody deeds occur. A stern, unbending, unflinching administration of the penal laws, without regard to position or sex, as it is the highest mark of civilization, is also the surest mode to prevent the commission of offenses.

Judgment affirmed.

AN ACT MORE EFFECTUALLY
TO PREVENT PROFANE CURSING AND SWEARING
Statutes of The Realm of England
12 George II, Ch. 21 (1746)

FORASMUCH as the horrid, impious, and execrable vices of profane cursing and swearing (so highly displeasing to Almighty God, and loathsome and offensive to every Christian) are become so frequent and notorious, that unless speedily and effectually punished, they may justly provoke the divine vengeance to increase the many calamities these nations now labour under;

And whereas the laws now in being for punishing those crimes, have not answered the intents for which they were designed, by means of difficulties attending the putting such laws in execution;

For remedy whereof, may it please your most excellent Majesty, that it may be enacted; and be it enacted by the King's most excellent Majesty, by and with the advice and consent of the lords spiritual and temporal, and commons, in this present parliament assembled, and by the authority of the same, That from and after the first day of June, one thousand seven hundred and forty six, if any person or persons shall profanely curse or swear, and be thereof convicted on the oath of any one or more witness or witnesses, before any one justice of the peace for any county, city, riding, division, or liberty, or before the mayor, justice, bailiff, or other chief magistrate, of any city or town corporate, or by the confession of the party offending, every person or persons so offending, shall forfeit and lose the respective sums herein after mentioned; (that is to say)

Every day labourer, common soldier, common sailor, and common seaman, one shilling; . . .

And every other person under the degree of a gentleman, two shillings; . . .

And every person of or above the degree of a gentleman, five shillings.

And in case any such person or persons shall, after conviction, offend a second time, every such person shall forfeit and lose double; and for every other offence after a second conviction, treble the sum first forfeited by an offender, for profane cursing and swearing as aforesaid. . . .

And be it further enacted by the authority aforesaid, That in case any person or persons shall profanely swear or curse, in the presence and hearing of any justice of the peace for any county, riding, division, or liberty; or in the presence or hearing of any mayor, justice, bailiff, or other chief magistrate of any town corporate; every such justice, mayor, or other chief magistrate as aforesaid, shall, and is hereby authorized and required to convict every such offender of such offence, (in the form and manner herein after set forth) without any other proof whatsoever. . . .

And be it further enacted by the authority aforesaid, That in case any person or persons shall profanely swear or curse, in the presence and hearing of any constable, petty constable, tythingman, or other peace officer, and they and each of them are hereby authorized and required (in case any such person shall be unknown to such constable, petty constable, tythingman, or other peace officer) to seize, secure, and detain such offender or offenders, unknown to him or them as aforesaid; and such offender or offenders forthwith to carry before the next justice of the peace for the county, riding, division, or liberty, or before the mayor, justice, bailiff, or other chief magistrate of the town corporate, wherein such offence was committed; and the said justice, mayor, or other chief magistrate, is hereby authorized and required, on the oath of such constable, petty constable, tythingman, or other peace officer, to convict the offender in manner and form herein after directed:. . .

And be it further enacted by the authority aforesaid that. . . In case such offender or offenders shall not immediately pay down the respective sum so forfeited, or give security to the satisfaction of such justice, mayor, or other chief magistrate, before whom such conviction is made, it shall and may be lawful for such justice, mayor, or other chief magistrate, to commit the offender to the house of correction for the county, riding, division, liberty, city or town corporate, where such offence shall be committed, there to remain, and be kept to hard labour, for the space of ten days. . . .

Provided always, and it is hereby enacted by the authority aforesaid, That in case any common soldier belonging to any regiment in his Majesty's service, or any common sailor or common seaman belonging to any ship or vessel, shall be convicted of profane cursing or swearing as aforesaid, and shall not immediately pay down the penalty by him forfeited, or give security for the same as aforesaid, and also the cost of the information, summons, and conviction, as in and by this act is directed, every such common soldier, common sailor or common seaman, instead of being committed to the house of correction, as by this act is directed, shall by the said justice, mayor, bailiff, other head officer, be ordered to be publickly set in the stocks for the space of one hour, for every single offence; and for any number of offences, whereof he shall be convicted at one and the same time, two hours. . . .

Provided always, and it is hereby enacted, That no person shall be prosecuted or troubled for any offence against this statute, herein before or herein after mentioned, unless the same be proved or prosecuted within eight days next after the offence committed. . . .

And it is further enacted by the authority aforesaid, That this act shall be publickly read four several times in the year, in all parish churches and publick chapels, by the parson, vicar, or curate of the respective parishes or chapels, immediately after morning or evening prayer, on four several Sundays, (that is to say) the Sunday next after the twenty fifth day of March, twenty fourth days of June, twenty ninth day of September, and twenty fifth day of December, in every year;. . .

THE QUEEN v. SCOTT
Queen's Bench, Trinity Term, 26 Victoria
122 E.R. 497; 4 B. & S. 368 (1863)

SIR WILLIAM WIGHTMAN, J.

[Conviction by two justices of Buckinghamshire, removed by certiorari. The judgment was in the following form: "Bucks. Be it remembered, that on &c., at &c., John Mason Scott, of &c., mealman, is convicted before us, the undersigned, two of Her Majesty's justices of the peace for the said county, for that he, the said John Mason Scott, on &c., at &c., unlawfully did profanely curse one profane curse in these words, to wit (setting it out), twenty several times repeated. And we adjudge the said John Mason Scott, for his said offence, to forfeit and pay the sum of £2 to be paid and applied according to law; and also to pay James King, who prosecuteth in this behalf, the sum of 12s. 6d. for his costs. Given under our hands and seals," &c. . .

. . . In Easter Term, a rule was obtained calling upon the prosecutor to shew cause why the conviction should not be quashed on the grounds, first, that it included several offences, and was therefore bad for duplicity and in contradiction of Stat. 11 & 12 Victoria Chapter 43 Sec. 10.; secondly, that the penalty was not warranted by Stat. 19 George II, Chapter 21, Sec. 1; under which the conviction took place.]

I am of the opinion that this rule must be discharged. I will consider the case first without. . . This is a prosecution under Stat. 19 George II, Chap. 21., intituled "An Act more effectually to prevent profane cursing and swearing," by which it is enacted (Sect. 1) that "if any person or persons shall profanely curse or swear, and be thereof convicted &c. before any one justice of the peace, &c., every person or persons so offending, shall forfeit and lose the respective sums hereinafter mentioned; (that is to say,) every day labourer, &c., one shilling; and every other person under the degree of a gentleman, two shillings; and every person of or above the degree of a gentleman, five shillings. And in case any such person or persons shall, after conviction, offend a second time, every such person shall forfeit and lose double, and for every other offence after a second conviction, treble the sum first forfeited by an offender, for profane cursing and swearing as aforesaid."

And by Sec. 8 a form of conviction is given [his Lordship read it]. The conviction in the present case follows the form given in the statute; for the defendant is convicted, for that he "did profanely curse one profane curse in these words, to wit," (the curse is set out which without doubt is profane,) "twenty several times repeated," and he is adjudged "for his said offence" to forfeit and pay the sum of 2l., being at the rate of two shillings per curse.

It is objected that this is a conviction for several offences, and is therefore bad. But several cases of convictions under Stat. 6 William III, Chapter 11 were brought before us, and in all of them the defendant was charged with swearing several oaths which were included in one conviction, and he was adjudged to forfeit so much at the rate of two shillings for each oath; and though in all the instances the conviction was quashed, the present objection has never before been taken; . . .

. . . The conviction in form is indeed for the offence of cursing several profane curses; and it is said that it only warrants the imposition of one penalty. But the form given in the statute evidently shews that the Legislature contemplated that a person cursing or swearing one or more profane curses or oaths may be adjudged to pay a cumulative penalty in one conviction; and the profane cursing or swearing being the offence which the statute prohibits, as often as the person repeats such curses or oaths consecutively he forfeits the sum specified. Therefore, looking at the case independently of Jervis's Act, I am of opinion that on the terms of the statute and upon authority the conviction ought to be supported.

Then it is said that at any rate the conviction is bad since Jervis's Act, Stat. 11 and 12 Victoria, Chapter 43; because Sect. 10 enacts that every information for any offence punishable upon summary conviction "shall be for one offence only, and not for two or more offences." The offence here is the swearing on one occasion so many oaths, which subjects the defendant to a cumulative penalty of two shillings for each oath. It is said that the defendant is subject to one penalty only; but according to the construction which has been put upon Stat. 19 George, Chapter 21, and the form given by that Act, though the offence of swearing the same oath several times on one occasion is one, it seems to have been considered that the penalty was at the rate of so much for each oath sworn at the same time. Therefore, if the offence is one, and the question only as to the amount of penalty, Sect. 10 of 11 & 12 Victoria, Chapter 43. does not apply. . .

IN RE EVOTA AND FEMOTA OF CHIVINGTON
Assize Court of Northumberland County
Northumberland Assize Roll, 40 Henry III (1256)

ANONYMOUS, Judge

Evota, daughter of William of Chivington, and Femota, daughter of Nicholas of Chivington, were robbed in the Forest of Stobbeswood by unknown brigands as they were returning from the Midford Fair. It is not known who the culprits were. Since this happened in daytime, and the hue and cry was raised, the villages of East Chivington, Acklington, Eshott, and Bockenfield, who did not make pursuit, are accordingly to be fined.

COMMONWEALTH OF PENNSYLVANIA v. BROWN
Supreme Court of Pennsylvania
388 Pa. 613; 131 A. 2d 367 (1957)

JOHN C. BELL, JR. , Justice.

A narrow but very important question is raised in this case: Was it reversible error to charge the jury that a dying declaration in a homicide case has the same effect as if it were made under oath?

Mary E. Brown was indicted for murder but was convicted of voluntary manslaughter. Defendant and Vivian Gay, apparently in a fit of jealousy, attacked Dorothy Francis, the decedent, on the street. Dorothy Francis was killed by a knife wound in the breast. Who stabbed her was the crucial factual question, Vivian Gay blaming Mary Brown and Mary Brown blaming Vivian Gay. Two eyewitnesses testified that defendant, Mary Brown, attacked Dorothy Francis with a knife, while Vivian Gay beat her with a golf club. . . . Dorothy Francis, just before her death and at a time when she knew she was about to die, made a dying declaration that Mary Brown, the defendant, stabbed her. . .

A dying declaration should in our judgment be given the same value and weight as sworn testimony, and any statement to the contrary in prior cases will not be followed by us.

Judgment affirmed.

MICHAEL A. MUSMANNO, Justice (dissenting)

The Majority Opinion in this case helps to perpetuate the myth that dying persons always tell the truth. Despite history, general observation, and daily chronicles which record countless examples of evidence to the contrary, the fable persists that every person, including the worst villains of mankind, standing on the brink of eternity, allow only pearls of veracity to fall from their lips. Adolf Hitler told some of the most monumental falsehoods which ever disgraced the human race, (even for that congenital prevaricator,) as he prepared to kill himself in the subterranean bunker in Berlin in the closing days of his conscienceless life. Napoleon Bonaparte, with a fertility which surpassed Baron Munchausen's, invented memorabilia which still confuse historians, as he made ready for his last Waterloo. Nor is it recorded that Herod, Nero, Caligula, Tamburlaine, Attila, Genghis Khan, Alaric the Goth, Mithridates, Ivan the Terrible, Stalin or any of the other infamous scoundrels down through the ages regaled their entourages with stories on the moral verities as they were ferried across the river Styx.

The perpetrators of all the unsolved murders in the world are liars who go down to their grave wholly oblivious to the angels of truth crying for confession and revealment. Atheists who repudiate belief in a Supreme Being have no inhibitions against wagging their tongues in spurious tales as death rattles in their throats. Godless ruffians, feudists, bandits, gangsters, all bent on their greedy, rapacious and vengeful deeds, have no scruples about dying as they lived,--with hate, dishonesty, and deceit in their mouths.

In her recently published book on the life and times of Sir Edward Coke, Catherine Drinker Bowen relates how in Lord Cobham's accusation of treason against Sir Walter Raleigh it was generally accepted that, because Lord Cobham was himself soon to be executed, his charges could only represent truth: "Impossible that a man with death so close upon him would lie thus to the Lords. What had he to gain thereby?" Yet it developed later that Cobham had lied because he hoped thereby to receive sovereign clemency. He in fact later did escape the death penalty.

To say that the world can invariably depend on the truth-speaking accuracy of a dying person is to ignore the most fundamental, physiological facts. Putting aside for the moment the undependability of knaves in their last, gasping moments, it should be manifest on the slightest reflection that even the statements of the most honorable persons on their deathbeds are not necessarily reliable. A dying person is at the ebb of his physical and mental resources. With every corpuscle struggling for survival, with every brain cell ringing in alarm, with the lungs fighting for that extra breath of air which may prolong the buoyancy of the ship of life sinking rapidly in the dark waves of oblivion, the mind is not always capable of assembling the forces of memory, concentration, and lingual control so as to guide speech into the channels of rational utterance. To juridically announce that a dying statement is the superlative demonstration of revealed fact is to glorify error, honor fallacy, and place the seal of infallibility on the most fallible of human assertions.

Moreover, it is not always certain that a person in extremis is consciously aware that the candle is about to be extinguished or will admit to himself that his body is reverting to mortal dust. It is an assumption which has never been proved, nor can it be proved, that when a moribund speaks, he knows his minutes are numbered. He may declare that he is dying, but with the exception of those who are preparing for suicide or execution, it cannot be established that with the very acknowledgment of anticipated death, he is not hoping and expecting that an untapped reservoir of strength may prolong what no one surrenders voluntarily.

These observations are so obvious and so irrefutable that one cannot help but wonder why the phantasy has grown that the last words heard above the tumult of the last battle for survival should be the last word in precision, accuracy, and trustworthiness. This illusion has come floating down the centuries, with each generation further inflating its ever-expanding balloon proportions, and the time had arrived to burst the age-ridden fallacy which almost amounts to superstition. I was hoping that, with the excellent opportunity before it to do so, this Court would with the lance of logic pierce the bag of this spurious dirigible and bring it down to the terra firma of realism from which it should never have ascended.

It is bad enough to assert that a dying declaration represents the highest expression of certitude but to say, as the Majority of this Court says in the case before us for review, that dying words must be invested with all the solemnity and sanctity of a statement made under oath, approaches credulousness. More than that, such a ruling is unjust because it clamps about the neck of the accused a yoke which he cannot possible shake off. He is accused by a person he cannot see, he is charged with words he cannot refute, he is attacked with an accusation he cannot counter-attack through cross-examination. Such a ruling requires juries in effect to accept fallible evidence as infallible proof; it calls upon juries to look upon dying speeches as if they were delivered at the altar of forthrightness when in fact they may have been concocted in the laboratory of cunning and deceit.

That there is something awesome about final pronouncements is not to be questioned, but the awesomeness does not assure that an incense lamp of integrity has been lighted at the bedside of the pronouncer. It could just as well be that the gasping speaker is projecting his voice through the smoke of dissimulation. An expiring murderer could have as much motive to falsify as he had to kill. If the

Sixth Commandment did not deter him from slaughtering his fellow-man, the Ninth Commandment would present no barrier to his bearing false witness. One who has already smashed the temple of life would find no difficulty in upsetting the pedestal of truth. Hence, the absolute need in treating of dying declarations to present the facts as they are, unvarnished with preconceived notions of sanctity and dependability.

Let the jury know just what occurred and let them decide whether the declarant, in the calm, dispassionate atmosphere of a tribunal of law, would have testified in the same manner as he spoke amid all the passions, fears, and pain which assailed him at the moment of his fatal utterance. Let the jury decide whether the declarant would be as categorical in his statements if he were in a courtroom, where he is subject to the laws of perjury as he was when he was beyond the reach of the law and the reprisal of refutation.

Of course, it could happen and it does happen, that at the very breaking of the thread of life one will speak gospel even if he never spoke it before. It can happen and does happen, that as one's soul departs on the flood tide of perpetuity he may wish to leave on the shores behind him only the chapel of haloed truth, but there is nothing in the chronicles of the human race which warrants the conclusion that this is a common experience of man. The probity or falsity of what is left on the shore can only be determined by probing the circumstances which surround the launching of the craft of infinity on the seas of everlastingness. . .

The Majority Opinion fears that a jury could not distinguish between the weight of an unsworn dying declaration and the weight of sworn testimony in court. What is the difference between a statement given as part of the res gestae and sworn testimony in court? Judges do not charge that the jury must accept the spontaneous utterance of the victim of an automobile accident at the time of the accident as if it were spoken before a judge and jury. Why should they invest a dying declaration, which is also in the nature of a spontaneous utterance, with the solemnity of a jurat? A dying declaration would have no standing at all in court were it not that it is an exception to the hearsay rule. To now pile on that exception an additional exception by calling it a sworn statement when it is not a sworn statement at all comes, as I view it, close to depriving a defendant of due process of law. It is already too much that he is denied the constitutional right to confront an accusing witness without magnifying, beyond reality, the nature of that accusation.

The Majority Opinion says:

> " Some authorities which limit the value and weight
> to be given to dying declarations, point out that
> the declarant may be influenced by hatred or
> revenge or similar unworthy motives, but this is
> equally applicable to any despicable character
> who takes the witness stand."

CHAPTER VII: SCOUNDRELS, CROOKS & OUTLAWS

But there is this difference which the Majority overlooks. The "despicable character who takes the witness stand" must face the batteries of cross-examination. He may, it is true, be influenced by hatred or revenge as the dying person may be, but he cannot conceal his lies, if he is lying, under the impermeability of a shroud.

The Majority says that:

> "When a person is faced with death which he knows
> is impending and he is about to see his Maker face
> to face, is he not more likely to tell the truth than is
> a witness in Court who knows that if he lies he will
> have a locus penitentiae, an opportunity to repent,
> confess and be absolved of his sin?"

The answer to this is Yes. But not all persons are like the person the Majority here describes. If they were, iniquity, injustice, tyranny, and inhumanity would disappear from the confines of the earth. It is because there are persons who defy goodness and honor and who accept the cut rates of Mr. Satan at his sulphuric supermarket rather than pay the just price which decency and justice demand, that evil still walks the earth.

In the case at bar it appears that two women, Vivian Gay and the defendant Mary Brown, armed with a golf stick and a knife, set upon one Dorothy Francis with the intention of doing her no good. Jealousy and criss-cross love affairs had fired the passions of this termagant trio and they fought desperately on the street. The arena of battle encompassed a street, a lawn, a flower garden, and a truck, around which the shrewish combatants chased one another, as testified to by the husband of Vivian Gay, apparently one of the heart-interests in the quadrangle. This pivotal figure testified that on August 16, 1954, he was walking on the Old Lincoln Highway in Malvern, with Dorothy Francis when Mary Brown and his wife Vivian came running toward them. At this point Vivian Gay announced: "The party is on." And it was. . .

The testimony as to what actually happened during the fatal melee was contradictory, conflicting, and generally confusing; one of the witnesses testified: "Three of them all tussling there." But at the hospital, in answer to questions put to her by a police officer Francis replied that it was Mary Brown who stabbed her. In his charge the Trial Judge said to the jury that the statement made by Dorothy Francis was "to be received by you and considered by you just as though it were made under oath by Dorothy Francis." Later he also said: "If you so find [that Dorothy Francis believed she was dying] then you give that statement the same effect as though it were made under oath in your hearing."

There can be no doubt whatsoever that the Trial Judge's instruction -- that the jury was to consider Dorothy Francis' statement as if made under oath in their hearing -- considerably influenced the jury and probably dictated to them their verdict. The instruction relieved the jury of the worry and anguish of seeking to ascertain the actual culprit amid the tangle of testimony as to just what did occur in the gory struggle which raged and spent its fury over the suburban expanse mentioned. The jury could well have concluded that if Dorothy Francis' statement had to be accepted by them as sworn testimony, and she did say that Mary Brown killed her, who should know better than she who killed her? The Judge simplified the case for the jury, but the situation was not so simple as the Trial Judge made it. When one speaks of a dying declaration the average listener assumes that the declarant, in full possession of his faculties, coolly and clearly announces: "X shot me" or "Y stabbed me." But the picture is rarely so clearly etched, and it certainly was not so etched in this case. Mary Scott, a student nurse, who was present at the hospital when the police officer was questioning Dorothy Francis, testified that "She [Dorothy Francis] was mumbling all the time, but there were times when the mask was off when she was examined." (Emphasis supplied.)

While Dorothy Francis' life blood drained, and her lips mumbled as the officer questioned her, did her answers mirror the irrefutable realities of the battle and flight in which she sought to flee, hide, fight back, and escape? Did the mortal wound come from the jagged metal end of the golf stick or from the blade of the knife? These were questions which the jury should have resolved, untrammeled by the command of the presiding Judge that the muttering answers of Dorothy Francis in the hospital were to be accepted as if spoken in court with all the solemnity, dignity and guarantees vouchsafed every accused.

Even so, the jury must have still had some grave doubts because they convicted Mary Brown only of voluntary manslaughter although she had been indicted for murder. Moreover, this was her second trial. The first jury was unable to agree on a unanimous verdict.

Apart from the injustice which may have happened to Mary Brown, I fear for the fate of other defendants who may be innocent but yet be convicted because this Court has placed its anticipated imprimatur of sworn testimony on what may be a mere matter of muttering, mumbling moribundity.

IN RE THOMAS OF HOBURN
Assize Court of Northumberland County
Northumberland Assize Roll, 7 Edward I (1279)

ANONYMOUS, Judge

When Thomas of Hoburn was slicing up mullets in the village of Seaton de la Val, a certain beggar-woman came begging for alms in God's name; unwittingly, he accidentally struck her on the head with the knife with which he cut the aforesaid fish, so that she died. The aforesaid Thomas is not suspected; accordingly, he may return if he wishes, but his property is confiscated on account of his flight. Value of his property: 18 pence, for which the sheriff is answerable. The villages of Seaton, Hertelawe, and Horton falsely assessed the value of his aforesaid property; accordingly, they are fined.

AN ACTE FOR PUNYSSHEMENT
OF PYROTES AND ROBBERS OF THE SEE
Statutes of The Realm of England
28 Henry VIII, Chap. 15 (1536)

WHERE Traitours Pirotes Theves Robbers Murtherers and Confederatours uppon the See, many tymes escape unpynysshed because the triall of their offences hath heretofore ben ordered judged and determyned before the Admyrall or his Lyeutenante or Commissary, after the course of the civile Lawes, the nature wherof is that before any judgement of Death canne be yeven ayenst the Offendours, either they must playnly confess their offences (which they will never doo without torture or paynes) or els their offences be so playnly and directerly proved by witness indifferente, suche as sawe their offences commytted, which cannot be gotten but by chaunce at fewe tymes by cause such offendours commytt their offences uppon the See, and at many tymes murder and kill suche persons being in the Shipp or Bote where they commyt their offences which shulde wytnes ayenst them in that behalfe, and also suche as shulde bere witnes be commonly Maryners and Shipmen, which by cause of their often viages and passages in the Sees departe without long tarying and protraction of tyme of the great costs and charges as well of the Kynges Highnes as suche as wolde pursue such offendours:

For reformacion wherof be it enacterted by the aucteroritie of this present parliament, That all treasons felonyes robberies murders and confederacies, herafter to be c mytted in or uppon the See, or in any other haven ryvere creke or place where the Admyrall or Admyralls have or pretende to have power aucteroritie or jurisdiction, shall be enquired tried harde determyned and judged in such Shires and Places in the Realme as shall be lymtted by the Kynges Commission or Commissions to be directered for the same, in the fourme and condicion as if any such offence or offences hadd ben commytted or done in or uppon the lande;

And such Commissions shall be hadd under the Kinges greate Seale directered to the Admyrall or Admyrals, or to his or their Lieutenaunt Deputie [or[1]] Deputies, and to iii or iiii such other substanciall persons as shall be named or appoynted by the Lorde Chauncellour of Englande for the tyme being from tyme to tyme and as often as nede shall require, to here and determyne suche offences after the common course of the lawes of this Lande, used for tresons felonies robberies murders & confederacies of the same done and commytted upon the lande within this Realme.

---

[1] and O.

And if eny pson or psons happen to be indited for eny such offence done or herafter to be done upon the Sees, or in any other places above lymytted, that then suche order processe judgement and execucion shall be used hadd done and made, to and agaynst every such pson and psons so being indited, as agaynst traytours felons and murderers for treason felony robbery murder or other such offences done uppon the lande, as by the lawes of the Realme is accustomed;

And that the triall of such offence or offences, if it be denyed by the offendour or offendours, shall be had by xii laufull men inhabited in the Shere lymytted within such Commission which shall be directered as is aforsaid, and noo chalenge or chalenges to be hadd for the Hundred; and such as shall be convyctered of any suche offence or offences, by verdite confession or processe by aucteroritie of any such Commission, shall have and suffer such paynes of Death losses of landes goodes and catalles, as if they hadd ben atteynted and convyctered of any treasons felonies robberies or other the said offences doon uppon the landes.

AND be it enacterd by aucteroritie aforsaid, that for treasons robberies felonies murders and confederacies, doon upon the See or Sees or in any place above rehersed, the offendours shall not be admytted to have the benefite of his or their clergy, but be utterly excluded therof and from the same, and also the privilege of any Sayntuary.

PROVIDED always that this Actere extende not be prejudiciall or hurtfull to any pson or psons, for takyng any vitaile gables ropes ancars or sayles which any such pson or psons, (compelled by necessitie,) taketh of or in any Shipp which may conveniently spare the same, so that the same pson or psons paye out of hande, for the same vitaill gables ropes ancars or sailes, money or money worth to the valew of the thing so taken, or to the delyvere for the same a sufficient bille obligatori to be payed in fourme folowyng; that is to say, if the takyng of the same thinges be on this side the Straytes of Marroke then to be paide within iiii monethes, And if it be beyond the said Straites of Marroke then to be paide within xii monethes, next ensuyng the makyng of such billes; and that the makers of suche billes well and truly pay the same dett at the day to be lymytted within the said billes.

PEOPLE OF CALIFORNIA v. BENTON
Court of Appeal of California, 4th District
77 Cal.App. 3d 322; 142 Cal. Rptr. 545 (1978)

ROBERT GARDNER, P. J.
After an unsuccessful motion to suppress under Penal Code section 1538.5, the defendant was found guilty of robbery in the first degree.

THE ROBBERY

Mrs. Barnhill and her daughter, Sainna Okeson, were seated at the kitchen table in Mrs. Barnhill's apartment on Keel Street in Anaheim on the evening of August 2, 1976. Around midnight, a black man entered. With pistol in hand, he said, "Don't say a word, don't say a mother-fucking word."[1] Two more black men entered, one of whom was the defendant. He was wearing a knit-type watch cap. The men robbed Mrs. Barnhill. One of them then announced that he ought to rape the ladies. He was dissuaded by the other robbers, not for any humanitarian reasons but because the robbers heard police approaching. In addition to taking $70 from Mrs. Barnhill, $2 or $3 were taken from Mrs. Okeson. One of the robbers carried away Mrs. Barnhill's radio.

THE MOTION TO SUPPRESS

With that as a background, we proceed to the evidence adduced at the section 1538.5 hearing which is the basis for the defendant's sole contention on appeal that his constitutional rights were violated during his apprehension by police.

Around midnight of August 2, Officer Petersen of the Garden Grove Police Department was patrolling on Keel Street when he was approached by a Mr. Perez. Mr. Perez was extremely excited. He said that some male Negro subjects were causing a disturbance in apartment No. 5 (Mrs. Barnhill's apartment) of a nearby apartment complex. Officer Petersen got as far as the stairway to the apartment complex just as the defendant was descending the stairs following the robbery. The officer said he wanted to talk to him. As he reached for the defendant, he saw a second black man standing on the stairs holding Mrs. Barnhill's radio. A third black man appeared at the top of the stairway. The man holding the radio threw it away and ran up the steps. The defendant broke away from the officer and took off with Officer Petersen in hot pursuit. The defendant escaped and Officer Petersen returned to apartment No. 5. There he secured the above story of the robbery and a description of the robbers. This was radioed to surrounding police units.

---

[1] It is a sad commentary on contemporary culture to compare "Don't say a word, don't say a mother-fucking word" with "Stand and deliver," the famous salutation of Dick Turpin and other early English highwaymen. It is true that both salutations lead to robbery. However, there is a certain rich style to "Stand and deliver." On the other hand, "Don't say a word, don't say a mother-fucking word" conveys only dismal vulgarity.

The speech of the contemporary criminal culture has always been a rich source of color and vitality to any language. Yet, when one compares the "bawds," "strumpets," "trulls," "cut-purses," "knaves," and "rascals" of Fielding and Smollett to the "hookers," "pimps," "Narcs," "junkies," and "snitches" of today's criminal argot, one wonders just which direction we are traveling civilization's ladder. "Hooker," at least, has traceable historical antecedents--although the descendants of General "Fighting Joe" Hooker would probably prefer that their famous ancestor be remembered for something other than his army's camp followers--such as the slaughter at Chancellorsville.

Officers Severson and Konieczny of the Garden Grove Police Department heard the broadcast. They were in the neighborhood. They saw a 1964 Chevrolet coming from Keel Street. Two male blacks were in the car, one of whom was wearing a watch cap. The officers started to overtake this vehicle using red lights and siren. The car began to run red lights, went down the wrong side of the highway and attained speeds of 80 to 85 miles per hour. It finally spun out of control near an apartment complex in the 800 block of South Fairview Street. The two suspects fled with the officers in pursuit. One of them was the defendant. Officer Konieczny fired at him. The defendant continued to run and finally climbed a brick wall with Konieczny still in pursuit. Konieczny climbed the wall and fired at the defendant a second time as the defendant ran into the apartment complex. Officer Severson had chased the driver but lost him when he ran into the apartment complex. The officers radioed to several converging units what had occurred and that shots had been fired.

Officer Hamann of the Santa Ana Police Department heard the broadcast and responded to the apartment complex on South Fairview Street. He was briefed on the direction the suspects had taken. He was told by a security guard that he, the security guard, had chased one of the suspects along the building and saw someone leaping the fence at the southwest corner of the building. He, the security guard, stayed there and did not see anyone leave. Officer Hamann then peeked over that fence into an apartment backyard. He saw that a screen door had been torn away from a sliding glass door of an apartment. Officer Hamann went over the fence, approached the sliding glass door and opened it two or three inches to establish that it was not locked. He looked through the kitchen window and saw the defendant and another black man sitting on a sofa watching television. He opined that this was somewhat unusual in light of the fact that shots had been fired, sirens were wailing, a large number of officers were in the area yelling back and forth and patting-down individuals in the apartment complex. Still, these two were watching TV. They were either stone deaf or it was a remarkably absorbing television program.

At Officer Hamann's request, Officer Taylor went with him to the front door of the apartment. Both were in uniform. They knocked on the door. It was opened by a Ms. Barns who appeared frightened and said, "Let me out of here, I'm not involved." She pushed past the officers and gestured with her hand in such a way as to indicate that she wanted them to go into her residence for some reason. She was extremely nervous and appeared frightened of something within her apartment. She told the officers that a third uninvolved retarded man was in the bathroom of the apartment.

The officers entered without further compliance with Penal Code section 844 and saw the defendant and the other black man seated on the couch. They were ordered to stand up. When the defendant did, his pants fell off. This remarkable phenomenon occurred because the pants were several sizes too big for him. He was sweating and his breath was labored as though he had been running. Officer

Taylor asked him where he was staying and he said, "I'm staying right here." Taylor asked him what the address was and defendant said he did not know. The officer picked up an envelope on a coffee table and it carried the name of Ms. Barns. The officer then asked defendant who else lived in the apartment. The defendant then turned to his companion and asked, "What's your name, man?" The officer asked defendant what his name was and defendant said, "Jim Long." At that point, defendant and his companion corobber, Nash, were arrested.

The officers then asked Ms. Barns if they could search the apartment. She said they could, that she did not know the defendant and that she was uninvolved and that they could look anywhere they wanted. In a search of the back bedroom, there was found, tucked under the mattress, a man's green corduroy jacket, a reddish colored watch cap, a man's blue long-sleeved shirt, a pair of Levis and a blue T-shirt. These apparently were the defendant's. By reasonable inference one may deduce that the defendant had jettisoned his own pants and put on some pants he found at the apartment. Unfortunately for the defendant, the owner of these pants was a considerable larger man -- or at least had a greater girth. These items were wet with perspiration and officers recognized them as being worn by the suspects when they fled the car. Officer Petersen identified the defendant as the man who fled from him at the foot of the steps. Officer Konieczny identified the defendant as the man he chased from the car and at whom he had shot.

Defendant's sole contention on appeal is that there was a violation of his constitutional rights in the pursuit, detention, arrest and the search of Ms. Barn's apartment.

It is rather apparent from the above statement of facts that the exigent circumstances created by the defendant's armed robbery and flight warranted the actions taken by the officers in arresting them. "The law recognizes that fresh pursuit of a fleeing suspect who has committed a grave offense and remains dangerous to life and limb may constitute 'exceptional circumstances' sufficient to justify a search without a warrant." . . .

Here, the officers were dealing with a very serious offense -- an armed robbery. The pursuit of the car was completely reasonable. The intrusion into Ms. Barns' backyard was completely reasonable. As of that time, the officers knew they were in fresh pursuit of two armed robbery suspects with whom they had been involved in an dangerous high-speed chase. It was noted that the screen door of the apartment had been ripped off its mount. The attention to the television program while all hell was breaking loose outside was a most peculiar circumstance. The officers were thus reasonable in their suspicion that the suspects were hiding in the apartment and possibly endangering the residents of the apartment. . .

Additionally, Ms. Barns the apparent householder, had, by her actions, invited the officers in. The actions of the officers in entering the apartment were reasonable and in no way violated any constitutional or statutory rights of the defendant.

We conclude that there was no violation of any constitutional rights of the defendant in his pursuit, detention and arrest.

Judgment affirmed.

GILBERT v. THE STATE OF GEORGIA
Supreme Court of Georgia
90 Ga. 691; 16 S.E. 652 (1892)

LOGAN E. BLECKLEY, Chief Justice.

Without a specific intent to kill as charged in the indictment, the offence of assault with intent to murder cannot be committed. The existence of such intent is matter of fact to be ascertained by the jury from all the evidence before them, and not matter for legal inference or presumption from only a part of the evidence, or even from the whole of it. . . . The law will certainly charge an evil doer with all the natural consequences of his unlawful act which the act produces, but why should it impute to him, by mere presumption, an intention to add a consequence which was not produced? . . .

The charge of the court in the present case treated the specific intent to kill as prima facie a conclusion of law, provided certain enumerated facts were found by the jury to exist; whereas the instruction should have been, in substance, that the enumerated facts (taking care to enumerate enough) if found to exist, and if not rebutted or qualified by other facts in evidence, would warrant them in finding the intent; that is, that these facts would be sufficient to manifest the intent if the jury, viewing them in the light of the whole evidence, were convinced beyond a reasonable doubt that an intent to kill existed in fact. . .

Both briefs furnished us in the case at bar are sufficiently striking to deserve mention. That of Mr. McLester is intensely classical. It opens thus: "When the mother of Achilles plunged him in the Stygian waters his body became invulnerable, except the heel by which she held him, and afterwards when he and Polyxena, the daughter of the King of Troy, who were lovers, met in the Temple of Apollo to solemnize their marriage, Paris, the brother of Hector, lurking behind the image of Apollo, slew Achilles by shooting him in the heel with an arrow."

The brief of the solicitor-general is less poetic, but equally irrelevant. It cites seven cases from the Georgia Reports, not one of which has any bearing on the question, for in each of the cited cases the attempt to kill was unsuccessful. When a homicide actually occurs from the voluntary use of a deadly weapon, an intention to kill is very much more certain than it is when the man assaulted is not killed but only shot in the toe.

Judgment reversed.

CHAPTER VII: SCOUNDRELS, CROOKS & OUTLAWS

HENDERSON v. STATE OF MISSISSIPPI
Supreme Court of Mississippi
445 So. 2d 1364 (1984)

JAMES L. ROBERTSON, Justice

I.

This case presents the question whether the rules of English grammar are a part of the positive law of this state. If they are, Jacob Henderson's burglary conviction must surely be reversed, for the indictment in which he has been charged would receive an "F" from every English teacher in the land.

Though grammatically unintelligible, we find that the indictment is legally sufficient and affirm, knowing full well that our decision will receive of literate persons everywhere opprobrium as intense and widespread as it will be deserved.

II.

On May 15, 1982, the Maaco Paint Shop in Jackson, Mississippi, was burglarized. Jacob Henderson was arrested immediately thereafter, four items of stolen merchandise still in his possession.

On July 6, 1982, Henderson was formally charged with business burglary in violation of Miss.Code Ann. § 97-17-33 (1972) in an indictment returned by the Hinds County Grand Jury. . . .

. . .the circuit court sentenced Henderson to serve a term of seven years without eligibility for probation or parole. From this conviction and sentence, Henderson appeals.

III.

A.

The primary issue presented on this appeal regards the legal adequacy of the indictment under which Henderson has been tried, convicted and sentenced. That indictment, in pertinent part, reads as follows:

The Grand Jurors for the State of Mississippi, . . . upon their oaths present: That Jacob Henderson . . . on the 15th day of May, A.D., 1982.

The store building there situated, the property of Metro Auto Painting, Inc., . . . in which store building was kept for sale or use valuable things, to-wit: goods, ware and merchandise unlawfully, feloniously and burglariously did break and enter, with intent the goods, wares and merchandise of said Metro Auto Painting then and there being in said store building unlawfully, feloniously and then and there being in said store building burglariously to take, steal and carry away; And

One (1) Polaroid Land Camera,
One (1) Realistic Am/Fm Stereo Tuner
One (1) Westminster AM/FM radio
One (1) Metal Box and contents thereof, . . .

the property of the said Metro Auto Painting then and there being in said store building did then and there unlawfully, feloniously and burglariously take, steal and carry away the aforesaid property, he, the said Jacob Henderson, having been twice previously convicted of felonies, to-wit: . . .

The remainder of the indictment charges Henderson with being a recidivist. Henderson, no doubt offended, demurred. In support, he presented an expert witness, Ann Dreher, who had been a teacher of English for nine years. Ms. Dreher testified that, when read consistent with accepted rules of English grammar, the indictment did not charge Jacob Henderson with doing anything; rather it charged that goods, ware and merchandise broke and entered the paint store. The trial judge overruled the objection and the motion, but not without reservation. He stated:

[T]his same objection has been made numerous times. It is one of Mr. Hailey's pets. [B]ut as far as I know no one has elected to appeal and I'm going to follow the decision whether it is grammatically correct or not. I have repeatedly begged for six years or five years for the district attorney not to use this form. It is very poor English. It is impossible English. . . . In addition to being very poor English, it also charges him with the crime of larceny, which is not necessary to include in an indictment for burglary. I never did understand the reason for that. I again ask the district attorney not to use this form. It's archaic. Even Shakespeare could not understand the grammatical construction of this indictment. But the objection will be overruled. Maybe it will take a reversal on a case of a similar nature where there is a serious offense as this one is by the fact that he is indicted as a habitual to get the district attorney's attention.

B.

1.

In the trial court and on this appeal, Henderson insists that the meaning of the indictment may be obtained only within the straitjacket of accepted rules of grammatical construction of the English language. From this point of view, we are asked to examine the indictment and concentrate on the words ". . . unlawfully, feloniously and burglariously did break and enter . . . ." Who, we are asked, when the rules of good grammar are employed, did this alleged breaking and entering?

There are two possible answers (again, looking at the indictment as would an English teacher). "Goods, ware and merchandise" are the most obvious choice. Those nouns proximately precede the verb(s) "did break and enter" (separated only by the familiar string of adverbs "unlawfully, feloniously and burglariously" -- the district attorney, like other lawyers, never uses one word when two or three will do just as well). Thus read, the indictment charges that Goods, ware and merchandise, not Jacob Henderson, burglarized the Maaco Paint Shop on May 15, 1982.

More properly, however, the words "Goods, ware and merchandise" are seen as the tail end of a largely unintelligible effort to describe something else: the store building. A perceptive English grammarian would conclude that it is "the store building there situated. . . ." which is charged with the burglary, for those words seem to constitute the subject of the nonsensical non-sentence we are charged to construe.

Even so, whether the indictment charges that "Goods, ware and merchandise" or "The store building there situated" . . . "unlawfully, feloniously and burglariously did break and enter. . . ." matters not to Jacob Henderson. His point is merely that the indictment does not charge that he did the breaking and entering.

Were this a Court of nine English teachers, Henderson would no doubt prevail.

The indictment does contain at the outset the charge "That Jacob Henderson . . . on the 15th day of May, A.D., 1982." We have another non-sentence. The unmistakable period after 1982 is used by astute defense counsel to nail down the point -- that the indictment fails to charge that Jacob Henderson did anything on May 15, 1982. Again, we must concede that grammatically speaking counsel is correct. The period after 1982 grammatically precludes the possibility that the indictment charges that Jacob Henderson did break and enter. Either the words "did break and enter" would have to precede the period, or the name Jacob Henderson would have to appear following it. Neither is the case.

Recognizing that the period is important, the State argues that in reality the indictment consists of one long sentence, written albeit in legalese instead of English. The State argues that "the period grammatically disjoined the first part of the sentence from the second", conceding that we are indeed confronted with "a patently inappropriate period". This, of course, prompts Henderson to analogize the state's argument to Lady Macbeth's famous "Out damned spot! Out, I say!"[1] W. Shakespeare, Macbeth, Act V, sc. 1, line 38. The retort would be telling in the classroom or in a court of the literati. Alas, it has meager force in a court of law.

2.

With no little temerity, we insist that the correct statement of the question before this Court is: Does the indictment conform to the requirements of Rule 2.05, Uniform Criminal Rules of Circuit Court Practice? That rule provides:

Rule 2.05

FORM OF THE INDICTMENT

> The indictment upon which the defendant is to be tried shall be a plain, concise and definite written statement of the essential facts constituting the offense charged and shall fully notify the defendant of the nature and cause of the accusation against him. Formal or technical words are not necessary in an indictment, if the offense can be substantially described without them. . . .

---

[1] It cannot be gainsaid that all the perfumes of Arabia would not eviscerate the grammatical stench emanating from this indictment. Cf. W. Shakespeare, Macbeth, Act V, sc. 1, lines 56-57.

For better or for worse, nothing in Rule 2.05 requires any adherence to correct grammatical form. We know of no constitutional or natural law that might supplement Rule 2.05 with the rules of good grammar.[2]

Rule 2.05 states that "formal or technical words are not necessary". Correct grammar, however desirable, is similarly unnecessary. So long as from a fair reading of the indictment taken as a whole the nature and cause of the charge against the accused are clear, the indictment is legally sufficient.

The instant indictment, however inartfully worded, clearly charges Jacob Henderson with the crime of business burglary. It informs Henderson that the burglary is alleged to have occurred on May 15, 1982. The indictment names the business burglarized as Maaco Paint Shop operated by Metro Auto Painting, Inc. It charges that the crime occurred within the First Judicial District of Hinds County. Further, the indictment identifies the items of property said to have been stolen in the course of the burglary.

Viewing the indictment under Rule 2.05, we find it legally adequate. It provides Henderson with a "written statement of the essential facts constituting the offense charged" in language which is "plain, concise and definite", albeit grammatically atrocious. Beyond that, the indictment notified Henderson of "the nature and cause of the accusation against him".

Establishment of a literate bar is a worthy aspiration. 'Tis without doubt a consummation devoutly to be wished. Its achievement, however, must be relegated to means other than reversal of criminal convictions justly and lawfully secured.

The assignment of error is rejected.

IV.

Before trial Henderson filed a motion in limine wherein he sought to restrict questioning of prospective jurors during voir dire examination. Specially, Henderson urged that the prosecutor be barred from inquiring, in the presence of the entire panel, regarding a prospective juror's involvement with criminal acts as either victim or perpetrator. On appeal, Henderson claims that the failure to grant the motion prejudiced the defendant in that the questioning created an aura of rampant crime in the streets in the minds of the jury panel.

Henderson argues that the rule of evidence, which prohibits the discussion of other criminal behavior of the defendant, is based on the same logical premises as is this assignment of error. We beg to differ. Suffice it to say that we divine no reason in common law or common sense that would support Henderson's point.

The assignment of error is denied.

AFFIRMED.

---

[2] This is not the first time this Court has placed its collective head on the grammarian's chopping block by insisting upon the clarity of a meaning clearly untenable under correct grammatical construction of language. We did this with an inartfully drafted regulation of the State Tax Commission, *Columbia Gulf Transmission Co. v. Barr*, 194 So.2d 890, 894 (Miss. 1967).

JACOBS v. STATE OF MARYLAND
Court of Special Appeals of Maryland
45 Md.App. 634; 415 A.2d 590 (1980)

CHARLES E. MOYLAN, JR., Judge.

This appeal, in its most significant aspect, requires us to stand far back and observe some fundamental characteristics of the criminal justice system that are too easily lost sight of when we get in so close that we lose perspective. It requires an appreciation of the functional difference between the common law of evidence. It requires a sensitivity to the distinct traditions, purposes and rules of procedures surrounding those basically different limitations upon the fact-finding process. Macroscopic vision is sometimes as needed as microscopic vision. But first the backdrop:

On the evening of February 5, 1978, Robert Lashley was murdered by four gunshot wounds to the head and one to the neck, two of the shots at point-blank, contact range. A Baltimore City jury, presided over by Judge David Ross, convicted all three appellants, Randy Jacobs, Lawrence Rufus Jackson and Robert Lewis (a/k/a Robert Galloway and Robert Lewis Jackson) of murder (Jacobs and Lewis of first-degree murder and Jackson, by way of obvious compromise, of second-degree murder) and related handgun charges. Their respective appellate contentions diverge as widely as did their trial tactics.

Legal Sufficiency of the Evidence
(As to Appellant Jackson Only)

Lawrence Rufus Jackson alone challenges the legal sufficiency of the evidence, claiming that Judge Ross erred in ruling that there was enough proof to go to the jury on the issues of murder in the second degree and the use of a handgun to perpetrate a crime of violence. In this regard, Jackson does not contest the adequacy of the proof to establish the corpus delicti of the two crimes. He challenges only the sufficiency of the evidence to establish his own criminal agency in those crimes. His challenge is without merit but will serve to place the contentions that follow in factual context.

Curtis Carter, a close friend of the murder victim, received via telephone ongoing "spot reports" on the progress of the murderous evening. He knew both the appellant Jackson and the appellant Lewis and knew, as well, that they were both acquainted with the victim Lashley. All of the actors in this case were homosexual acquaintances of each other. Both appellants Jackson and Lewis as well as Lashley had been together on one occasion in Carter's home within a week prior to the murder. On the evening of the murder, the victim Lashley was expecting an imminent visit from the appellant Jackson, and he communicated that expectation to Carter.

The first call came from Lashley to Carter relatively early in the evening (the times of the various calls were established with less than pinpoint precision) wherein Lashley informed Carter that Lashley expected the appellant Jackson to "pay him a visit that night." While the conversation was in progress, Carter overheard a knock at Lashley's door and heard Lashley say, "Oh, hi, Robert." Carter then had a brief conversation with the appellant Lewis, whose voice he recognized. Lewis then hung up the phone. This occurred at some point between 8:30 and 10:00 p.m.

Approximately 20 minutes later, the victim Lashley called Carter back. Lashley indicated to Carter that he, Lashley, had taken Lewis and Jackson to the bus stop. He indicated further that he was angry at the appellant Jackson for having brought his brother (the appellant Lewis) along on the this visit. The conversation concluded with Lashley saying, "I don't feel like talking. I guess I'll talk to you later."

Carter, in the meantime, was also in telephone contact with Ronald Whitfield, a mutual friend of Carter and the victim Lashley, keeping Whitfield apprised of his growing sense of dread. At one point, following Carter's second telephone conversation with Lashley, Whitfield called Lashley and determined that all was well. Whitfield communicated that reassurance to Carter, but Carter was not reassured. Carter called Lashley again. A voice answered which Carter recognized to be that of the appellant Lewis. The answer, however, was to the effect that Carter had the wrong number, and the phone was then hung up at Lashley's end. Carter immediately called back. The appellant Lewis again picked up the phone but this time identified himself. The appellant Lewis told Carter that Lashley and the appellant Jackson had gone out to get some beer. Carter heard background noises similar to those made when furniture is being moved. Following this conversation, Carter telephone the police and asked them to check out Lashley's apartment. The call to the police was made at approximately 11:40 p.m.

In the meantime, one David Bavis, a neighbor of Lashley's, heard the sound on Lashley's television set or stereo suddenly turned up very loud at approximately 11 p.m. Bavis interpreted this as a signal from Lashley to stop the band rehearsal which Bavis had been conducting in his own apartment. Bavis testified further that some five to ten minutes later, he heard a thumping noise come from Lashley's apartment, along with noises which he interpreted as emanating from a fight.

In response to Carter's call, Officer Charles Scharmann of the Baltimore City Police Department responded to check out Lashley's apartment at 11:42 p.m. On the parking lot outside, he found the appellant Jackson and the appellant Jacobs cleaning snow off an automobile registered to the victim Lashley. Although the two appellants were cooperative in other regards, the appellant Jacobs falsely identified himself as one Michael Jones. Officer Scharmann observed a Philco television set sitting on the back seat of the automobile. Both appellant Jackson and appellant Jacobs explained to the officer that Lashley had already left the area and that they, at the request of Lashley and as an accommodation to him, were delivering his automobile and the television set to Carter's apartment. Officer Scharmann insisted that the two accompany him to Lashley's apartment. The officer knocked on the door several times but received no response. He inquired of neighbors as to whether they had heard or seen anything unusual and learned that they had not. Solicitous of the murder victim's Fourth Amendment rights, the officer did not enter the apartment. He left the scene, and the appellants Jacobs and Jackson were free to go.

While Officer Scharmann had the appellant Jackson and the appellant Jacobs "in tow," two of Lashley's neighbors made significant observations to which they testified in court. Deborah Sammons observed that after the officer and these two appellants entered the apartment building, a third man crawled out from underneath a car parked beside the one from which the two appellants had been cleaning snow. Another neighbor, Marie Carter (no apparent relationship to Curtis Carter) testified that she saw one of the individuals who entered the building with the police officer later come outside, walk down to the corner of the building, stand there a second and then go back into the building. The next day, Marie Carter's husband, John Carter, found the victim Robert Lashley's wallet on the ground at the spot where his wife had noticed this man standing on the night before.

Shortly after this police visit, Curtis Carter received two interesting phone calls from the appellant Jackson. In the first, Jackson informed Carter that Jackson was calling from Jackson's home. Jackson then said, "Curtis, I don't know what's wrong with your buddy, he took me to the No. 5 busline and he act as though he wanted Robert Galloway to go back to his house." Carter, skeptical as to whether the call had been placed from Jackson's home, then called Jackson at home. A young man answered. Carter asked to speak to Jackson but was unable to make contact. Approximately ten minutes later, Jackson called Carter again, this time saying, "Carter, if anything happens to your buddy, I don't want you to think I had anything to do with it."[1] Carter inquired of Jackson as to why Jackson would say something like that. Jackson replied, "Because he gave me the keys to his car." Carter asked Jackson what Jackson was supposed to do with the car keys and the television, and Jackson replied that he did not know.

Just before receiving these two calls from Jackson, Carter had called his friend Whitfield and the two determined to go and make their own investigation of Lashley's apartment. En route, they stopped and informed a police officer of their concern. When they arrived at the apartment, Carter found the door unlocked and Lashley's body lying in a pool of blood. His television set was missing, and his bedroom appeared to have been ransacked. The phone rang. Carter picked it up and heard the appellant Jackson's voice on the other end. Carter hung up

---

[1] Qui s'excuse, s'accuse. [He who excuses himself, accuses himself.]

without responding. He immediately had a neighbor call the police, who arrived at Lashley's apartment at 1:43 a.m. There were no signs of a forced entry.

A lookout was immediately broadcast for Lashley's car and for the three appellants. At approximately 3:10 a.m., Lashley's automobile was found in the 500 block of W. Lafayette Avenue, within a block of the homes of all three appellants. All three appellants were shortly thereafter found in the same area where the car was found and were placed under arrest. A crime laboratory technician, at 3:52 a.m., performed a leucomalachite test on the hands of the appellants and found the probable presence of blood on the hands of the appellant Jackson and the appellant Lewis.

It is simply to state a self-evident truth to hold that this massive web of circumstantial evidence is legally sufficient to have permitted the jury reasonably to infer the involvement of the appellant Jackson in the murder and that Judge Ross, therefore, did not commit error in permitting the case to go to the jury. . .

Leading Questions
(As to Appellant Jackson Only)

Before proceeding to the significant legal issues raised on this appeal, we may dispose of summarily the other two contentions raised by the appellant Jackson.

He claims that Judge Ross committed error in permitting the State to ask leading questions of its witness Curtis Carter. He fails to lay any predicate whatsoever for this contention. However, he fails to direct our attention to a single instance of an arguably leading question, let alone an instance where timely objection was made and the objection was overruled. We have no way of knowing what rulings of the trial judge the appellant Jackson questions or, indeed, whether there were any rulings sought and made in this regard. There is obviously nothing preserved for review. [citation omitted]

Admissibility of Tape Recording of Telephone Call
(As to Appellant Jackson Only)

It is difficult to fathom the appellant Jackson's point in this regard except as an understandable desperation effort by a convicted defendant to grasp at any straw, no matter how frail and insignificant it may be.

The State's witnesses Curtis Carter and Ronald Whitfield were unable to pinpoint the precise times when events occurred on the evening and early morning of February 5-6, although they were able to establish the sequence of those events. The telephone calls they made to the Baltimore City Police Department, however, were taped and were logged in with precise timing. Tape recordings of those calls were played to the jury both to establish the times when they were made and to corroborate the testimony of Whitfield and Carter as to having made the calls. The appellant Jackson does not take issue with the playing of those tapes of those calls.

He does take issue with the playing of one additional tape recording of one additional telephone call made to the police by a neighbor who called in to report that someone had been killed. The appellant Jackson's complaint is that this "was hearsay and served no necessary purpose." In holding against the appellant Jackson on this issue, our response is twofold: 1) How do we know it was hearsay? and 2) What difference does it make?

The court reporter did not transcribe the tape-recorded conversation of the telephone call as the tape was played to the jury. The tape itself was, to be sure, introduced in evidence. No transcript of it has been made, however, and included in this record. The burden in this regard is clearly upon the appellant . . . In view of this failure of the appellant to perfect the record, we have no way of knowing whether the telephone call in question contained an out-of-court assertion offered in court for the proof of the thing asserted or not.

Although this is totally dispositive of the contention, we cannot help but note its frivolous nature even if a perfected record were here to establish everything the appellant Jackson seeks to establish. In view of the undisputed testimony by Curtis Carter and by the investigating officers that the victim's lifeless body was found in his apartment and in view of the indisputable testimony of the medical examiner that four bullets were taken from the victim's brain, the out-of-court declaration, even be it hearsay, to the effect that "someone had been killed," is as harmlessly redundant as anything could ever be. The appellant himself argues that this hearsay "served no necessary purpose." Where then was any arguable prejudice?

Declarations Against Penal Interest Made to a Private Person
(Appellants Lewis and Jacobs)

There is a curious "reverse English" to this case. The appellants Lewis and Jacobs vehemently challenge the introduction of two declarations against penal interest made by them to a private person and offered at the trial by their codefendant Jackson. The declarations were mutually consistent and served to inculpate Lewis and Jacobs but to exculpate Jackson. It was Jackson who offered them as part of his defense. Although the ultimate admissibility of the declarations would not have been affected if the State had offered them, the twist in this case is that the State did not. Indeed, the State objected to the introduction of these declarations. The State's tactical situation was such that it deemed the declarations redundant for purposes for further inculpating Lewis and Jacobs, but was fearful of the declarations because of their potentially exculpating influence as to Jackson. On balance, the State simply did not want these declarations against interest to go to the jury.

As we approach this central issue of the case, we must observe that analysis would be so much cleaner if all parties could discuss such matters in the neutral language of algebra instead of in the frequently emotionally charged language of English. Although the declarations in issue are full acknowledgements of guilt, they are "declarations against penal interest" and not "confessions." The very word "confession" carries too much highly charged connotative baggage, with its images of police interrogation, of third-degree sessions under naked lightbulbs, of question and answer formats, of Miranda and its progeny, of the right to counsel, and of the privilege against compelled self-incrimination.

The fact that the writings resemble, in terms of the arrangement of the text upon the page, the more familiar police "confession" is beside the point. The fact that the declarations were notarized is beside the point. The fact that the declarations were made within prison bars than without prison bars is beside the point. Had the same events occurred with all three codefendants out on bail, the legal posture would not be otherwise.

As a recognized exception to the rule against hearsay, the declaration against interest is admissible if the trial judge deems it trustworthy.[2] This is true whether the forum is civil or criminal; whether the declaration is offered by a plaintiff, a civil defendant, the State or a criminal defendant; whether it is offered for inculpatory or exculpatory purposes. If it is trustworthy, it comes in for all purposes; if it is not trustworthy, it may not come in for any purpose. The trial judge rules upon the question of admissibility. The fact finder gives such weight to it as he thinks appropriate in precisely the same way that he weighs all other types of evidence.

The indispensable major premise undergirding the defense argument in this regard is that the rules and procedures controlling the admissibility of a declaration (of any sort) made to a private person are precisely the same as those controlling the admissibility of a confession made to a police investigator. Nothing could be farther from the truth, but an appreciation of the vast difference between the two phenomena requires us to back far off and to view the whole criminal justice system in historic perspective before renarrowing the focus to the precise issue at hand. We need to approach the problem with a keen sense of the difference between the common law of evidence and the constitutional law of evidence.

From the earliest beginnings of human society, as people bound themselves together under a variety of social contracts, they promulgated rules of behavior for the group and they provided for the enforcement of those rules. Whenever the tenets of acceptable behavior were transgressed, men bound themselves together as a *posse comitatus* [power of the county]--first as families, then as clans, then as tribes, than as nation-states--and demanded an answer to the

---

[2] The trustworthiness in issue in this regard is the trustworthiness of the declaration, assuming it to have been made and to have been made in the form recounted from the witness stand. The trustworthiness of the witness who serves as the mere conduit for the out-of-court declaration is, on the other hand, tested by other devices such as the oath and cross-examination at the trial itself. All too frequently, we allow our distrust of the witness on the stand to be transmuted into a mistrust of the out-of-court declaration, and this frequently subconscious transfer serves only to blur analysis.

question, "WHO-DUNIT?: Who killed the boy?, Who stole the pig?, Who burned the cottage?" Once the transgressor had been identified, a variety of sanctions might be imposed. As this process manifested itself in Anglo-American common law, we early surrounded the process with safeguards to insure that we were "Getting the Right Man."

The service of this is the quintessential function of the common law of evidence. In essence, evidentiary law is a set of sieves and devices that pass through to the fact finder data that is competent, relevant and material but screen out all data that is incompetent, irrelevant and immaterial. The common law of evidence is interested fundamentally in the integrity of the fact-finding process. We keep out all that might obscure the truth; we allow in all that will further the search for truth. The prime concern is the trustworthiness, the reliability, the accuracy of the process by which we seek the answer to the ultimate riddle of Whodunit.

In the American quadrant of Anglo-America, we have in recent decades super-imposed a second limiting condition on the process. Aware of the awesome power of the State, acting in our collective name, to investigate and to prosecute those who break our laws, we seek additional safeguards to insure not simply that we are "Getting The Right Man," but also that the State is doing it "By the Marquis of Queensberry Rules." The service of this additional goal is the quintessential function of the constitutional law of evidence. Just as the body of a constitution sets out what government may do, a bill of rights sets out those things that government may not do. The exclusionary rule implements these limitations on governmental behavior. The prime concern is the fairness of the process by which we seek the answer to the ultimate riddle of Whodunit.

Thus, we circumscribe the process of identifying outlaws by two basic limiting conditions:

1) Getting The Right Man
2) By The Marquis of Queensberry Rules.

The first condition concerns the accuracy of the answer. The second condition concerns the fundamental fairness and decency of governmental conduct in obtaining the proof of the answer. The bitter irony is that the two purposes do not always dovetail; sometimes they are in opposition. This is why the exclusionary rule is described by Wigmore and McCormick and others as serving the purpose of an "extrinsic policy." We deny the fact finder probative evidence that would enhance the literal, objective search for truth to express disapproval of the means by which government obtained that evidence. We deliberately diminish the accuracy of the process in order to enhance the fairness of the process. The very existence of this second limiting condition is aimed at governmental behavior alone. The Bill of Rights and the Fourteenth Amendment, by express terms, regulate the behavior of government and not of private persons. The attendant rules of procedure that have grown up in this context--special burdens allocated to the State, etc.--are applicable to the regulation of governmental behavior via the constitutional law but do not regulate private behavior. With respect to evidence procured by private persons, we ask the questions that are the concern of the common law of evidence--Is it competent?, Is it trustworthy?, Will it enhance the accuracy of the verdict?

In the case at bar, the State completed its case against all three defendants without offering any inculpatory statements made by any of them. The State rested, and motions for judgments of acquittal were made and denied. It was only then, in the course of defense testimony, that the appellant Jackson called to the stand one Harry Anthony Conyers, a social worker assistant at the Baltimore City Jail and, more significantly for present purposes, a notary public. Through Conyers, there were introduced four statements, two of them declarations against penal interest made by the same two appellants on March 14, 1978. The latter two really concern us here.

In both sets of statements, the versions of the crime given by the two confessing appellants are consistent with each other. In both sets of statements, they take full responsibility themselves and exculpate totally the appellant Jackson. The key difference between the two sets of statements is that in the first set, both appellants confessed to having beaten the victim to death. In the second set, they both confessed to having shot him. According to Mr. Conyers, the statements had been typed in advance but were signed in his presence. They were, furthermore, made under the following oath:

"Do you solemnly swear and affirm in the presence
of Almighty God that the statements made in this
motion are true to the best of your knowledge?"

Judge Ross found against the appellants Lewis and Jacobs on the question of authentication and also on the question of whether these statements violated a lawyer-client privilege. They had been made apparently at the request of Roland Walker, Esquire, attorney for the appellant Jackson. No issue is being taken with respect to these rulings by Judge Ross.

Judge Ross further found, under the common law of evidence governing exceptions to the rule against hearsay, that these declarations met the criteria of admissibility as declarations against penal interest. Under the common law of evidence, the three critical questions for admissibility of any evidence are: 1) Is it material?, 2) Is it relevant? and 3) Is it competent? In a trial of three defendants for murder, the issue of who committed the murder is quintessentially material. Declarations by two of the accused defendants implicating themselves and exculpating their codefendant are quintessentially relevant on the issue of who committed the murder. The only question remaining to be asked is: Are the declarations competent evidence?--Are they worthy of belief and, therefore, likely to enhance the ultimate accuracy of the fact finding?

A declaration against penal interest is now recognized as competent upon the theory that the statement against interest is a sufficient guarantee of trustworthiness. Although Maryland earlier followed the common law tradition to the *Sussex Peerage* case, 11 Cl. & F. 85, 8 Eng. Rep. 1034 (1844)[3] that a declaration against penal interest was not admissible although a declaration against pecuniary interest was, it now has joined the modern trend holding that declarations against penal interest are admissible.

In V *Wigmore on Evidence* (Chadbourn Revision 1974), Section 1476, pp. 350-351, Dean Wigmore looked to the "arbitrary limitation" of the *Sussex Peerage* case:

> [A]cceptance was gained, after two decades, for the principle that all declarations of facts against interest (by deceased persons) were to be received. What is to be noted, then, is that from 1800 to about 1830 this was fully understood as the broad scope of the principle. It was thus stated without other qualifications; and frequent passages show the development of the principle to this point.

> But in 1844, in a case in the House of Lords, not strongly argued and not considered by the judges in the light of the precedents, a backward step was taken and an arbitrary limit put upon the rule. It was held to exclude the statement of a fact subjecting the declarant to a criminal liability, and to be confined to statements of facts against either pecuniary or proprietary interest. Thenceforward this rule was accepted in England, although it was plainly a novelty at the time of its inception; for in several rulings up to that time statements of criminal facts had been received.

---

[3] The monumental joke--that has haunted us for 150 years--is that the *Sussex Peerage* case was never taken seriously by anyone--taken seriously for precedential purposes, that is. The pre-existing law on declarations against interest had never subdivided interests into the pecuniary variety versus the penal variety. The strange notion that a man might cavalierly risk the gallows for a friend but would never risk financial loss for that friend had never occurred to anyone. If ever a hard case was blatantly result-oriented in making bad law, it was *Sussex Peerage*.

Young Victoria was but six years into her reign. Her favorite uncle--Augustus Frederick, the 70-year-old Duke of Sussex--had died in June, 1843, apparently without legitimate heir. The dukedom, with numerous lands and manors and an income of £21,000 per annum plus a seat in the House of Lords, would normally have reverted to the Crown. There suddenly appeared, however, a claimant, Augustus D'Este, holding himself out to be the late Duke's legitimate son by a private marriage contracted between D'Este's mother and the Duke in Rome over 50 years before. Upon the advice of the Attorney General, the Queen referred the matter to the House of Lords. At issue before them were both the validity of the Royal Marriage Act of 1772 and the question of whether the Roman marriage ever in fact took place. D'Este was put to his proof.

He went on to criticize the limitation in Section 1477, at pp. 358-359, referring to it as a "barbarous doctrine:"

> It is plain enough that this limitation, besides being a fairly modern novelty of judicial invention, is inconsistent with the broad language originally employed in stating the reason and principle of the present exception. . . as well as with the settled principle upon which confessions are received. . .

> But, furthermore, it cannot be justified on grounds of policy. The only plausible reason of policy that has ever been advanced for such a limitation is the possibility of procuring fabricated testimony to such an admission if oral. This is the ancient rusty weapon that has always been brandished to oppose any reform in the rules of evidence, viz., the argument of danger of abuse. This would be a good argument against admitting any witnesses at all, for it is notorious that some witnesses will lie and that it is difficult to avoid being deceived by their lies.

The Duke was dead; D'Este's mother was dead; all witnesses to the questioned marriage were dead; the Anglican clergyman who ostensibly performed the ceremony was dead--BUT, prior to his death, the clergyman had confided to his son that he had performed the wedding. D'Este offered this declaration through the mouth of his son. The Crown objected that the evidence was hearsay. D'Este responded that it was a declaration against interest in that the clergyman, by performing the marriage, would have violated the Royal Marriage Act of 1772 and subjected himself to its penal provisions. Ignoring precedents to the contrary (according to Wigmore) and giving the whole issue the most cursory of glosses, the Law Lords rejected the evidence by announcing for the first time a distinction between declarations against pecuniary interest, which are trustworthy, and declarations against mere penal interest, which are not. Their lofty phrases lived on long after the stark reasons of state which had predictably compelled those lofty phrases were forgotten. More realistic is the appraisal of the trial in the *London Times* of May 25, 1844:

> Really the House of Peers must be gifted with incredible decorum; for our reporter does not note down a single instance of 'loud and continued laughter' from the beginning to the end of the trial. If this were in a comedy, it would be the making of Haymarket; if in a police report, London would be in fits the next morning. Dickens and Ainsworth are flat compared with it.

A century later, judges on five continents looked to the disembodied words of Sussex Peerage as if listening to the Oracle of Delphi, without the remotest recollection of the bizarre scenario in which those words were uttered. If one wonders whether royal judges, sitting in the House of Lords, might ever be tempted to bend a rule of evidence to achieve a desired result, it must be remember that if Augustus D'Este had been declared to be the legitimate first cousin of the Queen, he would also have been, as of 1844, second in line to the throne itself.

In dissent in *Donnelly v. United States*, 228 U.S. 243, 277, 33 S.Ct. 449, 57 L.Ed. 820 (1913) Justice Holmes excoriated the *Sussex Peerage* limitation:

> [T]he exception to the hearsay rule in the case of declarations against interest is well known; no other statement is so much against interest as a confession of murder. . .

In *Brady v. State* [citation omitted], Chief Judge Brune chipped away further at the *Sussex Peerage* rule, pointing out that the rule "has been severely criticized;" again citing the Wigmore and Holmes criticisms with approval; and cataloguing the various limitations on the rule. . .

In *Dyson v. State*, [citation omitted] Judge Hammond continued the erosion, pointing out that such declarations against penal interest are admissible where there is "no evidence of collusion" and where the declaration is "not on its face obviously untrustworthy."

. . . At that point, the exceptions to the special limitation had swallowed up the limitation. We begin with the principle that declarations against interest are admissible as exceptions to the rule against hearsay. A limitation is placed on that principle, exempting declarations against penal interest from the admissible category. The latter-day exceptions to that limitation are that such declarations against penal interest will be admissible where there is "no evidence of collusion" and where the declaration is "not on its face obviously untrustworthy." This is the rule with respect to all declarations against interest, pecuniary or penal, if not indeed with respect to all proffered evidence of any variety. No judge, in the wise exercise of his discretion, would receive evidence where there is evidence of collusion or where the proffered evidence is on it face obviously untrustworthy. The special rule of evidence has thus remerged into the general rules of evidence.[4]

It but remained for Judge Morton to deliver the *coup de grâce* in *Harris v. State*, 40 Md.App. 58, 62-63, 387 A.2d 1152, 1154, 1155:

> Maryland is one of the so-called 'progressive' states that allows the admission of a declaration against penal interest, although some limitations have been placed thereon. . .

---

[4] Interestingly, no Maryland decision has ever overruled a trial verdict because a declaration against penal interest was received in evidence. The only reversals have come where such declarations were erroneously rejected. Interestingly as well, all of the Maryland cases deal with third-party confessions in criminal cases offered to exculpate the defendant on trial. This is not the critical factor, however, for the issue that matters in the common law of evidence is whether the proffered evidence is or is not worthy of belief, not the purpose or party which the proffered evidence is intended to serve.

CHAPTER VII: SCOUNDRELS, CROOKS & OUTLAWS

Although the Supreme Court of the United States had earlier adhered to the tradition of not recognizing the inherent trustworthiness of the declaration against penal interest, *Donnelly v. United States*, supra (but see the Holmes dissent), it has now joined the modern trend by virtue of the new Federal Rules of Evidence, Rule 804.

The rationale for admissibility was well articulated by the Supreme Court in *Chambers v. Mississippi*, 410 U.S. 284, 298-299, 93 S.Ct. 1038, 1047-1048, 35 L. Ed. 2d 297, 311 (1973), a case in which the Supreme Court held that the declaration against penal interest there in question was not only permitted but was indeed compelled in terms of its admissibility:

> Out-of-court statements are traditionally excluded because they lack the conventional indicia of reliability; they are usually not made under oath or other circumstances that impress the speaker with the solemnity of his statements; the declarant's word is not subject to cross-examination; and he is not available in order that his demeanor and credibility may be assessed by the jury. . . A number of exceptions have developed over the years to allow admission of hearsay statements made under circumstances that tend to assure reliability and thereby compensate for the absence of the oath and opportunity for cross-examination. Among the most prevalent of these exceptions against interest-an exception founded on the assumption that a person is unlikely to fabricate a statement against his own interest at the time it is made. . .

When dealing with the rule against hearsay and its exceptions according to common law evidentiary principles, admissibility is a question addressed exclusively to the discretion of the trial judge, and the fact finder then gives evidence which is admitted whatever weight it deems appropriate in its prerogative. For a declaration against penal interest to be admissible, it is required that the declarant be presently unavailable. The law is well settled that the invocation of the privilege against compelled self-incrimination is a sufficient showing of unavailability. . .

In terms of the guarantee of trustworthiness, the declarations in this case were further buttressed by the administration of the oath. When dealing with the common law of evidence, our predominant consideration is the accuracy of the proffered evidence. In this regard, the statements made by the appellants Lewis and Jacobs, certainly insofar as they implicated themselves, were well corroborated. This is all that is required by the common law of evidence.

The Inapplicability of Special Constitutional Strictures
Where Evidence Is Not Procured by the State
(Appellants Lewis and Jacobs)

The appellants Lewis and Jacobs, however, make the further claim that these admissions should have been tested by the same constitutional law of evidence that would be applicable if the statements had been taken by governmental agents and offered in evidence by the State. In this regard, they fundamentally misperceive the distinction and the constitutional law of evidence. In insuring not simply the accuracy of the fact-finding process but the fairness of governmental behavior, the constitutional law, to the extent that it goes further than the common law, is directed at State action. Far more than the reliability of the evidence and the accuracy of the verdict is at stake. Due process generally and the privilege against compelled self-incrimination specifically require that even unequivocally accurate confessions be suppressed if the rights of a citizen were trampled upon by the agents of government in procuring the confession. . .

There is a residual sense, of course, in which the jury will consider voluntariness, if evidence of voluntariness or involuntariness is offered by either party. Part of the jury's prerogative is to weigh all evidence and to decide how persuasive it is. With respect to admissions, confessions and declarations against interest (pecuniary or penal), that core aspect of voluntariness that goes to the trustworthiness of the statement is very relevant to the weighing process. That additional, latter-day dimension of constitutional voluntariness, however, that looks beyond trustworthiness to be propriety of governmental behavior has no relevance to the weighing function. It is not the job of a jury "to police the police."

In this regard, the assessment of the weight to be given a declaration against interest is no different from the assessment of the weight to be given any piece of evidence, exception to the hearsay rule or otherwise. The jury may always ask, "Was the utterance truly spontaneous?;" "Was the admission ambiguous?;" "Was the declaration truly against interest?;" "Did the interest threatened outweigh the benefit to be gained?;" "Did the dying declarant know he was about to die?"

In dealing with all such issues, the State is always entitled, in the exercise of its tactical judgment, to offer whatever it thinks will enhance the weight of its own evidence and will diminish the weight of the defense evidence. By the same token, a defendant is always entitled, in the exercise of his tactical judgment, to offer whatever he thinks will diminish the weight of the State's evidence and will enhance the weight of his own. This is but a routine incident of the trial process, civil or criminal. It does not involve the superimposition of those additional constitutional strictures, allocations of the burden of proof and of the special procedures aimed at the regulation of governmental behavior. . .

In all of the foregoing cases, the challenged statements were introduced by the State in furtherance of the State's case but were held to be beyond constitutional challenge because no State action had been involved in the initial procurement of the evidence. The case before us is even stronger in terms of the remoteness of any constitutional implications. The State here did not introduce the declarations of Lewis and Jacobs. The State went further and actually objected to the introduction of those declarations. Were the appellants to prevail in this contention, the logical implications would be absurdities. If the burden, which they contend for, had been upon the State and the State had deliberately failed to carry such burden, the State would have been delighted and only the defendant Jackson would have been harmed by denying the jury his key defensive evidence. If the burden, on the other hand, had been upon the codefendant Jackson, what would that constitutional burden consist of? Is one defendant to be required to furnish counsel to his codefendants before interrogating them? If so, what does an indigent defendant do before interrogating indigent codefendants? Must a defendant give Miranda warnings before interrogating a codefendant? Must a defendant even refrain from threatening or making promises to a codefendant?

The answer, of course, is that the universal solvent into which all such constitutional considerations dissolve is the Fourteenth Amendment. That Amendment, by its very terms, is addressed only to State action:

"No State shall. . . "

Lawrence Jackson is not the State. The special obligations imposed upon the State are not imposed upon Lawrence Jackson. . .

The Severance Problem
(Appellants Lewis and Jacobs)

The severance contention made by the appellants Lewis and Jacobs falls with the failure of their contentions. . . Their contention that their trial should have been severed from that of Jackson falls with our holding that their declarations against penal interest were generally admissible.

They add a nuance to this contention. They urge that even if their declarations against penal interest were admissible for purposes of exculpating Jackson, they were nonetheless, inadmissible for purposes of inculpating themselves. When dealing with the common law of evidence, as we are here, we know of no such one-way streets. The question with respect to those challenged declarations was not Who would be helped or hurt by their admission? but Were they competent? The law of evidence is neutral. If the evidence is unworthy of belief, it may not come in for any purpose, either to exculpate or to inculpate. On the other hand, if the evidence is worthy of belief, it comes in for all purposes, inculpatory as well as exculpatory. Blind Justice does not manipulate her scales according to whose interests are being served.

JUDGMENTS AFFIRMED; COSTS TO BE PAID BY APPELLANTS.

CHAPTER VIII

WILLS, TRUSTS, PROBATE AND RELIGION AND OTHER MATTERS CONCERNING THE HEREAFTER

. . . Why may not that be the skull of a lawyer? Where be his quiddities now, his quillities, his cases, his tenures, and his tricks? Why does he suffer this mad knave now to knock him about the sconce with a dirty shovel, and will not tell him of his action of battery? Hum! This fellow might be in's time a great buyer of land, with his statutes, his recognizances, his fines, his double vouchers, his recoveries. [Is this the fine of his fines, and the recovery of his recoveries], to have his fine pate full of fine dirt? Will his vouchers vouch him no more of his purchases, and double ones too, than the length and breadth of a pair of indentures? The very conveyances of his lands will scarcely lie in this box, and must th' inheritor himself have no more, ha?

- Hamlet[1]

The lawyers, Bob, know too much.
They are chums of the books of old John Marshall.
They know it all, what a dead hand wrote,
A stiff dead hand and its knuckles crumbling,
The bones of the fingers a thin white ash.
The lawyers know a dead man's thoughts too well.

In the heels of the higgling lawyers, Bob,
Too many slippery ifs and buts and howevers,
Too much hereinbefore provided whereas,
Too many doors to go in and out of. . .

- Carl Sandburg[2]

---

[1] William Shakespeare, *"Hamlet Prince of Denmark"*, Act V, Scene i.
[2] From "The Lawyers Know Too Much" reprinted in *Masterpieces of American Poets* by Mark Van Doren, Garden City Publishing Co., p. 448 (1932).

IN RE JOHN OF KERNESLAWE
Assize Court of Northumberland County
Northumberland Assize Rolls, 7 Edward I (1279)

ANONYMOUS, Judge

A certain unknown woman, a sorceress, entered the house of John of Kerneslawe at the hour of vespers, and assaulted John in such a way that John signed himself with the sign of the cross. This occurred during the evening when the "Benedicite"[1] was being recited. And this same John, in defending himself, as if from the Devil, struck the sorceress with a staff, so that she died. Afterwards, by decision of the entire clergy, her body was burned. John went insane following this incident. Later, when John regained his senses, he remembered the incident, and thinking he might be punished because of it, fled to the diocese of Durham. He is not suspected of any felony; hence, he may return if he wishes; but his property is confiscated on account of his flight. Value of his property: £4 5s.

LYONS v. THE PLANTERS' LOAN & SAVINGS BANK
Supreme Court of Georgia
86 Ga. 485; 12 S.E. 882 (1890)

LOGAN E. BLECKLEY, Chief Justice

. . . Treating the debt as unpaid, can the church edifice and the premises on which its stands, the same being a city lot in the city of Augusta, be subjected by a court of equity, or rather by a court of law exercising equitable powers, to its payment?

The church as an organization is the Antioch Baptist church, and the equitable ownership of the property is in it or in the trustees which represent it in this action. The formal legal title is outstanding in the Perkins Manufacturing Company, which once had claims upon the premises as security for a debt now satisfied. Here then is a debtor having some property, perhaps sufficient property, to discharge the debt. Why should it not be so applied? If any debt ought to be paid, it is one contracted for the health of souls -- for pious ministrations and holy services. If any class of debtors ought to pay as matter of moral as well as legal duty, the good people of a Christian church are that class. No church can have any higher obligation resting upon it than being just. The study of justice for more than forty years has impressed me with the supreme importance of this grand and noble virtue. Some of the virtues are in the nature of moral luxuries, but this is an absolute necessary of social life. It is the hog and hominy, the bacon and beans of morality, public and private. It is the exact virtue, being mathematical in its nature.

---

[1] [Ed. Note: The "Benedicite" is a canticle, a biblical song of praise.]

Mercy, pity, charity, gratitude, generosity, magnanimity, etc., are the liberal virtues. They flourish partly on voluntary concessions made by the exact virtue, but they have no right to extort from it any unwilling concession. They can only supplicate or persuade. A man cannot give in charity or from pity, hospitality or magnanimity, the smallest part of what is necessary to enable him to satisfy the demands of justice. It is ignoble to indulge any of the liberal virtues by leaving undischarged any of these imperative demands against us.

On the credit side of justice we can make any sacrifice of it that we will, but on the debit side we can make none whatever. I may burn as an offering my own bull or lamb, but not that which rightfully belongs to another owner.

There is nothing more exalted than a strict duty and its performance. What we freely give cannot be better bestowed than what we pay in discharge of a perfect obligation. The law grants exemptions of property to families, but none to private corporations or collective bodies, lay or ecclesiastical. These must pay their debts if they can. All their property legal and equitable is subject. [citation omitted] We think a court may well constrain this church to do justice. In contemplation of law, justice is not only one of the cardinal virtues, it is the pontifical virtue.

Certainly it is an energetic measure to sell the church to pay the preacher, nor would it be allowable to do so, if other means of satisfying the debt were within reach. But the plain implication from the facts alleged is that the church has no assets other than this property, and on looking into the answer, we find that the answer makes no suggestion of any other assets. . .

. . . The verdict of the jury was as follows: "We the jury find verdict for plaintiff, principal $278.75, interest $97.60." On this verdict the court entered up a decree to the effect that the debt is that of the Antioch Baptist Church; that the property is subject thereto; that the debt be a lien upon it; that the sheriff levy upon it under and by virtue of the decree, expose it to sale according to law and execute title to the purchaser; that out of the proceeds of sale the debt and all costs be discharged, and that the overplus, if any, be paid over to the trustees of the church; also that the defendants be perpetually restrained and enjoined from disturbing or in any way interfering with the title of said property or the sale thereof, until the debt and costs be paid off and discharged. . .

. . . The decree devotes the property to the payment of the debt by judicial sale through the sheriff, and directs the surplus proceeds, if any, to be paid over to the trustees of the church. We think the decree as a whole was a proper one.

Judgment affirmed.

CUMMINS v. BOND

Supreme Court of Judicature, Chancery Division

[1927] 1 Ch. 1967

SIR H. T. EVE, J.

[This was an action by plaintiff, Miss Geraldine Dorothy Cummins, against defendant, Frederick Bligh Bond, seeking to establish plaintiff's right to the copyright in a literary work entitled "The Chronicle of Cleophas," and for an injunction to restrain the defendant from publishing this work in any manner.

The plaintiff, Miss Cummins, was a journalist and writer and was also engaged in psychic research, acting as a spiritualist medium at séances and for some years had practiced automatic writing. In early 1924 plaintiff regularly engaged in automatic writing in the company of a friend, Miss Edith Beatrice Gibbes. The method of writing was as follows: The plaintiff covered her eyes with her left hand, took a pencil in her right hand and rested it on a wad of foolscap paper. After a while she passed into a sort of dream state, and her hand commenced to write very rapidly, sometimes over 2000 words in an hour and a half without any pause.

The defendant Mr. Bond, was an architect and much interested in recent discoveries at the Abbey of Glastonbury and in automatic writing. He was invited by Miss Gibbes to join the plaintiff and herself at the time that the automatic writing in "The Chronicle of Cleophas" commenced in May, 1925. After each sitting Mr. Bond took away the original script with the plaintiff's consent and transcribed it, punctuated it, and arranged it in paragraphs, and returned a copy of it so arranged to the plaintiff. From time to time during the séances the defendant placed his fingers upon the back of the plaintiff's hand when she was writing, but it made no difference to the mode of writing, except that it became somewhat slower.

There was some conversation in the course of the sittings as to possible publication of "The Chronicle," and the defendant in July, 1925, suggested that any profits arising from such publication should be divided equally between the three--i.e., the plaintiff, Miss Gibbes, and Mr. Bond. There was no conversation at first with regard to the ownership of the copyright. Miss Gibbes subsequently informed the defendant by letter that she understood the copyright of the writings belonged to the plaintiff, and he did not then dispute it.

Attempts were made to have an agreement drawn up between the parties, but no agreement was ever reached. There was evidence by Miss Gibbes, who was present at every sitting at which "The Chronicle of Cleophas" was being produced, that it was on June 14, 1925, that the plaintiff first chose and wrote the title to the work as "The Chronicle of Cleophas" (the name Cleophas appears twice in the New Testament as one of the followers of Christ).

It was proved that the whole of the manuscript of the work was written by the plaintiff alone in her own automatic writing, and none of it was dictated by the defendant or any other living person. The nature of the writing was archaic, of the sixteenth and seventeenth centuries. No written assignment of the copyright was ever made. Before 1925 none of the script had been published, but later on, about February, 1926, certain extracts from the script were published by the defendant, Mr. Bond, in the *Christian Spiritualist* paper.]

The issue in this action is reduced to the simple question who, if any one, is the owner of the copyright in this work. Prima facie it is the author, and so far as this world is concerned there can be no doubt who is the author here, for it has been abundantly proved that the plaintiff is the writer of every word to be found in this bundle of original script. But the plaintiff and her witness and the defendant are all of opinion--and I do not doubt that the opinion is an honest one--that the true originator of all that is to be found in these documents is some being no longer inhabiting this world, and who has been out of it for a length of time sufficient to justify the hope that he has no reasons for wishing to return to it.

According to the case put forward by those entertaining the opinion I have referred to the individual in question is particularly desirous of assisting in further discoveries relating to the ancient Abbey of Glastonbury, and he chooses the Brompton Road as the locality in which, and the plaintiff as the medium through whom, his views as to further works to be undertaken on the site of the Abbey shall be communicated to the persons engaged in the work of excavation. He is sufficiently considerate not to do so in language so antiquated as not be to understood by the excavators and others engaged in the interesting operations, but in order not to appear of too modern an epoch he selects a medium capable of translating his messages into language appropriate to a period some sixteen or seventeen centuries after his death.

I am not impugning the honesty of persons who believe, and of the parties to this action who say that they believe, that this long departed being is the true source from which the contents of these documents emanate; but I think I have stated enough with regard to the antiquity of the source and the language in which the communications are written to indicate that they could not have reached us in this form without the active co-operation of some agent competent to translate them from the language in which they were communicated to her into something more intelligible to persons of the present day. The plaintiff claims to be this agent and to possess, and the defendant admits that she does possess, some qualification enabling her, when in a more or less unconscious condition, to reproduce in language understandable by those who have the time and inclination to read it, information supplied to her from the source referred to in language with which the plaintiff has no acquaintance when fully awake.

From this it would almost seem as though the individual who has been dead and buried for some 1900 odd years and the plaintiff ought to be regarded as the joint authors and owners of the copyright, but inasmuch as I do not feel myself competent to make any declaration in his favour, and recognizing as I do that I have no jurisdiction extending to the sphere in which he moves, I think I ought to confine myself when inquiring who is the author to individuals who were alive when the work first came into existence and to conditions which the legislature in

1911 may reasonably be presumed to have contemplated. So doing it would seem to be clear that the authorship rests with this lady, to whose gift of peculiar ability to reproduce in archaic English matter communicated to her in some unknown tongue we owe the production of these documents. But the defendant disputes the plaintiff's right to be considered the sole author, alleging that he was an element and a necessary element in the production, and claiming, if the authorship is to be confined to persons resident in this world, that he is entitled to the rights incident to authorship jointly with the plaintiff. . .

He [Mr. Bond] is an individual upon whose memory little reliance can be placed--he is of an imaginative temperament and regards the alleged supernatural incidents connected with this work with a reverence that is almost fanatical, and he has, I think, in more than one incident shown that he is occasionally subject to hallucinations. His claim to be considered a joint author is suggestive of hallucination, for it is based upon the assertion that by his presence at the séances where the writing took place he in some way transmitted from his brain to the unconscious brain of the medium the classical and historical references which are to be found in these documents. He frankly admits that he does not appreciate how it was done, or to what extent he did it; but he has evidently brought himself to believe that he did contribute materially to the composition of the work and that his contribution was made by means of some silent transfer from his brain to that of the unconscious medium of phrases and allusions with which he was familiar but of which she knew nothing.

But inasmuch as the medium is credited with a power to translate language of which she knew nothing into archaic English, of which she was almost equally ignorant, and at a phenomenal pace, it does not appear necessary to fall back on the defendant's presence in order to explain the classical and historical references which he maintains must have emanated from his brain. They may well have originated in the brain of the medium herself. In these circumstances I am quite unable to hold that the defendant has made out any case entitling him to be treated as a joint author. I think he is labouring under a complete delusion in thinking that he in any ways contributed to the production of these documents. . .

I am quite unable to hold that the plaintiff ever abandoned the position she took up in the latter part of the year 1925 or ever so conducted herself as to preclude her from insisting on the claims put forward in this action. Accordingly I hold she is entitled to the declaration for which she asks, that is to say, a declaration that she is the owner of the copyright in this work--it must be identified in some way--delivery up of such parts of the original manuscript as have not already been handed to her, and the defendant must pay the costs of the action. The counterclaim by which the defendant seeks a declaration that he is entitled to the copyright is dismissed with costs.

GLEASON v. JONES
Supreme Court of Oklahoma
79 Okla. 191; 192 P. 203 (1920)

JOHN H. PITCHFORD, J.

This case comes on appeal from the district court of Okmulgee county in denying to probate the will of Frances Swartz. The record discloses that Frances Swartz resided in the city of Henryetta, Okla. Some time prior to and at her death she was engaged in conducting a house of prostitution. For some time preceding the execution of the instrument sought to be probated as her will she had been under the care of Dr. Robinson, suffering from an attack of jaundice. Early Sunday morning, April 9, 1916, the doctor was called in and found that the disease had reached an acute stage, and informed her of her serious condition, and further impressed upon her the fact that there was no hope for her recovery.

Some one in the house telephoned Mr. Axline, an attorney of Henryetta, and informed him that his services were wanted in the preparation of a will. He immediately responded, and the will was executed devising to Marguirite Gleason and W.E. Peak, two of the inmates of the house, certain real estate, the same being the house occupied by the deceased, together with the furniture therein contained, of a total value of $3,968.75, and real estate of the value of $600 was devised to Wesley Jones, a brother of the testatrix, residing in Peoria, Ill.

The testatrix died on the following morning. Claims filed against the estate amount of $3,200. When the will was offered for probate in the county court of Okmulgee county the brother filed a contest, and the court, after hearing the evidence, admitted the will to probate. An appeal was taken by the contestant to the district court of Okmulgee county, and judgment there rendered in favor of the contestant, on the ground that the will was procured by undue influence exercised by the proponents over the testatrix. . . . error in finding that the associations of the testatrix with the proponents in an immoral environment, and the presence of the proponents of the will in the room at the execution of the will, were sufficient to infer undue influence. . .

The second proposition contended for by the appellants is that a devise to one associated with testatrix in an immoral environment does not, because of the immorality of the association and the presence of the beneficiaries at the time the will is executed, give rise to an inference of undue influence exercised by the devisees over testatrix.

. . . He found that such undue influence arose a great deal because of the illegal and licentious relationship existing among the inmates of the house; that at the time of her death her mind was in such condition as to be easily influenced by suggestion; and the court was of the opinion that under the particular circumstances of this case, taking everything into consideration, the relationship of the parties, the character of the business in which they were engaged, the fact that both of the principal beneficiaries and proponents of the will were present. . .

the court was of the opinion that at the time of the execution of the will the testatrix was unfairly and unduly influenced in making it by the two principal beneficiaries and therefore that the instrument presented for probate was not the will of Frances Swartz.

Conceding that the environments of the decedent and the proponents were immoral, that fact did not deprive Frances Swartz of the right to say in life what the disposition of her property should be after death. The property was her own; she had the right to sell it or give it away. The court did not find, neither did he base his judgment in refusing to probate the will, upon the ground that the testatrix was not of disposing mind, but upon the ground that she was influenced by the suggestions of the proponents.

We have made a careful search of the record, and have been unable to find where either of the proponents ever at any time used the least influence on the testatrix to induce her to execute the will as she did, not even the remotest suggestion on their part is shown. Therefore we are confronted with this proposition: Does the fact that the testatrix was the mistress of a house of ill fame deprive her of testamentary capacity in the event the beneficiaries of her will happen to be inmates of the house conducted by her as such? Does the lack of morality forfeit her right to devise her property as conferred by statute? And if her occupation does not deprive her of this right, is she limited to those who are respectable members of society?

It is true that the testatrix and the proponents of the will had become social outcasts, and had wandered far from the paths of rectitude; brought to this condition, in all probability, by the passions of some lecherous, unprincipled lying man. Here we are reminded that a man may wander afar from the paths of virtue and right living; he may commit many offenses against the moral law; he may feed upon the husks of degradation; but when we see evidence of reformation on his part every one delights in giving him a word of encouragement.

On the other hand, when a poor unfortunate woman, in almost every instance the victim of misplaced confidence in some man, makes an effort to reform, attempts to regain a respectable position in society, we find the back of almost every hand turned against her. They are shunned by people of respectability, they have no one to associate with except those who, like them, have departed from a life of virtue. Is it to be expected then, when they come to their deathbeds and their spirit takes its flight to appear before the Infallible Bar where we hope that mercy will be shown them because of the fact that their sins are largely brought about by a confiding trust in some man, that the pillars of society will be present to administer to their last wants or close their eyes in death?

Must we say that because the proponents of this will were at the bedside of the testatrix at the time of her death, drawn together by their common social ban, compelled to administer, each to the other, that this is a circumstance from which alone we must draw a conclusion of undue influence exercised over the testatrix? The testatrix had cast her lot among these kind of people; they were of her world;

her days were lived among them; she died among them. Under all the circumstances of the instant case, we are not prepared to say that the proponents would be the unnatural objects of the bounty of the testatrix, Frances Swartz. . .

Reversed.

POTTS v. HOUSE
Supreme Court of Georgia
6. Ga. 324 (1849)

JOSEPH H. LUMPKIN, J.

This was an issue of *devisavit vel non* [Did he dispose of the property in his will, or not?] originating in the Court of Ordinary of Troup County, to try the validity of an instrument purporting to be the last will and testament of James Potts, senior, deceased. That Court having decided in favor of the will, an appeal was entered, and the final trial had in the Superior Court of that county, before Judge Hill, in November, 1898.

The Jury returned a verdict affirming the judgment of the Court of Ordinary, and declaring that the paper propounded, was the last will and testament of James Potts, senior, deceased. . .

I have endeavored, in this analysis of the case, to condense and simplify it as much as possible. The real question to be decided in both Courts in this case was, whether [or not] there was a valid will. The executor and those who claim under it, hold the affirmative. They must not only prove, therefore, that the instrument purporting to be a testamentary paper, was formally executed, but, also, that the testator was of sound and disposing mind and memory. . .

We will now, in conclusion, examine some of the general doctrines involved in the charge respecting wills; and I must say His Honor, Judge Hill, discharged this portion of his arduous functions with equal skill and perspicuity, and we are not prepared to say that he underrated the degree of testamentary capacity necessary to make a will, in maintaining that imbecility of mind did not disqualify, provided it stopped short of idiocy or lunacy. Before investigating this case, I had supposed that more capacity was required to make a will than I now find warranted by the authorities; and in remanding this cause to the Circuit for a new trial, with instructions, I am inclined to think, that we rather overrated the amount of mind which this exacts of the testator. At any rate, I have myself more clear and definite views respecting this subject than I have hitherto entertained.

Still, I find no acknowledged standard of "weights and measures" by which to regulate this as well as all similar investigations. We apprehend that this thing, from its very nature, is incapable of being fixed and determined. All attempts to draw the line between capacity and incapacity have ended where they began, namely: in nothing. All agree that there must be a sound and disposing mind and memory, but to define the precise quantum, *hoc opus, hic labor est*. [This is a task, this is a deed requiring effort[1]].

One thing is certain -- that eccentricity, however great, is not sufficient, of itself, to invalidate a will. . . Mason Lee, the testator in this case, supposed himself to be continually haunted by witches, devils and evil spirits, which he fancied were always worrying him. He believed that all women are witches. (In this, perhaps, he was not so singular!) He lived in the strangest manner -- wore an extraordinary dress, and slept in a hollow log. He imagined that the Wiggin's relatives, whom he desired to disinherit, were in his teeth; and to dislodge them, he had fourteen sound teeth extracted, evincing no suffering from the operation.

He had the quarters of his shoes cut off, saying that if the devil got into his feet he could drive him out the easier. His constant dress was an osnaburg shirt, a negro cloth short coat, breeches and leggings. His wearing apparel, at his death, was appraised at one dollar. He always shaved his head close, as he said that in the contests with the witches, they might not get hold of his hair, and also, to make his wits glib. He had innumerable swords, of all sizes and shapes, to enable him to fight the devil and witches successfully; they were made by a neighboring blacksmith.

In the day-time, neglecting his business he dozed in a hollow gum-log, for a bed, in his miserable hovel; and at night, kept awake fighting with his imaginary unearthly foes. He fancied, at one time, that he had the devil nailed up in a fireplace, at one end of his house, and had a mark made across his room, over which he never would pass, nor suffer it to be swept. He would sometimes send for all his negroes to throw dirt upon the roof of his house, to drive off ghosts. He had no chair, or table, or plate in his house. He used a forked stick. His meat was boar and bull beef and dumplings, served up in the same pot in which it was boiled, and placed on a chest, which answered him for both table and chair. He made his own clothes; they had no buttons; his pantaloons were as wide as petticoats, without a waistband, and fastened around him with a rope. His saddle was a piece of hollow gum-log, covered with leather, and of his own make. His kennel, on which he ate, slept and dozed away his time, was three feet wide, five feet long, and four feet high. He suffered no bull or boar, on his plantation, to be castrated. He cut off all the tails of his hogs and cattle, close to the roots; he said the cows made themselves poor, by fighting the flies with their tails, but cut them off and they would get as fat as squabs. He once brought a horse from home, cut off its ears, and mounted it instantly while bleeding. He mutilated in the same manner, all his horses and mules. He hoed his corn after frost, saying it would come out green again.

His bargins were peculiar, and generally losing. He gave long credits, without interest. He sold one place for $7,000, to be paid in 17 years, without

---

[1] [Ed. Note: From Vergil's *Aeneid*, Book VI, line 129.]

interest, and if the purchaser did not like the bargin at the end of that time, he was at liberty to give it up, without paying rent. He said that the land at the expiration of that time, would be worth ten times as much as when he sold it. He purchased a large body of poor flat pine land, without seeing it, and put his negroes there, without a hut to live in. They cleared and girdled the trees of 2,000 acres, for the purpose, he said, of planting it in pinders (ground nuts,) by which, he said, he should make a fortune.

He never went to church, nor voted, nor was required to do patrol or militia duty. He had a sulky made; his directions were, to have the shafts exactly nine feet long, and the chair and seat to be square--the sticks of which were to be worked with a drawing knife -- not turned -- and the cross-bars were to be square.

But enough of these whimsicalities. The will was established; and upon the appeal, the supervisory tribunal, through its organ, Judge Nott, declared that "the evidence, (a part of which only I have quoted,) seems very well to have authorized the verdict which the Jury rendered."

If the maxim be sound, that what is against reason, cannot be law, one might, I think, well doubt the principle of this case, without being branded as a skeptic. I subscribe, however, to the doctrine, that it is not every man of a frantic appearance and behavior, who is to be considered *non compos mentis* [not of sound mind], either as it regards contracts, obligations or crimes; and that one may be addicted occasionally or habitually to the strangest peculiarities and yet possess a testable capacity. . .

. . . but old age does not deprive a man of the capacity of making a testament; for a man may make a will, how old soever he may be, since it is not the integrity of the body but of the mind, that is requisite in testaments, provided the understanding has not become destroyed, by surviving the period that Providence has assigned to the sanity and stability of the mind.

The want of recollection of names, is one of the earliest symptoms of the decay of memory, by reason of old age; but it is not sufficient to create incapacity, unless it is quite total, or extend to the immediate family and property of the deceased. I once walked more than a hundred yards with Luther Martin of Maryland, for the purpose of being introduced to his grand-son, whom he had brought to college, without his being able to recall to his mind the name of his son-in-law, the father of the young man. And yet, I have no idea that his faculties were so far gone and shattered, as to have lost their testamentary power. If the testator be capable of doing an act of thought or memory, it is enough.

Jacob Bennet, the testator, was between 90 and 100 years old, when he made his will, disposing of his negroes, (New York!!) furniture and stock, on his farm. His will was executed -- Chancellor Kent holding, that neither age, nor sickness, nor extreme distress, or debility of body, will affect the capacity to make a will, if sufficient understanding remains. He feelingly observes, that, "it is one of the painful consequences of extreme old age, that it ceases to excite interest, and is apt to be left solitary and neglected. The control which the law still gives to a man, over the disposal of his property, is one of the most efficient means which he has, in protracted life, to command the attention due to his infirmities. The will of such an aged man ought to be regarded with great tenderness, when it appears not to have been procured by fraudulent acts, but contains those very dispositions which the circumstances of his situation, and the course of natural affections dictated." *Van Alst v. Hunter* [citation omitted]. . . .

Upon the whole case, we are satisfied that there was reasonable ground for prosecuting this writ of error; and that in view of all the circumstances, it would best comport with the ends of justice to order a new trial.

STAMBOVSKY v. ACKLEY
Supreme Court of New York, Appellate Division
572 N.Y.S. 2d 672 (1991)

ISRAEL RUBIN, J.

Plaintiff, to his horror, discovered that the house he had recently contracted to purchase was widely reputed to be possessed by poltergeists, reportedly seen by defendant seller and members of her family on numerous occasions over the last nine years. Plaintiff promptly commenced this action seeking rescission of the contract of sale. Supreme Court reluctantly dismissed the complaint, holding that plaintiff has no remedy at law in this jurisdiction.

The unusual facts of this case, as disclosed by the record, clearly warrant a grant of equitable relief to the buyer who, as a resident of New York City, cannot be expected to have any familiarity with folklore of the Village of Nyack. Not being a "local," plaintiff could not readily learn that the home he had contracted to purchase is haunted. Whether the source of the spectral apparitions seen by defendant seller are parapsychic or psychogenic, having reported their presence in both a national publication ("Readers' Digest") and the local press (in 1977 and 1982, respectively), defendant is estopped to deny their existence and, as a matter of law, the house is haunted.

More to the point, however, no divination is required to conclude that it is defendant's promotional efforts in publicizing her close encounters with these spirits which fostered the home's reputation in the community. In 1989, the house was included in a five-home walking tour of Nyack and described in a November 27th newspaper article as "a riverfront Victorian (with ghost)." The impact of the reputation thus created goes to the very essence of the bargain between the parties, greatly impairing both the value of the property and its potential for resale. . .

. . . While I agree with Supreme Court that the real estate broker, as agent for the seller, is under no duty to disclose to a potential buyer the phantasmal reputation of the premises and that, in his pursuit of a legal remedy for fraudulent misrepresentation against the seller, plaintiff hasn't a ghost of a chance, I am nevertheless moved by the spirit of equity to allow the buyer to seek rescission of the contract of sale and recovery of his downpayment.

New York law fails to recognize any remedy for damages incurred as a result of the seller's mere silence, applying instead the strict rule of caveat emptor. Therefore, the theoretical basis for granting relief, even under the extraordinary facts of this case, is elusive if not ephemeral. "Pity me not but lend thy serious hearing to what I shall unfold" (William Shakespeare, Hamlet, Act I, Scene V [Ghost]).

From the perspective of a person in the position of plaintiff herein, a very practical problem arises with respect to the discovery of a paranormal phenomenon: "Who you gonna' call?" as the title song to the movie "Ghostbusters" asks. Applying the strict rule of caveat emptor to a contract involving a house possessed by poltergeists conjures up visions of a psychic or medium routinely accompanying the structural engineer and Terminix man on an inspection of every home subject to a contract of sale. It portends that the prudent attorney will establish an escrow account lest the subject of the transaction come back to haunt him and his client--or pray that his malpractice insurance coverage extends to supernatural disasters.

In the interest of avoiding such untenable consequences, the notion that a haunting is a condition which can and should be ascertained upon reasonable inspection of the premises is a hobgoblin which should be exorcised from the body of legal precedent and laid quietly to rest.

It has been suggested by a leading authority that the ancient rule which holds that mere non-disclosure does not constitute actionable misrepresentation "finds proper application in cases where the fact disclosed is patent, or the plaintiff has equal opportunities for obtaining information which he may be expected to utilize, or the defendant has no reason to think that he is acting under any misapprehension" (Prosser, Law of Torts § 106, at 696 [4th ed, 1971]). However, with respect to transactions in real estate, New York adheres to the doctrine of caveat emptor and imposes no duty upon the vendor to disclose any information concerning the premises [citation omitted] unless there is a confidential or fiduciary relationship between the parties [citation omitted] or some conduct on the part of the seller which constitutes "active concealment" [citation omitted] (dummy ventilation system constructed by seller); [citation omitted] (foundation cracks covered by seller.) Normally, some affirmative misrepresentation [citation omitted] (industrial waste on land allegedly used only as farm); [citation omitted] (land containing valuable minerals allegedly acquired for use as campsite) or partial disclosure [citation omitted] (existence of third unopened street concealed); [citation omitted] (escrow agreements securing lien concealed) is required to impose upon the seller a duty to communicate undisclosed conditions affecting the premises [citation omitted].

Caveat emptor is not so all-encompassing a doctrine of common law as to render every act of non-disclosure immune from redress, whether legal or equitable. "In regard to the necessity of giving information which has not been asked, the rule differs somewhat at law and in equity, and while the law courts would permit no recovery of damages against a vendor, because of mere concealment of facts under certain circumstances, yet if the vendee refused to complete the contract because of the concealment of a material fact on the part of the other, equity would refuse to compel him so to do, because equity only compels the specific performance of a contract which is fair and open, and in regard to which all material matters known to each have been communicated to the other." [citation omitted] Even as a principle of law, long before exceptions were embodied in statute law (see, e.g., UCC 2-312, 313, 314, 315; 3-417[2]e), the doctrine was held inapplicable to contagion among animals, adulteration of food, and insolvency of a maker of a promissory note and of a tenant substituted for another under a lease [citation omitted].

Common law is not moribund. *Ex facto jus oritur* (law arises out of facts). Where fairness and common sense dictate that an exception should be created, the evolution of the law should not be stifled by rigid application of a legal maxim.

The doctrine of caveat emptor requires that a buyer act prudently to assess the fitness and value of his purchase and operates to bar the purchaser who fails to exercise due care from seeking the equitable remedy of rescission [citation omitted]. For the purposes of the instant motion to dismiss the action . . . plaintiff is entitled to every favorable inference which may reasonably be drawn from the pleadings [citation omitted] specifically, in this instance, that he met his obligation to conduct an inspection of the premises and a search of available public records with respect to title. It should be apparent, however, that the most meticulous inspection and search would not reveal the presence of poltergeists at the premises or unearth the property's ghoulish reputation in the community. Therefore, there is no sound policy reason to deny plaintiff relief for failing to discover a state of affairs which the most prudent purchaser of it would not be expected to even contemplate [citation omitted].

The case law in this jurisdiction dealing with the duty of a vendor of real property to disclose information to the buyer is distinguishable from the matter under review. The most salient distinction is that existing cases invariably deal with the physical condition of the premises [citation omitted] (use as a landfill); [citation omitted] (sewer line crossing adjoining property without owner's consent), defects in title [citation omitted] (remainderman), liens against the property [citation omitted] expenses or income [citation omitted] (gross receipts) and other factors affecting its operation. No case has been brought to this court's attention in which the property value was impaired as the result of the reputation created by information disseminated to the public by the seller (or, for that matter, as a result of possession by poltergeists).

Where a condition which has been created by the seller materially impairs the value of the contract and is peculiarly within the knowledge of the seller or unlikely to be discovered by a prudent purchaser exercising due care with respect to the subject transaction, nondisclosure constitutes a basis for rescission as a matter of equity. Any other outcome places upon the buyer not merely the obligation to exercise care in his purchase but rather to be omniscient with respect to any fact which may affect the bargain. No practical purpose is served by imposing such a burden upon a purchaser. To the contrary, it encourages predatory business practice and offends the principle that equity will suffer no wrong to be without a remedy.

Defendant's contention that the contract of sale, particularly the merger or "as is" clause, bars recovery of the buyer's deposit is unavailing. Even an express disclaimer will not be given effect where the facts are peculiarly within the knowledge of the party invoking it. [citation omitted] Moreover, a fair reading of the merger clause reveals that it expressly disclaims only representations made with respect to the physical condition of the premises and merely makes general reference to representations concerning "any other matter or things affecting or relating to the aforesaid premises". As broad as this language may be, a reasonable interpretation is that its effect is limited to tangible or physical matters and does not extend to paranormal phenomena. Finally, if the language of the contract is to be construed as broadly as defendant urges to encompass the presence of poltergeists in the house, it cannot be cannot be said that she has delivered the premises "vacant" in accordance with her obligation under the provisions of the contract rider. . .

In the case at bar, defendant seller deliberately fostered the public belief that her home was possessed. Having undertaken to inform the public at large, to whom she has no legal relationship, about the supernatural occurrences on her property, she may be said to owe no less a duty to her contract vendee. It has been remarked that the occasional modern cases which permits a seller to take unfair advantage of buyer's ignorance so long as he is not actively misled are "singularly unappetizing" (Prosser, Law of Tort s 106, at 696 [4th ed 1971]). Where, as here, the seller not only takes unfair advantage of the buyer's ignorance but has created and perpetuated a condition about which he is unlikely to even inquire, enforcement of the contract (in while or in part) is offensive to the court's sense of equity. Application of the remedy of rescission, within the bounds of the narrow exception to the doctrine of caveat emptor set forth herein, is entirely appropriate to relieve the unwitting purchase from the consequences of a most unnatural bargain.

Accordingly, the judgment of the Supreme Court, New York County (Edward H. Lehner, J.), entered April 9, 1990, which dismissed the complaint . . . should be modified, on the law and the facts and in the exercise of discretion, and the first cause of action seeking rescission of the contract reinstated, without costs.

ROGERS v. HOSKINS
Supreme Court of Georgia
14 Ga. 166 (1853)

JOSEPH H. LUMPKIN, J.

[Harrison D. Hoskins, of Houston county, having departed this life, his widow, Malinda A. Hoskins, made her application to the superior Court of the county, for the assignment of dower. The notice to the executors was objected to, because it did not state the name of the person in whose behalf the application was to be made; and because it was served on only one of the two executors of the deceased. The notice was in the following form:

GEORGIA, HOUSTON COUNTY
To Shepherd Rogers and James Alford, Executors upon the estate of Harrison D. Hoskins, deceased:

You are hereby notified that I shall apply to the next Superior Court, to be held in and for said county, on the fourth Monday in April next, for the appointment of Commissioners to admeasure, lay off and assign Dower to me, in and to lots of land Nos. 237 and 248, in the lower fifth district of said county, agreeably to the Statutes, in such cases made and provided.

WARREN & HUMPHREYS,
Petitioner's Attorneys.
March 24, 1853.

The notice was served on Shepherd Rogers, but not on the other executor, James Alford. The court overruled the objections and granted the order appointing commissioners. The executors appealed.]

A notice in the name of nobody, is no notice.

Both executors are joined in the notice. This was right. Both should have been served--they were not. This was wrong.

Judgment reversed.

OBICI v. THIRD NATIONAL BANK & TRUST COMPANY OF SCRANTON
Supreme Court of Pennsylvania
381 Pa. 184; 112 A. 2d 94 (1955)

ALLEN M. STEARNE, J.

The sole issue raised by this appeal is whether or not the signatures of the settlor on the purported Amendment to an inter vivos deed of trust were forgeries. The learned Chancellor who heard the testimony found that the signatures were genuine. He dismissed the complaint in equity which sought to set aside the document.

Appellants charge that settlor's name on the trust Amendment is forged. To overcome the force of Mr. McNickle's testimony that he saw settlor affix his signature to the paper, appellants point to many matters which they regard as suspicious. Furthermore, they produced a handwriting expert and several lay witnesses who testified that, in their opinions, the signatures of settlor were forged.

Defendants also produced a handwriting expert and all witnesses who testified that the signatures of settlor were genuine. The Chancellor found as a fact that settlor did execute the documents in his own handwriting. He accepted as credible the testimony of defendants' witnesses. . .This Court has held that the credibility of witnesses is a matter resting with the finders of fact. . .

[T]he Chancellor in the present case believed the testimony of Mr. McNickle who testified that he saw settlor affix his signatures to the documents. This overcame any opinion evidence of expert and lay witnesses. . .In accepting as credible defendants' evidence and rejecting that of plaintiffs', the learned Chancellor states:

> "The signature of Amedeo Obici purported to be made on the amendment to the 'Friends and Relatives Trust' of April 19, 1946, is challenged as forgery. In order to find such a fact the Chancellor would have to hold (1) that McNickle is a liar; (2) that McNickle is a forger, or (3) that Mackie, Attorney, is a forger, * * *

> "The Chancellor can find no warrant in the evidence to make any such finding. To make such a finding would be to assume the existence of the most fantastic, improbable and senseless plot imaginable. * * *"

This Court has repeatedly held that suspicion and conjecture do not take the place of evidence. . .

The decree is affirmed.

MICHAEL A. MUSMANNO, Justice (dissenting).

As the little acorn can rear a mighty oak, the lowly peanut in this case created a commercial empire of plantations, factories, offices, warehouses and stores. Its guiding genius was Amedeo Obici who arrived in this opportunity-blessed land of America from Italy circa 1888 and died in 1947.

On January 13, 1945, Amedeo Obici created a "Friends and Relatives" trust whereby his brother Frank A. Obici with Frank's children were to enjoy a substantial part of Amedeo's estate upon his death. After his death, there came to light a paper known as an Amendment to the trust (reputedly signed April 19, 1945) wherein all benefits theretofore payable to Frank Obici and his children were wiped out. Frank Obici and his children protested this Amendment, claimed that it was a forged document and filed a Complaint in Equity seeking to restore unimpaired the original provisions of the Trust of January 13, 1945.

The learned Chancellor in the Court below dismissed the Complaint and said that he could not declare the Amendment to the Trust a fraudulent paper because to make such a finding "would be to assume the existence of the most fantastic, improbable and senseless plot imaginable." Such a plot could hardly be characterized as "senseless." The estate left by Amedeo Obici amounted to six million dollars! There have been fabulous plots and fantastic scheming for sums less than that handy treasure chest.

The learned Chancellor found it difficult to believe that Amedeo Obici would not disinherit his only brother with whom he had been associated for forty years in the building of the fortune which is the subject of this lawsuit. As I read the testimony I find it more than difficult to believe that he would. The record reveals that Amedeo Obici was a man of sturdy character, straightforward in his dealings, devoted to his brother with strong bonds of affection and family love, and generous to him and his family. This warmth of feeling for them was evident throughout the lives of all the plaintiffs and continued unabatedly even after the date on which he supposedly struck them from the sphere of his munificent bounty. It is almost impossible to believe that a brother who had been so good to his blood kin could wear a cloak of unmitigated hypocrisy to be removed only when the shrouds of death took its place.

Amedeo showed a particular fondness for Susan Obici, daughter of his brother Frank. He always greeted her affectionately and with a kiss. He lavished gifts on her (among others a diamond necklace) and at the time of her wedding, he paid for the wedding celebration which took place in his home. When confined to the hospital at the birth of her child, he sent her flowers. (This after the purported Amendment.) When the child was to be christened, Susan postponed the christening date because of the following letter she received from Mr. Obici who was at the time in California:

"Please wait because it not only will be an honor
but ... it will make me very happy if you waited

until I return from California Why? Because I
christened you when you were a little baby, I
stood up at your wedding, and now I want the
honor to christen your baby."

It could only be a person of the most brutal instincts (which no one ever
ascribed to Amedeo) who could stand up by his grand-niece at her baptism while
planning to exclude her from the sunshine of the tremendous wealth which he
could not take with him. There is absolutely nothing in the record which would
rationalize Amedeo's repulsion of Susan and her baby to whom he was devoted
in every way that one can show affectionate devotion. Up to the date of his death
he continued to speak of his intention to take care of Susan. She testified:

"Well, one day he looked very good, and I said
'Uncle, you look wonderful today. I'm so happy.'
'Yes,' he says, 'that's what you think, but your
uncle is going to die,' and then he turned to me,
'Don't you worry, don't forget what I told you in
1944.' He said, 'You are well taken care of, you
and your family. You will never have to worry
when my eyes are closed."

But, according to the defendants, Amedeo was scheming to disinherit
Susan and her baby while his eyes were still open. In the absence of evidence that
Amedeo completely lost his senses, there is a certain evidentiary obligation on the
part of the defendants to show how and why Amedeo could do something so
diametrically opposed to what is natural and normal. If Amedeo had any reason
to disinherit his blood relatives he also had the character to tell them that reason.
Why would he wait to inflict a sardonic revenge in the tomb?

The learned Chancellor offers the explanation that Amedeo became angry
because Joseph, his nephew, had decided to open a peanut store in Wilkes-Barre.
That the owner of a six-million-dollar peanut business would be angry because the
son of his brother would sell a few peanuts is to me inconceivable. And that this
wrath could reach such monumental proportions that Amedeo would, because of
it, disinherit not only Joseph, but Joseph's sister and brothers and his own brother
as well, is so bizarre and fantastic an idea that it can find lodgment only in the mist
land of uninhibited imagination.

Constancy of character, short of mental derangement, is as objective of
reality as a snow-capped mountain. The noxious tree of inhumanity does not bring
forth poison apples overnight. To make believable the idea that Amedeo could
proffer such poisoned fruit, there must be some evidence of the seed of malevolence, misanthrope and deceit, none of which, it is conceded, was sown in the life
of Amedeo Obici.

This Court has frequently said that a Chancellor's findings will not be reversed if they appear to be supported by evidence. However, we have also said that the appellate courts may "draw their own inferences and make their own deductions and conclusions from that evidence." Applying that rule to the instant situation, it is my conviction that it is more logical to conclude that Amedeo Obici did not disinherit his flesh and blood because of a supposed affront over the opening of a new peanut stand than that he did disinherit him for that reason.

I would draw the inference, based upon the granitic foundation that Amedeo Obici was a reasoning and honest man, that he would not strike down the son of his own father and mother with whom he had never quarreled as he stood on the brink of eternity where he was to meet that same father and mother. Odd and peculiar as at times seem the ways of the world, irrationalization has not so seized the human race that rivulets of anger control glaciers of thought and that flea bites destroy intellect. At any rate, we should not found decisions on what is extremely improbable when the proved possible is ours to build on.

The plaintiffs called as an expert handwriting witness a J. Howard Haring who, with 25 years experience in studying questioned documents, examined the signature which appeared on the purported Amendment, compared it with admittedly genuine signatures of Amedeo Obici and pronounced the former signature a forgery. . . .

The defendants called to the witness stand Alonzo M. McNickle who at the time of the transaction in litigation was assistant trust officer of the Third National Bank & Trust Company of Scranton, one of the defendants in the case. He testified that he visited Amedeo Obici on April 19, 1946 and submitted to him the Amendment which had been prepared by Matthew D. Mackie, attorney for the defendants, and that he saw Amedeo sign the amendment. If Mr. McNickle's testimony is to be believed, the Chancellor was justified in dismissing the plaintiff's claim. But is he to be believed?

No witness attested in writing to the signature of Amedeo Obici. Why? According to McNickle he was present when Amedeo signed the document. Why didn't McNickle sign the document as a witness? McNickle testified he told Amedeo that he expected trouble to follow when Obici signed the Amendment. If he anticipated trouble why did he not call people who were available to witness the signature and sign as having witnessed it? This obvious question was not answered by the Court below, nor has it been answered by the Majority here. The Chancellor's decision to accept the Amendment as a genuine document must stand on McNickle's testimony alone. I repeat: Is he to be believed?. . .

Attorney Mackie received $125,000 for handling the proceedings of the estate. He turned over 10% of this amount, $12,500, to McNickle. Why? The fee incidentally was not paid by check, the normal vehicle for transfer of funds, but by bearer bonds not easily traceable. When asked on the witness stand for whom he had performed his services, McNickle testified that he was paid as an agent of the executors. But he was not paid by the executors, nor does his fee appear on the executors' account.

This case can be decided for the defendants only on the supposition that Mr. McNickle's testimony is absolutely and trustworthily reliable. The Chancellor regarded McNickle as the upper turret of the tower of evidence, but who supported the turret? The Chancellor says that the defendant's expert witnesses supported McNickle. But who supported the expert witnesses? The Chancellor says McNickle. Strange as this sounds, here are the Chancellor's words:

> "The credibility of McNickle as a witness was
> bolstered up by the testimony of the expert and
> other opinion witnesses and in turn the credibility
> of their testimony was supported by the direct
> evidence of McNickle."

Thus we have McNickle as the strong man in the act holding up the expert witnesses and they in turn holding up McNickle! This makes McNickle not only a Samson of strength but a contortionist as well. There should be little difficulty in believing, after reading his extraordinary testimony, that the latter is true.

Is it fair and equitable to disinherit a whole family on such slippery and contorted testimony?

My answer is in the negative, wherefore I Dissent.

HOLCOMBE v. THE STATE OF GEORGIA
Court of Appeals of Georgia
5 Ga.App. 47, 62 S.E. 647 (1908)

ARTHUR GRAY POWELL, J.

The defendant and other ministers had been carrying on a series of revival services in what is known as "the tabernacle," in Cartersville. On the concluding day, which was Sunday, a large number of people were in attendance. Services were held at eleven o'clock in the morning, and it was announced that early in the afternoon (either at 2:30 or 3 o'clock) a preacher named Oliver would deliver a lecture "to men only." The day was rainy. Many of the people had come from the country and even from surrounding counties, and a large number of women either remained in the building or sought shelter there from the rain; so that when the time arrived for the lecture "to men only" the audience was mixed. It is conceded that more than 2,500 persons were present. The defendant himself estimated the audience as between 2,500 and 3,000 in number. The defendant, when the time arrived for the lecture to begin, asked the ladies to retire. On account of the rain they were slow in leaving, and a considerable number, variously estimated, remained.

It seems that in the audience there was a large woman with her back to the rostrum. The defendant, upon being requested by the other preacher to get the ladies out, advanced to the front of the platform, and, in the presence of the congregation, said, as the State charged and the witnesses for the prosecution testified, "You woman with the big fat rump pointed towards me, get out of the way."

The language, according to the defendant's statement, was: "Gentlemen, there is a big old woman weighing about 400 pounds with her rump turned this way. If she would turn around and let me speak to her head, I might explain to her the object of this meeting, and we might go on."

He was indicted and convicted for violating section 396 of the Penal Code, which provides that "any person who shall without provocation .. use obscene and vulgar or profane language in the presence of a female .. shall be guilty of a misdemeanor." . . .

The indictment charged that the defendant did, without provocation, use, in the presence of females, whose names are to the grand-jurors unknown, the following profane, vulgar, and obscene language: "You woman with the big fat rump pointed towards us, get out of the way." The defendant demurred, because the language was not profane; also because it was not obscene and vulgar.

The language was not profane, and therefore the use of that word in the indictment was pure surplusage. "Defective allegations do not impair an indictment if, on their being rejected, what remains fully covers the law." . . . The word "profane," as used, is merely epithetic of the general nature of the offense, and does not fall within the rule that where the facts of the transaction are alleged with needless particularity, the unnecessary allegations cannot be rejected as surplusage. . .

The language charged was, in our judgment, clearly obscene and vulgar, within the purview of section 396 of the Penal Code. As was said in *Dillard v. State* [citation omitted]:

> "This statute does not stand upon the footing of statutes against public indecency. Its object is not to keep pure the public morals. It is to be found in that chapter of the Code which punishes private wrongs, and forms a part of the same clause which makes it a penal offense to use opprobrious and abusive language to another.

> "It is intended to protect females from insult; to furnish to the friends of a female whose modesty has been unlawfully shocked, or whose feelings have been wounded, by the use in her presence of obscene and vulgar language, some other remedy than that which nature dictates, to wit, club law. And the statute is to be construed and understood in the light of its object."

We can not adopt the suggestion of counsel that it is aimed alone at language suggestive of sexual intercourse, or tending to excite lewdness or to debauch the public morals. The word "obscene" means "offensive to the senses, repulsive, disgusting, foul, filthy, offensive to modesty or decency, impure, unchaste, indecent, lewd." *Century Dictionary*. We think that the phrase "obscene and vulgar language," as used in the statute, includes any foul words which would reasonably offend the sense of modesty and decency of the woman or women, or any of them, in whose presence the words were spoken, under all the circumstances of the case.

It would be absurd to tolerate the suggestion that to speak of a woman's rump in a loose or jocular connection would not be offensive to the modesty and decency of the ordinary woman. As a matter of common knowledge, we know that such language would shock any decent and modest woman. In other statutes, having different objects from the one before us, the word "obscene" may not be entitled to so broad a signification... Ours is a statute adapted to the temperament of the people of this State. It is to be understood in the light of our well-known sensibilities on certain subjects. Modesty, that "kind of quick and delicate feeling in the soul, the exquisite sensibility that warns a woman to shun the first appearance of everything hurtful," is, according to the mind of the average citizen of Georgia, as needful and legitimate a subject-matter of protection from invasions as those more familiar subjects of protection through the criminal statutes, --life, liberty, and property.

Of course, language tending to incite illicit sexual intercourse is obscene and vulgar; and in most of the reported cases in this State (where the words were not profane, so as to fall within the other portion of the statute) the prosecutions were for using words suggestive of sexual intercourse; but it does not follow that no other language is obscene and vulgar. . .

Any gross reference to the private parts of a woman, or to any of the surrounding portions of her person, is, by common consent of mankind, indecent and shocking to feminine modesty. Such a reference might, however, be made in the presence of a female, and not be per se criminal -- for instance, in a brothel. But where the language is gross and *prima facie* indecent, and such that common consent condemns it as unfit, by reason of its obscenity, to be used in the presence of women, -- that is, if it is so universally recognized to be obscene and vulgar that the court can assume its *prima facie* obscenity and vulgarity, through judicial cognizance as a matter of common knowledge, -- and the conceded time, place circumstances, and intent are such as to show no reason making or tending to make its use on the particular occasion less obscene and vulgar than it normally would be, there is no issue as to the obscene and vulgar quality, to be submitted to the jury. . .

In the present case the reference, whether we take the State's version or the statement of the defendant himself, was gross. The language was *prima facie* obscene and vulgar; in form and in substance the allusion was indecent. The time, the place, and the circumstances, instead of making or tending to make its use on the particular occasion less likely to offend the modesty of any woman who might hear it than normally it would be, tended distinctly to the contrary.

It was not the ribaldry of some low-grade comedian, in some second-class theater; it was the indecent jest of a minister of the gospel, made in a house devoted to the service of God, in the presence of some three thousand worshipers, aimed at a female member of the congregation, whose excess of adipose upon an unmentionable part of her person happened to excite his attention. His own statement concedes every element of this characterization, except that the words of his jest were indecent; and as to that we have decided against him.

We do not say that even a minister in the pulpit is precluded at all times and under all circumstances from making reference to things which are not usual subjects of conversation in polite society, if he couches his language in an inoffensive context (though, even as to these things, decency commands that he should be extremely cautious in the choice of his language), and we recognize that real modesty, and not prudery, and not pruriency, is the object of the law's protection; but we do say unequivocally that an indecent jest, couched in language ordinarily considered obscene and vulgar, is never permissible from the sacred desk, and that if it be made in the presence of females it is a criminal act. Our women certainly have a right to come to our places or religious worship without fear of shock or insult by reason of indecent language used by the minister in charge. . .

. . . The defendant had stated, on the trial, that his remark was not addressed to the woman in question, that he had used the language innocently and as a mere side remark for the hearing only of the men near him, that he used the work "rump" because he was thinking of the word "hump," and the word "rump" rhymed with it. To rebut this explanation Judge Fite was called as a witness. He testified that on the next day after the language was used, the defendant was called before a committee of the trustees of the tabernacle, and told that offense had been taken on account of his statement, and that he ought to make an apology, to which the defendant stated that he declined to apologize, as he thought that he had a right to say what he did; Judge Fite then said to him that the language, as he considered it, was vulgar and obscene; the defendant replied that he didn't think so, and said, in this connection, "That's the way I have got of moving them, and I move them."

By this and the further details of the conversation, as narrated in this testimony, it was made to appear that the defendant did not deny that he used the language, or that he intended for the woman to hear it, but sought to justify his conduct, on the ground that it was his usual way of moving recalcitrant female members of his congregation. It will be seen, therefore, that as a part of the *res gestae* of the conversation, the statement objected to was admissible. . .

Judgment affirmed.

IN RE MILLAR
Court of Appeal for Ontario
[1936] 1 O.R. 554

WILLIAM EDWARD MIDDLETON, J.A.:

Charles Millar, a barrister practicing in the City of Toronto, and one of His Majesty's Counsel learned in the law, died on or about the 31st day of October, 1926, having first made and published his will bearing date the 7th day of June, 1921, which was duly admitted to probate by the proper Surrogate Court on the 9th day of December, 1926.

Mr. Millar in his will prefaced his benefactions by this recital: "This will is necessarily uncommon and capricious because I have no dependents or near relations and no duty rests upon me to leave any property at my death and what I do leave is proof of my folly in gathering and retaining more than I required in my lifetime".

Mr. Millar then gave $10,000.00 to Mr. Gourlay, whom he described as one who had lost approximately that sum in a business transaction with him, Millar; $500.00 to Mrs. Wilson, his housekeeper; $1,000.00 to Mr. Kemp, and to Mr. West of Edmonton one-half of his shares in the British Columbia Express Company. Then followed a number of gifts which may well be described in the language of Mr. Millar as uncommon and capricious.

The residuary gift is the only one now before the Court for construction. This clause provides:

> " All the rest and residue of my property wheresoever situate, I give, devise and bequeath unto my Executors and Trustees named below in Trust to convert into money as they deem advisable and invest all the money until the expiration of nine years from my death and then call in and convert it all into money and at the expiration of ten years from my death to give it and its accumulations to the mother who has since my death given birth in Toronto to the greatest number of children as shown by the registrations under the Vital Statistics Act. If one or more mothers have equal highest number of registrations under the said Act to divide the said moneys and accumulations equally between them."

Remote next-of-kin of Mr. Millar now attack the validity of this clause upon the ground that it is illegal in that it is against public policy. . .

There are now filed affidavits of the Reverend C. E. Silcox [and] Dr. W. B. Hendry. . . and an application was made for an enlargement of the motion or for a direction for a trial upon oral evidence based upon these affidavits.

The affidavit of the Reverend Mr. Silcox states that he is the General Secretary of the Social Service Council of Canada, a body which includes representatives of the Church of England, the United Church, the Baptist Church, the Salvation Army, the Y.M.C.A. and the Y.W.C.A. and he has been engaged in various forms of social research in Canada, United States, Switzerland, and Latin America. He has read the clause of the will in question and he thinks that the clause would tend to encourage and cause mothers to have children in rapid succession, and that it is common knowledge among sociologists and social workers that the infant mortality rate is increased by this.

Further, that it is common knowledge of sociologists and social welfare workers that the having of many children in rapid succession impairs the mother's health, and by the same knowledge, the children have not a fair opportunity either physically, mentally, morally or otherwise for development. He also states that it is common knowledge and recognized among sociologists and social workers that the maintenance of a family where children are born in rapid succession imposes a heavy burden upon the father.

Dr. Hendry, an eminent obstetrician, gives his opinion that anything that encourages rapid births is extremely detrimental to the health of the mothers and to the well-being of the children.

Turning then to the serious inquiry as to whether this will offends against public policy, I find a guiding principle laid down by Parke B. in his opinion given to the House of Lords in the case of *Egerton v. Earl Brownlow* (1853), [citation omitted].

"This is a vague and unsatisfactory term, and calculated to lead to uncertainty and error, when applied to the decision of legal rights; it is capable of being understood in different sense; it may, and does, in its ordinary sense, mean political expedience, or that which is best for the common good of the community; and in that sense there may be every variety of opinion, according to education, habits, talents, and dispositions of each person, who is to decide whether an act is against public policy or not. To allow this to be a ground of judicial decision, would lead to the greatest uncertainty and confusion.

"It is the province of the statesman, and not the lawyer, to discuss, and of the legislature to determine, what is the best for the public good, and to provide for it by proper enactments. It is the province of the judge to expound the law only; the written from the statutes; that unwritten or common law from the decisions of our predecessors and of our existing courts, from text-writers of acknowledged authority, and upon the principles to be clearly deduced from them by sound reason and just inference; not to speculate upon what is the best, in his opinion, for the advantage of the community.

"Some of these decisions may have no doubt been founded upon the prevailing and just opinions of the public good; for instance, the illegality of covenants in restraint of marriage or trade. They have become a part of the recognized law, and we are therefore bound by them, but we are not thereby authorized to establish as law everything which we may think for the public good, and prohibit everything which we think otherwise. The term 'public policy' may indeed by used only in the sense of the policy of the law, and in that sense it forms a just ground of judicial decision. . .

"Prima facie, all persons are free to dispose of their property according to their will and pleasure, and are free to make such contracts as they please, and are morally and legally bound by them, provided, in both cases, they adopt the formalities required by the common and statute law. . .

"In treating of various branches of the law learned persons have analyzed the sources of the law, and have sometimes expressed their opinion that such and such a provision is bad because it is contrary to public policy; but I deny that any Court can invent a new head of public policy; so a contract for marriage brokerage, the creation of a perpetuity, a contract in restraint of trade, a gaming or wagering contract, or, what is relevant here, the assisting of the King's enemies, are all undoubtedly unlawful things; and you may say that it is because they are contrary to public policy they are unlawful; but it is because these things have been either enacted or assumed to be by the common law unlawful, and not because a judge or Court have a right to declare that such and such things are in his or their view contrary to public policy."

Mr. Hellmuth contends that this will offends against public policy because the tendency of the gift is to induce the mothers to have offspring in rapid succession and, secondly, because the gift is not in terms confined to the mothers of legitimate children and so would encourage illegitimate births.

In my opinion the contention of the next-of-kin fails.

I would like to say a word concerning Mr. Millar. He rightly described his will as necessarily uncommon and capricious and his estate as proof of his folly in "gathering and retaining more than I required in my lifetime". He evidently regarded his remote relatives as having no claim upon him, for he states that "I have no dependents or near relations and no duty rests upon me to leave any property at my death."

I would regard the clause in question as prompted rather by sympathy for the mothers of large families, who are often extremely poor people, not unmingled with a grim sense of humour.

The argument by the next-of-kin purports to be based on high motives of public policy and not upon mere greed, but the next-of-kin have waited until all the harm possible has been done, instead of prosecuting their claim immediately after Mr. Millar's death, when the evils, which it is said result from the tendency detrimental to public policy set forth, might have been prevented.

Order accordingly.

MIXON v. POLLOK
Supreme Court of Georgia
55 Ga. 322 (1875)

LOGAN E. BLECKLEY, Judge.

A sister sued her brother and sister and recovered against the brother alone. The sole complaint is, that the verdict was contrary to law and evidence and the charge of the court. On these grounds the brother moved for a new trial, and it was refused.

The cause of action alleged, was the promise to pay a fixed sum for withdrawing a caveat to a will. Defendants denied the contract as declared upon; averred that none was made to which the brother was a party; and alleged that the one in fact made between the two sisters was broken by the plaintiff, whereby the consideration totally failed.

The brother was not sworn as a witness, but the sisters both testified, and, for women, they swore hard. One of them must have been in deep error, for they disagreed widely. The plaintiff's husband corroborated her fully. . .

We should have been rather better satisfied with the verdict if it had been in favor of both defendants, instead of for the plaintiff against one of them. But if anything is for the jury, it is the credibility of witnesses, and as they have thought proper to believe the plaintiff and her husband, we will not disturb the verdict. . .

Judgment affirmed.

BASS v. AETNA INSURANCE COMPANY
Supreme Court of Louisiana
370 So. 2d 511 (1979)

JOHN A. DIXON, Jr. Justice.

Mr. and Mrs. Loyd Bass sued Aetna Insurance Company, insurer of Mr. Kenneth Fussell under a homeowner's policy, and Southern Farm Bureau Casualty Insurance Company, insurer of Shepard's Fold Church of God, seeking damages for personal injuries suffered by Mrs. Bass when Mr. Fussell, a member of the Shepard's Fold Church, ran down the church aisle and collided with Mrs. Bass, also a member of the church, who was in the aisle praying.

The defendants denied all allegations of negligence of the part of their insureds, and, alternatively, pleaded the affirmative defenses of assumption of the risk and contributory negligence. After trial on the merits, the Twenty-Second Judicial District Court for the Parish of St. Tammany dismissed plaintiffs' suit and on appeal the dismissal in an unpublished opinion. Upon plaintiffs' application we granted writs.

On the evening of February 12, 1974, during a revival service, the Shepard's Fold Church of God was very crowded with not enough seats to accommodate all the parishioners. Consequently, Mrs. Bass and other parishioners who would not find seats were standing in the aisles of the church. Reverend

Rodney Jeffers, in the course of preaching to the congregation, stated that the doors of the church should be opened and referred to the possibility of "running." Immediately afterward, Mr. Fussell began running up the aisle and ran into Mrs. Bass, who was in the aisle praying with her head bowed. As a result, Mrs. Bass fell and was injured.

The issues are whether Mr. Fussell was negligent, whether the Shepard's Fold Church of God was negligent, and, if so, whether the plaintiffs' action is barred by either the defenses of assumption of the risk or contributory negligence.[1] Although Mr. Fussell testified that he was "trotting" under the Spirit of the Lord and does not remember actually running into Mrs. Bass, another witness testified that she saw Mr. Fussell run into Mrs. Bass and knock her down.

If Fussell's defense is that he was not in control of his actions, it can be compared with voluntary intoxication, which will not exonerate one from delictual responsibility. A worshiper in church has no more right to run over a fellow worshiper in the aisle than a passerby on the sidewalk. Mr. Fussell breached his duty and was negligent when he trotted or run down the aisle of the church without regard for the safety of other parishioners in the aisles.

Actionable negligence also results from the creation or maintenance of an unreasonable risk of injury to others. In determining whether the risk is unreasonable, not only the seriousness of the harm that may be caused is relevant, but also the likelihood that harm may be caused [citation omitted]. In the instant case, according to both Mrs. Bass and Reverend Jeffers, there were approximately three hundred seventy-five parishioners in the church on the night of the accident, and many of the parishioners were standing in the aisles.

Reverend Jeffers recognized the likelihood that harm might be caused by this crowded condition because he testified that he asked that the aisles be cleared, that he encouraged "open response to the Spirit," and that running or moving "in the Spirit" were common forms of religious expression in Shepard's Fold Church. Another defense witness testified that Reverend Jeffers, recognizing the crowded aisles, asked if somebody would run for him[2] (which apparently is what Mr. Fussell did). Reverend Jeffers did not stop the service to clear the aisles, but continued to maintain an unreasonable risk of injury to the parishioners. The Shepard's Fold Church is responsible for the negligence of its pastor, Reverend Jeffers, under these circumstances [citation omitted].

---

[1] The "Act of God" defense cannot be seriously considered. An "Act of God" means "force majeure." See Stone, "Tort Doctrine", § 45 in 12 *Louisiana Civil Law Treatises* (1977).

[2] In response to defense counselor, Mr. Cassidy's questions, Mr. Fitzgerald testified on direct examination:

"Q. Did you hear Reverend Jeffers make any statement about opening the doors?

A. Yes, he said to open the doors.

Q. Tell the Court what he said, as best you recall.

A. The best I recall he said to open the doors, he felt like running and he didn't have room because of the crowd and would somebody please run for him."

Concluding that both Mr. Fussell and the church were negligent, we next consider the defenses of assumption of the risk and contributory negligence. The Court of Appeal, in affirming the trial court, concluded that Mrs. Bass assumed the risk by remaining in the aisle with her eyes closed, and that she was contributorily negligent by remaining after having been alerted that running might occur.

Assumption of the risk and contributory negligence are affirmative defenses [citation omitted] and as we stated in *Langlois v. Allied Chemical Corp.* [citation omitted]:

> "The determination of whether a plaintiff has assumed a risk is made by subjective inquiry, whereas contributory negligence is determined objectively under the reasonable man standard. . .

. . . Assumption of the risk therefore is properly applicable to those situations where plaintiff, with knowledge of the peril, voluntarily enters into a relationship with defendant involving danger to himself because of defendant's contemplated conduct.

We cannot agree with the Court of Appeal's conclusion that Mrs. Bass assumed the risk. Although Mrs. Bass had belonged to the Church of God faith for approximately fifty-five years and the Shepard's Fold Church for approximately twenty-five years, neither she nor any other witness had seen or heard of any injury or collision in any Church of God church. Before the accident, no one, including Mrs. Bass, felt endangered by worshiping in this church. Mrs. Bass unequivocally testified that she had never seen anyone run in the church. The evidence fails to persuade us that Mrs. Bass actually, subjectively[3] comprehended that by praying in the aisle she was incurring a risk of being run over [citation omitted] or that she could or should have known or understood that she was incurring such a risk as, for example, in *Schofield v. The Continental Insurance Co.* [citation omitted] where the spectator at a Zulu parade at Mardi Gras was hit by a coconut thrown from a float.

The defense failed to prove that Mrs. Bass voluntarily assumed or exposed herself to this risk. Movement in the aisles was not an extraordinary condition in this church because worshipers frequently went to the altar, "the very central focal point in the church," for prayer. Heedless running in the aisle was an unusual and extraordinary hazard, to which plaintiff did not knowingly expose herself [citation omitted].

---

[3] Although there is testimony that Reverend Jeffers asked the people to clear the aisles, Mrs. Bass and at least one other parishioner, a defense witness, testified that they did not hear this request. Mrs. Bass and several witnesses did hear Reverend Jeffers ask that the doors be opened and mention running, but almost immediately afterward, according to Mr. Fussell's own testimony, Mr. Fussell began running down the aisle and into Mrs. Bass.

Contributory negligence is also an affirmative defense; the defendants bear the burden of proving contributory negligence by a preponderance of the evidence. Contributory negligence is objectively determined under the "reasonable man" standard. [citation omitted] It is not contributory negligence to bow one's head when praying in church, whether in the pew or in the aisle.

The plaintiffs also ask this court to award damages, or, in the alternative, remand this case for a determination of quantum. As a matter of policy this court usually does not fix damages when neither the trial nor the intermediate court has passed upon this question. [citation omitted] Instead, we remand the proceedings for such purpose.

For the reasons assigned, the judgments of the district court and of the Court of Appeal are reversed; the case is remanded . . .

HARPER v. LOVELL
Supreme Court of Tennessee
105 Tenn. 614; 59 S.W. 337 (1900)

JOHN S. WILKES, J.

This is a bill by the administratrix of John F. Harper to recover from his former guardian [Lovell] a sum of money which it is alleged is, or ought to be, in the hands of the guardian, belonging to the ward at the time of his death. The chancellor, upon an adjustment of the guardian's accounts, gave judgment for $737.96 in favor of complainant, and the guardian appealed. Upon hearing in the court of chancery appeals the judgment of the chancellor was reversed, and complainant's bill was dismissed, and she has appealed to this court.

The complainant is the mother as well as the administratrix of her son, and is entitled to whatever estate the son has, and recovery is sought in both rights. The ward, John F. Harper was the bastard son of A. Ramsey, who died after making his will, never having been married. In his will he gave to John F. Harper $2,500 upon certain terms, and with certain limitations, as follows: "The interest on the share of John F. Harper shall be paid to him only when he becomes 21 years of age, . . . the interest to be paid annually for his benefit. . . Lovell qualified as guardian of John F. Harper in 1892, and received from the executor of Ramsey $666.86 in March, 1894. . .

. . . It is assigned as error that the court of chancery appeals should have held that this fund was paid to the guardian. . . as part of the principal of the legacy given to the ward, and only the interest on it could be legitimately consumed for the ward's expenses without first obtaining the sanction of the chancery court to trench on the corpus, if the corpus could be reached at all; that the expenditures made were not proper, and that no allowance should be given the guardian for his services. This is a summary of several of the assignments made.

It appears that the ward had no other property than this amount coming to him from the estate of Ramsey; that he was a reckless, dissolute character, who would not work, and was killed before he reached 21 years of age. It also appears that the guardian had a store, and furnished to the ward articles out of it until he consumed in amount more than the guardian ever received; that the ward was due him in some amount before he ever received any fund.

The court of chancery appeals report that many of the articles furnished were or could be considered necessaries, and some should not, but upon an examination of the entire list that court was satisfied that the legitimate expenses of the ward, together with a reasonable compensation for his services, more than cover the amount received from Ramsey's estate, and, this being apparent from an inspection of the account and list of expenses a reference was not necessary. It appears that the guardian sent the boy to school so far as he could prevail on him to go, and paid some school bills, and for books and clothes.

A petition to rehear was filed in the court of chancery appeals, in which that court was requested to make part of its report an itemized account of the articles furnished to Harper from Lovell's store. The court of chancery appeals declined to do so, stating that there were over 200 items in it, and that it covered seven legal record pages, and it did not consider it proper to set out in so much detail the evidential facts upon which it based its conclusions, but only the result of its finding.

That court gives however, a sort of summary of the articles furnished, as follows: Tobacco was furnished 86 times, smoking tobacco 9 times, pipes 3 times, candy 48 times, sardines 24 times, knives 9 times, neckties 9 times, canned peaches 11 times, cheroots 10 times, oysters 46 times, apples 5 times.

That court reports also that it is impracticable to get the exact charge for separate items, as several would be grouped in one entry. For instance, oysters and sardines, 20 cents. How much was for oysters and how much for sardines that court cannot tell. Fifteen cents for sugar and snuff. How much for each could not be stated. Sugar and crackers, 10 cents; candy and tobacco, 15 cents; candy and oysters, 15 cents. They find, however, that $9.15 is charged for tobacco, $5.65 for oysters, $3.75 for sardines, $4.50 for candy, $2.90 for canned peaches, $3.37 for cigars and cheroots, $3.35 for neckties, $3.35 for pocketknives, $2.10 for a double-barrelled gun, $3.66 for shot, powder, and shells, 20 cents for cologne, 30 cents for hair dye, $1.25 for fish hooks, $1.00 for kid gloves, $1.50 for a pair of slippers for his sister, bay rum 30 cents, water melons 43 cents, hair oil 15 cents.

The court reports that the boy was about 18 years old; that he had no home, and no business, and would not work, and could not be controlled, and was generally worthless and reckless. The court of chancery appeals report that among the necessaries might be classed oysters, sardines, crackers, canned peaches, and a moderate supply of candy, as they were food, though not of the most wholesome kind. Also the gun, ammunition, and handkerchiefs, and a small amount of cash, schooling, clothes, etc., and other items were classed as necessaries, as to which no serious question is made.

That court protests against the following articles as not articles of necessity: Cigars and cheroots, hair dye, hair oil, and bay rum, breastpins; that neckties, pocketknives, and candy were furnished too lavishly. Kid gloves and slippers were placed under the ban, as were also tobacco, two quarts of chestnuts, cinnamon oil, onions, and honey. On this last item that court says that separately they might be allowed, but in combination they cannot. Chewing gum, cologne, rat poison, two watermelons in one day. The court was of opinion one might be allowed, but two were not necessaries, but extravagancies.

The court of chancery appeals was divided or in doubt as to the following items: Fish hooks, a trot line, tobacco in even moderate quantities, one box corn salve, and some other items of less importance. That court, however, repeats its former holding that, eliminating all improper charges, and allowing a reasonable compensation for services, there were legitimate credits for enough to cover all the funds received by the guardian.

Under the view that we take of the case it is not necessary that we pass upon the correctness of the classification made by the court of chancery appeals as to what are or are not necessaries. The language of the will of Ramsey, under which the legacy was raised, is quite crude and inconsistent, and not altogether intelligible; but we think that, under a proper construction of the item giving this legacy, neither the principal sum of $2,500 nor any part of it was to become the absolute property of John F. Harper until and unless he reached his majority of 21 years, and in the event of his death prior to that time the principal of the legacy was to revert to the estate of Ramsey, the testator. This being so, the guardian could consume no more than the interest upon the legacy for the benefit of the ward, and the principal would revert to the estate of Ramsey. . .

. . . It follows that we reach the same result as to complainant's rights as did the court of chancery appeals, but upon different grounds, and the complainant's bill must be dismissed, at her costs.

GILBERT v. THE CRYSTAL FOUNTAIN LODGE
Supreme Court of Georgia
80 Ga. 284; 4 S.E. 905 (1887)

LOGAN E. BLECKLEY, Chief Justice.

The plaintiff, a minister of the gospel, (and as we construe his declaration, a most worthy and upright man,) brought his complaint for words against a mutual aid association of which he was a member, alleging the uttering by that association, as a partnership (the suit being against it as a partnership), of certain words imputing to him, as he alleges, the offence of obtaining money by false pretenses from the association,--cheating and swindling, and certain other words importing that he was afflicted with a loathsome and contagious venereal disease.

He alleges that in consequence of the use of these words, he was suspended from the benefits and privileges of the association for five years; and he lays general damages in a large sum for his grievances. The declaration was demurred to; the demurrer was sustained, and the action was dismissed. We are now to determine, upon this writ of error, whether there is a cause of action set forth in the declaration. . .

. . . Upon principle, we do not see how he could charge the partnership assets with the damages that might be recovered, he having an interest in the assets as part owner of the same. Nor can we see how he can escape the general rule that, in an action at law against a partnership, all the partners, so far as the partnership assets are involved, must be defendants. That rule, applied to this case, would require the plaintiff to sue himself. . .

. . . Turning from the remedy to the wrong itself, there is much doubt whether the facts alleged make out the imputation of a crime or misdemeanor. . . But the case as a whole cannot be ruled upon this distinction, because the venereal disease was not a partnership malady. That was individual property. . .

. . . The difficulty in the present case is, not alone that the partnership could not slander anybody, but that it could not slander a member of the firm, he being so united to the partnership that there could be no partnership tort that would not involve him as a tort feasor; and he could not be both agent and patient in the infliction of an injury. Cases of defamation growing out of jars and bickerings amongst the members of associations, religious as well as secular, are, unfortunately, too numerous. Many of them are summarized and discussed in Shurtliff vs. Stevens [citation omitted] itself a case of much interest, and quite instructive on the literature of the subject. Such actions are not to be encouraged, but rather discouraged, and we are not sorry to mete out strict law against them. . .

AN ACTE FOR THADVAUNCEMENT OF TRUE RELIGION AND FOR THABBOLISSHMENT OF THE CONTRARIE
Statutes of the Realm of England
34 Henry VIII, Ch. 1 (1542)

WHERE the Kinges moste royall Majestie our gracious and naturall Soveraigne liege Lorde supreame head of the Churche of Englande and allso of Irelande, and his honorable Counsaill, perceyveth the ignoraunce fonde opynions errours and blindenes of divers and soondrye his Subjects of this his Realme, in abusing and not observing nor folowing the commaundements precepts and lawes of Almightie God nor the verye true and perfecte religion of Christe, notwithstanding suche holesome doctrynes and documents as his Ma^te hathe heretofore caused to be set forthe for that purpose, besydes the greate libertie graunted to them in having amonges them and in theyre handes the Newe and Olde Testament, whiche notwithstanding, many sedicious people arrogant and ignoraunt persones, wherof some pretending to be learned and to have the profite and true knowledge understanding and judgement of the sacred and holye Scriptures, and soome others of theyre perverse frowarde and malicious myndes willes and intents intending to subverte the veraye true and perfect exposition doctryne and declaration of the saide Scripture, after theyre pervers fantasies, have taken upon them not oonelie to preache teache declare and set foorthe the same by woords sermons disputations and arguments, but allso by printed bokes printed balades playes rymes songes and other fantasies, subtellye and craftelye instructing his Hieghnes people and speciallye the youthe of this his Realme, untruelie and otherwyse thanne the scripture ought or shoulde be taught declared or expounded, and contrarye to the veraye sincere and godlye meaning of the same, wherupon diversitie of opinions sayengs variaunces arguments tumults and scismes have been sprung and arisen among his saide Subjects within this his Realme, to the great inquietation of his saide people and greate displeas^r of his Majestie, and contrarye to his Graces true meaning good intention and moste godlie purpose.

FOR REFORMATION wherof his Majestie most vertuouslye and prudentlye considereth and thinketh, that it is and shalbe most requysite expedient and necessarye not oonelie by lawes dredfull and penall to take awaie purge and clense this his Highnes Realme terrytoryes confynes domynions and Countreys, of all suche bokes wrytings sermons disputactions arguments balades playes rymes songes teachings and instructions, as be pestiferous and noysoome with all the causes and instruments [and[1]] meanes of the same, but allso to ordeyne and establisshe a certaine forme of pure and sincere teaching, agreable with Godds woorde and the true doctryne and catholicke and apostolicall Churche, wherunto men maye have recourse for the true decysion of some such contraversies as have in tymes past and yet doo happen and aryse amongs them:

And thefore be it enacted ordeyned and establisshed by our saide Soveraigne Lorde the King, the Lordes spirituall and temporall and the Commons in this present parliament assembled and by thauctorytie of the same, that all maner of bokes of the Olde and Newe Testament in Englishe, being of the craftye false and untrue translation of Tyndale, and al other bookes and wrytings in the English tongue teaching or comprysing any matiers of Christen religion articles of the faithe or holye scripture, or any parte of them, contrarye to that doctryne whiche sithens the yere of our Lorde a thousande fyve hundred and fourtie is or at any tyme during the Kinges Majesties lief our saide Soveraigne Lorde that now is King Henrye theight, whiche our Lorde long preserve, shalbe set foorthe by his Hieghnes with suche supscription and subscription as herafter shalbe declared, shalbe by auctorytie of this present Acte clerelie and utterlie abolished extinguished and forbidden to be kepte or used in this Realme or elswhere [within[2]] any the Kings Domynions.

AND allso be it enacted by thauctorytie aforesaide, that if any printer boke bynder bokeseller or any other persone or persones shall after the first daie of Julye

---

[1] O. omits.

[2] in O.

next ensuing, printe or cause to be printed, or utter sell give or deliver within this Realme or elswhere within any the Kings Domynions any of the bokes or wrytings afore abolisshed or prohibited, or plaie in interludes sing or ryme any matier contrarye to the saide doctrine whiche sithens the saide yere of our Lorde a thousand fyve hundred and fourtie, is or at any time (as is aforesaid) shallbe set foorthe by the Kings Ma^{te} our saide Soveraigne Lorde that now is, and be of anye of the offences aforesaide convicted by sufficient witness before any twoo of the Kings Counsaill or the Ordinarye of the dioces where any suche offence shalbe commytted, and twoo Justices of Pease of the same Shyre where any suche Ordinarye shall sit within his diocesse for that purpose, or before any other persone or persones whome for this purpose the Kings Majestie shall appointe by his Hieghnes Commision, shall have and suffre for the first tyme, imprysonement of his bodye for three monethes, and allso lose and forfaicte for everye suche boke or wryting prynted uttered solde gyven or delivered as is aforesaide the soome of tenne pounds Sterling; and for the seconde tyme so offending in any of the saide Offences, and being thereof conviced as is aforesaide, shall lose and forfaicte all his goods, and his bodye to be commytted to perpetuall prysone. . .

PROVIDED allwaies that the Chauncellour of Englande, Capitaines of the Warres, the Kings Justices, the Recorders of any Citie Boroughe or Towne, Speaker of the Parliament and all other Justices Officers and Mynisters whiche heretofore have been accustomed to declare or teache any good vertuous or godlie exhortations in any assembles, maie use any parte of the Byble or Holye Scripture as they weere wont and have been accustomed, so allwaies it be not contrarye to the doctryne set foorthe or to be set foorthe as is aforesaide; Any thing in this Acte to the contrarye therof notwithstanding.

PROVIDED allso that it shalbe lawfull to every noble man and gentleman being a householder to reade or cause to be read by any of his famylie or servantes in his house orchard or gardeyne, and to his owne famylie, any texte of the Byble or New Testament, so the same be doone quietlie and without disturbance of good order. And allso that it shalbe for every marchaunte man being a householder and occupying the seate of merchaundyse, to reade to himself privatelye the Byble and New Testament: Any thing in this contrarye hereof notwithstanding. . .

. . . PROVIDED allwaies that everye noble wooman and gentlewooman maie reade to themselves alone and not to others any [Textes³] of the Byble or Newe Testament; anything in this Acte to the contrarye therof notwithstanding. . .

. . . AND be it further enacted by auctorytie aforesaide, that no persone or persones other thenne be above lymited, shall take upon him openlye to dispute or argue, to debate discusse or expounde Holye Scripture or any parte therof, whiche with all Reverence ought to be communicated amonge Christen men, upon the paynes of oone monethes imprysonement. . .

---

³ Text O.

... And be it further enacted that if any spirituall persone or persones shall after the firste daie of Julye nexte cooming, preache teache defende or mainteyne any matier or matiers thing or things contrarye to the godlie instructions or determynations whiche sines the yere of our Lorde aforesaide, is or shalbe set foorthe by his Ma^te as is aforementioned, that thenne everye suche Offendour being therof convicted before the Ordinarie of that diocesse within the whiche the saide Offence shalbe committed, and twoo Justices of Peace as is aforesaide, or before twoo of the Kings Majesties counsaill, or suche Commissioners as his Majestie shall apointe for that purpose, shalbe for the firste tyme admytted to recante and renounce his saide erroures, after suche maner and forme as shalbe appointed by the Ordinarye or Judges afore whome suche Offendour shalbe convicte: And if suche Offendour refuse to recante in suche forme as is aforesaide, or if he recante and after eftsones offende, that [thanne[4]] he shall for the seconde tyme and for refusall to recante, abjure and beare a faggot, after suche maner and forme as shalbe assigned by the Ordinarye or Judge and twoo Justices of Peace as is aforesaide, afore whome suche Offendour shalbe so convicte; And if suche Offendour refuse to abjure and beare a fagot as is aforesaide, or if he abjure and beare a fagot as is aforesaide, and after offende the thirde tyme contrarye to this Acte, and be therof convicte in maner and forme as is aforesaide, that thenne everye suche offendour for the thirde tyme or for refusall to abjure, shalbe deamed and adjudged an heretyke and shall suffre therfor paines of deathe by burning, and losse and forfaictures of all his goodes and catalles.

... And be it further provyded by auctorytie aforesaide, that the Kings Ma^te our saide Soveraigne Lorde that now is King Henrye theight, maie at any tyme hereafter at his Hieghnes libertie and pleasure chaunge and altre this present Acte and provisions of the same, or any clause or article therin conteyned, as to his Hieghnes moste excellent wisedome shall seme convenient; Any thing in this acte to the contrarye therof notwithstanding...

CATHOLIC CEMETERIES ASSOCIATION OF THE DIOCESE OF PITTSBURGH ZONING CASE
Supreme Court of Pennsylvania.
379 Pa. 516; 109 A.2d 537 (1954)

ALLEN M. STEARNE, Justice.

The appeal of the Township of Upper St. Clair is from the order of the court below directing the Board of Adjustment of Upper St. Clair Township to grant a certificate and permits to the Catholic Cemeteries Association of the Diocese of Pittsburgh... for the use of approximately 185 acres of land in the Township as a cemetery. It is contended that the court below did not properly exercise its reviewable powers within the scope statutorily prescribed for appeals from a zoning board of adjustment.

---

[4] then O.

On December 27, 1952, the Catholic Cemeteries Association of the Diocese of Pittsburgh, an appellee, acquired an option to purchase an area of approximately 185 acres of land in the Township as a Farm in the southwestern part of the Township containing in all about ten square miles. The Association then filed with the Board of Supervisors its application for a permit to lay out and establish a cemetery.

At a regular meeting of the Board, a public hearing was held on a proposed ordinance which would amend the zoning law to allow non-profit cemeteries within the area "at such location as shall be permitted by the Board of Supervisors". The Board of Supervisors, by vote, refused to pass or adopt the proposed ordinance. An appeal was then taken to the Board of Adjustment. The permit was again refused. . . This decision was reversed by the County Court of Allegheny County upon appeal and the Zoning Board of Adjustment was ordered and directed to grant the desired certificate and permits.

The court below held that a literal enforcement of the provisions of the Ordinance would result in unnecessary hardships; that the variance is not contrary to the public interest; that the neighboring property owners are not sufficiently offended or hurt by the use of the land as a cemetery; and that the action of the Zoning Board of Adjustment was arbitrary, capricious and could not be sustained. . .

. . . The single question, however, properly before the court below was whether or not the Board of Adjustment, in refusing the variance requested, was guilty of a manifest and flagrant abuse of discretion: . . . Such request was, in effect, an application for re-zoning. Furthermore, there is no evidence to support the finding of the court below that a denial of the use as a cemetery would result in unnecessary hardship. It was error to direct the issuance of the requested certificate and permits.

The order of the court below is reversed. . .

MICHAEL A. MUSMANNO, Justice (dissenting).

It is almost a waste of paper to write that there is nothing more certain than death. It is equally superfluous to say that no one wants to die. And it follows with the same inevitability that proper interment of the dead has an important bearing on the survival of the living. During action in the field in World War II, I always noted (with awe) that one of the vital items in battle directives carried the saddening words: "Burials will be prompt." In civilian life, reasonably prompt burials are also necessary. As death is certain and sepulture is imperative, the question propounded in this appeal is not one that can be disposed of by technical legalistic formulae and procedural rites. Values which cannot possibly be surpassed in the whole scheme of life are involved here, and we must study the record meticulously to see if law has supported reason and judicial decision has confronted fact.

Margaret E. Houston, Florence C. Riles and John R. Houston own some 185 acres of farmland in Upper St. Clair Township, Allegheny County. They have entered into an agreement with the Catholic Cemeteries Association of the Diocese of Pittsburgh to sell this acreage to the Association for use as a cemetery. The Majority says this cannot be done.

Why?

Fundamentally, the Houstons can sell their property to whomever they wish. Basically, the Catholic Cemeteries Association has the right to purchase what it may pay for and to use it as it desires, so long as the use is a legal one. No one contends that there is anything illegal about a cemetery.

The Houston farm is located in what is known, under the Zoning Ordinance of Upper St. Clair Township, as District U-1. The Board of Adjustment of the Township, to which application has been made for the necessary certificate and permits which would authorize the use of the land as a cemetery, held that District U-1 limited permitted uses to: single family dwellings with appurtenant buildings, and accessory uses incident thereto and not involved in the conduct of a business. . .

. . . The need for a Catholic cemetery in the area known as the South Hills is acute. There are 22 parishes in the South Hills with 19,634 known Catholic families. On the basis of an average of 4 persons to a family, cemetery space for some 78,000 inhabitants must be anticipated. Rev. Daniel A. Gearing, assigned by the Bishop of Pittsburgh to the task of finding suitable ground for a Catholic cemetery in the area under discussion, testified:

> "In order to serve those Catholics there are seven small Parish cemeteries which have a total of only seventeen and one-half acres of unused ground, which is woefully inadequate to provide for the future cemetery needs of the Catholic members of the Community."

Proper burial among civilized people, and even among the most primitive tribes as well, has a spiritual significance which is as important to the survival of the human race as the hygienic considerations which call for orderly interment. Into the closed heart of the most absolute atheist and into the mind of the most uncompromising agnostic there comes, as he stands before the grave of a loved one, the promise of another springtime and the assurance of a reunion that no winter will blight.[1]

---

[1] Standing at the bier of his brother, the justly famed Ingersoll mused: "In the night of death, hope sees a star and listening love can hear the rustle of a wing."

CHAPTER VIII: WILLS, TRUSTS & RELIGION

Even without articulation, faith in immortality is natural to man. When that support fails, something weakens inside. Decent burials, comforting ceremony, scenic and restful surroundings with flowering shrubs and friendly trees are all part of the therapeutics which assuage the pain and eventually cure the wound of bereavement. All this is civilization. Thus, a well-cared-for cemetery is as necessary to the inhabitants of any community as a well-equipped hospital.

As already stated, District U-1 allows for churches, and it is not to be disputed that anything which forms part of a church's function is thus necessarily within the compass of permitted religious uses authorized in District U-1. A cemetery, which is made part of a church organization, is, because of that attachment, a religious institution in itself, even though the cemetery is not physically attached to the church. . .

. . . The Opinion of the Majority declares "That it may probably be impossible to find another suitable tract is not the necessary hardship envisioned by the Act." Why can it not be? It would be difficult to visualize a more intolerable hardship striking at a community than that it should be deprived of proper burial facilities. The Majority Opinion goes on to say: "The same is true of the other argument that the seller is being deprived of his sale and the corporation of the right to use the land as burial grounds. The equivalent argument could be made by one desirous of establishing a slaughter house or a fertilizer manufacturing company." Here the Majority Opinion completely inters logic in a deep grave and buries precedent in a bottomless crypt. A slaughterhouse or fertilizer plant is prima facie a nuisance, especially where it is operated in a residential district, but by no conceivable stretch of jurisprudence, obiter dictum or imagination, is a cemetery a nuisance per se. . .

. . . It is to be noted that the contemplated cemetery will have the appearance of a beautiful sylvan park. Earl O. Blair, landscape architect and graduate in Engineering and Forestry from the Ohio State University, identified pictures of the Chicago Cemetery and testified that the present cemetery would be built on exactly the same plan as that venerated burial place. The pictures which were introduced in evidence depict a panorama of evergreens, shade trees, small exquisite stone bridges, spired chapels, flower gardens and the sails of a windmill with wings silhouetted against the background of the sky. Marble and bronze markers flush with the ground identify the graves which, contrary to old custom, are not mounds of earth but depositories covered by a living lawn level with the surrounding terrain.

There can be no cognizable fear that the presence of the cemetery contemplated in this litigation could in any way depreciate surrounding real estate values. . .

. . . To prohibit the use of land of this character for so exalted, healthful and necessary a purpose as an estimable cemetery of the type described, can be described only in the words of Justice Kephart as the "arbitrary, unnecessary, or unreasonable intermeddling with the private ownership of property". . .

. . . Does this decision end the current litigation? Apparently it does because, rightly or wrongly, all legal controversies eventually reach the point of no return. That, however, does not necessarily place an immovable tombstone on the living body of a living cause. Perhaps through legislative action, since judicial processes sometimes temporarily barricade the entrance to the cemeteries which will one day open to all, a way may be found to utilize the neglected farmland in Upper St. Clair Township for the most sacred purpose to which land may be dedicated--a repose for the sainted dead.

ZIM v. WESTERN PUBLISHING COMPANY
United States Court of Appeals, Fifth Circuit
573 F.2d 1318 (1978)

IRVING L. GOLDBERG, Circuit Judge:

I

In the beginning, Zim[1] created the concept of the Golden Guides.[2] For the earth was dark and ignorance filled the void. And Zim said, let there be enlightenment and there was enlightenment. In the Golden Guides, Zim created the heavens (STARS) (SKY OBSERVER'S GUIDE) and the earth (MINERALS) (GEOLOGY).[3]

And together with his publisher, Western, he brought forth in the Golden Guides knowledge of all manner of living things that spring from the earth, grass, herbs yielding seed, fruit-trees yielding fruits after their kind, (PLANT KING-DOM) (NON-FLOWERED PLANTS) (FLOWERS) (ORCHIDS) (TREES), and Zim saw that it was good. And they brought forth in the Golden Guides knowledge of all the living moving creatures that dwell in the waters, (FISHES) (MARINE MOLLUSKS) (POND LIFE), and fowl that may fly above the earth (BIRDS)

---

[1] Dr. Zim is a noted science educator with a Ph.D. in science education from Columbia University. His special expertise is in the presentation of scientific subjects to popular audiences. The major focus of his efforts has been the development of a multivolume series of books on scientific subjects, the "Golden Guides." Dr. Zim, the plaintiff in this suit, is a citizen of the state of Florida. Since the amount in controversy is in excess of $10,000, diversity jurisdiction exists under 28 U.S.C. § 1332.

[2] The listing of titles in the following account is neither exhaustive nor chronologically accurate.

[3] Zim's actual role in the preparation of the books in the Golden Guide Series varied from book to book. Zim was the principal author of some of the books; other books were prepared jointly by Zim and an expert in the particular field. The expert supplied the technical knowledge which Zim assembled and presented in a form suitable for lay readers.

BIRDS OF NORTH AMERICA) (GAMEBIRDS). And Zim saw that it was good. And they brought forth knowledge in the Golden Guides of the creatures that dwell on dry land, cattle, and creeping things, (INSECTS) (INSECT PESTS) (SPIDERS), and beasts of the earth after their kind (ANIMAL KINGDOM). And Zim saw that it was very good.[4]

II

Then there rose up in Western a new Vice-President who knew not Zim. And there was strife and discord, anger and frustration, between them for the Golden Guides were not being published or revised in their appointed seasons. And it came to pass that Zim and Western covenanted a new covenant, calling it a Settlement Agreement. But there was no peace in the land. Verily, they came with their counselors of law into the district court for judgment and sued there upon their covenants.

And they put upon the district judge hard tasks. And the district judge listened to long testimony and received hundreds of exhibits. So Zim did cry unto the district judge that he might remember the promises of the Settlement Agreement. And the district judge heard Zim's cry, but gave judgment for Western. Yea, the district judge gave judgment to Western on a counterclaim as well. Therefore, Zim went up out of the court of the district judge.

III

And Zim spake unto the Court of Appeals saying, make a sacrifice of the judgment below. And the judges, three in number, convened in orderly fashion to recount the story of the covenants and to discuss and answer the four questions which Zim brought before them.[5] . . .

IV

A. Parol Evidence

And the parties came before the district judge for an accounting of the royalties of Zim. Under Sections 3 and 4 of the 1970 Settlement Agreement, Zim was entitled to payments of royalties and bonuses for books in the "Golden Guide Series." . . . The parties agree that Zim is to earn royalties and bonuses only on those books "published or to be published or distributed by Western. . ." They

---

[4] According to Zim's brief before this court, well over 100 million of the Golden Guide books have been printed under Zim's name, earning him "millions of dollars" in royalties.

[5] The trial below was long and involved a host of exceedingly complex issues. The district judge's rulings on most of the difficult questions presented for resolution below have not been appealed. We restrict ourselves to discussion of those rulings challenged on appeal and note that we have been materially aided in our consideration of these issues by the district court's careful memorandum opinion and his skill, displayed at many points in the trial, in encouraging counsel to focus questions on specific issues before the court.

disagree sharply, however, on the correct construction of "Western." Zim offered parol evidence, the testimony of the attorney who represented him during the contract negotiations, to support his view that "Western" means not only Western Publishing Co., the defendant here, but its affiliates and subsidiaries as well.

The district judge excluded the testimony on the grounds that "Western" was unambiguous as a matter of law in view of the first recital in the contract. There the parties to the contract were stated to be Zim and "Western Publishing Co., Inc. (a Wisconsin Corporation), its successors and assigns, herein referred to as 'Western' . . ." In the district court's view, the contract provided its own definition of "Western" and that definition was not itself subject to ambiguity, i. e., Western Publishing Co., Inc. (a Wisconsin Corporation), its successors and assigns, meant that jural entity and none other. Zim contends that this ruling denies him his "day in court" and is inconsistent with the Wisconsin parol evidence rule. . .

. . . The law in Wisconsin appears to be that parol evidence is not admissible to contradict or vary the terms of an agreement, but may be considered in interpreting an ambiguous term. . .

. . . In the case at bar, the parties made an effort in the written instrument to define the term whose meaning they now contest. They defined "Golden Guides" by reference to another term, "Western," the meaning of which the agreement also provides explicitly. "Western," the recitals tell us, is to stand for "Western Publishing Co., Inc. (A Wisconsin Corporation) its successors and assigns." Western Publishing Co., Inc. (a Wisconsin Corporation), is a definite entity, created by the law and legally distinct from separately incorporated affiliates or subsidiaries.

Here, then, counseled parties made a deliberate effort to define a crucial term in the agreement. They defined that term in words with a quite definite legal significance. When they wished to give that term some special meaning different from its definition in the agreement, they so provided in unmistakable terms. We think the district court was correct in its conclusion that the intent of the parties was unambiguously evidenced by the writing itself. Under Wisconsin law, the parol evidence was properly excluded.

B. The Contract Claims

Zim next contends that Western breached the 1970 Settlement Agreement by publishing revised versions of two of the Golden Guides, STARS and SKY OBSERVER'S GUIDE, without his approval. Zim bases his claim on Subsection 6.5 --Zim releases to Western all Zim's right, interest and claim under all programs heretofore agreed upon or now under way for the revision of books published prior to the date hereof. It is agreed, however, that Western will not publish any revision, change, correction, alteration or updating of any book published prior to October 1, 1970 on which Zim is entitled to a royalty or bonus, without Zim's prior approval.

It is undisputed that both STARS and SKY OBSERVER"S GUIDE has been published prior to October 1, 1970. It is also undisputed that projects for the revision of both books were "under way" when the contract was executed. It is also undisputed that Western failed to obtain Zim's approval of the revisions prior to publication of the revised versions of the books. Zim vigorously contends that these facts establish a breach of contract by Western and that he was entitled to damages and an injunction against further publication without his approval.

Western counters by pointing out that the district judge found that Western had submitted all proposed changes to Zim for his approval, but that Zim "unreasonably withheld" his approval of the changes. Western contends that Zim's failure to make a meaningful response to the proposed changes excuses Western's publication of the revisions.

Zim's power of approval under subsection 6.5 cannot, however, be construed to be an unlimited power to prevent publication of revised versions of the Guides covered by 6.5. Zim bargained for the retention of his power to exercise his judgment as a science educator with enormous experience in the presentation of material in the Golden Guides format. That judgment, once exercised, was to be decisive; Western could not publish revisions of which Zim disapproved.

Nonetheless, justice and fairness considered in the light of the parties interests here require that Zim's power not extend to holding Western hostage to dilatoriness, obstructionism, or greed. . . Zim's retained power to disapprove changes, therefore, has to be exercised within a reasonable time and in a reasonable manner, i.e., in a manner which makes it possible for Western to rework the manuscript in order to obtain his approval. Necessarily, this requires reasonable specificity in the statement of Zim's objections to any proposed changes. . .

. . . Under these circumstances, we have no hesitation in concluding that Zim failed to exercise his power of disapproval within the time and in the manner required, and in so doing effectively waived his right to reject the proposed revisions. Zim's approval conditioned on execution of a new contract was an abusive use of his power and an attempt to reform the Settlement Agreement.

This is not to say that Zim was not honestly motivated by a desire to maintain and improve the quality of SKY OBSERVER'S GUIDE. It is to say, however, that conditioning his approval in this manner was beyond the scope of his contractual power. Zim's failure to exercise his power properly operated to authorize Western's publication of the revised work. The district court's holding as to SKY OBSERVER'S GUIDE must be affirmed.

The situation with STARS is quite different. Although proposed revisions were sent to Zim in 1972, a final set of revisions was first sent to Zim in September of 1974. Western at that time demanded that Zim examine the revisions and report within sixty days his approval or disapproval together with suggested changes. Western stated that it would consider his suggestions and advise him whether the changes would be made. Western stated it would then ask Zim whether he wished to be shown as co-author, original project editor, or have his name removed entirely from the book. Western proceeded to publish the book notwithstanding Zim's express disapproval communicated within the sixty day period.

It is apparent that Western breached the agreement here. Western's 1974 letter confused Zim's rights under subsections 6.4 and 6.5 of the agreement. Zim's prior approval of the revised version of STARS was a prerequisite to lawful publication by Western, absent waiver by Zim. Since there had been no waiver as to STARS, Western's publication of the book without Zim's approval constituted a breach of contract. . .

C. The Tort Claims

. . . The third count of Dr. Zim's complaint alleged an unauthorized and wrongful appropriation of Zim's name, a claim sounding in tort under Florida law. Zim's claim again grows out of the publication of revised revisions of STARS and SKY OBSERVER'S GUIDE. Zim's name appeared on the spine of both books even though he never approved the revisions. Moreover, Zim's initials appeared beneath a foreword added to STARS which expressed his gratitude to the authors hired by Western to revise the book. Zim never approved this foreword either. . .

Thus, Zim's complaint alleged a cause of action with respect to the use of his name in SKY OBSERVER'S GUIDE and STARS. We have already concluded, however, that Western was entitled under the contract to publish SKY OBSERVER'S GUIDE without Zim's actual approval in view of Zim's default. Western's right under the contract to publish the book in these circumstances operates as an authorization sufficient to privilege Western's use of Zim's name as a matter of tort law as well. . .

. . . Just the opposite result obtains with respect to STARS. Paradoxically, if repeatedly in this case, he who observes the skies does not see the STARS. Western's use of Zim's name in STARS was unauthorized by the contract and was, therefore, tortious. Although Zim failed to prove any actual damages from the publication of the revised version of STARS, under Florida law, nominal damages, at least are recoverable; the plaintiff need not plead or prove actual damages. . .

V

And when the judges of the Court of Appeals had passed through the wilderness of Zim, they recapitulated the history of their journey.

The ruling of the district judge regarding parol evidence on the meaning of "Western" is AFFIRMED. The court's conclusion that Western did not breach the Settlement Agreement or commit a tort by publishing the revised version of SKY OBSERVER'S GUIDE is also AFFIRMED. We REVERSE, however, the court's conclusion that Western committed no breach of the contract by publishing the revised version of STARS. We REMAND for a determination and award of nominal damages for the breach of contract. . . We REVERSE the judgment for Western on its counterclaim. And it therefore shall come to pass that the district judge shall write another chapter in the chronicle of Zim.

AFFIRMED IN PART, REVERSED IN PART AND REMANDED.

HALL-MOODY INSTITUTE v. COPASS

Supreme Court of Tennessee
108 Tenn. 582; 69 S. W. 327 (1902)

JOHN S. WILKES, J.

This is an action for damages arising out of the discharge of the plaintiff, Frances Copass, as a teacher in the Hall-Moody Institute, of Martin, Tenn. It was commenced before a justice of the peace of Weakley County. On appeal to the circuit court there was a verdict and judgment for $275 in favor of the plaintiff, and the institute has appealed to this court and assigned errors.

It is said that it was error in the court below to instruct the jury that the institute could be held liable by judgment for the discharge of the plaintiff by the trustees of the school. The argument is that the institute is an eleemosynary charity,[1] and hence not liable to judgment. The contention might, and probably would, be correct, if this were a suit for a tort committed by the trustees; but the action is not one of tort, but for a breach of a contract whereby the trustees agreed, upon the part of the institute, to pay the plaintiff a stipulated salary for her personal services as teacher. . .

It is said the court committed affirmative error in charging the jury as follows: "If you find that when the original contract was made there was no express stipulation that she was to keep the study hall, but that she was afterwards assigned to the position and work, and that the disorder and confusion, if any there were, in the study hall, was not due to her neglect or inattention to her duties, but that it was due to the fact that she was a lady, and a young lady, and that many of the pupils were young men or large boys, and that they were unruly, and could not be restrained by plaintiff, as a young lady, without fault on her part, then, under these circumstances, she would not be liable for such disorder."

We think there was no error in this charge. The plaintiff was put in charge of the study hall, in which there were some 65 pupils of both sexes, many of them young men and young ladies of her own age. She was required to hear eight classes a day in this hall, which each consumed 45 minutes. In addition, she was required to tap the bell for the different hours and classes. She could not be held as an insurer of good order under such circumstances. As tersely stated by herself, "she could not see behind herself." While she was engaged in hearing a class recite and in demonstrating on the blackboard, the unruly boys would take advantage of her

---

[1] [Ed. Note: a non-profit charitable organization.]

occupation, and do things which would create disturbance in the room. It would be beyond the reach of human possibilities to expect a young lady to preserve entire good order in such an assemblage of young people, full of life and fun, and often wanton mischief.

Even in this court, composed of mature, not to say old, men, devoted to the enforcement of law and order, with a chief justice ever on the alert, and a marshal ready and watchful to check any disorder, and with very rare occasion for any fun and pleasantry, occasionally a slight ripple of disturbance will arise; and that notwithstanding that the court is armed with a process of contempt to preserve and enforce order. We are judicially informed that some disorder occasionally occurs in the trial courts, notwithstanding the efforts of the trial judge and sheriff. It is requiring too much to hold the plaintiff as an insurer against any and all disturbances in a school room. . . .

The trial judge properly charged that she would be responsible for inattention and neglect only, and could not be held to keep order at all hazards. This would be requiring more diligence and a higher degree of control than is required of common carriers in the shipment of mules and other live stock, where the carrier is excused from such injury as results from the native unruly disposition of the stock, and we cannot require of this young lady, in the management of boys and girls congregated in a schoolroom, a higher degree of control than is applied to shippers of live stock crowded into cars and subjected to many inconveniences. . . .

It is said there is no evidence to support the verdict. This assignment raises two questions of primary importance, -- one, whether the plaintiff properly discharged her duties as hall or chapel teacher; and the other, whether she indulged excessively, and to the detriment of the school, in social recreation or dissipations. Upon these questions quite a large volume of proof is taken, and all of the minute details of the school and the social life of the plaintiff are laid bare. The testimony bearing upon her derelictions of duty in the schoolroom and her demeanor and conduct in society is given almost altogether by the trustees of the institution and their families.

The school was a new one, founded but a short time previously, and it was during its first term that this controversy arose. The board was a new one, and the teacher was new. There can be no doubt, from this record, that the trustees were devoted to what they thought were the best interests of the school, and they were extremely solicitous as to the conduct and demeanor of its teachers. Their zeal and devotion and attention to the school and its interests cannot be too highly commended. It was a denominational school, under the care and dominion of the Missionary Baptist Church. The plaintiff, as well as the other teachers and principal, belonged to this denomination, and so did the trustees. They were selected from the business men of Martin, -- some of them being merchants, some bankers, some grocers, and others engaged in other occupations; and among them the minister of the Baptist Church. That they were sincerely and devotedly interested in the welfare of the school cannot for a moment be doubted. If they made any mistake in the management, it arose, not from a want of zeal, but from a want of experience and knowledge of the requirements of the situation.

The plaintiff was a young lady of excellent education, having received the degree of M.A. and B.A. from the Southwestern Baptist University of Jackson, Tenn., -- an institution of high standing and repute. She had previously spent three years in Clinton College, Ky. She was strongly recommended by the presidents of these institutions, and no imputation is made against her educational and scholastic attainments. She had just reached her majority, and was for the first time engaged in teaching.

The record shows she was a young lady, handsome in appearance, attractive in bearing, gifted in conversation, and of a cheerful and social disposition. The trustees were of the opinion that she was too much devoted to society, and had too much company for the best interests of the school. She says that, being a "new girl in Martin," she had temporarily attracted attention, which she expected would soon cease, as is usual in such cases. As before stated, the record does not bear out the contention that she had agreed not to receive company, but the fact, as established by the record, is that it was the policy of the management that there should be no excessive indulgence in social pleasures.

She, as well as the other teachers, demurred to being bound by any rigid rule upon this subject, and insisted that they be left a rule unto themselves, with the assurance that their efficiency and influence should not be impaired thereby. One teacher, it is true, thought a more rigid rule should be adopted, basing her view upon what she knew of the surroundings in the city of Martin; but she was in a hopeless minority, and the rule of individual discretion prevailed, with a caution from the principal to be very discreet.

The court, at the very threshold, is confronted by the most difficult and delicate question that has ever been presented for its consideration; that is, what is excessive indulgence in social functions and recreations? The court has no judicial knowledge whatever on the subject, and but little experience and observation. The evidence in this case is very conflicting. The trustees, with their wives and children, have ranged themselves on one side, while the plaintiff and her friends have lined up on the other. The court is not disposed to lay down any rigid rule. What would be excess in a lady of retiring, domestic habits and views might not be in the case of one of a lively, social disposition, coupled with a handsome appearance and attractive manner. Perhaps no two could be measured by the same standard. It appears that the plaintiff was, to some extent, supplied with a boarding house by the trustees, generally in their own homes, and while there she was under their watchful care, -- so much so that the number of her visitors and the dates of their visits were impressed on the memories of the trustees, or else jotted down in memoranda, so that we are furnished with the names and number of visitors plaintiff had, the dates of their calls, and the hours they kept. In fact, we have before us almost a diary of plaintiff's life as a teacher, even to the minutest details.

The trustees' statements as witnesses are to the effect that they watched over her not only as a teacher, in the interest of the school, but as fathers, in her own interest, and we have no doubt of the truth of their statements. While they talked among themselves as to her demeanor, and indulged in some criticisms, they do not appear at first to have talked to her.

After a time, however, the board took action, and appointed a committee to wait on her, and remonstrate with her, and notify her that unless she changed her conduct they would be compelled to discharge her, as her mode of living was detrimental to her efficiency and influence. This committee consisted of the pastor and another trustee, and they agreed to call on her and talk it over. They planned their mode of operation before coming into her presence. The minister was to open the interview. He proceeded to talk to her, and she defended her action in a forcible manner; that is "she talked back," as ladies are sometimes prone to do. The other committeeman says that, after the minister had spent some 60 minutes or more in an earnest appeal, he saw that he was about exhausted, and thereupon intervened himself and continued the lecture. He says he told her that the minister had reasoned with her to no avail, and that he would talk plain, and stated his ultimatum that she must quit having company from Monday morning till Friday night, but that from Friday night until Sunday night, if she wanted company, to go ahead, -- it was all right; but she must not sit up after 10:30, as that was the retiring hour at her boarding house. The witness adds that after laying down this ultimatum, and giving this explanation, he and his brother committeeman sat there for quite a while and "looked at each other." He says that the board had directed them to say to her that she would be discharged if she did not comply with their demands, but the plaintiff very cordially and politely thanked them, and agreed to comply with their demand, and talked so pleasantly, and said she was a "new girl in the town," and had a young lady visitor, and that the matter would be all right, and they were thoroughly beguiled by her manners and ways. This was on the 10th of December.

On the Saturday following, Barlow's Minstrels struck the town; and the plaintiff, having received a free ticket and an invitation from a gentleman to attend, went to this committeeman and asked if she could attend, and if there was any impropriety in her going. He told her she could go, and there was no impropriety; that, if ever there was a good minstrel show, Barlow's was; and that, if he was well enough, he would go himself, and take his wife. He cautioned her again not to have any company during the week, and she assured him she had not seen a man since the former interview.

On Sunday evening after this minstrel show on Saturday, this committee-man called on plaintiff at her boarding house, and talked to her about keeping better order in the chapel, -- a matter which, for want of time, physical capacity, or some other cause, had been neglected at the first interview. He said he left, thinking he had the plaintiff "going his way," and was pleased with the interview, and so reported to the president. But she failed to lecture the pupils on Monday morning as she promised, and he learned she had company on Sunday night until about 12 o'clock. He thereupon reported to the board that she had talked so nicely and fairly to the committee that they had failed to notify her, as the board directed, that she should be discharged if she failed to comply with the demands. Thereupon the same committee was appointed to visit her again, and give her the ultimatum of the board as to her discharge.

He says they followed up the same plan of attack as on the first occasion; that the minister talked first, until he exhausted himself, and he then took it up, and told her in plain terms what the board demanded. She states that she protested that she had done nothing wrong, and again thanked the committee, and they retired. This trustee who had been so active was then attacked with *la grippe*,[2] and went to bed. However, he had conferences with the board, and they decided it would be useless to temporize further. He also saw plaintiff, who insisted that she had done nothing wrong; and, as a result of the interview with her, he expressed regret that she had not been discharged two months earlier, as her conduct was injuring the school, and said that in New York, Louisville, or Nashville the "four hundred" could do such things, "but in Weakley county it wouldn't work."

Soon after this, plaintiff was summoned before the board of trustees, and was informed they desired her resignation, because she had failed to comply with their demands. She asked for an explanation, and was told that the board had taken action, and asked her to resign; if not, she would be dismissed. She asked for time to think, when the reply was: "We will not discuss the matter. We have acted, it is settled, and you must resign or be dismissed." She asked for specifications as to wherein she had failed, but was given the same answer, -- that it was settled, and she had her choice to resign or be dismissed. One after another advised her to resign, the principal saying, "Knowing the brethren, Miss Copass, I believe it best for you to resign." She replied she had no grounds to base her resignation on, and they replied, "We give you your choice." And she rejoined "I have no choice."

The secretary undertook to read an order of dismissal, but was interrupted by various members urging plaintiff to resign. At last he succeeded, after some half hour, in reading an order of dismissal, as follows: "We hereby dismiss Miss Frances Copass from Hall-Moody Institute on account of failing to comply with the demands of the trustees." She then requested to be informed what demands she had refused, and the reply was "You understand." She persisted in further explanations as to the demands, but was refused, and the interview closed.

She requested another meeting after one of the trustees returned to the city, who was not present at the former meeting, and, after the conference had progressed, she again asked for a definite statement of the charges against her, when, on motion of the secretary, it was resolved they would not state definitely the grounds of their action; and, after assuring her that they acted with great deliberation, they adjourned.

She sought and was granted another interview with the board, and expressed great regret at the result of the matter, and wanted to get at the bottom

---

[2] [Ed. Note: a viral illness resembling influenza.]

of it; said that, if she had done anything wrong, she was sorry, and wanted to be reinstated. She told them that she had no doubt that, from their standpoint, they had acted conscientiously, and she was anxious to adjust the matter. They promised to take the matter under further consideration, but on the next day notified her that the decision was final, paid her up to date of her discharge, and imposed her duties on other teachers. She attempted to get other employment there and elsewhere, and failed, and then brought suit for the balance due her for the unexpired term.

It appears that plaintiff was in the institute for 4 1/2 months, and her testimony, as well as the weight of the evidence, is that she had callers and visitors about 16 times, or about one a week. There is much conflict on this point, however. The jury had the plaintiff before them, and saw her appearance and demeanor, as well as that of other witnesses; and they were of the opinion that she had not damaged the school in this way, or they could not, under the charge, have found in her favor. Under this feature of the case, there is a conflict of testimony; but the jury have seen proper to believe the plaintiff's view of the case, and there is evidence to sustain their finding.

There is some evidence that upon one or two occasions, when she had been to an entertainment, she sat up and had company until near 12 o'clock. The jury did not believe she was in such error in so doing as to impair her influence or warrant her discharge. The members of this court have been known to sit up until 12 o'clock at night. It is true, they have the company of very entertaining records, and in the consideration of contingent remainders, executory devises, and the class doctrine, the time passes by without any note, so that we cannot (at least, over the verdict of the jury) say that an occasional staying up until 12 o'clock with pleasant company is excessive. We are not aware that we have been rendered less efficient by such hours. Indeed, this seems to be the settled policy of the state, and we have heard of no criticism on this account; and there seems now to be a disposition to allow such members of the court as desire to do so to continue the practice.

Upon the other feature of the case (that is, the efficiency of the plaintiff) there is also much proof, and it is also contradictory. The chief complaint is that she could not maintain order in the study hall. We have already adverted to the difficulty attending this part of her duties. It appears that on two occasions marbles were rolled across the floor. They evidently came from the boys side. The girls were dismissed and the boys lined up and put on honor, when it was revealed that none of them did it. The marbles evidently got loose and rolled themselves while the teacher's back was turned.

A lap rug was thrown across the hall, but this was also done surreptitiously. The boys would look at the girls, and the girls would look at the boys, and both would smile, when there was no apparent occasion for such conduct, and when the teacher's back was turned. Other things of like character were done, but the teacher was always kept uninformed of these matters until after they had happened. It is evident she had not small task before her, -- to keep 65 boys and girls in order, some large and some smaller, but all imbued with the sense of fun and mischief. The court charged, in substance, that she was bound to due diligence to keep order, but could not be held to be a guarantor; and the jury were evidently of the opinion she did all she could, as she states, and there is evidence to sustain this view.

The plaintiff was required to teach a class in zoology. In order to do this, it was directed by the principal that the pupils should go out into the open fields, with the plaintiff in charge. The principal reported that, after they had gone, he followed, and found the plaintiff and pupils paired off by couples, eating watermelons. The plaintiff's version of this is that the plan of operations was to take a mosquito bar, and, holding it by the corners, use it as a dragnet to catch all the bugs, worms, butterflies, grasshoppers, frogs, and other objects they could, and take them to the institute for dissection and study at leisure, -- a practice similar to medical students in search of subjects for dissection. It seems that some of the boys, in carrying the dragnet through the field of Mr. Farmer, one of the trustees, caught some watermelon. They gallantly shared them with the girls, and while the melons were being dissected on the ground (being too heavy to carry to the institute) the principal appeared.

It appears that there were three girls and six boys in this zoological class. The only criticism the principal made at the time was that perhaps it would be best to divide the class thereafter. The jury thought, undoubtedly, no great injury had been done in this matter.

All these matters, and many others of like character, were placed before the jury, and commented on with great eloquence by counsel; and the jury, after a deliberation of five minutes, returned a verdict for the plaintiff. The charge of the court is correct and lays down a proper rule. There is evidence that the young lady was diligent; that she was not derelict in her duties; that she did the best she could with the material she had; and we can see no ground to disturb the verdict of the jury.

It appears that most of the disorder in the school was caused by the sons of trustees, and they are the principal witnesses against the plaintiff as to these disorders, of which they were well posted, but plaintiff knew nothing, and one of them, notably (Mr. White), was a witness as to his improper visits socially to the plaintiff, when she supposed he had a permit to come. No imputation is cast upon the character of the young men who paid attentions to the plaintiff. It is agreed that they are the cream of Martin society, intelligent and refined, and one polished by years of foreign travel, and one of them a prominent member of the bar and a practitioner in this court. It was attempted to show that one of them was an insurance agent, and that the plaintiff was never introduced to him, but nevertheless talked to him and walked with him. Plaintiff explained her relation to him, no doubt satisfactorily to the jury, as it is to this court. Besides, the well-known modesty and retiring disposition of insurance agents is prima facie evidence that he was a gentleman, as the proof demonstrates he was.

It is insisted that a new trial should have been granted because of undue pressure and influence brought to bear on the jury by the public at the trial. The motion for new trial was supported by the affidavits of six trustees, who were also witnesses in the case. Their affidavits state, in substance, that the case attracted a great deal of attention and interest in Weakley county, and that the court room was crowded with partisan adherents of the plaintiff; that they filled up the space allotted for the spectators, and also the bar, and crowded around the jury; that they manifested their approval of plaintiff's case by applauding her attorneys by hand-clapping, and other means, in the presence of the jury; that they shook their heads, and smiled and frowned, and by other facial expressions manifested their approval or disapproval as the case progressed; that on the close of the speeches of counsel for plaintiff there was a vigorous applause, by hand-clapping and otherwise, and this tended to influence the jury; that inflammatory utterances were made by her counsel; that the case was talked about in the presence and hearing of the jury by the friends of the plaintiff, both ladies and men, and the hope and belief were expressed that the plaintiff would win her case; that the shops and stores, the offices and public places, streets and business houses, the court house and hotels, were filled with her friends, male and female, talking and commenting about the case; that the jury, in consequence, did not take time to consider the verdict, or read the charge, or weight the evidence, but returned with a verdict for plaintiff within five minutes after retiring; that its delivery was loudly cheered, and she and her attorneys were openly and profusely congratulated on the result; that the public sentiment was molded in plaintiff's favor by public comment on the streets and in the press, so that a fair and impartial trial was not had.

The sworn statements of the clerk of the court and of the jury were introduced, to the effect that while there was a large crowd present, and much interest manifested, no remarks were made by spectators in the presence of the jury. There was applause by both parties in the court room and in the presence of the jury, which the court on each occasion suppressed, and on each occasion rebuked the audience. The jury state that they were in no wise and to no extent influenced by these manifestations. Some of them stated that they knew public feeling was high, but could not tell whether it preponderated in favor of one side or the other; that they were not approached or talked to by the friends of either; that the trustees, some of the witnesses, and many of the friends of the institution appeared in court with the badge of the institution displayed on their bosoms or collars; that they based their decision on the law and the facts; that they were not influenced by public sentiment or manifestation; and that they disapproved of the applause, and considered it out of place.

Counsel for plaintiff states that first applause occurred at a sharp answer to plaintiff's attorney; that there was no applause during speeches, but some laughter; that there was never any applause but hand-clapping, and no cheering at any time, and that the applause was promptly checked and rebuked whenever it occurred; that no exception was taken to any of it at any time by defendant's counsel.

We are satisfied that the efforts of counsel on both sides merited, if the propriety of the case would permit, a great deal more applause than was in fact given. Faint echoes of their eloquence have even reached this court, and on this feature of the case the parties are well balanced. The trial judge overruled the motion for a new trial, and we must assume that he properly exercised his discretion in so doing. He was present and saw the entire proceedings, and, being satisfied that a fair trial had been had, he did not grant a new trial, and we cannot see that he was in error.

The judgment of the court below is affirmed.

CHAPTER IX

ACCIDENTS, SLIPS, FALLS, CRASHES, CRUNCHES, WRECKS, BUMPS, THUMPS AND LUMPS.

"Law is law" wrote the satirist who decided not to adopt it as a profession. "Law is like a country dance; people are led up and down in it till they are tired. Law is like a book of surgery--there are a great many terrible cases in it. It is also like physic--they who take least of it are best off. Law is like a homely gentlewoman--very well to follow. Law is like a scolding wife--very bad when it follows us. Law is like a new fashion--people are bewitched to get into it. It is also like bad weather--most people are glad when they get out of it." [1]

---

[1] From George A. Morton, and D. Macleod Mulloch, *Law and Laughter*, p. 1 (1913).

CHAPTER IX: BUMPS, THUMPS & LUMPS

FISHER v. LOWE
Court of Appeals of Michigan
122 Mich. App. 418; 333 N.W. 2d 67 (1983)

JOHN H. GILLIS, Judge.

> We thought that we would never see
> A suit to compensate a tree.
> A suit whose claim in tort is prest
> Upon a mangled tree's behest;
>
> A tree whose battered trunk was prest
> Against a Chevy's crumpled crest;
> A tree that faces each new day
> With bark and limb in disarray;
>
> A tree that may forever bear
> A lasting need for tender care.
> Flora lovers though we three,
> We must uphold the court's decree.

Affirmed.[1]

ROBINSON v. PIOCHE, BAYERQUE & CO.
Supreme Court of California
5 Cal. 460 (1855)

SOLOMON HEYDENFELDT, J.

The Court below erred in giving the third, fourth and fifth instructions. If the defendants were at fault in leaving an uncovered hole in the sidewalk of a public street, the intoxication of the plaintiff cannot excuse such gross negligence. A drunken man is as much entitled to a safe street, as a sober one, and much more in need of it.

The judgment is reversed and the cause remanded.

---

[1] Plaintiff commenced this action in tort against defendants Lowe and Moffet for damage to his "beautiful oak tree" caused when defendant Lowe struck it while operating defendant Moffet's automobile. The trial court granted summary judgment in favor of defendants pursuant to GCR 1963, 117.2(1). In addition, the trial court denied plaintiff's request to enter a default judgment against the insurer of the automobile defendant, State Farm Mutual Automobile Insurance Company. Plaintiff appeals as of right.

The trial court did not err in granting summary judgment in favor of defendants Lowe and Moffet. Defendants were immune from tort liability for damage to the tree pursuant to § 3135 of the no-fault insurance act. M.C.I. § 500.3135, M.S.A. § 24.13135.

The trial court did not err in refusing to enter a default judgment against State Farm. Since it is undisputed that plaintiff did not serve process upon State Farm in accordance with the court rules, the court did not obtain personal jurisdiction over the insurer. GCR 1963, 105.4.

SCHWARTZ v. WARWICK-PHILADELPHIA CORPORATION
Supreme Court of Pennsylvania
424 Pa. 185; 226 A.2d 484 (1967)

MICHAEL A. MUSMANNO, Justice.

It was a wedding banquet and the guests were enjoying themselves in the traditional custom of nuptial celebrations. There was dining and dancing and then dancing and dining. Fork work interspersed with footwork. The banquetters would enjoy a spell of eating and then amble out to the dance floor to dance. When the music suspended, the dancers returned to their tables and became diners again. The mythical playwright who prepares the script for the strange and sometimes quixotic episodes which eventually end up in court, mixed his stage properties and characters in this presentation because he placed in the center of the dance floor a quantity of freshly cooked asparagus and ladled over it a generous quantity of oleaginous asparagus sauce. In this setting it was inevitable that something untoward would happen, and it did. One of the performers in the unrehearsed play described what occurred.

Joseph Rosenberg, tall, weighing 185 pounds and wearing a tuxedo suit, was dancing with his sister-in-law, Mrs. Ruth Schwartz who was wearing a gold lame' dress, made of a metallic brocade material when, as he described it, "I went up in the air and flipped on my back, my buttocks, and I pushed her down, and as I pushed her down, I let go, and she hit the floor, and my feet went up in the air."

Were is not for what he testified later, the casual reader could assume Joseph Rosenberg was merely describing one of the modern dances which, in acrobatic manipulations and grotesque gyrations, sound no less exotic than the wild movements narrated above. Rosenberg explained, however, that the terpsichorean maneuver he executed was involuntary. He said he was a veteran of the ball room with some 35 years of successful dancing behind him and he had never previously done such a flip as he described. He said that his excursion into space rose from an asparagus pad in the middle of the floor, and that after got up he noted his pants were "green and white, like sauce."

His dancing partner, Mrs. Schwartz, confirmed Rosenberg's testimony and stated that as a result of the squashed asparagus floundering, her dress was covered with "strings of like green asparagus," and that the stain was 8 inches wide and 15 inches down from the side. In addition, the floor was wet for a distance of 3 feet with asparagus and sauce. Mr. Schwartz, the husband of Mrs. Schwartz, testified that immediately after the tumble occurred, "I rushed over and there they are sitting in a spill of green substance and sauces, and it was spread over quite an area * * * the area seemed to be full of liquid and asparagus." He saw that Rosenberg's shoe was full of the "green substance," that the sole of the shoe was green and "there seemed to be something sticking to it near the heel."

Twenty minutes after the dine-and-dance debacle, Mr. Rosenberg and Mrs. Schwartz left the hotel, bruised, sore, and asparagus-laden, and in due time brought an action in trespass against Warwick-Philadelphia Corporation, the caterers of the wedding feast.

At the end of the ensuing trial, the judge entered a compulsory non-suit, asserting that the plaintiffs had not established a prima facie case of negligence or proximate cause. There was evidence that the waiters carrying food to the tables not only walked over the dance floor, but did so while the dance was in progress. Since the dancing space was not large, it happened that the dancers and waiters sometimes competed for passage and, while no one testified to actually seeing asparagus slide from an uplifted tray, the jury could easily have found that in the gridiron clashes between dancers and waiters the asparagus fumbled out of the trays and onto the floor. How else did it get there?

The trial judge, an ex-veteran congressman and thus a habitue of formal parties and accordingly an expert in proper wearing apparel at such functions, all of which he announced from the bench, allowed testimony as to the raiment worn by the banquetters. All the men were attired in tuxedos, the pants of which were not mounted with cuffs which could transport asparagus and sauce to the dance floor, unwittingly to lubricate its polished surface. Ruling out the cuffs of the tuxedo pants as transporters of the asparagus, the judge suggested the asparagus, with its accompanying sauce, could have been conveyed to the dance floor by "women's apparel, on men's coats or sleeves, or by a guest as he table hopped." The Judge's conclusions are as far-fetched as going to Holland for hollandaise sauce. There was no evidence in the case that anybody table hopped; it is absurd to assume that a man's coat or sleeve could scoop up enough asparagus and sauce to inundate a dance floor to the extent of a three-foot circumference; and it is bizarre to conjecture that a woman's dress without pockets and without excessive material could latch on to such a quantity of asparagus, carry it 20 feet (the distance from the tables to the dance floor) and still have enough dangling to her habiliments to cover the floor to such a depth as to fell a 185 pound gentleman with 35 years' dancing experience who had never before been tackled or grounded while shuffling the light fantastic.

A non-suit must be based on fact and not on supposition, on testimony and not conjecture, on realities and not guesses. Since no one questioned the presence of asparagus and sauce on the dance floor where assuredly it should not have been, since there is no evidence it was carried there by guests because the Trial Judge's hypothesis that it could have gotten there hanging on to the men's coattails or women's dresses must be dismissed as visionary, since there was direct evidence that waiters transported asparagus across the floor aloft on trays and there was evidence that waiters physically jostled dancers and, since it is not difficult to conclude that in a clash between a hurrying waiter and a dancer writhing in the throes of a watusi, frug, twist, jerk, or buzzard, the resulting jolt would tilt the tray, cascading asparagus and sauce to the floor to throw the terpsichorean gymnasts off balance, it is reasonably proper, and fair to conclude that this concatenation of circumstances made out a prima facie case of negligence against the establishment running the wedding feast. It requires no citation of authority to demonstrate that a waiter with a tray balanced on an uplifted arm is out of place on a ballroom floor during a late twentieth century dance which would make the Apache war dance seem tame in comparison.

It can be stated as an incontrovertible legal proposition that anyone attending a dinner dance has the inalienable right to expect that, if asparagus is to be served, it will be served on the dinner table and not on the dance floor.

Nor are the plaintiffs in this case required to rule out every possible hypothesis for the happening of the accident, including the coathanging asparagus flight of fancy of the Trial Judge, except the thesis on which they base their cause. This Court said in Smith v. Bell Telephone Co. [citation omitted] .

> " It is not necessary, under Pennsylvania law, that every fact or circumstance point unerringly to liability; it is enough that there be sufficient facts for the jury to say reasonably that the preponderance favors liability * * * The facts are for the jury in any case whether based upon direct or circumstantial evidence where a reasonable conclusion can be arrived at which would place liability on the defendant * * * The right of a litigant to have the jury pass upon the facts is not to be foreclosed just because the judge believes that a reasonable man might properly find either way."

In Liguori v. City of Philadelphia, [citation omitted] we said:

> "* * * since proof to a degree of absolute certainty is rarely attainable in any litigated factual controversy, the law requires only that the evidence as to the operative cause of the accident be enough to satisfy reasonable and well-balanced minds that it was the one on which the plaintiff relies."

The law applicable to a case of this kind was expounded as recently as 1961 in a case where the facts were somewhat similar to the ones at bar. Lederhandler v. Bolotini, [citation omitted]. The plaintiff there was injured when she fell on an apple strudel which had fallen to the floor also used for dancing. The defendant maintained he could not be held liable for the appearance of the strudel on the floor because it could not be linked to any of his waiters, arguing specifically:

> "To find as a fact that the strudel got there as a result of defendant's negligence one must resort to the use of an inference viz., strudel was served at the dinner, hence one of the waiters must have dropped a piece."

We affirmed a judgment in favor of the plaintiff, stating:

> " A caterer who serves meals and has charge of the premises in which they are consumed has the responsibility to clear the premises of food which he or his staff allows to escape to the damage of others; or, if it gets to the floor through the intervention of someone else, the caterer is liable for any resulting damage if it remains on the floor a sufficient period of time for him to be aware of its presence, actually or by constructive notice. * * * We have held that the time of constructive notice depends on the particular circumstances of the case. . . . we said that there could conceivably be a situation where 5 minutes would be adequate notice and where 5 hours would be inadequate notice."

Moreover, if it is established that the alleged tortious act was the result of the defendant's active negligence, constructive notice need not be proved. The waiters here were admittedly employed by the defendant and if they negligently dropped asparagus to the floor, their acts, under the principle of respondeat superior, were the acts of the employer. . .

The evidence presented at the trial in the instant case made out, if accepted by the jury, a prima facie case of negligence, and the plaintiffs were entitled to have the jury pass on the issues involved.

Judgment reversed with a procedendo.[1]

DISSENTING OPINION

JOHN C. BELL, Chief Justice.

One cannot help wondering if plaintiffs had, in the alleged 35 years of dancing, ever been to any dance, let alone a wedding banquet dance. There was no evidence of constructive notice; moreover, plaintiffs undoubtedly voluntarily assumed the risk of this banquet dance floor which was obviously periled with

---

1 [Ed. Note: A "procedendo" is a writ by which a cause which has been removed from an inferior court to a superior court is sent down again *to be proceeded in* there. *Black's Law Dictionary*, 4th Ed. (1968).]

asparagus sauce, winding waiters, and grotesque exotic tribal dancing under modern names. A dancer cannot, with legal sanction, look only into the captivating eyes of his lovely partner.

I certainly dissent.

GUTHRIE v. POWELL
Supreme Court of Kansas
178 Kan. 587; 290 P. 2d 834 (1955)

WILLIAM W. HARVEY, Chief Justice.

At all times mentioned herein defendants were partners in and the proprietors of a business known as the Winfield Sales Company located at the Cowley County Fair Grounds in or near the west edge of the city limits of Winfield, Kansas, and engaged in and operating what is generally known as a community sale business, buying and selling for their own account and the account of various patrons and customers diverse kinds of livestock and used and new merchandise, and holding forth said premises as a place of public resort to all interested persons.

On April 15, 1953, plaintiff and her husband, S.R. Guthrie, came to and attended the premises of said Winfield Sales Company for the purpose of being customers and patrons at the sale held there on that day. . .

The premises used and occupied by said defendants as a place of business consists of several frame buildings and livestock pens and runways, of which the principal building where most of said sales activities are conducted consists of a large room at the south end of said building in which patrons interested in buying and selling merchandise and inanimate personal property were congregated on said day, the business office of said defendants, a lunch stand, and a livestock pavilion located on the second story and reached by way of a ramp leading up from the first floor of said principal building. Said livestock sale pavilion is a recessed semi-circle of board seats surrounding a pit or sales arena approximately 30 feet long and 15 feet wide in which livestock is exhibited for sale. . .

At about 1 p.m. of said day plaintiff was seated in a chair at the north end of the south main floor room engaged in visiting and conversing with women friends and acquaintances, most of whom were the wives of patrons attending said sale. Suddenly, there was a loud commotion and noise overhead and simultaneously bits of plaster and debris began to fall from the ceiling onto plaintiff and others standing or sitting near her which was followed instantaneously — as plaintiff later learned — by a six hundred pound steer falling through the ceiling immediately over and approximately twelve feet above her position, said beast falling and landing upon plaintiff as she sat in said chair, knocking her unconscious, flattening the chair and plaintiff to the floor and under said steer and causing painful, serious and permanent injuries to her as hereinafter set forth. . .

. . . the plaintiff states and alleges that the fact that the steer fell through the ceiling onto the plaintiff causing the resulting injuries to plaintiff, was an occurrence which would not have taken place except for some act or acts of negligence of the defendants, their agents, servants or employees in the proper and safe operation, maintenance, conduct and handling of said premises and livestock being exhibited therein, . . .

Plaintiff is entitled to a trial in this case. . . affirmed.

TEAGLE v. CITY OF PHILADELPHIA
Supreme Court of Pennsylvania.
430 Pa. 395; 243 A.2d 342 (1968)

MICHAEL A. MUSMANNO, Justice.

A few minutes before midnight on July 2, 1961, Mrs. Beatrice Teagle, plaintiff here, while crossing Leland Street in Philadelphia, stepped into a hole in the street and sustained injuries. At the trial of the lawsuit instituted against the City of Philadelphia by the plaintiff, she testified that the hole into which she fell was 36 inches long, 2 feet wide, from 4 to 5 inches deep and was filled with black water. She explained that she could tell the depth of the hole by the wet mark on her stocking.

A Mrs. Dorothy Gross testified that on the night in question she was in her home, she heard a scream and ran out to the street where she saw two persons helping Mrs. Teagle out of the hole in which her foot was immersed. Mrs. Gross knew this defect in the pavement since she had reported it to the City authorities a year before.

The jury returned a verdict for the plaintiff and the defendant asks for judgment n. o. v. or a new trial "at least." Reason? A photograph of the offending hole introduced at the trial inexplicably showed a ruler stuck into it, its measuring indicating the surface of the fortuitous pond to be 1-1/2 inches above the supposed bottom. No one explained who inserted the ruler, no one testified as to whether the measuring rod was punched into the deepest part of the crater, its shallowest part, or somewhere in between. The photographer who took the picture was not called as a witness.

The defendant claims that the City should not be liable for a trivial depression in its public thoroughfares. The Courts have not declared what absolute minimum depth is required in a fissure in the street to establish negligence on the part of the municipality for allowing it to remain unrepaired. Nor can there be a judicial pronouncement on the subject because obviously negligence invariably depends on a number of concatenating circumstances.

The defendant argues that the measure appearing on the ruler in the photograph "must be accepted as conclusive evidence of the true depth." This is an argument of less depth than that measured on the ruler. As already stated, the ruler does not specify that the depth of the concavity was uniform throughout its length of 36 inches and its breadth of 2 feet, nor that it was at the precise point where the ruler stood guard that Mrs. Teagle's foot disappeared into the murky hollow.

In addition, photographs cannot be said always to be an undeviatingly accurate reproduction of the scenes they presumably depict. It is said that figures do not lie, but that liars can figure. It can also be said that while photographs do not lie, there can be pictorial legerdemain which transforms a ramshackle house into a mansion, a city dump into a panoramic vista, and an ugly duckling into a swan. Everyone has experienced the surprise of seeing for the first time a person whose photograph he had previously witnessed and noting how different the real person looks from the photographed individual. It is indeed the boast of some photographers that they can do more for a person with the camera than can be done for him or her in a barber shop, beauty shop, and/or a tailor shop.

In Beardslee v. Columbia Township, [citation omitted] this Court sagely observed:

> "Photographs are competent evidence, and, when
> properly taken are judicially recognized as a high
> order of accuracy * * * But in careless, or inexpert,
> or interest hands they are capable of very serious
> misrepresentation of the original."

Sometimes a photograph may be admitted for the limited purpose of showing "physical aspects" of a location rather than for the purpose of demonstrating that what is in the picture represents the situation at the time of the happening of the controverted episode. . .

The plaintiff here was not present when the photographs were taken, she never saw the photographer, and, at the trial, did not vouch for the measurements supposedly indicated by the ruler. We repeat that there is not a syllable in the record to indicate that the plaintiff fell at that point in the photograph where the ruler lifted its measured head.

Nor did anyone come forward to say that the bottom of the ruler rested on terra firma. In fact, the photograph shows that it was held in position by a transverse beam, the latter extending from the curb to the adjoining pavement.

The Trial Judge presented both sides of the controversy to the jury in a charge luminous with clarity. He said, inter alia:

> "You have to consider all the surrounding circum-
> stances in regard to this hole. This is an alleged
> defect, and before liability attaches to the City,
> you should consider the depth of the hole, the size
> of an obstruction constituting the impediment,
> and consider whether all the particular facts of
> this case are sufficient to indicate that an unsafe
> condition was existing here, and that this was due
> to the negligence of the City of Philadelphia."

Nothing could be fairer. The jury took the photographs with them into the jury room, they studied them and concluded there was more credibility in the sworn testimony of the plaintiff and Mrs. Gross than in the unaccounted-for, unexplained, phantom ruler dipping its lower extremity into the dark depths of the haphazard puddle.

This is the hole case, and we see nothing in the appellant's argument of such depth that it submerges the jury's verdict into such a cavern of unreliability that it compels this Court to send the parties back for a retrial, when it is very clear that justice, wisely measured by the ruler of common sense, has been fairly done.

Judgment affirmed.

MURPHY v. STEEPLECHASE AMUSEMENT CO., Inc.
Court of Appeals of New York.
250 N.Y. 479; 166 N.E. 173 (1929)

BENJAMIN N. CARDOZO, C. J.

The defendant, Steeplechase Amusement Company maintains an amusement park at Coney Island, N.Y. One of the supposed attractions is known as "the Flopper." It is a moving belt, running upward on an inclined plane, on which passengers sit or stand. Many of them are unable to keep their feet because of the movement of the belt, and are thrown backward or aside. The belt runs in a groove, with padded walls on either side to a height of four feet, and with padded flooring beyond the walls at the same angle as the belt. An electric motor, driven by current furnished by the Brooklyn Edison Company, supplies the needed power.

Plaintiff, a vigorous young man, visited the park with friends. One of them, a young woman, now his wife, stepped upon the moving belt. Plaintiff followed and stepped behind her. As he did so, he felt what he describes as a sudden jerk, and was thrown to the floor. His wife in front and also friends behind him were thrown at the same time.

Something more was here, as every one understood, than the slowly moving escalator that is common in shops and public places. A fall was foreseen as one of the risks of the adventure. There would have been no point to the whole thing, no adventure about it, if the risk had not been there. The very name, above the gate, "the Flopper," was warning to the timid. If the name was not enough, there was warning more distinct in the experience of others. We are told by the plaintiff's wife that the members of her party stood looking at the sport before joining in it themselves. Some aboard the belt were able, as she viewed them, to sit down with decorum or even to stand up and keep their footing; others jumped or fell. The tumbling bodies and the screams and laughter supplied the merriment and fun. "I took a chance," she said when asked whether she thought that a fall might be expected.

Plaintiff took the chance with her, but, less lucky than his companions, suffered a fracture of a knee cap. He states in his complaint that the belt was dangerous to life and limb, in that it stopped and started violently and suddenly and was not properly equipped to prevent injuries to persons who were using it without knowledge of its dangers, and in a bill of particulars he adds that it was operated at a fast and dangerous rate of speed and was not supplied with a proper railing, guard, or other device to prevent a fall therefrom. No other negligence is charged.

We see no adequate basis for a finding that the belt was out of order. It was already in motion when the plaintiff put his foot on it. He cannot help himself to a verdict in such circumstances by the addition of the facile comment that it threw him with a jerk. One who steps upon a moving belt and finds his heels above his head is in no position to discriminate with nicety between the successive stages of the shock, between the jerk which is a cause and the jerk, accompanying the fall, as an instantaneous effect.

There is evidence for the defendant that power was transmitted smoothly, and could not be transmitted otherwise. If the movement was spasmodic, it was an unexplained and, it seems, an inexplicable departure from the normal workings of the mechanism. An aberration so extraordinary, it is to lay the basis for a verdict, should rest on something firmer than a mere descriptive epithet, a summary of the sensations of a tense and crowded moment. . . . But the jerk, if it were established, would add little to the case. Whether the movement of the belt was uniform or irregular, the risk at greatest was a fall. This was the very hazard that was invited and foreseen.

Volenti non fit injuria [an injury is not done to a consenting person]. One who takes part in such a sport accepts the dangers that inhere in it so far as they are obvious and necessary, just as a fencer accepts the risk of a thrust by his antagonist or a spectator at a ball game the chance of contact with the ball. . . . The antics of the clown are not the paces of the cloistered cleric. The rough and boisterous joke, the horseplay of the clown, evokes its own guffaws, but they are not the pleasures of tranquillity. The plaintiff was not seeking a retreat for meditation. Visitors were tumbling about the belt to the merriment of onlookers when he made his choice to join them. He took the chance of a like fate, with whatever damage to his body might ensue from such a fall. The timorous may stay at home.

A different case would be here if the dangers inherent in the sport were obscure or unobserved [citation omitted] or so serious as to justify the belief that precautions of some kind must have been taken to avert them [citation omitted]. Nothing happened to the plaintiff except what common experience tells us may happen at any time as the consequence of a sudden fall. Many a skater or a horseman can rehearse a tale of equal woe.

A different case there would also be if the accidents had been so many as to show that the game in its inherent nature was too dangerous to be continued without change. The president of the amusement company says that there had never been such an accident before. A nurse employed at an emergency hospital maintained in connection with the park contradicts him to some extent. She says that on other occasions she had attended patrons of the park who had been injured at the Flopper, how many she could not say. None, however, had been badly injured or had suffered broken bones. Such testimony is not enough to show that the game was a trap for the unwary, too perilous to be endured. According to the defendant's estimate, 250,000 visitors were at the Flopper in a year. Some quota of accidents was to be looked for in so great a mass. One might as well say that a skating rink should be abandoned because skaters sometimes fall.

There is testimony by the plaintiff that he fell upon wood, and not upon a canvas padding. He is strongly contradicted by the photographs and by the witnesses for the defendant, and is without corroboration in the testimony of his companions who were witnesses in his behalf. If his observation was correct, there was a defect in the equipment, and one not obvious or known. The padding should have been kept in repair to break the force of any fall. The case did not go to the jury, however, upon any such theory of the defendant's liability, nor is the defect fairly suggested by the plaintiff's bill of particulars, which limits his complaint. The case went to the jury upon the theory that negligence was dependent upon a sharp and sudden jerk.

The judgment of the Appellate Division and that of the Trial Term should be reversed, and a new trial granted, with costs to abide the event.

FREER v. PARKER
Supreme Court of Pennsylvania
411 Pa. 346; 192 A.2d 348 (1963)

MICHAEL A. MUSMANNO, Justice.

Leroy Parker, the defendant-appellant in this case, moved for a new trial in the court below on two grounds: (1) that the verdict was against the weight of the evidence; (2) that there was a variance between the allegata and the probata. He has since dropped his claim that the verdict was against the weight of the evidence and argues for a new trial on the second ground alone.

The plaintiff, Harry B. Freer, averred in his Complaint that, as a result of the automobile collision, for which the defendant was responsible, he sustained various hurts, injuries and disablements, one of them being "loosening of teeth." At the trial the plaintiff's dentist testified that prior to the accident the plaintiff suffered from some loosening of teeth but that the violence of the collision, of which he was a victim, had further loosened his teeth, that they were "mobile," that "you could shake them with your fingers," and that he "splinted the teeth together to try to allow the bone to regenerate and tighten the teeth."

The defendant argues that there was thus demonstrated a variance between allegata and probata and that this variance entitled him to a new trial. The reason why the probata is required by law to concur with the allegata is that otherwise the defendant in a lawsuit would not know what he might be confronted with at the trial and he thus could not properly prepare for it. If, for instance, a plaintiff avers that his left arm was severed as a result of the litigated event and then stamps into court on a wooden leg, his arms intact, the defendant can well object because he has been caught by surprise. But if the plaintiff, as is the fact in this case, states in his Complaint that as a result of the legal bone of contention his teeth were loosened and the lay as well as medical evidence addresses itself to teeth loosening, it is difficult to see how the defendant can reasonably argue that he was left in the dark as to what to expect at the trial of the cause.

The defendant maintains that the plaintiff should have averred in his Complaint that the condition of his loose teeth was aggravated by the accident. But even if the plaintiff had so averred, the defendant would have known no more than what he was advised of in the Complaint as filed, namely, that the plaintiff's teeth were loosened by the vehicular violence of which the defendant reputedly was the author. Even if the plaintiff already chewed on loose teeth prior to the accident but the teeth were made looser by the accident, what still happened was that his teeth were loosened. A loose tooth can always become looser. In fact, that is more or less the melancholy story of teeth.

A tooth first manifests the slightest variation from perpendicularity; then it leans a little more, but, like the Leaning Tower of Pisa, it is still firmly imbedded in the terra firma of the jaw bone. One day, however, the tooth bearer will note, as he masticates a tough steak or bites into a bit of gravel in his oyster sandwich, that the tooth under surveillance wobbles a little more, but it is still useful and still resolute for further masticatory assaults on foods of a stronger constituency than mush. A person may have a number of teeth in that state; they may even resemble a slightly pushed-over picket fence but they are still good teeth, still serviceable tusks. If, because of violence applied to the mandibles, the whole dental battery is jostled and the individual molars, bicuspids, grinders and incisors are shaken in their sockets, it is certainly proper to say that there has been a loosening of teeth. A further loosening, it is true, but still a loosening.

In whatever stage of looseness a man's dental pearls may be, he is entitled to keep them in that state, and if they are tortiously subjected to jostling, jarring and jouncing, the tortfeasor may not be excused from responsibility for the further chewing dilapidation of his victim on the basis that he had bad teeth anyway.

If a Complaint avers that the plaintiff suffered a shortening of his left leg and it develops at the trial that the injured left leg was already, prior to the accident, 2 inches shorter than his normal right leg, he may not be denied compensation for the increased shortening from let us say, 2 inches to four inches because he did not specify in the Complaint what was the length of his leg prior to the accident. Once leg shortening is mentioned in the Complaint, the defendant is put on notice what to expect in the way of evidence at the trial and it is expected that he will come to the trial at least armed with a tape measure.

The defendant here suffered no surprise, and was in no way deceived by the phraseology in the Complaint. If he felt himself uninformed as to what the plaintiff intended to prove under the rather obvious heading of "loosening of teeth," he could have asked for a more specific Complaint. If he still remained perplexed, there was available to him a pre-trial discovery which would have permitted him to count and examine every tooth in the plaintiff's head and ascertain its stability, mobility and state of general welfare.

The appellant cites Littman v. Bell Telephone Co., [citation omitted], as authority for new trial on the basis of the allegata-probata clash. The situation in that case was wholly different. There, the Court charged the jury that the plaintiff could recover for the aggravation of a pre-existing arthritis, of which there was not the slightest intimation in the Statement of Claim. There the defendant could not prepare for claims of arthritis because he had no way of knowing that the plaintiff ever had or had acquired arthritic decrepitude. Here, the defendant could not possibly plead ignorance to knowledge of the plaintiff's "loosening of teeth." If a man's teeth are 10 per cent loose before an accident and 60 per cent loose after an accident, "loosening of teeth" accurately describes the deplorable dental deterioration, and adequately acquaints the defendant with what he must face at the trial in the way of claimed damages.

In Gibson v. Stainless Steel Corp., [citation omitted] the Superior Court stated:

> "If the proof corresponds to the substance of the allegation, a variance is not established; in determining this question, the entire pleadings and evidence must be considered, and, if the latter substantially proves the former, a variance does not exist."

That standard was certainly met in the case at bar. It was "loosening of teeth" all the way through.

Judgment affirmed.

CORDAS v. PEERLESS TRANSPORTATION CO.
City Court of New York, New York County
27 N.Y.S.2d 198 (1941)

FRANK A. CARLIN, Justice.

This case presents the ordinary man-that problem child of the law-in a most bizarre setting. As a lowly chauffeur in defendant's employ he became in a trice the protagonist in a breath-bating drama with a denouement almost tragic. It appears that a man, whose identity it would be indelicate to divulge was feloniously relieved of his portable goods by two nondescript highwaymen in an alley near 26th Street and Third Avenue, Manhattan; they induced him to relinquish his possessions by a strong argument ad hominem couched in the convincing cant of the criminal and pressed at the point of a most persuasive pistol. Laden with their loot, but not thereby impeded, they took an abrupt departure and he, shuffling off the coil of that discretion which enmeshed him in the alley, quickly gave chase through 26th Street toward 2nd Avenue, whither they were resorting "with expedition swift as thought" for most obvious reasons.

Somewhere on that thoroughfare of escape they indulged in the stratagem of separation ostensibly to disconcert their pursuer and allay the ardor of his pursuit. He then centered on for capture the man with the pistol whom he saw board defendant's taxicab, which quickly veered south toward 25th Street on 2nd Avenue where he saw the chauffeur jump out while the cab, still in motion, continued toward 24th Street; after the chauffeur relieved himself of the cumbersome burden of his fare the latter also is said to have similarly departed from the cab before it reached 24th Street.

The chauffeur's story is substantially the same except that he states that his uninvited guest boarded the cab at 25th Street while it was at a standstill waiting for a less colorful fare; that his "passenger" immediately advised him "to stand not upon the order of his going but to go at once" and added finality to his command by an appropriate gesture with a pistol addressed to his sacroiliac. The chauffeur in reluctant acquiescence proceeded about fifteen feet, when his hair, like unto the quills of the fretful porcupine, was made to stand on end by the hue and cry of the man despoiled accompanied by a clamorous concourse of the law-abiding which paced him as he ran; the concatenation of "stop thief," to which the patter of persistent feet did maddingly beat time, rang in his ears as the pursuing posse all the while gained on the receding cab with its quarry therein contained.

The hold-up man sensing his insecurity suggested to the chauffeur that in the event there was the slightest lapse in obedience to his curt command that he, the chauffeur, would suffer the loss of his brains, a prospect as horrible to an humble chauffeur as it undoubtedly would be to one of the intelligentsia. The chauffeur apprehensive of certain dissolution from either Scylla, the pursuers, or Charybdis, the pursued, quickly threw his car out of first speed in which he was proceeding, pulled on the emergency, jammed on his brakes and, although he thinks the motor was still running, swung open the door to his left and jumped out of the car. He confesses that the only act that smacked of intelligence was that by which he jammed the brakes in order to throw off balance the hold-up man who was half-standing and half-sitting with his pistol menacingly poised.

Thus abandoning his car and passenger, the chauffeur sped toward 26th Street and then turned to look; he saw the cab proceeding south toward 24th Street where it mounted the sidewalk. The plaintiff-mother and her two infant children were there injured by the cab, which, at the time, appeared to be also minus its passenger who, it appears, was apprehended in the cellar of a local hospital where he was pointed out to a police officer by a remnant of the posse, hereinbefore mentioned.

He did not appear at the trial. The three aforesaid plaintiffs and the husband-father sue the defendant for damages predicating their respective causes of action upon the contention that the chauffeur was negligent in abandoning the cab under the aforesaid circumstances. Fortunately the injuries sustained were comparatively slight.

CHAPTER IX: BUMPS, THUMPS & LUMPS

Negligence has been variously defined but the common legal acceptation is the failure to exercise that care and caution which a reasonable and prudent person ordinarily would exercise under like conditions or circumstances. It has been most authoritatively held that "negligence held in the abstract, apart from things related, is surely not a tort, if indeed it is understandable at all." Cardozo, C.J., in Palsgraf v. Long Island Railroad Co. [citations omitted]. In Steinbrenner v. M. W. Forney Co. [citations omitted] it is said, "The test of actionable negligence is what reasonably prudent men would have done under the same circumstances"; Connell v. New York Central & Hudson River Railroad Co., [citation omitted] holds that actionable negligence must be predicated upon "a breach of duty to the plaintiff. Negligence is 'not absolute or intrinsic,' but 'is always relevant to some circumstances of time, place or person.'"

In slight paraphrase of the world's first bard it may be truly observed that the expedition of the chauffeur's violent love of his own security outran the pauser, reason, when he was suddenly confronted with an unusual emergency which "took his reason prisoner." The learned attorney for the plaintiffs concedes that the chauffeur acted in an emergency but claims a right to recovery upon the following proposition taken verbatim from his brief: "It is respectfully submitted that the value of the interests of the public at large to be immune from being injured by a dangerous instrumentality such as a car unattended while in motion is very superior to the right of a driver of a motor vehicle to abandon same while it is in motion even when acting under the belief that his life is in danger and by abandoning same he will save his life."

To hold thus under the facts adduced herein, would be tantamount to a repeal by implication of the primal law of nature written in indelible characters upon the fleshy tablets of a sentient creation by the Almighty Law-giver, "the supernal Judge who sits on high." There are those who stem the turbulent current for bubble fame, or who bridge the yawning chasm with a leap for the leap's sake or who "outstare the sternest eyes that look, outbrave the heart most daring on the earth, pluck the young suckling cubs from the she-bear, yea, mock the lion when he roars for prey"[1] to win a fair lady and these are the admiration of the generality of men; but they are made of sterner stuff than the ordinary man upon whom the law places no duty of emulation.

The law would indeed be fond if it imposed upon the ordinary man the obligation to so demean himself when suddenly confronted with danger, not of his creation, disregarding the likelihood that such a contingency may darken the intellect and palsy the will of the common legion of the earth, the fraternity of ordinary men, — whose acts or omissions under certain conditions or circumstances make the yardstick by which the law measures culpability or innocence, negligence or care. If a person is placed in a sudden peril from which death might ensue, the law does not impel another to the rescue of the person endangered nor does it condemn him for his unmoral failure to rescue when he can; this is in recognition of the immutable law written in frail flesh.

---

[1] [Ed. Note: From Shakespeare's "The Merchant of Venice."]

Returning to our chauffeur. If the philosophic Horatio and the martial companions of his watch were "distilled almost to jelly with the act of fear" when they beheld "in the dead vast and middle of the night" the disembodied spirit of Hamlet's father stalk majestically by "with a countenance more in sorrow than in anger" was not the chauffeur, though unacquainted with the example of these eminent men-at-arms, more amply justified in his fearsome reactions when he was more palpably confronted by a thing of flesh and blood bearing in its hand an engine of destruction which depended for its lethal purpose upon the quiver of a hair? When Macbeth was cross-examined by Macduff as to any reason he could advance for his sudden despatch of Duncan's grooms he said in plausible answer "Who can be wise, amazed, temperate and furious, loyal, and neutral, in a moment? No man". Macbeth did not by a "tricksy word" thereby stand justified as he criminally created the emergency from which he sought escape by indulgence in added felonies to divert suspicion to the innocent. However, his words may be wrested to the advantage of the defendant's chauffeur whose acts cannot be legally construed as the proximate cause of plaintiff's injuries, however regrettable, unless nature's first law is arbitrarily disregarded.

Plaintiff's attorney in his brief cites the cases of Grunfelder v. Brooklyn Heights Railroad Co. [citations omitted] and Savage v. Joseph H. Bauland Co., [citations omitted] as authorities for a contrary holding. Neither case is apposite in fact nor principle. In the classic case of Laidlaw v. Sage, [citations omitted], is found a statement of the law peculiarly apropos:

> "That the duties and responsibilities of a person confronted with such a danger are different and unlike those which follow his actions in performing the ordinary duties of life under other conditions is a well-established principle of law. * * * 'The law presumes that *an act or omission done or neglected under the influence of pressing danger was done or neglected involuntarily*.' It is there said that this rule seems to be founded upon the maxim that self-preservation is the first law of nature, and that, where it is a question whether one of two men shall suffer, each is justified in doing the best he can for himself". (Italics ours.)

Kolanka v. Erie Railroad Co., [citation omitted] says: "The law in this state does not hold one in an emergency to the exercise of that mature judgment required of him under circumstances where he has an opportunity for deliberate action. He is not required to exercise unerring judgment, which would be expected of him, were he not confronted with an emergency requiring prompt action". The circumstances provide the foil by which the act is brought into relief to determine whether it is or is not negligent. If under normal circumstances an act is done which might be considered negligent it does not follow as a corollary that a similar act is negligent if performed by a person acting under an emergency, not of his own making, in which he suddenly is faced with a patent danger with a moment left to adopt a means of extrication.

The chauffeur-the ordinary man in this case-acted in a split second in a most harrowing experience. To call him negligent would be to brand him a coward; the court does not do so in spite of what those swaggering heroes, "whose valor plucks dead lions by the beard," may bluster to the contrary. The court is loathe to see the plaintiffs go without recovery even though their damages were slight, but cannot hold the defendant liable upon the facts adduced at the trial. Motions, upon which decision was reserved, to dismiss the complaint are granted with exceptions to plaintiffs. Judgment for defendant against plaintiffs dismissing their complaint upon the merits. Ten days' stay and thirty days to make a case.

IN RE WALTER OF NEWCASTLE
Assize Court of Northumberland County
Northumberland Assize Rolls; 40 Henry III (1256)

ANONYMOUS, Judge
The jurors report that a number of persons got onto a certain boat laden with herrings and overloaded the aforesaid boat to such an extent that the boat sank; all got out of danger except for Walter of Newcastle, who drowned. No one is suspected in this incident. Verdict: misadventure. They also say that the boat in question belonged to a certain Flemish man who fled with his boat forthwith, before he could be attached; accordingly, there is nothing to decide about the boat.

IN RE UNKNOWNED DROWNED PERSON
Assize Court of Northumberland County
Northumberland Assize Roll; 40 Henry III (1256)

ANONYMOUS, Judge
A certain unknown person was found dead on the beach near Shoston. The first person to find him is present and is not suspected, nor is anyone else. The person drowned. Verdict: misadventure. The village of Shoston buried him without warrant; accordingly, it is to be fined.

SHIMER v. BANGOR GAS COMPANY
Supreme Court of Pennsylvania
410 Pa. 92; 188 A.2d 734 (1963)

MICHAEL A. MUSMANNO, J.

On August 11, 1961, Mrs. Donald Riley, living at 425 William Street in the borough of Pen Argyl, smelled gas, always an ominous sign because gas being an inflammable and explosive substance, is supposed at all times to be imprisoned within containers which prevent its odors from being released into the open air. She cautiously made an investigation in her house and found nothing which would explain the sinister symptom. The next morning at 6 o'clock she opened the door leading into the cellar and was struck by an even stronger emanation than the one she had smelled the night before. Hastily closing the door, she made an attempt to call the Bangor Gas Company, which supplied the gas for her house.

She was unable to reach anyone at the gas company offices until 8:30, at which time she reported the gas leak and urged that someone be sent to her place at once to check conditions. The operator, who took the report rather casually, suggested she call one or two other numbers. The person answering at one of the numbers given by the bored operator said with the same casualness Mrs. Riley had encountered at the gas company's office that he was not on duty but that she might call the second number given her by the gas company. The person answering at the second number said that this was indeed the home of a gas inspector, Edwards by name, but that he was not at home. Mrs. Riley related to this person at the second number the hovering menace in her dwelling, whereupon, with the same nonchalance which had characterized the languid girl at the gas company's switchboard and the uninterested person answering the first number, this person at the second number said that Edwards might be returning home for lunch, and if so, she would tell him that Mrs. Riley had called. In the meantime Mrs. Riley's home was filling with more detonating gas.

Eventually, at about 11:55 a.m., a man called Edwards appeared at Mrs. Riley's home and, in self-identification, called out that he was the "gas man." He entered into the kitchen, as he later testified, and smelled gas "right away." He descended into the unilluminated cellar, being careful, as he subsequently described the event, not to turn on the electric light switch because "there was too much gas," and even snapping the switch might create a spark which would ignite the explosive compound. Continuing his extreme vigilance and caution he went out to his truck to pick up a flashlight with which he could reconnoiter through the dark because a flashlight produces no flame, spark or scintilla which could cause an explosion. However, he discovered that he had failed to bring along a flashlight and so he returned to the house, this time entering through the cellar door.

He could not see his way around because of the wholly enveloping gloom. He reflected on the situation and then arrived at the conclusion that since he could not turn on the electric light because this might instantaneously precipitate an explosion, he would find his way around by lighting a match. And that is what he did.

> He was asked at the trial: "What happened when
> you lit the match?"
> His reply was "One awful boom."
> He got out of the hospital eight weeks later.

As the result of this "boom", the house of Harry V. Shimer, the plaintiff in this case, who lived next door at 427 William Street, was demolished. He brought suit in trespass against the Bangor Gas Company and the Kirk Construction Company, allegedly responsible for the gas leak. The jury returned a verdict against both defendants. The Kirk Construction Company appealed to this Court for judgment n.o.v., maintaining that the evidence did not establish that it was responsible for the leak and that, in any event, the act of Edwards in striking the catastrophic match was an intervening and superseding act which relieved the Kirk Company from liability for any resulting damages.

The Kirk Company, which had been engaged in installing a sewer system in Pen Argyl, was, on August 11, 1961, excavating ditches for sewer laterals in the 400 block of William Street. Sometime during that day, a Mrs. Knecht said to one of the Kirk employees that she smelled gas. The Kirk foreman informed her that what she was smelling was the newly turned earth. The next day, when the catalytic Edwards appeared on the scene, the ensuing eruption proved that her olfactory sense was more reliable than that of the Kirk foreman.

After the explosion, it was observed that the service line leading to the Shimer house had become separated from the gas main at the point of connection. What had caused this separation? The Bangor Gas company, which resisted in the court below the motion of the Kirk Construction Company for judgment n.o.v., and continues to resist it here, argues that the jury was justified in concluding that in excavating earth in front of the Shimer house, one of the machines being used by the Kirk Company damaged the gas line.

It was shown at the trial that at 10:55 a.m., on August 11, 1961, the gas pressure in Bangor's main had dropped from a normal of 7 1/2 to 8 inches to 6.8 inches and as low as 6.3 inches. This significant drop in pressure would be consistent with a break of the service line on William Street. The lower Court pointed out in its Opinion affirming the jury's verdict:

> "The service line pipe was bent at a point close to
> the main and 'in the locality of the arched posi-
> tion' was a 16 inch boulder. The earth in the
> immediate vicinity of the break was lighter in
> color than the surrounding earth which escaped
> from the break. The area of this burned ground
> would have been enlarged if the break had preex-
> isted for more than three days prior to the
> explosion."

The Kirk Company maintains that there is no direct evidence that it broke the gas line, arguing that the only evidence in this case is circumstantial. It has been demonstrated in myriads of cases that circumstantial evidence can be as revealing, under certain conditions, as the testimony of on-the-spot witnesses, especially when the concrete realities are not disputed. Irrefutable circumstances are like bricks, and, when they join, one with another, to form a solid wall of fact, inseparably wedded by the mortar of nature's laws and inevitable cause and effect, the resulting barrier excludes fanciful hypotheses, airy guesses and uncontrolled imaginings as to how a given event occurred.

The lowering of the gas pressure, the discoloration of the earth at the point of the excavation, the smell of gas in the immediate area, all coinciding in time, combined to form a formidable arrow of accusation which pierced and shattered the feeble shield of theory raised by the defendant Kirk. The jury was not only justified but was practically ordered by the law of physics to reach the conclusion at which it arrived, with regard to the responsibility of Kirk for the pipe breakage which filled the Riley and Shimer houses with potential explosion.

The Kirk Company then argues that, even if it did negligently tear the service line from the gas main, its act of negligence spent itself with that untoward happening and it was not responsible for the disaster which followed because of what the preoccupied Edwards did.

It argues that Edward's act was an intervening and superseding cause of negligence which "would insulate the negligence, if any, of Kirk Construction Company." Section 447 of the Restatement of Torts, declares:

> "The fact that an intervening act of a third person is negligent in itself or is done in a negligent manner does not make it a superseding cause of harm to another which the actor's negligent conduct is a substantial factor in bringing about, if:

> (a) the actor at the time of his negligent conduct should have realized that a third person might so act. . . "

The appellant argues that under this Section, it should not be held liable because it could not have realized that the gas company employee would light a match. But actionable foreseeability was not limited to the gas company employee striking a match. Others may have struck a match. There were many foreseeable acts which could equally have detonated the gas-charged atmosphere. The throwing of an electric switch before the thrower could have had time to note the presence of gas might have caused the same demolition which resulted from the act of the wool-gathering Edwards.

Once a tortfeasor releases a destructive agency, he is responsible for the damage which follows as long as that destructive force remains at loose and is uncurbed. A circus attendant who allows a tiger to escape from its cage into the streets may not plead non-liability if a passerby, in fright and panic, runs into the path of the tiger instead of seeking refuge in some building or other available shelter. . . .

Judgment affirmed.

CHRISTY BROS. CIRCUS v. TURNAGE
Court of Appeals of Georgia
38 Ga. App. 581; 144 S.E. 680 (1928)

ALEXANDER W. STEPHENS, J.

There may be a recovery of damages for mental suffering, humiliation, or embarrassment resulting from a physical injury of which they are inseparable components. . . Any unlawful touching of a person's body, although no actual physical hurt may ensue therefrom, yet, since it violates a personal right, constitutes a physical injury to that person. . . The unlawful touching need not be direct, but may be indirect, as by the precipitation upon the body of a person of any material substance. . .

Where a petition alleged that the plaintiff was an unmarried white lady, and that while in attendance as a guest of the defendant at a circus performance given by the defendant, and while seated in one of the seats provided by the defendant for the defendant's guests at the circus, a horse, which was going through a dancing performance immediately in front of where the plaintiff was sitting, was by the defendant's servant, who was riding upon the horse, caused to back towards the plaintiff, and while in this situation the horse evacuated his bowels into her lap, that this occurred in full view of many people, some of whom were the defendant's employees, and all of whom laughed at the occurrence, that as a result thereof the plaintiff was caused much embarrassment, mortification, and mental pain and suffering, to her damage in a certain amount, that the damage alleged was due entirely to the defendant's negligence and without any fault on the part of the plaintiff, the petition set out a cause of action and was good as against a general demurrer. . . .

The court, fairly to the defendant, submitted all the issues presented. The evidence authorized the inference that the plaintiff was damaged, by reason of humiliation and embarrassment, in the sum of $500, and the verdict found for her in that amount was authorized.

STOOPS v. MULHORN
Supreme Court of Pennsylvania
383 Pa. 132; 117 A.2d 733 (1955)

MICHAEL A. MUSMANNO, Justice.

The plaintiff in this case, E. Frank Stoops, wisely followed the sage counsel offered by traffic safety committees everywhere, namely, that in walking along a highway one should invariably face the oncoming traffic -- but he was hit just the same. The car came up on him from the rear.

On the night of November 28, 1952, Stoops visited a friend in North Vandergrift, whose home bordered on the left side of Route 66 as one faces Leechburg. He had parked his car at a service station on the right side of the highway (facing Leechburg) several hundred feet away from his friend's home. Thus, after the visit, it became necessary for him to return over this same Route 66 in order to reach the service station. As before stated, he prudently walked along the highway, facing traffic -- because a pedestrian can more quickly and adroitly avoid a car which he can see in front of him than one which comes up in his wake. Route 66 at this stretch of the road is 24 feet wide.

After travelling some distance in the direction of Leechburg (with North Vandergrift behind him), Stoops readied himself to cross the highway over to the right side where his car awaited him. He stopped and looked in both directions. Two cars were proceeding toward Leechburg on the right side of the highway and they moved by without mishap. Moving in that same direction, Stoops now prepared to move obliquely from the left edge of the road so that he could continue to keep under surveillance all traffic which might approach from Leechburg. He had taken only two short diagonal steps which carried him but three feet away from the left edge of the highway, still facing Leechburg, when a car coming from *North Vandergrift* struck him in the rear. Since Stoops was yet in the lane accommodating traffic *from* Leechburg, and this car was headed *toward* Leechburg, the inevitable conclusion was that the offending car was travelling on the wrong side of the road.

The motorist was Clarence Mulhorn, a policeman for the Township of Parks. The plaintiff sued him and the Township and recovered a verdict against both defendants in the sum of $30,000. The defendants filed motions for judgment n.o.v., which were refused in the Court held below, and this appeal followed.

The appellants urge reversal of the lower Court's action on the ground that Stoops committed contributory negligence. They assert that if the plaintiff had looked as he said he did, he could not fail to see Mulhorn's car. But the answer to this contention is that Stoops did look in both directions before committing himself to the highway, and as he walked he continued to look in the direction from which traffic would normally come -- in the lane in which he was advancing toward his objective. There would be no reason for him to look behind.

Even if the law imposed the cautionary standards of a Milquetoast which it does not, a pedestrian is not required to apprehend that a motorist may steal up on him from his postern side on the contrary half of the road. . .

Certainly no rule of common sense or fundamental fairness would saddle upon a pedestrian the responsibility of expecting a motorist to outrightly ignore the law of the Commonwealth. Driving on the wrong side of the road, if it so dominates facts and action as to precipitate injury, is an act which in itself constitutes negligence.

It is also to be noted particularly that at the time of the actual collision that plaintiff had not committed himself to the definitive movement of *crossing* the highway. He was still *left of the center of the road* and had not reached the point where to traverse the thoroughfare he might be required to turn right angularly to traffic moving from North Vandergrift, whence came the defendants' car.

There would be no justification under the decisions to hold Stoops culpable in contributory negligence as a proposition of law, and, as the record amply manifests, there would scarcely be any justification for the jury to find him guilty of contributory negligence on the facts. The negligence of Mulhorn cannot be doubted; he was driving on the wrong side of the road at such a velocity that his car hurled the plaintiff's body 25 feet, inflicting injuries which merited an award of $30,000 damages.

It is contended by the appellant Township of Parks that although the accident occurred during the time that Mulhorn was assigned to policy duties, his activities at the moment of the collision were without the scope of his employment. It appears that some time during the evening Mulhorn had purchased groceries and that he was on his way home to deliver them when he ran down Stoops. This circumstance would not absolve him employer from liability, for it is clear that Mulhorn was at the time still in the area of his patrolling jurisdiction and he had not arrived at the point where he would leave the highway in order to get onto the subsidiary road which led to his home, which was one mile off Route 66. . .

Judgment affirmed.

IN RE WILLIAM SPENDE
Assize Court of Northumberland County
Northumberland Assize Rolls; 7 Edward I (1279)

ANONYMOUS, Judge

William Spende was crushed by a certain wheel of a water-mill, so that he died therefrom. No one is suspected in this case. Verdict: misadventure. Value of the wheel: 12 pence, for which the sheriff is answerable. The village of Weetwood did not come to the inquest; accordingly, it is to be fined.

IN RE WILLIAM, SON OF WALTER DE ALDEBIR
Assize Court of Northumberland County
Northumberland Assize Rolls; 7 Edward I (1279)

ANONYMOUS, Judge.

William, son of Walter de Aldebir, intending to throw a stick at a rooster, did so in such a way that it accidentally struck a certain boy in the head, so that he died. The aforesaid William is not suspected in the aforesaid death; accordingly, he may return if he wishes.

GASH v. LAUTZENHEIZER
Supreme Court of Pennsylvania.
405 Pa. 312; 176 A.2d 90 (1961)

MICHAEL A. MUSMANNO, Justice.

On February 7, 1955, Eugene Gash, the plaintiff in this case, was driving his car, a 1953 Chevrolet, northwardly on Mosside Boulevard between Wilkinsburg and Monroeville when an accident occurred which resulted in his bringing suit in trespass against William A. Lautzenheizer, the defendant, the action resulting in a compulsory non-suit. He appealed.

The bizarre accident which produced the litigation evolved briefly as follows. Mosside Boulevard at the point of the untoward occurrence is about 18 feet wide and made up of "blacktop composition." The weather on the day of the unusual happening was cold but clear, the road not perceptibly icy except perhaps in some rare spots. Suddenly the plaintiff, Gash, beheld a car coming toward him on his own side of the road.

To avoid the obviously impending collision he cut abruptly to the right. He hit the berm which, because of deep frozen ruts, became an unpassable barrier. The continuing momentum of the car, finding no outlet forward, swung the rear end toward the left, sweeping in a clockwise direction. The car skidded across the road and then, hitting the left berm, it tilted, toppled and fell 15 feet into a gully at the bottom of the embankment. Through the gully ran a creek, the water carrying on its surface particles of ice.

At the end of his tumultuous journey Gash found himself lying on what he at first thought was the floor of the car but which turned out to be the inside of the roof, the car having completely capsized in this precipitous descent. Taking inventory of his situation, amid the broken glass and wreckage of his car, Gash concluded that despite the calamity he might have suffered he had sustained only an injury to his right leg. However, another possible calamity now obtruded. The car was wedged in the gully in such a fashion that neither door (it was a two-door car) could be opened and the creek was flowing through it, with its particles of ice.

CHAPTER IX: BUMPS, THUMPS & LUMPS

Gash could hear automobiles passing on the highway above, but despite his continued blowing of the horn of his car, he could attract no one to heed his plight. As his perilous state continued and augmented in gravity, something quite extraordinary happened. He felt a sudden jolt and his car spun around in the creek, releasing him from the imprisoning wreck and icy jailor. He looked to see what had occurred and found that another car had come to join him in the creek. It was because of this almost miraculous and certainly fortuitous visitation that possibly his life was saved, even though in the succoring process he sustained another injury, this time to his back.

As a result of this second injury he sued William A. Lautzenheizer, the man who, willingly or unwillingly, had provided the means for extricating Gash from the watery trap which might eventually have cost him his life. But we are here not concerned with the morals or ethics of the situation. We are passing only on the legal aspects of the strange event. Moreover, it is by no means fatefully written that the arrival of Lautzenheizer in his own way constituted a wholly Samaritan interposition. What turned out to be a providential rescue of the plaintiff could also have been his coup de grace because had Lautzenheizer's car struck Gash in some manner other than the way in which they met in the aqueous arena, Lautzenheizer's car could have done what so far the creek had not accomplished, that is to say, killed Gash.

It is certainly within the realm of possibility that Gash could have extricated himself from his dilemma without the intercession of Lautzenheizer, or he could have been rescued by others through less unorthodox methods.

Be that as it may, at the trial, after the plaintiff had related what we have abbreviatedly set out above, the Trial Judge entered a compulsory non-suit on the basis that the plaintiff's narrative did not offer a suitable premise upon which to base a charge of negligence against the defendant. The Trial Judge summed up the situation in the following pseudo-syllogism:

> "The plaintiff says: I was in the creek, I got there without any fault of my own. The defendant came into the same creek and hit me. I don't know how he got there or why but I want you to say that it was because of his fault. This amounts to a sort of Gertrude Stein, I was, I was not, I was, I was not. He was, He was, He was. Equals $10,000, please."

The literary allusion is interesting but the argument presented is erratic. The imagined soliloquy does not conform to the proved facts. The plaintiff not only said he was not at fault,--he proved he was not at fault. In considering the taking off of a non-suit we, of course, read the evidence in the light most favorable to the plaintiff. We, therefore, accept as undisputed, which asserted fact was in verity not denied, that Gash got into the gully through no fault of his own.

He had been traveling on his own right side of the road, a car aiming at his destruction loomed without warning ahead of him, and he swerved to avoid the potential destroyer. From that point on, the law of gravitation, the nature of the the terrain, and the geography of the locale all combined to take Gash into the bed of the creek which, as uncomfortable as it was, did provide him sanctuary from the aggressor on the road; and, under the circumstances, he had the right to occupy it undisturbed by the second aggressor.

If, instead of entering the creek, the plaintiff's car had come to rest, let us say, on the ample berm (10 to 15 feet wide) and Gash was thus entirely free of the traveled portion of the highway, and he had been struck by the defendant's car while there, the defendant would undoubtedly have had the legal duty to explain what he was doing off the highway.

Strange as it might sound, the plaintiff, again in the singular conditions related, had the right to be in the creek as much as a swimmer on a summer's day would have the right to be natatorially enjoying the creek. Certainly it could not be argued that if the plaintiff's car had stopped at the very edge of the embankment, with half of it hanging over the brink, that the defendant would have been entirely divorced of blame had he ploughed into it and sent it crashing into the chasm below.

Had the circumstances been reversed and had Gash been charged with impropriety in entering the creek and striking Lautzenheizer's car already in the creek, Gash could have exculpated himself from the charge of negligence by explaining that he was catapulted into the creek by the action of a motorist who forced him off the highway. The defendant here, however, offered no explanation of the grotesque condition of affairs which took him into an area where certainly normally, he had no right to be. Since his violent arrival in the creek inflicted injury on the plaintiff, the defendant incurred the obligation to explain why he departed from the roadway, and it would then be a question for the jury to determine if he also was without fault for his headlong leap into the glacial watercourse.

The defendant argues that he did not have any duty to show how he got into the creek because there were many possibilities that he got into the creek legitimately. That is true, but there would also be the reasonable inference he got into the creek illegimately, in which event, of course, he would be liable. Where there can be a reasonable inference that an unwitnessed accident could have been caused in a tortious manner, the jury is the tribunal to unscramble the facts and determine where liability rests, if at all.

In Smith v. Bell Telephone Co. of Pennsylvania, [citation omitted] this Court said:

> "We have said many times that the jury may not be
> permitted to reach its verdict merely on the basis
> of speculation or conjecture, but that there must
> be evidence upon which logically its conclusion
> may be based. . . .

"It is not necessary, under Pennsylvania law, that every fact or circumstance point unerringly to liability; it is enough that there be sufficient facts for the jury to say reasonably that the preponderance favors liability. The judge cannot say as a matter of law which are facts and which are not unless they are admitted or the evidence is inherently incredible."

It will be recalled that the Trial Judge conjured up an equation in which he said that "I was" and "I was not" equaled $10,000, but the Judge had no right, under the circumstances revealed, to dispose of the case on a fanciful equation. . .

If, merely being on the wrong side of a road, but still on the road, allows for the inference, *ipso facto,* of negligence, how much more so would that inference logically arise when the motorist is far from the road in a cornfield, in somebody else's front yard, or in a creek? . . .

Judgement reversed with a procedendo.[1]

THE NIOBE
United States District Court, S. D. Georgia
31 F. 164 (1887)

EMORY SPEER, J.

On the twenty-third day of March, 1886, a small sloop with a batteau bottom might have been seen beating her way up the Savannah river. It was March, and its conventional wind was blowing a pitiless gale from the northwestward, and the tide was pouring its turbid volume down the broad reaches of the Savannah, and, altogether, there was nothing in the weather which indicated that the sloop called the Pleasant Day should be out upon the waters, and yet there she was. She had, under the skillful pilotage of two mariners, threaded the sinuous and intricate waters that trend from Savannah to the neighboring port of Thunderbolt, or, more accurately, Warsaw.

When the Pleasant Day came abreast the Savannah, Florida & Western wharves, whether a gust of unusual violence blew down the river, or whether she sought instinctively her accustomed anchorage in the Bilbo canal, the evidence is silent; but certain it is that she "pulled for the shore," and made fast to the wharf. The weather-beaten crew without delay betook themselves to a neighboring house of entertainment, having first requested a lone fisherman, who, in despite of the severity of the weather, was angling from the wharf, to give an occasional eye to the Pleasant Day.

---

[1] [Ed. Note: See footnote to *Swartz v. Warwick Philadelphia Corporation*, supra.]

About that time the Norwegian bark Niobe, in charge of two tugs, one towing her with a hawser from her bow and the other made fast to her starboard side, came up the river against the same stress of wind and tide which had embarrassed the Pleasant Day. Further down the Niobe had been hailed by the harbor-master, Kennedy, and the pilot in charge directed by that official to put the bark on that particular spot of the mile and a half of wharf at which the Pleasant Day was peacefully lying. The Niobe accordingly was towed up the stream above that spot, the tug ahead cast off the hawser which held her against the stream, and the north-west wind, the downpouring tide, together with the impulse of the tug fastened alongside, swept the Niobe rapidly inshore. These preliminaries adjusted, it seemed to flash upon the Niobe's people that there was an inevitable collision ahead of them.

There was much shouting and "running to and fro" by the pilot and officers of the Niobe, and "Move that boat!" was the cry; but the shouting was directed at no one in particular. There was nobody to move her. The lone fisherman was engrossed with the finny inhabitants of the Savannah, — presumably at that moment had a bite; in any event, he was pre-occupied, or in reverie, and listened with a callous and indifferent ear to the outcry of the pilot and the Scandinavian objurgations hurled at him by the master and crew of the Niobe. The harbor-master came running up, but it was all too late. The Niobe dropped her anchor, but notwithstanding, swung in with full momentum against the little sloop, which disappeared under the water; and that was the end of the Pleasant Day.

The owner of the latter brings his libel to recover damages for her destruction. Undoubtedly, the crews of both the Pleasant Day and of the Niobe were guilty of negligence. It was in broad day; the Niobe had passed up the river in full view of the berth where the Pleasant Day was moored. It was the duty of the Niobe to see that the berth was clear. There in full view lay the sloop, apparently with no one on board. She was very perceptible. She was thirty feet in length; eight tons. The Niobe's people had no right to presume that she could be, or would be, instantly removed; they knew the consequence of a collision, and yet they cast off the hawser from the leading tug with the full knowledge and intention that the Niobe would swing in the berth. Then to shout and scream to "move the boat" was not enough (nor to drop the anchor) to relieve them from the consequences of their recklessness.

If the Pleasant Day crew had not been also at fault, I would give a much larger sum as damages, but they were also negligent. They left the sloop without any one in charge, which is contrary to the harbor regulations. The undertaking of the fisherman to watch her was a mere *nudum pactum* [bare promise], and carried with it no legal obligation. She was not lying where boats of her class properly belonged; but this does not give any right to a vessel entitled to that berth to crush into her, and sink her, when that result could be easily avoided.

What is the value of the Pleasant Day is a question difficult of determination. Her *disjecta membra* [scattered parts] were rescued from beneath the wave, but the Niobe had left her with a shattered constitution. Opinions as to her value vary pretty much anywhere from five hundred to fifty dollars, and one witness thought she would be dear at any price. The truth is, the Pleasant Day was not a very valuable craft. She had been moored for quite a while in the Bilbo canal, an artery which performs the same functions for the city of Savannah that the Cloaca Maxima did for ancient Rome,[1] and was as a consequence not so pleasant as her name imported. All the sails and rigging were saved. On the whole I award $150 to Wilson, the owner of the Pleasant Day, and decree that he pay half the costs.

LEDERHANDLER v. BOLOTINI
Supreme Court of Pennsylvania
402 Pa. 250; 167 A.2d 157 (1961)

MICHAEL A. MUSMANNO, Justice

Mrs. Yetta Lederhandler slipped on a piece of apple strudel, fell and broke her hip. She and her husband sued Harry Bolotini, doing business as Bolotini's Catering Service charging him with negligence in the manner he managed the dinner and reception where the accident occurred. The plaintiffs recovered a substantial verdict. The defendant moved for judgment n.o.v. and a new trial. The motions were refused, and from the judgment entered on the verdicts, the defendant appealed.

Reviewing the evidence in the most favorable light for the verdict winners, the following narrative emerges. On the evening of December 8, 1956, Yetta Lederhandler and her husband attended a dinner at the Overbrook Park Congregation Hall, 76th and Woodbine Avenue, Philadelphia, in honor of a Bar Mitzvah which had been celebrated that morning. The auditorium in which the dinner was served was laid with linoleum over a cement floor. At about 8 p.m., the guests, numbering some 200, sat down at tables accommodating from 4 to 12 persons each. For two hours the guests dined, the menu being ample and diversified enough to satisfy almost any appetite, namely, mixed fruit cocktail, olives, celery, nuts, mushrooms in patty shell, different kinds of fish, chopped liver, soup, roast turkey, cranberry sauce, a couple of vegetables, and hot apple strudel, topped off with baked alaska and demitasse. The food was carried to the tables by the waiters employed by the defendant catering firm.

At 10 p.m., the meal ended and some of the tables were moved to make room for dancing. During the dinner, fragments of food and trickles of beverage had spilled to the floor without any of the cater's staff making any effort to pick up or sweep away the liquids and articles underfoot.

---

[1] [Ed. Note: i.e., the function of municipal sewer.]

Harry Schur, one of the guests, noticed on the floor "a spot of wetness and debris," and he warned one of the waiters: "You better clear this up before an accident happens or someone slips." Helen Winokur, another guest, testified that after the dinner the floor was "pretty sloppy." The plaintiff testified that she saw food, water, and "some vegetables on the floor."

At about 11 p.m., Mrs. Lederhandler noticed a "puddle of water" located about 3-1/2 feet from the chair on which she was sitting next to her mother. By midnight this water had spread, and it was now touching the toes of her shoes. Seeking to avoid the mobile puddle, Mrs. Lederhandler thrust her feet under her chair, pushed backwards and stood up. As she did so, her feet came into contact with "something hard and slimy like," she slipped, fell heavily, and fractured bones which necessitated her being hospitalized and operated on.

One of the men who went to Mrs. Lederhandler's assistance after she fell observed a piece of mashed strudel at her feet. We are indebted to the learned Trial Judge in the Court below for a definition of strudel. He describes it as a "delicacy made from pastry dough, apples and raisins." After it has fallen from a certain height to the floor, is stepped upon, and churned over, it ceases to be a delicacy and turns into a potential menace for pedestrians or sitters unaware of its presence. Mrs. Lederhandler did not know of this strayed strudel lurking under her chair.

The defendant argues in this appeal that he cannot be held liable for the rambling strudel because it cannot be linked to any of his waiters. He says in his brief:

> "To find as a fact that it [the strudel] got there as a
> result of defendant's negligence one must resort
> to the use of an inference viz., strudel was served
> at the dinner, hence one of the waiters must have
> dropped a piece."

But the plaintiff's case is not based on the claim that a waiter dropped strudel. Her point is that, regardless of how the strudel crept under her chair or how the chair canopied the strudel, the defendant was at fault in not seeing the strudel and taking it away.

The defendant had at least two hours in which to do this because if the dinner terminated at 10 p.m., and no strudel was served after that hour, the particular strudel which is the central figure of this case had to be on the floor no later than that same 10 o'clock. There is no proof or even suggestion that a diner or stranger placed the offending strudel under Mrs. Lederhandler's chair just before the invading pool caused Mrs. Lederhandler to retreat from her stabilized position overlooking the dance floor and the general festivities of the evening.

The negligence attributed to the defendant is not that one of his waiters dropped strudel, but that after this particular strudel fell from the table or through one's slippery fingers or off an unanchoring fork, the defendant did not clean up the resulting mess when the strudel splashed to and over the floor.

As caterer of the evening, the defendant had charge not only of the dinner but of the premises. Thus, while he was not insurer of the safety of his invitees, he had "the affirmative duty of maintaining his premises in a reasonably safe condition for the contemplated use thereof and for the purpose for which the invitation was extended, or to give warning of any failure to maintain them in that condition."

The only real question in this case is whether the tortious strudel was on the floor a sufficient length of time to inform the caterer of its presence. As already indicated, since the dinner ended at 10 o;clock and the accident occurred at midnight, a period of two hours intervened during which a reasonable exercise of caution, care and a broom would have detected and expelled the threatening strudel.

The caterer, however, made no effort to clear the floor of strudel or any other one of the theretofore edible substances which had graced the table and now decorated the floor, impeding free and safe movement over it. . .

. . . Judgment affirmed.

DAVIS v. THE CENTRAL RAILROAD
Supreme Court of Georgia
60 Ga. 329 (1878)

LOGAN E. BLECKLEY, Judge.

[Plaintiff, Rebecca B. A. Davis, a minor, by her next friend, brought an action against the defendant railroad for $10,000 damages, alleged to have been sustained on account of a collision of two trains, upon one of which she was riding. In addition to other injuries sustained, she contended that she had been made permanently deaf and dumb. The defendant denied the allegations.

There was no dispute as to the collision having been caused by the negligence of the defendant. The controversy was as to the amount of damages to which plaintiff was entitled. At the time of the injury she was two months old. At the time of trial, she was deaf and dumb. Both her parents were deaf mutes. It was asserted, and evidence was introduced, that the train injury caused her condition. This was denied, and contrary evidence offered. Voluminous and conflicting expert testimony was introduced.

The jury awarded plaintiff $700. The plaintiff then moved for a new trial upon the grounds that the court erroneously gave the following jury instruction:

> "By our law, the parties litigant in a case are
> permitted to be witnesses. The interest of a party
> to a case affects his credit. But this does not mean
> that the jury should disbelieve a witness who is a
> party to, or interested in, a suit, but that to a certain

extent the witness is affected, and the jury are the
judges of his evidence as thus affected. Weigh
and compare it with all the testimony in the case,
and give to it the value which his relation to the
case satisfies the jury it ought to receive."]

. . . Strictly speaking, the court should not instruct the jury that the interest of a witness affects his credit. The better instruction is, that it *may* affect his credit. Interest and truth may go together. Is there, in the world, an honest man who does not know that he can tell the truth against his interest? Interest is felt as a temptation; but corruption reaches to an excess if, yielding to temptation, it succumbs on every occasion. We suppose it does not.

Where there is possible doubt as to the effect of villainy upon veracity, the jury ought to be left to decide it. As coming from the average of society, they know best what to think on such a question. Interest is a great rascal; but is not an absolute reprobate. Its doom is not perdition at all events. It has a chance of salvation. It is not obliged to commit perjury. Doubtless the court meant nothing to the contrary of this, the inaccuracy being merely verbal.

The jury were not misled.

The love of Justice! What a great love it is?

The verdict was warranted. It is satisfactory to this court, as it was to the court below. . .

Judgment affirmed.

LAYMAN v. DOERNTE
Supreme Court of Pennsylvania
405 Pa. 355; 175 A.2d 530 (1961)

MICHAEL A. MUSMANNO, Justice.

On June 17, 1957, Clement P. Layman, the plaintiff in this case, was seriously injured when the bus in which he was riding was struck in the rear by another bus. In the ensuing trespass action which he brought against the Doernte Bus Lines, owner of both buses, the jury returned a verdict in favor of the plaintiff in the sum of $25,000. The defendant seeks a new trial on the sole asserted ground that the verdict is excessive and should not be allowed to stand.

When bus No. 1, in which the plaintiff was a passenger, was struck by bus No. 2, the plaintiff was thrown with great force against the back of the seat which he occupied, his head coming into violent contact with the hand rail above the seat. This whiplash blow fractured the plaintiff's sixth and seventh vertebrae and, in consequence, he sustained disabilities and incurred ailments from which he had not recovered up to the time of the trial in October, 1960. . .

CHAPTER IX: BUMPS, THUMPS & LUMPS

The doctor found that the plaintiff had "two definite fractures or broken bones in two of the spinal processes." He recommended physiotherapy, a cervical collar, a cervical pillow, a brace for his back, muscle stimulation and home traction.

The plaintiff testified that he suffered from constant headaches. He described the symptoms: "You would swear your head was going to bust." He said further that his head "gets full of knots." When his wife was asked as to Layman's sleeping habits after the accident she replied: "Twisting and turning and groaning."

The doctor testified the plaintiff received physiotherapy 144 times; he saw him at his office about 175 times. Even after three years of medication and treatment, the plaintiff's prognosis was not a bright one:

> "I am of the opinion after having examined him and
> followed him not once or twice but for three (3)
> years, I am convinced in my opinion he will never
> get completely better. . . ."

The plaintiff's wife testified that her husband "seems to be getting what you call weaker." Also that "his condition is becoming progressively worse."

Dr. Pantalone said that the two fractures "have not hooked together":

> "the two pieces that are broken off the two verte-
> brae are still there in the muscles of the neck. If
> he doesn't get any better and tends to get worse,
> they will have to be removed because they are just
> like something that doesn't belong there * * * He
> has a lot of muscle turned into gristle. . . ."

The plaintiff's total out-of-pocket expenses up to the date of the trial amounted to some $2,100. If the operation is performed, the surgical bill will amount to $500, plus hospital bills, and then there will be the further expense for the therapy treatments. . . . The appellant's principal argument in support of the asserted excessiveness of the verdict rests on the fact that the plaintiff lost no time from his occupation because of his injuries.

It is true that the plaintiff did not remain away from his job the day after the accident and that he continued to be gainfully employed when work was available, but this, *ipso facto*, is not proof that he was not physically disabled. There are many reasons why a person would continue at his employment and still be suffering from the effects of severe trauma.

The plaintiff, at the time of the accident, was 51 years of age. He is married and has four children, two of whom (a son 23 years of age and another 16) live with him at home. The 23-year old son is a permanent cripple, whose total helplessness is reflected in the fact that he must be spoon-fed. The younger son attends school. When the plaintiff was asked why he went to work after the accident he replied: "Because I couldn't keep the family going not working."

One who has been injured as the result of a tortious deed, and is legally entitled to recovery for his injuries, should not be penalized because he works in pain, and toils in agony, in order not to suffer the great torment of seeing his family in want. . .

A benevolent employer may make allowances for a faithful employee and assign him to comparatively easy jobs so that the pay envelopes may, like an unbroken assembly line, continue to carry the necessities of life to the employee's family. Thus, if Layman received the same rate of wages after the accident as before, this was due to the generous attitude of the employer, which benevolence does not lessen the responsibility of the tortfeasor. One who is responsible for an accident is required to make the victim of that accident whole to the extent that money can accomplish this, regardless of the intervening philanthropy of third persons.

Twenty thousand dollars is not an excessive sum for the pain, suffering and inconvenience which the plaintiff has endured and to which he will continue to be subjected as the result of his injuries. Because of those injures he had to wear a cervical collar, one of those devices which gives to the wearer the rigidity and the possible appearance of a tribal chieftain wearing numerous iron necklaces. Aside from the pain and discomfort of such a contrivance, the wearer experiences the humiliating sensation of being in a pillory; he walks about in a mobile stock. There is the suggestion of a medieval felon.

Layman wore this apparatus, which he called a "dog collar", for a year--night and day, removing it only when he had to wash it because "the heat of your body would cause sweat, and it would run down the front of your shirt."

Even three years after the accident he still had to adopt the collar on occasion because, he said: "When you don't have the support, you sit down and your head just seems to want to fall down."

The plaintiff must also continue to use the "home traction," a device of pulleys, ropes, weights and chin cup described by the doctor as a contrivance which "goes and stops, goes and stops." The plaintiff is required to wear his brace every day; at night he must use the "cervical pillow," and he sleeps with a board beneath his mattress. When the weather changes, he experiences excruciating pains in the head and neck. . .

The plaintiff's pain is intense and constant, and his suffering is penetrating and severe. This type of hurt creates a disability of its own, which loses none of its compensatory scope because the sufferer, for reasons already stated, continues to be gainfully employed at the same wage paid him prior to his disablement.

The static nature of one's stipend may in this day of constantly increasing wages be evidence in itself of remunerational impairment. . .

The appellant has cited various cases in which asserted high verdicts were reduced by this Court and the Superior Court. The mere height of a verdict, however, is in itself no evidence of excessiveness because height is always a matter of relativity. Even the Empire State Building in New York is but a toadstool when placed against the image of Mt. Everest. Thus, the $25,000 verdict in this case must be placed against the mountain peaks of inflation, as well as the hills of the years the plaintiff must climb before he reaches the climacteric of life. A verdict of $25,000 of today is certainly not equivalent to a verdict of that sum twenty years ago, much less is it like a similar verdict of thirty and forty years ago...

Nostalgic and sweet as may be the memory of the American dollar of 1940, 1930, and 1920, the inexorable fact remains that *that* dollar has gone forever. It would require a search of sea-diving or archaeological intensity to find an article whose price has not doubled, tripled, or quadrupled during the last two or three decades. Hence, a comparison with verdicts of the past can only be meaningful if we assume in unrestrained fantasy that we can still purchase a five-cent ice cream cone, a five-cent hamburger, a five-cent shoe shine, a good five-cent cigar, a 35-cent haircut, a 15-cent shave, beef steak at 15 cents a pound, a good theatre seat for 50 cents, a seven-course dinner for a dollar, a pair of shoes for two dollars, and a 12-ounce glass of beer for a buffalo nickel, both buffalo and nickel having now, for practical purposes, almost disappeared...

In view of all these circumstances, the verdict of $25,000, instead of shocking the conscience of the court, convinces the Court that it is fair and reasonable and should be sustained.

The judgment is accordingly affirmed.

WEAVER v. WARD
Court of Common Pleas, Easter Term, 14 James
80 E.R. 284; Hob. 134 (1617)

ANONYMOUS, Judge

Weaver brought an action of trespass of assault and battery against Ward. The defendant pleaded, that he was amongst others by the commandment of the Lords of the Council a trained soldier in London, of the band of one Andrews captain; and so was the plaintiff, and that they were skirmishing with their musquets charged with powder for their exercise in *re militari*, against another captain and his band; and as they were so skirmishing, the defendant *casualiter & per infortunium & contra voluntatem suam* [by accident and by misadventure and against his will], in discharging of his piece did hurt and wound the plaintiff, which is the same, &c. *absque hoc*, [and by this], that he was guilty *aliter sive alio modo* [otherwise or in another way].

And upon demurrer by the plaintiff, judgment was given for him; for though it were agreed, that if men tilt or turney in the presence of the King, or if two masters of defence playing their prizes kill one another, that this shall be no felony; or if a lunatick kill a man, or the like, because felony must be done *animo felonico* [with felonious intent]: yet in trespass, which tends only to give damage according to hurt or loss, it is not so; and therefore if a lunatick hurt a man, he shall be answerable in trespass: and therefore no man shall be excused of a trepass (for this is the nature of an excuse, and not of a justification, *prout ei bene licuit* [that it was legally permissible for him]) except it may be judged utterly without his fault.

As if a man by force take my hand and strike you, or if here the defendant had said, that the plaintiff ran cross his piece when it was discharging, or had set forth the case with the circumstances, so as it had appeared to the Court that it had been inevitable, and that the defendant had committed no negligence to give occasion to the hurt.

HAUSHALTER v. WOODLAWN AND SOUTHERN MOTOR COACH COMPANY
Supreme Court of Pennsylvania
407 Pa. 65; 180 A.2d 10 (1962)

MICHAEL A. MUSMANNO, Justice.

The plaintiff in this case, Charles Haushalter, was struck by a bus belonging to the defendant, Woodlawn & Southern Motor Coach Company, and recovered a verdict of $26,000 for injuries sustained in the accident. The defendant moved for judgment n. o. v. The motion was refused and the defendant appealed.

The issue in this case was simply one of fact. Did the circumstances show that the driver of the involved bus was negligent in the manner he operated his bus which ran down the pedestrian? Was the plaintiff guilty of contributory negligence in the manner he started across a street? The jury answered the first question in the affirmative and the second in the negative. The record amply substantiates these findings.

It was 6:40 in the morning on January 15, 1953, when the plaintiff, a crane operator, walked across the Ambridge Bridge spanning the Ohio River and continued eastwardly on Eleventh Street, a continuation of the thoroughfare on the bridge. Close to the bridge, Ohioview Street, running north and south, intersects Eleventh Street. Haushalter proceeded to cross Ohioview Street at this point, but before doing so he looked to the left which would be north on Ohioview, he looked to his right which would be south on Ohioview and then, when he got to the center of Ohioview he paused and again looked to the right. At each of these viewings he saw no approaching vehicle. . .

The bus moved east on Eleventh Street after leaving the bridge and then began to make the turn north on to Ohioview. Here is where the collision occurred. At this point Ohioview is thirty feet wide. The plaintiff testified that he had traversed twenty-five feet of this width when he was struck from the rear with such force that he was thrown twenty-five feet north on Ohioview.

CHAPTER IX: BUMPS, THUMPS & LUMPS

The defendant company insists that the plaintiff walked himself out of court when, as he walked east on Eleventh Street he did not turn around to see what might be following him. Wide-angled, and miraculously so, as is one's vision, man is not equipped for direct rear viewing without turning his head in that direction. And for a pedestrian, in the middle of a street, to swivel his head toward the west while his feet are propelling him toward the east, is not a practice recommended for longevity. As this Court said in Bovell v. Dubrusky, "A person facing east cannot without periscopic assistance divine what is happening in the west."

The record reveals clearly that the accident would not have occurred had the bus driver been attentive to his responsibilities of looking ahead for pedestrians in his path of travel. . .

But the defendant argues that it is unfair to hold the bus company driver negligent for failing "to see an unlighted [sic!] pedestrian, wearing dark clothes against the dark background of an unlighted, dark surfaced street," and yet not hold the pedestrian negligent for failing to see a bus with its ample lighting. But there is this cogent difference in the requirements of the parties. A pedestrian is not directed by law to be illuminated, whereas the owner of a vehicle is obliged by statute to provide his vehicle with an adequate amount of incandescence as it travels through darkness.

The defendant quotes the familiar rule that "it is vain for a man to say that he looked and failed to see that which he must have seen had he looked." This is a good rule but it has no application here. Even if the plaintiff had seen the bus at the bridge portal he was not charged with the responsibility of knowing that the bus would turn into Ohioview. When the bus was stopped at the bridge it was facing the same direction in which the plaintiff was traveling. It was after the plaintiff committed himself to the crossing on Eleventh Street that the bus began making the turn from Eleventh into Ohioview, executing this maneuver entirely in the rear of the crane operator moving steadily ahead on his way to work. The Appellant urges that the plaintiff had the duty to turn around, but a pedestrian crossing a street, if he values his safety, must concentrate on watching where he is going and not looking back to study where he has been.

The appellant emphasizes that the bus was lighted, but this does not black out the all-controlling feature of the case, namely that the bus struck the plaintiff from the rear. What happens behind one's back when one is engaged in facing perils ahead can never be a ground for contributory negligence in law.

Judgment affirmed.

SPARKS v. THE EAST TENNESSEE,
VIRGINIA AND GEORGIA RAILWAY
Supreme Court of Georgia
82 Ga. 156; 8 S.E. 424 (1888)

LOGAN E. BLECKLEY, Chief Justice.

The action was by Sparks for a personal injury received whilst coupling cars. He was his own witness, and the evidence which he gave to the court and jury showed clearly that he had put himself under the orders of the conductor to work his way instead of paying fare as a passenger, and that without any express instructions from the conductor he took orders from a brakeman, and while engaged in the execution of these orders was injured.

He was a mere volunteer, and not in the service of the company. . . Moreover, his injury resulted, not from the negligence of the company or any of its employes, but from the unknown and unforeseen fact that the coupling was frozen in a way to prevent it from working freely. He testified that had not the coupling proved to be in that condition the injury would not have occurred. He knew the state of the weather, and had many years' experience as a railroad man, and it was as easy for him to anticipate the effect of frost upon the coupling as for the servants of the company to do so. He was a volunteer in the work he undertook and his failure to accomplish it successfully was due to accident.

He complains that the car to be attached was moved too rapidly, yet says that the speed was not unusual, and that he had formerly made couplings when it was three times as great. He complains also that no brakeman was on top to work the brake, yet he saw there was none before he exposed himself. He was unfortunate and is therefore entitled to sympathy, but the victim of a mere casualty has no cause of action. . . The court did not err in granting a nonsuit.

It is complained that the counsel was not fully heard in resistance to the motion for a nonsuit. As the decision of the court was correct beyond doubt or question, we cannot send the case back merely to have an unfinished argument concluded, unless we could know from the record how long or to what extent the counsel had been heard. We are not informed what length of time had been consumed, or at what precise stage of the discussion the counsel was obliged to suspend his remarks. . .

The order granting the nonsuit declares that argument had been heard. . . The bill of exceptions recites that "counsel for plaintiff proceeded to reply to the argument in favor of the nonsuit, but was, almost at the outset, interrupted by the court, who stated that it was unnecessary for counsel for plaintiff to take up the time of the court, as the court was 'dead-head' against him, and the court then passed the order." The interruption was not in the outset, but almost at the outset. . . How long did he speak, and how much longer should the court have listened? It seems to us that a very few minutes would have sufficed for saying all that could be said in support of so weak a case.

We know it is frequently the habit of counsel to make the speech long because the case is weak, yet we agree with the circuit judge in thinking it needless to do so. We really believe that the best and strongest argument that the present case admitted of on either side might have been brought to a conclusion "almost at the outset." That the judicial head was in the mortuary state described by its possessor was a necessary result of the evidence.

Judgment affirmed.

COLE v. LLOYD
Supreme Court of Pennsylvania
392 Pa. 33; 139 A.2d 641 (1958)

MICHAEL A. MUSMANNO, Justice.

Route 52 was covered with snow to a depth of from 6 to 8 inches as Harry S. Cole, on the afternoon of January 24, 1954, crossed the Delaware state line and moved northwardly into Chester County, Pennsylvania. His wife and 4-year old son occupied with him the front seat of his Chevrolet coupe. At a point in Pennsbury Township, the wheels of his car fell into ruts in the center of the road and beneath the surface of the snow. He attempted to get out of them by cutting his front wheels sharply to the right. The depth and the slipperiness of the sub-surface grooves were such that he could not reach his own lane of travel, so he proceeded forward, continuing all the time to escape the imprisoning ruts beneath, without ever succeeding in doing so.

Although he had originally been traveling at the rate of from 35 to 45 miles per hour, the frozen barriers reduced his speed considerably until at last he could only move at the rate of 5 miles per hour. While fighting the ruts and the snow, Cole saw a truck a quarter of a mile away, advancing toward him on its own side of the highway. As Cole inched forward in jerks and spurts, the truck, which was being driven by John H. Lloyd, approached unimpededly and without diminution in speed.

When the truck was about 150 feet away, Cole sounded his horn to emphasize what must have been quite apparent to the truck driver. During the time that the truck covered a quarter of a mile, Cole had progressed only one car length. The truck driver ignored the distress signal, ignored what his eyes must have told him, and ploughed ahead into the Chevrolet, hurling its three occupants into the snow and ice, inflicting certain injuries on all of them, which it is unnecessary to discuss here.

The Coles sued Lloyd and the Court below entered a non-suit. The Coles appealed. . . .It was the opinion of the Trial Court that Harry Cole and his wife were guilty of contributory negligence. The lower Court said of Margaret Cole:

"The plaintiff, Margaret E. Cole, knew that there were ruts made invisible by action of a snow plow and that the car had settled into and was proceeding along the same in the center of the road. She was aware of her husband's efforts to leave the course of the ruts and to get over to the proper side of the road and that he continued moving unsuccessfully in those efforts after she first saw the truck approaching on its proper side of the road, when she was 'about half way between the line and the bottom of the hill.' During the interval between her first view of the truck and the collision she made no objection to the continued forward movement of the car, nor request of her husband to stop the car. Therefore, she too, assumed the risk and tested the apparent danger of a collision without the remonstrance that a reasonably prudent person would have made. We are of opinion that she is precluded from recovery by her contributory negligence."

What the Court said was that the wife plaintiff was required, as a matter of law, to protest to her husband that, failing to do so, she was legally guilty of contributory negligence. But here we have a question of fact. The Jury could find in the particular circumstances of this case if there is one thing a wife should do when her husband is at the wheel is to do what Mrs. Cole did, and that is to remain silent.

The authority of a husband has undergone considerable shrinkage since Common Law days when he was accorded the respect and obeisance usually associated with that offered royalty. Married women's rights and the great freedom given and taken by children have made a householder something less than an absolute monarch. But the husband-father is still king at the wheel of his car. For a wife to criticise, order, and satirize her husband as he pilots the car in which she is a passenger; to issue ultimatums to him that if he does not desist his present course she will get out; to command him to stop so she may leave him is not only a rather poor way to increase family harmony but it may accentuate the difficulties the husband is already encountering and accelerate the very happening of the accident he is with might and main endeavoring to avoid. . . A wife passenger is not required to challenge a husband's control of a car when it is obvious to her that he knows, as well as she does, of an existing potential danger. . . .

Mrs. Cole knew that her husband was aware of the danger which confronted both of them. She knew that her husband was blowing the horn of his car and thereby seeking to prevent a collision. As was said in Azinger v. Pennsylvania R. Co., [citation omitted] "an interference on her part would not only have been useless but might have tended to increase the danger." . . .

CHAPTER IX: BUMPS, THUMPS & LUMPS

It would not be unreasonable for one to conclude that what Cole did was advisable under the circumstances. It was apparent to him that it was impossible to lift his wheels out of the icy grooves at the place where he then was. He had to decide whether to remain stationary, hoping that a St. Bernard dog, in the shape of a man or vehicle, might happen along to dig him out of the snow, or to proceed forward with caution, looking for a rutless stretch of highway where he could get over to the right side of the road. Whether he chose a course that evinced lack of due care was a question for the jury to decide under instructions from the Court. . .

According to Cole's testimony, Lloyd had a clear view for 150 feet of the situation in which Cole found himself. Cole also blew his horn to accentuate the evidence of his dilemma. It was a question for the jury to decide whether one in possession of his normal senses would not have seen Cole and have not concluded that unless Lloyd stopped or decelerated his approach a collision was inevitable since Cole was in such a position in the road that obviously Lloyd could not pass unimpededly. . .

Reversed with a *venire facias de novo* [cause to come again.]

CHAPTER X

SCURRILOUS, SCANDALOUS, ARBITRARY, CAPRICIOUS, WILLFUL, DELIBERATE, INTENTIONAL, MALICIOUS, OPPRESSIVE, OBSTINATE, DESPICABLE, OUTRAGEOUS, LOATHSOME, EGREGIOUS, AND REPREHENSIBLE TORTIOUS ACTS AND CONDUCT.

. . . may not a judicial wayfarer, travelling in the dry and dusty highways of the law, at spells lighten his labor without lowering the dignity of his case by gathering a nosegay for use as do other wayfarers, so long as he does not loiter afield and miss the main traveled road to ultimate justice? . . .

- Henry Lamm, J.[1]

---

[1] From *Stumpe v. Kopp*, 201 Mo. 419; 99 S.W. 1073 (1907).

CARVER v. PIERCE
Kings Bench, Michaelmas Term, 23 Charles I
82 E.R. 534; Sty. 66 (1648)

ANONYMOUS, Judge

Carver brings an action upon the case against Pierce for speaking these words of him, "Thou art a thief, for thou hast stollen my dung," and hath a verdict. The defendant moved in arrest of judgement, that the words were not actionable; for it is not certain whether the dung be a chattel, or part of the free-hold, and if so, it cannot be theft to take it, but a trespass, and then the action will not lye. Bacon Justice, Dung is a chattel, and may be stollen. But Roll Justice answered, Dung may be a chattel, and it may not be a chattel; for a heap of dung is a chattel, but if it be spread upon the land it is not, and said, the word thief here is actionable alone, and there are not subsequent words to mitigate the former words: for the stealing of dung is felony if it be a chattel. Bacon Justice said, It doth not appear in this case of what value the dung was, and how shall it then be known, whether it be felony or pety larceny? To this Roll answered, The words are scandalous notwithstanding and actionable, though the stealing of the dung be not felony...

DISON AND BESTNEY'S CASE
King's Bench, Easter Term, 8 James I
77 E.R. 1480; 13 Co.Rep. 71 (1611)

ANONYMOUS, Judge

Humphry Dison said of Nicholas Bestney, Utter Barrister and Counsellor of Gray's-Inn, "Thou a Barrister? Thou art no Barrister, thou art a Barretor; thou wert put from the bar, and thou darest not shew thyself there. Thou study law? Thou hast as much wit as a daw.[1]" Upon not guilty pleaded, the jury found for the plaintiff, and assessed damages to £23 upon which judgment was given; and in a writ of error in the Exchequer-chamber, the judgment was affirmed.

ANONYMOUS
King's Bench, Michaelmas Term, 15 Charles II
82 E.R. 1152; 1 KEB. 629 (1663)

ANONYMOUS, Judge

Of a justice of peace, that he is a logger-headed and a sloutch-headed bursen-bellied hound, is no cause of indictment before justices of peace in their sessions, partly for want of jurisdiction, partly because the words are not actionable: and after judgment, this was by Jones assigned for error. *Adjornatur* [it is adjourned].

---

[1] [Ed. Note: "daw" is short for "jackdaw," a bird resembling a crow; daw is itself a common word meaning "fool."]

IN RE KIRK
Supreme Court of New Jersey
101 N.J.L. 450; 130 A. 569 (1925)

JAMES F. MINTURN, J.

The observant traveler, leaving the dizzy cliffs of Manhattan, in his progress up the Rhine of America, will inevitably have obtruded upon his expectant vision the bold outlines of a precipitous cliff of basaltic rock of glacial origin, which Gibraltar-like projects its giant outlines into the rolling waters of the majestic Hudson, guarding as it were the erstwhile fancied entrance of the visionary pioneer to the fabulous wealth of the Indies.

Inquiry will elicit the information that this projection was intended by a natural prehistoric cataclysm to mark the gateway to the famous Palisades, and that stretched at its feet in bucolic simplicity are the remnants of the beautiful emerald slopes, termed by the primeval natives "awiehawk," and by the modern residents "Weehawken." Of these scenes the poet Fitz-Greene Halleck in ravishing transport wrote:

> *When life is old, and many a scene forgot,*
> *The heart will hold its memory of this.*

Upon these arboreal slopes, the traveler will be told, was enacted one of the greatest tragedies in American history, for there the scintillating Burr, in the days of the duel, took from human existence the erudite and heroic Hamilton, and to that extent sadly impoverished American public life.

Although a century of national existence has passed, no stately monument graces the site of that national tragedy, but, hidden away out of the vision of public observation, there has been erected by some public-spirited hand an attenuated inclosure that might be visualized as an adequate conception of Ibsen's "Doll House," which contains a miniature carving of what we are informed, in apologetic tones, is intended to serve as a bust of the lamented Hamilton. But, like all modern self-concentrated townships, this municipality shares the unique distinction, peculiar to the dress of modern modish femininity, that it possesses neither distinctive bodily lines, nor perceptible corporeal boundaries; so that the anxious traveler, intent upon seeking its historic landmarks, is unable without expert assistance to determine its terminus a quo or its terminus ad quem.

However, like all townships worthy of the name, it prides itself upon the possession of a town hall, which, like the Acropolis at Athens or the Forum at Rome, is the *Deus ex machina* [God from a machine] for all municipal lucubration, the fount of all public inspiration, and the Mecca of all political ambition. It also enjoys the spiritual distinction of the early church, in that it is built upon a rock, from which adamantine tenure neither the iconoclastic hand of time nor the progressive evolutionary arguments of municipal ambition have been able to dislodge it, but, enshrouded in an atmosphere of modern mysticism, retirement, and modesty, it stands, like the rock of ages, unmoved and immovable.

Upon stated evenings, amid the quietude of an environment which makes for serious reflection and dignified procedure, the business of the township was transacted without ostentation, and yet with becoming dignity, decorum and dispatch, until the memorable night of June 3, 1925, when in the quietude of their homes the confiding inhabitants were startled, astounded, humiliated, and shocked to learn that one of their honored representatives, in the solemn conclave of a public session, had been called a "bootlegger" and a "souphead."

Such a flagrant contempt of the dignity of the town and its representatives was properly met by a proceeding under section 3 of the Disorderly Act (2 Comp.St. 1910, p. 1927) against this defendant, and in due time he was found guilty before the recorder, and sentenced to imprisonment, which, however, like the sword of Damocles, is hanging over him while he behaves himself within the unobservable and indistinguishable limits of the township.

The defendant, upon this review, insists that, if there be such an offense as is charged against him, it was not committed in a public place. This contention is certainly unique, for, if any place be public, the hall erected by the public for the transaction of public business, like a public park, is peculiarly within that designation State v. Lynch [citation omitted].

But his strenuous contention is, and this connotes serious pause and no little bewilderment, that his utterances were terms of compliment and distinction, rather than offensive epithets, so as to be comprehended within the term "disorderly conduct." Thus it is argued that, while the bootlegger, like some of the early saints, may have had an unholy beginning, he has risen like the Phoenix, and stands to-day as the chivalric Bayard, *sans peur et sans réproche* [without fear and without reproach], the cynosure of every eye, and the hope of every heart, wherever liberty unrestrained possesses an admirer, and license unchallenged commands a champion. In various social circles, where bibulousness is ever the dominant thought, and the proverbial hip pocket is seldom a vacuity, is he not recognized like Robespierre as the saviour of popular liberty?

In financial and business circles, does he not command extensive credit, when the ordinary purveyor of dry goods receives scant accommodation? Does he not boast of his estates and acquisitions, when the ordinary laborer in the vineyard struggles like Sisyphus to maintain his never-decreasing burden? Does not the government, in recognition of his potentiality and prowess, spend princely sums to padlock him on land and suppress his activities upon the raging main? Like the publican, does he not often occupy a prominent pew in our temples of worship; and are not the faithful publicly exhorted to pray for his deliverance from the bondage and prosecutions of the merciless minions of the law? Surely, to quote Holy Writ, "By their fruits shall ye know them." But, with all its plausibility and force, this alluring picture of modern success and godliness presents another side. Reared above it all, like the condemning hand which consigned the Babylonian to disaster and oblivion,[1] is the handwriting of the Constitution and the law, which condemns this unique malefactor as a criminal, and consigns him to the same moral and legal category as the pirate and the outlaw.

No financial, social, or religions recognition can remove the brand of Cain from the brow, or place a heroic halo upon the head of one who stands as a common felon before the law. When, therefore, this defendant publicly charged a member of the council in a public place with being a bootlegger, he charged him in legal effect with being a criminal, and thereby subjected himself to the charge leveled against him in this compliant.

The mystical term "souphead," however, stands in another category, and awakens delectable memories of the early well-kept home, fast disappearing, like many other cherished American institutions, before the tinsel invasion of that birdlike roost, appropriately termed a flat. This euphonious appellation seems to have had a local application peculiar to the days when that attractive dish was made and consumed with relish and avidity, by the habitués of that ancient comfort station known as a barroom.

The libraries and lexicons of neighboring municipalities furnish no clue to its origin, doubtless due to the fact that, in those less-favored localities, the canned variety fulfilled the local needs. Nor are we in any wise assisted in this research by the erudite researches of learned counsel, possessed as they are with a large and varied experience in the sociological conditions of the past. The difficulty of classification and etymology is therefore quite manifest, and as in all such researches, when modern learning fails, recourse must be had to the ancient founds of inspiration. The antique genus "souphead" was doubtless the proud possessor of a mentality surcharged, among other things, with the diluted essence of succulent garden products, not radically indistinguishable from the modern vegetarian, whose dietary code has its genesis in soup as a fundamental substratum.

[The] *"Magnum caput"* [big head] of the luxurious Roman was possessed by a character *sui generis* [of his own kind, unique], a product of the rich Etruscan vineyards, not unlike the overstimulated graduate of the embossed barroom of later times, and subjected its possessor alternately to pity, ribaldry, and ridicule, but in no proper sense could this proud product of inebriety be classed as a "souphead."

When souphouses existed as a social safety valve, assuming the status in modern life occupied by the Toman "panem et circenses,"[2] the master mind controlling the institution might well be termed a "souphead." So, also, it may be accepted as a matter of judicial observation that, during the lightning-like rapidity with which some judges and lawyers alike, with equal rapidity betake themselves to the nearest boniface, and there discard everything edible for this attractive and toothsome decoction, as though to evince that in some esoteric manner the rapid

---

[1] [Ed Note: see Daniel 5:5ff.]

[2] [Ed Note: "bread and circuses": a phrase from the Roman poet Juvenal, Satires X. 81]

administration of the work typified by the blindfolded goddess is dependent upon the momentary acquisition and rapid ingestion of that ever ready and most inviting dietetic staple. If, therefore, we apply the legal maxim, "*noscitur a sociis*," [one is known by the company one keeps] to the situation, the "souphead" maintains respectable and satisfactory relationships in all the dignified walks of life, and proverbially one is known by the company he keeps.

In the light of these circumstances it will be quite universally conceded that the head which invented this popular gastronomic edible, like the genius who discovered the attraction of gravitation, or the rotundity of the earth, is entitled to the applause and gratitude, rather than the condemnation, of mankind. Obviously, therefore, the term cannot be deemed either undignified or offensive, and the defendant, whether conscious of his complimentary ebullition or not, cannot be adjudged guilty of disorderly conduct.

The conviction, however, must be sustained upon the ground first stated.

AYERS v. MORGAN
Supreme Court of Pennsylvania
397 Pa. 282; 154 A.2d 788 (1959)

MICHAEL A. MUSMANNO, Justice.

On April 20, 1948, the plaintiff in this case, Chester A. Ayers underwent, in the Wilkes-Barre General Hospital, an operation for a marginal jejunal ulcer. He was discharged from the hospital on May 4, 1948, but the operation did not afford him the relief he had anticipated. On the contrary, he experienced pains in his abdomen which continued for several years. On January 3, 1957, he returned to the hospital for a series of tests, hoping that science might discover the cause for his unceasing discomfort. It did. At the spot which seemed to him to be the fountainhead of his suffering and misery, there was found a foreign substance, that is, a sponge. It had been left there by the surgeon, Dr. Philip J. Morgan, who had performed the operation nine years before.

Ayers sued Dr. Morgan in trespass, charging him with negligence in that, having opened him up to remove an ulcer, he then sealed the aperture without first removing a metallic gauze sponge which had been used in the surgery. The defendant filed an answer denying the charge of negligence and then asked for judgment, raising the affirmative defense of the bar of the Statute of Limitations. . . The Court of Common Pleas of Luzerne County granted the motion and entered judgment for the defendant. The plaintiff appealed. . .

The only question we have before us is: Did Ayers wait too long to bring his action of malpractice against Dr. Morgan? The plaintiff contends that the Statute of Limitations could not take effect until it became a matter of knowledge to him that the surgeon had buried a sponge in his entrails. This he did not learn until January 3, 1957. Was the running of the statute, in view of the circumstances related, tolled until that date? The pertinent feature of the statute reads:

> ". . . Every suit hereafter brought to recover damages for injury wrongfully done to the person, in case where the injury does not result in death, must be brought within two years from the time when the injury was done and not afterwards ***"

This statute, as all statutes, of course, must be read in the light of reason and common sense. In its application to a given set of circumstances, it must not be made to produce something which the Legislature, as a reasonably-minded body, could never have intended. The Statutory Construction Act. . . states that in ascertaining the intention of the Legislature of the Courts may be guided by the presumption that:

> "The legislature does not intend a result that is absurd, impossible of execution, or unreasonable."

With so wholesomely logical and intelligent a standard of interpretation, it would be illogical and unintelligent to say that a person who does not know, and cannot know, for example, that a surgeon has negligently left a rubber tube in his body, would be denied damages because his claim for damages was filed, due to delay in learning of the presence of the tube, more than two years after the operation. . .

Thus, in the instant case, the negligence charged was not the use of a sponge but the failure to remove it at the proper time. Surgeons employ all manner of implements in performing their magic of restoring health and well-being to ailing humanity. Able, solicitous and ever-caring as nature is in rebuilding broken bones, restoring wrecked tissue, and rehabilitating flaccid muscles, the expert hand of the surgeon guides the restorative procedure and, in doing so, he often must use such things as nails, screws, sponges, metallic clips and rubber tubes. If he overlooks removing the nails, unscrewing the screws, taking out the clips, withdrawing the sponges and extracting the tubes, his negligence dates from the time the extraneous item was to have been removed and continues throughout the period he fails to perform his obvious duty. An operation is not completed until the surgeon takes away the tools with which he operates. . .

The plaintiff in the case at bar could hardly have launched his lawsuit on the day Dr. Morgan performed the operation because, at that time, no injury was yet inflicted. The injury became a reality when the sponge began to break down healthful tissue within the body of the plaintiff. . .

. . . a right of action accrues only when injury is sustained by the plaintiff, -- *not when the causes are set in motion which ultimately produce injury as a* consequence. Pollock v. Pittsburgh, Bessemer & Lake Erie R. Co. [citation omitted].

In another case, Scranton Gas & Water Co. v. Lackawanna Iron & Coal Co. [citation omitted], the [court] said:

> . . . The question in any given case is not, what did the plaintiff know of the injury done him? but, what might he have known, by the use of the means of information within his reach, with the vigilance which the law requires of him? * * * When knowledge is impossible, because of the laws of nature, or because of the actual fraud of the wrongdoer, the statute runs from the time of discovery.

Did the laws of nature prevent Ayers from ascertaining what was causing the pain in his abdomen? Certainly he could not open his abdomen like a door and look in; certainly he would need to have medical advice and counsel; certainly he would have to be dependent upon those who with appropriate instruments and devices could pierce the wall of flesh which hid from his own eyes the cause of his wretchedness. . .

The defendant says further that the "injury wrongfully done to the person" of the plaintiff occurred on April 20, 1948. He argues that "as soon as the plaintiff's incision had been sewn up, plaintiff had been injured as a result of the alleged negligence of the defendant." But it was not the sewing up of the incision which constituted the defendant's negligence; it was his taking off the gauze mask, putting away the rubber gloves, removing his white apron, and walking away, leaving a sponge in his patient's anatomy -- and not taking it out. That was the negligence.

A plumber who abandons a wrench or other sizable impediment in a water main, which three years later bursts because of the presence of that impediment, may not successfully argue that the person injured from the bursting may not bring a trespass action since two years passed since the wrench was forsaken. While the plumber's careless abandonment of the wrench was the original act which led to the eventual damage, it did not of itself cause the bursting. The accident was caused by the relinquishment of the wrench, plus the incrustation of rust, plus other changes wrought by the passage of time, plus the failure of the plumber to remove the wrench.

The man who buries a time bomb would argue futilely that he could not be held responsible for a resulting death because the explosion and death of his victim did not occur until more than a year after he had placed the bomb. . .

The defendant argues in his brief that there was no concealment on the part of the defendant, but what greater concealment could there be than hiding a foreign substance within the folds of a patient's intestines while he is asleep and not telling him of this malady-incubating cache for nine years? Of course, it is not contended by the plaintiff that Dr. Morgan purposely and fraudulently interred the sponge within living tissues, nor is it necessary that there be any proof to that effect. The charge against Dr. Morgan is negligence, which only rarely (so far as personal injury cases are concerned) encompasses criminality.

If, as Mr. Ayers charges in his complaint, Dr. Morgan deposited a sponge in his body and failed to remove it in therapeutically good time and, because of the nature of the concealment, the plaintiff was unable to learn of the hidden sponge until after the two year period had expired, he is entitled to proceed with his action.

The judgment of the Court below is reversed with a *venire facias de novo* [cause to come again].

DICKES v. FENNE
King's Bench, Michaelmas Term, 15 Charles II
82 E.R. 411; March, N.R. 60 (1640)

PER CURIAM (including ROLLS and BARCKLEY, JJ.):

In an action upon the case for words; the words were these: The defendant having communication with some of the customers of the plaintiff, who was a brewer, said, that he would give a peck of malt to his mare, and she should piss as good beer as Dickes doth brew. And that he laid *ad grave damnum* [to the extreme damage], &c. Porter for the defendant; that the words are not actionable of themselves, and because the plaintiff hath alleged no special damage, as loss of his custome, &c. the action will not lie. Rolls; that the words are actionable; and he said, that it had been adjudged here, that if one say of a brewer, that he brews naughty beer, without more saying, these words are actionable, without any special damage alledged. But the whole Court was against him (Crooke only absent) that the words of themselves, were not actionable, without alledging special damage; as the loss of his custome, &c. which is not here. And therefore not actionable. And Barckley said, that the words are only comparative, and altogether impossible also. And he said, that it had been adjudged, that where one says of a lawyer, that he had as much law as a monkey, that the words were not actionable; because he hath as much law, and more also. But if he had said, that he hath no more law than a monkey, those words were actionable. And it was adjourned.

HEAKE v. MOULTON
King's Bench, Trinity Term, 4 James
80 E.R. 61; Yelv. 90 (1606)

PER CURIAM (including FENNER, J.):

Thou art a common barretor, and deservest to be hanged: And, *per curiam* no action on these words: For the words (common barretor) are no slander;

for the offence is only made finable, and he is to be bound *de se bene gerendo* [for good behavior]; And to say that a man has broke the peace, or is a common rogue, or a common hunter of deer in parks, and a breaker of forests, are not actionable; for they are not slanders, but sound only in disgrace. The same law to say, J.S. would have killed me, is not actionable, because no act is done, but rests merely in conjecture; Otherwise to say, he did lie in wait to kill me; for the lying in wait is punishable, and a slander, as being an introduction to a more wicked intent. The same law to say, he prepared poison to kill J.S. although he never gave the poison, yet the very preparation is a slander. And for the other words (he deserveth to be hanged) they are too general and extravagant to ground an action upon them; because it is not shewn what act was done to deserve hanging: And, per Fenner justice, it was adjudged, that to say, thou art as very a thief as any is in Warwick gaol, will bear an action, with a particular averment that such a one by name at the time of the words was a thief in Warwick gaol; but, because the plaintiff in such case had alleged the averment of such a one who was not in the gaol for felony, but only as accessory to felony, for that reason there was entered *nil capiat per billam* [that he receive nothing by the bill].

MARRUCHI v. HARRIS
Supreme Court of South Africa,
Orange Free State, Provincial Division
[1943] S.A. 15

FRANCOIS PETRUS VAN DEN HEEVER, J.

In this action plaintiff claims £1,000 as damages in respect of defamatory statements about him, which he alleges defendant made and published. The declaration contains three counts. The first, as supplemented by further particulars, avers that between the 1st and the 7th of August, 1941, and in the Machine Shop of the South African Railways at Bloemfontein, defendant, speaking to and in the hearing of Georg Johann Cary Stoop and Johann Lambrecht du Plessis, used the following defamatory words concerning the plaintiff: "That Maccaroni Bastard is always in a hurry. He should have been in an internment camp long ago." The *innuendo* pleaded is that "Plaintiff was of illegitimate birth, that he, though employed by the South African Railways, was disloyal to the Government of the Union.... and that he was a danger to the country and the community and as such should be interned."

In the second count it is alleged that during the period from the 7th to the 14th of August, 1941, and at or near the defendant's office in the Brass shop of the South African Railways at Bloemfontein, defendant, speaking of plaintiff to and in the hearing of Andries Gerhardus Labuschagne, made and published the following words: "Die bastaardse Italianer rob die Goewernement." An *innuendo* is laid to the effect that "plaintiff was guilty of dishonest, dishonourable and fraudulent dealings and was of a despicable character in that he robbed and/or stole from the Government of the Union of South Africa and also from his employers, the South African Railways and Harbours."

In the third count it is alleged that, at the time and place stated in the first count, defendant published to Johann Lambrecht du Plessis the following defamatory words concerning the plaintiff: "What, that Italian Maccaroni Bastard! How can you call him your brother-in-law?" Plaintiff claims £500, £300 and £200 respectively on the three counts.

The defence is a denial that the words were uttered, that the words mean or could reasonably have been understood to mean what the *innuendos* aver and that they are incapable of bearing such meanings.

Plaintiff and defendant are both employed by the South African Railways; they are equal in *status* and emoluments, being chargemen or assistant foremen, each drawing £531 *per annum* plus remuneration for work done overtime.

Marruchi is of Italian stock. He was born in Northern Italy in 1887 where he qualified in a branch of engineering, viz., toolmaking. He came to this country in 1910 and was naturalised as a British subject in 1913. At the outbreak of the first world war he joined the South African forces and took part--in the Air Force--in the campaigns in East Africa and Egypt, winning the Distinguished Conduct Medal in 1917. He has a bent for invention; to the extent of about ninety per cent. of his working hours his time is spent in tooling for munitions work for the Government and he has contrived to reduce certain operations which formerly took 78 minutes to 15 minutes. His superior officer says that his loyalty is beyond question.

At the time when Italy overran Abyssinia plaintiff and defendant held opposite views on the wisdom or expediency of applying sanctions. When sanctions were withdrawn, plaintiff apparently adopted an attitude of "I told you so" towards defendant, which led to an argument and ultimately to a fight. The contestants were unevenly matched: Marruchi knew something about wrestling and applied his science to Harris, nearly strangling him. The latter retaliated by using his fists and knocking Marruchi down. The honours, I understand, were more or less even, with the result that relations between the two were strained or reserved. I mention this brawl to illustrate the spirit between the parties from then onwards.

Except in so far as it reflects upon the credibility of the parties, the origins of this clash are unimportant. Marruchi complains that defendant wanted to be more loyal than the King. He accused Harris of being a racialist and twitted him with the remark that he was not even English, since his mother was Dutch. According to Marruchi, Harris, who was vice-chairman of the Sons of England at the time, was angered by this taunt, which led to the fight.

According to defendant Marruchi adopted a provocative pro-Italian attitude, beating his chest and that "WE", i.e. the Italians, "will fight the whole bloody world"; that plaintiff then used filthy language concerning his mother, which led to the fight.

The truth, I think, lies somewhere in the middle, appreciably closer to Marruchi's version of what transpired than to Harris's relation of events. It is freely admitted that the litigants and their circle habitually use strong language, spiced with salacious terms subolent of the sewer. It is probable, therefore, that Marruchi applied an unseemly epithet to defendant's mother merely by force of habit. On the other hand it is probable that Marruchi's taunt about a Dutch admixture in Harris's blood was a contributory, if not the principal cause of the latter's anger. It is significant that Harris claims to be of Danish descent on his mother's side--she was a Weideman.

On the 7th August, 1941, the armed neutrality between the parties was terminated with explosive force, possibly due to an unfortunate misunderstanding. Marruchi was engaged in an experiment and urgently required some sal ammoniac. He came to Harris's department, but was told by defendant that the commodity he wanted was not stocked. After having been sent, as he thought, on a wild-goose chase, some sal ammoniac was produced from some coign in the shop. Plaintiff accused Harris of purposely and maliciously withholding the salt. Threats of violence were exchanged interposed with the usual pleasantries. Harris called Marruchi a sanguinary Dago and told him to get out in language in which a word signifying the sexual act was substituted for a verb of motion. Marruchi retorted with equal lack of restraint and exactitude, adding that Harris was an epithetised bastard, no white man, but bred between a bastard and a yellow belly. This exchange of civilities is important since plaintiff sought to use it, in the light of subsequent litigation between the parties, as a measure of damages and to prove the defamatory nature of the word "bastard".

Harris instituted action against Marruchi for slander claiming £1,000 damages. The words complained of in the summons in that case were "You lying bastard" and "You're a white Kaffir". This fact shows the futility of attaching too much weight to discrepancies and inconsistencies, seeing that Marruchi admits having on that occasion used more injurious language. Marruchi settled by paying £50 damages and £25 towards costs. On the same date the letter of demand initiating the present action was sent.

It was argued on behalf of defendant that this fact renders plaintiff's case in this action suspect. It is an aspect of the case which has to be considered; the long-standing feud between the parties may have induced Marruchi to take revenge for the round lost to Harris. I do not think, however, that he sought to gain this end by bringing a fictitious charge against Harris or that he managed to persuade others to join him in such a conspiracy.

The making and publication of the statements complained of have therefore been proved. It becomes necessary then to consider whether the *innuendos* have been established. The *innuendo* on the first count is set out to be, in the first instance, that plaintiff was of illegitimate birth. Now, of course, that is the primary meaning of the word "bastard". I think, however, that I must take cognisance of the King's English not as something static and immutable but as a medium of expression constantly subject to change. In South Africa, at least, the word "bastard" to denote illegitimacy, is somewhat archaic. Most people, like Labuschagne, are persuaded that the word signifies a halfbreed.

In abstracto a word has no meaning; it conveys a meaning only when used in a certain society in which a convention exists as to its connotation. In the Rehoboth Gebied, for example, "Bastard" is an appellation which burghers apply to themselves with pride. Dewberry stated in evidence--and it was freely admitted by others--that in the Railway workshops the word "bastard" is frequently used as a term of endearment. Du Plessis and Stoop did not at first attach the meaning set out in the *innuendo* to the expression; it is clear from their evidence that they did so as an after thought--perhaps when better instructed as to its meaning.

Then it was argued that Harris himself nailed the meaning of the word by suing for damages in respect of its use in relation to him. The circumstances were entirely different, however, since in that instance Marruchi admittedly paraphrased the expression, stating in lieu of an *innuendo* that Harris was bred between a bastard and a yellow belly. In all the circumstances I have come to the conclusion that the expression "bastard" was used to convey, and was understood to mean, nothing in particular. It was meaningless abuse adopted for the explosive sound of the word rather than for any other reason.

An attempt was made to distinguish between meanings of the word when used in anger or otherwise. To my mind this contention carries no weight.

There remains the statement that Maccaroni should have been in an internment camp long ago. Du Plessis states that he understood the phrase in relation to Marruchi's war work in the Railway workshop. It conveyed to him that Marruchi, an Italian, an "Uitlander", in such a position was dangerous to the country and the Government and should not be trusted. As a consequence of the statement he thought less of Marruchi and doubted his loyalty. Stoop understood the phrase to convey that in regard to our country and Government Marruchi was an undesirable and disloyal in his work; or, as he said in cross-examination, because we were at war with Italy and that in his work Marruchi was disloyal. . .

In the case of an individual our law certainly does protect the imponderable goods of life. The detractor is made to pay composition not only for the mental hurt suffered by the person maligned but for the reactions of the slander upon the latter's co-citizens. It is undoubtedly defamatory to say of an individual that he suffers from a contagious disease as the law considers that the effect would be that the person slandered would be avoided by his fellow citizens. The law therefore protects such amenities of life as the individual's enjoyment of the society and comfort of his kind.

There will be judgment for plaintiff in the amount of £80 with costs.

RICHARDSON v. ROBERTS
Supreme Court of Georgia
23 Ga. 215 (1857)

JOSEPH H. LUMPKIN, J.

[Plaintiff, Mary Jane Roberts, filed a suit for slander against defendant, William Richardson, alleging that the defendant had accused her of fornication with one Nathaniel Griggs, by speaking the following false, scandalous, malicious and defamatory words about her:

> "John Barnes would have married Mary Jane Rob-
> erts, if it had not been for me, I prevented him; her
> child was Nathaniel Griggs'."

Plaintiff alleged that by speaking these words, defendant intended to charge and accuse plaintiff of illicit intercourse and fornication with Nathaniel Griggs, and of having a bastard child by him.

Another count alleged that defendant spoke the following other words about plaintiff, "that the said Nathaniel Griggs was keeping her, unmarried, for his own purposes," meaning that the plaintiff had been, and was guilty of fornication with the said Griggs. The jury awarded the plaintiff, $400.00 damages. Defendant moved for a new trial, contending that the damage award was excessive.]

. . . As to the excessiveness of the damages, they are small at best; much too small if the charge be false. And Courts can feel but little sympathy for a *man* who will go about through a neighborhood prating about such matters. It is bad enough in women. But women will talk, for God has made them so. It is *unmanly* in a man thus to tattle, and suppose it be true, that this woman was seduced by her step-father, under the advantages which he possessed for that purpose, the compassionate SAVIOUR of the world, who said to one taken in adultery, "go and sin no more," would have covered her fault with the mantle of his silence. Let his erring, fallible creatures imitate his divine example, otherwise they need not resort to this tribunal to get relief from the just penalty of their own unpitying persecutions.

Judgment affirmed.

TRICOLI v. CENTALANZA
Supreme Court of New Jersey
100 N.J.L. 231; 126 A. 214 (1924)

JAMES F. MINTURN, J.

"Run away, Maestro Juan, I am going to kill you." Such was the ferocious threat that disturbed the atmosphere, not of prehistoric Mexico, where upon desolate plains the savage coyote still bays at the moon, nor yet of classic Verona, where dramatic memories of the houses of Montague and Capulet still linger to entrance the romantic wayfarer, but from the undiluted atmosphere of Bloomfield avenue, where it winds its attractive course through the prim rococo shades of modern Montclair, which upon the day of succeeding Christmas in 1923 sat like Roman immortals upon its seven hills, and from its throne of beauty contemplated with serene satisfaction the peace and tranquility of the modern world.

The Maestro, however, with true chivalric disdain, refused to retreat, but determined at all hazards, like Horatius, to hold the bridge, or rather the stoop, upon which he stood. Like a true Roman, inoculated with the maximum percentage of American patriotism, he turned defiantly to the oncoming house of Centalanza, and proclaimed in the bellicose language of the day, "You too son of a gun."

In the days of the Montague and Capulet, aristocratic rapiers and swords defended the honor of their respective houses; but in this day of popular progress the Maestro and the Centalanza sought only the plebian defense of fists and a shovel. As a result of a triangular contest, the physician testified that the Maestro was battered "from head to buttocks" — a distribution of punishment, it may be observed, which, while it may not be entirely aesthetic in its selection of a locum tenens, was to say the least equitably administered and distributed. Indeed, so much was the Maestro battered that his daily toil lost him for 12 days, and the trial court estimated that this loss, together with his pain and suffering, and the aggravation of the trespass, entitled him to receive from the house of Centalanza $210.

The latter, however, has appealed, and alleges that the Maestro proved no substantial cause of action against them. But the learned trial court, upon this contested state of facts, concluded, and we think properly, that there was an issue of fact thus presented, since the suit was for assault and battery in the nature of trespass *vi et armis* [with force and arms]. But the defendants Centalanza insist that two distinct encounters took place, one by both defendants, and the other by one only, and they ask: How can such a physical contretemps be admeasured, so as to impose upon each member of the house of Centalanza his fair share of compensation for his physical contribution to the melee? The inquiry possesses its latent difficulties, but, since it is an admitted rule of law that the court will not distribute the damages between tort-feasors, upon any theory of equitable admeasurement, the house of Centalanza obviously must bear the entire loss, without seeking a partition thereof. *Ex turpi causa oritur non actio.* [An action does not arise from a base (illegal or immoral) consideration.] [citation omitted].

Indeed, it would prove to be a rare feat of judicial acumen, were the court to attempt to give due credit to Donato Centalanza for the prowess he displayed in his fistic endeavors, and to assess to Raffale Centalanza his meed of financial contribution for the dexterity with which he wielded his handy implement of excavation. In it doubtful, even in these days of the mystic prize ring, whether such a metaphysical test may be included among the accredited mental accomplishments of a quasi militant judiciary, which, while it occasionally indulges in a caustic punch, still strenuously endeavors to maintain the proverbial respectability and regal poise of its ancestral prototype. In such a situation we are not inclined to impose this extraordinary and novel field of jurisdiction upon our inferior courts. The occurrence of trespass *vi et armis* confers upon the trial court the right to assess exemplary damages as smart money, and this the trial court properly did under the circumstances of the case. [citation omitted]

It is contended, however, that the actual damage sustained by the Maestro was inconsequential, and that the rule, *De minimis non curat lex*, [the law is not concerned with trifles] applies. It must be obvious, however, that damage which to the attending physician seemed to penetrate the Maestro "from head to buttocks" may seem trivial to us as noncombatants, but to the Maestro it manifestly seemed otherwise, and doubtless punctured his corpus, as well as his sensibilities. Indeed, he well might declare in the language of the gallant Mercutio of Verona, concerning the extent of his wound: "It is not as wide as a church door, or as deep as a well, but 'twill serve."

The judgment will be affirmed.

PIERCE v. HICKS
Supreme Court of Georgia
34 Ga. 259 (1866)

IVERSON L. HARRIS, J.

[In January 1860, the defendant kept a retail liquor shop in the town of Irwinton. The plaintiff had been drinking there one day, and late in the afternoon, being drunk got into a quarrel in the shop, with a Dr. Hudson. He cursed, was noisy, and had a small knife open in his hand. The defendant, saying it was his duty to keep order in his house, spoke to the plaintiff kindly, and told him he must stop his fuss or leave the house. The plaintiff refused to go out, and a bystander, taking hold of him, pulled him out, and tried to keep him from going back. He did return, however, and with his knife drawn and raised in his hand, advanced towards defendant, in the house, threatening to cut him. When he was just inside of the door, and still advancing, defendant struck him with a stick, giving him a severe injury over the eye, and knocking him down, or, at least, making him stagger back. Defendant was sober, and was larger and more powerful than the plaintiff.

The plaintiff sued the defendant for battery. The jury found for the defendant. The plaintiff then moved for a new trial on the grounds that the court erroneously, charged the jury that the dwelling house and business house of every citizen was his castle; that no person, after leaving such house upon request, or being, after request to leave, ejected, had any right to re-enter unless armed with legal authority, and he does so at his own risk; and that if defendant's house was a licensed grocery, the law put him upon the same footing with other citizens in controlling his house. Plaintiff's motion for a new trial was denied.]

It is related in a biographical sketch of the celebrated Lord Ellenborough--when simply Mr. Law--that during the trial of Warren Hastings, Mr. Sheridan, one of the managers conducting the impeachment, in the fervor of his speech, said: "That the treasures of the Zenana of the Begum was an offering laid by the hand of piety upon the altar of the saint." Mr. Law, in a sarcastic tone, inquired "How the Begum could be considered a saint, and how the camels, the better part of her treasures, were to be laid on an altar." Mr. Sheridan replied, "That it was the first time in his life that he had ever heard of special pleading on a metaphor, or a bill of indictment against a trope."

Has not our brother DeGraffenreid--whose chief ground of complaint against the charge of Judge Reese, is, that he submitted to the jury as law that defendant's shop was "his castle," and as such its inviolability--done precisely what the distinguished lawyer mentioned did,--make war on a metaphor?

I am fully sensible how very difficult it is for a gentleman of refined literary cultivation, by any effort of the will, to bring his senses into such subjection to an abstraction, an ideality, so as to regard a shop redolent with the perfume of corn whisky--*quo semel est imbuta recens servabit odorem "casa" diu* [Once it has been imbued with this odor, a house will retain it for a long time]--as a royal or baronial castle--a fortress, like the proud keep of Windsor, rising in the majesty of proportion, and girt with the double belt of its kindred and coeval towers--an awful structure, defended by power, and overseeing and guarding a subjected land.

He must strip this shop of its accessories, and learn to contemplate it not in the concrete.

How, otherwise, could the patriot scholar glow with enthusiasm when he listened to the vehement and boldly figurative illustration, by Lord Chatham, of that undoubted maxim of the English law, "That every man's house is his castle"- "The poorest man may in his cottage bid defiance to all the forces of the crown. It may be frail--its roof may shake--the wind may blow through it--the storm may enter, but the king of England can not enter! All his force dares not cross the threshold of the ruined tenement."

Can a principle be less law because it is enunciated in such splendid declamation?

It enforces, not in the stolid and jejune style of many of the venerated common law writers, (worthy of immortality in a Dunciad) but in burning eloquence, the sacredness and inviolability of home--the uncontrollable dominion of the tenant of the cabin, alike with that of the lord of the castle.

We will not elaborate this idea further.

The record furnishes us with the testimony of an uncontradicted witness, who says, that after plaintiff had been mildly rebuked by defendant for his disorderly conduct, plaintiff arose very much offended, cursing and threatening, and advanced with a small drawn knife upon defendant, as if intending to cut him. Defendant gave back. In such a case, is there any principle of law which required the defendant to flee from his own house--to wait until the plaintiff had struck with his knife, before attempting to disable him? We think not. Even on the public square, or in the street, the defendant would have been justified, under the provisions of our penal code, in doing what he did.

The defendant, moreover, was bound by the requirements of statute to keep an orderly shop, and was liable to prosecution for a failure. Does not this requirement sanction the use of all means that are proper, and not excessive, to accomplish so salutary an end? The plaintiff, upon the testimony in the case, was not entitled to damages.

Let the judgment be affirmed.

MORGANROTH v. WHITALL
Court of Appeals of Michigan
161 Mich. App. 785; 411 N.W. 2d 859 (1987)

DAVID H. SAWYER, Judge.

"Truth is a torch that gleams through the fog
without dispelling it."
Claude Helvetius, *De l'Esprit.*

In this heated dispute, the trial court granted summary disposition in favor of defendants on plaintiff's claims of libel and invasion of privacy by false light. Plaintiff now appeals and we affirm.

Plaintiff alleges that she was libeled and cast in a false light by an article written by defendant Whitall which appeared in the Sunday supplement of the Detroit News on November 11, 1984. The article was entitled "Hot Locks: Let Shila burn you a new 'do." The article was accompanied by two photographs, one depicting plaintiff performing her craft on a customer identified as "Barbara X" and the second showing Barbara X and her dog, identified as "Harry X," following completion of the hairdressing. Central to the article was the fact that plaintiff used a blowtorch in her hairdressing endeavors. According to the article, plaintiff's blowtorch technique was dubbed "Shi-lit" and was copyrighted.[1]

---

[1] Sic. While this is not an intellectual property case, we note in passing that it would seem more reasonable that the blowtorch technique would be subject to patent law and the term "Shi-lit" would constitute a trademark, rather than coming under the terms of copyright law. However, we leave it to a more appropriate forum to decide this burning issue if it should ever become relevant.

The article also described two dogs, Harry and Snowball, the latter belonging to plaintiff, noting that the canines have had their respective coats colored at least in part. The article also indicated that the blowtorch technique had been applied to both dogs. Additionally, the article described plaintiff's somewhat unusual style of dress, including a silver holster for her blowtorch and a barrette in her hair fashioned out of a $100 bill. Much of the article devoted itself to plaintiff's comments concerning her hairdressing and the trend of what, at least in the past, had been deemed unusual in the area of hair styles.

Plaintiff's rather brief complaint alleges that the article, when read as a whole, is false, misleading and constitutes libel. More specifically, the complaint alleges that the article used the terms "blowtorch lady," "blowtorch technique" and the statement that plaintiff "is dressed for blowtorching duty in a slashed-to-there white jumpsuit" without any factual basis and as the result of defendants' intentional conduct to distort and sensationalize the facts obtained in the interview. The complaint further alleges that the article falsely portrayed plaintiff as an animal hairdresser, again as part of a deliberate action by defendants to distort and sensationalize the facts. In her brief on appeal, plaintiff also takes exception to her being cast as an animal hairdresser and claims as inaccurate the portrayal in the article that she does "mutt Mohawks for dogs" and the reference to "two canines who have been blowtorched." . . .

The elements of defamation were stated by this Court in *Sawabini v. Desenberg,* [citation omitted]:

> The elements of a cause of action for defamation are: "(a) a false and defamatory statement concerning plaintiff; (b) an unprivileged publication to a third party; (c) fault amounting at least to negligence on the part of the publisher; and (d) either actionability of the statement irrespective of special harm (defamation *per se*) or the existence of special harm caused by the publication (defamation *per quod*)". . . .

The *Sawabini* court further commented on the appropriateness of dismissing a defamation claim by summary disposition:

> The court may determine, as a matter of law, whether the words in question, alleged by plaintiff to be defamatory, are capable of defamatory meaning. . . .

In determining whether an article is libelous, it is necessary to read the article as a whole and fairly and reasonably construe it in determining whether a portion of the article is libelous in character. . . .

CHAPTER X: SCURRILOUS, MALICIOUS, DESPICABLE CONDUCT

Reading the article as a whole, we believe that it is substantially true; therefore plaintiff's complaint lacks an essential element of her defamation claim, namely falsity. In looking at plaintiff's specific allegations of falsity, for the most part we find no falsehood. Considering as a group the various references to plaintiff's using a "blowtorch" in hairstyling, we note that *The Random House College Dictionary*, Revised Edition (1984), defines "blowtorch" as follows:

> [A] small portable apparatus that gives an ex-
> tremely hot gasoline flame intensified by air
> under pressure, used esp. in metalworking.

In looking at the photographic exhibits filed by defendants, we believe that the instrument used by plaintiff in her profession can accurately be described as a blowtorch.[2] Accordingly, while the use of the term "blowtorch" as an adjective in connection with references to plaintiff or her hairdressing technique may have been colorful, it was not necessarily inaccurate and certainly not libelous. As for the reference that plaintiff was "dressed for blowtorching duty in a slashed-to-there white jumpsuit," we have examined the photographic exhibits submitted by defendant at the motion hearing and we conclude that reasonable minds could not differ in reaching the conclusion that plaintiff did, in fact, wear a jumpsuit "slashed-to-there."

Finally, while having disposed of the allegedly libelous claims contained in the complaint, we briefly turn to the additional allegations of false statement listed in plaintiff's brief on appeal. In her brief, plaintiff claims that defendants inaccurately described her as being a hairdresser for dogs, giving dogs a Mohawk cut, and using a blowtorch on the dogs. While it appears that plaintiff did do hairdressing on dogs, it is not necessarily certain at this point that she did, in fact, use the blowtorch on the dogs. . . .

Moreover, inasmuch as it appears undisputed that plaintiff at least dyed the fur of the dogs, which would constitute hairdressing of dogs, we are not persuaded that the article, when read as a whole, becomes libelous because of an inaccurate reference to using the blowtorch on the dogs. This is particularly true since, by plaintiff's conduct, she asserts that blowtorching is a safe practice when performed on humans. Therefore, it would appear that, from plaintiff's perspective, blowtorching would also be safe on dogs, even if she did not engage in such a practice. Furthermore, her claim that she was libeled by labelling her as both a dog hairdresser and a human hairdresser is unsupported in light of the tinting of the dogs' hair. Since the undisputed factual showing indicates that plaintiff did blowtorch her human clientele and style her pooch's fur, we will not split hairs at

---

[2] We acknowledge that *The Random House Dictionary's* definition did not list hairdressing as an example. However, we are not persuaded that the dictionary's editors intended their examples to be exclusive. See also "blowtorch," *Webster's New World Dictionary* 2nd College Edition, (1976).

this point to conclude that the statement that she used her blowtorch on dogs, even if inaccurate, is libelous.

For the above-stated reasons, we conclude that, when reviewing the article and accompanying photographs as a whole, the article was not libelous.

On appeal, plaintiff also argues that the article invaded her privacy by casting her in a false light. . . .False light invasion of privacy is described in *Ledl v. Quik Pik Stores*, [citation omitted] as:

> "[p]ublicity which places plaintiff in a false light in
> the public eye". . . .

In discussing what is necessary to state a cause of action for invasion of privacy, this court stated in Reed v. Ponton [citation omitted]:

> "When there has been no misappropriated use of, or
> physical intrusion into, the private life, employ-
> ment, property, name, likeness, or other personal
> place or interest, so that the privacy action is
> premised solely upon a disclosure of secret or
> confidential matter or upon being put *publicly* in
> a "false light", then if (without deciding) mere
> words of mouth can never be actionable (except
> by a slander action) the oral communication must
> be broadcast to the public in general or publicized
> to a large number of people.'" . . .

As indicated in the above discussion under the theory of defamation, with the exception of certain references to hairdressing dogs, none of the conduct attributed to plaintiff in the article was false. Therefore, it could not place plaintiff in a false light. With reference to the assertions concerning her hairdressing of dogs, we do not believe that a rational trier of fact could conclude that, even if inaccurate, those references are unreasonable or put plaintiff in a position of receiving highly objectionable publicity.

The article did not indicate that plaintiff harmed, injured or inflicted pain upon the dogs. Rather, at most, the article inaccurately stated that plaintiff used techniques on the dogs, such as blowtorching, which she also used on humans. While the article may have overstated the techniques that she uses on dogs, inasmuch as she advocates those techniques for use on humans, we cannot conclude that plaintiff would believe it highly objectionable that those techniques also be performed on dogs.

Similarly, she cannot have been placed in false light as being both the hairdresser of dogs and humans inasmuch as the tinting of the canines' fur would constitute hairdressing. Thus, it would not be placing plaintiff in a false light to indicate that she served both dog and man. Accordingly, we believe that summary disposition was also properly granted on the false light claim.

In summary, although the manner in which the present article was written may have singed plaintiff's desire for obtaining favorable coverage of her unique hairdressing methods, we cannot subscribe to the view that it was libelous. We believe that the trial court aptly summarized this case when it stated that "this Court is of the Opinion that the Plaintiff sought publicity and got it." Indeed, it would appear that the root of plaintiff's dissatisfaction with defendants' article is that the publicity plaintiff received was not exactly the publicity she had in mind. While the publicity may have been inflammatory from plaintiff's vantage point, we do not believe it was libelous. At most, defendants treated the article more lightheartedly than plaintiff either anticipated or hoped. While this may give plaintiff cause to cancel her subscription to the *Detroit News*, it does not give her cause to complain in court.

Affirmed. Costs to defendants.

BOLAY v. BINDEBERE
Court of the Bishop of Ely at Littleport
reprinted in 4 Selden Society 133 (1321)

ANONYMOUS, Judge
Littleport. Court there on Wednesday next after the feast of S. Luke in the fifteenth year of King Edward the Second.

It is found by inquest that Rohese Bindebere called Ralph Bolay thief and he called her whore. Therefore both in mercy. And for that trespass done to the said Ralph exceeds the trespass done to the said Rohese, as has been found, therefore it is considered that the said Ralph do recover from the said Rohese 12d. for his taxed damages.

DAVID FREDERICK'S INC. v. MCNALLY
Court of Appeals of Georgia
168 Ga. App.503; 308 S.E. 2d 635 (1983)

MARION T. POPE, Judge.
Appellee William J. McNally brought this action against appellants David Frederick's Inc. d/b/a Brenda Allen's and Sam's Style Shops, and Connie Barefield, alleging malicious prosecution and false imprisonment and seeking actual and punitive damages. The trial court directed a verdict in favor of appellants as to the false imprisonment claim; on the remaining claim, the jury returned a verdict in favor of appellee in the amount of $5,500 actual damages and $75,000 punitive damages. Appellants' five enumerations of error challenge adverse rulings by the trial court on their motions for directed verdict, judgment n.o.v. and new trial.

To paraphrase from former Chief Justice Bleckley's opinion in *Wells v. Mayor &c. of Savannah*, [citation omitted] some cases task the anxious diligence of this court not by their difficulty but by their simplicity. The case at bar is one of these. Because the case seemed too plain for controversy, we have had some apprehension that we might decide it incorrectly. Impressed by the ability and learning, the wide research and earnest advocacy of the distinguished counsel for appellants, we have experienced a vague dread that we might stumble over legal obstacles which, if they exist, a treacherous darkness conceals.

We have examined the enumerations of error thoroughly, read authorities cited and not cited, deliberated, meditated, considered and reconsidered. As the result of all this, we have found nothing debatable in the issues presented for resolution here, fringed though they certainly are with technical niceties of great delicacy and much interest. To which side the artificial logic of these niceties would incline the scale is immaterial, for the issues presented attack only the sufficiency of the evidence to support the verdict; thus, we must apply the "any evidence" test in reviewing appellants' enumerations. . .

. . . As noted by appellants throughout their brief, the evidence of record was in sharp conflict as to appellee's claim of malicious prosecution. Appellee presented evidence in support of his contentions and appellants presented evidence in support of theirs. Appellee's testimony, if believed by the jury, authorized the verdict in his favor. . . Accordingly, appellants' motions for directed verdict, judgment n.o.v. and new trial were properly overruled by the trial court.

Judgment affirmed.

FRANK v. NATIONAL BROADCASTING CO., INC.
New York Supreme Court, Appellate Division
119 A.D.2d 252; 506 N.Y.S.2d 869 (1986)

SYBIL HART KOOPER, Justice.

We have occasion today to address the issue of when humor or jest at the expense of an identifiable private person becomes defamation. It is an issue that since the turn of the century has arisen but rarely in New York's Appellate Courts, and never at all with respect to the medium of television. . .

The facts, which are not disputed, are fairly simple. The plaintiff, Maurice Frank, a resident of Westchester County, is described in his amended complaint as being "engaged in business as an accountant, tax consultant and financial planner". The defendants Richard Ebersol and Lorne Michaels are the producers of the late night television comedy program "Saturday Night Live". Saturday Night Live (hereinafter SNL) is broadcast weekly throughout New York and the United States by the defendant National Broadcasting Company, Inc. (hereinafter NBC).

CHAPTER X: SCURRILOUS, MALICIOUS, DESPICABLE CONDUCT

The plaintiff's complaint concerns an SNL broadcast initially aired nationwide on April 14, 1984, the day before the general deadline for the filing of 1983 income tax returns. The program that evening included a segment known as the "Saturday Night News", the name of which implies a parody of standard, televised news broadcasts. It is a skit contained within the "Saturday Night News" which is the subject of the instant defamation suit.

The plaintiff refers to the objectionable skit as the "Fast Frank Feature". In the skit a performer was introduced to the audience as a tax consultant with the same name as the plaintiff, Maurice Frank. The performer allegedly bore a "noticeable physical resemblance" to the plaintiff. This character then gave purported tax advice which the plaintiff described in his complaint as "ludicrously inappropriate". Specifically, the complaint recites the following monologue as defamatory:

> "Thank you. Hello. Look at your calendar. It's April 14th. Your taxes are due tomorrow. You could wind up with your assets in a sling. So listen closely. Here are some write-offs you probably aren't familiar with--courtesy of 'Fast Frank'. Got a houseplant? A *Ficus*, a *Coleus*, a Boston Fern--doesn't matter. If you love it and take care of it--claim it as a dependent.

> "Got a horrible acne? ... use a lotta Clearasil ... that's an Oil-Depletion Allowance. You say your wife won't sleep with you? You got withholding tax coming back. If she walks out on you--you *lose* a dependent. *But* ... it's a home improvement--write it off.

> " Should you happen, while filling out your tax form, to get a paper cut--thank your lucky stars--that's a medical expense *and* a disability. Got a rotten tomato in your fridge? Frost ruined your crops--that's a farm loss. Your tree gets Dutch Elm Disease ... Sick leave--take a deduction. Did you take a trip to the bathroom tonight? If you *took* a trip ... and you did *business*--you can write if off. Wait, there's more. Did you cry at 'Terms of Endearment?' That's a *moving* expense. A urologist who's married to another urologist can file a joint return.

> "Got a piece of popcorn stuck between your teeth? ... Or a sister who drools on her shoes? ... You got money comin' back-- and I can get it for your *fast*, because I'm Fast Frank. Call me. I have hundreds of trained relatives waiting to take your call. At Fast Frank's, we guarantee your *refund* will be greater than what you *earned* ..."

In June 1984, the plaintiff's attorney wrote to the defendant Ebersol requesting both a public apology and compensation. It appears, however, that only a private, written apology was offered. Thereafter, in August 1984, the April 14, 1984 SNL program, including the "Fast Frank Feature", was rebroadcast nationwide.

The plaintiff commenced the instant action in November 1984 and served an amended complaint in March 1985. The first two causes of action in his amended complaint sought damages for defamation as a result of the two broadcasts of the "Fast Frank Feature". As the alleged defamation was broadcast by television, it is therefore classified as a libel. . .

In reviewing defamation cases, it is the principal duty of the courts to reconcile the individual's interest in guarding his good name with cherished First Amendment considerations. This balancing of interests is evident in the requirement that "actual malice" must be demonstrated before a public official can recover damages in defamation, a stringent standard necessitated by the "profound national commitment" to "uninhibited, robust and wide-open" debate upon public issues. . . In some instances, the protection of the First Amendment approaches the absolute: for example, the expression of one's opinion, no matter how pernicious, distasteful or unpopular it may be, is not actionable on the theory that defamation requires falsity, and in this country "there is no such thing as a false idea". . .

The terms "humor and comedy" are not and cannot be synonymous with the term "opinion". As forms of expression, humor and comedy have never been held to be entitled to absolute or categorical First Amendment protection. . . Indeed, the danger implicit in affording blanket protection to humor or comedy should be obvious, for surely one's reputation can be as effectively and thoroughly destroyed with ridicule as by any false statement of fact. "The principle is clear that a person shall not be allowed to murder another's reputation in jest". . .

But it is equally clear that not every humorous article, comedic routine or antic performance will subject its author or performer to liability for defamation. As Judge Learned Hand once observed, "[i]t is indeed not true that all ridicule * * * or all disagreeable comment * * * is actionable; a man must be not too thin-skinned or a self-important prig". . . Frequently too, courts, including those of this State, have requested claims of damages for defamation where the allegedly defamatory statements were patently humorous, devoid of serious meaning or intent and impossible of being reasonably understood otherwise.

The principal factors distinguishing humorous remarks that are defamatory from those that are not appear to be whether the statements were intended to injure as well as amuse and whether they give rise to an impression that they are true. This is the standard that was established in New York in *Triggs v. Sun Printing & Publishing Assn.* [citation omitted]. There, the defendant published a series of newspaper articles concerning the plaintiff, a professor at the University of Chicago. In each of the articles, the plaintiff was portrayed as egotistical in the extreme, a man who believed, among other things, that his own brand of colloquial language and slang would be a vast improvement upon Shakespeare.

CHAPTER X: SCURRILOUS, MALICIOUS, DESPICABLE CONDUCT

The articles also cast aspersion on Triggs' patriotism; told how he had taken "a year of solemn consultation" before naming his new son; and referred to Triggs as "the god", who was "born great, discovered himself early and has a just appreciation of the value of this discovery". With thinly veiled contempt, the articles closed, stating that it had been one of the pleasures of life to introduce people to the "shrine" of the plaintiff, a "true museum piece". . . [The Court in *Triggs* held, *inter alia*, as follows]:

> We are of the opinion that one assaulting the reputation or business of another in a public newspaper cannot justify it upon the ground that it was a mere jest, unless it is perfectly manifest from the language employed that it could in no respect be regarded as an attack upon the reputation or business of the persons to whom it related.

How laughter-provoking statements are viewed will depend in large part upon the context in which they are delivered. A recent case in California involved the well known television personality and comedian Robin Williams. A stand-up comedic routine performed by Mr. Williams at a San Francisco night club was recorded, and the video and audio tapes were thereafter distributed. A video tape of the performance was also carried over the Home Box Office cable television channel. Part of Williams' routine concerned wines, and, in one version, ran as follows:

> "There are White wines, there are Red wines, but why are there no Black wines like: REGE A MOTHERFUCKER? It goes with fish, meat, any damn thing it wants to (comment from a member of the audience) * * * Thank you Lumpy * * * Isn't it nice, though having someone like Mean Joe Green advertising it--You better buy this or I'll nail your ass to a tree" (*Polygram Records v. Superior Court* [citation omitted]).

A suit seeking damages for personal defamation, among other things, was thereafter brought by a Mr. David H. Rege, the distributor of "Rege" wines from his San Francisco store, Rege Cellars. The California court examined the statements using a standard similar to our own, to wit, if the offensive words were "not fairly susceptible of a defamatory meaning," the action should be dismissed. . .

In that case, there was an additional question, not present here, of whether Mr. Williams had intended to refer to Mr. Rege's product. In dismissing the action, the court relied upon the fact that the statements were unquestionably uttered as part of a comedy routine, and could not be interpreted in any other way.

Williams's descriptions of "Rege wine" were "obvious figments of a comic imagination impossible for any sensible person to take seriously"... The court noted that the audience "knew [Williams] as a comedian, not a wine connoisseur"...

In the instant case, it can also be asserted without hesitation that no person of any sense could take the so-called tax advice of "Fast Frank" seriously. If anything, the statements here are even more plainly the obvious figments of a comic imagination. A wine might possibly be made dark enough to look black. It might also taste bad, and unquestionably persons who might be regarded as ruffians can and do advertise many products. Income taxes, on the other hand, and persons connected with their collection and even preparation, have been a fertile source of the comic imagination since their adoption.

No person who has ever had the dubious pleasure of filling out a 1040 Federal tax form would, in his most extravagant fantasies, believe that he could claim his favorite Boston Fern as a dependent. No person exists who is so gullible as to believe that his acne medication entitles him to an oil-depletion allowance or that the departure of a spouse from the marital premises--however welcome-- may be listed as a deductible "home improvement". Moreover, just as it is inconceivable that anyone hearing Robin Williams's monologue would thereafter avoid Mr. Rege's wines in the belief that they were possessed of an unnatural wine color, or had other peculiar qualities, no one who saw the "Fast Frank Feature" could believe that the plaintiff was inclined to prepare income tax returns claiming paper cuts as medical expenses.

The contested statements here were so extremely nonsensical and silly that there is no possibility that any person hearing them could take them seriously. Neither were the statements themselves so malicious or vituperative that they would cause a person hearing them to hold the plaintiff in "public contempt, ridicule, aversion or disgrace"... We believe that the lunacy of the statements themselves, presented as they were as a small comic part of a larger and obviously comic entertainment program, coupled with the fact that they were neither a malicious nor vicious personal attack, requires a finding that they were not defamatory as a matter of law. Rather, this case involves just that sort of humor which is "of a personal kind that begets laughter and leaves no sting," and it thus cannot form the basis of a lawsuit...

Certainly, this is an area in which cases will stand or fall on their own peculiar facts. We hold today that in certain situation and under some circumstances the authors of humorous language will be insulated from liability in defamation cases even where the comic attempt pokes fun at an identifiable individual. The line will be crossed, however, when humor is used in an attempt to disguise an intent to injure; at that point a jest no longer merits protection, because it ceases to be a jest. As was the case in *Triggs (supra),* the defense of humor will not immunize the authors of a malicious or abusive attack upon a plaintiff's character or reputation. In this case, no such malice or abuse can be found in a comic dialogue that offers a *Coleus* as a tax-deductible dependent...

Order affirmed.

CHAPTER X: SCURRILOUS, MALICIOUS, DESPICABLE CONDUCT

KING v. BURRIS
United States District Court, D. Colorado
588 F. Supp. 1152 (1984)

JOHN L. KANE, JR., District Judge.

If I were capable of complete judicial restraint, I would begin this opinion by stating that this is an action for damages based upon allegations of intentional infliction of severe emotional distress and defamation. Then I would say that the matter is before me on the defendants' motion for summary judgment. I would summarize the doctrines governing summary judgment and make due obeisance to the unshakable precept that to grant summary judgment there may not exist any genuine issue of material fact. Then, to show I know where it is I am about, I would recount that I must resolve all doubts in favor of the nonmoving party before deciding whether an actionable claim is set forth.

But this is not just a case about damages; this case is about baseball! Even the Supreme Court of the United States cannot restrain itself when confronted with mankind's noblest achievements on "Hoboken's Elysian Fields."[1] I think it too much to expect a mere tyro on the district bench to cleave to the issues in the face of that august example.

For almost a century, baseball has been America's national pastime. From Babe Ruth's "called shot" to Carlton Fisk's twelfth inning home run to win the sixth game of the 1975 World Series, baseball has sparked the imaginations of generations of Americans. Though changes have occurred which make grown men cry, its essence remains unchanged.[2] Baseball is uniquely unconstrained by

---

[1] *See Flood v. Kuhn,* U.S. 258, 92 S.Ct. 2099, 32 L.Ed.2d 728 (1972), where Justice Blackmun wrote:

It is a century and a quarter since the New York Nine defeated the Knickerbockers 23 to 1 on Hoboken's Elysian Fields June 19, 1846, with Alexander Jay Cartwright as the instigator and the umpire. The teams were amateur, but the contest marked a significant date in baseball's beginnings. That early game led ultimately to the development of professional baseball and its tightly organized structure.... The ensuing colorful days are well known.... [O]ne recalls the appropriate reference to the "World Serious," attributed to Ring Lardner, St.' Ernest L. Thayer's "Casey at the Bat"; the ring of "Tinker to Evers to Chance"; and all the other happenings, habits, and superstitions about and around baseball that made it the "national pastime" or, depending on the point of view, the "great American tragedy."

[2] The designated hitter rule and artificial turf have succeeded the lively ball and night games as the game's pre-eminent controversies. Sparky Anderson said of the "designated hitter rule" "I've changed my mind about it. Instead of being bad, it stinks." After a solid career, Dick Allen is most renowned for his comment: "If horses don't eat it, I don't want to play on it." Dave Lemonds of the Chicago White Sox once said that playing on artificial turf "is like playing marbles in a bathtub."

Despite the changes and complaints, visitors to modern ballparks witness a sport that has maintained its noble fascination since the nineteenth century. Bill Veeck, baseball's notorious promoter, said that "Baseball is almost the only orderly thing in an unorderly world. If you get three strikes, even the best lawyer in the world can't get you off."

clocks and timekeepers.[3] Perhaps as a result, baseball's memories are the most vivid, and many of our fondest recollections are of afternoons and evenings at the ballpark.

Baseball mirrors our foibles and fallibilities. The game has survived the Black Sox scandal of 1919, striking umpires, striking players, drug and alcohol problems, and even perhaps George Steinbrenner.

The matter before the court stems from one of the less memorable events in the history of the game--an argument at the 1981 winter meetings of the American Association of Professional Baseball Clubs. Plaintiff Dick King and defendant Jim Burris attended the meetings in their capabilities as president and general manager of the Wichita Aeros and the Denver Bears, respectively. King and Burris did not agree on several issues, including league expansion and scheduling for the upcoming season. At one point in the December 5 session, Burris lost his temper and hurled a barrage of verbal beanballs at King. The parties agree that the epithets included: "damn fat fag," "fatso," "liar," "I ought to hit you in the mouth," and "why don't you do the game of baseball a favor and resign?" According to King, Burris then swore at him and threatened him with a Sprite bottle.[4]

King alleges that as a direct result of Burris' actions, he resigned from his position and was forced to seek medical consultation and counseling. He gave up a salary of $40,000 per year plus 25% of the Aero's profits. He is suing Burris, the Denver Bears, and Gerald and Allan Phipps, general partners of the Denver Bears, for defamation and negligent and intentional infliction of severe emotional distress. He asks for $2,000,000 compensatory damages and $5,000,000 punitive damages.

INTENTIONAL INFLICTION OF SEVERE EMOTIONAL DISTRESS

The parties have agreed and I find that Florida law applies. The Florida Supreme Court has yet to award damages for emotional or mental injuries standing alone. It has recognized, however, that a cause of action for negligent or intentional infliction of severe emotional distress may exist:

> There may be circumstances under which one
> may recover for emotional or mental injuries, as

---

[3] "You can't sit on a lead and run a few plays into the line and just kill the clock. You've got to throw the ball over the goddamn plate and give the other man his chance. That's why baseball is the greatest game of all." Earl Weaver.

[4] The pleadings and supporting affidavits clearly specify that the bottle was a Sprite bottle. They are unclear as to whether Burris' intended delivery was overhand, sidearm, or submarine style, or whether Burris was gripping the bottle properly, label side up. Had Burris gripped the bottle properly, so that he could read the label, it would have been difficult for King to see it as well. The propriety of Burris' grip, however, does not affect the gravity of his threat. When Henry Aaron, one of the sport's most formidable hitters, was razzed for his improper grip, he replied, "I ain't up here to read--I'm up here to hit." Who can argue with 755 home runs and 3,771 career hits?

> where there has been a physical impact or when they
> are produced as a result of a deliberate and calculated
> act performed with the intention of producing such
> an injury by one knowing that such acts would
> probably--and most likely produce such an injury,
> but those are not the facts in this case. *Gilliam v.*
> *Stewart*, 291 So. 2d 593, 595 (Fla. 1974). . .

King makes no allegation of direct physical impact, so I must dismiss his charge of negligent infliction of severe emotional distress. I turn now to the charge of intentional infliction of severe emotional distress. . . . In an earlier case, *Slocum v. Food Fair Stores of Florida,* [citation omitted] the court affirmed the dismissal of a complaint by a customer who sued a store after a clerk told her "If you want to know the price, you'll have to find out the best way you can ... you stink to me."

Florida courts have been slow to allow recovery for emotional distress. The five Florida District Courts of Appeal are split on whether an independent tort of intentional infliction of severe emotional distress exists. The courts allow recovery only in extraordinary circumstances. They are generally stringent in their damage awards. In light of Florida's case law, I must decide whether defendant's conduct, reading all disputed facts against him, was extreme enough to state a claim beyond the defamation charges and any charges that plaintiff could bring for assault. . .

In this case, King's claim for severe emotional distress is a restatement of his defamation claims bolstered by the charge that Burris assaulted him with a Sprite bottle. Following Florida's application of Section 46 of the Restatement (Second) of Torts, I cannot find that King has alleged enough in his pleadings, depositions, and affidavits to maintain a cause of action for intentional infliction of severe emotional distress. In light of the charges dismissed in . . . *Food Fair,* I find that Burris' behavior, however unsavory even in sporting circles, was not "so outrageous in character, and so extreme in degree, as to go beyond all possible bounds of decency, and to be regarded as atrocious, and utterly intolerable in a civilized community. . . .

The parties have stipulated that Burris called King a "damn fat fag,"[5] "fatso," and "liar," and said "I ought to hit you in the mouth" and "Why don't you do

---

[5] King is particularly upset with the use of the word "fag":

"[T]o me this is the lowest blow that was ever struck at me, to have ugly words like that come out of a man's mouth. I know we're in a different world today, but I have nothing but detest for homosexuals, just--the mere mention, if I shook hands with a homosexual, then somebody told my that, I'd go out and wash my hands right away. So if a guy were to talk baseball language and we were in a room and there wasn't any women and it was strictly American Association directors, and he'd have said to me, "You dirty CS," now, that's baseball language, but when you refine it to faggot and fag and repeat it and repeat it and you go berserk, so to speak, pick up a sprite [sic] bottle and go wild, had to be restrained by a couple of people, I don't--I don't see this is--it's easy for a man to take." Deposition of Dick King at 92. It was Jacques Barzun who said, "Whoever wants to know the heart and mind of America had better learn baseball."

the game of baseball a favor and resign," but dispute any further comments that may have been made.[6] Burris comments, while hardly reminiscent of Cyrano de Bergerac's nose speech among baseball's contributions to the ancient art of insult,[7] do state a cause of action for defamation. The pleadings raise many interesting issues such as whether the term "fag" constitutes defamation *per se* or *per quod*[8] whether King is a public figure, and whether the Denver Bears or its General Partners ratified Burris' statements.

I need not, however, decide any of these issues because King never notified Burris of his intent to sue. Fla.Stat.Ann. § 770.01 reads:

> Before any civil action is brought for publication
> in a newspaper, periodical, or other medium, of a
> libel or a slander, the plaintiff shall, at least five
> days before instituting such an action, serve no-
> tice in writing on the defendant, specifying the
> article or broadcast and the statements therein
> which he alleges to be false or defamatory.

---

[6]Their disputes range from the serious, such as whether Burris actually threatened King with a bottle, to the petty, such as Burris' word choice. Burris claims: "I don't think I specifically said fat head, faggot. I had never used the word faggot in my life. When I saw these Minutes, I even looked it up. I think I did say you fat fag or fat boy or, I'll hit you in the mouth, but the word faggot I never used." Deposition of Jim Burris at 31.

[7]*See, e.g.,* "There is no reason why the field should not try to put the batsman off his stroke at the critical moment by neatly timed disparagements of his wife's fidelity and his mother's respectability." George Bernard Shaw.

"[H]is head was full of larceny, but his feet were honest." "Bugs" Bear on outfielder Ping Bodie, 1917.

"Call me anything, call me M_____ F_____ but don't call me Durocher. A Durocher is the lowest form of living matter." Harry Wendelstedt, 1974.

"The more we lost, the more Steinbrenner will fly in. And the more he flies, the better chance there will be a plane crash." Graig Nettles, 1977.

"(Charles Finley) would want to know why there were fourteen uniforms dirty when only ten men got in the game." Frank Ciensczk, Oakland equipment manager, 1972.

"I have often called Bowie Kuhn a village idiot. I apologize to all the village idiots of America. He is the nation's idiot." Charlie Finley, 1981.

"The best way to test a Timex would be to strap it to [Earl] Weaver's tongue." Marty Springstead, umpire.

"As a lifetime Cubs fan, I was used to players who, as the sportswriters say, 'can do it all.' In the case of the Cubs, 'doing it all' means striking out, running the wrong way, falling down, dropping the ball." Mike Royko, writer.

[8]The words "fag" and "faggot" have many uses in the English language. "Fag" can mean a tuft of grass, a cigarette, or toil. A faggot can be a bundle of sticks, or a spicy meatball. *Webster's New International Dictionary*, 2d Ed., 1950. Nonetheless, one use of both terms predominates in American culture, and this court will follow that interpretation.

[T]he sole occasion upon which the word "fag" is commonly used in the United States, in the form of a noun and to connote an adult human being, is with reference to a homosexual. To suggest otherwise serves only to further test the gullibility of the credulous and require this court to espouse a naivete unwarranted under the circumstances. *Moricoli v. Schwartz*, 46 Ill. App. 3d 481, 361 N.E. 2d 74 (Ill. App. 1977).

King argues that I should apply the maxim *"ejusdem generis"* [of the same kind] to limit the meaning of "other medium" to forms of mass communication. I believe it prudent, however, to follow the interpretation of a recognized expert in Florida law. In 1976, the legislature amended the statute, adding both "other medium" and "slander" to the wording. In view of the added language, a United States District Judge sitting in Florida wrote that "[t]he better interpretation of the statute's applicability ... is that the provision is applicable to all defendants in actions for libel or slander." . . .

Accordingly, the defamation claims are dismissed without prejudice; summary judgment is granted for the defendants and against the plaintiff on the negligent and intentional infliction of emotional distress claims. Each party shall bear his or its own costs. This civil action is dismissed.

KIRCHOFF v. FLYNN
United States Court of Appeals, Seventh Circuit
786 F.2d 320 (1986)

FRANK H. EASTERBROOK, Circuit Judge.

Arrested for feeding the pigeons and walking her dogs in the park, Anita Kirchoff recovered $25,000 from the police. The defendants gave up, but Kirchoff's lawyers did not. They wanted some $50,000 in fees under 42 U.S.C. § 1988. The district court gave them $10,000 on the ground that their contingent fee contract with the Kirchoffs entitled them to 40% of any award. The case requires us to decide whether the contingent fee is the appropriate rate under § 1988 when the case resembles private tort litigation in which contingent fees are customary. First, however, we pause for the facts.

Anita Kirchoff regularly allowed her dogs to roam without leashes in Washington Park in Chicago, about a half block from her home. While in the park with the dogs, she would feed the pigeons.[1] Michael Flynn, a sergeant of the chicago Police, twice told her that the dogs must be leashed and the pigeons left to their own devices. On May 8, 1982, Flynn saw Kirchoff, her unleashed dogs, and a pigeon enjoying Kirchoff's largesse. As Flynn tells the tale, he and officer Mary Siwak tried to give Kirchoff a citation. To find out who they were citing, they asked Kirchoff her name and address. She balked, and they arrested her, maintaining that when a person being cited will not provide the necessary details, regular procedure requires the arrest. As Kirchoff tells the tale, the police knew who she was, so it was unnecessary for her to provide identification.

---

[1] Anita Kirchoff will never be confused with the 30th Earl of Mar, whose hobby was kicking pigeons. See his entry in *Who Was Who 1971-80*, 520 and his obituary by Auberon Waugh in *Private Eye* (1975). Hear, e.g., Tom Lehrer, *Poisoning Pigeons in the Park* (1959).

Because the police did not have a cell suitable for the two dogs, and the parakeet Kirchoff happened to have in hand, they escorted Kirchoff home, so that she could park her menagerie. At her home they found William Kirchoff, Anita's husband. Anita told her husband that she had been arrested; he responded with some unprintable remarks and punched officer Siwak. (Who started the scuffle will remain a mystery.) Apparently both William and Anita Kirchoff are skilled in karate (the police state that they have black belts), and the officers called for help. By the time help arrived in the person of Lt. Chausse and his paddy wagon, Flynn and Siwak had William Kirchoff in handcuffs. He had been kicked in the groin (self-defense, according to Flynn) and was bleeding about the head. William says that he was clobbered by a pair of handcuffs; Flynn maintains that the Kirchoffs' red macaw drew the blood when it landed on William's head during the fracas and started pecking.[2]

William was trundled to the squadrol, and the police turned their attention back to Anita. All the police had left the house with William; while they were gone, Anita locked the door and refused to let them back in. The police say (and Anita denies) that they twice asked her to open the door. The police ultimately kicked in the door and took Anita into custody. They left a neighbor and an unknown number of dogs, birds, and other animals to guard the Kirchoffs' house. William refused treatment at the hospital to which the police took him. Both Kirchoffs were booked and stayed in jail until the wee hours of the next morning. William spent ten hours in jail, Anita nine.

Anita was prosecuted for littering (dropping bird seed on the ground), feeding a bird, allowing her dogs to run unleashed, and resisting arrest (by locking herself into the house). The state judge convicted Anita of omitting the leash but otherwise acquitted her. The charge of feeding the pigeons had no legal basis. Section 30-7.6 of the park regulations states that "[n]o person shall feed animals in any zoo area except unconfined squirrels, sparrows, pigeons and ducks." Even if Washington Park is a "zoo area," Anita was on safe ground unless some robins or perhaps the parakeet hopped in for a meal.[3] The charge concerning the dogs was more substantial. Section 30-7 requires dogs and cats in the parks to be "continuously restrained by a leash not exceeding six (6) feet in length...." The penalty for allowing dogs to run unleashed in the park is time in the pound (for the dogs only), see Section 30-7.10. The prosecutor asked for 30 days, but the judge apparently sentenced these dogs to time served.

William Kirchoff was charged with obstructing the police in their arrest of Anita and with battery of officers Flynn and Siwak. He was acquitted on all counts.

---

[2] Predatory birds rarely attack large animals whose eyes they can see, 11 *Harv.Med. School Health Letter* 8 (Feb.1986), and perhaps William's eyes got distracted, to his macaw's glee.

[3] Flynn was carrying a booklet of park regulations dated 1973, which included a rule against feeding birds in the park. The police apparently did not have copies of the new book of rules dated 1981.

This suit under 42 U.S.C. § 1983 turned the tables. The complaint charged the officers with assault, battery, false arrest, and malicious prosecution, all in violation of the fourth, fifth, and fourteenth amendments, and with several pendent state claims. Without stating reasons, the district court granted Anita's motion for summary judgment with respect to liability. About a month before the trial the defendants offered $42,000 to settle the matter; the Kirchoffs held out for more. The jury fixed Anita's damages at $25,000 and ruled for the defendants on William's claims. [citation omitted] Neither side has appealed on the merits, so we shall not need to inquire why the court granted summary judgment in a case that apparently turns on whose story one believes. We also need not examine the $25,000 verdict, which is $2,778 for each hour Anita spent in custody.

The defendants missed a good bet when they neglected to make an offer of judgment under Fed.R.Civ.P. 68. The Kirchoffs recovered less than $42,000, so under *Marek v. Chesny*, -- U.S.--, 105 S.Ct. 3012, 87 L.Ed.2d 1 (1985), an offer would have stopped the running of attorneys' fees. They did not, however, and the Kirchoffs' lawyers asked for fees of $49,732.50, representing 331.55 hours of work at $150 per hour. More than 180 of these hours came after the offer of settlement. The defendants argued that the request was excessive. William Kirchoff had lost outright, and Anita had won on liability without a trial. The time spent on William's claims should be excluded, the defendants contended. The case was marginally successful from the plaintiffs' perspective; no plaintiff is happy to take home only 60% of the last settlement offer. The defendants also challenged the hourly rate of $150 and the need to devote 332 hours (more than eight weeks of full time work) to litigating the events of May 8. One lawyer would have done; the plaintiffs used two for parts of the case. The defendants recomputed the hours and hourly fees, coming up with a proposed award of about $5,000.

Although the positions with respect to fees differed by an order of magnitude, the district court did not hold a hearing. Instead the judge decided the matter from the bench. After first remarking that he had not seen the agreement between the Kirchoffs and their lawyers concerning fees, he asked whether the agreement provided a contingent fee. One lawyer replied that it did: one-third if settled before the pretrial order, 40% if things went farther. The court then observed that the "beginning point ... should be a determination of the market value for the services" and concluded that the market value in a case such as this is the contingent fee.

Treating the case as a personal injury matter in which the constitutional foundation was window dressing, the court thought the state of the law "well settled ... for a number of years. These cases are today to the jurisprudence of the Federal Courts what FELA cases were forty, fifty years ago. They are personal injury cases with a Federal law underpinning. The marketplace for this type of litigation throughout my career at the bar has been the contingent fee contract."

The judge went on to explain that $50,000 was at all events an unsupportable request. William lost, so "[t]he time should be divided in half." More, "this was an easy case to try, an easy case to try.... [T]here just is no need for the two of you to try this case.... This was a fist-fight case and, indeed, you lost that aspect of it." The judge summed up:

> When I take all of these factors into account, I believe that the contingent fee agreement which you reached with your clients is the fair measure of the fee in this case. You recovered a $25,000 award for Mrs. Kirchoff. She agreed to pay you forty percent of that. The philosophy of the Civil Rights Attorney's Fee Act is that she should recover her damages without incurring fees. That the defendant should pay her fees, if those fees are reasonable. So she shifts that forty percent of $25,000, or $10,000 to the defendants.

II.

A court awarding fees under § 1988 is supposed to compute the "market rate" for the attorneys' work and assess that reasonable fee against the defendants. . . . The rate should "simulate the results that would obtain if the lawyers were dealing with a paying client." [citation omitted] The district judge thought that 40% of the award is the "market rate" for cases of this type; it was, after all, the rate the Kirchoffs themselves negotiated. What could be a better gauge of the market than an actual transaction in it?

The judge never did read the contingent fee contract, and he got its provisions wrong. True, it entitled the lawyers to 40% of the award if the case went to trial. But this was the lawyers' entitlement against the Kirchoffs, not against the defendants. The contract also provided that if the court should award more than 40%, the lawyers would keep the excess; if the court should award less than 40%, the Kirchoffs' net recovery would be reduced. In other words, the 40% in the contract was a floor; there was no contractual ceiling. The district court made the 40% into a ceiling and thereby modified the contract.

There is a more fundamental question: why should we care about this contract? In ordinary tort litigation the contract fixes entitlements. If the plaintiff recovers $25,000, the lawyer gets $10,000 and the plaintiff $15,000. The plaintiff, with money on the line, takes care when negotiating. The Kirchoffs' contract is not about the disposition of their money. As the district court said, the (or a) policy behind § 1988 is to ensure that the plaintiffs keep the whole recovery. So in negotiating a contract such as this, the Kirchoffs were dickering about the defendants' money, not their own.[4] If the contract had said that the fee is to be 60%, would it then be appropriate to award $15,000 to counsel here? The

---

[4] If the Kirchoffs has lost, they would have paid nothing. If they had won and the judge had awarded less than $10,000, they would have owed money to their lawyers. So it is not strictly

contingent fee may be the market's way to price legal services for this sort of claim, but there is nothing magical about the percentage when the plaintiff expects the defendants to pay the freight.

One logical response would be to say that 40% is the customary fee in tort litigation in which plaintiffs are looking out for their own wallets, and the bargains these other plaintiffs strike offer vicarious protection to defendants in cases under § 1988. A court need only match these private bargains to arrive at the "market rate." This would be too facile, however, because the risks plaintiffs face in § 1983 litigation are greater and the rewards smaller. A § 1983 case is not like FELA litigation, in which all but a few defenses have been stripped away. . . . It is not even like ordinary tort litigation. Although § 1983 creates "a species of tort liability".

The market for legal services uses three principal plans of compensation: the hourly fee, the fixed fee, and the contingent fee. The contingent fee serves in part as a financing device, allowing people to hire lawyers without paying them in advance (or at all, if they lose). It also serves as a monitoring device. In any agency relation, the agent may pursue his own goals at the expense of the principal's. A fixed fee creates the incentive to shirk; a lawyer paid a lump sum, win or lose, may no longer work hard enough to present his client's case. Fixed fees therefore are used only in cases where the client can monitor the results and the lawyer's work (did the lawyer secure the divorce or not?) or where the client (or the client's general counsel) is sufficiently sophisticated to assess what the lawyer has accomplished.

An hourly fee creates an incentive to run up hours, to do too much work in relation to the stakes of the case. An hourly fee may be appropriate where it is hard to define output (in litigation, for example, the outcome turns on the merits and not simply the lawyer's skill and dedication), so the hourly method measures and prices the inputs, the attorney's hours. Again, however, it is necessary to monitor the lawyer's work. The general counsel of a corporation or a sophisticated client may measure inputs well, but in litigation under § 1988 the plaintiff usually has little ability to monitor and also has little incentive to do so, knowing that the defendant will pay the bill. So the court rather than the plaintiff must do the supervision. This in turn creates complex, secondary litigation about fees.

Judicial monitoring also is necessarily imprecise. The judge cannot readily see what legal work was reasonably necessary at the time; the judge first sees the application for fees after the case is over, and hindsight may obscure the difficult decisions made under uncertainty as much as it illuminates them. The Supreme Court's oft-repeated wish that litigation about fees not turn into a second

---

accurate to say that *none* of their money was at stake. The point, however, is that plaintiffs in § 1983 litigation ordinarily expect the defendants to pay enough that the plaintiffs do not compensate their own lawyers, and the plaintiffs' incentive to drive a hard bargain with their lawyers is correspondingly reduced.

major lawsuit [citation omitted] is an unattainable dream. The computation of hourly fees depends on the number of hours "reasonably" expended, the hourly rate of each, the calculation of the time value of money (to account for delay in payment), potential increases and decreases to account for risk and the results obtained, and a complex of other considerations under the heading of "billing judgment." The stakes -- in this case the request for fees was double the judgment, in others the request for fees may be millions of dollars -- ensure that the parties will pursue all available opportunities for litigation. . . . The fuzziness of the criteria (what is a "reasonable" number of hours?) ensures that people seeking opportunities to contest the fees will not need to search hard.

There is no wholly satisfactory way to employ hourly rates when the plaintiff can not or will not monitor his own attorney and the defendant has both incentive and ability to turn the request for fees into a second major litigation. The "lodestar" method makes of the court a public utilities commission, regulating the fees of counsel after the services have been performed, thereby combining the difficulties of rate regulation with the inequities of retrospective rate-setting.

When the use of hourly rates is the norm in the private market, § 1988 requires courts to follow. This will be so, for example, when the litigation does not have a fixed money value, as when the plaintiff principally seeks injunctive relief. The same forces that drive private parties to monitor inputs of attorneys' time rather than particular results must drive the legal system in the same direction. But when private litigants have found that it is more useful to give the lawyer a monetary stake in the recovery through the contingent fee than to monitor inputs of time, courts should be willing to learn from that accumulated experience.

The contingent fee uses private incentives rather than careful monitoring to align the interests of lawyer and client. The lawyer gains only to the extent his client gains. This interest-alignment device is not perfect. When the lawyer gains 40 cents to the client's dollar, the lawyer tends to expend too little effort; unless concern for his reputation dominates he would not put in an extra $600 worth of time to obtain an extra $1,000 for his client, because he would receive only $400 for his effort. . . . But imperfect alignment of interests is better than a conflict of interests, which hourly fees may create. The unscrupulous lawyer paid by the hour may be willing to settle for a lower recovery coupled with a payment for more hours. Contingent fees eliminate this incentive and also ensure a reasonable proportion between the recovery and the fees assessed to defendants. Except in grudge litigation, no client, however wealthy, pays a lawyer more than a dollar to pursue a dollar's worth of recovery. Nothing in the legislative history of § 1988 suggests that Congress meant to give civil rights plaintiffs a sort of representation that wealthy people would not purchase for themselves. . . .

At the same time as it automatically aligns interest of lawyer and client, rewards exceptional success, and penalizes failure, the contingent fee automatically handles compensation for the uncertainty of litigation. Hourly fees usually are fees that lawyers charge to clients who pay promptly when billed. These fees translate poorly to § 1988 cases, where payment is contingent on success and is delayed until after the end of the litigation. Courts have wrestled with questions concerning multipliers for risk, multipliers for exceptional success, and the treatment of the time value of money. One common concern with compensation for risk is that the multiplier should rise as the probability of success falls, soaking the unlucky defendant who had a good case (more than a 50% chance of prevailing) but lost anyway and therefore faced a huge multiplier. . . .

. . . The contingent fee contract takes care of this adjustment automatically, yet it never presents defendants with a bill many times the stakes of the underlying litigation. So long as the percentage is set by category of case (as it should be), rather than case by case, defendants with good cases pay no more than defendants with poor ones. The adjustment for risk takes place not in the judge's chambers but in the private market--under a contingent fee system, potential litigants with poor chances simply cannot find counsel. Weak cases stay out of court.

For all of these reasons, we agree with the district court that when the private market for legal services employs the contingent fee for "similar services by lawyers, of reasonably comparable skill, experience, and reputation" [citation omitted] so may a court making an award under § 1988. The private market uses the contingent fee for personal injury cases, including torts such as battery, false arrest, and malicious prosecution, the subjects of this case. The district court was entitled to employ a contingent fee as a bench mark, even though for reasons we have explained it was wrong to stop the inquiry with the 40% minimum fee in the Kirchoffs' contract. The district judge must ascertain the appropriate rate for cases of similar difficulty and risk, and of similarly limited potential recovery.

To sum up: the district judge was entitled to compute the attorneys' fee in this case as a percentage of the total award. The court was mistaken, however, to lift that percentage out of the contingent fee contract. The 40% was to be a minimum, not a cap. The contract was not bargained between the lawyer and the real parties in interest - the defendants. It also may not provide the percentage that is used in similarly risky tort litigation with moderate stakes. We therefore remand the case to the district court for further consideration of the reasonable attorneys' fee.

REVERSED AND REMANDED.

STATE OF NORTH CAROLINA v. OLIVER
Supreme Court of North Carolina
70 N.C. 44 (1874)

THOMAS SETTLE, J.

[Defendant, Oliver, came home intoxicated one morning after breakfast was over; got some raw bacon, said it had "skippers" (maggots which infest meat) on it, and scolded his wife for not cleaning it. He sat down and ate a little, then threw the coffee cup and pot into the corner of the room and left. While outside he cut two switches, brought them in, and told his wife that he was going to whip her, because she and her "damned mother" had aggravated him near to death. He then struck her five licks with the switches, each of which was about four feet long. One of the switches was about half as large as a man's little finger and the other was slightly smaller. The attack inflicted bruises on her arm which remained for two weeks, but did not disable her from work. Defendant was charged with assault and battery. The Court found defendant guilty and assessed a $10 fine. The defendant appealed.]

We may assume that the old doctrine that a husband had a right to whip his wife, provided he used a switch no larger than his thumb, is not law in North Carolina. Indeed, the Courts have advanced from that barbarism until they have reached the position that the husband has no right to chastise his wife under any circumstances.

But from motives of public policy, and in order to preserve the sanctity of the domestic circle, the Courts will not listen to trivial complaints. If no permanent injury has been inflicted, nor malice, cruelty nor dangerous violence shown by the husband, it is better to draw the curtain, shut out the public gaze, and leave the parties to forget and forgive. No general rule can be applied, but each case must depend upon the circumstances surrounding it.

Without adverting in detail to the facts established by the special verdict in this case, we think that they show both malice and cruelty. In fact it is difficult to conceive how a man who has promised upon an altar to love, comfort, honor and keep a woman can lay rude and violent hands upon her without having malice and cruelty in his heart.

Let it be certified that the judgment of the Superior Court is affirmed. Judgment affirmed.

SMITH v. PITTSBURGH RAILWAYS COMPANY
Supreme Court of Pennsylvania
405 Pa. 340; 175 A. 2d 844 (1961)

BENJAMIN R. JONES, Justice.

On January 28, 1957, appellant Roselyn K. Smith, and her sixteen year old daughter, Carol Smith, were passengers on an uncrowded street car owned and operated by the Pittsburgh Railways Company, appellee. Appellant and her daughter were seated on a long seat located lengthwise in the extreme right front portion of the street car. According to appellant, the street car ride was "rough" and the car "was jerking just as though he [the motorman] was playing with the pedal" and, as the street car approached the so-called Bloomfield stop, passengers expecting to alight at that stop came forward and "he [the motorman] jerked that street car again" and a man, standing near where appellant was seated, was thrown off balance by the jolt and "the heel of his foot just stomped right down on the great toe of [appellant's] left foot" causing severe injuries. Furthermore, according to appellant, the street car was about to stop when the jolt occurred.[1]

As the car approached the Bloomfield stop, Carol Smith left her seat to ask the motorman for a street car schedule and she "had [her] hand on the railing when the motorman started the car real fast" and she fell to the floor.[2] Except for the statement that other passengers were "thrust back" there is no evidence that the alleged "jolt" or "jerk" affected any other passengers in the street car.

At trial in the Court of Common Pleas of Allegheny County that court entered a compulsory nonsuit and, from its refusal to remove this nonsuit and the entry of judgment, this appeal was taken. . .The applicable law is clear. In Staller et al. v. Philadelphia Rapid Transit Co., [citation omitted] we stated:

> "It is well established by a long line of decisions that testimony indicating that a moving trolley car jerked suddenly or violently is not sufficient, of itself, to establish negligence in its operation. There must be a showing of additional facts and circumstances from which it clearly appears that the movement of the car was so unusual and extraordinary as to be beyond a passenger's reasonable anticipation, and nothing short of evidence that the allegedly unusual movement had extraordinarily disturbing effect upon the other passengers, or evidence of an accident, the manner of the occurrence of which or the effect of which upon the injured person inherently establishes the unusual character of the jolt or jerk, will suffice." . . .

An examination of the testimony produced by appellant failed to show that the movement of this street car was so unusual and extraordinary as to be beyond the reasonable anticipation of the passengers therein and it is clear that the evidence falls far short of the standard of proof required to fasten liability upon the appellee. . . .

Judgment affirmed.

MICHAEL A. MUSMANNO, Justice (dissenting).

On January 28, 1957, the motorman of the Pittsburgh Railways Company street car involved in this litigation, who was apparently angry with himself and

---

[1] According to the complaint, the "jerk" or "jolt" occurred when the street car was "started up without warning" by the motorman.

[2] Carol Smith stated: "I wasn't holding on to it [the railing] but I had my hand on it" and "I put my hand on the pole just to brace myself while I was going forward * * *."

the world in general, picked up passengers on the northside of Pittsburgh and then furiously headed across the Allegheny River into downtown Pittsburgh and out to Bloomfield. His speed was such that from time to time the trolley pole jumped the overhead high voltage wire, whereupon he would jerk the car to a stop, leap off to reengage the trolley, swearing all the while and intermixing with his profanity a variety of indelicate and indecent phrases. As he bounded over the rails he applied the power in fits and starts as if playing the pedals of a pipe organ, thereby shaking up the passengers to such a degree that one of them exclaimed: "This is the roughest ride we have ever had." Other passengers described the rough trip as a "terrible ride."

As the car approached the Bloomfield stop, the motorman slowed down and the alighting passengers prepared to disembark. Suddenly the motorman, possibly realizing that he was moving into the stop too uneventfully, threw on a sudden burst of power and jolted the car forward as if he had decided not to stop after all. In consequence, *all* the passengers were thrown backward and one of them, a sixteen-year-old girl, measured her length on the floor. Her mother testified that the girl was "terribly embarrassed because her dress went up when she fell."

Still another passenger, a large, heavy six-foot gentleman, went into an involuntary jig to maintain equilibrium and balance. He executed a few steps backwards and then eventually braked his anticipatory fall by anchoring one foot firmly to what he thought was the floor. It turned out to be the foot of another passenger. The weight of his body and the violence with which he bore down fractured the big toe of the left foot of the startled passenger, who is the plaintiff in this lawsuit which terminated with a jolt in the Court below in a Court-imposed non-suit.

This court has affirmed that non-suit in an Opinion which would suggest that the Court assumes that the ride of the momentous street car was as smooth and tranquil as that of a gondola moving over the Grand Canal of Venice. The Majority Opinion states:

> "An examination of the testimony produced by appellant fails to show that the movement of this street car was so unusual and extraordinary as to be beyond the reasonable anticipation of the passengers therein and it is clear that the evidence falls far short of the standard of proof required to fasten liability upon appellee [the street car company]."

Are passengers to anticipate that a street car will be operated in such headlong fashion that the trolley pole does a St. Vitus dance on the roof? Are they to foresee that an angry and mysteriously infuriated motorman will do a dance on the power pedal? Is a trip on a street car to be considered a usual one when one passenger is hurled to the floor, another does an impromptu ballet, and *all* of them are thrown back?

CHAPTER X: SCURRILOUS, MALICIOUS, DESPICABLE CONDUCT

How unusual must a street car ride be when a passenger suffers a fractured toe from the pirouetting of a six-foot passenger before there may be a recovery for the injury? Even the attorney for the street car company admitted the jolt, of which the plaintiff complains, was a "*violent* jolt." Is violence now so much a part of daily existence that it no longer arouses surprise and cannot stir the law into enforcing redress for injuries suffered as a result of the violence?

The personal characteristics of the motorman in this case would have no bearing, generally speaking, on the manner in which he operated his car. However, since the whole street car was under his absolute domination and control, his conduct may help the legal observer to determine whether he did operate the car in a manner to cause the result suffered by the plaintiff. In describing the motorman, the plaintiff employed a phraseology of her own which would not be without meaning to the jury. She said that the motorman was "snotty." The dictionary defines this colloquial and slangly work as meaning contemptible, dirty, offensive, nasty, snooty, offish and supercilious. A motorman who could be nasty and snooty would be just the kind of motorman who would slam on his brakes and precipitately throw on his power regardless of what happened to his passengers.

The plaintiff added that the motorman was also "snippy." This is not as pungent a description as "snotty," but, added to everything else said about the motorman, reveals an operator given to impetuosity. The dictionary defines "snippy" as being short-tempered, tart, and snappish. It would not be too much to assume that a motorman who is nasty, snooty, snappish, short-tempered, and supercilious would be just the kind of motorman who would operate his car with such angry abandon and unconcern over the safety of his passengers that he would lose his trolley three or four times in a short run and then slam on his brakes with such instantaneous violence as to produce the toe-smashing event heretofore narrated.

The plaintiff's counsel in his brief cites all three cases, all of which support his position that this case should have been submitted to the jury. In Sanson v. Philadelphia Rapid Transit Company, [citation omitted], the plaintiff-passenger signalled the motorman he intended to get off at the next stop. The motorman acknowledged the signal and began to slow down. As the plaintiff, however, rose from his seat and took hold of the handle of the door the motorman suddenly increased the speed of the car, causing the plaintiff to be thrown to the platform. Verdict for the plaintiff was sustained.

In Tilton v. Philadelphia Rapid Transit Company, [citation omitted], the plaintiff was non-suited after testifying that the car suddenly stopped and he was thrown forward striking the seat ahead of him. This Court removed the non-suit, . . .

In Angelo v. Pittsburgh Railways Company, [citation omitted], the plaintiff was injured when the bus in which she was riding suddenly swerved to one side and made a violent and unusual stop throwing her against a pole in the car to her injury. She recovered a verdict and the defendant appealed. The Superior Court affirmed the verdict, . . .

In the case at bar, the defendant company should have been required to show that the motorman could not have avoided the extraordinary circumstances in the car when, because of his operation, the car jolted, jerked and otherwise so carried on that a large passenger was thrown off balance and came down heavily on the foot of the plaintiff who was innocently sitting in the car minding her own business and now has a disabled foot, which will impede her walking, even if she determined she would never ride street cars again.

The Majority does not attempt to analyze these three cases or show how they differ in principle from the principle controlling the facts in the case at bar. It merely says that these cases "are clearly *inapposite*." [Emphasis supplied.] Even the brief treatment I have given them demonstrates that they are quite *apposite*, and certainly far more apposite than the cases which, like a long train of cars, have been cited by the Majority.

And thus, because of all this inappositeness, Mrs. Smith is out of court. She boarded a street car, she paid her money and accordingly had the right to be taken to her destination with the care that a common carrier is required to exercise in accordance with the law of the land. A motorman who, from the evidence adduced at the trial, revealed to himself to be masterfully incompetent and superbly insolent, and with personal traits inapposite to the skill required properly to run a street car, so operated the car as to fracture her foot. She hobbled into court for a redress of her grievance and she was compelled to hobble out with her grievance unredressed.

And she will now hobble through life still unredressed, not because a jury passed on her rights, but because a long series of inapposite cases passed over her.

EPILOGUE

. . . And for a farewell to our jurisprudent, I wish unto him the gladsome light of jurisprudence, the lovelinesse of temperance, the stabilitie of fortitude, and the soliditie of justice.

- Edward Coke[1]

The man of firm and noble soul
No factious clamours can control:
No threatening tyrant's darkling brow
Can swerve him from his just intent;
Gales the warring waves which plough,
By Auster on the billows spent,
To curb the Adriatic main
Would awe his fixed determined mind in vain.

Aye, and the red right arm of Jove,
Hurtling his lightning from above,
With all his terrors there unfurled,
He would unmoved, unawed behold.
The flames of an expiring world.
Again in crushing chaos rolled,
In vast promiscuous ruin hurled,
Might light his glorious funeral pile,
Still dauntless 'mid the wreck of earth he'd smile.

- Horace[2]

---

[1] From Epilogue: Edward Coke, *The First Part of the Institutes of The Laws of England or a Commentary upon Littleton*; 17th ed., Vol. II p. 395a (1817).

[2] Horace, Ode III.3, Byron Translation, as reprinted in *Oxford Book of Latin Verse*, p. 482-483 (1912).

INVITATION TO
CONTRIBUTE AND REFER
ADDITIONAL CASES AND MATERIALS

A follow-up volume, CORPUS JURIS HUMOROUS II, is currently being compiled and edited. All readers are invited and encouraged to contribute and refer any information concerning additional humorous, extraordinary, outrageous, unusual, colorful, infamous, clever and/or witty reported judicial opinions and related materials from any source whatsoever. Please direct all such contributions, referrals and other communications to:

MAC-MAT
c/o
McCLAY & ALANI
A Professional Law Corporation

1630 East Palm Avenue
Santa Ana, California 92701

Telephone: (714) 558-1535

Telecopier: (714) 558-8024

McCLAY & ALANI
1991

McCLAY & ALANI, a Professional Law Corporation, emphasizes real property litigation and commercial asset management law, representing developers, commercial landlords and asset management companies throughout Southern California. John B. McClay has practiced law in Orange County, California since 1980 and is co-founder and co-lead counsel of McCLAY & ALANI, a Professional Law Corporation. John B. McClay is a graduate of the University of California at Berkeley (B.S., Business Administration, 1976) and Pepperdine University School of Law, (J.D., 1979) where he was named to the Dean's Honor List and served on the Pepperdine Law Review.

McCLAY & ALANI
A Professional Law Corporation

1630 East Palm Avenue
Santa Ana, California 92701

Telephone: (714) 558-1535

Telecopier: (714) 558-8024

INDEX OF CASES AND MATERIALS

90000>

9 780963 148803

ISBN 0-9631488-0-X